AMERICAN "POLONIA" AND POLAND

A Sequel To *Poles In America: Bicentennial Essays*

Edited by
FRANK MOCHA

EAST EUROPEAN MONOGRAPHS, BOULDER
DISTRIBUTED BY COLUMBIA UNIVERSITY PRESS, NEW YORK
1998

EAST EUROPEAN MONOGRAPHS, NO. CDXCVI

Printed in the United States of America

EDITOR'S NOTE AND ACKNOWLEDGEMENTS

This book, written in the pain of post-surgery convalescence, is the third, and last, in a series I like to call my "Trilogy" of books edited by me (and shorter works entirely written by me) dedicated to American Polonia and Poland in the last twenty years, during which I largely abandoned my principal research specialty while summing up the accomplishments and contributions of American Polonia in *POLES IN AMERICA: Bicentennial Essays* (1978), evaluating Solidarity in *POLAND'S SOLIDARITY MOVEMENT* (1984), and bringing Polonia and Poland together in *AMERICAN "POLONIA" AND POLAND* (1998). The last book is different from the earlier ones in two respects, first, by resorting to the device of the so-called "alternate history" with the help of the "What If?" deliberation. (For example: What if Casimir Pulaski hadn't died at Savannah, Władysław the Jagiellonian at Varna or, for that matter, Casimir the Great and Stephen Batory prematurely?) A new book has just arrived on my desk with precisely the title, *WHAT IF? Strategic Alternatives of WWII*, showing that it is a legitimate device.

The second difference in the last book from the earlier ones is its resorting to the first-person singular narrative (very legitimate now according to the Publications of the Modern Language Association) in chapters describing my own activity in connection with the Polish American Congress and the Polish Institute of Arts and Sciences, as well as the Kosciuszko Foundation and, of course, in Poland and in Russia, each of these chapters (or subchapters) requiring a "Personal View"* (asterisked in at least one case) obtained by the use of the first person. But there is more to it. Brought up in an atmosphere of Poland's lost opportunities and spoiled potential, due to many causes, but probably fate (Norman Davies' *God's Playground* comes to mind) and bad luck—hence my tendency to resort to alternate history for a retroactive compensation—I viewed my own lost opportunities in the same vein, and this could not be well conveyed from the distance of a third-person narrative.

iii

In the final analysis, illness was a determining factor in the book, its structure and its voice. There was the ever-present fear that there wouldn't be time for other books: to continue the memoir *Choices in War and Peace*, so far brought only to the September 1939 campaign in Poland before the need for the present book arose after the fall of Communism, leaving at least half a dozen chapters of the memoir in typescript, unpublished; as well as unfinished projects in Polish-Russian literary relations, my research specialty. There are echoes of and allusions to these projects in the book, where they probably don't belong, but friends, associates, and members of the academic community are entitled to know about the status of my writings that they were once familiar with, and frequently enquire about. In this sense, next to its main motivation—concern about Poland—the book is an instrument of communication for its author with the outside world, as every book is, or should be.

• • • •

In my labors, mostly in isolation except for my helpful wife, Doreen, and daughter Jane with her young son Mathew, and an equally helpful assistant Michael Kaniecki on frequent occasions, I relied on my own materials and resources, but received also outside help in various forms, which I want to acknowledge with gratitude and thanks.

I wish to thank Ms. Kate Wittenberg, Editor in Chief, Columbia University Press, distributor of the book, for directing me to Dr. Stephen Fischer-Galati of East European Monographs, publishers, and thank him and his aide, Ms. Nancy Tyson, for their encouragement and patience.

A different kind of thanks go to David Gonzales of *The New York Times* for mentioning the book in his column "About New York" in an Independence Day 1996 interview with me entitled "Silver Zlotys And a Dream of America"; to M. Kaniecki, a Polish-American writer and performer, for responding to the interview with a fine letter expressing gratitude for what I was doing and offering help, becoming my assistant, with the blessings of his Slovak-American ballerina-wife Sarah; to Rafał Olbiński for designing the cover of the book; and to Professor Wieńczysław Wagner for acting as liaison with the book's contributors in Poland.

Special thanks are due to people who contributed to the success of the project in various ways: Robert Bonsignore by ordering 12 copies for the Polish National Library in Warsaw; Małgorzata Dymek-Ćwiklińska, a journalist, by providing translation and other help; Janusz Krzyżanowski of the Polish Combattants by being a reliable source of information; Dr. Stanley Stein, a specialist on Germany, by sending clippings of pertinent articles and acting as liaison with the Deutsches Polen Institut in Darmstadt, Germany; and Prof. Mark von Hagen, director of the Harriman Institute in New York, by bringing a photograph of the Zagorsk Monastery plaque from Russia (see p. 431).

Words of appreciation are due to some people for just being there, by participating in the planning meetings (the veteran Henry Archacki and his son John, Stanley Naj, Michael Jacewski, Alina Kędzierska, Dr. Edmund Osysko, Joseph Wardzala, and the other veteran, Edward Pinkowski) or offering the best excuse in the world, baby-sitting their grandchildren (Walter Lasinski and Anthony Podbielski), and others by expressing readiness to help (Ewa Gierat, Bolesław Łaszewski, Wiktor Sawicki, Władysław Zachariasiewicz, and the Patton veteran Czesław Bolesław Wróbel, founder later of the Polish Museum in Port Washington, who suddenly and disturbingly fell silent, like many others.) Of the many wealthy Polish women only one responded, the always reliable Lady Blanka Rosenstiel, busy now endowing a Polish chair at the University of Virginia.

One acknowledgement I make without thanks—of the Editors (Lester R. Brown et al.) of *State of the World 1998* (A Worldwatch Institute Report on Progress Toward a Sustainable Society) simply because for the second time Poland is absent from it. Like before, I will complain, and like before, demand a refund and an explanation, and like before, get just the refund and *no* explanation!

I was more fortunate with the many maps illustrating the book. The most "dramatic" of them (p. 338) comes from Iwo C. Pogonowski's book, *Jews in Poland* (Hippocrene Books, 1993), reproduced here with the author's permission. Other maps come either from Oskar Halecki's *History of Poland* (Roy Publishers, 1961), long out of print, or were provided by colleagues and associates. More specialized maps, dealing with Prussia, were sent by Dr. Andreas Lavaty (a specialist) from the Deutsches Polen Institut in Darmstadt, and the lone US map was prepared by Michael Kaniecki. Thanks!

Words of thanks are also due to those who came, or were prevented from coming, to the last meeting connected with the book, on June 27, 1998, at the Pilsudski Institute. The mainstream editors were probably notified too late, while contributors from Poland would have to have been provided with transportation and lodgings, but the Kosciuszko Foundation was not cooperating on what was also to be a farewell to the older generation. It turned out that it was already too late for that. For some, it was too hard to get down (Ewa Gierat), others were too ill (Henry Archacki) or recovering from surgery (David Wapinsky, an American Jew in love with Polish culture, and Edward Pinkowski, but he at least sent somebody to speak for him—Peter Obst, desktop publisher). There was nobody from the Polish media, nobody from the Polish Institute and from the host institute, except the refreshments people. So much for organized Polonia!

It would have been good to hear from Stanley Blejwas what his plans were for the endowed Polish Studies program in New Britain, beside the lecture series so far, which had been done much more extensively without costing a cent, by the income-producing Literary Section of the Polish Institute in the mid-70s (see p. 164).

Despite these absences, the meeting was an unqualified success. Prof. Czerwiński spoke about his 8-year labor producing the much-needed *Dictionary of Polish Literature*. Mr. Obst reported about his trip with Pinkowski to the Pulaski Museum in Warka, and Victor Sawicki, besides filming the whole program, delivered a patriotic speech about Poland, with my daughter taking pictures and my grandson Mathew handing me a story he had written about me and my strivings. But it was Robert Bonsignore who surprised me and everybody else by distributing a little essay explaining the origins of his interest in Poland. Excerpts can be found in the book on p. 258.

The next day I received a card from Ed Czerwiński with a brief message:

Dear Frank,

Thank you again for being the Leader of the Good League.

Sincerely, Ed

and it is to the "Good League" that I dedicate this book.

Frank Mocha
July, 1998

PREFACE

Twenty years ago I edited and co-authored a large volume, *POLES IN AMERICA: Bicentennial Essays*, which was a collective effort to sum up the total experience of the Polish ethnic group in America (American "Polonia"). In that sense, the book was a gift to Polonia and, by association, a gift to America, too. In the Preface to the book I called America "a gift of history to our planet" cautioning in the same sentence that "there shall never be another." During his most recent visit here Pope John Paul II defined America somewhat differently when he declared upon arriving, "Thank God for the extraordinary human epic that is the United States of America," urging America to live its ideals.

In his infinite wisdom, the Holy Father seems to be saying that America's destiny is not in organizing the world according to its own economic and strategic designs while Americanizing it in the process, after becoming the sole superpower a few years earlier, but in first putting its multi-cultural house in order, an ongoing process that could still be derailed by the unfolding drama on America's doorstep, in Mexico. America's future is tied to Mexico's progress. Failure of democratic reform in Mexico would bring about an economic collapse which, in turn, would send millions of Mexicans fleeing north across the border, adding to the illegal immigrants already here, and placing a heavy burden on the American economy. The resulting disruption would be felt by every segment of American society, including the Polish American community, just when American Polonia was straining to help Poland.

The purpose of the present book, a sequel, is to re-assert Polish contributions to America, to re-evaluate the strength and weaknesses of American Polonia, and to re-examine the ways Polonia can help Poland.

The Polonia-Poland special relationship goes back to World War I, when Polonia even raised an army (part of the "Blue Army") to help Poland regain its independence after 123 years of Partitions and then to defend that independence in a victorious war the new Poland had to fight against the new enemy, the Soviet Union, in 1920. Some of the Polonian soldiers remained in Poland to help settle the uneasy Eastern territories. During the interwar period there was a lively Polonia-Poland interchange interrupted by World War II, in which Polish Americans served in great numbers in the US Armed Forces, while Polish American organizations conducted charitable activity on behalf of refugees from war-torn Poland. This charitable activity continued on personal and organizational levels throughout the 45 years of Communist rule when Poland was a member of the Warsaw Pact during the Cold War.

Charitable activity was not the only Polonia-Poland interaction during the Cold War. Representatives of both communities took part in celebrations of Poland's great anniversaries: the 600th of the University of Cracow (1964), the Millennium of Poland's Christianity (1966), and the 500th anniversary of the birth of Nicholas Copernicus (1973). Polish American scholars took part in all three Congresses of Scholars of Polish Descent in Poland (1973, 1979, 1989), and scholars from Poland participated in programs of the Kosciuszko Foundation and of the Polish Institute of Arts and Sciences in America. The election of a Polish Pope (John Paul II, 1978) did a lot to bring the two communities closer, and the rise of Solidarity (1980) foreshadowed the end of Communism.

1980 was a watershed year in Polonia's attitude toward Poland. It was the year of the Gdansk Agreements when the Solidarity movement had the Communist regime on the run. It was also the year of the emergence of Lech Walesa, the leader of Solidarity, as a world figure. If we looked for the precise moment when concern for Poland among the rank and file Polonia outweighed strictly domestic concerns, it would probably be the September-December 1980 issue (No. 5) of the faculty-advised Chicago Polish students publication *Echo*, a collector's item today, which carried a centerfold spread dedicated to Solidarity, with the Solidarity monument in the middle, a poem about Solidarity by the poet Tymoteusz Karpowicz on the left, and a translation by Frank Mocha on the right (see Appendix).

The *Echo* issue was followed by no fewer than six scholarly panels or symposia organized by this writer, who had witnessed the birth of the Solidarity movement while on an academic assignment in Poland in the summer of 1980. Upon return to the United States, he set about studying the movement further and informing the public about it. Three of the panels took place at regional and national Slavic conferences and the remaining three at Loyola University of Chicago, the last of which, an International Symposium, "Poland's Solidarity Movement," resulted in a book of the same title in which the philosopher Leszek Kołakowski foretells the disintegration of the Soviet Empire. But it was Solidarity that was liquidated first, by the imposition of brutal martial law in Poland (December 13, 1981), and all American Polonia could do was to intensify its charitable activities. The rest is history.

The Pope's second visit to Poland (June, 1983; the first took place in 1979) helped end the martial law, while Gorbachev's "perestroika" ironically speeded up the disintegration of the Soviet Empire beginning with the dissolution of the Warsaw Pact, an act which restored Poland's independence in 1989. In another irony, General Jaruzelski, the mastermind of the martial law, became the first President of the newly independent Poland as a result of roundtable agreements between post-Solidarity activists and Communists, but his term was reduced to one year in order to have a general election. It was held in 1990 and Lech Walesa became the first Polish President elected in a free and general election. He served a full term, with his popularity steadily declining, and was narrowly defeated by a former Communist, Aleksander Kwaśniewski, in 1995.

To many Polish Americans the defeat of Lech Walesa was a painful shock. They wanted to see him re-elected. To them, he was and still is a living symbol and a link with a memorable chapter of Poland's recent history. But to young Poles, that history was already old, something that was happening when they were children, and they wanted someone who was closer to their generation and their lifestyle. Kwaśniewski, 41, was an answer to their prayers. The fact that the new President was a former Communist may have been be a shock to Polish Americans but not to the Poles. Their thinking was probably best explained in an editorial of *The New York Times* (January 5, 1996):

> Poland, after economic reform, has been the fastest growing country in Europe over the past few years. But even there, voters were frustrated by their overblown expectations, turned out reformers and brought Communists back into office. The remarkable fact, however, is that Communists have stuck with market reforms, which offer the only realistic path to growth. Perhaps the Poles can serve as a model for Russia.

This thinking was confirmed by President Kwaśniewski in his inaugural speech when he said that he was a man of the "Polish left" and a "representative of a country of frustrated hopes, unfulfilled promises, bitterness and doubts," but that such frailties should not obscure the achievements of the last six years since the collapse of Communism. He also repeated his pledges to take Poland into NATO and the European Union.

These two pledges are what unites Poland and American Polonia. Just as the Poles can think of nothing more important than membership in NATO and the European Union, in that order, so do the Polonians. This writer would reverse that order, putting the European Union first and leaving NATO alone until Russia's fears of extending NATO closer to its borders are somehow lessened. Perhaps future elections in Russia will produce a leader with a broader outlook than Yeltsin, someone like Grigory A. Yavlinsky, a reformer without superpower aspirations for Russia, who would understand that as long as the Russians remain right on top of Poland in the isolated Kaliningrad enclave, which under the name of Koenigsberg was once a part of Ducal Prussia and a Polish dependency, the Poles feel more strongly about being in harm's way than they care to "serve as a model for Russia."

Kaliningrad is somehow a taboo subject, judging by the fact that in a symposium, "NATO and the East," at the Institute on East Central Europe of Columbia University on November 20, 1995, none of the participants raised it until the present writer pointed it out to them for the record and for the benefit of the featured speaker, Janusz Onyszkiewicz, member of Parliament and former Minister of Defense of Poland. Kaliningrad must become the main Polish foreign policy problem to be pursued relentlessly until a satisfactory solution is reached, a solution beneficial to both Poland and Russia, as will be discussed in the "Poland and Russia" chapter of this book.

For American Polonia there are other problems to get involved in Poland. In many respects, Poland is a success story, but at what cost? There is the perennial housing shortage and, above all, environmental pollution and poor health, especially among children. Just as American Polonia, under the leadership of the Polish American Congress, lobbies energetically for Poland's inclusion in NATO, it should lobby as energetically for help in improving the environment and the nation's health, which is assuming catastrophic proportions. To provide help, Polonia has been using its own resources, but they are not nearly adequate for the task. Above it all hovers a demographic specter, in which Poland is approaching zero population growth. If the trend is not reversed, Poland will start declining as a nation. From one of the highest birthrates in the world only a few years ago, even during martial law, Poland is suddenly facing depopulation. Here is where education can help, education stressing the joys and importance of extended family as a moral and physical support system, and as a safeguard against the prospect of the declining population of Poland being surpassed by the number of people of Polish descent living abroad, chiefly in America, a possibility discussed further elsewhere in this book.

Nota Bene: The 1997 parliamentary elections, resulting symbolically in the defeat of former Communists just before the November 11 Independence Day, seem to indicate that Poland is at last getting on the right track.

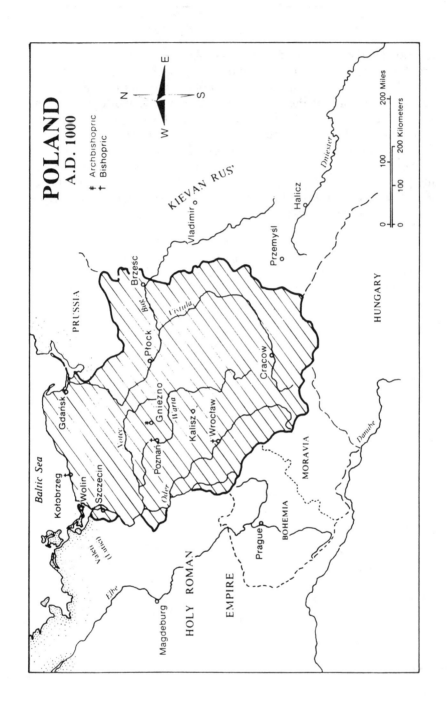

POLAND
A.D. 1000

‡ Archbishopric
† Bishopric

N   E   S   W

200 Miles
200 Kilometers

KIEVAN RUS'

Dniester

Halicz ○

Vladimir ○

Przemysl ○

Brzesc ○

Bug

Vistula

HUNGARY

PRUSSIA

Płock ○

Cracow ○

Danube

Gdańsk ○

Gniezno ○

Warta

Wrocław †○

MORAVIA

Baltic Sea

Kołobrzeg ○

Wolin ○

Szczecin †○

Notec

Poznań †○

Kalisz ○

Oder

BOHEMIA

Prague ○

Vistula (lmia)

Elbe

HOLY ROMAN

EMPIRE

Magdeburg ○

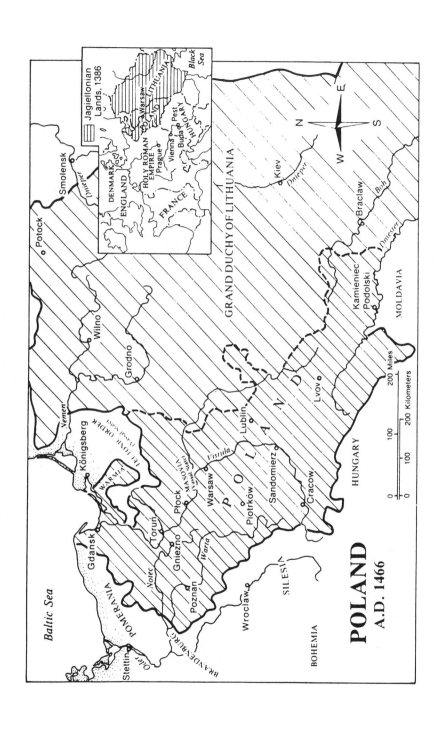

POLAND
A.D. 1466

Baltic Sea

GRAND DUCHY OF LITHUANIA

Jagiellonian
Lands, 1386

Black Sea

DENMARK
ENGLAND
HOLY ROMAN
EMPIRE
Prague
Vienna
Buda
Pest
HUNGARY
POLAND
LITHUANIA
Warsaw
FRANCE

Smolensk

Dniepr

Potock

Wilno

Grodno

Nemen

Königsberg

TEUTONIC ORDER (Prussia)

WARMIA

Gdansk

Toruń

Gniezno

Płock

MASOVIA

Warsaw

Vistula

Lublin

Piotrków

Sandomierz

Cracow

Lvov

Kamieniec
Podolski

MOLDAVIA

Braclaw

Kiev

Dnieper

Boh

Dniester

HUNGARY

SILESIA

Wroclaw

BOHEMIA

POMERANIA

BRANDENBURG

Stettin

Oder

Notec

Warta

Poznan

200 Miles

200 Kilometers

100

100

0

0

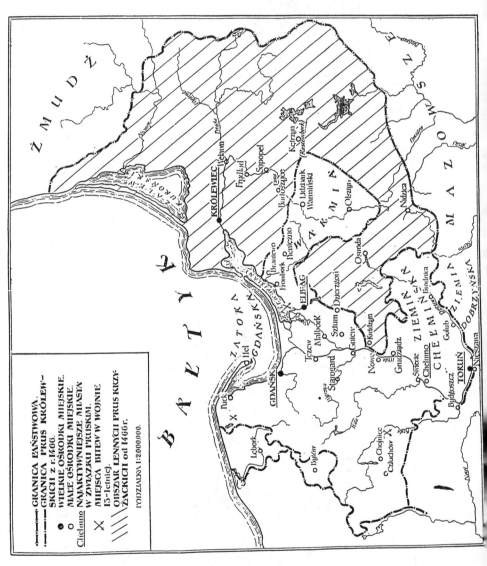

POMORZE WSCHODNIE W OKRESIE WALKI O ZJEDNOCZENIE Z POLSKĄ

GRANICA PAŃSTWOWA.
GRANICA PRUS KRÓLEW-
SKICH z r.1466.
WIELKIE OŚRODKI MIEJSKIE.
MAŁE OŚRODKI MIEJSKIE.
Chełmno NAJAKTYWNIEJSZE MIASTA
W ZWIĄZKU PRUSKIM.
MIEJSCA BITEW W WOJNIE
13-letniej.
OBSZAR LENNICI PRUS KRZY-
ŻACKICH od 1466 r.
PODZIAŁKA 1:2.000.000.

TABLE OF CONTENTS

INTRODUCTION

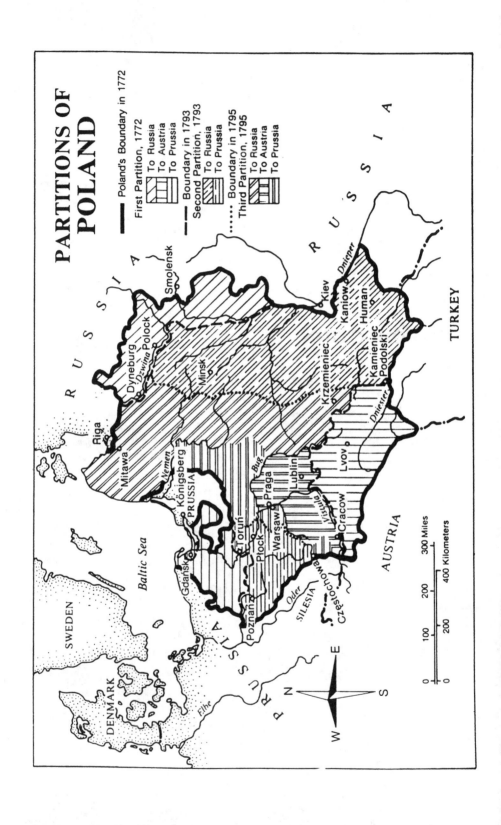

PARTITIONS OF POLAND

— Poland's Boundary in 1772

First Partition, 1772
- To Russia
- To Austria
- To Prussia

- - - Boundary in 1793
Second Partition, 1793
- To Russia
- To Prussia

· · · · Boundary in 1795
Third Partition, 1795
- To Russia
- To Austria
- To Prussia

RUSSIA

RUSSIA

Smolensk

Dyneburg
Dźwina Polock

Minsk

Kiev
Dnieper

Kaniow

Human

Krzemieniec

Kamieniec
Podolski

Dniester

Lvov

Riga

Mitawa

Niemen
Königsberg
PRUSSIA

Bug

Lublin

Toruń

Praga
Warsaw
Vistula

Płock

Poznań

Gdańsk

Oder
SILESIA

Cracow

Częstochowa

Baltic Sea

SWEDEN

DENMARK

Elbe

P R U S S I A

AUSTRIA

TURKEY

| 0 | 100 | 200 | 300 Miles |

| 0 | 200 | 400 Kilometers |

N
W E
S

1

Małgorzata Dymek-Ćwiklińska, Ed.
Editor and Publisher, *GP Light*

WHO OWES WHO?
FIRST POLES IN AMERICA

The only time when there was no need for Poles to emigrate was before 1776, when Poland was free and still strong, and America did not yet exist as a state.

A study of the pre-1776 period would show that, for Poles, America was not just a haven from political and economic oppression inflicted on their country by its neighbors, but that Poles were coming here originally in search of adventure, to satisfy their curiosity about a new continent, and, like the English Pilgrims, to seek religious freedom.

By some counts, there were 21 Polish family names in New Amsterdam alone. Daniel Litscho, whose name was spelled in various fashions but was probably Liczko, served in the rank of sergeant and then as an officer in Governor Peter Stuyvesant's small army before becoming a prosperous and active member of the community. Alexander Carolus Curtius (name also variously spelled, but most probably a Latinized version of Kurcz or Kurczewski), a physician, resided in New Amsterdam chiefly as its first secondary school master. Albert (or Albrecht or Olbracht) Zabriskie (most likely Zaborowski, or perhaps Zborowski) was a land owner and progenitor of a remarkably large and successful clan, and Anthony Sadowski was a frontiersman and pioneer (his sons were companions of the legendary American frontiersman and pioneer, Daniel Boone). They all represent a cross section of early Poles in America: soldiers, educators, landowners and pioneers.

Why should men, representing occupations in which Poland in the 17th century, and even the 18th, still had much to offer, come to America in such meaningful numbers?

The time of the first Polish settlement in Jamestown, Virginia, was also the time of Poland's greatest expansion, culminating in no less than the occupation of Moscow. It does not matter here how ill-fated or how short-lived the occupation was; what matters is that at

3

that time Poland controlled an area larger than the combined settled area of the European colonies in America and that Poland's population was many times larger than the combined European population of America. It was still at least five times larger—approximately ten million to two—before the First Partition of Poland in 1772.

What it all adds up to is the fact, hardly realized today, that before 1776 Poles were coming to America from a large country to a small one, from a nation with established traditions of civil liberties and religious tolerance to a frontier society of great potential but still uncivilized. The idea of America as a land of unlimited opportunities, strongly impressed upon the minds of late 19th-century Polish immigrants, or "a paradise for everybody," as one writer would have it, did not apply to their pre-1776 predecessors for whom having to leave Poland amounted to leaving paradise, not going to one.

Early Polish immigrants to America were, in the main, Protestants. To explain this phenomenon in view of Poland's Catholic tradition, we have to go back to the 16th century, to Poland's Golden Age.

The discovery of America in 1492 coincides roughly with the beginning of Poland's Golden Age, the period of nearly two centuries during which the country was at the zenith of its power and culture. Poland's Golden Age coincides with another event of great significance and importance in world history: the Reformation. While in most European countries the Reformation led to bloody persecutions and religious wars, in Poland its adherents were left undisturbed. Religious freedom under the last two Jagiellonian kings, Zygmunt I and Zygmunt II (August), was such that the Poland of the 16th century was known as Paradisus Hereticorum (a "paradise for heretics").

The Counter-Reformation, ushered in by the Council of Trent (1545-1563) and resulting in the re-establishment of tribunals of the Holy Inquisition in most Catholic countries, did not affect religious freedom in Poland. King Zygmunt August simply refused to sanction in secular courts verdicts passed in ecclesiastical courts, thus assuring continuous safety for the Protestants (Calvinists, Czech Brethren, Lutherans). Their influence was, on the whole, positive, particularly on education and literature. It expressed itself in excellent schools and in the increased use of the vernacular in spoken and written language. Many Polish writers were either Protestant (like the celebrated Mikolaj Rej) or sympathetic to the idea of a reformed church in Poland (like Jan Kochanowski, the greatest poet of the Polish Renaissance). The idea of a reformed national church in Poland was, furthermore, very attractive to the nobility, and even the king was partial to it. Under these circumstances, the Counter-Reformation arrived in Poland just at the right time.

Since violent means to combat Protestantism were out of the question in Poland, the Church resorted to another method: Cardinal Stanisław Hozjusz (Hosius) brought the Jesuit Order to Poland in 1564, after the Council of Trent. The Jesuits began by founding schools to compete with Protestant schools. Not overly concerned with the religious beliefs of the older generation, the Jesuits concentrated on the young; after only one generation they were victorious and Protestantism was on the retreat.

The decline of Protestantism in Poland had other causes beside the Jesuit counteroffensive. A complete Catholic victory came, ironically, during a critical moment in Polish history. While Poland managed to stay away from the Thirty Years War between Catholics and Protestants (1618-1648), it was attacked by anti-Catholic forces following the war's completion, among them the chief Protestant power of that time, Lutheran Sweden (1655). During the protracted war with the Swedes, the Arians ("Polish Brethren") were accused of collaborating with them. Consequently, a law was passed in 1658 banishing the Arians from Poland and severely restricting the other Protestants in their civil liberties, forcing many of them to leave, too. 1658 marks the temporary end of Polish religious toleration and civil liberties, which were not completely restored until 1768, when the Sejm (Diet) granted dissidents equal rights with Catholics. 1658 also marks the first significant exodus of Poles from Poland, an exodus which brought many of them to America.

There is scant literature on the subject of the first Polish exodus. The one work which poignantly depicts the difficulties and hardships the exiles felt, and is thus in keeping with the "Paradise Lost" theme, is to be found in *Nauka Polska* (Polish Scholarship) in an article titled "Anglo-Polonica" by Stanisław Kot. The author describes the considerable contacts of the Polish dissidents abroad, particularly ties in England and Holland. Before 1658, such contacts revolved around plans for a United Protestant Church in Poland; after 1658, they became a matter of survival for the expelled dissidents. We read about their attempts to find protection in England, or simply help;

we read letters asking for alms, or simply begging. But it was not easy to find a suitable situation in England and, failing to do so, many exiles ended up going to America.

This was one route. Another was via Amsterdam, Holland, ending in New Amsterdam, New Holland. There was also a third route to America, via Sweden, for dissidents who left Poland with the defeated Swedes. This route ended in New Sweden. In each case America was receiving educated and often talented men, who were ready to contribute to the new nation's future genius.

Evidence points to the fact that most of the early Polish arrivals to America settled in Protestant-held colonies which, even if they changed hands, remained Protestant, such as New Holland and New Sweden, which were eventually absorbed by the English. There is no evidence of an early Polish presence in Catholic French and Spanish colonies, to the north and south, respectively, an absence which strengthens the Protestant character of early Polish immigration. At any rate, after the Treaty of Paris in 1763, ending the Seven Years War (French and Indian War in America), when "half of the American continent had changed hands at the scratch of the pen," the entire eastern half of North America (east of the Mississippi) came under Protestant English rule.

The new reality in America did not make much difference to Protestants in Poland. In a few years (1768), they were going to have their civil rights and religious freedom restored, and there would be no need for them to emigrate on religious grounds. But the end of religious emigration marked the beginning of political emigration.

In 1768, the Confederacy of Bar began as a reaction against Russia's interference in Poland's internal affairs. One of its leaders was Kazimierz (Casimir) Pulaski, a hero of Poland and soon also of America. His arrival in America was preceded by that of another Polish political émigré and future hero, Tadeusz Kosciuszko. Both contributed, amply and outstandingly, to America's independence, while witnessing the decline and fall of their own country. Pulaski did not witness the fall. He died in battle at Savannah, his death a sacrifice for America but a disaster for Poland. With so many essential Polish contributions and sacrifices, America remains Poland's beneficiary to this day.

This article has been adapted from the "Introduction" to the volume, *Poles in America: Bicentennial Essays*, Frank Mocha, ed., Worzalla Publishing Company, Stevens Point, Wisconsin, 1978.

2

Frank Mocha

A CENTURY OF PROGRESS

1768 is a watershed year in the history of Polish emigration to America. It marks the end of emigration on religious grounds and the beginning of political emigration. Its two first and greatest representatives, Kosciuszko and Pulaski, beside having statues erected in their honor and places and institutions named after them, started a tradition of making America the place to go whenever Poland was in trouble. Kosciuszko himself returned to America (temporarily) after his failed insurrection of 1794. Later catalysts of emigration included the insurrections of November (1830) and January (1863), and, of course, World War II and its aftermath. The idea for these political emigrants was to return to Poland to fight another day. When this became impossible, they merged with others in a new pattern of Polish emigration—economic.

The one man who would have returned to fight another day in Poland but didn't, because he fell in battle in America, was Pulaski, and here it serves a good purpose to engage in a bit of alternate history, the "What If" history so popular nowadays. Had Pulaski lived, he would have joined Kosciuszko in the Insurrection of 1794 and, between them, they would have won. Why would one man have made the difference? There is evidence that Kosciuszko had been approached by the Don Cossacks who proposed that they switch sides and join the Insurrection in exchange for certain privileges, and that he turned them down. For some reason, Kosciuszko did not want to turn the Insurrection into a revolution. Pulaski, a deadly enemy of Russia and an experienced recruiter, would have had no such scruples. The extra help would have made the difference in the close battle of Maciejowice, which would have been won instead of lost, and the stage would have been set for a battle of Warsaw, where the two heroes would have faced the great Suvorov, whom Empress Catherine had recalled from retirement, that's how important the battle was. But the odds would have been different, and that battle, too, could have been won, saving Poland and changing history.

Friedrich Engels, co-author with Marx of the *Communist Manifesto*, is alleged to have said that had Kosciuszko gone all out,

7

encouraging peasant and Cossack risings outside of Poland, particularly in Russia, where the memory of the Pugachev Rebellion was still fresh, he would have brought about a violent downfall of autocratic monarchies in Europe (Pulaski would have been instrumental because he was feared by the monarchs for his attempt to kidnap the Polish king), resulting in the rise of only two states in continental Europe: France and Poland. It did not happen, and history proceeded the way we know it.

Polish emigrants after the January 1863 Insurrection consisted of people leaving for economic reasons. This emigration was a slow but determined century-long progress for a place in the sun, mainly in America. Lack of education was their greatest obstacle, but also their most important need. The new immigrants (more than two million between the 1860's and 1920's) were mostly peasants, and mostly illiterate. To remedy this sad but understandable situation, Polish schools were started almost immediately in Polish parishes. It is a historical fact of some significance that when Poland was entering its darkest period following the January 1863 Insurrection, Polish immigrants in America were beginning their education.

The history of Polish education in America is discussed in two chapters (by Ellen Marie Kuznicki, CSSF, and Thaddeus C. Radzialowski, Ph.D., parochial and higher, respectively) of *Poles in America: Bicentennial Essays*. It is an impressive history. From the first schools: in Panna Maria, Texas (1867 officially, but started earlier); Stevens Point, Wisconsin (1864); Milwaukee, Wisconsin (1868); and Chicago, Illinois (1869), the system grew to a network of 50 schools by 1887, 300 by 1911, and 500 by 1921 educating 219,711 children, while 110,148 Polish children attended American public schools, according to a recent study by Zygmunt Sibiga in Poland. At the same time, there already existed the Cyril and Methodius Polish Seminary in Detroit, Michigan, founded in 1885-1887 (moved to Orchard Lake in 1909) to train Polish priests for Polish parishes.

With time, the number of Polish children in American public schools increased at the expense of the parochial schools. Declining enrollment had to do initially with the primitive conditions of the parochial schools and later with their educational level which, according to some other researchers (Józef Miąso, Andrzej Brożek, Ryszard Kucha) was low. It was raised with the arrival from Poland of the Felician Sisters in 1874 who, together with other teaching Orders, improved the educational level of the parochial schools immensely. But the schools themselves were changing, together with the character of the parishes, which were becoming multi-ethnic. The children themselves began to realize the advantages of going to school where the language of instruction was the language of the dominant culture, English. An outstanding example of this perception is the late JOHN GRONOUSKI.

The American-born economist John Gronouski is a symbol of Polish American achievement, an achievement made even more significant by the extraordinary coincidence that it came exactly a century after the first wave of economic emigration from Poland following the January Insurrection of 1863. In 1963 John Gronouski was chosen by President John F. Kennedy to be Postmaster General.

As a tough-minded administrator he had revamped the Wisconsin tax system. But he had what many saw as an even more important political credential: his Polish background (this is a quote from his obituary in *The New York Times*, January 10, 1996). He was not only the first person of Polish origin to serve in the Cabinet in America, he was also the first Cabinet officer to have earned a Ph.D. in America.

Following his World War II service as an Air Force navigator, Gronouski served America in many prestigious posts, the most significant of them, for the purposes of this essay, as President Johnson's Ambassador to Poland and President Carter's chairman of the Board of International Broadcasting, which ran Radio Free Europe and Radio Liberty. But perhaps the most significant, and symbolic, was his service as President of the Polish Institute of Arts and Sciences in America, an institution founded in 1941 by Polish émigré intellectuals to preserve Polish culture. This was John Gronouski serving Poland.

John Gronouski is a symbol of Polish American achievement in the professions, which took a century to accomplish. It wasn't easy. At the beginning of the process the immigrants worked and their children learned, not without some resistance on the part of their parents, because child labor was quite common among the early Polish immigrants, who sought economic improvement and advantages. They worked for the most part in agriculture and coal mining, and later also in heavy industry (steel and car manufacture). They served in all American wars, beginning with the Civil War in which, however, it was predominantly the veterans of the Polish November 1830 and January 1863 Insurrections who did the fighting, on both sides. In one military action, the ill-advised American intervention in the Russian Revolution (1917), Poles from Michigan were recruited for the American landing in Northern Russia because of their presumed familiarity with the language and adaptability to the terrain and its severe climate.

Thus, the Polish economic immigrants and their descendants were becoming part of America: as farmers helping to feed the rapidly growing population; as builders of industry working as coal miners, car makers, and steel workers; and, most importantly, as defenders of America, serving in disproportionate numbers to protect its interests and in the process becoming Polish Americans.

Their social life revolved around and within the parish and it is no wonder that their first organization was the Polish Roman Catholic Union of America (PRCU), founded in 1873, when the number of Polish immigrants in America was estimated at 200,000. At its peak, the PRCU alone had more than 200,000 members organized in hundreds of lodges across the United States, and considerable assets. Among its many social, humanitarian, patriotic and educational causes was laying the foundations for St. Mary's College, which still exists at Orchard Lake, Michigan.

The 1880's, a remarkable decade in the evolution of the Polish American ethnic group, gave rise to another organization, the Polish National Alliance of the United States of North America (PNA) which, from modest beginnings grew into the largest and the most influential fraternal organization of Americans of Polish descent. Among its multitude of activities and accomplishments, too numerous to be discussed in this chapter, its proudest achievement was the founding of Alliance College, whose opening ceremonies in 1912 were attended by US President William H. Taft, and whose director in 1920-1928 was a well-known Polish historical novelist, Wacław Gąsiorowski. The college closed down in 1987 for lack of students.

Another remarkable organization should be mentioned here, the Polish Women's Alliance of America (PWA), founded in 1898-1899 in Chicago. It became a nationwide Polish women's association with about 80,000 members at its peak. From the beginning of its existence, the PWA dedicated itself primarily to a woman's role as custodian and guardian of Polish family life, a dedication which could be very important if applied to family life in Poland now.

A special mention must be made of an organization which originated not in America but in Poland in 1867, and whose offshoot reached these shores 20 years later, namely the Polish Falcons. Because of their dedication to the liberation of Poland, most of their members volunteered for military service in France when America entered World War I, and served in Gen. Haller's "Blue Army" first in France and then in Poland, contributing to its liberation.

After the liberation of Poland, following the war among its partitioners that Polish poets and patriots had prayed for since the loss of independence, a whole new area of cooperation between Poland and American Polonia opened up, spearheaded by the Polish Falcons on the battlefield and continued by new institutions in the cultural field. The new contacts were coordinated by the World Alliance of Poles Abroad (Światowy Związek Polaków z Zagranicy) in Poland and by The Kosciuszko Foundation in America. But the contacts were short-lived just as Poland's independence, which was ended after barely two decades by the outbreak of World War II when Germany invaded Poland in September 1939.

World War II was the biggest catastrophe for Poland in its entire history. Yet, as if to compensate for the threatening extinction of the nation at home, it was a "good war" for the Polish Americans, as will be seen, when America entered the war two years later.

The threatening extinction triggered a massive exodus from Poland, first of soldiers for the new Polish Armed Forces in France and, after the fall of France in 1940, to England; and then also of intellectuals, some of whom reached America in 1941. The latter exodus can be compared to the "Great Emigration" of 1831. True, there was no Mickiewicz this time, but there were poets like Wierzyński, Tuwim, Lechoń, and Wittlin; there was no Lelewel or Prince Czartoryski, but there were Halecki, Lednicki, and others, who joined the world's foremost anthropologist, Bronislaw Malinowski, already here, and founded the Polish Institute of Arts and Sciences, dedicated to the preservation of Polish learning after the German onslaught. The Kosciuszko Foundation, founded earlier, was very helpful in this endeavor, as was also the Joseph Pilsudski Institute, founded later (1943).

By then, Germany was beginning to lose the war, first in North Africa and then in the Soviet Union, and as the victorious Soviet armies were approaching Poland, there was strong apprehension among Poles everywhere about the fate of their homeland. The Soviet Union was, after all, a co-aggressor with Germany in 1939. An uneasy ally when itself attacked in 1941, it broke the alliance and withdrew recognition from the Polish Government-in-Exile in London at the first opportunity (the Katyn Forest massacre controversy). Then there was the highly ambiguous behavior when the Soviet armies reached the Vistula in the summer of 1944. They watched, from across the river, the heroic romantic Warsaw Uprising, and the methodical and nearly total destruction of the city by the Germans, without lifting a finger in its defense. It was at this point that American Polonia came to the aid of Poland for the second time, or at least intended to, this time by organizing itself into the Polish American Congress (PAC).

The main stimulus for the rise of the Polish American Congress, which was to consist of representatives of all Polish organizations in America and thus become a potent instrument of political pressure, was the restoration of free and independent Poland, a goal by no means certain. There was much ignorance in the Polish circles about the agreements reached by Roosevelt, Churchill, and Stalin in their Allied summit conferences, first in Teheran (1943) and then at Yalta (1944), agreements concerning Poland, the fourth biggest contributor to the war effort and, because of that, deserving a fair treatment, especially by England. Poland was England's *only* ally during the Battle of Britain in 1940, when Polish pilots contributed decisively to winning it. Polish soldiers and sailors were present in all the theaters of combat. As the war was turning around in favor of the Allies, the presence of large Polish forces in England was becoming an inconvenience souring its relations with the Soviet Union, which wanted to play down Poland's contributions. Against this background, the "accidental" death of the Polish Prime Minister, the highly regarded General Władysław Sikorski, in an air crash in Gibraltar in 1943, looks highly suspicious.

The Polish American Congress did not have the knowledge and experience to gauge the power plays. Its first President, Karol Rozmarek, trusted Roosevelt, who had assured him during a Chicago stop in his reelection campaign in 1944 that Poland would be free and independent. Rozmarek did not know that in a private meeting at the Teheran conference the previous year, Roosevelt had agreed with Stalin that the Soviet Union should keep the eastern part of Poland it had annexed in 1939.

Roosevelt needed the Polish vote (about its strength Stalin had allegedly warned him at Teheran), but he also wanted to secure Soviet help in the war with Japan, hence the concessions to Stalin, confirmed later at the Yalta Conference which placed East Central Europe in the Soviet sphere of influence. Whether the Polish American Congress should have talked with the other Presidential candidate, Thomas Dewey, who is alleged to have said that there would have been no Yalta had he been elected, is debatable, since there is no record of Dewey courting the Polish vote.

When the Soviet armies entered Poland they installed a Provisional Polish Government first in Lublin, where it was at first called a "Committee," and then in Warsaw. The promised coalition government never materialized, and neither did the promised free elections. As the war ended, Poland was ruled by Communists, including briefly a Soviet Marshal (Rokossowski), a situation which with some tremors prevailed for 45 years, with incalculable damage to the Polish national character and traditional Polish values.

When the war in Europe ended, it left about a quarter of a million Polish servicemen stranded in the West, not to mention an army division interned in Switzerland (the II Division from the 1940 French campaign), former inmates of prisoner-of-war camps (including POW's from the 1939 Polish September campaign), and former inmates from labor and concentration camps (one of the latter, Zbigniew Kruszewski, eventually became Vice-President of the Polish American Congress). Most of them returned to Poland, the rest either remained in England or emigrated to Canada, South America, South Africa, Australia, and Pakistan (Polish pilots built the Pakistani Air Force), with the majority, including this writer, going to the United States, courtesy of Senator Henry Cabot Lodge Jr.'s special amendment to the US Immigration Law admitting 20,000 Polish ex-servicemen.

The saga of the Polish ex-servicemen in America deserves a separate study. Suffice it to say that some joined an already existing (since World War I) veteran organization, the Polish Army Veterans Association of America; others organized a new association, a namesake of the London-based Polish Combatants Association. Their vitality was such that together with Polish ex-servicemen from all over the world they took part in 1992 in a World Reunion of Polish Combatants in Poland, *post-Communist Poland*, marching in Warsaw's Victory Square before President Lech Wałęsa and other dignitaries, as well as the applauding public. The reunion (the last hurrah of a dying breed), still 10,000 strong almost half a century after the war, is, in the opinion of this writer and participant, unparalleled in the annals of military history.

But it is in the educational field that the ex-servicemen left the most beneficial mark.

Education was a password in postwar America, as it was also for the newly-arrived Poles. Professional soldiers with officer training in Poland now sought a civilian profession, among them Włodzimierz Drzewieniecki, a true soldier's soldier who, as a young officer in Poland, stood guard by the catafalque of Marshal Pilsudski in 1935. He now entered the University of Chicago, earned a doctorate in East European History and went on to teach at the State University of New York in Buffalo. Those who had completed their higher education in Poland, now sought an American doctorate, among them Marian Dziewanowski, who earned it in Russian an East Central European History at Harvard University and went on to teach at Boston University and at the University of Wisconsin, Milwaukee. There were others, all supported by various scholarships and all following in the footsteps of established scholars from the Polish Institute of Arts and Sciences who were already teaching: Oskar Halecki, Polish and East European History, Fordham University; Waclaw Lednicki, Polish and Russian Literature, University of California, Berkeley; Wiktor Weintraub, Polish and Russian Literature, Harvard University. They were all strengthening the Polish presence at American universities, and attracting students from the Polish American community: both Eugene Kusielewicz, the future President of the Kosciuszko Foundation, and Thaddeus Gromada, the future Secretary General of the Polish Institute of Arts and Sciences, were doctoral students of Professor Halecki at Fordham.

Three more chairs of Polish were created: at the University of Pennsylvania, Philadelphia; at Pennsylvania State University, College Park; and at the University of Wisconsin, Madison, occupied by Professors Giergielewicz, Birkenmeyer, and Zawacki, respectively. All three are dead now, making it difficult to verify their respective backgrounds. There was also a chair of Polish at Columbia University, New York, occupied by Professor Manfred Kridl but funded by the Polish Communist Government, a move which led to the resignation of Professor Arthur Coleman, the future President of Alliance College at Cambridge Springs, Pennsylvania. Columbia University had a lively Polish Students Club, frequented among others by the poets Wierzynski and Lechon. One of the Club's members, Albina Swierzbinska, is still active today.

A special mention must be made of the late Professor Ludwik Krzyżanowski, a symbolic figure in many respects. A non-combatant because he was on a Kosciuszko Foundation scholarship in America when the war broke out, he later taught Polish at the Monterey Language School in California before moving to New York to become the Editor-in-Chief (lifetime, as it turned out) of *The Polish Review*, a quarterly published by the Polish Institute of Arts and Sciences, where Krzyżanowski also became its Secretary General and Secretary of its Literary Section. Beside these duties, he also taught East Central Europe Area Studies at New York University, and Polish at Columbia University. One of his students, Joseph Wieczerzak, is the current Editor-in-Chief of *The Polish Review*.

Then there were those who entered specialties that were not Poland-centered, such as law (Wieńczysław Wagner) or sociology (Richard Kolm and Eugene Kleban). Kleban became Executive Director of the Polish Institute of Arts and Sciences during the ethnic awakening in America, when sociology became important for Polish Americans.

The drive for education and professions among the ex-servicemen was praiseworthy and beneficial, but it involved only a small number of them. For the rest there was the problem of finding employment, which was not easy because of language difficulties, resulting in low-level jobs such as elevator operators, doormen or porters, and as assembly line workers in factories. Only with improvement in language skills was the road open to better jobs.

My own experience was at first a compromise between the scholars and the workers, but with a difference. Having studied for two years after the war under a British grant in a London university and then married an English girl, I was fluent in English when I arrived in America. Because of that, I wanted it all: business, academics, and family. As quoted in a *New York Times* column (David Gonzales, "Silver Zlotys And a Dream Of America," July 6, 1996), I wanted to be a success in the American sense.

Out of these strivings for success, and direction, there emerges a picture of the remarkable decade of the 1950's, not only in America, but also in Poland, where I kept in touch with my relatives, and in England, where I kept in touch with old friends. These strivings make the narrative more palpable, but also very extensive, which would affect the structure of the book and detract from its main purpose. For this reason I had decided to place my personal experience at the end of the book, as an appendix, but when it became too extensive, to publish it separately as a book, with the title *One Man's Saga*, submitted to Farrar, Straus & Giroux and Twayne Publishers for consideration.

• • • •

In my personal strivings I never lost sight of the wider view, of Polish America, and I gradually became a chronicler of its accomplishments and progress. Of great interest to me was the participation of Polish Americans in the G.I. Bill, which after World War II was sending a whole generation of veterans to college and pointing them to a brighter future. To what extent Polish American veterans took advantage of the G.I. Bill would be an apt subject for research by the Polish American Historical Association, or the Polish Institute of Arts and Sciences.

Called the "good war" by Studs Terkel because it not only ended the Depression but provided Americans with an upward mobility, the Second World War afforded that same mobility to Polish Americans. To what extent that mobility was facilitated by the G.I. Bill is a question whose answer would tell us whether Polish Americans were getting their due or had to rely on their own resources to get ahead.

To answer this question, I did some occasional investigating on my own. When I first visited Columbia University I was astonished to see the campus dotted with Quonset huts housing the former G.I.'s and turning the campus into a veritable army camp, where the ex-soldiers had their studies financed by the G.I. Bill. That Columbia was a magnet for the soldiers because its new President was their former Commander-in-Chief, General Dwight D. Eisenhower, seemed reasonable, but it was more likely that similar situations prevailed on all campuses across the nation, with Columbia simply more conspicuous on account of its new President. As I walked among the huts talking to the G.I.s, some of whom still had their uniforms on, asking and looking for Polish American G.I.'s among them, I did not find a single one. Whether the situation was different on other campuses I was not able to find out.

On the other hand I found one Polish American with a G.I. Bill loan for business. He was a captain, whose father owned a small printing place downtown near William Street. When the son returned from the war, he took over the business, but decided to expand, leaving his father in charge of the composing room, and securing a G.I. loan. The captain reminded me of Fred, the soda-jerk turned captain in the movie "The Best Years of Our Lives." Unlike Fred, who took longer to find his future via the demeaning return to his old soda-jerk job (and would no doubt be securing a G.I. loan for his prefabricated housing business from his father-in-law, Al, a G.I. and a prime example of post-war upward mobility in the movie), the Polish American captain acted faster, which tells us something about his resolve.

While the traditional occupations (farming, coal mining, factory jobs) still applied to most of the Polish Americans after World War II, men who returned from the war as officers or even NCO's were not likely to return to the Ford assembly line in Detroit. If they didn't go to school they would start their own business, expand their father's (like the captain), or buy land with G.I. loans (like the ex-serviceman Novak in "The Best Years of Our Lives" who so impressed Al, vice-president for loans in the bank, with his resolve, that the latter accepted it as collateral).

Others would enter sports, and here something remarkable was taking place. While "gentleman" Frank Parker, America's top tennis player, was still hiding his Polish name, Pajkowski, when he represented America at Wimbledon in 1948, this was not the case when the Polish Americans made their assault on baseball, America's pastime. Soon the likes of Stan Musial (St. Louis), Carl Yastrzemski (Boston) and Bill Mazeroski (Pittsburgh), took the place of Babe Ruth, Lou Gehrig and Joe DiMaggio as America's idols. As for America's other pastime, football, Polish Americans had dominated it since even earlier. Bigger and heavier than their fathers and grandfathers, they excelled both as professionals (Bronko Nagurski, America's first football hero, of the Chicago Bears, and Dick Modzelewski of the New York Giants) and in college football (Heisman trophy winners Vic Janowicz of Ohio State and Johnny Lujack, who won fame at Notre Dame, football's cradle).

There is a well-known anecdote about Notre Dame, where the football immortal Knut Rockne (the inventor of the forward pass) was said to have remarked when trying out new players: "If their names end with -ski don't even try them out, take them." This would indicate that second- and third-generation Polish Americans were prime candidates for coveted athletic scholarships, and in good colleges, too. But it was George Halas, an NFL founder and Chicago Bears' coach, who made it in the managerial ranks of football.

It was not only in sports that Polish Americans excelled. Many served in politics with distinction, among them Clement Zablocki, Congressman from Wisconsin, who was greatly respected in Washington, as was, until recently, Dan Rostenkowski, Congressman from Chicago. Ed Derwinski, another Congressman from Chicago, was later elevated to Secretary of the Department of Veterans Affairs, a Cabinet post under President Bush. Another Cabinet post, even earlier, under President Carter, was occupied by Zbigniew Brzezinski, the National Security Adviser. Polish Americans also headed the Federal Reserve Bank (M.S. Szymczak) and the Small Business Administration (Mitch Kobelinski).

Two more names ought to be mentioned: Jankowski and Jaworski. The former was an eminent executive who had climbed the American corporate ladder to become President of CBS; the latter, a peerless jurist about whom the transplanted Polish-Jewish writer and intellectual, Leopold Tyrmand, wrote admiringly in a brilliant Op-Ed article ("Jaworski and Sirica") in *The New York Times* in connection with the Watergate affair.

But perhaps the most outstanding Polish American next to the late John Gronouski or even more so, was Edmund Muskie. Their passing on so close together marks the end of an era of political prominence for Polish Americans. Muskie was the first Polish American Governor of a state (Maine), then a Senator and, briefly, Secretary of State in Carter's administration. Widely respected for the qualities of his character and supported by a growing influential segment of America, including the writer James Michener, Muskie was an important Presidential candidate until he was derailed by President Nixon's infamous hatchet men in 1972.

Muskie belonged to a brilliant post-war flowering of Polish American talent, in sports, business, law, and politics. To the last all-important segment of America belonged also young Roman Pucinski, a rising Congressman from Chicago until he was talked by Mayor Daley into running for Senate against an unbeatable incumbent. There was also the bearer of an anglicized name, Thomas Gordon, chairman of Congressional Foreign Affairs Committee, a very important post regarding Poland. But none was as respected and as popular as Thaddeus Ma(j)chrowicz, "gentleman from Michigan," as

Congressman and then a member of the state's Supreme Court. A legal scholar, he was the author of treatises on the Oder-Neisse line (Odra-Nysa) as a new border between Poland and Germany protecting Poland's interests and reflecting new realities.

Most are gone now, dead or retired (except that "Stan the Man" Musial served a term after retirement from baseball as President Johnson's Commissioner of Sports). Of those still in office, the formerly prominent Barbara Mikulski, Senator from Maryland, is rarely if at all heard from, and Frank Murkowski of Alaska (like Muskie in Maine serving as Governor and Senator but in reverse order) is surrounded by controversy concerning his environmental policies. Only Zbigniew Brzezinski is active nationally and globally (Kobelinski, active locally in Chicago, died in 1998), both as an eminent professor and a universally regarded writer and commentator on world affairs, but he is approaching 70 and already slowing down. When he falls silent, Polish Americans will have reached a new low. There is only one way this low can be avoided.

There is a persistent rumor that Jack Kemp, Bob Dole's running mate as the Republican Vice-Presidential candidate, is of Polish descent. It doesn't matter if he does not identify with the Polish American ethnic group, the fact that out of this group came a man on the scale of Muskie, but far stronger because he arrived by way of football as a star quarterback of the Buffalo Bills, would in itself be a success story emblematically reflecting the rise of that group. There is much symbolism in this, and should the rumor be based on fact it would go a long way toward restoring to Polish Americans their sense of accomplishment, which is usually ignored, and expose the way the Polish Americans are taken for granted, except in an election year.

American Polonia has been too big to be taken for granted. Its numerical strength is something to reckon with. Stalin pointed it out to Roosevelt in Teheran on the eve of the American Presidential elections, but it was the Kennedys who paid proper attention to it. During the Presidential campaign in 1960, the Kennedys, in an effort to determine the strength of the Polish vote and to decide whether to go after it—especially after acquiring a Polish brother-in-law, Prince Radziwill—went to the expensive trouble of counting the potential vote. The figures were published in *The New York Times* and showed that the number of Poles in America was then between 9 and 13 million. We should be grateful to the Kennedys because their figures were larger than most official statistics, including the census. By projecting the Kennedy figures, allowing for normal increase, one can arrive at a more believable estimate. I did just that for my book *Poles in America* in 1976, arriving at between 12 and 17 million (p. 728).

That was twenty years ago. Yet, during all that time the figure most often heard and quoted defined the American Polonia as 10-million strong. But Polish descent is a more inclusive term. The Kennedys knew it, and that knowledge won the Presidency for them. It seems that the Clintons, the Kennedys' wannabe clones, have learned from them. The presence of Poland's First Lady in the White House on the eve of the 1996 Democratic Convention must surely have been calculated to win Polish American votes.

It is important to keep the population figures accurate in view of what has been happening in Poland in that respect since independence in 1989. Ten years earlier, at the II Congress of Scholars of Polish Descent in Warsaw and Cracow, I was able to make a statement, unchallenged and echoed, that "one third of the Polish nation lives abroad, mostly in America." This was 1979, the year Poland regained its pre-war population of 35 million-plus.

The population kept increasing in Poland during the Solidarity period and even during the darkest years of martial law, reaching one of the highest birthrates in the world. When Bill Kurtis, CBS's ace reporter, visited Poland during martial law to make a videotaped film and then write a book (*Bill Kurtis: On Assignment*, Rand McNally & Company, 1983), in which he quotes many statistics, the birthrate statistic must have worried him, particularly that "there were 700,000 births in Poland in 1982," on which he commented that this was "an unwanted explosion in a country with a chronic food shortage" (p. 188).

The truth is it was not "an unwanted explosion" but a defense mechanism with which the nation has defended its existence in times of danger. Once the danger has passed, the mechanism stopped. In the late 1980's, with independence in the air, the birthrate in Poland began to decline, and it keeps declining, approaching zero growth. Poland is expected to have a population of only 39 million in the year 2000 and even that is unlikely. By contrast, in 1939 Poland had expected to have a population of 40 million by 1950, equal to France. Incidentally, just as Polish Americans are too modest about their numbers, the Poles in Poland are too optimistic. For years now,

Poland has been referred to as a nation of 40 million people, and not only by the Poles. Gorbachev liked to call Poland "the most populous country outside the Soviet Union in the Warsaw Pact." This is no longer so, one republic of the former Soviet Union, Ukraine, is more populous than Poland, and the 40-million nation is a myth, and will remain so unless a way is found to reverse the threatening depopulation of the country.

In the year 2000 Poland is more likely to be a nation not of 39 million but less than the present 38 million. By then, the Polish American population should be well over 20-million strong. Adding to it Polish communities in other Western Hemisphere countries (Canada, Brazil, Argentina), in West European countries (Germany, France, Belgium, Great Britain), and republics of the former Soviet Union with sizable Polish minorities (Russia, Kazakhstan, Ukraine, Belarus, Lithuania), I estimate a Polish diaspora well over 30 million and passing the home country early in the 21st century, when more than half of the Polish nation will be living abroad, mostly in America. This is something for Polish Americans to think about in order to raise their level of excellence and professionalism to meet the many challenges that the new reality will create, and which in some respects are already presenting themselves.

As if in support of this thinking, Polish names are again popping up in the media, just like after World War II, and again in sports, not baseball and football so much this time, but rather ice hockey and women's figure skating, with the legendary Wayne Gretzky, the best hockey player of all time, and young Tara Lipinski, on her way to become the world's best, topping the list of Polish names.

In one branch of popular culture, entertainment, a polka ensemble has won a Grammy Award, a sign that the music is being taken seriously. More importantly, Polish names appear as finalists in science competitions like Westinghouse and their bearers are recruited by leading colleges as indicated in a survey of "The Harvard Class of '00" by Bruce Weber, in which Anna Fudacz was featured, looking very Polish and sharing the front cover of *The New York Times Magazine* (April 28, 1996) with three other students.

Two names must be mentioned here, of writers and artists who would have brought much pride to the Polish American community even if only as bearers of Polish names had they not died prematurely. One, the writer Charles Bukowski (not to be confused with

Anthony Bukoski who often writes for *GP Light*), greatly admired by the American counter-culture as well as by the German director Barbet Schroeder, who made a successful movie out of Bukowski's novel *Bar Fly*; the other, David Wojnarowicz, a writer in the style of Jack Kerouac, and a painter. Both were part of the American mainstream but not as firmly as Jerzy Kosinski, who had greater exposure (books and media).

Early in 1996, while recovering from a bout with pneumonia, I gave myself an easy assignment of jotting down from *The New York Times* Polish names with jobs in the American mainstream. I was astonished at the number of names and the variety of jobs. Just a few examples: Mike Okhrent, theater director—"Big"; James Urbaniak, stage actor; David C. Wrobel, lawyer for Catherine Deneuve; Angel Kosinsky, actor in "Eye for An Eye"; Barbara Wilck, writer for *New York Magazine*; Garth H. Drabinsky, theatrical producer; Jules Olitski, painterly drawings; Lewis Bogacil, AMC's director of original programming; Mike Krzyzewski, the well-known Duke basketball coach; Joseph Helewicz, a spokesman for Brown & Williamson Tobacco Company; David Kocieniewski, a *New York Times* reporter (Pope's visit); Paul Kaminski, the Pentagon's top acquisition officer; Kris Janowski, spokesman in Bosnia for the UN High Commissioner for Refugees; Dan Kozlowski, chief of the cargo plane program at McDonnell Douglas; Robert Lipka, arrested for spying for the Soviet Union in the 1960's; Lawrence A. Sowinski, a naval historian and the Intrepid Museum's Executive Director; Jeffrey Gural, president of Newmark & Company, the owners of the Paramount Building.

The last name on my list was Jude Wanninski (8/11), identified briefly in the *Times* as Jack Kemp's supply sidekick. In view of what is said about Jack Kemp above, it is a good name to finish the list and the chapter, with the final thought that people on the list know who they are: their names tell them.

Part I

ORGANIZATIONAL STRUCTURE OF POLONIA

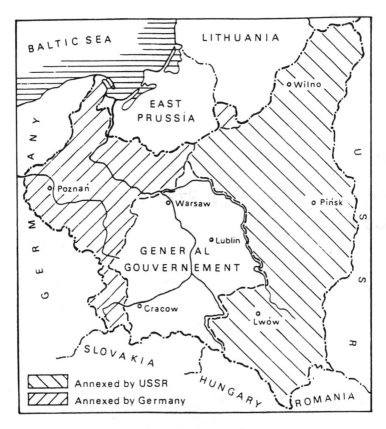

Poland in October 1939

3

Frank Mocha

THE POLISH AMERICAN CONGRESS (PAC)
A PERSONAL VIEW*

In the New World Order which America has been imposing since the disintegration of the Soviet Union in 1991 (and Poland became part of after the dissolution of the Warsaw Pact in 1989 resulting in independence) and the almost simultaneous "Desert Storm" war in the Persian Gulf, Polish Americans have to rethink their traditional concerns vis-à-vis Poland, as practiced by the organization representing them, the Polish American Congress, which, in turn, has to rethink its attitude toward its own community.

As discussed in the previous chapter, the Polish American Congress was established in 1944 to protect Poland against Soviet post-war designs, an admirable idea, but impossible to carry out. Poland remained Polonia's chief concern for the entire period of Communist rule to the neglect of almost everything else. Fifty years after the establishment of the Polish American Congress, Polish Americans are taking up Poland's cause again. This time the PAC is championing membership in NATO, a highly uncertain proposition,

---

* There are good reasons why this chapter was written from a personal point of view. First, this is a book of ideas, not a collection of facts and figures, which can be found in other books. As a book of ideas, which are personal creations, it calls for a first-person narrative, in which the "I" is no longer frowned upon but has the blessing of no less an authority than the Publication of the Modern Language Association (PMLA, October, 1996).

Second, the ideas, from "Casimir Pulaski University" to the "Certificate in Polish," were of such magnitude that writing about them from the distance of a third-person narrative would not convey the euphoria or drama that had gone into them. Adding details from everyday life meant to show that the person working on the ideas was not a fanatic but a normal family man enjoying food, music, and sports, and expressing the enjoyment in his own voice.

Some of the activities are described in greater detail than necessary for the purposes of the book and properly belong in the *One Man's Saga* companion book if or when it is continued beyond the projected first volume's time span (1951-1959), which is by no means certain, in which case this chapter is the best place for them, if only because of its location—mainly in Chicago.

and probably not needed in the absence of any clear threat to Poland, whose needs are more acute in health, education, and the environment.

Examples of neglect of the Polish American community were quite frequent during the tenure of PAC's first two presidents, Karol Rozmarek and Aloysius Mazewski, beginning with the case of Private Slovik.

In my Conclusion to *Poles in America*, bearing in mind the occupations the great masses of Polish immigrants entered upon landing on these shores, I called them "farmers," helping to feed a growing America; "builders of industry," as coal miners, car makers, and steelworkers; and, most importantly, "defenders of America," serving in greatly disproportionate numbers in every American war since Independence. There is an unintended irony in the last label, if one considers that the only American soldier tried and shot for desertion since the Civil War was a Polish American, Eddie Slovik, in the Second World War.

The late-1944 case of Private Slovik (the name means "nightingale" in Polish) still raises questions mainly because of its date, which coincides with the establishment of the Polish American Congress. This means that when President Roosevelt was seducing PAC's President Rozmarek with promises about the future of Poland, Private Slovik was being sacrificed. In a desertion-prone army of raw recruits, Slovik was to serve as an example and a warning, a sacrificial lamb, when one word on his behalf from Rozmarek to Roosevelt would have saved him.

Why was Slovik not defended by the Polish American Congress? Was Rozmarek simply in awe of Roosevelt to such an extent that he did not dare to make any demands? Yet, he was the head of an umbrella organization for the by-then multi-million Polish American community which since the 1880's had four big fraternals plus a network of smaller organizations and parishes stretching from Panna Maria in Texas to New Britain in Connecticut and representing big votes. Roosevelt wanted the votes so badly that he would have ordered Eisenhower to commute Slovik's sentence.

Yet, Private Slovik was not defended (at least not until after the fact), as if the life of a confused Polish boy meant nothing. Only his mother stood by him from the beginning, just like another mother in another case at about the same time, that of Frank Wiecek, who was tried for murder and sentenced on false testimony, and was languishing in jail. He was lucky. His mother, a cleaning woman, saved all her money to keep the case alive until it was picked up by a big newspaper reporter who proved him innocent. The case stirred enough interest to be made into a movie, "Call Northside 777" (1948), with James Stewart as the reporter, and Richard Conte playing Frank Wiecek. The movie shows some of the seamy sides of Polish Chicago and makes no secret that the false testimony was given by a Polish American woman from that milieu.

Under Aloysius Mazewski, President of the Polish American Congress after Rozmarek, the neglect of the Polish American community was of a different kind, concerning Polonia's wider interests and its standing in America. The most outstanding example in this respect was the failure of the Congress to mark in a meaningful way the approaching Bicentennial of America, by summing up the Polish contributions to this country, contributions going back even beyond the well-known participation of Kosciuszko and Pulaski in the War of Independence. There was talk of commissioning a historian for the project, but whether the young man, who will remain unnamed here, was not up to it, or the Congress was not pursuing it seriously, the project came to nothing. It fell to the present writer to take it up and do it, and do it in a big way.

As it happens I was teaching at that time at New York University a sequence of courses dealing with the Bicentennial, courses which the university permitted me to introduce, "Poles in America: A Bicentennial View," which as far as I know were the only courses on that subject in America. To prepare myself, I read at the Polish Institute of Arts and Sciences, where I was active at that time, its entire set of *Polish American Studies*, a publication of the Polish American Historical Association (PAHA), and all the literature on ethnicity available then. I also had guest speakers, among them Mazewski, who however delegated the task at the last moment to Magda Ratajski from the PAC's Washington office, and she gave a great talk about the Polish American Congress. She had the potential to become its President, according to the then-Vice President, Kazimierz Łukomski.

The NYU courses, the second of which was widely supported with tuition scholarships by the Polish American community including the Polish National Alliance of Brooklyn and the Polish American Congress, New York Division, introduced something new in university teaching: its guest speakers were recruited from both

academic and non-academic circles, which means that next to speakers like Ludwik Krzyżanowski, Eugene Kusielewicz, Stanley Blejwas
and Maria Święcicki, there were Henry Archacki, Col. Anthony
Podbielski, Edward Pinkowski, and Walter Zachariasiewicz, who
were invited in recognition of their knowledge or expertise. It was
this breadth of talent, suddenly available, and the fact that the course
was recognized by the City of New York as an official Bicentennial
event with a special Certificate issued, that gave me the idea for the
Poles in America book.

As for Magda Ratajski, who was the most impressive of the
speakers (Madeleine Albright reminds me of her today in some
respects) even if very young and only a substitute for Aloysius
Mazewski, her subsequent departure from PAC's Washington office
represented a serious shortcoming of the Polish American Congress:
its inability to hold on to a talented employee by providing her with
a salary she needed and deserved.

Once the decision on the book had been made—not an easy
decision, since it amounted to a digression from my doctoral and
post-doctoral research on Polish-Russian literary relations—I
approached Mazewski, whom I had met at a ceremony at West Point
honoring Kosciuszko, with a request of support for the book project.
He handed me the text of the speech about Kosciuszko he had just
delivered. When I pointed out that it was not the support I had in
mind, that the Kosciuszko (and Pulaski) assignment had already been
given to Dr. Metchie Budka, Mazewski's speech ended up in the
hands of Bolesław Wierzbiański, editor of the Polish *Daily News*
(*Nowy Dziennik*), where it properly belonged, and a meeting about
the extent of PAC's support of *Poles in America* with Kazimierz
Łukomski was scheduled in Chicago, where I was coming to discuss
a job offer with the Chicago branch of the University of Illinois.

By then my NYU courses and the emerging book had made me
into a national figure, and a one-man institution in a sense. My office
at the Polish Institute in New York became a hub of editorial and
promotional activity, including an interview with J. Dubicki of the
Nowy Dziennik for a biographical essay (published June 6, 1976)
and with Tom Buckley of *The New York Times* for his "About New
York" column. The column, entitled "The Revival of a Heritage,"
announcing the book, was published on June 23, 1976, virtually on
the eve of the Bicentennial, resulting in an avalanche of mail, including an enthusiastic letter and an order for 20 copies from Mrs. Lewis

S. (Blanka) Rosenstiel, President of The American Institute of Polish Culture, Inc., in Miami, Florida. The book was, in effect, launched, and heading for success on its own momentum.

The initial momentum had been provided by two $500 contributions to the book's publishing fund, from the always helpful Joseph Głowacki, President of the Polish National Alliance of Brooklyn, and Dr. Eugene Kusielewicz, President of the Kosciuszko Foundation, enabling me to open a bank account for the book.

The help of the Kosciuszko Foundation was crucial. Not only did Dr. Kusielewicz agree to be part of the book by contributing an essay about the Foundation (on its 25th anniversary) he also suggested another author, his doctoral student at St. John's University, Zofia Sywak (a Ukrainian who wrote about Ignace Paderewski). But it was his decision to insert an announcement of the book in the Foundation's mail to members, resulting in an unprecedented 50% return, which made the book a bestseller in the K.F. Bookstore for years, aside from other bookstores. A different kind of help came from Kusielewicz's assistant, Mary Van Starrex, whose knowledge of the members resulted in four contributions from the new generation of native Polonian scholars, among them Anthony J. Kuzniewski, S.J. and Theodore Zawistowski, who wrote about the Church (Roman Catholic and Polish National, respectively); and Sister Ellen Marie Kuznicki, CSSF, and Thaddeus C. Radzialowski, who wrote about Polish American schools (parochial and higher, respectively). Together they make up Part II of the book: RELIGION AND EDUCATION, the most symmetrical part of the book.

By the time of my meeting with the Polish American Congress in Chicago, represented by its Vice President, Kazimierz Łukomski, the book was already well on its way. In addition to Gene Kusielewicz, two other guest lecturers from the course had been invited to become part of it: the knowledgeable Walter Zachariasiewicz, writing about the organizational structure of Polonia, and Edward Pinkowski, perhaps the most thorough researcher of its early history. Other essays, in addition to those secured with the help of Mary Van Starrex, were to come from personal acquaintances: the Yale historian Piotr Wandycz ("The United States and Poland: An Attempt at Historical Synthesis"); the tireless researcher Maria J.E. Copson-Niećko; the sociologist and anthropologist Konstantin Symmons-Symonolewicz; the young journalist Bernard Pacyniak; the eminent librarian and translator Jerzy (George) J. Maciuszko; the recently arrived musicologist from Poland Leon Thaddeus Blaszczyk; the former diplomat Michael Budny (the Jozef Pilsudski Institute), and myself.

Łukomski was clearly impressed by my report and handed me a check for $1,000 which he had on him, the judgment having been apparently left to him whether to give it to me or not. The money was an advance payment for a 100 copies of the book, an arrangement which was entirely satisfactory to me. It made the Polish American Congress one of the sponsors of the book, as duly noted in its ACKNOWLEDGEMENTS, a 6-page document listing all sponsors, all advance purchasers, and all who helped, including my students and family members who helped with the INDEX.

I told Łukomski, with whom I had established a good rapport, that as a result of my success in New York, I was the top candidate for the only two faculty positions in America for Polish that year, one in Michigan and the other in Chicago, and that I had chosen Chicago, where the book would be finished and the Polish American Congress would receive the first copies. This was my last contact with the Congress until I started teaching in Chicago.

The Poles in New York did not relish my departure, and those in Michigan my choice of Chicago, but there were things about the city that attracted me, beside the fact that it was the capital of Polonia, and therefore a proper place for my energy, as Łukomski had pointed out. As for the university, its modern campus attracted me too, to my surprise, because it had first-class athletic facilities. The neighborhood itself was a bit disheartening. The university had been built by Mayor Daley to rehabilitate a high-crime area around Racine and Carpenter Streets, the locale of the con-movie "The Sting" (1973) starring Paul Newman and Robert Redford, which I recognized immediately by the street names. Whether it was because of the locale, the university was a 9-5 school, what I immediately called a "proletarian university." The absence of an evening division and of late library hours rendered the area a no-man's land in the evenings and eliminated the school as a research university which did not seem to bother the faculty consisting for the most part of low-level opportunists seeking an easy tenure in a new university.

It was with mixed feelings that I attended the reception for new faculty at which the Chancellor made a point of welcoming Ph.D.'s from Ivy League universities, which made a good impression on me, and even more so when my turn came to meet Dr. Crawford and he greeted me:

"Welcome to Chicago Circle. How do you like it?"
"I have seen the future, and I hope it works."
"It will, it will. We will make it work."

I could see that Dr. Crawford was a first-rate Chancellor in a second-rate university. It did not surprise me when he left, soon to accept the presidency of the prestigious MacArthur Foundation (the "genius grants" foundation) to the serious detriment of the university and for me a loss of someone who would have backed my ideas for the school.

Not all these ideas concern the Polish American Congress and the Polish community directly, and they should be discussed in a different context, but some do, and they shall be discussed here. To begin with, I was elected faculty adviser to the Polish American Student Association (PASA), replacing (unwillingly) the venerable Professor Tymon Terlecki, and I undertook immediately to edit (and write) PASA's "Student Chronicle" replacing (willingly) its previous editor, Anna Rychlinski, who had just graduated. I had big plans for PASA.

Then I joined the Polish Arts Club with a mandate from Walter Zachariasiewicz, the then-President of the American Council of Polish Cultural Clubs (ACPCC), at its national convention in Philadelphia earlier that year (1976) to revive the Chicago Club, a charter member gone sour. I was soon elected its President and moved its headquarters to my office at the university and its monthly meetings to a conference room across the corridor. At the first meeting I moved that the Arts Club remain a member organization of the Polish American Congress, beating a contrary proposal.

As in New York, my office in Chicago became a hub of activity, with its doors always open. My first official caller was Attorney Thaddeus Kowalski, Public Defender but also President of the Polish American Congress, Illinois Division, with an invitation to give a series of lectures, at a nominal fee, on topics raised by my book-in-progress. This was my New York course in miniature and it soon became popular, especially after a run-in between Ted Radzialowski who was on a visit from Minnesota, and the widow Rozmarek, who objected to his remark that the way to count the number of Poles in

Detroit was to count all the basement windows and multiply them by 10. Another meeting was revealing in a different sense when several members of the Polish Arts Club came to hear Bishop Rowinski speak about the Polish National Catholic Church and it turned out that they were all members of it. Throughout the series consisting of about ten meetings, there was never anybody from the upper echelons of organized Polonia present, not even the host, Thaddeus Kowalski, which says something about the lack of communications within the Polish American community.

My school work (preparing for classes) and work on the book (correspondence with authors) was done mostly in the evenings in my spacious office with a western exposure: marvelous sunsets over the plains stretching toward Iowa and the Mississippi. It was a sight for sore eyes. I could see the front of my second-floor apartment on Carpenter Street above the grocery store of the Fontana family, an apartment I had taken over, buying its furniture, from the poet Tymoteusz Karpowicz, a professor of Polish at the university who had gone to Germany as a visiting scholar. Since I used the apartment only to sleep in and for occasional cooking, I rented rooms to scholars from Poland on Kosciuszko Foundation grants, sending the money to my wife in New York, who was pursuing a career at Columbia University while supervising our children's education and visiting me and vice-versa on long weekends and holidays.

My days were full of activity. My well-attended classes made the Polish enrollments catch up with and then pass the Russian, which was what the chairman had wanted, but within limits. I had my lunches not in the faculty lounge but at the "Polish table" in the student cafeteria, often preceded by a swim in a pool in the same building, displaying my still considerable form in beating the students in sprints.

I beat them also in ping-pong, except one, and in tennis, which we played on Saturdays on nearby courts, with my wife joining us when visiting and then serving refreshments in the apartment. She was there when I won the faculty tournament, with my students egging me on.

There was a sport I paid special attention to, namely volleyball, and for a good reason. Among the Polish students, particularly recent immigrants, there were excellent players, Poland having just become the best in the world in volleyball as demonstrated by a gold medal in the Montreal Olympic Games in 1976, beating the Soviet

Union in a spectacular final, which I had to watch on TV, unable to secure tickets. I organized a volleyball team, which soon became the best in intramural competition, a success which did not pass unnoticed in the university and in the Polish American press, where a commentator called me "the best volleyball player among professors, and the best professor among volleyball players." But my ambition reached higher. Since America was not yet a volleyball power (Karcz Kiraly, its future star captain, was probably still in kindergarten) there was a chance that my team, if properly trained (it already had two stars, a Pole and a Polonized German) could qualify for the Olympic Games, or at least for the trials (both pipe dreams, since the next Olympic Games were the unwisely boycotted by America Moscow Games). Such prominence reflecting on the university would go a long way in my ultimate idea for it.

My ultimate idea for the Chicago Circle campus was to rename it the Casimir Pulaski University, a great idea, but.... One of my Chicago students, the grandson of Congressman Annunzio, once told me that his grandfather could not understand why Poles in Chicago were unable to dominate it politically by electing a Polish Mayor. Like Fontana and his Italian customers, Annunzio had great respect for the potential of the Polish organizations in Chicago, reflected in annual parades, but not in the realization of important goals, as evidenced by the disastrous campaign for Mayor by Alderman and former Congressman Roman Pucinski.

The grandson also told me that his grandfather had done more for the Poles in Chicago than all the Poles and their organizations put together. It was this perception, irrespective of how true it was, and Pucinski's defeat by a virtual nobody, that had made me touch all the bases for my idea. I spent many hours in the PASA (the Polish Student Association) office, encouraging its members to persuade their friends in other Chicago universities to switch to Chicago Circle, which some of them had already been doing, in order to make the Polish ethnic group the largest on the campus, which it probably already was. I also encouraged them to try and run for offices in the Student Government thus to have a larger representation in it than one, in order to influence the Student Government to petition the university to add to its program an evening division, which would attract Polish students who had to work during the day.

The next base was to place a Polish American on the university's Board of Trustees, someone who would at a proper moment make the motion to rename the university. In this I had an unexpected ally, even if for an entirely different reason. My departmental chairman, a calculating Serb, had been planning to introduce a doctoral program, a totally irresponsible idea, but I went along with it once he told me that it would help to have a Polish American on the university's Board of Trustees because Polish was the most important part of the new program, which the Board would have to approve, and that Attorney Thaddeus Kowalski was his candidate and he wanted me to talk to him.

As it happened, Kowalski was also my candidate. Past President of the American Council of Polish Cultural Clubs (ACPCC), current President of the Polish American Congress, Illinois Division (and alleged candidate of Karol Rozmarek for the Presidency of the national body), and Public Defender, he had the star qualities for any office. Because he accepted the invitation to the ceremony of my installation as President of the Polish Arts Club, I would have a chance to talk to him. The ceremony, in a reserved dining room of one of Chicago's better restaurants, was attended by several Polonian notables, among them the past President of the Polish Women's Alliance, the conservative Adela Łagodzinska, who objected to the proposal in my acceptance speech to organize a consortium of Polish organizations in Chicago, a proposal to be aired on a Polish television program the following Sunday.

Unexpectedly, my chairman came to the ceremony, no doubt to gauge my standing among Chicago's Polonia which he must have found strong. This was also the impression of my wife, who had combined the ceremony with one of her visits. Afterwards Thad Kowalski, pleased to make her acquaintance, invited us to his home for a glass of wine and to meet his Anglo-Saxon wife and his two children. The women had much in common, and while they talked I told him about the Board of Trustees membership. To my surprise, he wasn't very eager, as if he had no desire to get involved, but would let me know. His wife harped a little about the Presidency of the Polish American Congress which, according to her, had been coming to him at some point. He had no comment, but he did ask my advice about inviting Zbigniew Brzezinski to be the recipient of a Heritage Award which the Illinois Division would be making at its annual autumn banquet. I told him to first write to Brzezinski asking whether he would accept such an invitation while a National Security Adviser in the White House. Kowalski thanked me for the advice which told me that had he indeed become President of the Polish American Congress, he would have relied on people from the academic world more than Mazewski.

There remained just one more base to touch, namely to establish contact with Thaddeus "Lech" Lechowicz, Illinois State Representative and a strong voice in the Legislature, which would have something to say about changing the name of a State University. I was preparing a statement on it.

The draft of the statement for Lechowicz justifying the change of name of the university from "UICC" (University of Illinois–Chicago Circle) to "Casimir Pulaski University" was as follows:

> Of all the outstanding foreign heroes in the American Revolution (Kosciuszko, Lafayette, von Steuben), Casimir Pulaski was the only one who died in battle on American soil, his death a sacrifice for America but a disaster for Poland. What better way to honor him than to name a university after him which would be a repository of all his mementos and all the books and papers devoted to his memory, and where scholars would meet once a year, on the anniversary of his death, to refresh and enrich that memory.

I never met Lechowicz, which was a great pity, because as an early subscriber to my book, and listed in it, he would have been an invaluable ally. Lechowicz never spoke in the Illinois Legislature on Pulaski's behalf (how could he, when we never met), but he did speak on my behalf, as I had heard, when in my second year in Chicago, instead of shaping what would, in effect, be a Polish University in the most Polish city outside of Poland, I found myself in harm's way, and with me all my ideas and plans.

The signs of harm came at first imperceptibly, but soon intensified, coinciding with the departure of the Chancellor and Vice Chancellor for Academic Affairs, both of whom were succeeded by lesser men, the former by the President of the College of Criminal Justice of CUNY (City University of New York), a bad connotation, and the latter by a little man with the demeanor of a clerk rather than a university VIP. As for my three bases, to use baseball language, I was stuck on them. The much-vaunted volleyball team rarely attended practice sessions in full force. The Polish star and his friends preferred to tinker with radio, although the reach of the student radio station was only 500 yards, and nobody lived that close to the university except me (a choice expected of faculty in other schools), but I still obliged by appearing on it, catering to their exercising the right of freedom of expression, denied to them in Poland. As for the lone Polish member of the Student Government, backing and promoting me, he actually did me a disservice by spreading a rumor (if it was only a rumor) that I was to be the next chairman of the department, a position I did not crave, because it would have involved time released from teaching, and I much preferred classroom work to administrative duties.

But it was exactly the opposite with the chairman, who *had* to be one to exist, not having enough expertise as a holder of a degree in Comparative Literature to teach a variety of courses in a Slavic department. To him it was a matter of life and death and, alarmed by the rumor, he reacted by creating one of his own, about my leaving the university at the end of the academic year, and used the Polish American Student Association (PASA) to spread it.

A seemingly legitimate question could be asked why a university fight should be discussed in a chapter about the Polish American Congress, and the answer is that it not only should but must, because at stake was not just my job but the fate of an important stronghold of Polish (and American) history and culture, the Casimir Pulaski project, which would have attracted worldwide attention to itself, just as the various Conrad projects have (the most recent meeting of Conrad scholars in Philadelphia, for example), with great benefit to Polish culture, a fact the Polish American Congress should be aware of if it wants to represent Polonia and protect its wider interests.

When the President of PASA approached me with an invitation to a farewell party for me, I was at first taken aback, but only briefly, because I had already known what was going on. A few days earlier I had a visitor, a certain Mr. Strugielski who had just returned from a trip to Moscow sponsored by the Foreign Affairs Council of Chicago, and he told me that my chairman, his fellow traveler, had been telling everybody who would listen that I would be leaving Chicago. This was going too far, affecting my reputation even in Moscow, where during my stay there in 1971 I had made a few professional acquaintances whom I hoped to meet at the International Slavic Conference in Zagreb in a few weeks. Mr. Strugielski offered to make me a notarized statement which he thought could be useful to me. I agreed.

The "farewell" party was held at the "Last Chance" restaurant run by the family of one of my female students. I asked them to consider it just a nice get-together after classes, and that I would reciprocate during my wife's next visit, and I made the necessary arrangements, receiving a good price of $100 and inviting all those present to come. To my questioning what made them think I was leaving, they replied that the chairman had told them.

The next day I visited Thaddeus Kowalski at his office to inform him of the situation and ask his advice. He didn't know what to make of it and suggested that I seek legal advice, not his, but rather of a specialist in such problems whom he was prepared to recommend. As for the candidacy to the Board of Trustees, Kowalski told me he had decided against it, unwilling to add to his busy schedule.

With Kowalski's decision, the support system for my great idea was gone. There was still Lechowicz, but he would act only after the proposal to change the name of the university had been made by the Board of Trustees, which was not likely to happen without someone making the motion. The irony of the situation was that even without the Pulaski idea this was to be a great summer for me: the Kosciuszko Foundation had asked me to lead a group of students to a summer school in Poland; I was preparing a paper for the International Conference of Slavists; I had just mailed corrected proofs of my book to the publisher, waiting for final proofs, and I was working on an important letter/article to *The Polish Review*. I couldn't allow myself to be railroaded, and I decided to see Mr. Mazewski.

This was my first visit to the new headquarters of the Polish National Alliance at 6100 North Cicero Avenue, where Mr. Mazewski had his office as President of both the PNA and the Polish American Congress. I was impressed by the building but also sad about PNA's flight from the "Polish Triangle," weakening that formidable Polish stronghold despite a master plan according to which the entire area was slated for major development by the city.

For the appointment with President Mazewski I took a witness, Richard Łysakowski, a long-time employee of the Chicago Board of Education and, like me, an ex-serviceman. The resulting meeting told something about the Polish American Congress at that time. Mr. Mazewski not only refused to employ the legal arm of the Congress in my case but flatly declared that it wasn't its concern. At that time the phone rang and he turned to us and told us the call was from Washington, indicating that *this* was the Congress' concern. While he talked on the phone, one of his associates, Mr. Moskal, showed us around the building, including the impressive office of the Vice

President, Helen Szymanowicz, with a clear desk and a secretary in an anteroom. We also visited the plant of the Polish *Daily Zgoda (Dziennik Związkowy)*, and the fortnightly *Zgoda.*

On our way back Łysakowski and I discussed the inability of the Poles to work together, which is a trait of the Polish national character. An intelligent man and a doctoral candidate at the university, Łysakowski was very supportive of my position and warned me about my chairman.

This was precisely what I had on my mind lately, to enter the mind of my adversary, for whom I had been a catch two years earlier, "head and shoulders above all the other candidates for the position," as he brazenly told one of them, who had relayed the statement to me. Barely a few years after my doctoral dissertation at Columbia, I already had it published (*and* my M.A.) and several articles, including a well-received one in *Slavic Review*, while serving on the Board of Directors of the Polish Institute of Arts and Sciences, as Chairman of its Literary Section and Associate Editor of its quarterly, *The Polish Review*, and teaching at New York University a sequence of courses on the Bicentennial which became the germ for the book I was now finishing. My background was such that had I asked for tenure and more money I would have received it because without me the department would have stagnated. I knew it, the chairman knew it, and his minions knew it, but while I, an officer and a gentleman, was not in the habit of asking for rewards in advance, I did not reckon with the perverse mind of a man I had at first regarded as a descendant of the noble Belgrade Military Academy cadets I had befriended in Stalag XVIIB, but he was just a street-smart imitation.

As I was finding this out, my first reaction was to leave without undergoing a humiliating tenure hearing, with its outcome probably already decided, but I remained for the sake of my summer obligations and a desire to see how academic manipulators abuse a once-revered procedure.

What happened next belongs in an essay or a book on American universities and their bankrupt tenure system. As I suspected, the tenure hearing was a mere formality, with the new Vice Chancellor for Academic Affairs presiding and the chairman, who was by then striking me as a clown, feeding him with sly remarks, such as why did I leave NYU. I could have replied that I didn't want the famous New York witticism about a Columbia man moving to NYU and thereby raising the standard of both universities applied to me, but I didn't, knowing that they would not appreciate the wit or misunderstand it entirely, yet it was apt, since one of the chairman's minions was an NYU man. I had a witness with me, who didn't say a word, and neither did the five faculty nobodies (I had never laid eyes on them, they were not my peers). All the time in front of me were fruits of my two-year labors: programs of three scholarly conferences (two organized by me), a joint article with contributions by members of the department (all tenured now), and the final proofs of *Poles in America*, a 781-page book, with an Index of 5,400 names, but nobody paid attention to it, one of only two books by a faculty member at the university that year. Before leaving, I crossed out the chairman's name from the Index, as not belonging among heroes.

What happened can serve as a lesson for the Polish American Congress about not getting involved protecting its own. But there were people who wanted to get involved even unasked, among them esteemed members of the Polish American community in Chicago, who knew about the chairman's devious ways, Mr. Strugielski for example, and Lechowicz. Thaddeus "Ted" Lechowicz, Illinois State Representative, railed on the floor of the State's Legislature at Springfield that a Polish Professor was being railroaded at a State University and demanded to withhold funds from it. There was fear at the university, and I wanted briefly to play on it even if that was not my way, but a chance to penalize the chairman was worth the compromise, and Strugielski's statement could have done it, proving that the tenure hearing had been a sham, to which other charges could have been added which so far I had kept to myself. But the chairman knew me too well and what I would, or would not do, and ultimately I stopped short. Still afraid, he called Congressman Rostenkowski, who allegedly assured him that he would not get involved in the case.

Rostenkowski's assurance (if true) was a shock to me, and I reminded him of it when I turned down his request to take a copy of *Poles in America* to the White House (Brzezinski did it). But by then I had already decided to move on to Loyola University of Chicago, a fine Jesuit school, to help introduce a Polish program, a welcome opportunity. But the damage to my reputation and the disruption of my academic career was unforgivable. Of my summer obligations, I found it necessary to cancel two: the trip to Poland and the Conference of Slavists in Zagreb. I was expected in both and my absence damaged my reputation further. At least in Zagreb, the later of the two, *Poles in America* was already on display, and as a result I was receiving orders for it from participants, some from as far away as Wellington, New Zealand, and Hokkaido, Japan.

Poles in America: Bicentennial Essays, of which the Polish American Congress was one of the sponsors, was the last of my scheduled obligations in the summer of 1978, and the only one I had been able to bring to a conclusion, since it was my book that was being presented to the public in a Symposium organized by the Polish Arts Club on Sunday, August 6, on the Lake Shore campus of Loyola University. The Symposium was well attended, but the Polish American Congress was not represented when the then-President of the Illinois Division, who was one of the scheduled speakers, did not show up, marking another case of neglect of worthy and significant events by the Polish American Congress.

Among unexpected but welcome Symposium guests was a representative of the Polish University in Exile (London) Chicago Division, who invited me to teach Polish and Slavic Philology on Saturday mornings and be Dean of Humanities. This was a welcome development, generating some income which I needed to make up the difference between my salary at UICC and the initially part-time earnings at Loyola. A big help in that respect came from my wife, who had arrived from New York to act as hostess and be in charge of the book's sale, and reported that hundreds of copies were sold during a post-Symposium reception as well as other hundreds picked up by pre-publication purchasers, and I autographed them all in a festive atmosphere that the Polish American Congress would have done well to be part of.

An uninvited guest arrived during the reception, having ignored the Symposium and not purchased a book (my wife kept a record, partly because she was going to take half of the money with her to New York). It was my former chairman, who came to look. I noticed him in an animated conversation with the host, chairman of Loyola's Department of Modern Languages, Fr. Lawrence Biondi, S.J. Who knows what he was telling him, but I know that this insecure man was afraid again (it showed), this time of competition from me at Loyola, and with good reason. He must have noticed several of my former students, some thinking of switching to Loyola.

I succeeded in making Loyola an important center of Poland-oriented activity, a fact totally ignored by the Polish American Congress, as if it inhabited another planet. I started the process with a course called "Polish Culture and Civilization," taught by me on both campuses of Loyola, Lake Shore and Water Tower, while a Polish language course was at first taught by a doctoral candidate from Chicago University. Then I added two literature courses, "History of Polish Literature" and "Polish Drama," which soon reached the highest enrollments in the country for such courses, with close to 50 and 30 students, respectively. Leszek Kolakowski, the philosopher, was touched, while on his way to a Symposium at Loyola, to see students reading *Undivine Comedy* (Krasinski) on the lawn of Lake Shore campus. At the same time I introduced Polish language mini-courses in the School of Continuing Education, which Dean Malecki of the University College (evening division) had talked me into, and I discovered a gold mine in the quality of students, mostly young professionals superior to UICC students.

Shortly after I had joined Loyola, Father Biondi broke the department into several mini-departments, Polish among them, which I was in charge of, with a full-time salary which became available when a Spanish professor had returned to Madrid. I was now teaching Polish language and literature on both campuses and the mini-courses at the School of Continuing Education, and supervising several part-time instructors. At the same time I helped Father Biondi to organize an International Symposium, "Poland's Church-State Relations," with Mons. Szczepan Wesoly, the Pope's liaison with Polish communities abroad (this was not long after the visit to Chicago of His Holiness Pope John Paul II) and Chicago's Bishop Alfred Abramowicz attending, but again nobody from the Polish American Congress to give the Symposium a stamp of approval of organized Polonia.

The proceedings from the Symposium were published in book form, with Father Biondi writing the Introduction, and I, the Conclusion. It was the second book to come out during my association with Loyola and close cooperation with the chairman. There was to be a third soon, but in the meantime I was creating programs or taking initiatives on my own, either in cooperation with the Polish American community or the assistance of my students. There was an exhibition, "Polish Books in America," with books provided by the Curator of the Polish Museum of America, Fr. Bilinski, the Chicago

Public Library, and private collectors. Prof. Terlecki, on a tour from England, was the speaker. But it was my next program, "Poland Today," inspired by Solidarity, that really put the Polish program at Loyola on the map.

The extremely well-attended event, sponsored by Continuing Education, consisted of a "Prayer Service for Poland" in the University chapel and a videotaped film, "Poland: The New Spirit," made in Poland by Bill Kurtis of CBS and shown with comments by him in the University auditorium, followed by papers on the situation in Poland by scholars from Loyola University, University of Wisconsin, University of Windsor, Canada, and statements by members of the media (CBS, *Chicago Tribune*) and me, as moderator and commentator on the display of historical maps of Poland (placed with care on display stands by recent immigrants from Poland). The standing-room-only audience included the two "Polish" deans (Wozniak of Education and Malecki of University College), members of the Polish American community and of the Polish Consulate (and, because of that, no fewer than five FBI agents), and many students, but nobody from the Polish American Congress.

It was as a result of this successful event that my literature courses ballooned to 80 students, the biggest Polish literature courses anywhere. Among those students were several who had assisted me in the launching of *Echo*, "A Publication of Polish Student Clubs in Chicago," edited and published by my students at Loyola. Its prized issue, No. 5, September-December 1980, with a Solidarity spread, is a collector's item today.

With such accomplishments accompanied by summer assignments in Poland (always mentioned in the faculty column of *Loyola World*) and frequent appearances in regional and national scholarly conferences, two of them in Chicago, giving much publicity to Loyola and its Polish program, I was on top of the world, so soon after the UICC debacle. It was too good to be true, nothing ever came to me so easily, something had to happen to ruin it. And something did happen, actually two things, two personnel changes affecting people important to keeping my career in high gear with even greater accomplishments to come.

First, the President of the Kosciuszko Foundation who had visited me at Loyola (we had had lunch with Father Biondi who was very impressed by him) and given me the summer assignment in Poland, knowing the plans I had for it, was voted out of office by the

KF Board of Trustees and succeeded by a real spoiler who treated the assignments as perks to be handed out as returns for favors rendered. I was pessimistic about the future of my assignment.

Even worse, Father Biondi, my chairman, became Dean Biondi, and his place as head of Modern Languages was taken by a Hispanic woman with a mandate to develop and expand the Spanish program. At her first faculty meeting she declared that she would eliminate the mini-departments, leaving just what she called the "major" languages (French, German, Italian, Spanish) and phasing out the minor, which she called "an experiment that did not work out."

I listened with amazement. My Polish department was a success by any standards, and others were beginning (Russian, Arabic, Japanese) to attract to Loyola students who wanted or needed them. This was "an experiment that did not work out"? I understood the woman's preference for "major" Western languages, but Polish was one of Chicago's "major" languages, and Polish American students were the largest ethnic group at Loyola. When the implication of it hit me I glanced at the Polish instructor and when our eyes met we both knew that it was Polish that was going to be the target of our new chairperson. But why?

The woman was a fanatic, and fanatics are capable of any violations, especially when they have a mandate. But mandate was not enough in a city whose Hispanic population was for the most part illiterate in English and no material for college (Chicago was a goal of unskilled Mexicans who were arriving by a new kind of "underground railway"). Bona fide students were needed, and the biggest pool of them at Loyola were the Polish American students. Eliminate the Polish department and a large part of its students would end up in Spanish courses since they had to take a language to meet the foreign language requirement, and literature to satisfy the core curriculum. (When a Polish summer course was eliminated, the victim was Rozmarek's granddaughter!) It was like taking away a national heritage from an ethnic group, and in this the sinister plot reminded me of Bismarck's *Kulturkampf* in Prussian Poland in the second half of the 19th century. But there was more to it.

I noticed how controlled the Hispanic students were and how they were told what courses to take or not to take. I played soccer with some of them and they wanted to take my literature course. Yet, when in that huge class I was able to identify students from 14 (fourteen!) different nationalities or ethnic groups (Dean Biondi was impressed when told about the count by a student-informant) there was not a single Hispanic student among them. Likewise, the students were herded to any guest lecture by a Hispanic speaker, filling the lecture hall to capacity. After one of the lectures, about Nicaragua, I had a mild run-in with the speaker, the Mexican writer Carlos Fuentes, when he declared that "there would be no Jaruzelski in Nicaragua." Comparing the situation in Nicaragua to Poland at the time of Solidarity, and Manuel Ortega to General Jaruzelski was unrealistic, and I was going to tell him so, but the chairperson hovering around him prevented me.

The worst of it was that a devious woman was placing me in conflict with a culture of which I had the highest opinion. I was familiar with Spanish history and literature and I had known interesting people, among them the great matador Manolete, who had dedicated a bull to me when, as a young soldier I was passing through Spain on my way to England from occupied Europe. At Loyola my closest colleague was a young professor from Madrid who wanted to buy my Manolete souvenirs (my ticket stub and a program with a picture) and gave me a framed portrait of King Juan Carlos before returning to Spain (I was a beneficiary of his salary). Also, a Jesuit professor had introduced me by chance to a waterworks engineer from Veracruz and asked me to put him up. I did, and Oliver Arieta shared my apartment with me, with a visit one day by his soccer player brother from Mexico with two young sons who knew the entire Polish national soccer team by heart!

The frail-looking chain-smoking woman's hostility toward me was known on both campuses of the university. It took the form of petty harassment (my office space being assigned in rooms progressively further back, harder to find; editorial meetings with the *Echo* staff at Water Tower reported by spying faculty women to the office at Lake Shore; no access to departmental typewriters; having to pay for xeroxing of Polish course material), which I never reported because that's not my way. I expected Dean Biondi to hear about it through the grapevine but there was no reaction of any kind except his remark at a party that it was a "relationship of love and hate." In reality it was the case of an unprincipled woman whom I viewed with revulsion and fear of what such a person could do if placed at an even higher level of academic power. Pity the Polish American students! That is why the Polish American Congress has to keep its eyes open and develop a mechanism to monitor the training of Polish cadres, especially at Loyola where much Polish American money had gone (from George Halas, for example) or been generated by Polish Americans (Dan Rostenkowski, an illustrious loyal alumnus).

When I next saw Dean Biondi, instead of discussing the behavior of his predecessor, he asked me whether I was going to Poland in summer, which made me wonder whether he knew something I didn't know. I immediately called the Kosciuszko Foundation and asked to speak to the President who, just as I had expected, had given the assignment to someone else, a person who would "take care of something" for him. This was just after the great "Poland Today" event and I was beginning to wonder whether this was a peak from which a downward movement would start for me, but when my courses skyrocketed I felt reassured, though only briefly.

The enrollment in my Polish literature courses adversely affected the enrollment in other, non-Polish literature courses, and I could sense the hostility toward me of their teachers, mostly women, and almost all of them singularly plain. The chairperson was visibly worried because I was in a position to tell her that my courses were a proof that Father Biondi's "experiment" *was* working out and that she should resign for mishandling the department but, again, that's not my way, it was up to the Dean to address the situation. When he didn't, and when she decided to eliminate my literature courses, I didn't say anything because I noticed how tense she was telling me "their" decision. A Cuban friend from *Opus Dei*, a psychoanalyst whom I had brought once to a lecture she was chairing to take a look at her and at samples of her handwriting, declared her mentally (and physically) ill and in need of treatment, and told me that had I exploded angrily then, she would have had a stroke, probably fatal.

I went home to my family for Christmas, which was the Christmas of martial law in Poland. There was a Slavic conference in New York between Christmas and New Year, as in every other year, in which I took part, as I always did. A Ukrainian colleague, once a fellow-doctoral student at Columbia, told me there was an opening in Polish there, my dream, which she was aware of. Another colleague, a fellow-lecturer at my "Poles in America" course at NYU, suggested that I might try to repeat my success there in 1976 with another success in 1982, this time with a course about Solidarity. Because during my summer's assignment in Poland I had acquired first-hand knowledge about Solidarity I was enthusiastic about the suggestion, and my enthusiasm soon brought to my side a crowd of

Solidarity activists and specialists, and I took all their names and addresses.

During the New Year's holiday I wrote to the President and Vice President of Loyola, resigning from my job. Then I applied to Columbia, where my former instructor was now chairman, and I visited NYU, where there was a new Dean now, a woman. My wife and children (young adults now, soon to have their own children) were happy about my coming return to New York, and I left them with that feeling.

At Loyola nobody mentioned the resignation. I was met with silence all around, except from Dean Biondi, who told me he had secured a Mellon grant for me for an International Symposium on Solidarity. When I told him I had twelve speakers lined-up, he was flabbergasted.

"The Polish Solidarity Movement" International Symposium was organized in record time, and was held on April 24, 1982, in the same auditorium as "Poles in America" in 1978 and "Poland's Church-State Relations" in 1980, in two-year intervals. Its proceedings were published in 1984 as a 236-page book, *Poland's Solidarity Movement*, edited by Lawrence Biondi, S.J. and Frank Mocha.

The Symposium was preceded by a meeting of students and participants with Attorney Aloysius Mazewski, President, Polish American Congress, a meeting which I was very happy to bring about. Mr. Mazewski, attended smartly by the grandson of Congressman Annunzio (who had political ambitions), was in a good form and answered all questions addressed to him including questions from recent refugees, to whom he was a kind of legend. It was different when I had a brief private meeting with him during recess. When I informed him of the new developments at Loyola, threatening the Polish department with elimination, thus harming the wider interests of Polonia, Mr. Mazewski replied firmly that it was no concern of the Polish American Congress.

The Symposium itself was a success, featuring speakers like Leszek Kołakowski, George J. Lerski, Jerzy Thieme, Andrew S. Targowski, Irene Dubicka-Morawska, with the entire proceedings recorded by "Voice of America."

The success of the Symposium gave me something to do. While finishing my last literature courses and acting as President of the Polish American Educators Association, I was busy correcting and editing the Symposium papers and handing them to Dean Biondi's secretary to type. There was no thought of leaving Loyola until the book was finished, especially when both my applications in New York turned out to be too late, which did not disappoint me as much as I had thought it would, because after an initial letdown I again had great ideas, perhaps the greatest yet, with the exception of the Casimir Pulaski idea, which would have been carved in stone if it had come to pass.

Of the new ideas the first had to do with Chicago Polish teachers, an idea only marginally inspired by the Educators. In brief, Chicago had, and still has, two kinds of Polish teachers: those trained in Poland, who teach in the Polish Saturday schools, and those, trained in America, who teach Polish in the public and parochial schools. The first group is deficient in English and in American history and culture, and its training has left some residue of their Communist-dominated education. The second group is deficient in Polish and in Polish history and culture. To remove the deficiencies and the residue, and in effect to retrain the teachers, I applied to the National Endowment for the Humanities (NEH) for a grant in support of an ambitious two-pronged summer program. My students were going to participate in the program's second group. By "my students" I mean my language students, the young professionals I was encountering in the mini-courses. It was these students to whom my second idea applied to.

The idea had occurred to me when at a Polonian meeting I saw Mr. Mazewski, in his capacity as President of the Polish American Congress, giving a Polish American woman, in a typical patronage manner, an appointment to an important job of ethnic adviser to the Governor. The woman was illiterate in Polish and her only action on behalf of Polonia that I knew of was to arrange for the sightseeing bus to include on its rounds a portion of the Kennedy Expressway with a virtual procession of Polish churches, a famous landmark in Chicago which had to be included anyway.

I realized then that jobs were available on the local, state and federal levels where knowledge of Polish should have been a must. My students would obtain that knowledge in my mini-courses and, having finished the series, transfer to regular language courses I was teaching then in place of literature, and complete the sequence to perfection and fluency in a special "total immersion" summer program in Poland. This was not the traditional "minor" or "major" in Polish, neither of which applied to my nucleus group of students all of whom were already college graduates and, besides, the chair-person would not allow it anyway. It was something new, a project that I pursued at first as a hobby, intending to write an official proposal after it became sufficiently advanced but already referring to it by its proper name, "Certificate in Polish."

In my mind, the Certificate in Polish was far more important than just a means of getting a government job. Unlike its namesake at Columbia University which was part of academic "area" studies, my certificate was to be an instrument to create a new Polish American intelligentsia which would be comfortable in both languages and cultures in a generation which was losing, or had already lost, the knowledge of Polish. If my certificate program was a success, and the dedication of the nucleus group was a good indication of it, it could become a blueprint for similar programs in cities like Detroit, Cleveland, Buffalo, New Britain, Binghamton, creating jobs to run the programs as well as training leaders to succeed Mazewski's generation.

The Certificate project became an obsession with me, just as the Casimir Pulaski project had been before. The work connected with it, requiring individual attention in some cases, trips to Washington in connection with the NEH application (and visiting Congressman Clement Zablocki, an important reference), stopping in New York on my way back to see my first grandchild (a boy), all that feverish activity, added to the chairwoman's obstructions, began to take its toll, and I started losing weight. I asked Dean Biondi to arrange a CAT-scan for me at Loyola's Medical School, but he turned me down despite my offer to donate my collection of historical maps to the university as payment. The worst outcome, however, was the rejection of my NEH application, on a technicality, when one of my partners (the historian, Prof. Lerski) sent his materials not with my package, but directly to NEH, which is a no-no! When I fired an angry letter to NEH, its chairman, Dr. William Bennett replied, including an opinion from a referee:

> *"This man is a human dynamo."*
> *"He is a one-man promotion team."*
> *"We don't think his partners will be able to keep up with him."*

Despite the disappointment, I rather liked the opinion, which described me accurately. To make up for the NEH institute, I set up a mini-institute of my own, consisting of two courses only: one semester of advanced Polish, the first time advanced Polish was offered at Loyola, and Polish Culture and Civilization, not for the teachers, because there was no stipend money for them, but for my students, with both courses counting for the certificate.

Surprisingly, the chairwoman scheduled the courses (probably because they were the only courses offered in the department that summer, a bad reflection on her and the effect of my large enrollments on the non-Polish courses) and very conveniently, too. On the same floor as my office in the Humanities Building, next to a music room, the two evening courses followed each other in the same classroom, which was convenient for those students who were taking both, but also for me, enabling me to make out of the break between them a pleasant creative coffee break, augmented by starting the first course five minutes earlier and ending the second five minutes later. The coffee was provided by me and prepared in my coffee urn in my office; the students took turns bringing pastries and frequently guests, for whom for a magic half hour this was a home-away-from-home.

There was an always-helpful Blue Cross man who arrived early as he had to all the classes he had taken with me, bringing paper coffee cups and napkins, making the coffee, and otherwise acting throughout as my assistant, up to and including cleaning up at the end. I never found out what his background was, but I thought it was Ukrainian. Then there was the Polish Jew, Izrael Taubenfligel, who hailed from Kalisz, a town rich in the history of Polish-Jewish relations, and whom I often used in my Polish class as an assistant because of his excellent Polish. He was to die soon of a weak heart, but not before I had designated him as my successor for Polish language (and had this last wish printed on my farewell luncheon program). Another guest who made it a habit to come to the coffee break, often with his mother, was a young black self-taught pianist who played Chopin for us in the next-door music room. I gave his name as a candidate for the annual Chopin Competition of the Kosciuszko Foundation, and his mother invited me to his graduation party, to be conducted in the format of the "This Is Your Life" television program, with me as one of the surprise guests. It was partly his presence that makes me use the adjective "creative" when referring to the coffee break. He added considerably to its magic atmosphere which made that summer at Loyola a memorable one, compensating for the disappointments and disasters engulfing me in their web.

Next to the NEH disappointment (not a disaster yet because it could be corrected if other things worked out), caused by a professor objecting to be rushed and, like a typical Pole, not understanding the meaning of the word "deadline," came the disasters, involving first the all-important Kosciuszko Foundation's Poland connection.

While a big NEH grant would have probably resulted in a named professorship for me at Loyola, since it was renewable, bringing in big money while at the same time revolutionizing the teaching of Polish in America, it *had* to be granted soon, before disaster struck killing the Certificate in Polish project and making my further stay at Loyola irrelevant.

I called the Kosciuszko Foundation and, not finding the President in, I spoke to one of his assistants, who told me that the Lublin assignment in Poland had already been made, probably to the same person who had gotten it when I had lost it. This was the disaster I had feared, and another blatant example of the inability of the Poles to put their best foot forward and cooperate for the common good. In retrospect, there could have been a Polish Government veto this time because of my Solidarity Symposium.

But even then I was not yet defeated. While my not going to Poland to continue a Polish language program for Loyola students (three of whom had already applied to the Foundation) would have removed the last obstacle for the chairperson to eliminate Polish in the department, and eliminate me, too, in the process, there was a way to go around it. I could continue to teach Polish outside the department, namely at the School of Continuing Education, the main supplier of candidates for the Certificate.

Just as I had conceived the idea, I read in the university newspaper that the School of Continuing Education was discontinuing its language courses, which for me were a source of superior students. Without them there was no meaningful future for me at Loyola. This was the final disaster (engineered to get me out?) and I decided to leave after the summer courses, on Independence Day.

Among all the disappointments and disasters there was one piece of good news, something to take to New York with me: the book, *Poland's Solidarity Movement*, finally came out and was prominently displayed in the university bookstore. Dean Biondi, who in his "Introduction" to it praised my concluding chapter ("Conclusion:

Solidarity—A Movement Unlike Any Other"), spoke about getting more money for me when I picked up a box of the books from his office. Perhaps this was the time to save the Polish department, especially since the hostile chairperson was being replaced after scuttling Biondi's departments (the "experiment," as she called the brilliant idea, ahead of its time), but that was not to be. It was at that time that my offer of maps for CAT-scan was made again and rejected, and I decided that my health came first and it was more likely to improve with my family around me and a second grandchild on the horizon.

On Friday, the day before a farewell luncheon the Educators were throwing for me, my wife arrived from New York. I met her at O'Hare Airport and we went by subway to a mid-town garage to rent a medium-sized U-Haul truck (to be surrendered in New York) which we drove uptown (stopping on the way in the bank to close my account) and parked behind my small but comfortable apartment in a town house near the campus. Doreen, my wife, immediately plunged into cleaning, as usual, while deciding what to put into the U-Haul over the weekend to take to New York with us. We had a late lunch, and then I left her alone, picked up my Columbia University canvas bag with books and examination papers, and proceeded to the campus. This was the final examination day in my courses, which I combined with a discussion of the Solidarity book during my customary coffee break, for which I had asked Doreen to join me.

On my way, I stopped at the financial office to inquire about my last pay and leave instructions to send it to New York. One of the clerks, a Polish American, gave me an amazing piece of news, that there was a million-dollar scholarship fund in Chicago (left by a rich widow) for Polish American students, half of it at the Illinois Institute of Technology and half at Loyola, where it had been sitting idle for several years, earning interest, and was about to be activated. Why hadn't I known about it?

This was a whole new ball game. I understood now the loose remarks by the chairwoman which I had overheard in the department about needing a "test," presumably to test the knowledge of Polish of the applicants, but the devious woman was addressing the remarks to the women professors who had close ties with Northwestern University, which had no Polish. A terrible suspicion seized me that the scheming woman was laying her hands on the scholarship money, by making it somehow benefit her Spanish program in the coming absence of Polish courses. This time I was going to take action. I thanked the man and rushed to the Dean's office, remembering his talk about more money for me (for giving the tests? But why be so secretive about it?).

Dean Biondi wasn't in his office and wasn't expected. This was a big disappointment for me, and I immediately called Aloysius Mazewski, the President of the Polish American Congress, and caught him just before he, too, left early. I told him about the Polish scholarship money and how there was little I could do to find out how it was being used. This time he listened patiently and expressed genuine regret about my leaving Chicago, but he still had no idea what the Congress could do about the scholarship. I suggested that he create a mechanism to monitor such cases for the benefit of the Polish American community, and that he consult with Dr. T. Radzialowski, the most knowledgeable Polish American about such matters. Mazewski promised he would look into it. He even took notes, but I had doubts about his resolve and intentions. This was the last time I spoke with him. His record in the educational field was summed up later in Donald Pienkos' *For Your Freedom Through Ours* (East European Monographs):

> ...The Congress' inability, or unwillingness, to systematically work in the educational field for the enlightenment of Polonia proved to be a major negative on the otherwise generally favorable balance sheet summing up Mazewski's twenty year stewardship of the PAC (p. 165).

The assessment is vague and makes no mention of Mazewski ever venturing (not even "look[ing]" as he had promised) outside of pseudo-educational and largely ineffective fields for the "enlightenment" of Polonia (Plonski) into the strongholds of real education, the universities, where battles were raging to build Polish strongholds within the establishment citadels. Some were successful, such as the long battle of Stanley Blejwas (who had studied Polish under me at Columbia as a Fulbright scholar) to establish an endowed chair of Polish in New Britain, largely thanks to the support of the Polish American community, but others were not, such as mine at Loyola, largely because of the lack of that support in what was evolving as a destructive inter-ethnic rivalry, of which Polonia was not even aware.

The lack of support was evident in my last meeting with my students and guests from the Pol/Am community, of whom only six arrived, but I treated them to an experience they would never forget: my creative coffee break. The students and guests mixed well together, and with abundant coffee and the Blue Cross man's excellent pastries, this, the last, was, fittingly, the best coffee break of all. The guests watched with amazement the easy informality which prevailed, with small groups socializing in my office or in the hall outside, or looking into the now-empty classrooms, deciphering the writing on some of the blackboards in Spanish, French, German, Italian, but mostly Polish. As the coffee break was ending, students who had just had their exam, proctored by Izrael Taubenfligel, and were preparing to leave, mixed with those about to have theirs in the second course, also to be proctored by Israel, the young musician gave us his best: Chopin's "Revolutionary," the triumphant climax of which describes the Polish spirit well.

With Izrael and the Blue Cross man in class, Doreen was in charge of the party but, having tidied up a bit after the first departures, left me with my guests and, with a professional's eye, took a first, and last, look at a place in which I had worked the last six years. She thought that, unlike the compressed Columbia University, where she was an officer, Loyola was blessed with space.

My guests and I easily and comfortably fitted into my office. I told them how disappointed I was at the small turnout for a discussion of an important book, with even my Dean and co-editor declining, and the *Chronicles of Culture* editor, Leopold Tyrmand, having a previous engagement. One of the guests, an active member of the Polish American Congress, knew something about the "previous engagement": it was a meeting in Chicago with the philosopher Leszek Kołakowski, one of the contributors to the book, with at least one other Polish contributor also participating. I was puzzled. What kind of cabal was this. Was it a boycott of my book, and if so, why…?

Our discussion was interrupted by the arrival of Izrael Taubenfligel with the exams and by the students. They all had a cup of coffee, we talked a little and said good-bye and then they left, followed by the guests. The last to leave were Izrael and the Blue Cross man, the last in my mini-institute and in the creative coffee break.

The farewell luncheon the next day—given by the Polish American Educators Association, whose presidency I was going to resign, and held in the State Room, Mertz Hall on the bucolic Lake Shore campus of Loyola University—was attended by a mixed audience of acquaintances from the Polish American community (some from outside of it—Jewish and German), by fellow members of the host organization, and students, mostly those associated with the student *Echo* publication, who were genuinely sorry to see me go, knowing that without me the publication would cease to exist. They had high hopes to use it to help reinstate an old Polish fraternity, about which a small article had appeared in the memorable issue of September-December 1980:

> As an interesting sidelight, the 1937 *Loyolan*, Loyola University's student yearbook, revealed a fraternity composed of Polish-American students. The fraternity, Sigma Pi Alpha, founded in 1932, was probably the only Polish college fraternity in the U.S.A. The fraternity is arousing a great deal of interest, making it possible to bring it back to life after an interval of over forty years. Sigma Pi Alpha, if reinstated, may be the future vanguard of Polonian students at many universities if chapters developed.

Instead, independently of *Echo*, a new fraternity had been founded at Loyola, a Pre-Professional Fraternity Pi Omicron Lambda (POL), which asked me to be its Faculty Adviser. I soon grew impatient with it, seeing it as a self-serving vehicle for a few students who put their own narrow interests above the wider goal of recognition for Polonian students which would have been better served by reinstating the old fraternity.

Musing about lost or unfulfilled opportunities while circulating with Doreen before we took our seats in the middle of the head table, I was also thinking about my fellow-Educators whom, despite my best efforts, and those of the indefatigable Sue Strand, I was not able to steer to genuine educational goals, and whose main claim to recognition on the Chicago cultural scene was as sponsors of polka dances. While the education-oriented programs, initiated by me, were poorly attended, the polka dances organized by the program chairman were successful. I attended one of them, *ex officio*, reaching the conclusion that entertainment is good as a reward, but not as a goal.

Still, it was good to hear one speaker after another extolling my virtues and contributions to Polonia, beginning with the jovial but suddenly serious new President Ken Gill: "Frank Mocha walked among us...," followed by others in the same vein ("Stop them," my wife whispered in my ear, embarrassed), especially students, for whom I was not only a popular teacher but a tennis partner, a playing-captain of a volleyball team, writer of a student chronicle column in the Polish American press, and adviser to their clubs, fraternities, and publications, especially *Echo*, represented by its Production Director, Alicia Adams (Alicja Adamczewska). I couldn't help thinking about the great ideas I had had torpedoed on my watch in Chicago: the renaming of UICC into The Casimir Pulaski University, and the Certificate in Polish project. Who was to blame...?

An unexpected guest entered the State Room, a shifty student who, though listed on the masthead of *Echo*, never contributed anything to it. He just wanted to be in on the staff meetings, I thought. He entered, looked around as if checking something, refused to sit down in an empty chair at a table, exchanged a few awkward words with me, and left, as if satisfied with what he had seen and heard.

"He is spying on you," my wife said.

"Spying on me? Whoever for?"

"How should I know? The School? The woman?"

It made sense. The young man's sniffing around looked like spying. But for whom? I didn't think the "woman" even knew him. I had seen him on some occasions acting as Biondi's factotum, and I also suspected he had a drinking problem. It's just possible that upon being notified that I had looked for him and then made what must have sounded like an urgent call, Biondi had sent somebody to find out what I was up to. But if that was the case and he did find out, the next thing he would have wanted to know was who was the Master of Ceremonies, and if it was Bill Kurtis. I recalled how after the Kurtis-inspired "Poland Today" program, Biondi had asked me if Kurtis was Polish. There was something about Kurtis that inspired respect, and so it was on this occasion. Kurtis wasn't the emcee, but he could have been, and here lies one of those little blunders that can change a man's life and affect an entire group he is part of.

The emcee at the luncheon *was* to have been Bill Kurtis, who had by then been transferred by CBS to its New York headquarters as co-anchor on the "Morning News" with Diane Sawyer but maintained his residence in Chicago, where he returned for weekends. He readily accepted the invitation, and spoke of having me on his program in New York, which made me think: knowing how inquisitive Diane Sawyer, former White House reporter could be, I worried that she would try and get things out of me I didn't wish to speak about, such as the reasons for my leaving Chicago.

I didn't want the media to get involved in my problems and I suggested to Kurtis that he share the emcee spot with Thaddeus Kowalski, knowing that he would refuse, which he did, going to Rome instead. This, of course, meant that there would be no "Morning News" appearances for me in New York, which in retrospect I see as a big mistake.

What Biondi would have done upon finding out that Kurtis was indeed the emcee is a matter of speculation. He might have walked over from the Jesuit Residence to Mertz Hall and tried to talk me out of leaving. Like me, he also wouldn't want the media to get involved in my problems. But if Kurtis were the emcee, it would mean that I wanted to be on his "Morning News," and why not? Since I would not be able to keep Diane Sawyer from getting the truth out of me, let the truth be told, in one stroke humbling and stopping a sick woman in Chicago and, with the help of the book, doing more for Poland and Polonia than the PAC could. At the same time, I would be preparing the groundwork for what I was dreaming to be after teaching: Ambassador to Poland.

This, a piece of my alternate history, was not what I was thinking about (it came to me later) when sitting at the head table, sipping wine, autographing copies of *Poles in America* and *Poland's Solidarity Movement* and listening to Thaddeus Kowalski talking to Doreen about his children, seeking her advice. Then the luncheon came to an end and real farewells began. A woman, whom I had noticed collecting signatures, approached our table and handed me an envelope. I slipped it in my briefcase but Doreen took it out and discreetly showed it to me. Inside was a large photo of me standing in front of a blackboard and writing something with chalk on it in Polish (the declensions of Polish personal pronouns, quite legibly). The front of the photo had several bills clipped to it, (a $100, a few

$50's, and several $20's). The back had the signatures of my hosts, and written beneath them, in beautiful calligraphy:

"We will always be in your debt."

This was on par with the new President's opening sentence.

It was packing from then on. First, the books I had on display at the luncheon, of which half had been sold, and presents I had received, mostly valuable books. A former student from UICC drove us to the apartment where we talked about ways to dispose of my things.

In the evening our son, Paul, called from Seattle, asking if we would like to meet on the Continental Divide in Colorado the next day. It was tempting. To stand on the Divide was something to tell one's grandchildren about, but it was precisely they who were a factor against the trip, with our second expected in New York any day. But Paul insisted: if we took an early morning plane, we could meet at the Denver airport, drive to the Divide, take pictures, return to the airport, and be back in Chicago by midnight. I felt I was not up to it, and I regret it to this day.

We needed the extra time gained by not going to the Divide to sort my things out and pack, a formidable job as it turned out. With Doreen busy with the furnishings and utensils, discarding any damaged and chipped items, I had the major part of the job, sorting out my papers, which had accumulated over the years and had not been sorted out properly even during my move from Carpenter Street in the vicinity of UICC to the Lake Shore townhouse close to Loyola. The irony of my leaving was that after the book on Solidarity was finally out I would have had more time for my other papers. Instead, I was taking them to New York.

The volume of the papers was the main problem. They were in file folders suspended from filing cabinet racks resting on the floor under the wall in the bedroom, where they were also in neat piles on top of the desk and under the TV table. They were also in boxes that were clearly marked and placed on the shelves of the storage bin in the basement. In other words, despite the great volume, I knew exactly what I had, and when I could not find something I knew I had, the only explanation was that it had been removed, or stolen, by my guests or lodgers from Poland, a sad phenomenon which I will return to when I discuss the erosion of morals and manners in Poland.

The next day, Sunday, not wanting to shop for any perishables, we went to the campus for breakfast, sliding on our way under the door of the Dean's office an envelope with the graded exams and a copy of an exam for an absent student, to be administered in the Dean's office and mailed to me. After breakfast we stopped by my office to see if there was anything we had forgotten. The only thing left behind were boxes of *Poland's Church-State Relations* which I had wanted to donate to the Kosciuszko Foundation for a course under that name that the Foundation was offering in Poland, but I withheld the offer under the new president.

On our way back to the apartment we stopped at my neighbor's across the street, a young Polish giant with a black belt in karate who had blazed his way across Western Europe and England to America, becoming a maintenance and building contractor, often doing work in and around Loyola. I was very fond of him, and he had invited me long ago to his Fourth of July barbecue at the back of his house, when he wanted me to test his American wife for one of my Polish language courses. He was a successful man with great potential, and I would like to have seen him involved in serious Polish American projects. I came to ask him to help me load a heavy bed on the U-Haul tomorrow, and tell him he could keep the things I was leaving behind, if not for himself then for his men. He promised, and in turn asked that before leaving we drop in to his barbecue; it was to feature a roasted pig. He was genuinely sorry to see me go.

When we returned to the apartment, the former student (he was a teacher of Polish in Lane Tech public school) was already waiting. He took some cartons of my books, telling me he was storing them in his protected garage. I felt uneasy about the arrangement, but alas....

During the entire afternoon various people came to say good-bye but also to see what I could part with. I was not in the giving mood—yet—except for some of my course materials and outlines, especially of *Polish Culture and Civilization*, for the archives of the Dmowski Institute. I sold a four-volume German edition of the Linde Dictionary of Polish Language, a Russian typewriter that was likely to get damaged in the truck, and the larger of my two desks, Doreen insisting on keeping the smaller one, which had an unscratched mahogany top and a row of small green drawers under it to put some of my papers in. She also wanted to take my brown flat telephone sitting on the desk, the table lamp next to it, and the brown couch in the living-dining room. She didn't want the television and the dining table with four chairs, but she would take all the utensils.

By evening we were tired and hungry, so hungry that we didn't trust the campus cafeteria and went shopping to a friendly Palestinian's store (he once gave me a copy of the Koran, which I still have and read occasionally). We bought two big lamb chops, a few potatoes (just enough for supper), a small lettuce and cucumber (there was still some El Diablo salad dressing in the refrigerator and a tomato, plus some Quaker Oats, milk, sugar, butter, jam, bacon and eggs, just enough for breakfast), a small loaf of rye bread and a box of Lorna Doones for dessert (and for the road). This was to be our last supper in Chicago.

With Doreen doing the lamb and the potatoes, I prepared the salad (I even rinsed the El Diablo bottle to take some of the bite off the dressing for Doreen's sake). The chops were great, no wonder, they had come from lamb eaters, and so was the salad. While we ate, coffee was perking on the stove, its aroma filling the room. I had a slice of the rye bread with butter and jam instead of the cookies with my coffee, relaxing finally with a second cup and a Marlboro on the apartment's balcony as was my habit on warm evenings. On that one, there were distant sounds of firecrackers but no-one to hear them on a Sunday night.

We were up early the next day. While Doreen was preparing breakfast—and I asked her to use up all that was left in the refrigerator, turn it off and start defrosting—I walked over to my office to see if there was a note from my absent student. I had trouble opening the door, until I realized that the lock had been changed. This was a final insult, and an indication of the degree of hostility the sick woman had for me. Anger welled up in me. For the first time I regretted not following the advice of my Cuban from *Opus Dei* on how to handle her. I started walking toward her office in the hope that maybe, just maybe, she was in, weaving her web, so I could kill her with anger and invective. But no, no such luck, so I just put a curse on her, an awesome oath I learned in Spain during the war.

There was a lone letter in my mailbox next to her office. It opened surprisingly easy (tampered with?). It was an invitation to a project honoring Czeslaw Milosz but it was more, a sad reminder of the perfidious spider's web.

Because of the large correspondence I maintained at Loyola on account of my activities (invitations to speakers, confirmations, editing of papers, all in a hurry) I had an arrangement with the mailroom that I would bring my mail directly to it, bypassing the departmental mailbox. It was an irritating disappointment when John, the Polish "mountain man" in charge of the university's mailroom, had refused at some point to take my letters for quick mailing, the result of the chairwoman's devious meddling (she wanted my letters to be dropped in the departmental box next to her office, for obvious reasons).

John was one of the many Poles who served Loyola with utmost loyalty, but he was also loyal to things Polish by talking longingly about his native mountains and some delicious cheese (*osypka*?), by scrupulously placing copies of the *Echo* publication in faculty mailboxes; and by even attending the "Poland Today" event (true, it was just across the hall from the mailroom). He was being a good soldier by obeying an order (a request, really), but a bad soldier by obeying a bad order, and this was a bad order. I am sure the distinction was lost on him. As for me, this was the last straw....

Unable to enter my office to decide what to do with the books, I returned to the apartment, taking a last look at the campus, and joined Doreen for breakfast, our last there, which was ready and consisted of leftovers. A steaming bowl of porridge with sugar and milk, followed by bacon and eggs on rye for a change, with mustard and a few slices of a fried potato saved by Doreen, and coffee with two forgotten doughnuts. The refrigerator was empty, defrosting. I had my second cup of coffee with a Marlboro on the balcony, enjoying a brilliant Independence Day morning. After that, things moved fast.

As if by pre-arrangement, the giant and the former student arrived together, freeing me from heavy lifting. The loading was supervised by Doreen, who knew exactly what to take with us and what to leave behind. Within an hour the apartment was empty, with the giant taking the table and the chairs, and the TV set. He told us to come at noon, and although the barbecue was scheduled for later, we would have some early farewell roast.

After the two men left, with the former student saying good-bye and helping the giant by carrying the TV set, we had some coffee and a bath, Doreen first, to change and to take our discarded laundry to be washed in the basement. We were going to travel in comfort, in our most casual outfits and sneakers. When Doreen came up, I was sitting comfortably in one of the landlord's beach chairs on the balcony, sipping coffee and smoking. She joined me, and we both relaxed, talking....

It was now 11 o'clock. Doreen put the leftover coffee on the gas and, while it was heating, she swept the apartment. Then she poured the coffee in my thermos, with the rest in two cups for us, for a last sip, touching cups. Then she washed the coffee pot and the cups, put the coffee grounds and the sweepings in a garbage bag, the pot and cups in the box with the cutlery, and, carrying the box and the garbage bag, we left the apartment temporarily.

A perfectionist to the end, with merciless attention to detail for which people admired and hated me, I now checked an old bullet indentation on the garbage bin lid while disposing of our garbage bag. The indentation was still visible after two years, remaining there as a mark of a near and unsolved tragedy when a shot was fired in my direction (while also then disposing of garbage), ricocheted and hit me flat (luckily) on the forehead just above the left eye, causing temporary blindness and perhaps other after-effects, making me wonder to this day about the reasons for this act, if I was indeed its intended victim. Was it the Solidarity Symposium, or something else?

Moving to the basement, where Doreen was folding our laundry, I checked the storage bin, empty now except for some loose sheets in a box to be discarded, and I removed my lock. We moved to the U-Haul truck. Doreen put the clean laundry in my clothing suitcase on the bed, and I put the box with the pots and pans and cutlery in the back of the truck and locked it. We put the thermos and the box of Lorna Doones in the truck's cab. When we returned to the apartment the landlord was there, waiting for us.

He came for the keys, to say good-bye, and to express his regrets at losing me as a tenant. He was amazed to see the apartment in the condition we were leaving it on moving day. I told him how I enjoyed living in the house which had all the conveniences I wanted and needed. As we talked, the phone rang. It was the giant telling me he was ready for us. I disconnected the phone, slipped it in a plastic bag and into my briefcase.

It was exactly noon when we climbed into the cab of the U-Haul truck and started backing out of the alley behind the house, with the landlord guiding us along. We parked right in front of the giant's house, noticing the smoke in the backyard and seeing our host, coming out to meet us, strike up a conversation with the landlord about getting work for his firm. He got it, and turned to me:

"You brought me business. All Poles should be like you."

"We Jews are better at that," the landlord remarked.

He said good-bye, shook hands all around and excused himself, wishing us a good journey.

We followed our host into the backyard and there, a small pig was roasting on a spit over a slow fire built in a ditch on one side of the yard, in the middle of which was our old table and four chairs. There was a platter of pork on it, horseradish, brown bread, rolls, a jug of juice, a pot of coffee, and a bottle of Polish vodka. Presiding over this abundance was a young woman, the giant's wife. She filled our glasses and proposed a toast:

"To Independence Day!"

We raised our glasses but Doreen asked for water to dilute her drink. The hostess apologized, ran into the house, brought out a jug of water, and said something very clever: "On a Polish table there is never water, only 'little water' [vodka]."

What followed was—of all the "last" things we had been experiencing in Chicago in the last few days, like the protagonists of Mickiewicz's epic *Pan Tadeusz*—the best. But while Mickiewicz's feast was the *bigos*, which in its modern version contains a great amount of pork (sausage), our feast harked back not to the Lithuanian forest but to the German farmland, and from there to Silesia, and even to a German restaurant in Chicago which advertised a special meal after a pig slaughter (*Schweinschlacht*), because that was what the feast was all about. My giant friend combined the European ritual with the American barbecue ritual, and we ended the feast with another American tradition.

Apple pie and coffee was a perfect ending to a perfect meal on a perfect day, which was also Independence Day. I allowed myself a little luxury and bad form by having a Marlboro with my second cup, the only person smoking at the table, and by withdrawing into myself and thinking how this was the real farewell luncheon, the rituals of which were not of the common kind. Then I heard the host proposing a last (another "last") toast:

> *"To Professor Mocha and his charming wife—*
> *the best of luck to them,"*

and we were on our way.

The hosts escorted us to the U-Haul, where we said good-bye, with the hostess handing Doreen a brown paper bag which contained some roast pork and two slices of apple pie. The resourceful young woman advised us to have the food warmed up wherever we stopped for coffee, and the giant told us how to best reach the highway. I took a last look at the house, at "our" townhouse, waved back to our waving hosts, then sat in silence until we maneuvered our way to the highway and got into the proper lane, when I heard Doreen: "This was something! Are you sorry you are leaving?" I told her I needed proper rest to restore myself.

Rest was still far away. First we had to cross one third of America in holiday traffic, from Illinois to New York, across Indiana, Ohio, Pennsylvania, New Jersey. Drinking coffee from my thermos and nibbling cookies we were already deep in Ohio when we stopped at a roadhouse, parked in a truck lot, had split pea soup while waiting for our food to be warmed up in the cafeteria, had the pork and the apple pie with coffee, had the thermos filled, bought sandwiches and fruit for the road, then slept until dawn in our U-Haul, hearing the trucks come and go all around us.

We discovered that the cafeteria was an all-night establishment, where we could refresh ourselves and have an early breakfast, which meant that the supplies we already had and the candy we added to it would last us until we got home, with no need for longer stops. On previous trips along the same route, we would make various detours (to the Michigan Dunes; to give a lecture in Indianapolis; to see a friend in Cleveland; to see the Delaware Water Gap), but not this time. We just drove, stopping only to refresh ourselves, stretch our legs, and have a snack of one of our sandwiches, bananas, or candy with the rolls or bread from our Chicago hosts, washing it down with our own coffee. At this rate we crossed the George Washington Bridge in the early evening, entering New York and parking in front of our home soon after. Our daughter Jane was waiting for us, signifying the beginning of a family-oriented interval.

Mark's baby hadn't been born yet, which was good news, because we would be around when it happened; space had been cleared in the storage room in the basement for my books, which was also good news, because I could unload the U-Haul and return it. Steve, Jane's husband, came with a hand-truck from his store to help me, but insisted on doing all the work himself, saying it was his job, and he did. I had him put the books on a skid, in case the basement became flooded in bad weather, and then put the furnishings in the apartment. When my big comfortable bed was in place I knew I was home. I was also very tired, and left the return of the U-Haul to the garage to Doreen and Steve.

Our second grandchild was born on July 6. It was a girl, and Mark and Adina had a pair now, Justin and Jackie. Doreen rushed over to see how she could help, but Mark was very efficient looking after Justin, and Adina's mother was there to look after her and the baby. This freed Doreen to look after me, to help me regain weight, as she was firmly determined to do. I didn't want to put myself in a position of dependence, but when I almost fainted at Woolworth's on a particularly hot day and Doreen was summoned by the store manager to come for me, I began to worry again about the bullet and about what kind of medical help I should seek. Just when I was deciding to see a young black doctor in my neighborhood, something was taking place that gave me the relaxation I needed—the 1984 Los Angeles Olympic Games. A candidate for the 1948 London Olympic Games, I relaxed best when watching world-class sports. After watching the entire TV broadcast of the Olympics and eating and sleeping well, in two weeks I had regained my normal weight, 144 pounds, perfect for a six-foot tall runner (2 pounds per inch), according to sports medicine.

While I watched, I wrote about the Olympics, and afterwards I sold the lengthy article. For some reason, it was not published, probably because I criticized the United States' decision to boycott the 1980 Moscow Games which had caused the Warsaw Pact's boycott of the 1984 Los Angeles Games, the boycotts preventing America from winning both, victories which would have contributed to the decline of the Soviet Union in view of its stress on sports.

Since this was not an academic paper, I didn't care about it not having been published. The important thing was that I was able to sell my writing. I decided to write my memoir, as already imprinted on the program for the farewell luncheon in Chicago, *Choices in*

War and Peace, and because my early years and war service revolved around Germany, I registered for Advanced German at Columbia University. This decision had far-reaching consequences.

As a student of German, I was entitled to use the facilities of *Deutsches Haus* and encouraged to attend its *Kaffee Stunde* (Coffee Hour) on Wednesday afternoons. It was a favorable hangout of what my German woman-instructor called "culture vultures" (mostly elderly Central European Jews) but my presence soon changed that perception, and it became an elite club, very much like my "Coffee Break" at Loyola, but consisting of three members only: the Czech intellectual Leo; Joe, my former fellow Ph.D. candidate at Columbia, still hoping to finish his dissertation; and myself. All three of us were engaged in serious writing and reading each other's works, and because of that, we became objects of interest as writers. When I wrote something for *The New York Times* about Kurt Waldheim, it became a sensation at the Coffee Hour meetings. It was an even bigger sensation when the editor of the periodical *Modern Age*, after reading the piece, invited me to write for his quarterly. I accepted the invitation, but under the condition that I could start from the beginning. He agreed, and I became a writer for *Modern Age*. My first chapter, "Choices in War and Peace," about my family's evacuation from Germany to Poland after the Silesian Uprisings and my early school years in Poland, came out in the Summer/Fall 1986 issue, and the second, "In Sight of Crisis," covering my secondary school years (1935-1939), appeared in the Summer/Fall issue of 1987. Then problems started.

The publisher of *Modern Age* was eager to promote my memoir as a means to win subscribers to his quarterly from the Polish American community. He devised a special promotional flyer for the memoir, offering new subscribers a special discount. When mailed out to individuals and clubs, the flyer did indeed attract new subscribers, among them several former fellow-students, colleagues from academia, and total strangers who found the memoir not only fascinating but also important as a vehicle to remind the world about Poland. I received letters of support and encouragement, but also concern that the chapters were not coming out often enough. This was also my concern. By then I already had a chapter outline of a two-volume memoir consisting of five chapters each of *"War"* and *"Peace"* parts, the first focusing on the '40s in Europe and the second on five decades in America, from the '50s ("Working and Raising a

Family") through "Studying," "Teaching," "Writing," and "Dying in America in the '90s," preceded by a two-chapter introductory part, "Between the World Wars," altogether twelve chapters, some of which ("Stalag XVIIB") could be expanded to book length. There was a good chance I could publish all the chapters in *Modern Age*, but they would have to be printed in almost every issue for the entire memoir to be finished in two to three years, as I intended. But this was not the editor's intention. When I sent him the next chapter, "September 1939," the first of the *"War"* part, he returned it for more work (it looked perfect when I read it over coffee and *Kuchen* [pastries] to my associates at *Deutsches Haus*), and pointed out that I would have to just wait for my turn like everybody else. Apparently the publisher and the editor did not see eye-to-eye.

I sent the war piece to *The New Yorker* where the editor (Gottlieb, I think, at that time) sent it back with a thank you letter and a note that "it wouldn't work" in the weekly. Then I submitted it to *The New York Times Magazine*, where I thought it would have to work as an article marking the 50th anniversary of the outbreak of the Second World War, considering how many readers of *The Times* were participants in, victims of, and witnesses to the war. But here I ran into a real piece of bad luck.

Getting no reply, I called one late afternoon the following week and, after a long wait, someone who sounded like a cleaning woman answered the phone. (What does a cleaning woman sound like? Background sounds betray her.) She replied to my inquiry that *The New York Times Magazine* uses only its own writers for its articles. Knowing this not to be true, I became angry, told her off, and wrote a letter to the Editor of *The Times*, mentioning the cleaning woman. I received a long letter from Max Frankel, telling me that my article was lost and a search for it had not produced it. In the meantime, a similar assignment had been given to the military editor of *The Times*, and would appear on the first Sunday of September. It did appear, written from the vantage point of London, as if the war began there and not in Poland. The author died shortly afterwards, and I couldn't help wishing that he had died earlier.

By then I had to go to Poland to take part in the observances of the 50th anniversary, and to read excerpts from my article in Polish translation. Before leaving, I wanted to submit the article to one more American publication, *Harper's* magazine, not because of its reputation about which I knew very little at that time, but because of its Editor, Lewis Lapham, the host of the television programs "The American Century," *and* "Bookmark, an excellent program on which authors discussed their books, and which I was hoping to join one day with writers like Studs Terkel and John Lukacs. The article was to be my introduction. I typed a letter to Mr. Lapham, listing the twelve chapters of my memoir, but I discovered that, unfortunately, I had no copy of the third chapter (the article) and it was too late to make one. I mailed the letter on my way to the airport, adding that I would be back in New York on September 6.

I found Poland emerging from 45 years of Communist control, slowly groping its way into an uncertain future. This was after the visit by President Bush, and there was some disappointment about the extent of American help. As for the anniversary observations, I found the discussions of the causes and the conduct of the war rather naive and faulty. When I interrupted one long-winded professor and asked why the Poles hadn't taken General Gamelin's advice to abandon the Western provinces which were indefensible, and withdrawn to the South East bordering on Rumania, in order to secure a corridor to the Black Sea through which French help might come, he replied "Why should Poland listen to France which let it down by not attacking Germany?" I found such thinking incomprehensible, as if Poland had been in a position to dictate to France. Before leaving, I visited my relatives in Upper Silesia, including my three surviving sisters and an older brother, and found the same uncertainty, fueled by rising inflation. In this, as in our earlier meeting, we celebrated the 100th anniversary of our late parents' birth. Their children, grandchildren and great-grandchildren were present.

On September 6, still feeling the effects of jet lag, I received a call from *Harper's*, not from the Editor, but the Associate Editor, who was following up on my letter to Mr. Lapham. From the first words of the young man I detected a certain coolness toward me and my project. I realized that not sending the article with the letter had been a mistake, because its very first sentence contained a revelation not encountered so far in any histories of, or books on, the September campaign, namely why the Germans had begun their attack on the first Friday of the month. Even glancing at the article, Mr. Lapham (who had some knowledge of Poland, if only from hosting on "Bookmark" Lawrence Weschler, a staff writer from *The New Yorker* who wrote extensively on Solidarity) would have noticed the significant revelation, and I would be hearing from Lapham, not from his underling. My streak of bad luck was apparently continuing, and I sent the article to *Harper's* with some reluctance, feeling it was a waste of time.

My encounter with *Harper's* deserves a separate treatment. Suffice it to say now that it taught me a lot about publishing in pretentious American magazines, particularly how difficult it was to publish something Poland-oriented, unless it was sensational, chiefly because of the arrogance (ignorance) of the underlings handling the preliminaries. Once the Laphams are gone and there are no Tina Browns to step into their shoes, the magazines will go down because, among other things, they suffer from a common disease in American publishing: the lack of good copy readers. One example: after reproaching the Associate Editor for ignoring history by returning my article, I sent him a chapter about the humiliating French defeat in 1940 ("The Fallen Idol"). He returned it with a note that it was "paced for a book" and a remark, which sounded like a boast, that *Harper's* was printing something about 1940 by a Dutchman. I was curious and read the article until I got to a passage in which the author (Koenig) refers to Holland as a "poor" country. Nobody at *Harper's* knew that Holland was one of the richest colonial powers, and that until after World War II, Indonesia, the fourth largest nation in the world at the time of the writing, was Holland's colony! So much for *Harper's*.

By comparison, my chapters, each covering a separate topic, such as "The Passage to France" following "September 1939" and preceding "The Fallen Idol," were read twice, by my associates at the Coffee Hour in the *Deutsches Haus* and by me in the lecture/ discussion series at the East Central Europe Institute at Columbia University. I kept on writing and reading them. There were two readings for the Metropolitan Chapter of the Kosciuszko Foundation and one for the Polish Institute of Arts and Sciences. "The Fallen Idol" was followed by the grim "Europe Marching to German POW Camps," followed by "Stalag VIIA" preceding the already mentioned immense "Stalag XVIIB," to be followed by "Road to England" and "V-E Day." "To be followed" because the sequence was interrupted by the novelistic "Novgorodian Rubles," a treasure quest cutting across these and future chapters. Its writing was somehow suggested by the approaching Millennium of Christianity in Russia (which passed almost unnoticed) and by something else—bad news from Poland about neglected schools, underpaid teachers, and a generally unsatisfactory educational situation, which made me pay attention to these problems and seek remedies.

"Novgorodian Rubles" was a treasure quest which, if successful, could have taken care of many problems, but it was not completed yet. Something else was needed.

Absorbed by my writing and the arrival of three more grandchildren, I hadn't been paying attention to anything except my family and Poland (and, increasingly, America, in connection with Poland). I canceled all my memberships and subscriptions, keeping just two (or being kept by them as member emeritus after 30 years): the MLA (Modern Language Association) and AATSEEL (the American Association of Teachers of Slavic and East European Languages) and their publications. I also subscribed to *The New York Times* to keep track of current events. It was in *The Times* that I read an article which gave me an idea.

The idea was a book dedicated to the teachers of Poland. It came to me on New Year's Day, 1992, while reading an article defining the true purpose of education: *to prepare the next generation to inherit society*. I was struck by the simple wisdom of the definition, applicable to the whole world but particularly to the ex-Communist countries of Eastern Europe which had to be re-educated, a process that would last until the generation now in school, or entering it, completes its education. What a tremendous responsibility for teachers, and what a great need on our part to recognize it and help!

My book was meant to help by pointing to a period in twentieth century Polish history when teachers also had a responsibility to re-educate the nation, after a century of Partitions, accomplishing the task with great success. The task for today's teachers is not so formidable, but it is by no means simple. There is only half a century of foreign or alien rule to undo, but for 45 years the aliens were Poles, seduced by a foreign ideology.

The surviving Communists must not be allowed to interfere with the educational process of the country, but there was another problem, of a new kind: a spiritual danger of materialism expressed in free market consumerism and Poland's inability to satisfy the long suppressed expectations of its citizens. If the teachers find a way to deal with the problem in schools (by stressing traditional values?) while suppressing their own expectations, they will win for themselves the respect and social standing their predecessors enjoyed in the period described in my book.

The book itself was easy to produce. All that was needed was to expand (and illustrate with photos) my two articles in *Modern Age* and provide them with a brief "Preface" and an extensive "Introduction" showing that it was a part of a larger work. It also needed a new title: *Between the World Wars: The Education of a Polish Schoolboy* and financial support, for which I turned to my present and former associates, to the always reliable Lady Blanka Rosenstiel, to the equally reliable Polish Combatants Association, and to the fraternals. The slim volume was produced by Polstar Publishing in Greenpoint in time for part of its edition to be taken along with me while going to Poland to participate in the 1992 World Reunion of Polish Combatants, a memorable event with an inspiring parade that I hoped at least some of teachers in Poland were able to see to tell their pupils about. While in Warsaw, I discovered that it was not so simple to meet with anybody from the Ministry of Education or from the Polish Teachers Union to give them the books; that strange work ethics prevailed in Poland and that people seemed constantly to be taking vacations; so I just left the books on my way from the airport in the building of the former "Polonia" Society in the care of an employee of its present tenant, "Wspólnota Polska" (Polish Community?).

While seeking support for the book from the fraternals, I found out that Aloysius Mazewski, President of the Polish National Alliance and, as such, President of the Polish American Congress, had died in 1988, and that his successor in both offices was Edward Moskal, former Treasurer. Mr. Moskal supported the book, and I watched his initiatives, with a new interest in the PAC.

At first there was no initiative where there should have been. When former Congressman Ed Derwinski was being dropped as Secretary of the Department of Veterans Affairs (for which, incidentally, my son Paul works), a cabinet post, he was defended by the influential journalist William Safire in his incisive column in *The New York Times* but not, to my knowledge, by the Polish American Congress. It would seem that in this case the PAC continued its neglect of the Polish American community, despite the fact that Derwinski had some good ideas for the VA, while his successor was surrounded by controversies, including his self-serving statements concerning his accumulated pension (close to a million as President of a veteran organization) which he had taken with him, saying he "deserved it."

It was cases like this that made me pay close attention to America and to Polonia, especially since by then my creative writing had virtually stopped, due partly to the deaths, close together, of my two associates at the *Deutsches Haus* Coffee Hours, which were soon discontinued. I was still writing, but mostly "Letters to the Editor," many of them published, and some unpublished but privately distributed articles like "Quo Vadis, America?" during the 1992 Presidential elections.

I began drafting a sequel to my *Poles in America: Bicentennial Essays,* with the subtitle *Twenty Years Later.* But my colleagues in the preliminary editorial meetings, as well as professors Wieńceystaw Wagner and Janusz Zawodny, were advising me to change it, as it was too narrow, being aimed at the first book's audience, now largely gone, and I saw their point.

Because of its stress on Poland, absent in the first book, the new book was to be one of my vehicles to the Ambassador's job in Warsaw, soon to be vacant, and I began to seek the support of New York's Senator Patrick Moynihan, first by sending him some of my books to start correspondence, then visiting his office in Washington. The second vehicle was to be money, which I was hoping to get by playing in all kinds of sweepstakes and lotteries, with very little luck, but I continued, determined to go to Poland with enough money to help in the most vulnerable areas, education and the environment in my native Silesia, which I call the "Three Big E's" along with economy.

Then, cancer struck (a belated result of my Chicago burnout and harassment, including possibly the bullet), and all my later activity, including my further contact with, and observation of, the Polish American Congress, was to be as a convalescent.

A few months after my surgery and radiation treatment I tested my fitness for further activity by reading a paper, "Polish Contributions to the Battle of Normandy (and World War II)," at the East Central Europe Institute at Columbia University on the 50th anniversary of D-Day. Declared fit by those present at the reading, and later in my apartment where we had refreshments and played ping-pong, I plunged into planning how to help Poland but with a difference. Since going to Poland was out of the question, I drafted a program for a mini-Institute for Polish Affairs in the School of International Affairs at Columbia, where young potential leaders from Poland would study advanced English and American work ethics. The program would need an endowment of at least a million to get it started, and I am still trying to raise it.

Later that same year (1994) Mr. Moskal presided over the 50th anniversary meeting of the Polish American Congress in Buffalo. It was attended by leaders from Poland and from the American establishment, making it one of the biggest, if not the biggest, meetings in the history of the Congress, and a good opportunity for Mr. Moskal to assert his leadership. I wrote to him before he departed for Buffalo, requesting some statistical data about the Congress and the four most prominent fraternals. The request was ignored, which made me wonder whether the statistics did not compare favorably with 1976, but that is to be expected. Nineteen seventy-six was a banner year for Polonia, a year of taking stock (by me, with others), and if the stock has gone down somewhat since, it is part of a national trend, affecting Polish Americans less than other groups, the Jews, for example.

As it happens the Jews were the reason I heard and read about Mr. Moskal's "initiatives" again. I am referring to the exchange of letters between the President of the Polish American Congress and the President of Poland, initiated by Mr. Moskal on April 25, 1996, with a letter in which he accuses Polish authorities of being too submissive in the face of Jewish demands in Poland, and he cites a few examples of it. The letter became a source of controversy here and in Poland, where President Kwaśniewski's awkward handling of his reply, which the media saw before Mr. Moskal, prompted another letter from him, adding to the quite unnecessary controversy. Although I do not agree with the resulting attacks on Mr. Moskal by several self-styled Polonia "leaders," some going as far as to ask for his resignation (I even like his firmness), I nevertheless question the need for his letter.

As if anticipating the question, Mr. Moskal explains the need in his letter:

> It is the duty of the Polish American Congress to properly care for Polish interests and to react whenever they are violated.

That's just my point. Is it still the same "duty" it was in 1944 when Poland was being raped and the Polish American Congress was called into being "to react" to the violence, or shouldn't the Congress, half a century later and Poland fully independent, rethink its traditional concerns vis-à-vis Poland and its attitude toward its own community as pointed out in the beginning of this chapter? The end of this chapter is a proper place to dwell on this question, and if the answer is "yes" because this was the guiding principle at the founding of the Congress, it would also be necessary to strengthen its voice by caring about the interests of the Polish American community, to make it stronger, because it is, after all, the Polish *American* Congress, and to determine, once and for all, how many of us there are here, and how strong we are numerically.

In his letter, Mr. Moskal anticipates criticism that the Polish American Congress meddles in the internal affairs of Poland by justifying his action:

> My letter is an expression of opinion, which we always have the right to express as the voice of a 10-million strong American Polonia, this symbolic, almost one fourth part of the homeland.

This is a good argument, but the figure is too modest. For one thing: 10-million is more than "almost" one fourth of Poland's 38-million, but I am concerned with the total figure which has always been troublesome, and always, for various reasons, too low. (Nowak Jeziorański once wrote about a 5-million Polonia). In the previous chapter, "A Century of Progress," I do some estimating based on the projection of figures obtained by the Kennedys during the 1960 Presidential campaign. The results are startling, but not unexpected. It is possible now to speak about Americans of Polish descent as a group 20-million strong, equal to more than half of the population of Poland.

At the end of that same chapter, I do some speculating about Polish names in the American mainstream as encountered on the pages of *The New York Times*, and how the bearers of the names know who they are: their names tell them. As for people of Polish descent with altered or outright non-Polish names, the entertainment world is full of them. To name two: Loretta Swit (Świt is a Polish word, but pronounced differently) and Stephanie Powers (Federkiewicz). It is useful to read the monthly *GP Light* (English language supplement to *Gwiazda Polarna* of Stevens Point), where one often encounters such people, including the famous Martha Stewart and the Chief Justice of Wisconsin, Shirley Abrahamson.

It is important to keep the population figures accurate, irrespective of the official statistics, not only to have a stronger voice and a better informed audience in Poland, but for our own satisfaction and ethnic politics in America. A 20-million strong ethnic group is bigger than most countries in the world, as many as thirty of them in Europe alone, and there is no reason to be modest about it. After the far more numerous descendants of the English, Irish, and German immigrants, Polish Americans belong among the middle ethnic groups (the Italians are in between) together with the blacks (Afro-Americans) and Hispanics (Latin Americans). This closeness, both statistical and geographical (the latter gradually disappearing) has its own problems. Both blacks and Hispanics view the Polish Americans (and Poland!) as an obstacle to their progress. This perception among the blacks goes even beyond America, as when Archbishop Tutu complained during the Solidarity crisis that so much was being done by the West for Poland and nothing for South Africa. Rev. Jesse Jackson echoed this accusation by citing a baseless story that Poland had been rebuilt by America after the war with a virtually interest-free 6-billion-dollar loan [!] so why not rebuild America? In America itself, it was a black who replaced Ed Derwinski, and what is one to think of the attack on the Polish fighter Andrew Golota in Madison Square Garden by the black entourage of Riddick Bowe, a black fighter? (There was no outburst when Magda Grzybowska beat Venus Williams.)

As for the Hispanics, who are only beginning to compete in America, I know of only one instance of outright hostility toward Polish Americans, from my own experience, when a devious Hispanic chairwoman destroyed a trail-blazer department of Polish at Loyola University of Chicago. I have described this incident extensively as a warning of things to come and to alert the Polish American Congress.

Interestingly enough, there is no collision course between Polish Americans and American Jews, only strong reactions to everything perceived as anti-Polish or anti-Semitic, as when Polonia rushes to the defense of Poland, because it is Poland and not Polonia that is being attacked. Many American Jews have done much for Poland, among them Abe Rosenthal, *The New York Times* correspondent in Warsaw in the 1950's, who was expelled for his critical reports from Poland, but continued them from Vienna, winning the Pulitzer Prize. As Managing Editor of *The Times* and now a columnist ("On My Mind"), he returns to Poland occasionally in his writing, with a sentimental article "The Trees of Warsaw" (1983) after a visit, and admiring pieces about Poland's ability to get up after every fall. Another example occurred recently with William Safire defending Edward Derwinski.

Defending Poland from bitter Jewish attacks is a thankless and unproductive task when the time could be better spent on defending Polonia's strongholds in America and helping Poland where help is really needed, as will be shown in the next chapter ("The Big Fraternals"). That's why it was refreshing to read that in the talks at the meeting of the President of Poland with the President of the Polish American Congress at the United Nations, Polish-Jewish relations were put on a back burner, replaced by "more important" topics, such as the significance of Polonia's activities for the future of Poland (good start) and the expansion of NATO (does Poland *really* need it?).

To conclude the discussion of the troublesome and never to be resolved problems of Polish-Jewish relations, two points have to be made by one who has given them much thought and is no longer bothered by them. One concerns a line in the Talmud about places where Jewish blood was spilled. It is Poland's tragedy that most of the concentration camps were located there, turning the country into a huge Jewish cemetery. It is of some consolation that Auschwitz, the site of the biggest camp, was in Germany during the Holocaust, having been incorporated into the Third Reich, a fact largely unknown.

My second point concerns something even less known about what some Jews call "unrequited love." It was related to me with some emotion by a rabbi born in Poland who is the father-in-law of my younger son. The "unrequited love" is the love of Polish Jews for Poland, love that was allegedly never returned, causing bitterness, feelings of rejection and, in many cases, hostility. These points should be of help to the Polish American Congress in future discussions, if any, of Polish-Jewish relations.

Worthy of notice before closing the chapter is the "Political Memorial" sent by the Polish American Congress in 1996 to both the Republican and the Democratic Party Conventions in San Diego and Chicago respectively, spelling PAC's views on the most important problems of the internal and foreign policy of the United States. The Memorial did not show any party allegiance; it did not endorse either of the presidential candidates; it protested Jesse Jackson's statement, about Poland being rebuilt after World War II with American money, demanding its correction in the media.

Also worthy of notice is President Moskal's growing stature in Poland, reflected in honorary doctorate from the Medical Academy in Poznan in October 1997, and before that, in April, in "Honorary Citizen of Krakow." On that occasion, Mr. Moskal wrote a highly appreciative article in *Zgoda* (June 15) but spoiled it by railing about some unnamed people who do not understand "the principle of fraternalism." He is even more opinionated in the interview with *Nowy Dziennik* (November 18) concerning mostly Poland's chances of joining NATO, displaying much optimism, but also allowing that there are problems to solve beside NATO, and lawyers are employed to solve them, which is good news, which should be followed by one about the expansion of the Education Commission's responsibilities. As for the NATO expansion, President Moskal was one of the Polish Americans testifying before the Senate Foreign Relations Committee on behalf of the Central and East European Coalition.

4

Frank Mocha

THE BIG FRATERNALS:
HOW TO HELP POLAND

INTRODUCTION

Although not established until 1944, the Polish American
Congress functions as an umbrella over Polish American organizations, including those founded much earlier, the big fraternals, the
oldest of which dates from 1873 (The Polish Roman Catholic Union).
The fraternals are the backbone of Polonia and the source of
strength of the Polish American Congress (PAC), which they had
organized and are its most important member organizations. Their
local lodges or divisions and districts, together with veterans organizations, cultural societies, and other groups affiliated with PAC, as
well as organizations not affiliated or no longer affiliated with it,
plus PAC's State Divisions, stretch across the United States, forming
a network of Polish presence in America.

The term "network" applies just to well-known and well-
established organizations. There are a great many others, which will
be discussed in the "Introduction" to the next chapter ("Other Organizations and Institutions"). The present chapter is concerned only
with the fraternals which, being insurance societies, control great
amounts of money, an important factor in any undertaking on behalf
of Poland, which needs American Polonia's help.

By all standards of a free market economy, Poland is a success
story among the new emerging post-Communist democracies. There
is even talk of an "economic miracle" about to take place there, and
of Poland becoming the "Japan of Europe." But at what cost? With
all efforts directed at privatization and income-producing ventures,
other sectors are neglected, such as health, education and, above all,
the environment, as are also the elderly, children, and those unable
to keep up with new technologies. Of course, these are not just Polish
problems. Even America, the richest country in the world, has them,
and those who watched the last Presidential campaign must have

heard the Republican candidate's battle-cry: "Nobody must be left behind!" which, like all campaign slogans, is easier said than done. Even so, this is a problem in Poland where, according to reports, five million people have been "left behind," which means that one in seven Poles lives in poverty.

But it is not the biggest of Poland's problems. There is another one, which threatens the very existence of the nation, namely the fact that more people die in Poland than are born, which means depopulation of the country. This is the result of one of the dubious "blessings" of a free market economy: higher cost of living without corresponding higher wages, a situation in which having children is beyond the means of an average couple, and abortion becomes a solution, which is recommended by the "democratic left" (former communists).

It is imperative for Poland to reverse the process of depopulation, just begun, before it becomes irreversible. With the economy growing, today's unemployment may change into tomorrow's shortage of labor and reliance on migrant workers, with all the disruptions that *that* involves. There is also another reason: Poland, squeezed between the two largest populations in Europe, the German and the Russian, cannot exist as a midget between two giants. Who knows what either of them will turn into? "History hasn't ended yet," as *The New York Times* columnist, David Gonzales, quoted me. Even Ukraine, part of the old Polish Commonwealth, has a larger population than its former mother country.

These population problems were well understood in prewar Poland, which had a natural increase on the average of half a million a year. But in Marshal Pilsudski Poland had a leader who could inspire the nation, a leader with a worldwide reputation. It is difficult not to speculate what would have happened if Pilsudski had lived longer. He could have probably prevented World War II or at least delayed it, which would have been quite enough.

This is a book of ideas, and the present chapter contains the most pressing one: How to help Poland *now*. Of the eleven fraternal insurance societies affiliated with PAC, four are uniquely qualified to help by tradition and experience. Their combined assets are considerable (the Polish National Alliance alone has assets of $310 million, as quoted in the latest interview with its President, Edward Moskal); they are also the oldest and the largest:

- Polish National Alliance (1880)
- Polish Roman Catholic Union (1873)
- Polish Women's Alliance (1898)
- Polish Falcons of America (1887)

We will look at each one of them beyond the thumbnail sketches we had already drawn of them, but in the context of the best way for them to help Poland. This help is not to be confused with help under the auspices of the Polish American Charitable Foundation, which goes back to 1971.

A. POLISH NATIONAL ALLIANCE (PNA)

The Polish National Alliance of the United States of North America (PNA's full name) is the most important support mechanism of the Polish American Congress (PAC), whose President is also President of PNA and has his office at PNA's headquarters at 6100 North Cicero Avenue, Chicago. (PAC's national office is also no longer at the "Polish Triangle" but at 5711 North Milwaukee Avenue).

With its local lodges, its councils, and districts, the PNA is by far the strongest organization in Polish America. As a fraternal, it ranks high nationally among similar organizations. It is no wonder then that all three presidents of PAC so far have also been presidents of PNA. The fact that PNA has two widely read newspapers, the Chicago-oriented *Dziennik Związkowy* ("Polish Daily *Zgoda*") and the bilingual fortnightly *Zgoda* with a high circulation nationally, is of importance in the arrangement.

The united presidency is not an official arrangement. Started in 1944 by Karol Rozmarek who, as President of PNA, was instrumental in founding the Polish American Congress and became its first president, it worked well during most of his 24-year tenure, until he was challenged, first for the presidency of the PNA (1967) and then of PAC (1968) by Aloysius Mazewski. The transfer of leadership in two stages meant that the changing of the guard was not amiable and that for one year (1967-1968) the two organizations had two presidents until Rozmarek's term at PAC expired and Mazewski was elected. He presided over both organizations for the next twenty years.

Mazewski's sudden death of heart failure at 72 in August of 1988 threw both organizations into confusion, which was dispelled thanks to responsible action on the part of potential presidents. Helen Szymanowicz, First Vice President of PNA, took over temporarily as President and was succeeded by Edward J. Moskal, who was elected to complete Mazewski's term in October; Kazimierz Łukomski, Vice President of PAC, took over temporarily as president, but like Szymanowicz, immediately made known his decision not to seek the presidency. Instead, he called a meeting of the PAC National Council of Directors to decide how to fill Mazewski's place. At the November 11, 1988 meeting, most of the nominees for the presidency withdrew, leaving only Chicago Alderman Roman

Pucinski (former US Congressman), President of PAC Illinois Division, and Moskal, who won over Pucinski, thus maintaining the tradition of one president.

Looking at the three presidents, we see Rozmarek gaining office at one of the darkest hours of Poland's history, and valiantly wrestling with it. With the cloud hanging over him of having been duped by Roosevelt, Rozmarek neglected domestic problems. Mazewski, on the other hand, took over in a spirit of activism and renewal, manifesting itself in the formation of 18 "commissions," most of them focusing on the domestic problems or issues facing Polonia; and a "PAC Talent Bank" was created.

But Poland's problems were never far away. Among Mazewski-created "commissions," one of the most active was the "Polish Affairs" (headed by Łukomski), which concerned itself with Poland. In 1971 the Polish American Congress Charitable Foundation was established as a reaction to the bloody riots along the Baltic seacoast to protest a thirty percent increase in the prices of most foods and consumer goods on the very eve of the 1970 Christmas holiday season. This interference with cherished Christmas in Poland showed more than anything else the alien nature of the regime, and there was no reconciliation possible after that. The riots put an end to the long rule of Władysław Gomułka, who was replaced by Edward Gierek and his new plan to improve the stagnant economy with a modernization program based on foreign loans. The program failed because of wasteful planning and Soviet exploitation of the loans. By then an organized opposition to the regime already functioned in Poland, culminating in the rise of Lech Walesa's Solidarity in 1980 (helped by the visit of the newly elected "Polish" Pope in 1979) and the subsequent fall of Edward Gierek. In Polonia, the focus of its spokesman, Aloysius Mazewski, shifted from domestic problems to problems in Poland, to the neglect of the former.

When Edward Moskal became the PNA/PAC President in 1988, he was, like Rozmarek had been, plunged into Poland-centered problems. Unlike Rozmarek, who had no predecessor, Moskal followed Mazewski's policies, but unlike either of his predecessors, he could see light at the end of the tunnel, being just one year away from the victory of the democratic opposition in Poland.

How can the Polish National Alliance, the subject of this sub-chapter, help Poland in this new scenario? As the most important support mechanism of the Polish American Congress, of course, but also in line with its own traditions, among which education has always stood out, as shown by the continued support of Alliance College in Cambridge Springs, Pennsylvania, founded in 1912. Alliance existed until 1987, when it was closed down for lack of students, as was to be expected from the youngest generation's flight from ethnic roots in the 1980's. How important the College was in its beginning could be seen when President William H. Taft attended its opening ceremonies. What it left behind we can read today in a report about its impressive library:

> The Alliance College Polish Collection is honored with an exhibit and reception by the University of Pittsburgh's library system on October 12 at the Hillman Library. The collection is one of the most prestigious in the nation and consists of 35,000 books and 10,000 journals, newspapers, yearbooks, records, slides, maps, movies, calendars, musical scores, all chronicling Polish culture, history and politics. The exhibit has established the university as one of the largest repositories for work of this kind (*GP Light*, October 1996).

It is too late to enrich Poland with the Alliance College Polish Collection. It is where it should be, in its home state, Pennsylvania, and in a traditional Polish ethnic town, Pittsburgh, where it can do some good for the Poles, and in a good university, where it can attract young Polish American students, who need a reminder of who they are.

But there are other ways in which the PNA can continue its tradition. Before Alliance College was founded, its members supported, with a 5 cents a month assessment, the Seminary in Orchard Lake, Michigan, the first Polish school of higher learning in the USA. More recently, PNA was one of the sponsors of my book about schools in pre-war Poland and how they can serve as a model for today (*Between the World Wars: Education of a Polish Schoolboy*). PNA can help Poland, at no cost, in the present state of its education, where help of a particular kind is needed.

Here is an idea for consideration. To begin with, let the PNA adopt a school in Warsaw, a good secondary school, with a good program in foreign languages, including English, the type of school in which future elites are studying. The adoption process, arranged with the Polish Ministry of Education, would be limited at first to one respectable and respected Polish American visiting the school once a week for a meeting with students interested in America and

American Polonia. These meetings would be extra-curricular and strictly voluntary. The only problem with the arrangement would be the choice of the person conducting these meetings. It would have to be somebody at home both in America and in Poland, somebody perfectly bilingual, and willing and eager to donate his time to the idea. The person I have in mind is Professor Wieńczysław Wagner, a resident of both countries the last time I heard from him, perfectly qualified for such an assignment.

Professor Wagner is a renowned jurist and as such, is unlikely to create any controversies. His assignment would be not teaching, but *informing*, after regular school hours in order not to interfere with its curriculum and to attract only those really interested in what he has to say as demonstrated by their willingness to give up some of their free time to it.

Professor Wagner would inform the students about America, expanding and correcting its image in Poland. Like most of Europe and the world, Poland is a country where an average teenager knows more about Madonna and Michael Jackson than about presidential candidates, and almost nothing about anything else. Knowledge about America is derived mostly from entertainment—movies, television, rock concerts—and not from good literature and objective press. Students learn more about America outside of school than in it, which is a pity because teachers are bound to have at least some legitimate preparation about America. American Polonia is not held in high esteem in Poland, with old stereotypes still in existence. Someone of Wagner's stature is needed to project a proper image of Polonia.

If the experiment with this first pilot school is a success, other schools should be adopted by the PNA, and more speakers involved, drawn perhaps from the ranks of visitors. Professor Wagner would, of course, need an office and a secretary to help him coordinate the program. Before any office space is rented, the Ministry of Education and Wspólnota Polska (Prof. Stelmachowski) should be approached with a request for office space, using as an argument that the evolving program was in Poland's best interest.

This would not be the first office of a Polish American organization in Poland.

There is yet another reason why the program should have an office instead of operating out of Professor Wagner's apartment (provided, of course, that Prof. Wagner takes up the idea): an office would endow the PNA program with an air of professionalism and efficiency. It would also be a starting point for specific activities in Poland by the three other big fraternals: Polish Roman Catholic Union, Polish Women's Alliance, and Polish Falcons of America. Together with the Polish National Alliance they would become Polonia's unofficial Embassy in Poland, under the aegis of the Polish American Congress.

B. POLISH ROMAN CATHOLIC UNION (PRCU)

The Polish Roman Catholic Union of America (PRCU's full name) is the oldest Polish American fraternal (1873), and the second largest after the Polish National Alliance. Its members are organized in hundreds of lodges across the country. Its headquarters are in the "Polish Triangle" at 984 North Milwaukee Avenue in Chicago, which is also the address of the Polish Museum, PRCU's proudest creation (to be discussed separately, in the next chapter, "Other Organizations and Institutions").

To carry its message, and that of the President (currently Edward Dykla), the Polish Roman Catholic Union publishes an official organ, a bi-weekly *Naród Polski* ("Polish Nation"), the 24,000 copies of which go to family groups of paid-up members. Its slogan, "Fraternalism, Patriotism, Service" and the years 1873 and 1996 [replaced since by 'Your Window to the World of Polonia' Celebrating 100 Years under the Masthead of 'Naród Polski' and 1997] on top of the masthead, as well as the round emblem between the two words of the publication's title, reflect PRCU's origins and mission.

The emblem itself is a little masterpiece. Inside two circles, of which the outer one, red, contains the full spelled out name of PRCUA, and the inner one, black, the slogan, but with "Benefits" replacing "Patriotism" as a reminder that PRCU is an insurance society, the emblem is full of symbols, beginning with crossed flags of America and Poland, and the Polish white eagle on red background in the lower section between the poles of the flags, and a red symbol (difficult to identify) between the flags, above.

As Kathryn Rosypal, Executive Editor of *Naród Polski* explained to me over the phone, the symbol shows the Sacred Heart of Jesus, the patron, with flames above it and a crown of thorns around it, and black letters "P.R.C.U.A." on top of it, next to the black, inner circle. This mixing of religious and lay symbols is reflected in the PRCUA name with its religious ("Roman Catholic") and lay ("Polish," "Union," and "America") parts, which is how the founders, equally divided between priests (Theodore Gieryk, Leopold Moczygemba) and laymen (Jan Barzyński, Peter Kiolbassa) saw the fraternal, as a fusion of clergy and laity.

Walter Zachariasiewicz, who wrote about the Polish fraternals in the forerunner of the present book twenty years ago, goes into

great length when discussing the PRCU. Just to quote one passage
from his fine essay:

> Founded to preserve Catholic and Polish traditions and culture
> among Polish immigrants and to inspire them with true American
> ideals, the Union played a significant role in the development of
> Polish communities, instilling among its members a pride of their
> Polish heritage as well as high moral and civic values.

Founded to serve the interests of the entire Polish community,
then estimated at 200,000, the PRCU had that many members at its
peak, and a history to be proud of.

During its long existence, the PRCU expended great sums of
money not only in benefits to its members, but also for humanitarian, social, educational, as well as patriotic causes on behalf of
Poland. According to Zachariasiewicz:

> The Union's concern for Poland was best manifested during the
> First World War. Members contributed generously to the Polish
> Central Relief Committee, which helped victims of war in
> Poland. Politically the Union supported the Polish National
> Committee, whose dominant figure was Ignacy Jan Paderewski.
> The largest recruiting station for the Polish Army of volunteers
> (known as Gen. Haller's Blue Army) was in the Union's build-
> ing. The membership of the organization at that time topped
> 100,000.

Concern for Poland in crisis returned with the outbreak of the
Second World War with the end of the brief period of independence
that permitted social and cultural relations. Once again, the PRCU
became a center of activity, first as the headquarters of Polonia's
relief efforts, and then of the Catholic League organized for postwar
religious help to Poland. The religious aspect of PRCU's concern for
Poland lasted over the entire 45-year span of Communist control. It
is an irony of history that the concern needs to be even stronger after
the defeat of Communism, because of what the regime left behind—
the most serious problem facing Poland then—uncontrollable (but no
longer legalized) abortion.

For many years the Polish Roman Catholic Union has taken a
pro-active stance against abortion, under President Edward Dykla.
According to *Naród Polski* (April 18, 1996):

Taking advantage of its unique location, the Polish Roman Catholic Union of America is proud to make its unwavering support of the Catholic Pro-Life position known to all Chicago—plus the thousands of tourists from all over the world who travel on the Kennedy Expressway—with a huge **Respect LIFE** sign painted on the headquarters building.

The Polish Roman Catholic Union should take its message to Poland, as part of the program proposed for the Polish National Alliance. It should be talking to the graduating seniors, telling them about the dangers, individual and group, of now illegal (but resorted to) abortion, and of the joys of family life, the latter ideally in concert with the Polish Women's Alliance.

C. POLISH WOMEN'S ALLIANCE (PWA)

The Polish Women's Alliance of America (PWA's full name) is the largest Polish women's organization in the US. Its members, who at is peak numbered 80,000, are organized in districts (*Obwody*), commissions, and reportedly several hundred groups nationwide (the Lira Ensemble, for example, is Group 816). After a move from its historic headquarters in the "Polish Triangle," the PWA is located at 205 South Northwest Highway at Park Ridge, near Chicago. It still has its own organ, the bi-weekly and bilingual *Głos Polek* ("The Voice of Polish Women"), which tells its message of the woman's role as the staunch custodian and firm guardian of Polish family life, a message which should be voiced in Poland, where family life is beginning to unravel.

From its founding in 1898-99, the association was fortunate to attract remarkable women, from its founder, Stefania Chmieliński, through women capable of standing up to Roosevelt when Poland's fate hung in the balance in 1944, to fine postwar presidents Adela Łagodzinska, Helen Zieliński and Helen V. Wójcik. About its current president I know little except her inspiring first name, Delphine (Lytell). The PWA list of Honorary Members is even more impressive, including such prominent Polish women as Maria Konopnicka, Eliza Orzeszkowa, Maria Rodziewiczówna, and three Helenas: Modrzejewska, Paderewski, and Sikorska. Very appropriately, the PWA has a museum and a library.

At some point the PWA worked with Senator Barbara Mikulski of Maryland on women's issues in America, but its main goals, as spelled out by Zachariasiewicz, are

> ...to foster a permanent national spirit, preserve Polish ideals among the younger generation by cultivating within it knowledge of Polish history and literature, and impressing upon it the need of maintaining a constant relation with Poland, thus developing within it the cultural values that are inherent in the Polish people.

To preserve Polish values among the younger generation of Polonia, PWA established a special Youth Department, which conducts its activities through the network of hundreds of youth groups called *Wianki*. Every two years the PWA sponsors a youth convention in each of its districts.

The lessons learned by the Youth Department of the Polish Women's Alliance of America could be applied in the old country,

Poland. It would be a remarkable and unique reversal. Values once brought to America by the ancestors of the present younger generation from Poland (where they are now, for various reasons, disappearing in a disturbing process spreading in a widening circle from the capital to the provinces), would be returning in symbolic repayment after a century. If the Polish Women's Alliance should join the Polish Roman Catholic Union in a program spearheaded by the Polish National Alliance under the aegis of the Polish American Congress (provided such a program becomes a reality, as it should), it must be well prepared.

Since, like the PRCU, the PWA would address itself to young women who are soon-graduating seniors, its office should be supplied with appropriate publications dealing with health, family life, work, and motherhood. There are good American magazines dealing with the topics, including:

* *American Health, Fitness of Body and Mind*, $12.97 yearly
* *Family Life*, $9.97 (6 issues);
* *Working Mother, New Ways to Work from Home*, $12 annually
* *Parenting, What's in a Name?* $15 per year.

Among books on these topics, the most recent is *Fruitful: A Real Mother in the Modern World* by Anne Roiphe (260 pp.; Boston: Houghton Mifflin Company. $22.95).

The purpose of the Polish Women's Alliance mission in Poland should be the restoration of family values and the preparation of young ladies for responsible motherhood which, in Anne Roiphe's words, is the "center of the soul" when it is not just motherhood as a discharge of a woman's duty, but what she calls a truly rewarding "mothering." Such a motherhood excludes abortion, which is causing a declining birthrate, currently below replacement level in Poland, with all the consequences that this implies.

The three fraternals could be instrumental in starting a reversal of the evil and threat to Poland, while the fourth, by virtue of its history and stress on fitness, would raise the nation's health according to the motto "Mens sana in corpore sano" of its guardians, the Falcons.

D. POLISH FALCONS OF AMERICA

The Falcons, a national fraternal and physical fitness organization with headquarters in Pittsburgh, Pennsylvania, has a history going back to Poland, where organized sports began in 1867 (four years after the disastrous January Uprising against Russia in 1863) with the founding in Galicia, Austrian Poland (freer after "Ausgleich") of the Polish Gymnastic Association "Sokoł" ("Falcon"), a paramilitary and sports organization which was extended to Prussian Poland in 1885, to Russian Poland (illegally) in 1905, and to Polish émigré groups abroad, chiefly in America.

The falcon was adopted as the official emblem of the organization to symbolize strength, fearlessness, and independence, qualities the Falcons needed in their sworn dedication to the liberation of Poland. The first Falcons chapter in America was organized in 1887 in Chicago by Felix Pietrowicz, who became the chapter's first physical fitness instructor. A few years later, representatives of several already existing Falcons groups met to form a national organization, which eventually became incorporated under its present name, "Polish Falcons of America."

Under its new charter, the Falcons became a fraternal benefit organization, with a membership of close to 30,000 in 17 states at its peak, divided into a dozen districts and more than a hundred nests. They publish an official organ, the monthly *Sokoł Polski* ("The Polish Falcon"). However, despite the new status, the Falcons remained faithful to their long patriotic tradition, but dividing their loyalty between Poland—their homeland, and America—their adopted country. To quote Zachariasiewicz:

> The Falcons passed their highest test of patriotism during World War I. From among 12,000 well-trained members, 7,000 answered President Wilson's first call for volunteers when war was declared against Germany. Later on, 5,000 Falcons joined the Polish Army organized on French soil. These men, joined by 27,000 other Poles, fought under the command of General Haller first in France [where, unlike after World War II, the Polish Army, including the Falcons, took part in the Victory Parade in Paris, creating a highly favorable impression...*F.M.*] and subsequently in Poland, thus contributing to its liberation. During World War II, many members of the Falcons organization and most of their instructors, all well-drilled, again answered the call to arms.

The Falcons continue to exert much effort for the physical mental, and cultural welfare of its members. Their athletic programs include gym classes; volleyball, basketball, and baseball competitions; swimming; golf tournaments, etc. Biannually, track and field meets are held in some states, while national competitions take place every four years in conjunction with the Falcons national conventions.

The Falcons have summer camps which are used for children's colonies, for various sports, and for cultural and patriotic events. The Falcons also maintain a Special Scholarship Fund for deserving college students who major in Physical Education.

Because of their stress on fitness and physical education, the Falcons of America could play an important part in the proposed program in Poland aimed particularly at secondary schools. Physical Education begins in school, and since the Falcons help train specialists in it in America, why not in Poland?

Pre-war Poland had an excellent Central Institute of Physical Education (CIWF) which, by the 1930's, began to supply the schools with physical education instructors, who were replacing the existing ones, for the most part former junior officers in Pilsudski's Legions rewarded with the jobs for wartime service. The new instructors were not just monitoring volleyball or basketball games and conducting calisthenic exercises, they were active athletes frequently ranked among the best in the country in their specialties, bringing their experience and knowledge of the sports with them. On rainy days they would hold classes in hygiene and even dancing, crowning them with a mixed dance at the end of the year, to help develop the students' social graces. Games were moved from the regular classes to Saturday afternoon sessions when mini-tournaments were conducted.

As for the calisthenics, they were shifted to the first break, where, for 15 minutes every day the entire school assembled in the yard to take part in synchronized Swedish calisthenics, with the instructor leading the exercises from a raised platform to loud music broadcast nationally on the radio. This was a new concept in physical culture, a concept which the Falcons should seriously consider restoring in Poland as one of the pre-war ideas worth emulating, for obvious reasons.

There are other pre-war ideas the Falcons should think of restoring in order to raise the level of fitness and physical culture in Poland. Following Poland's dismal showing at the Berlin Olympic Games in 1936, four years after the euphoria of the Los Angeles

Games where Poland not only had the fastest woman in the world in the highly competitive "Stasia" Walasiewiczowna (Stella Walsh from Cleveland) and the best long distance runner in the highly popular Janusz "Kusy" Kusocinski, a sports movement was started in Poland and a membership pin produced in large quantity to be awarded to participants in sports festivals all over the country who achieved minimum results in track and field events. Winning the POS (Państwowa Odznaka Sportowa) pin would create a stimulus for more training and competition resulting in uncovering talent for the next Olympic Games to be held in Helsinki in 1940, which was the movement's goal. Since CIWF graduates were involved, the level of physical culture and fitness was raised considerably in Poland, which raises a question whether Poland's post-war successes in sports were due more to pre-war practices than the regime's support. Hence, why not a Falcons pin and Falcons-sponsored competition?

The postwar equivalent of the Central Institute of Physical Education (CIWF) was the Academy of Physical Education, the noun "Academy" presumably making a claim to an academic standard. I have no personal acquaintance with the Academy the way I had with CIWF (one of whose graduates saw in me a future Olympian), and I can't say how much it contributed to Poland becoming an athletic power within a decade after the war, but this is history now. The period of the Polish "Wunder Team" with Kirszenstein-Szewińska, the best woman sprinter of all time, and Pawłowski, the best fencer of all time, along with world class soccer, volleyball, fencing, boxing and weight-lifting teams is over, and only occasionally a star appears, like Wanda Panfil, winner of the New York City Marathon (living and training in Mexico). More often than not it's a tarnished star, like Niemczyk, the marathon runner disqualified in New York for substance abuse, and Andrew Golota, a high-ranking professional boxer with a criminal record and a disqualification in his last two fights for hitting below the belt, who now represent Poland. It is obvious that all is not well with physical culture in Poland, and help is needed, with the Falcons the ideal candidate to give it.

This is a surprising conclusion, considering the results in the last Olympic Games (in Atlanta), in which Poland finished in 11th place overall, almost, but not quite among the top ten athletic powers in the world, its customary place. Its 7 gold medals were equal to the best Polish starts, in Tokyo (1964), Munich (1972) and Montreal (1976). What doesn't quite add up is the high ratio (7:17) of gold medals in the overall number of Polish medals (in Barcelona in 1992 it was 3:19). This disparity was explained by a Polish critic in *Polityka* (August 16, 1996):

> Not to belittle our output, we triumphed in events in which it is easier to develop a champion than, for example in track and field events, which would call for a reform of the methods of popularizing physical culture, beginning with kindergarten.

This is just the point, and this is what the Falcons could do in Poland, popularize physical culture, beginning with the nationwide morning calisthenics exercises in schools across the country. Not any modern aerobics, but what we used to call "gimnastyka szwedzka" ("Swedish gymnastics") in the old days. Getting it installed would be a gift of technology from the Falcons to Poland, as there once was a gift of blood, which helped to liberate Poland. The gift of daily nationwide calisthenics would make every child in Poland healthier and fitter, dedicated to physical culture, and a potential athlete, a sum of benefits far exceeding the cost, which could probably be covered by a foundation.

The Polish critic concentrates on individual track events, but it is in team sports, such as volleyball and soccer, in both of which Poland was once Olympic champion, where the greatest decline has taken place, with Poland losing all of its five matches in volleyball in Atlanta, and for the first time not even qualifying in soccer.

The last time Poland excelled in both the track and the team events was in 1976 at the Montreal Olympics, where the great Irena Kirszenstein-Szewińska won her last gold medal, this time in the 400-meter run, not her usual 100 and 200-meter sprints; where the amazing Jacek Wszoła won the high jump, the first time a Polish athlete won that event; and when an inspired Polish volleyball team defeated the Soviet Union in the final, winning a gold medal for Poland. There were other gold, silver and bronze medals, but these three deserve special mention because of their stellar quality and the large crowds of patriotic Polish Americans and Polish Canadians present at the Games. Perhaps the Falcons will be able to restore some of the patriotism in a consumerism-obsessed Poland.

P.S. Poor showing in the recent World Championships in Switzerland, far behind the supposedly problems-beset Russia and even the hard-pressed Ukraine, both behind Poland as free-market democracies, is a call for action, as is also elimination in qualifying rounds of the World Cup.

HEADQUARTERS OF SELECTED INSTITUTIONS OF AMERICAN POLONIA

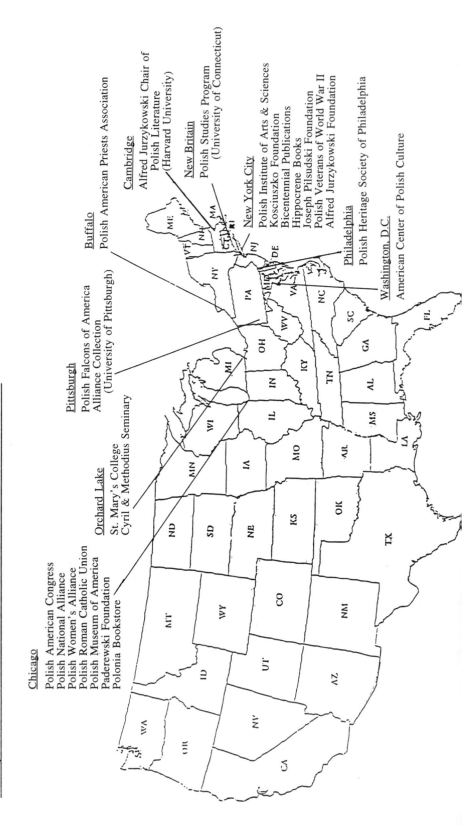

Chicago
Polish American Congress
Polish National Alliance
Polish Women's Alliance
Polish Roman Catholic Union
Polish Museum of America
Paderewski Foundation
Polonia Bookstore

Pittsburgh
Polish Falcons of America
Alliance Collection
(University of Pittsburgh)

Orchard Lake
St. Mary's College
Cyril & Methodius Seminary

Buffalo
Polish American Priests Association

Cambridge
Alfred Jurzykowski Chair of
Polish Literature
(Harvard University)

New Britain
Polish Studies Program
(University of Connecticut)

New York City
Polish Institute of Arts & Sciences
Kosciuszko Foundation
Bicentennial Publications
Hippocrene Books
Joseph Pilsudski Foundation
Polish Veterans of World War II
Alfred Jurzykowski Foundation

Philadelphia
Polish Heritage Society of Philadelphia

Washington, D.C.
American Center of Polish Culture

5

Frank Mocha

OTHER ORGANIZATIONS AND INSTITUTIONS

INTRODUCTION

No ethnic group in America has more organizations, institutions, foundations, clubs, leagues, circles, centers etc., than the Polish American group. This multitude can be explained by the tradition of taking the name of a Polish hero of the American Revolution, Kosciuszko or Pulaski, to start an organization, a tradition further explained by the Polish immigrants' desire to belong to something Polish in the absence of Poland, and in this way, like other groups, to feel connected to America, an alien country at first.

Other names were taken from Poland's cultural history, with the names (Chopin, Paderewski) reflecting the character of the organization (music, art), while more recent names (Pilsudski, Dmowski), reflecting Poland's long struggle for independence, pointed to the organization's politics inherited from the wartime and postwar exiles. The current name, of John Paul II, points to the religious nature of the foundations or centers named after him.

Unlike the big fraternals, not one of which was named after a famous person, having been organized, beginning with the Polish Roman Catholic Union, with the unrestricted idea of uniting the Polish immigrants in this country, none of the other organizations had a comparable nationwide character. The closest to this ideal came the American Council of Polish Cultural Clubs (ACPCC), started in August 1939 in a New York meeting of Polish American cultural leaders to discuss uniting the Polish Arts Clubs that had mushroomed in America during the interwar period of cultural relations with newly-independent Poland.

Like the ACPCC, other organizations have also achieved a measure of nationwide character by virtue of either membership and branches (The Kosciuszko Foundation and the Polish Institute of Arts

95

and Sciences), or membership and regiments or posts (the Polish Scouting Organization and Polish Veterans organizations). While the two former are essentially cultural and scholarly institutions (to be discussed in separate sub-chapters), the two latter are expressions of Polish patriotism and service to the Polish cause. Both had their start in America in and after World War I and World War II, but while the Polish Scouting is thriving under the watchful eye of Tadeusz Kozłowski, president, and his wife Danuta, secretary, in Clark, New Jersey, and Ewa Gierat, author of *History of Scouting in the US* and editor of Polish Scouting's quarterly *Znicz* ("Torch") and monthly "Newsletter" in Bethlehem, Connecticut, the Polish veterans are dying out and, with them, their organizations, ending an epic spanning a century climaxing in a Warsaw parade in 1992.

Several postwar institutions should be mentioned here, with special attention paid to the role of women in starting and running them, as in the case of The American Institute of Polish Culture, Inc., in Miami, Florida, whose founder and president, Blanka A. Rosenstiel, a patroness of Polish culture, will be discussed with other "Polish Women in America" in Chapter 6, "Individual Accomplishments." An almost exact namesake but younger than the Institute, which was probably its inspiration, The American Center of Polish Culture, Inc., in Washington, DC, tries to become a factor on the capital's cultural landscape through guest lectures, exhibitions, and fund-raising raffles. It is not clear in what way such activities could be of direct help to Poland, an imperative for American Polonia, unless the Center becomes also a lobbying stage on behalf of Poland. Of an entirely different nature is Chicago's Legion of Young Polish Women, no longer "young" and no longer "legion" but at its best a reliable fund-raiser, whose popular balls provided funds for a variety of worthy causes, including the cost of the addition of an Index of Names (5,400) to this writer's book, *Poles in America*, in 1978.

There is a Copernicus Foundation in Chicago and Jurzykowski Foundation in New York, the former started by Mitchel Kobelinski, former Small Business Administration head, a Cabinet post, and the latter by the industrialist Alfred Jurzykowski, a solid pedigree in both cases. While not much is heard from the Copernicus, the Jurzykowski, once the benefactor of the Polish Institute of Arts and Sciences, is heard from once a year, at the ceremony of the Alfred Jurzykowski Awards in literature, history, medicine and science. The awards, for better or worse, favor Poland.

There is a veritable plethora of smaller entities which are still awaiting a compilation. A step in the right direction is *Polonia Connections*, subtitled "A Regional Resource," compiled recently by Michael Pietruszka for a region comprising Western New York, Southern Ontario, and Western Pennsylvania. Its 41 pages of entries (pp. 3-43), each containing 8-10 entries, for a total of close to 400, are a mine of information on clubs, institutes, centers, committees, societies, associations, groups, foundations, alliances, auxiliaries, unions, councils, divisions, nests, homes, schools, programs, choirs, ensembles, shows, churches (67—Roman and National), congregations, posts (veterans), and even Polish government offices. Assuming that a similar situation prevails in the tri-state area in the East, in the Midwest and, to a lesser extent in the South (Florida), Southwest (Texas) and West (California), we are dealing with thousands of entities, not counting such individual Polonia activists as Henry Archacki, Ed Pinkowski, Col. Anthony Podbielski, and Joseph Wardzala. Visitors from Poland, not understanding the original necessity and present needs, would like to see them all unified for strength, but there is strength in diversity.

Among the multitude, four institutions stand out, two of prewar and two of postwar vintage. All four are powerful symbols, and they will be discussed separately.

A. THE POLISH MUSEUM

Despite New York Polonia's exaggerated claims, it is Chicago—for many years in the nineteenth century and during World War II and a few years after it the biggest Polish city in the world—that is the capital of American Polonia, and it is there that Polonia's—and Poland's in times of crisis—cultural repository belongs, in the Polish Museum. Here is what Walter Zachariasiewicz says about it in *Poles in America* in 1978:

> One of the PRCUA's [Polish Roman Catholic Union's] foremost achievements was the establishment and maintenance of a Polish Museum. In 1935 the PRCUA formed an "Archives and Museum" section to collect and preserve documents and other objects relating to Polish American history and Polish culture. The Museum was officially opened in 1937. Since then it has grown into an institution of national importance. Most of its valuable collections and art treasures have been donated as gifts. Of lasting value are, among others, the memorabilia of Ignace Jan Paderewski assembled in a beautiful room bearing his name. The Museum is constantly expanding, and long-range plans call for erecting of an appropriate Museum building in Chicago. As of now, the Museum occupies two floors in the PRCU building. Its curator is Father Donald Bilinski.

And here is what the Museum's illustrated brochure, "The Polish Museum of America," says about its status now:

> The Polish Museum of America, founded in 1935, is one of the oldest and largest ethnic museums in the United States of America. Located in the heart of the first Polish neighborhood in Chicago, it promotes knowledge of Polish history and culture, and especially promulgates Polish and Polish American art in its paintings, sculptures, drawings and lithographs by well-known artists.
> It offers numerous exhibits as well as cultural programs such as lectures, concerts, movie and slide presentations, theatre performances, meetings with scholars and artists dedicated to Polish Culture from all over the world.
> With its 60,000 volumes, 250 periodicals, collections of Polish music records and cassettes, the Museum Library ranks as one of the best outside of Poland.
> The archives preserve documents pertaining to Polish and Polish American history. Many scholars from varied parts of the country come here to complete their research and many students receive their first introduction to knowledge of Polish history and culture through the Museum archives.

Not everything is as rosy with the Polish Museum as the two quotations suggest. What is lacking is greater professionalism on the part of the curators, and tighter control over the Museum's holdings. Father Bilinski's lax supervision allowed some items to be removed, in most cases by recent arrivals or visitors from Poland, in at least one case by an employee.

After Father Bilinski came three curators trained in Poland, but the situation did not seem to improve. This writer came to the Museum on a Friday afternoon, but found it closed hours before closing time. The curator soon left for a job at the Holocaust Memorial Museum in Washington; the two who came after him did not stay long either. The new curator is a native Polish American, as he should be.

Jan Lorys is the son of Maria Lorys, a member of long standing of the Polish Women's Alliance and editor of its organ, but that should not be the main recommendation. How much does he know about art, about conservation and restoration, knowledge which a good curator should have? If he doesn't know enough, then perhaps a part-time guest residency at the Chicago Art Institute should be arranged to make him a professional.

The same goes for the president, who should be expected to do more for the Museum than organize a Summer Ball. Dr. Radzilowski told me that when he was a resident at the National Endowment for the Humanities, he prepared a grant application for the Museum, and all it needed was for the president to make an appearance at the NEH. If he had, perhaps the Museum would now have a building for itself.

The Polish Museum is too important to be handled haphazardly or used for a photo opportunity with Hillary Clinton in an election year as its claim to distinction. This is a new world order penetrating everything, when funds are getting scarce and competition for them deadly. The old ways no longer work. The president who ignored the appointment at the NEH shocked me by saying that Polish Americans don't need help!

How can an improved Museum help Poland, which is the gist of the book? Not materially, except indirectly as a place in which to make appeals for help, but spiritually, by simply being there? Amidst the generally low opinion of American Polonia in Poland, due mainly to old stereotypes and ignorance, the existence of a veritable jewel in its crown would go a long way toward mutual respect and productive cooperation.

B. THE KOSCIUSZKO FOUNDATION

A jewel in the crown, alluded to in the last sentence about the Polish Museum, is probably at present The Kosciuszko Foundation. But is it a perfect jewel?

Since its cautious founding seventy years ago The Kosciuszko Foundation has been striving to be just that, pushed by history and guided by its first two presidents.

Its four presidents so far present a revealing study in contrast reflecting the needs of the time and the personalities of the presidents:

• STEPHEN P. MIZWA, the Founding President, an academic but not a scholar in a strict sense. At home in academia and in the American mainstream, a quality which enabled him to attract important backers and trustees to the Foundation and later direct exiled Polish scholars to teaching posts. An extremely modest man, very careful with the Foundation's money, expecting the same care from the Foundation's staff and grantees. The Foundation was his life and he lived in it with his family, serving it almost half a century, and laying the groundwork for future expansion until his death in January of 1971. This writer retains the memory of a characteristic encounter with President Mizwa when buying books at the Foundation's bookstore for students in his two Polish courses at the University of Pittsburgh. Mr. Mizwa was impressed watching a client not only pay for the books but having them placed in a shopping bag and taking them to the airport for the flight back, thus saving the Foundation time and money for billing and shipping. He was even more impressed when told that the books would be used that same evening in the classroom. "How would you like to work for the Foundation?" he asked. "Thank you, I prefer teaching." The person who preferred working for the Foundation was the president's assistant and the next president.

• EUGENE KUSIELEWICZ—the Creative President, an academic and the only one of the four presidents with a promising career as a scholar. A history student of Professor Oskar Halecki at Fordham University he became an expert on Woodrow Wilson and had his early articles published in *Polish American Studies*, the publication of the Polish American Historical Association (PAHA). He was not born yet when his future workplace, The Kosciuszko Foundation, was already in place, but it became his obsession starting with his student days. He soon became assistant to the president, dividing his time between working at the Foundation and teaching history at St. John's University, with the Foundation progressively taking more and more of his time, to the detriment of his academic work, which was gradually sacrificed, but he did direct a few doctoral dissertations in Polish and Polish American history (among them on General Edward Rydz-Śmigły by a Jewish student and on Ignace Paderewski by a student of Ukrainian descent). With President Mizwa slowing down, Dr. Kusielewicz was taking more responsibility until, with Mizwa's death in 1971, he moved with his family into the Foundation and his identification with it became complete.

In total control of the Foundation, and easily confirmed by its Board of Trustees as the new President, Dr. Kusielewicz plunged into activity which fell into three main areas, the most important of which was cultivating potential donors to secure their bequests, an activity in which he was largely successful, soon multiplying the Foundation's endowment and thus increasing its operating fund and enlarging its staff. With larger staff came recruiting new members, accomplished by throwing the doors of the Foundation open to programs of other institutes, notably the Joseph Pilsudski Institute and the Literary Section of the Polish Institute, and more frequent mailings to members and potential members. The third main area of Dr. Kusielewicz's activity were exchange programs with Poland which, interrupted by the war, had not resumed until the early 1960's and mushroomed under his leadership. His contacts with Poland reached a high in a trip to Poland with the Foundation's Trustees to take part in a symposium (July 24-25, 1976) on "The Contribution of Poles to the Making of the United States" at the Polish Academy of Sciences in Warsaw, where he delivered an address, "Reflections on the Kosciuszko Foundation," which was subsequently printed in the Foundation's *Newsletter* and in an updated and revised version two years later in *Poles in America: Bicentennial Essays*. The essay is excellent, with a wealth of knowledge of the Foundation's early years, including participation in its various public programs of such figures as Albert Einstein, Artur Rubinstein, and the future President of the United States, Herbert Hoover. Why was it then that with this knowledge and with his record, Dr. Kusielewicz was voted out of office a few years later?

In retrospect, this writer looks upon the dismissal of Dr. Kusielewicz by the Foundation's Trustees as one of three calamities

(along with the death of Ludwik Krzyżanowski, the editor of *The
Polish Review*, and Aloysius Mazewski, the President of the Polish
American Congress) that afflicted Polonia in the 1980's. Just as *The
Polish Review* and the Polish American Congress suffered when
their top men were succeeded by lesser ones, so did The Kosciuszko
Foundation suffer when its president was succeeded by his assistant, a
choice as inexplicable as his predecessor's removal.

• ALBERT JUSZCZAK—the Transitional President, an academic but,
unlike his two predecessors, without any publications to his name. He
passed up an opportunity to write, with the help of the Polish
Library in London, a much needed work on Kazimierz Wierzyński,
and wrote instead an insignificant dissertation at the University of
Chicago under Professor Tymon Terlecki, for whom, after the
latter's retirement to London, The Kosciuszko Foundation sponsored
a lecture tour in America. Touted as the "Future of Polonia" by
some, a praise which was probably responsible for his elevation to
the presidency of the Foundation, Dr. Juszczak had, frankly speaking, only one important qualification for the job: perfect fluency in
both English and Polish. A vegetarian and a self-proclaimed poet, he
wanted to put his own stamp on the Foundation, but it's not certain
he had a clear idea what his mark was to be, and neither had anybody
else.

    As the new president, he started by firing some members of the
staff, including the hard-working manager of the book store, which
needed a hard worker. When, unlike his two predecessors, he chose
not to reside in the Foundation, he deprived it of its old warmth,
openness and accessibility, restored temporarily by Dr. Kusielewicz's
series of evening guest discussion meetings on Polish-Jewish
relations. As for meetings generated by the new president himself,
more often than not they were musical, which was all right, except
for one dealing with Jan Kiepura, Poland's famous tenor and a
highly controversial personality. Kiepura had been criticized before
the war for giving money to a German charity (*Winter Hilfe*) but he
could be excused by the great amount of money he was making in
Germany and the adulation he was held in by the Germans. It was
after the war that Kiepura disgraced himself, singing (literally)
praises of the famous Russian commander, Field Marshal Suvorov.
For Juszczak, a Slavist, not to know what Suvorov really meant to
Poland was a disgrace too, because it was Suvorov, the butcher of
Warsaw, who was brought back out of retirement by Catherine the

Great to put down the Kosciuszko Insurrection, which he did with a vengeance. Without Suvorov, a one-time victor over Napoleon (in the Swiss campaign), the Insurrection would have had a chance. But it was in the handling of Kusielewicz's pet project, the Summer Programs in Poland, that the new president not only hurt the Foundation, but also the future of Polish in America and even the cause and standing of Polonia itself. Since I was directly involved in the summer programs as a group leader, I knew how important they could be for the future of Polish in America, especially the free program in Lublin for teachers of Polish, which I was planning to use in conjunction with my own program at Loyola University of Chicago. My plans were set back when in 1981, three years after getting the Lublin assignment from Dr. Kusielewicz following his visit to Loyola as the Foundation President, his successor arbitrarily gave it to a professor of Slavic languages at Hunter College because, as he put it cynically "he will take care of something for me." That "something" was, I think, a chance to teach Polish at Hunter in exchange for a free vacation in Poland, because that was what the assignment would be for the professor, just as it had been for Juszczak as a group leader in Cracow in 1971, when his group, including my son, saw him only on arrival and departure. (My son looked in vain for him when summoned to the American Embassy in Warsaw to register for the draft on his 18th birthday and had to handle it on his own.)

This regrettable incident tells us something about the new president using the office as an instrument for his own gratification, and important Foundation's assignments as perks to be given in return for favors. It also tells us about the way things were done in Polonia that needed to be changed. Never defeated until the final shots are fired, I used the setback constructively by embarking—upon the discovery of a veritable gold mine of highly motivated adult Polish American students in the School of Continuing Education—on a new project, the "Certificate in Polish."

I have described the Certificate project in detail within the chapter on the Polish American Congress. I will add here that I had what the traditional area studies programs did not have, namely an unlimited supply of students. Also, my Certificate was to be different from the one offered by the Institute on East Central Europe of Columbia University in conjunction with the MA or Ph.D. programs in History or Slavic Languages for specialists in area studies, but whose language preparation was largely left to their own initiative. I was not interested in creating another Ph.D. factory in a field short of jobs. My Certificate was to lay stress on language preparation; it was intended for Polish Americans who were either working or were planning to work in jobs on the local, state or federal level where knowledge of Polish was, or should have been, a must. They would obtain that knowledge in my courses, and complete it to perfection in Poland itself. This was the project.

Three of my students from a nucleus group applied to the Foundation for the Lublin program. Two, outstanding women, were accepted, the third, George Rico, a fine music teacher of Mexican and, as he claimed, Polish descent, was rejected on the ground that he could not prove his Polish descent, a requirement for the all-expenses-paid program. Rejecting him, and thus eliminating him from the project despite his readiness to pay his way was a bad mistake. But the worst mistake by the Foundation was not restoring the key Lublin assignment to me. As a result, when the two women left for Lublin, I would not be there to adapt the program to theirs and future students' needs for the Certificate. And even though I received glowing reports from the Lublin program about my students' preparation and progress, it was not the same. As a perfectionist, I had to see the project every step of the way, and the Foundation made it impossible.

The consequences of the Foundation's irresponsible handling of the Lublin program were far-reaching. The Certificate program, which would have had its first two graduates the following year (1985) was a pilot program, to be submitted for adoption in other universities with substantial numbers of Polish American students (Wisconsin, Cleveland, Buffalo, Pittsburgh, Binghampton), in order to create an entirely new Polish American intelligentsia, fluent in both Polish and English, and at home in both Polish and American cultures. Because of the latter, candidates had to be products of the American educational system, with liberal arts degrees. The graduates of the Polish Certificate programs were bound to reinforce the big fraternals and eventually run and reform them, putting an end to patronage and initiating a new era of leadership in Polish America. This was the long-range plan, of such gigantic proportions that I refrained from making a formal complaint to the trustees of The Kosciuszko Foundation demanding Dr. Juszczak's dismissal for ruining it, for fear they would not grasp it, and he was allowed to vegetate a few more years. Perhaps his present duties at the Polish and Slavic Center can accommodate his ways.*

There are some footnotes to the Foundation's irresponsible ways under Juszczak's presidency. One concerns the Polish teaching position at Hunter, long before Juszczak laid his eyes on it, if that was indeed the root of the subsequent evil. Between teaching jobs in the mid-1970's I was active at the Polish Institute of Arts and Sciences as chairman of its Literary Section, member of the Board of Directors, and Associate Editor of *The Polish Review*, in which one of my responsibilities was writing a "Chronicle of Events." While doing it, I became aware that Polish was being taught at Hunter but not by a Polish teacher, which I considered an affront in view of the availability of teachers from the Institute nearby. I wrote to the president, a nun at that time (before Donna Shalala) and received a reply promising to rectify the situation. In a height of irony, Juszczak was probably the later beneficiary of my intervention.

The other footnote concerns Juszczak only by association in showing that he was not the only one using his position for personal reasons, and goes even further back, to 1971, to my son's return from the Summer Program mentioned earlier. (Incidentally, in a memorable double celebration, while my son, thanks to a fine gesture from Dr. Kusielewicz, was celebrating his High School diploma with an award from the Foundation to study Polish in Cracow, I was celebrating my Ph.D. with an award from IREX to study Russian in Moscow. By a remarkable bit of synchronizing we managed to meet at our relatives in Poland on our way back and returned together.) Upon his return to begin at Columbia College, he was urged by the freshmen adviser, Robert Maguire (remembered today as the translator, with Magnus Kryński, of Wisława Szymborska) to register for Polish, which he did with anticipation. But the man in charge of Polish at Columbia gave the language course for some personal reason (returning a favor?) to a Polish writer (Minkowski) who was an awful teacher, and my son dropped it in time to register for something else. I felt for him, and I was furious, but there was nothing I could do.

---

* It was not to be. According to a report in *Nowy Dziennik* (5/8/97) "Wojciech Juszczak, Executive Director of the Polish and Slavic Center...resigned...having been earlier dismissed by the Executive Board...."

There was both irony and tragedy in my son's situation. The irony stemmed from the fact that the regular instructor of Polish at Columbia, Ludwik Krzyżanowski, was retiring that year (1971), designating me as his successor, with a letter to that effect. There was a real chance that I would be teaching Polish at Columbia, which was my dream, and teaching my son, another dream, but when I showed the letter to the chairman of Slavic Languages, he told me that it would be up to the professor of Polish, and so it was, with disastrous results, especially for my son, who was just beginning a love affair with Polish poetry, as exemplified by the poet Zbigniew Herbert. He was able to get one of his professors in Columbia's famous Contemporary Civilization (CC) course interested in Herbert, thus doing in effect more for Polish at Columbia than the man in charge of it, whose bad handling of Polish at Columbia shall never be forgiven and forgotten, just as Juszczak's irresponsible handling of the Lublin program at the Kosciuszko Foundation.

Getting back to the Foundation, it would be good to think that the long search by the trustees for a new president was motivated by a desire to remove the irresponsibility and bring in strict account-ability to the office. There must have been something of that if only because the new president was not an academic, but a lawyer.

• JOSEPH E. GORE, Esq.—the Renewal-Oriented President. The renewal started with the Foundation's building, which was repaired where needed and its inside redecorated. The bookstore, hidden until then in a small cluttered basement space accessible by way of a steep staircase from the foyer was now a well-designed and well-furnished establishment sharing the floor below the foyer with clean and spacious washrooms accessible both by way of the elevator and down a wide staircase from the foyer. The receptionist's small room in front was upgraded too, as was also the back room serving as a place to have refreshments after programs and round-table discussion or business meetings. The lecture (or concert, as the case may be) room upstairs was also upgraded (with more paintings added to those on the walls already), and so were surely the offices past the staircase and on the upper floors, but I haven't seen them.

There was no significant turnover of staff except for Mary Van Starrex (Dembiak), longtime presidential assistant, who left the Foundation for reasons not entirely clear to me, and nobody was hired in her place as far as I know. She had been hired away by Dr. Kusielewicz from an equally longtime assistant's job with Ludwik

Krzyżanowski on *The Polish Review*, making room, incidentally, for Krystyna Olszer. The renewed Foundation became again full of lively activity and again a "Center of Polish Culture," keeping in touch with members and society-at-large by means of its improved and expanded *Newsletter* containing detailed reports. Rather than sift through its issues to determine the state of the Foundation today, I have decided to reprint from the fine journal, *2B*, with permission of its editor, Tomasz Tabako, a detailed report sent from the Foundation by Maryla Janiak, Assistant to the President for Educational Programs:

THE KOSCIUSZKO FOUNDATION™

The K.F. is a national organization founded in 1925 by a small group of educators and entrepreneurs who were inspired to create a lasting institution dedicated to the conduct and pro-motion of educational and cultural exchanges between the United States and Poland.

The Kosciuszko Foundation is led today by its President and Executive Director, Joseph E. Gore, Esq.

The Foundation's work reaches audiences throughout the United States and Poland, through its headquarters in New York City, its office in Warsaw, and regional Chapters in Buffalo, Chicago, Denver, Houston, Pittsburgh and Philadelphia. In addi-tion, the work of the Foundation is assisted by a National Advisory Council, composed of individuals residing in various parts of the United States who actively promote work of the Foundation in their localities. The Foundation owns an elegant townhouse at 15 East 65th Street in the historical landmark section of Manhattan's Upper East Side, a perfect setting for its many concerts, exhibits, lectures, and scientific conferences as well as for the richly-endowed Art Gallery collection of 19th and 20th century paintings by Polish masters.

The Kosciuszko Foundation's mission is being achieved through a variety of programs, one of the oldest (since 1926) and its most important is the Exchange Program between the United States and Poland, through which the Foundation annually sponsors approximately 50 Polish academics, scholars, professionals and artists in furthering their research studies at various institutions of higher learning in the United States. In exchange the Foundation selects and recommends to the Polish Ministry of National Education American students, scholars and academics for graduate and postgraduate studies/independent research at various institutions of higher learning in Poland, and undergraduate students for the Year Abroad Program of Polish

language, culture and history at the Polish Institute of the
Jagiellonian University.

The selection process for both programs is highly competitive. The applicants' credentials, including their publications and
references as well as research proposals, are evaluated by the
Foundation's two Academic Advisory Committees after an
initial administrative review. The candidates from Poland are
subject to a two-step evaluation process, one in the United
States and another in Poland. The United States Committee is
comprised of a board of Polish Americans and American aca-
demicians, scientists and professionals who review the research
proposals and recommend the best candidates for personal
interviews in Warsaw. The interviews at the Foundation's
Warsaw office are conducted by members of the Polish
Academic Advisory Committee comprised of Polish academi-
cians and professionals from many different academic institutions and representing a variety of disciplines. All academic
disciplines are included within the program.

In 1991 the Foundation opened an office in Warsaw, at
Nowy Swiat 4, in an effort to improve its services to the Polish
academic community, to the American students and scholars
engaged in independent research or study programs in Poland
under the auspices of the Foundation. Through its office in
Warsaw the Foundation develops and maintains close relations
with the universities, technical schools, medical academies and
other institutions of higher learning and various cultural
institutions in Poland.

Aside from the Exchange Programs the Kosciuszko Foundation offers the following programs:
* tuition scholarship to Americans of Polish descent;
* tuition scholarship to Americans pursuing Polish studies;
* Summer Sessions in Poland and Rome in language and
  culture;
* English Teaching Program in Poland in conjunction with
  UNESCO of Poland);
* National Chopin Piano Competition;
* Chamber Music Series broadcast from the Art Gallery;
* Book Service featuring mostly titles in English on Polish subjects;
* lectures, exhibits, authors' events, theatrical showings, films
  and concerts presented across the U.S.;
* Polish Studies Programs at various American universities and
  colleges.

In accordance with the Foundation's keen interest in the
promotion of Polish Studies Programs at American universities,
the Foundation has been sponsoring courses in Polish Language
and Literature at Hunter College, City University of New York,

for over 10 years. Additionally, in 1992, after a special category of grant called the Teaching Fellowship was created, the Foundation's support for Polish Studies was extended to various universities throughout the United States and it became a major element in the planning and budgeting of the Exchange Program. In the 1994/95 academic year the Foundation sponsored seven Teaching Fellowships from Poland at:

- Stanford University, California, courses in Polish Language, Literature, and Film;
- University of Connecticut at Storrs, courses in Polish Language and Literature;
- University of Buffalo, courses in Polish Language and Literature;
- DePaul University, Chicago, Illinois, courses in Polish Language and Literature;
- University of Illinois at Chicago, courses in Political Science;
- University of Central Florida, courses in Polish History;
- Hunter College, City University of New York, courses in Polish Cinema and Theater.

In the 1995/96 [?] academic year the Foundation will sponsor Polish Programs at two additional universities:

- Rice University in Houston, Texas, courses in Polish History;
- University of Rochester, New York, courses in Political Science.

I am grateful to Maryla Janiak for preparing this report (even if the Kosciuszko Foundation Annual Ball and some of the Foundation-cosponsored symposia are missing, one on the Warsaw Uprising, for example). It told me much I didn't know, and helped me answer the question asked in the first sentence of this essay, whether the Foundation was a jewel.

YES and NO! It is a jewel but not a perfect jewel. The Foundation is certainly a jewel in the physical sense, meaning its location, its building, and ample space inside, but this writer has doubts about, and criticism of, certain aspects of its academic programs, particularly the Polish Language and Literature courses at Hunter College and the "special category of grant called the Teaching Fellowship," both being probably funded unnecessarily or unwisely out of the Foundation's precious resources. Hunter College is a good starting point for the argument, but first, a few explanatory remarks for the benefit of those who do not understand properly the American educational system.

It is one thing for the Jurzykowski Foundation to endow a chair of Polish Literature at Harvard, a premier private university, and another thing for the Kosciuszko Foundation to sponsor courses in Polish at Hunter College, a part of the City University of New York (CUNY), a public institution whose business it is to provide New Yorkers with the best opportunities for relatively inexpensive education, which should also include, in a city like New York, courses in Polish. Yet, according to Ms. Janiak's report, it was "the Foundation [which] has been sponsoring Polish Language and Literature courses at Hunter College, CUNY, for over 10 years" (I assume "sponsoring" stands for funding), which means that the procedure was inherited from Juszczak's presidency, when it began in circumstances already discussed when a professor of Slavic languages at Hunter was to "take care of something" for Juszczak. Was that "something" connected with Polish at Hunter?

The whole Hunter arrangement is unclear but light must be thrown on it to help us understand how unwisely Poles in America are protecting their vital interests here. When I wrote to Hunter's President in the mid-1970's, Polish was already being taught there, as it should have been. The Modern Language Association Directory (PMLA, September 1996, p. 915) lists Polish at Hunter in two categories, in "Classical & Oriental Studies" alongside Ancient Greek, Chinese, Hebrew, Japanese, Latin, Russian, and in a smaller unnamed category "Russ, Polish, & Ukrainian, Alex E. Alexander." Which of the two is the Kosciuszko Foundation "sponsoring?" I assume the second (with students from the first taking advantage of it), because it was Professor Alexander who had been given my assignment in Lublin while taking care of "something" for Juszczak. He was probably at that time constructing a small department of his own and the Lublin assignment would look good on his resume (it would have looked even better on mine, in a far more important plan), making the addition of Polish that much easier, especially if it was graciously sponsored (funded) by the Foundation.

These are conjectures, but they are logical and based on precedent. Like the President of the Polish Museum (another of my candidates for "jewel" status) who shocked me by saying that "Polish Americans don't need help," the President of the Kosciuszko Foundation appears to agree, making it his business what is properly CUNY's/the business of the city.

I once attended the Polish Club's Christmas party at Hunter, and I was impressed by the number and quality of the students, making their club the best after the Chicago clubs I had advised, which even had their own publication, *Echo*, copies of which and of *Poles in America* I donated to the Hunter Club. Its very existence was the best security for the Polish courses, without the need to resort to any petitions should they be threatened. What need was there for the Foundation to enter the picture? "If it ain't broke, don't fix it," the saying goes. The money would be better spent on tuition scholarships for Polish students who need help, and concrete help is what's needed most here and in Poland, and not unproductive sponsorships.

The sponsorship idea at the Foundation goes back to Dr. Kusielewicz when he brought Dr. Andrzej Kaminski from Cracow to teach Polish history at Columbia University which, like Harvard, is a world-famous private university. My son, incidentally, took Kaminski's course and was happy in it. The sponsorship ended with the growth of Columbia's Institute on East Central Europe when Polish history became jointly part of the History Department and the Institute. The present instructor, Dr. John Micgiel, had completed his studies with the help of the Foundation's scholarship to pay Columbia's high tuition fees. (They were high even when I was a student, but I was able to win an exemption with high grades, and my son had a "family" exemption.) Micgiel is now the Institute's Director, his success due partly to the Foundation's concrete and productive help.

There was nothing of that striving at the time of Juszczak's sponsorship of Polish at Hunter when Poland had the attention of the world while Solidarity had captured its imagination, and Polish programs were available for the asking. In Chicago I was able to organize two international symposia, one on "Poland's Church-State Relations" and the other on "Poland's Solidarity Movement," both funded not by Polish American organizations whose funds were channeled to the Pol/Am Charitable Foundation to help Poland, but by the Mellon Foundation. As for Mr. Gore's continuing the sponsorship of Polish at Hunter, at a time when Poland is again in need of help in an altered world order (and the Foundation should seriously look into it), one wonders who is advising him on educational matters, whether the Council or Maryla Janiak, his Assistant for Educational Programs, when the ideal adviser would have been the late Metchie Budka, who was the only Ph.D. (Harvard) on the premises.

Polish at Hunter College is a drop in the bucket of the overall picture of the Foundation-sponsored programs and involves probably an insignificant amount of money, but important principles are at stake: of public versus private funding and University versus Foundation sponsorship. The confusion can lead to harmful disruptions as, for example, when Krystyna Olszer left the Polish Institute (where she had succeeded Mary Van Starrex) to teach Polish at Hunter. Somehow, becoming an Adjunct Assistant Professor was more important than teaching Polish at the Institute and serving as Assistant Editor of *The Polish Review*.

The violation of the principles is more serious in the Teaching Fellowship category in which the Foundation sponsored seven Teaching Fellows from Poland in the year 1994-95. Of the seven, the first four are examples where "the Foundation's keen interest in the promotion of Polish Studies Programs at American universities" is not only misguided but harmful on several grounds. For example, Stanford University (California) which houses the famous Hoover Institute of War and Peace has, probably because of that, a department of Slavic Languages and Literatures with Polish along with Czech, Russian and Serbo-Croatian (PMLA, *ibid.*, 926), so why sponsor something already in place? Besides, it is no good to use a different language teacher every year, unless it is Dr. Miodunka (whom I call "the second best teacher of Polish in the world"), and Miodunka went to teach Polish in Brazil (Kurytyba) from Stanford.

The same conclusions apply to the University of Buffalo, but for different reasons. It has Polish in the Department of Modern Languages and Literatures (PMLA, 920), so again why sponsor something already in place? But there are two universities of Buffalo in the PMLA Directory, and the other one has no Polish (and no other Slavic Languages, for that matter), in which case sponsoring a Polish program is highly justified in an ethnic city like Buffalo, except for two considerations, first, why not try to have the New York State or the City of Buffalo provide for the program, and second, why bring a Teaching Fellow from Poland when there are Polish American teachers without jobs? The second consideration is essential for another reason: the Fellows are likely to be not fluent enough in English and thus incapable of conducting a well-functioning program.

These considerations are crucial in Chicago, where there are more well-qualified Polish American teachers than anywhere else, and at least four universities, including DePaul (another Teaching Fellows program), offering Polish, as listed in the PMLA Directory (p. 913). This program too should go to a local instructor, in order not to create a situation in which The Kosciuszko Foundation is depriving Polish Americans of teaching jobs that are already scarce.

Storrs (University of Connecticut), the last of the four disputed Teaching Fellows programs, presents a different kind of problem, namely that Polish is not listed in the "Mod & Classical Langs" department of the university according to the PMLA Directory (p. 912). This means that the program either does not exist or is not judged viable enough by the university, thus depriving Polish in America of a vital statistic, and lowering its national standing in a shrinking field where statistics are all-important for the local, state, or federal educational authorities to determine which programs are to be funded and which not. My own credentials to voice an opinion in these matters are reflected in a leading article by Leonard A. Polakiewicz, "Teaching Polish in the United States: Past and Present" (*The Polish Review*, vol. XLI, no. 2, 1966: 131-155) which shows Polish language registrations in the highest enrolled programs, 1977-1994 (Table 5) to drop precipitously in the two I was instrumental in developing before my departure (at the University of Illinois, Chicago, and at Loyola University of Chicago, from 160 in 1977 to 60, and from 50 in 1980 to 10, respectively).

I have no quarrel with the remaining three Teaching Fellows programs, except for the courses in Polish History (University of Central Florida) which I would like to go to a Polish American historian, for obvious reasons already discussed. The same goes for one of the additional two Polish Studies Programs, for 1995-96, (Rice University in Houston, Texas). The professor at Rice who had probably engineered it has sufficient standing to have the History Department or the University invite a scholar rather than rely on sponsorship. I was impressed when, upon meeting the new President of Columbia University, formerly of Rice, and mentioning that a Polish colleague was a member of his former faculty, he replied instantly, Ewa Thompson (married name). Such name recognition means a lot in a university.

Otherwise The Kosciuszko Foundation's "conduct and promotion of educational and cultural exchanges between the United States and Poland" works well even for an occasional slip, as when a K.F. grantee is described in the *Newsletter* to be in the 6th (or 7th) year of his Ph.D. program. Such programs usually take a maximum of five years, and it does not speak well of the Foundation to support slow students.

The Annual Ball is a traditional celebration and an occasion to honor outstanding supporters and benefactors of the Foundation while indulging in the stately Polonaise.

Beside its own cultural programs, the Foundation cosponsors important events with other institutions, with the Institute on East Central Europe, the Jozef Pilsudski Institute, and others. Mostly they mark anniversaries, the most recent being the 50th of the Warsaw Uprising, and the 100th of the poet Józef Wittlin. This writer participated in both, took the floor in the first (with some difficulty, considering that he was recovering from life-threatening surgery) but did not get a chance in the second, which was a pity, because he would have reminded the audience that exactly twenty years ago (autumn 1976) when he was chairman of the Literary Section of the Polish Institute, he was able to organize, while already teaching in Chicago, a memorial program for the just departed Jozef Wittlin which took place in the very same room, with his wife as hostess, Prof. Zoya Yurieff presiding, and Prof. Tymon Terlecki from Chicago delivering the main address. With every Tom, Dick, and Harry (and the Consul) who knew something about Wittlin gathered for the anniversary symposium, there was just one person in the audience who remembered the previous occasion and two who remembered an even earlier one, when the same poet Wittlin, in the last public function of his long life, inaugurated the Literary Section as its first speaker, by introducing Zofia Romanowicz, its first guest, who had arrived from Paris to publicize her new book. This writer waited to be invited to say a few words about it but wasn't because the Director of Cultural Events didn't know him, and that's my last criticism of the Foundation.

With frequent turnover in the position of Director of Cultural Events, each succeeding one has a shorter memory of the Foundation's history and its more memorable events, of which the Foundation should have a permanent record for reference by just saving and filing a copy of each program. What is needed is someone of the older generation, someone close to retirement or retired, and a member or friend in long standing of the Foundation. It should be someone like me but younger, someone who cares deeply about Poland and Polonia, and this care should be reflected in the Foundation's future events.

Despite its economic successes (deceptive, because accomplished from still a low base), Poland's future is uncertain. It is a sick country, literally, with children the most vulnerable victims of poverty and sickness. New charities and ideas are springing up among American Polonia (the latest among them the "Society for Social Assistance, SOS") to help remedy the situation; the chief reason for this book was concern about Poland and ideas how to help. The most serious problem is that more people in Poland are dying than are born, which means that Poland is, in effect, a dying country, and will remain so until the low birthrate caused mainly by high rate of abortion, is reversed.

One of Poland's biggest drawbacks is its neglected environment. If Poland does not improve its environment, and can't solve its waste disposal, this could prevent it from joining the European Union, which has strict rules about the environment. Here is a chance for the Kosciuszko Foundation to enter the efforts to help. To be sure, most of its funds are earmarked for the Exchange Program, but perhaps within it, environmental scholars could come to America to study what's being done about the environment, and much *is* being done here with notable successes, like the cleaning up of the Hudson River or Lake Erie, and constant work on waste disposal dumps, precisely what needs to be done in Poland. There is much to be learned.

As for Polonia, according to the Polish American press, it has reached a new low in its evolution, mainly due to the absence of Polish Americans in Congress. But Senators and Congressmen are no longer elected in ethnic districts, which are a thing of the past, while Polish Americans have been increasingly joining the American mainstream, as shown elsewhere in this book but, unlike in the past, retaining their Polish names, which tell them who they are. With that knowledge, and no longer saddled with an inferiority complex, they will want to know more, and will turn to the institutions which are capable of providing that knowledge, the Kosciuszko Foundation among them. But they will want the Foundation to be more responsive to the needs of Polonia and Poland, not only in fancy slogans and reports, but in concrete deeds. It will then become a perfect jewel.

C. THE POLISH INSTITUTE OF ARTS AND SCIENCES (PIAS)

Is the Polish Institute a jewel? Unlike the Polish Museum and the Kosciuszko Foundation, founded before World War II with expectations of long-lasting existence, forever if necessary, the Polish Institute was a wartime temporary institution founded by a few exiled scholars determined to preserve Polish culture and civilization from annihilation by Germany-turned-fascist(Nazi) and bent on world conquest. In that respect the Polish Institute was a jewel, and had the war ended without Poland's other ancient enemy, Russia, also transformed into a deadly system with the world on its collective mind and Poland in its way, the Institute would have grown in Polish memory into a perfect jewel, instead of continuing its exile while seeing Poland fall under the sway of the Communist Soviet Union.

This writer had compiled the history of the Polish Institute from its beginning to 1973, the year of the first Congress of Scholars of Polish Descent, which took place in Warsaw and Cracow at a time of relatively lively exchanges between Poland and America following worldwide celebration of Poland's important anniversaries: 1964, the 600th of Cracow University; and 1966, the Millennium of Poland's Christianity. The year 1973 was chosen for the Congress because it marked another important anniversary, and a very apt one at that: the 500th of the birth of Nicolas Copernicus, Poland's gift to the world and a student in his youth of Cracow University where the Congress was taking place. Because of that, many members of the Institute accepted invitations to take part in the Congress, including this writer, who contributed his history of the Institute to the program, whose proceedings were published in a large volume by the Polish Academy of Sciences, with the history itself translated into English and included in his *Poles in America: Bicentennial Essays.*

By the time of the first Congress in Poland and the Bicentennial in America, the founders of the Institute were already dead, and the Institute itself was undergoing a temporary crisis because of that, especially the recent passing away of the great historian Oskar Halecki, whose finest contribution to the Institute's work was as the main speaker in 1969 at another anniversary, the 400th of the Union of Lublin which created the famous Polish-Lithuanian Commonwealth. The anniversary celebration was attended by representatives of the nations that once belonged to the Commonwealth. Professor Halecki, escorted by two of his former students, Professors Gromada and Kusielewicz, spoke for over an hour, getting stronger as he proceeded, on a topic that he knew better than anybody, sharing with his audience knowledge gained in the Vatican archives, about a proposal to the Lublin assembly by the envoy of the Ottoman Porte of such magnitude and benefit to the Commonwealth that the audience was shocked to hear that the assembly rejected it as coming from an "infidel." A standing ovation was Dr. Halecki's reward, as it was also in his last appearance, the celebration in 1972 of the 600th anniversary of the birth of Queen Jadwiga.

Professor Halecki's successors as Director and President—he held both positions at different times and was Honorary President until his death in 1973—were not his equals in intellect and national standing, but they did organize two highly successful congresses at Columbia University: Congress of Scholars and Scientists in 1966, and Second Congress of Scholars, Scientists, Writers and Artists in 1971. At the latter Professor Halecki spoke of the importance of making a clear distinction between East Central Europe and Eastern Europe, two different cultural, historical and geographical concepts, according to him. This writer considers Halecki's statement a pioneering effort to settle the question of Poland's place in Europe, just as the Institute was about to start paying attention to America by entering a period of critical transition in connection with the approaching crisis of the theory of the American melting pot brought about by the rise of ethnicity. The Institute's answer to the new phenomenon was to pay close attention to it by electing a sociologist, Dr. Eugene Kleban as Director in 1973, and by some Americanization, electing a Polish American, Dr. John Gronouski, President.

1971, the year of Halecki's watershed statement, for which he has not received enough credit, considering that the concept is on everbody's lips today, was also a watershed year for this writer. After teaching for five years at the University of Pittsburgh and returning to New York, I at last earned my Ph.D. at Columbia University (in Slavic Languages and Literatures) and became eligible for membership in the Polish Institute. Upon becoming a member, having been recommended by Prof. Ludwik Krzyżanowski to the then Executive Director Jan Librach (before Kleban), I gave a lecture on Polish-Russian literary relations, under the chairmanship of Krzyżanowski in his last year as Secretary General (and, unrelatedly, as Adjunct Professor of Polish Language at Columbia). That

same year I attended the Institute's Second Congress with
Krzyżanowski and we both heard and discussed Halecki's inspired
speech about East Central Europe. That same year I spent the
summer in Moscow (while my older son, a freshman at Columbia
College, studied Polish in Cracow) in an IREX program, completing
in many respects my professional education (like Henry Adams, the
subject of the last recommended reading in my American Lit. course
at Columbia) and finding out, like Halecki, that Russia was Eastern
Europe (nothing wrong with that) and that Poland, like Hungary and
Czechoslovakia, both well known to me, are East Central Europe,
and that any attempt to keep them together with Russia must end in
failure and bloodshed, as in Poland and Hungary in 1956 and
Czechoslovakia in 1968. Returning to New York I found out that I
would not be teaching Polish at Columbia as Krzyżanowski's designated successor, because the man in charge of the Polish program
treated the language classes as a kind of financial aid to random
acquaintances from Poland (or to a local woman friend who
"needed" to buy a Mercedes), thus preventing me from putting
Polish at a level on which it belonged at Columbia and teaching my
son in the process, making up for earlier neglect due to my perennial
lack of time. With time on hand for a change, I started frequenting
the Institute.

I was not a complete newcomer to the Institute. While still a
part-time student at Columbia, taking a full program with tuition
exemption for top grades, and working full-time with overtime in
the printing industry, trying to return to school seriously after the
Soviet Sputnik went up and America panicked, I was urged by my
Advanced Russian instructor to attend a Slavic regional conference at
West Point, where I met Ludwik Krzyżanowski and Magnus Jan
Kryński, the only two scheduled Polish speakers. When the chairman
of the conference, Arthur Coleman, formerly of Columbia University and then President of Alliance College, delayed the Polish
speakers while time was running out, I exploded and, seconded by
Nina Syniawska, a Ukrainian instructor of Russian at Columbia, I
demanded to hear the Polish speakers in the little remaining time.
They were immediately given the floor, President Coleman
introduced Professor Krzyżanowski who, in turn, very eloquently
introduced Mr. Kryński as a doctoral student at Columbia completing
a dissertation about Polish Literature after the "Thaw" of 1956, and
this was the subject of Kryński's talk, the last of the conference.

During refreshments, courtesy of West Point's Russian Department, Professor Krzyżanowski, grateful for my intervention, introduced himself to me as the Polish professor at Columbia and editor of *The Polish Review* and invited me to visit him in his office or in his class, and at the Polish Institute at East 66th Street. Later I described the stormy conference, including Arthur Coleman's offer of a job at Alliance when I was ready, and the return trip, when my fellow-student and driver, Peter Zilinsky, a Ukrainian teacher of Russian at Commack High School, Long Island, offered Krzyżanowski and Kryński a ride (they were joined in the back seat by Rebecca Domar, the best Russian instructor at Columbia but, unfortunately, leaving), giving me a chance to get better acquainted with them and marking the beginning of a long friendship with both. I was unable to find the narrative when the time came for a special issue of *The Polish Review* honoring "L.K."

Friendship with L.K., as he liked to refer to himself, was extremely valuable to me. His encyclopedic knowledge of all things Polish and his impeccable command of both Polish and English became an important resource for me. I was at that time preparing an article, "The Karamzin-Lelewel Controversy" (an expanded version of a chapter in my doctoral dissertation), for publication, and L.K.'s reading of it was very helpful. Its appearance in *The Slavic Review* resulted in "Letters to the Editor" and, what's more, coincided with the last lecture of Professor Halecki, the Queen Jadwiga anniversary lecture in November 1972. Professor Halecki praised my article and encouraged me to continue my research on Polish-Russian relations.

My entry into serious scholarship was not lost on Halecki alone. Slavists in the first Congress of Scholars of Polish Descent the following year in Poland recognized my name from the article, but they were mostly impressed that a Polish historian humbled a Russian historiographer when reviewing his *History of the Russian State*. It was on my way back, in London, that the article received a reward.

In London I visited the Polish Library whose director, Dr. Maria Danilewicz, having read my article surmised that it was part of a larger work, and when told so, offered to publish the dissertation in *Antemurale*, the organ of "Institutum Historicum Polonicum Romae," of which she was the London editor. She extended her offer to my M.A. thesis, also on Polish-Russian literary relations,

including the relationship between Pushkin and Mickiewicz. This was
my reward. Back in New York, I immediately mailed the two texts
and received 25 printed copies of each before the end of 1973, while
copies of *Antemurale* were finding their way to university libraries,
including those in Poland. Two years after my doctorate I was an
established scholar, having my Ph.D. dissertation and M.A. thesis
published, an article in a reputable journal and a highly regarded
review article ("History as Literature") about Wiesław Kuniczak's
The Thousand Hour Day (1966), probably the best book on the
campaign of September 1939 and my first assignment from L.K. for
The Polish Review. I was becoming a presence in the Institute,
looking for new worlds to conquer. An opportunity arrived that
same year.

The annual national convention of the American Association of
Teachers of Slavic and East European Languages (AATSEEL) was
held in 1973 in New York during the traditional time between
Christmas and New Year. As a member since my student days, I
attended it whenever it was held on the East Coast in alternate years,
but as I began teaching, my participation included a paper or a panel.
In 1973 it was a report on the Congress of Scholars in Poland but
with a twist, an idea I had conceived, of having the Polish Institute
involved in the convention with its own project. Only L.K. knew
about it and I asked him to be the host and to save a page for it in the
forthcoming issue of *The Polish Review*, and I also asked the excellent columnist "Bob" from the *Polish Daily News* (*Nowy Dziennik*) to
be the reporter. At the convention, I asked the chairman to make me
the last speaker on the late afternoon panel and, when I finished, I
made a special announcement of a meeting at the Polish Institute in
half an hour to discuss a new project. I was not surprised that most
of the audience at the panel discussion followed me, as we walked in
light snow from the midtown hotel to East 66th Street.

At the wide open door of the Institute Ludwik Krzyżanowski
was already waiting, directing everybody upstairs, where Maria
Modzelewska, former star of Polish theatre, was serving hot tea and
biscuits. After some circulating and getting acquainted, and after
L.K. came upstairs leaving the front door open for latecomers, we
took our seats in the lecture room to hear him open the meeting and
introduce me. I looked at the room which had about 20-30 people in
attendance and was still filling, and announced the purpose of the
meeting which was to reinstate the Institute's once active Literary

Section headed by the late Wacław Lednicki, with Ludwik Krzyżanowski, a link to the present, its Secretary. I added that with the Institute at a crossroads at present, it was a good idea to look for new directions, and I opened a discussion of the project.

What followed was a highly creative meeting, not devoid of clashes, as between Kuniczak and Kryński about the relative merits of creative versus academic literature, with Kuniczak voicing suspicions that the project was just a device to feed *The Polish Review* with articles, to the detriment of creative writing, and Kryński retorting that academic writing can also be creative. The best time was had by "Bob" who scribbled furiously to catch all the fine points of the dispute which ended with Kuniczak leaving and the meeting entering an orderly stage. Somebody moved that we should first vote, by show of hands, if the Literary Section should be reinstated in the first place, and all hands went up. Then Kryński, seconded by Edmund Zawacki of Wisconsin, made a motion that the meeting nominate Ludwik Krzyżanowski honorary chairman and Frank Mocha chairman, and again all hands went up. They went up again when L.K. proposed Tom Bird from Queens College for Secretary, and Jan Kryński from Duke for the Advisory Board, all the results to be reported the next day to the Executive Director, Eugene Kleban. With the meeting adjourning, L.K. invited everybody to a traditional "lampka wina," with the wine already poured and waiting. The social hour was full of high hopes and optimism, justified as it turned out.

Because it was Friday evening, December 28, 1973, the beginning of a long New Year's Day weekend, the next working day at the Institute, albeit a brief one, was on Monday, New Year's Eve. The Executive Director, Dr. Kleban, was overjoyed when Prof. Bird and I reported to him the news about the Literary Section, and handed him a copy of its rules for approval. He called it a perfect New Year's resolution and a good omen for 1974.

He was right, as we learned when we met again the following week, already in 1974, and this time it was he who had good news to report. By then "Bob" (Zdzisław Bau) had already published a brilliant and witty column in the *Nowy Dziennik* about the Literary Section's initial meeting, and Kleban was reading it when we came in. He realized the publicity value of such reporting, and wanted the same for his own piece of good news: the Sociological-Historical Research Project on the Polish American Ethnic Group proposed by

Vice President Feliks Gross two years earlier, finally received a grant ($32,000) from the Rockefeller Foundation (the fact that Michael Novak, an intellectual of Slovak origin, was then the head of the Humanities Division of the Foundation, was of some importance in getting the grant). At the same time, the Executive Director was hard at work opening or reinstating branches of the Polish Institute, and suddenly there were many things to report. I suggested that I could expand the "Chronicle of Events" which I had been compiling for *The Polish Review* with Dr. Bernard Ziffer in the 1960's (after the West Point meeting) and by myself on and off after Dr. Ziffer's death, into a larger unit, and Kleban liked the idea. He summoned Ludwik Krzyżanowski to the meeting, and we agreed that I should become Associate Editor in charge of half of the *Review* containing materials having to do with activities of the Institute, starting with the first issue of 1974.

The first issue of *The Polish Review* in 1974 was a catalyst for me and for the Institute. My "Chronicle" and the activity of the Literary Section described in it next to other events and developments (Leopold Tyrmand's talk on "How to Be an Influential Ethnic" on March 1; a symposium "Polish Americans and the New Ethnicity" on March 22 with the participation of Michael Novak, Russel Barta, Paul Wróbel, Feliks Gross, Eugene Kleban and Eugene Kusielewicz; the Rockefeller Foundation grant; ongoing work on branches) made me suddenly the most visible person in the Institute. I thought that for the sake of accountability I should be a member of the Board of Directors, but since the Institute already had its candidates for the next elections (the already mentioned Michael Novak and the publisher of *Nowy Dziennik*, Bolesław Wierzbiański), I decided to rely on a write-in vote, expecting members from the by then lengthy mailing list of the Literary Section to vote for me. My expectations were correct, and when the votes were counted during the Annual Meeting on April 12, 1974, I was elected by a landslide, as was also Michael Novak.

The 1974 Annual Meeting was notable for another reason. It was the meeting at which Dr. John Gronouski was elected President, an election if not exactly engineered then certainly favored by Professor Zbigniew Brzezinski, a Board member who was increasingly becoming a problem-solver for the Institute, offering what he saw as best solutions. Rising on the national scene (two years away from a Cabinet post), he would come to be called by his critics the "instant solutions" man, having seemingly ready answers to all problems. This brings to mind his decision a few years later, if indeed it was his decision as President Carter's security adviser, to boycott the Moscow Olympic Games in 1980. As an expert on sports, both in theory and in practice, I was shocked by the decision, which robbed America of the opportunity of not only winning the Olympic Games, but beating the Soviet Union on its own ground, *for the first time*, and in the year of triumphant "Solidarity" next door. I was in Poland during that summer of 1980, and the Poles were also shocked, expecting an American victory. The American decision to boycott, imposed on confident athletes spoiling for a fight, gave the Soviets a ready excuse to retaliate by boycotting the 1984 Los Angeles Olympics, in which they would have suffered another defeat. These two defeats in a row would have done more damage to the ailing (as seen in Afghanistan, the cause of the boycotts) Soviet Union than "Solidarity," NATO and the CIA combined, that's how important sports were in the Soviet Empire, a fact of life apparently not known in the White House.

As for John Gronouski, past holder of high posts, including Postmaster General under President Kennedy and Ambassador to Poland under President Johnson, the first Polish American to hold such high posts, his election was eminently sound. He started to "Americanize" further the Institute, proposing to change its name to Polish American Institute of Arts and Sciences of America, but there was not enough support for the change, and all that was left of it was a change of prepositions, from "in" to "of" America.

There was something in the air during the 1974 Annual Meeting, something I grasped only after the results of the election of new Board members were announced and all eyes turned in my direction. Even before, I was surprised when the usually discreet Francis Pusłowski, Dr. Kleban's assistant and on that day supervisor of the vote count in the next room, kept coming to the meeting room to tell me how well I was doing in the voting, and assuring me, with undisguised elation, of a huge victory. I was puzzled by his attitude, thinking that it must also reflect that of his chief, since the two of them were a perfect team. Two beautiful people, members of Polish nobility, formerly with the diplomatic corps ("Count" Pusłowski), and the officer corps (Kleban in the traditional career of petty nobility), they both valued my knowledge of Russia (an obsession with Pusłowski) and success with the Literary Section (Kleban). As the meeting adjourned for lunch, they both congratulated me on my election to the Board, remarking about my future in the Institute. Could it be that they saw in me the successor to Kleban when his term of office expired in a year? This was virtually confirmed when on my way out I stopped in the office downstairs by the desk of the third beautiful person in the Institute (actually fourth, with L.K.), the Financial Secretary, Mieczysław Sierpiński.

Sierpiński, the son of a famous mathematician, and a refugee like Librach and Pusłowski from the diplomatic fringe, was a pragmatist who treated the Institute not as a financial aid station for all kinds of refugees, but very seriously, as a Polish stronghold of unlimited potential, which was not being fulfilled. What it needed was someone to run it who knew how to generate income in order to make it self-sustaining and to get a clear title to the building as its chief asset. Like the late Mizwa at the Kosciuszko Foundation, Sierpiński admired the way I saved money by cutting corners and scrupulously handed him the receipts from the well-attended programs of the Literary Section at which, to save money, my wife served as receptionist and hostess; the relatively costly wine and biscuits were done away with in favor of good coffee brewed by my wife in our own coffee urn and excellent poppy seed pastries donated by a Polish bakery downtown and picked up by me personally.

Sierpiński appreciated all this, because in this respect he was just like me. As we talked, he invited me to lunch consisting of homemade ham and cheese sandwiches and excellent coffee which he had just brewed in the little kitchen behind the office. He even produced a little cognac with which we drank a toast to the future of the Institute about which he had been pessimistic until the elections. He told me that the irony of the situation was that the money the Literary Section was generating from dues and programs had to be spent in the same fiscal year, according to the rules the Institute was functioning under, meaning that it was wasted, just as other money was wasted on expenses for officers, on superfluous staff, and costly receptions, as if there were no tomorrow, while the Institute should rely as much as possible on voluntary services and donations.

I spent the afternoon part of the meeting, which consisted mainly of boring reports, thinking of what I had learned earlier. When my turn came to report, I couldn't help but notice how riveting the news of the activities of the Literary Section was to the audience, among which there were many who felt that with the passing away of the PIAS's founders, completed with the death of Professor Halecki the previous year, the institution had needed a shot in the arm, and the Literary Section was providing it. There was more to it. A few days after the Annual Meeting I was invited to the Joseph Pilsudski Institute, on Park Avenue at that time, ostensibly to look at its growing archives, but in reality for a private meeting with some of its prominent members, among them Jan Fryling, a writer and former diplomat, and Aleksander Korczyński, who remembered me as one of the youngest soldiers with whom he had served in the famed Reconnaissance Unit of General Prugar Ketling's Second Polish Division in France in 1940, where it screened the Division's successful retreat into Switzerland, all of which was important to my hosts, who wanted the Executive Director to be a soldier-scholar. Kleban came close to this ideal, but the years he spent in a German POW camp affected him physically and mentally, and he was fast deteriorating. On the other hand, the vigor I was displaying with the Literary Section augured well for the Institute, and made me a perfect candidate for the job of its chief executive officer, with all the support that the Pilsudski Institute could muster. Would I consider this possibility and treat it as a career? I said that I would be honored.

I was sorry to hear about Kleban's deteriorating condition, but I had my own ideas about what happened to people who spent the war years in POW camps: they became empty shells, and that's why when I became a POW in 1940 I tried to escape time after time until I succeeded on the third try. Besides, it is a duty to escape and rejoin the war. The 6,500 Polish officers from the September campaign were certainly not helping Poland and the Allied cause by spending the entire war in POW camps (mostly in Murnau). As for Kleban, there was a certain lightheadedness about him that made me wonder whether he could focus on important things, like the research project on Polish Americans that was supported by the Rockefeller Foundation, but nothing was being done on it except Kleban visiting Polonia leaders all over America during the summer of 1974, among them Aloysius Mazewski, President of PAC and PNA, in Chicago; John Cardinal Krol in Philadelphia; Walter Zachariasiewicz, President of the Council of Polish Cultural Clubs, in Washington; Jerzy Lerski, President of the Polish American Historical Association (PAHA), in San Francisco; Bolesław Wierzbiański and Bolesław Łaszewski, publishers of the new Polish daily, *Nowy Dziennik*, in New York City, all in the name of the Institute's research interest in Polonia. I spent the summer of 1974 in Poland, taking Mark, my younger son, to the Kosciuszko Foundation's Summer School in Cracow and doing some work of my own, resulting in a book, an article, and one of the finest programs of the Literary Section, conceived in unusual circumstances.

One of the reasons for my 1974 trip to Poland, funded by a special grant from the Kosciuszko Foundation, whose President, Eugene Kusielewicz, was interested in my project, was to read a manuscript about Queen Jadwiga by an excellent Polish historian Stefan Kuczyński, whose research for it was supported by the Kosciuszko Foundation. My task was to find Professor Kuczyński, read his manuscript, an excerpt of which I had come across in a Polish periodical and found it very good, determine whether the rest of it was just as good and, if so, prevail upon the prospective publisher to print it, if for no other reason than its author was a former student of Professor Halecki, and his book would enrich the Halecki collection at the Polish Institute in New York.

There began an odyssey, the trials and tribulations of which, or "twists and turns" as in Homer's *Odyssey*, deserved its own Homer, but it had only my son Mark as its witness. It serves a useful purpose to recall it here.

Arriving in Warsaw on an overnight Polish LOT flight from New York, we took a train to Łódź, where I had reasons to believe I would find Professor Kuczyński at the local university. I was too late. Kuczyński had just moved to Katowice, where he joined the Silesian University, but our trip to Łódź was not a total loss. Our host, Professor Skwarczyński, former Rector and now professor of literature, whom I had met the previous year at the Congress of Scholars of Polish Descent, was a gracious host who had a pleasant surprise for us. We were the first residents in a beautiful villa which once belonged to a local Jewish textile mogul, and had been given just before our arrival to the university. Later, I often wondered about the timing of the gift, but at that time Mark and I enjoyed the VIP treatment, which included university car with a driver, meals in the university restaurant, and use of coffee-making equipment in the villa's kitchen. Over coffee Professor Skwarczyński told me that his students were using my dissertation, just published by *Antemurale* in Rome, in their research. I was surprised that they had access to it.

Since I was a stranger to this part of Poland, knowing it only from Władysław Reymont's novel *The Promised Land* (*Ziemia obiecana*), Professor Skwarczyński offered to show us the countryside, some famous gardens of the former landed gentry, and the Łowicz region famous for its folklore where we had lunch in a country inn staffed by women in rich local clothes otherwise seen only in the famous Polish song and dance groups, like "Mazowsze." It was a pleasant drive.

In the evening I met with the faculty, quite a few considering it was the middle of summer. Our host introduced me as a former Assistant Professor and now co-editor of *The Polish Review*, which surprised the audience familiar with my research, but Skwarczyński explained that such shifts were not unusual in America, and I could next become Associate Professor (*profesor nadzwyczajny*) and he was right. Then I spoke for an hour about the American educational system, its unevenness explained by me in terms of liberal admissions.

On the drive to the station the next morning Prof. Skwarczyński told me that his predecessor as Rector had been the well-known historian Marian Serejski, father of Krystyna Olszer, whom he had known when she was a student at Łódź, and he asked me about her. I told him that she was assisting Prof. Krzyżanowski on *The Polish Review* and starting classes in Polish at the Institute in the fall, which pleased him. He helped us board the crowded train and I never saw him again or his young son, who had been very useful with Mark.

In Katowice, with a mutual friend, Dr. Józef Musioł, a judge from my hometown who met us at the station, we first paid a visit to Wilhelm Szewczyk, another Silesian and the publisher of the periodical *Poglądy* ("Views") which had printed the excerpt from Kuczyński's manuscript. He was happy that his sending me copies of his publication had resulted in my learning of the existence of an important manuscript, but cautioned me about difficulties with publishing it, since its subject, the union of Poland and Lithuania, was taboo in Russia.

Like Skwarczyński in Łódź, "Wiluś" Szewczyk was a gracious host. Having treated us to excellent (imported) coffee and fabulous Polish pastries of which I never had enough, he produced a half-full bottle of Napoleon brandy and we drank a toast to the success of my mission (with Mark's drink properly diluted by the host himself). On parting, he gave me thumbnail sketches of key people at the university and at the "Silesia" (*Śląsk*) publishing house. He also handed me a copy, just off the press, of his "Views."

The visit to the university was brief. A visibly disturbed professor, the acting Rector, informed us that, yes, Professor Kuczyński was a faculty member at the school but that he was away, undergoing a cure in one of Poland's spas, his wife would certainly know which one, and he gave us the address. A quick taxi ride brought us to the doorstep of a modest house in a suburb, where Pani Kuczyńska, also visibly disturbed, invited us in just long enough to tell us that her husband was in Krynica, Poland's most famous spa.

By then it was evening and, like the professor in Łódź, the judge had a pleasant surprise for us in Katowice. His neighbor, editor of the illustrated magazine "Silesian Panorama" had invited us to a late dinner to discuss taking some photographs for his magazine and an article by me. Our taxi, still waiting, took us to the judge's apartment. On our way we saw the editor's wife coming home with an armful of supplies and reminding us about the dinner date. We went in to refresh ourselves and to meet the judge's family.

The judge was tired. The morning session in the court had dealt with amnesties, which he had been pressured to grant against his better judgment. I warned him not to get too involved, since in his mid-forties he was ripe for a cardiac arrest. Mark offered him some American peanuts which cheered him up, and he reciprocated with a bottle of Russian wine. The children were sent to their room with fistfuls of nuts while we had a little celebration, with the wife, whose maiden name was the same as Kochanowski's—Podlodowska, as the judge proudly pointed out, joining us. Then it was time to go.

The editor was an opinionated young man; the dinner his wife served was quite sumptuous. This was a time when Poland lived off Western loans which were surprisingly easily obtained by Edward Gierek after the disturbances of 1970, and conditions improved. There were even boasts that Poland was among the ten most advanced countries in the world, an opinion voiced also by the editor, but I listened to it with a proper dose of skepticism, more interested in the unusual bottle out of which he was filling our glasses. The editor caught my gaze, handed me the bottle, pointed to its label and said: "This is *Soplica*, the best and hardest to get vodka in Poland. Let us drink it in your honor."

He knew all there was to know about me, having read my biography in a collection about outstanding Silesians, *People of this Land*

(*Ludzie tej ziemi*), written by the judge after our first meeting in 1972. He wanted to use my story in his magazine and illustrate it with photos from my visit. It was all right with me, but first I wanted to go to Krynica for a day or two. He suggested I go this very night, as there was a midnight train arriving in Krynica early in the morning. There was also a midnight train back from Krynica, arriving in Katowice early in the morning, which I should take back and come straight to his flat, to take the photos before work. As for my writing something for his magazine, I suggested an article about the Pulaski Parade in New York, which was fine with him.

We spent the rest of the evening talking about America (for which curiosity in Poland was always great), drinking coffee (imported, which told me again that editors lived well in Poland) with occasional *Soplica* (diluted in Mark's case), and tasting pastries made for the occasion by the hostess. She packed some for us for the journey, and when I produced our thermos, she filled it with fresh hot coffee. It was thoughtful of her and, as a coffee addict, I showed my appreciation with a pair of nylon stockings for her and a pack of Marlboros for her husband, both gifts greatly appreciated. Then we said good-bye, but the men insisted on escorting us to the station, a short walk, and since we were taking only my briefcase with our documents and a notebook, along with the smallest of our traveling bags, it was a pleasant walk. On our way the judge recalled that his sister-in-law and her husband were spending their vacation in Krynica, and told us how to find them and use them to help us find Professor Kuczyński.

Our hosts succeeded in finding an empty compartment for us with room to stretch and take a nap and a collapsible small table by the window to have coffee and practice bridge on, with a pack of cards which Mark, ever a resourceful manager, had brought with him. We waved from the window to our hosts as the train took off from the station's lights into the darkness of southern Poland. I regretted not being able to see the countryside, only some of which I knew from pre-war trips to Cracow and pilgrimages to Zebrzydowice Calvary. We made ourselves comfortable until Mark dozed off. I had coffee and a Marlboro, made notes, and watched for the names of the stations we passed in flickering lights.

I was fast asleep at dawn and so was Mark. The rays of the rising sun coming through the window awakened me, and I dashed to the washroom to refresh myself, returning almost immediately in order not to leave Mark unprotected. We were still about half an hour away from Krynica. The coffee was still hot, the pastries still smelled deliciously, and I had a royal breakfast, followed by an after-breakfast Marlboro. Only then did I give Mark his wake-up call. It wasn't easy to wake him up, but I had no choice. From the window I could see we were approaching Krynica, beautifully situated in the foothills of the Carpathians. I pointed Mark to the washroom and when he came back I had breakfast waiting for him on the little table by the window, same as mine minus the Marlboro. As he was finishing, the train came to a stop.

Despite the early hour, the station was crowded with people on a cure in Krynica—every one of them holding a small container and taking sips from it through what looked like a straw—greeting their visitors. Since nobody was greeting us, we proceeded to find the judge's relatives. Their cabin—a tiny hut, really—was near the small river Poprad, known to me from pre-war patriotic songs in which the Poles claimed its entire valley right up to the "blue" Wag in neighboring Slovakia. Our surprised "hosts" were just getting up and knew exactly what to do to help us, but first invited us to share their breakfast, which was standard Polish: sliced tomatoes, cucumber and spring onion salad in vinegar and cream, bread and sausage, and coffee (domestic). After breakfast we walked along the lovely Poprad, then turned to the largest hotel in Krynica and there, in the lobby, was a list of all the guest-residents in Krynica, among them Stefan Kuczyński.

Professor Kuczyński couldn't get over his surprise, and hide his pleasure when, after we had him paged in his boarding house, I told him the reason for our visit. "Only an American professor would be so resourceful!" he exclaimed upon hearing of my meetings with Skwarczyński, Szewczyk, the acting rector of his university and finally, his wife. He had the bulky manuscript with him in a folder with some other papers he was planning to work on, but he handed it to me immediately, not to delay my reading of it. He was in a hurry to get us settled, and we followed him to a bus stop where we took a bus to a secluded part of town with only a public park and a few boarding houses around it. He took us to one run by a religious order of nuns, whose Mother Superior led us to the dining room just in time for the time-honored ritual of "second breakfast," apparently not quite dead yet in Poland. She invited us to have tea, coffee, or milk, and some of the cakes and pastries on plates buffet-style, while she and the professor left for her office to make sure that a double room was available. It was, on the second floor up a soft carpeted staircase, with a bathroom on the same floor. Mark took a bath right away and then went to bed while I buried myself in what I had come for, the manuscript, with just a brief interruption when the professor dropped in on his way out with some more coffee to keep me awake and a parting remark, "You know where to find me when you finish reading."

Drinking coffee and smoking, I couldn't tear myself away from the manuscript, the main title of which was *Jadwiga i Jagiełło*, with a subtitle *Litwin i Andegawenka* (The Lithuanian and the Princess Anjou). Although I thought that I knew everything there was to know about these two renowned Polish-Lithuanian rulers at the end of the fourteenth century, the manuscript was a revelation to me, expanding my knowledge of the period to an expert's level.

It was with reluctance that I put the manuscript down when a call for lunch (dinner in Poland) sounded in the corridor, awakening Mark. We had nothing to change into, so we just brushed and straightened our casual clothing and proceeded to the dining room, which was full. A girl serving the tables had one reserved for us just for two by a window with a view of the park on one side and the entire dining room on the other. There was a family sitting a few tables away from us but watching us intently, especially a young girl of such classic beauty that I immediately named her "Angel" to amuse Mark, secretly thinking what a perfect wife she would make for him in a few years. But she seemed to have eyes only for me, flashing a brilliant smile every time our eyes met, which flattered me but also disturbed and disappointed me, because Mark was a very handsome boy.

After the meal which was excellent, especially the thick meat-enriched vegetable soup and plentiful fruit, I returned with a thermos full of coffee to our room to go on with my reading, while Mark was exploring the neighborhood. I went out only briefly, to smoke outside for Mark's sake. It was the same after supper, when I read into the small hours of the morning until I ran out of coffee. Reading at a slow pace of twenty pages an hour while also making notes, I needed a 24-hour reading time, which I accomplished by the time of the afternoon tea (another time-honored ritual left over from better days) the following day.

After tea I asked Angel to gather all the teenagers in front of the dining room around the blackboard on which the menu was usually written. At precisely that moment, one of my long-range ideas was born when I told the youngsters I was going to give them an introductory lesson of English and that they should, when they go back to their schools in the fall, ask for English, and continue learning it with a view of eventually getting a scholarship to study in America. As I was finishing my talk, the dining room filled up, all the nuns came in, even the girls serving the tables listened, and more chairs were brought in. Unlike teaching Polish in America, where I usually started with the vowels, teaching English in Poland I decided to start with the consonants, disposing first with those pronounced exactly as in Polish (vast majority—good news!), then moving to those pronounced differently (j, w,) or in more ways than one (c, g). Vowels were more difficult, since each one of them is pronounced in more ways than one, and I demonstrated it with a vocabulary of about 50 words covering greetings, family relationships, and everyday objects. At the end I taught them the simplest song, "My bonnie lies over the ocean," and when after a few tries it erupted like a volcano, everybody was clapping.

The famous long lesson lasted two hours. The Sister on duty announced, after the last singing of "My Bonnie," to remain seated, as supper was being served. Mark and I found ourselves sharing a table with the youngsters, next to Angel who showed me her voluminous notes from the lesson. I gave her a Kennedy half-dollar in appreciation of her help and as a reward for her ability, encouraging her to study English.

Things moved fast from then on. After supper Mark and I picked our things from our room and stopped at the office to settle our bill. The Mother Superior told us the professor would take care of it and, besides, if anybody owed anything, it was they, for the splendid English lesson. Could she, at least, fill our thermos with hot coffee and have some food packed for us for the journey? When I expressed our gratitude, she sent a Sister to the kitchen. While waiting, I parted with another Kennedy half-dollar as a souvenir, received with gratitude bordering on reverence, so great was the cult of the Kennedy family in Poland.

Half an hour later we found Professor Kuczyński in his room. While Mark excused himself to explore the town, as was his custom, the professor couldn't wait for me to tell him what I thought about his manuscript. I told him how impressed I was by it and how I would do everything to help get it published, which was what he wanted to hear. Then we plunged into a detailed discussion of the manuscript. I wanted to know if the facts in it were historically correct, whether immediately following the Polish-Lithuanian royal marriage it was indeed the Polish knights who defended Wilno (Vilnius, the Lithuanian capital), besieged by three armies of the Teutonic Order in the biggest war waged by it so far, a war that was to be the end of Lithuania, and Poland after it. He explained that all the facts were well researched and thus historically correct, and because of it, this type of historical novel was called "Literature of Fact" (*literatura faktu*), as explained by the sponsor of the book in an essay on file with the "Silesia" publishers.

I was also interested in how Kuczyński had obtained all the details of Jadwiga's life, and he told me that there was considerable literature devoted to her as well as literature in which she appeared marginally, and she was probably the most written about personality in Polish history. This was of great interest to me, and I decided there and then to organize a small symposium upon return to New York, and to include in it a paper by me on the subject of "Queen Jadwiga in Polish Literature." The information I obtained from Kuczyński plus the essay in "Silesia" would provide me with enough material to write a review article, "Literature as History," to complement my earlier "History as Literature," written in connection with Kuniczak's book.

By the time Mark returned, Kuczyński and I had covered all that needed to be covered for my meeting with the "Silesia" Publishers. I handed him back his manuscript, keeping just my much augmented notes, and we left for the station, Kuczyński seeing us off and wondering if we would ever meet again "in this life" as he put it.

We were back in Katowice early in the morning, after sleeping most of the night in a comfortable "private" compartment secured for us by the conductor for a few much appreciated Marlboros in their box, a prized item in Poland. Before dozing off we had some of the Sisters' pastries and coffee, still hot in the thermos, and we played cards on our little collapsible table by the window, outside of which a storm was raging in the darkness, putting us to sleep.

Brilliant sunrise awakened us just before Katowice; we watched the industrial Silesian landscape with interest. I regretted missing Wadowice, birthplace of Cardinal Wojtyła. From the station in

Katowice we took a slow walk, so as not to be too early. To our surprise, the "Panorama" editor was up, waiting for us, with his photographic equipment and light early breakfast ready. We left together soon afterwards, joined by the judge, who helped select suitable landmarks for the photos, among them the famous statue commemorating the post-World War I Silesian Insurgents, very apt, if one considers that before the Second World War I was a local commander of the Sons of the Insurgents.

At the statue we parted company with the editor, who was in a hurry to develop the pictures. As a parting gift he gave me the empty bottle of *Soplica* as a souvenir. I never found out if he ever published the article the photos were to illustrate, but I did receive a batch of them from the judge before leaving Poland, and they are in the family album jealously guarded by my wife because both Mark and I look good in them against a memorable background.

There remained the encounter with the "Silesia" Publishers. We returned with the judge to his apartment for our belongings, and then he drove us to the meeting, but did not go in, waiting in the car. The meeting was brief, the decision to publish Kuczyński's manuscript resting on the question of how much we, in America, wanted to see the book published. When I said "Very much," including the President of the Kosciuszko Foundation, "Silesia" was satisfied. We shook hands and I left the meeting with some books and the essay about Kuczyński's manuscript, promising to return it before I left Poland. I rejoined the judge, who dropped us off at the station on his way to work. We took a train to our relatives in that part of Silesia, appropriately, that the Silesian Insurgents had won half a century ago.

To fulfill my research obligation to the Kosciuszko Foundation (a $3,000 research grant), I spent the next few weeks on research at Wrocław (Breslau) University. The choice of Wrocław was eminently sound for two main reasons: I would have a chance to get to know one of Poland's ancient cities, separated from it for 600 years; also, Wrocław had an excellent library, with probably the largest collection on Polish-Russian literary relations, my specialty, and the best specialist in the field on its faculty. The few weeks I spent in Wrocław were my most satisfying and productive research undertaking until then. I found close to a thousand pertinent items in the card catalogue, and had most of them microfilmed before my time in Poland was up.

The day after returning to New York I resumed my activities at the Polish Institute, beginning with a report to the Executive Director. Dr. Kleban was glad to see me, and even more so when I gave him a bottle of Polish rye vodka as a present from Poland. He immediately summoned L.K. from the office below his, brought out glasses and ice cubes from the refrigerator, and we had vodka on the rocks. I was moved watching these two exiles sipping the Polish national drink reverently because it was not something bought in a liquor store but brought out of Poland, which they hadn't seen since prewar days. They asked me about Poland, and I told them that the country was in seemingly good shape and that there was much we could do there: I told them about my talk to the Łódź faculty, about Professor Kuczyński's book, about my English lesson in Krynica, and about my other encounters. They listened with great interest, particularly L.K., who was pleasantly surprised to hear that while in Cracow I had managed to meet his old schoolmate, Dr. Karol Estreicher, who helped me to find and meet L.K.'s sister and step-mother, two splendid Polish academic women who were very anxious to see him, just as L.K. was anxious to hear about them. Both L.K. and Kleban couldn't thank me enough for the vodka treat and the good conversation, and I saw in them kindred spirits who loomed prominently in my future plans.

The standing-room only success of the symposium built around Kuczyński's book, with Dr. Eugene Kusielewicz, President of the Kosciuszko Foundation chairing the program because it was the Foundation's money which made the book possible on two counts, and Dr. Thaddeus Gromada, Secretary General of the Institute talking about Kuczyński's mentor, Professor Oskar Halecki who had died almost exactly a year ago, had unexpected consequences. The fact that the program was sponsored by *my* Literary Section and not by the PIAS itself, and that its gist was *my* paper, "Queen Jadwiga in Polish Literature," did not go well with some people, a feeling strengthened further by the praise the paper received in the discussion that followed it, including a remark by a young professor from KUL (Catholic University of Lublin), Father Kondziela, that he could follow my English better than that of the other participants, both US-born. (Father Kondziela, while still a parish priest, had baptized my nephews, the sons of my sister Zosia in Upper Silesia.)

Disturbed that my activity seemed to be threatening to some people at the Institute, I tried hard to soften the impression but everything I touched turned to the proverbial gold. The best example of this came during the concert tour of the folk ensemble *Śląsk* ("Silesia"), brought to New York by Sol Hurok to coincide, whether by design or accidentally, with the annual Pulaski Parade in October. Suddenly I had something extra to write about for the "Silesian Panorama," because I was convinced, and so was the director of *Śląsk*, that the organizers of the Parade would take advantage of the presence in town of an ensemble reputed to be the best in the world (better than "Moiseyev") and have it march and perform in the parade (just as the Germans did for their own parade when Lufthansa flew in an ensemble from Berlin), but I was wrong and so was the director, Stanisław Hadyna.

The organizers of the Pulaski Parade would have nothing to do with an ensemble coming from a "communist" country. Should the Institute have intervened? Dr. Kleban was against getting the Institute involved. What Hadyna did was to call on the Institute, where Sierpiński and Pusłowski directed him to me. I admired the man, having heard much about his legendary dedication to the ensemble. He told me that since he could not march with his group in the parade, he wanted to talk about it, and the Institute was the most suitable place for it. The best time for the talk, and the only available time in his schedule, was Saturday after the matinee performance, and it was already Friday, no time to even announce the talk, except by word of mouth and by phone, and almost no time to secure equipment necessary to show films, slides, and other visual illustrations of it. That's where Dr. Janusz Ostrowski, chairman of the Natural Sciences and Technology Section (activated, with my help, about the same time as the Literary Section), entered the picture. He went to an electronics store, where he purchased on a trial basis all the equipment needed, and installed it to enable Hadyna to test it and leave for the theatre in time for the evening performance. Then he called all the members of his section in the metropolitan area, while I did the same with my section, and L.K., joining in the action, called some of his friends, all three of us asking everybody to call others. My last calls were to my personal associates who had been getting behind me offering voluntary help in my undertakings. The very last call was to the Polish bakery to have a large supply of poppy seed pastry ready to be picked up the next day (Saturday).

Saturday was a big day for the Institute, and a perfect example of what can be accomplished by a few good men. Going by car with my wife, Doreen, we made a detour to the bakery to pick up the pastry, still hot from the oven. The Institute was empty (as a board member, I had my own key) but it soon filled with the aroma of coffee (and tea, in a teapot, in its own English tea cozy) and the sweet smell of pastry. Soon Hadyna arrived and we had a snack, while putting last touches to the lecture room and waiting for the public. First to arrive was one of my associates, whom I placed at the wide open front door to direct people upstairs, where Doreen was posted at the entrance, behind a tiny table with some literature and a cash box (a Kosciuszko Foundation gift, a metal lunch box, really) for donations.

When the public began to arrive it was like a flood, filling the lecture room beyond its capacity imposed by fire regulations. We closed the front door and Hadyna told those outside that there would be a second presentation just for them, immediately after the first. Those who were too old or too tired to wait outside could sit in the reception room downstairs. Then he made his presentation, which was a real treat, especially the parts dealing with the search for and recruitment (verging on the illegal) of the "little girls with the big voices," as a *New York Times* critic called the amazing girls with the raw, untrained but powerful voices echoing hauntingly in their native hills.

There was a standing ovation after the presentation followed by Hadyna's announcement that there was no time for questions from the floor, that any questions should be asked during the brief refreshment period when the new public was coming in, while those who won't get a chance to ask should wait downstairs for the end of the second presentation which was about to begin. Doreen moved to the refreshments while I took her place at the entrance to control the flow of the public in and out the lecture room. The second presentation was just as good and just as enthusiastically applauded, and then Hadyna was surrounded by admirers and well-wishers many of whom had arrived from Poland only a few years ago (1968).

After the refreshments, which were praised by all in preference to the formerly traditional glass of wine, it was time for Hadyna to return to the theatre. Since Doreen and I intended to return the next day to restore the place to its former state on our way to the parade, she just put the leftovers in the refrigerator and we offered Hadyna a lift. He was very happy about it, telling me that he wanted me to come to the theatre because he had a surprise for me. After putting all the lights out and making sure that all cigarettes had been extinguished, I carefully locked up the Institute while Doreen was bringing the car in front. On our way we first dropped off Dr. Ostrowski who was returning the electronic equipment to the store (very resourceful of him) and, with him out of the car, I handed Hadyna an envelope stuffed with money, receipts from the second presentation (the cash box was in the refrigerator with the leftovers). With the help of an attendant we found a parking space near the theatre and Hadyna led us right in, where two isolated seats were reserved in the middle of the first row.

Having seen the ensemble before, in Pittsburgh, where it had been declared "hands down" winner over Moiseyev (an earlier visitor), I was paying less attention to the program than thinking about Hadyna's surprise. Then, just before intermission, there was a little pause, the entire ensemble regrouped, then moved forward to the edge of the stage, right opposite me, and after another pause exploded with one of my favorite Polish military songs, "The Sentry's Vision" (*Wizja szyldwacha*), beginning it with the explosive refrain and only then going to the soft beginning and the refrain again, during which I stood up, letting them know that I knew they were singing for me and that I was honored.

When the curtain came down to a deafening applause and the lights went up, Hadyna joined us. Seeing how moved I was, he said he was glad he had made the right choice. Then he thanked me for the money, the largest gift he had ever received. He said there was enough to give everybody ten dollars, which was more than their daily allowance, and still have enough left to buy a piece of American equipment. I told him we would not stay for the second part, which for me would be an anticlimax after the first, and he understood and was even pleased, because his Party "commissar" wanted to meet me, not a wise meeting for me. The man was a coward who, in a concert in Moscow, was afraid to put the Polonaise on the program, until Khrushchev asked for it saying it would not be the first time the Poles danced it in the Kremlin.

Hadyna saw us off to our car, where he first kissed Doreen's hand, thanking her for the reception (his English was functional), and then he and I embraced. Like Kuczyński before, he too wondered if we would ever meet again "in this life" and he was correct in his premonition. He died not long after. Premature death among good people in stressful situations was prevalent in Poland,

and it was a duty of the Institute to cultivate and help such people, because their ranks were growing thinner with every passing year.

We took our children (ages 21, 18, 17, "children" in name only) to the Pulaski Parade the next day (Sunday) stopping at the Institute first, to show them where their father spent most of his free time and their mother assisted him in events like yesterday's. We had a second breakfast of coffee, tea and the poppy seed pastry, and while Doreen was putting the lecture and reception rooms in order I acted as a guide, showing the youngsters the Institute, its fine library making an impression on Paul, a Columbia College senior then, just back from a Junior Year in Paris.

Putting our things in the car and leaving it parked near the Institute, we walked down Fifth Avenue all the way to St. Patrick's Cathedral, where the Cardinal, surrounded by clergy on the top step, was blessing the many contingents (parishes, schools, police, firemen, veterans, marching bands, social and cultural clubs, beauty queens in cars and on floats, and sanitation men at the end) passing by. The official reviewing stand was on the steps of the Public Library at 42nd Street, but we did not go there. I joined the veterans, with my family keeping up with me from the sidewalk right up to 65th Street, just before the parade veered off east to disperse. We got into our car and went home, where I immediately started writing about the parade.

Writing about the Pulaski Parade for the "Silesian Panorama," I could not help thinking that despite its huge size it was inferior to the von Steuben German Parade I had seen a few weeks earlier, and that Hadyna's ensemble would have made a difference. I was also thinking how the Poles were unable to put their best foot forward. Such musings were probably the reason that my article was not published by the "Panorama" (at least not to my knowledge) but I still have a copy which I intend to use on a suitable occasion.

When I came to the Institute on Monday, everybody was reading *Nowy Dziennik* (Polish Daily News) containing Bob's witty-as-usual critique of Hadyna's presentation and an illustrated report on the Pulaski Parade. When I handed Sierpiński the receipts from the Hadyna program, he was flabbergasted by the amount, especially when I told him that I had given Hadyna a similar amount for his second talk, and how much it had meant for the ensemble. By repeating it all to others, Sierpiński was clearly becoming my associate, and so was Pusłowski, who with his beautiful wife and L.K. had been at Hadyna's program on Saturday, with all three duly impressed by its mechanics. My not having had time for them impressed them even more. As for Kleban, he had not been well enough to attend, and I believed him.

At the next board meeting of the Literary Section I proposed a book project, *Dictionary of Polish Literature*, in addition to the by-now frequent lectures or discussions. The *Dictionary* was to follow the example of the popular and inexpensive paperback, *Dictionary of Russian Literature*, by Professor William Harkins of Columbia University, and it was to be produced quickly, to stimulate and satisfy the growing interest in Polish literature. A description of the project in *The Polish Review* brought responses from many members of the Literary Section, willing and eager to contribute an entry about a particular writer (the poet Julian Tuwim was the most sought after assignment) or literary period (with Romanticism the most popular), but from the beginning the project was being delayed because of a serious disagreement about its scope between me and Professor Tadeusz Błaszczyk.

Professor Błaszczyk, a relatively recent exile from Łódź University, where I had a chance to inquire about him, had brought with him a tendency for large, well-documented volumes better suited for libraries than for private use, which was what I wanted: to have something handy at one's fingertips. It is true that, having become a member of the Institute, Błaszczyk was then made academic consultant to its library and, as a board member of the Literary Section, he had a say about any proposed publications. But the truth is that he was not yet familiar with what was needed in a hurry, and how such needs were satisfied in America. Having spent a lifetime in a tightly controlled system in Poland, he was not accustomed to the kind of individual initiatives I excelled in and which would have prevailed in this case too but for some new developments in the Institute which caused me to temporarily postpone the *Dictionary* project (and a planned Polish language textbook) in order to acquaint myself with what was taking place on other fronts.

What was taking place was at last some progress on the research project on Polish Americans. In collaboration with Irwin T. Sanders, an allegedly prominent sociologist from Boston University, a working conference was held in its Conference Center on September 26-28, 1974. Having just returned from Poland and busy with the symposium inspired by the Kuczyński book, I was not consulted about the conference as I would have liked to have been in order to point out some glaring inconsistencies, namely why Sanders, and why Boston? Some works on ethnicity had already come out, the pioneering Moynihan/Glaser book among them, which should have been studied for guidance by our own sociologists instead of relying on strangers. The first hesitant steps should have taken place at the Institute, which had been slated at the annual meeting to be the center of Polish American research; so why run the expense of going to Boston, as if the answers were there, instead of seeking them in New York, with better participation than in Boston? My doubts were confirmed when Dr. Kleban handed me his report from the conference, to be printed in *The Polish Review*. I couldn't believe my eyes: it read like a society column, with walks and talks in the park in the moonlight. If there was one person I wanted no disagreement with, it was Dr. Kleban, but I had to reject his report.

The rejection of Dr. Klebans's report was my first painful experience in the Institute, but I had no choice. I knew that my half of *The Polish Review* was read faithfully by members and subscribers, and I could not include in it something as unsuitable as Kleban's report. It was written well, because Kleban's English was surprisingly good, but it was not a report, rather a romantic reminiscence, and I told him so, promising to use it at some point with similar reminiscences—a good idea that had just then entered my head, but not good enough to make up for his disappointment and slight. In retrospect, I feel that I should have used it the way it was, with just some editing; it would have been a productive compromise, and not a source of enmity.

After the uncomfortable encounter with Dr. Kleban I understood why he had ignored the Hadyna presentation which, with his love of everything Polish, he would have certainly attended. There was more to it. My rejection of the report implied doubts on my part about the conduct of the ongoing research project, as Kleban had accused me of in our meeting. He was right about that, and I decided to prove it to myself and to him. I read every article in the *Polish American Studies*, of which there was a complete set in the Institute's library, and every book on ethnicity I could lay my hands on. All of a sudden I was becoming an expert on Polish American ethnicity, a digression I hoped would not take me too far away from my academic research specialty. The only casualty so far was the *Dictionary* project, postponed indefinitely, and resumed independently twenty years later under entirely different circumstances by Professor Edward Czerwiński (separate chapter).

In the final analysis, the reasons for pursuing my own research on Polish Americans had less to do with doubts and disagreements inside the Institute than with what was taking place outside of it. Without my knowing it, my publications and my most recent symposium promising more publications on Eastern Europe, had resulted in inquiries about me from Polish academic circles in London acting on behalf of the Lanckoroński Foundation. Its representative, a certain Dr. Kirkor, saw in me a successor to Lednicki and Halecki, and a candidate for a long-term research grant. The inquiries were addressed to the Pilsudski Institute, specifically to Dr. Fryling, who passed them on to the one person who knew my qualifications best, L.K., who responded with a glowing recommendation, which he loyally showed to me. I asked him to add to it how this would be the best of all worlds for me, allowing me to continue my post-doctoral research while giving up translating from Soviet scientific journals articles on ichthyology for the Museum of Natural History, making good money, but acquiring useless, even if interesting, knowledge I could do without while serving the Institute and doing research. There was one reservation on my part. In my research I would not aim to become a Sovietologist, partly because it would be unwise on account of my many relatives in Poland, but mainly because my research would continue to be in the area of Polish-Russian literary and historical relations.

A letter arrived from the Lanckoroński Foundation shortly afterwards informing me regretfully that its investments in Switzerland had suffered big losses postponing the grant indefinitely. It was a big blow for me. Instead of staying with my post-doctoral research, I stayed with the research on Polish Americans, but by then there was a new factor that made the research not only necessary, but mandatory.

The new factor was the American Bicentennial, which was fast approaching. Preparations were being made all over the country to celebrate the great anniversary, which was to heal America after the disruptive 1960's and, coming on the heels of the Watergate scandal, mark a new beginning in a new century for America. There were ample reasons for the ethnic groups to celebrate too, especially in New York, the site of two meaningful symbols, the Statue of Liberty and Ellis Island. The Polish American Congress was planning a book for the occasion, a laudable project, but as it turned out neither the designated writer nor the Congress itself were quite up to it. Whether or not it was due to Dr. Kleban's growing disorientation, caused by the onset of a deadly illness as I found out later, nothing was being done in the Institute in connection with the approaching Bicentennial. Suspecting that nothing would be done, I broadened my research, a task in which I received much encouragement and help from L.K. As for Kleban, he reminded the Board of Directors that his term of office was expiring in May of 1975, and that his last official task would be to prepare the Third Congress of Scholars and Scientists which was to be hosted by the Canadian Branch of the Institute at McGill University in Montreal, when a new Executive Director was to be elected.

Kleban's imminent vacating of the Executive Director's chair fitted well within my plans. Since my return from Poland, and even while in Poland, I had been making notes about the future of the Institute, my vision of it, which I now divulged to a small group of associates to whom I referred as my "constituency" and who were ready to serve the Institute on a voluntary basis. I was also renewing contact with a lady in Pittsburgh who, when I was teaching there and cooperating with the local Arts League, had offered to give me part of her inheritance from her late husband (or lover?), a steel magnate, leaving the rest for me in her will if and when I would be in charge of an institution like the Kosciuszko Foundation or the Polish Institute. If the latter, there would be enough money to buy the building housing it on 59 East 66th Street, and put the Institute on a firm ground for the first time.

Getting elected was not a foregone conclusion, since only members of the board voted, rendering members of my team helpless, while they would be decisive in a general election. To make things more complicated, Prof. Thaddeus Gromada let it be known that he was interested in becoming Executive Director, a position which he claimed was coming to him as member of the old Polish American community. This claim created a situation that needed careful handling.

While Gromada was dreaming of becoming Executive Director, L.K. was dreaming of becoming Secretary General, a position he had once held and was persuaded to relinquish to Gromada in recognition of the growing membership from old Polonia. Gromada never equaled L.K.'s flair and skill in presiding over the Institute's programs (calming down the shy and nervous playwright Sławomir Mrożek), and with the rise in activities L.K. wanted to be part of the action again. Besides, he felt strongly that the time for the changing of the guard hadn't arrived yet, and I shared that feeling, but when I did some lobbying for him I discovered that two directors I was counting on had other ideas, and in the voting Gromada won 5:4 instead of losing 3:6.

The Third Congress, which took place as scheduled in Montreal on May 16-18, 1975, was a success. Chaired by Dr. Tadeusz Brzeziński, former Consul General of Poland in Canada and the father of Professor Zbigniew Brzezinski, who gave the keynote address, the Congress was attended by scholars and scientists from the United States and Canada, and from Europe (mostly England), South America, Australia, and Asia. It had eighteen disciplines, represented by 185 papers, among them mine, my first in an Institute Congress. However, the Institute's Board meeting was not a success.

There was tension in the room when we reached the point on the agenda calling for the election of Executive Director. I had been studying the Institute's by-laws, paying attention to the rules governing elections, and I could see now I was the only one in the room who knew that elections must not take place outside the United States. I got up and shared my knowledge with the other directors. Prof. Brzezinski asked me for the by-laws booklet, took one look at the underlined passage, agreed with me and, as was his custom, reached a quick decision to close the meeting. The election of an Executive Director was postponed, with Dr. Kleban agreeing to serve until then.

The turn of events at Montreal worked well for me. Since Dr. Fryling, my most formidable partisan, was too old to travel, it was just as well the election had not taken place. Upon returning to New York, I was not surprised to notice that my standing at the Institute was even stronger than before. The "Defender of Law and Order" my two noble constituents called me over coffee and brandy celebrating my initiative at the Third Congress, and Dr. Fryling, glad to see me, applauded the values of "old Silesian nobility."

Since I was planning another summer trip to Poland I plunged into work to finish materials for the next issue of *The Polish Review* and to begin something new that I had been already thinking of in Montreal. It was a design for a promotional flyer for the Polish Institute, but flyer is too weak a word for what I had in mind, pamphlet, brochure or booklet described it better, but still not completely. It was to be something new, something to catch the eye of the beholder, something without an iota of commercialism in it, just ideas unobtrusively but tastefully presented.

The work on the brochure became an obsession with me and soon attracted the attention of the whole Institute. I had by then managed to create for myself an ample office in an empty room in the back of the building across the hall from the editorial office of *The Polish Review*, by simply removing a quantity of bookshelves and having the librarian take the books. All that was left in the room was a simple desk with a phone and an old manual typewriter on it, a few chairs, an old but comfortable armchair, and next to it a small table on which my coffee maker kept it hot at all times to sustain me in what was for me a labor of love. In that splendid solitude I was interrupted only by phone calls, growing more frequent just like the number of curious visitors, all looking over my shoulder and all wanting to know what was it that I was creating. One of the visitors was the by-then visibly shuffling Dr. Kleban.

I offered him some coffee and motioned him to the armchair next to my desk. He told me that from the reports he had received from L.K. he assumed that I was working on an unusual fund-raising flyer for the Institute, and that I was doing it without discussing it with him. I pointed out to him that I was certainly not "working on a fund-raising flyer" but designing a literary-artistic piece, let's call it a pamphlet or a booklet on which my wife, who was good at drawing, was helping me, because I wanted it to be a collector's item, describing the Institute and illustrating its functions in such a way as to attract new members and wealthy patrons, beginning with a lady in Pittsburgh.

When I showed him what I had done so far, he was genuinely impressed, but hastened to say that he could not authorize the considerable expense of producing something so elaborate. My labor, like all my work for the Institute, was free, I told him, and I hoped that my former associates in the printing industry would do the printing for me for old time's sake as a kind of professional courtesy. To this he had no answer and he blurted out the real reason for his visit. It was to buy my sketch. I listened with disbelief turning into disgust mixed with sadness about the poor man.

It turned out that the glamorous Mrs. Blanka R. Rosenstiel, an heiress like the lady from Pittsburgh but more aggressive as a patron of Polish culture, chiefly as founder and president of The American Institute of Polish Culture, Inc. in Miami, Florida, had taken it upon herself to help the Polish Institute in the only way she thought she knew how, namely by advertising its existence. She had budgeted $3,000 for the campaign, with Kleban giving her a free hand and inviting no submissions out of which the best would be chosen. Knowing it would be mine he begged me to let him work with Mrs. Rosenstiel without worrying about my sketch, in other words sell it to him. L.K., who kept peeking into the room until I finally asked him in, took Kleban's side, even suggesting a price for the sketch: the cost of my trip to Poland, which that summer (1975) I would pay for myself. L.K. convinced me. I told them to expect me at noon the next day and to bring cash. I would have the sketch ready and the materials for *The Polish Review*. We would have vodka before my wife drove me to the airport.

At home, I had Doreen make a good copy of the sketch for my files. She didn't like the arrangement, and neither did I. We both felt that the trip to Poland was unnecessary. I could have microfilms from Wrocław sent by mail, especially since there was no burning need for them.

With the children occupied the next day in the St. John the Divine summer program, Doreen and I drove to the Institute. I wanted her to be present at the meeting as a witness, but probably because of that, and because it was in my office this time, the meeting was not a replica of last year's joyful libation. To be sure, both my guests greeted Doreen cordially, L.K. as her former instructor of Polish at Columbia, and Kleban as an admirer of her skills as hostess at my programs. She reverted to that role in this meeting, too, serving coffee and some biscuits she had brought with her. We drank only two vodkas, one at the beginning, with Doreen taking just a symbolic sip out of my glass, and a farewell drink at the end, after I had handed them the materials and taken the money, which was to be my spending money in Poland. Otherwise it was coffee we drank during the meeting, with Doreen putting the left-over in my ubiquitous thermos and leaving behind everything in perfect order as was her custom, and me handing the still half-full bottle of vodka to L.K. who knew how to appreciate it, and telling Kleban to feel free to use my ideas in the project.

On our way out we stopped at the reception room to say good-bye to Mr. Sierpiński and "Count" Pusłowski, with the latter greeting us with a charming compliment:

"Mr. Frank, you and I have something in common."
"And what would that be?"
"We both have beautiful wives."
"This deserves a toast. I left half a bottle of Polish rye vodka with L.K. If you hurry...."
"Have a good trip!"

and both vanished in the lift.

Getting into our car outside the Institute, Doreen had the last word, making a statement that I remembered on another memorable occasion. Looking back, she said pensively:

"This is really a nice building, a little palace, and you are leaving it in the hands of four old men, each of whom has a liking for Polish vodka."
"I know, and I feel uneasy about it, and about Poland."

With that feeling, we drove quickly to the airport. Since I was traveling light, Doreen dropped me off at the proper gate and left to rejoin the children. The last thing I did was to give her half of the money from the Institute.

Despite the uneasiness, Poland held many surprises for me. After sleeping through most of the flight, making up for working late the previous night, I realized upon landing in Warsaw that there were several acquaintances on the plane, and that they were expected, having their names checked off a long list spread out on a table around which Polish Army officers were sitting or standing. I discovered that my name was also on the list. I was told that there was a meeting of Polish veterans of World War II from all over the world marking the 30th anniversary of Poland's taking possession of its postwar northern and western territories. I recalled having heard about such a meeting, but the Montreal Congress had prevented me from following up on it. As it was, the Army was to conduct a guided tour of the territories, including famous battlefields, and the *Polonia* Society was to hold scholarly sessions about the Polishness of the territories, beginning with Wrocław. As Wrocław was my destination anyway, I joined the meeting.

The ride from the Warsaw airport to Wrocław, in a comfortable "Orbis" tour bus, was highly educational for me, having never viewed the Polish countryside except from a train window. I had a good companion sitting next to me, General Franciszek Skibiński, a veteran like me of the 1940 French campaign and presently commander of the local veterans organization. I treated him to coffee, still warm in the thermos, and a Marlboro, always prized in Poland. He was invaluable in pointing out to me the old Polish-German border, especially around the historic Oleśnica.

It was good to be back again in Wrocław, ancient city for which I had special affection for having been the oldest stronghold of Polishness, after Gniezno, and for having been the capital city of Silesia, *my* Silesia, whose unfortunate loss in the fourteenth century and failure to regain later despite numerous opportunities deprived Poland of one of its four vital provinces, abandoning it to German and then Prussian influences while seeking uncertain gains in the East, contributing to the country's decline and fall.

It was with thoughts like these that I got off the bus at the market place in Wrocław. Other buses had arrived before ours and were lined up out of the way, with their erstwhile passengers grouped together facing some officers and civilians standing on the steps of what looked like the town hall. The moment our group joined the other veterans, a general stepped up to a microphone and said briefly:

"Welcome to Poland! You defeated the Germans!"

After this electrifying greeting he saluted and stepped back, to be followed by a town official welcoming us to Wrocław, a colonel outlining the tour, and a strikingly handsome tall civilian describing tomorrow's session. This was Wiesław Adamski, Secretary General of the *Polonia* Society, whom I had met at the Meeting of Scholars two years before. He recognized me, too, and speaking above the heads of the gathering asked me to consider chairing the session. Then he invited us to our quarters.

The quarters turned out to be a brand new NOVOTEL, a motel built by a French firm on the outskirts of town in record time for the meeting, as we were told. Beautifully landscaped, with a swimming pool in the back, it was well appointed and elegantly furnished. The rooms were large and comfortable, and the food fine, as we found out at supper.

I shared my supper table with a companion-in-arms from my division in France, interned in Switzerland, where he had married and remained after the war, becoming an expert watchmaker. We were joined by Secretary Adamski, whom I had always thought to be a perfect candidate for Consul General in New York, where deportment in diplomats is highly regarded. He told me the session tomorrow was to be held at the town hall (the old Rathaus) from 10 o'clock til noon, and that I would be doing him a great favor by chairing it. I asked a favor in return, a car with a driver for the afternoon to visit my family briefly in Jastrzębie-Zdrój. At that point General Skibiński joined us, and made much of the fact that I was a native of Silesia, and what a marvelous symbolism there was in my participation in the session. But what the general really wanted was another Marlboro, and I gave him the pack with whatever was left in it, taking just one to join him while drinking the excellent coffee just being served. The old boy couldn't thank me enough, but I truly liked him, as if sensing that he did not have long to live.

There was a concert in the Officers Casino, where our buses took us after supper. One of the numbers was a beautiful young woman singing a song I had never heard before, ending each stanza with "You will defend me" addressed to a man. While singing, she had her eyes fixed on me, as if I were the defender. At the cocktail party afterwards I asked her about it, and she said I looked like a defender of the weak. Would she sing it just for me when I return to town? No, she won't be here, she would be on a tour, but would leave a record for me at the Casino.

Returning to the motel I was able to make up some of the money I had parted with before leaving New York. There was a group of veteran airmen from England having a party around the swimming pool, with one in, swimming.

"Mr. American, how about a race?" he called to me.

I looked at him and I could see I could beat him, but the pool was a problem. Wide enough for two without bumping into each other, its length would require constant turns. But I was still a strong swimmer, and I needed to unwind. I changed into swimming trunks, which I carried in my bag with my money and documents, and I was ready, even readily agreeing to a bet, any amount, and handed my bag to a man who acted as a referee. At a count from him we dived in, and swam the agreed number of laps, with me a clear winner.

"How did you know you could beat him?"
"If I couldn't beat him, I would know about him."

The man smiled knowingly and handed me my bag with pound notes filling its top, as many airmen had bet on their pal (Doreen will love to see so many pictures of the Queen). I had noticed the referee's professionalism and his grasp of sports, and I told him so. He said he was a former soccer player and now manager of the Glasgow Rangers. I was impressed. The Rangers were a top team, on par with any team in Poland, a world power in soccer at that time.

Fearing I had caught a chill in the midnight swim, I stopped at the bar and asked for a brandy and a pot of hot tea, which I sipped while taking an aspirin in my room, resting. The next day, Sunday, was a big day for me.

After a big breakfast our buses took us to the town hall, and we proceeded to a large room on the second floor called Knights Hall, the famous *Rittersaal* in German times. It was packed with veterans, townspeople, television crews and reporters, all beginning to perspire on what promised to be a hot day. There was a big clock on the wall opposite the end of the room with a raised floor and a large table around which the speakers were already sitting. Secretary Adamski led me into a little room behind the table, and took some data from me for the purpose of introduction. Then he turned to nobody in particular and said "Now let Professor Mocha sweat"; we had a brandy with excellent coffee as the big clock struck 10 times.

But I didn't sweat. On the contrary, I was getting into what I later referred to as my "finest hour" (two, really). After a factual introduction by Secretary Adamski in which he stressed that I was born in Upper Silesia in a village called Nendza ("Misery"), I turned to my panel and cautioned its members to stay within their allotted time limit which I would not allow to be extended. My first speaker was a bishop from former East Prussia whose paper I found extremely interesting and excellently timed. He was followed by long-winded academics who made it necessary for me to slip them a note to conclude their respective talks. As the last speaker was unable to abide by my rule, I took advantage of a pause in his delivery, thanked him, and glancing at the clock I thanked the panel and the public and closed the session. At that very moment the big clock began to strike 12 and the Rittersaal erupted in applause.

I was surrounded by reporters who couldn't believe what they had just witnessed. They didn't expect me to be so efficient. It never happens in Poland, they kept saying. One of them, from the official paper, kept harping on my birthplace, trying to make something out of its name, and whether through ignorance or by design he wrote an article that was to cause me a great deal of trouble. But that was still in the future, and now I was rescued by a husky young man who turned out to be my designated driver. "Ready?" "Ready!" On the town hall's steps a young boy was reciting:

"Who are you, boy?"—"A Polish schoolboy!"

I waited for him to finish, patted him on the head, told him I used to recite it, then hopped into the waiting car.

The young man drove as if possessed. I was lucky there was no traffic and the old Autobahn, now neglected, was still safe and fast. I soon settled down to watching the countryside, taking sips of coffee with which I had filled my thermos during the meeting with Adamski, and smoking my Marlboros. I resisted the temptation to leave the Autobahn for a look at Opole (Oppeln), another ancient city with a rich Polish-German history, where now one of my old girlfriends lived, whose daughter, a remarkable clone of her mother as I remembered her, I had met two years ago in England, when she had been visiting her uncle, a rector in Derby and chaplain of a Roman Catholic girls' school, on the occasion of his silver anniversary of priesthood and an elevation to Auxiliary Bishop of Derby for the spiritual needs of the local Polish community. The ceremony was conducted by Bishop Rubin, spiritual head in the Vatican of the Polish diaspora, and attended by another mutual friend from our hometown. My participation, a stop on my return from the Congress of Scholars in Poland in 1973 was loaded with symbolism. I was repaying Father Herbert for his participation in my family ceremony, when on another stop on another return he had baptized my children in London in 1959, a ceremony which had had a huge echo in our hometown, a magic place full of ties that bind and pull.

I felt that pull when we stopped in front of my sister Maria's house. I honked the horn and she appeared on the verandah raising her arms in surprise. I called out that I would be back and would she

have something to eat for us? "Just hurry," she called back. I guided
the driver to the local church where Herbert and I had been altar
boys in our youth and where friends met after Sunday's High Mass
for a little social gathering before Sunday dinner. Some were still
there, surprised to see me after watching me on television only a few
hours ago. I also met an old doctor who had seen the broadcast and
noticed that I was coughing a little. I told him about the midnight
swim and he warned me about such extravagances at my age, when
one is prone to pneumonia. Should I go on the guided tour? I asked
him. I shouldn't miss it, he said, but he wanted me before leaving to
stop in his office for a checkup and something else.

At my sister's there was a family gathering on my account.
They had all seen the broadcast from Wrocław and half expected that
I would show up, passing up the planned wreath-laying ceremony,
knowing that family always came first with me. I left them around
the table in the living room and asked my sister to give me something to eat in the kitchen. Great cook that she was, even her
leftovers were good. My driver maintained he hadn't eaten anything
so good in a long time, yet it was only the remainder of one of
Adam's (son-in-law) rabbits, but it was the preparation and seasoning
that mattered. It was the same with the soup and salad. For dessert
we moved to the living room. It was coffee for me and tea for
everybody else, with the usual Sunday afternoon pastries. I passed a
pack of Marlboros around, and it was then that my brother Maks
arrived from Racibórz across the Odra (Oder) with his wife Zosia.
Having seen the broadcast he too figured I would be visiting.

I gave my sister and my brother a pound note each for
souvenirs, or to spend if they wished in one of the hard currency
stores that were then springing up in Poland. For the others I left a
pack of Marlboros. I tried to calm down everybody's apprehension
about resurgent Germany, telling them that the Germans will never
make trouble again after the last war's atrocities which will not be
forgotten for a thousand years, especially by the Poles and the Jews.
Poland's problems lie elsewhere, I told them, at which point my
driver, probably a Party member, discreetly left the room, ostensibly to bring the car around.

Of course, it is possible that he was just letting me know that it
was time to start back, and it really was, especially since I wanted to
add a detour to give Maks and Zosia a ride home. Besides, I had
neglected to bring a supply of vodka, and there can be no satisfactory

Polish gathering without it. One of my nephews asked whether we were going to have a drink. I was embarrassed but Maks, who must have foreseen the situation, solved it by producing a bottle out of a small briefcase he carried with him, and asked for glasses. While he was pouring, I asked my sister whether she would refill my thermos with coffee for the road. She poured into a cup the remainder of the motel coffee, tasted it and declared that there was no coffee so good in the stores. She heated it up and shared it with her daughter while we drank the farewell toast with vodka.

It was time to go. To the question when would they see me again I replied that after the guided tour I should return to Wrocław from which I would come back for at least one long weekend. My sister handed me the thermos filled with her best coffee and a small package with sandwiches (*kanapki*). It was only then that I realized that she was a widow now, that Ludwik, her Karamazovian husband, had died since my last visit, and that I was missing something dear to me during the present brief visit. I told her how sorry I was and how I really missed him, promising to make up for my forgetfulness, proof that I wasn't well, by visiting his grave with her and paying for the gravestone, and we both shed a tear, with her telling me to take care of myself.

This was also the advice of the good old doctor whom we found in his office waiting for me and scribbling furiously on yellow sheets of note paper. He turned out to be a remarkable man. While finishing his notes, he stuck a thermometer under my left armpit, discovered I had a slight fever, gave me a pill to swallow and a supply for a week til my next visit, told me not to take any other medicine until then and in the meantime to take good care of myself. How? Eat well and sleep well, don't strain yourself, and when traveling in the comfortable "Orbis" bus, tell the officers accompanying you to make it even more comfortable by giving you the back seats that have no gap between them to serve as a bed on which you can rest and, having windows all around, watch the countryside and cut down on smoking. He gave me a thermometer and his phone number to call in case of fever, and I gave him a pound note with thanks. "And now to something else," he gravely declared.

The something else were his notes, a mind-boggling exercise in medical trailblazing. The doctor had long been interested in the medicinal qualities of honey, testing it on himself in various forms and preparations, using only pure raw honey, unfiltered and uncooked, in other words straight from the beehive. All the time he had kept a detailed record of his experiments and of their effects on him. He noticed first that his blood pressure became lower and his eyesight and hearing sharper. Most importantly, his level of energy was higher, as if the aging process had been arrested and even reversed. As a result, he kept working long past his retirement age, and working hard, as we could see for ourselves, watching him working on Sunday.

Satisfied with the results, he was at the point of deciding what to do with them. If he made them public, they would become the property of the state in Poland, unlike in Germany or America where they could make him a wealthy man. When he met me he saw in me the only person to be entrusted with his findings: my academic standing inspired trust; my perfect Polish precluded any misreadings of his notes; and my relatives in Poland were a guarantee of my meeting him frequently about the project. He handed me a clean copy of his notes, and we made a date to meet again next Sunday.

Before we parted company he offered to give us a taste of his medicine, and filled two small glasses out of a jar in his locked cabinet. Both Maks and I found it tasty which pleased him and he promised to give us both a checkup next Sunday. As we were getting into the car he asked me if I was likely to be in Cracow this time, because he would like me to meet his niece, the poet Wisława Szymborska.

With Zosia piloting the driver, and I in the back seat talking with Maks, we were in Racibórz in 15 minutes. I just had to sit down on the bench under the old apple tree and Zosia just had to heat up some *bigos* for us which we wolfed down in the old comfortable flat by the railroad tracks and off we went. At breakneck speed we soon passed Opole and reached Wrocław in time for supper at the motel. Not to be too extravagant, I gave the driver not a pound note, but a Kennedy half-dollar for a souvenir. At supper I learned the details of the afternoon ceremony (tiring in hot weather) and turned down a challenge from a local swimmer to the disappointment of the airmen who were hoping to get their money back (the Glasgow Ranger man just smiled knowingly). Instead, it was a hot bath for me and bed.

My temperature was still slightly high early in the morning, and I took a pill. At breakfast I found an article about me in the paper, in which the writer, playing on the name of my birthplace, contrasted its past "misery" with the present well-being, without mentioning that the past was in post-World War I Germany, which my family left for Poland after the Silesian Uprisings and the plebiscite. I showed the article to Secretary Adamski, demanding a correction, not for any political reasons but for the sake of accuracy, and to avoid any misunderstandings in America.

The guided tour was an extraordinary experience. After breakfast and an official sendoff at the town hall we left Wrocław which was still bearing traces of the fierce battle waged there toward the end of the war. On our way we stopped briefly at the old Jewish cemetery, a ghostly place whose gravestones told the history of a once prominent old Jewish community. From the cemetery we proceeded to Poznań.

Going straight up north we passed through formerly German territory until we reached the old border. The young officers traveling with us, among them colonels who were doctoral candidates in history, had to point it out to us, so indistinguishable the landscape was on both sides, clear testimony to the artificial nature of the old border. But there was nothing artificial about Poznań, a stronghold of Polishness and the capital of the premier province of old Poland, called Great Poland, which had successfully resisted all Prussian attempts at Germanization.

Having seen Poznań only once, during a night stop in one of the travels with my father, I couldn't help but notice the city's tidiness, its beautiful parks, and the hospitality of its inhabitants. There was only one instance that the admirable trait was broken, when in a stationery kiosk in our hotel a local woman refused to sell picture postcards to a Russian woman, a tourist in love with Poznań (having lived there as a young girl when her father was stationed there) as I found out when I intervened on her behalf telling the kiosk woman how stupid her behavior was and how important it was to cultivate Russians well-disposed to Poland. I bought the postcards the woman wanted and gave them to her, but she insisted that I accept a piece of Russian amber as a token of friendship.

Even more than by Poznań I was touched during an excursion by Gniezno, the cradle of Poland, whose legendary founder, Piast, had selected the site, according to legend, upon sighting a nest of eagles, from which the name of the town derives and the Polish national emblem originates (the name Gniezno derives from the Polish word for nest—*gniazdo*) and the cult of the eagle began then. My own image of Gniezno had been formed by reading Antoni

Gołubiew's books about Poland's first official king, Bolesław the Brave ("Chrobry"), who resided there, where he royally received his friend and champion, the young German Emperor Otto III, in one of history's magic moments, in the year 1000. It was difficult to imagine Gniezno of the year 1000 while seeing that of 1975, but it was documented history, not a legend. Musing about it in Gniezno, I resolved to make Golubiew's books a translation project for the Polish Institute, rather than another translation of Mickiewicz's "Pan Tadeusz" or a contemplated new translation of Sienkiewicz's "Trilogy," the holy cows of Polish literature.

I was tired when I returned to the hotel in Poznań and I called the good doctor in my hometown. He reiterated his recommendations, was glad to hear that the arrangements on the bus had been carried out, told me to forego evening activities and stay in after supper, drink hot tea, read his notes to pass the time and call him in the morning.

Reading the good doctor's notes was not a restful pastime, but I was convinced of their validity and of the huge future success of the remedy. There was a brief footnote addressed to me. The good doctor had found me in great shape except for a history of bronchitis, an invitation to pneumonia, which the remedy would cure. This was good news for me and for humanity. I realized it would take years to develop on that scale, but there was an immediate benefit on the horizon, closer to home, namely for the Polish Institute in America, my present concern.

First, leading pharmaceutical companies in America would be approached, without even a glance at the notes, with just a general presentation of the results so far. In the meantime small quantities of the remedy would be prepared, at home, and tried by volunteers, people with a definite need of medication, and a detailed record kept of the results, just as the doctor had done with himself. Once the results became conclusive, and this the good doctor guaranteed, the company most interested would be given an option to buy the patent for a sum in excess of a million and a proviso for a fixed percentage of future profits, which would make me independently wealthy and capable of strengthening the tenuous and uncertain arrangement between the Polish Institute and the Jurzykowski Foundation, or to terminate it and put the Institute on a firm ground.

In the morning my temperature was still slightly high, and I reported it to the organizers at breakfast. They came to my room with a doctor, who recommended, just in case, taking me off the tour. But then I remembered that my temperature was almost always a little above normal, and I immediately phoned the information to the doctor in my hometown, who considered it important. The two doctors had a brief consultation and agreed that I should continue, but with due caution, meaning no midnight swimming feats.

The colonels were happy to see me, and there was even a warm blanket on the back seats of the bus. Our first stop was an ancient battlefield where Bolesław's father had stopped the invading Germans under Otto's father. There was an impressive monument on a hill which, throwing all caution aside, I ran up to at the urging of a young camera girl who, standing on top with a camera, was filming my race because in my khaki jacket I looked like a warrior.

The next stop had some drama to it. This was a large cemetery containing thousands of Polish soldiers who died during a particularly gruesome crossing of the Odra. Reading the names on the headstones I noticed a large number of Russian names, all officers, and it puzzled me. One of the colonels explained that almost all officers above the rank of lieutenant in the Polish Army in Russia were Russian, because there were no Polish officers in Russia after General Anders took them out. To which I added "after Stalin had them killed in Katyn," a remark which made the colonel uncomfortable, and he drew my attention instead to some disturbance in the cemetery.

One of the participants from England was roaming the cemetery shouting what were Russians doing in a Polish cemetery? and even kicking the headstones trying to topple them, putting the hosts in a quandary how to deal with the outburst of misplaced patriotism. I knew this man, but he was no patriot. He was one of the hundreds of thousands of Poles who, willingly or unwillingly like my brother Maks, had served in the Wehrmacht, most of them ending up in a British POW camp in Scotland, where they were recruited into the Polish Army. That's where I had first met this man, then a young soldier. He was boasting in the barracks how on leaves in Warsaw with Wehrmacht friends they would pretend they wanted to sell weapons to Polish bandits, only to lure them into an alley and rob or kill them. I listened with astonishment. What bandits? "They called themselves the Underground Army...." Before he could finish, one of the "bandits," a young wounded lieutenant, a former POW, tore into him screaming "You traitor!" But he was no match for the young killer, who knocked him down and started kicking him. I rescued the young hero only to get into a fight with the young brute. When I finally subdued him I invited the lieutenant to kick him back. "I wouldn't touch this manure with my boots." The "manure" was transferred.

I saw him again when leaving the Knights Hall in Wrocław after my session and overhearing someone telling a group of Polish reporters about his exploits with General Maczek's First Polish Division in Normandy. I recognized the now twenty years older killer and quickly pulled aside one of the reporters telling him the man was a liar and a killer while in the Wehrmacht of Polish patriots in Warsaw. Looking back I saw the man abandoned by his listeners.

And here he was again, still with us. I told his story to the colonel and the Swiss watchmaker who had just joined us and was shocked by it. The colonel quietly stated he would take care of it and, as we watched, he joined a group of the organizers, spoke to them, then walked to the man, put his hand on his shoulder, and together they walked to a waiting car, to be driven away by a uniformed guard.

Back in the bus I thought about the incident and its disturbing background, including the indiscriminate recruitment into the Polish Army in England of POW's, even favoring them on the ground of their supposedly superior training, which I had personally found to be a myth. My class of the Officer Training Program toward the end of the war was 90% former Wehrmacht, yet I beat them all in every part of the training, from drill to shooting, swimming and running, becoming a leading candidate to finish first among 100. But I finished in 20th place, preceded by 19 former Wehrmacht soldiers, some of whom I suspected of being Polish-speaking Germans. It was easier to become a Polish officer in England during the war than a British citizen after the war, the English being more discriminate than he Poles. The airmen told me they doubted whether the killer was a citizen, and without a passport he could not become a member of the Veterans. They had no idea how he had managed to come to the meeting.

Such incidents and most of the guided tour don't belong in a chapter about the Polish Institute, and in this book, but rather in its projected companion volume, *One Man's Saga*, in the part devoted to the 1970s (Part 3), but they tell us something about what was happening to the Polish values during and after World War II. The same goes for the incident with the Russian woman in Poznań, but it reflects my attitude toward the Russians which I had developed during my extended stay in the Soviet Union in 1971. It was there that I learned there that there were 19,000 Russian officers, including 50 generals, largely of Polish descent, in the Polish Army in Russia, a fact which throws a different light on the incident in the cemetery.

As for me, the purpose of my trip was research, which was, or should have been, of interest to the Polish Institute. The Veterans meeting was incidental, but turned out to be most instructive. But I added two more tasks to the research, one dealing with the drinking problem in Poland, and the other with the good doctor's project.

When I returned to Wrocław, I first secured an assistant, instructing her to pull out all cards with titles dealing with Polish-Russian relations and then arrange a meeting with Professor Marian Jakubiec, a leading specialist in my area of research. The task was easy, finishing research begun the previous summer, yet the Wrocław library had never seen anybody going through so many books and articles with such speed. My graduate student-assistant was worn out when we stopped for lunch. She reported it to Professor Jakubiec when confirming our lunch appointment and he told me when we met that Americans work faster than Poles. I handed him proofs of my review of his impressive *History of Russian Literature* (started by Professor Samuel Fiszman before his departure from Poland), which had come out earlier that year, and he remarked, "You see what I mean." We had a rather abundant lunch (dinner, really, in Poland) in the dining room of his comfortable suburban house, probably belonging to the university, but I didn't pry, just as I didn't pry into the function of the woman serving the well-prepared food. I was able to observe how senior professors live in a major Polish university, but I was mostly interested in getting out of him ideas on Polish-Russian literary relations, and also on the struggle after Grunwald between Lithuania and Muscovite Russia for the lands of Old Rus, and I was amply rewarded.

The second task was not easy, but it was convenient. While in Wrocław I located a childhood friend whom I had looked after before the war for his father, my benefactor in many respects. In the panic of the first day of the war we became separated, he joining an exodus that was to end in Rumania and I staying behind to defend our hometown. My search for him deserves a separate treatment, but suffice to say here that when I finally found him, he was a man with a huge drinking problem, which I noticed immediately when we had a drink celebrating our meeting. I decided to help him, and I thought I knew how.

Having spoken to his doctor, I told my friend Janek that he was an incurable alcoholic, but that he could control his drinking without giving it up, and prolong his life. Just as I controlled my smoking by reducing it to below a pack a day and aimed at light smoking of half a pack, he should reduce his drinking to one small bottle a day, but augment it by diluting it with water or soda, at first in small amount but aiming at a ratio of one to one. Drink with food only, thus stimulating eating. If he were able to control his drinking, we should see each other again, which was the only reward I could promise him as we were saying good-bye at the Wrocław railway station. As we embraced, a moan escaped from his lips but I understood:

"Why didn't you come for me to Craiova?"

As I climbed aboard the train I saw Janek from the window waving, his face contorted with pain as the train started moving. This was the image of him I would retain for ever.

I was drained emotionally. I was thinking about the crippling drinking problem in Poland, and how we, Poles in America, could help. How could the Polish Institute, searching for new directions, now that its original function had ended with the death of Oskar Halecki, help? After all, members of the Polish Institute participating in the First Congress of Polish Scholars in Cracow in 1973, signed a resolution calling for restoration of Cracow's priceless architecture. This was mainly an environmental problem, caused by bad air but pointing the way to the human environment, poisoned by bad air but also by alcohol, which is mainly an educational problem, an area in which the Institute should excel.

Since this was my last weekend in Poland and I was spending it with my relatives in my hometown, I intended also to take care of the third task. Accordingly, with my brother Maks, who arrived specifically for that purpose, we had a long meeting with the doctor. First, he explained that the reason he had agreed to meet this Sunday and not last was his plan to have Szymborska visit him, and meet me, but he had failed because she was a very shy person. I told him that this was probably why I could not find her in Cracow, so we had both failed with the elusive poet.

From Szymborska the good doctor moved to Maks, warning him about kidney problems which he detected in his complexion, and giving him a prescription and a jar of his honey mixture. As for me, he found me in excellent condition, with all traces of the threatening pneumonia gone, possibly due, as he ventured to add, to the sampling of his mixture and its effect on a body very receptive to medications on account of infrequent use of them. I was impressed by his perception about my medication history and I hastened to tell him so, adding that after studying his notes and feeling great despite an extremely active month, I was convinced about his remedy, and ready to talk concretely.

We agreed that I should take a few jars of his honey mixture with me to be used by two or three volunteers including myself at a frequency specified in the notes with a detailed record kept of the experiment and its effect. If the effect were positive as expected (surge of energy, lowering of high blood pressure, increased ability to fight off colds and muscular pains), the project would pass into the hands of reputable lawyers who would arrange meetings with pharmaceutical companies to negotiate the sale of the idea and the percentage of future profits derived from it. Thus a fund would be started (foundation?) and a permanent income secured to revitalize the Polish Institute, put it on firm ground, and create an indestructible stronghold, with the means to help and serve both Poland and Polonia.

As for the good doctor, his present and future needs would be generously taken care of out of the fund, with Maks serving as an intermediary between us, a role which would allow him to visit me in America, perhaps even bringing the old doctor with him. Both were excited about the prospects, and in a surge of good feeling the doctor presented me with a mini-bicycle, a new product in Poland just then, which one of his grateful patients had gotten for him. What a perfect present for my English wife, I told him, and to reciprocate in kind, I gave him an English pound note, with the picture of the Queen on it, which he greatly appreciated, confessing that he was an avid collector. We drank a toast with the doctor's honey mixture to the three of us, and we parted company in high spirits, he placing Betty in a proper spot on his display wall, me carrying a package with his jars, and Maks the bike in its canvas bag.

With my by-now considerable baggage, Maks decided to help me transport it to the plane in Warsaw. It was just like him, coming to the rescue at the right time, and rescue was needed at the Polish International Airport, which was a disgrace on that particular Monday, with long unruly lines filled with sweaty people with huge suitcases getting in line hours before flight time as if afraid that the plane might leave without them. Since the Polish Airline LOT did not have seat reservation mechanism, I thought I might just as well get in line myself, to have at least some choice of a seat. That's where a photographer, who had accompanied the veterans on the tour, found me, handing me a promised copy of a picture he took of me firing a light machine gun with a sight for shooting in the dark. I promised him that the picture would be famous in America, and I kept my promise.

Just then a stewardess was calling for passengers with U.S. passports. I was first. While she dealt with my passport and the important pieces of my baggage, I thanked Maks for everything, giving him a 20-dollar bill and rushing him to an earlier train. Then I followed the stewardess to a choice window seat to work on my report.

I never had a chance to present to the Institute's Board and to the general public my detailed report from, and on, Poland. Instead, when I came to the Institute the day after my return from Poland (with my wife meeting me at JFK and excitedly receiving a large canvas bag containing a Polish mini-bicycle, which she called a "royal gift" and started assembling the moment we reached home, giving all the other presents barely a glance while testing the bike), it was I who found myself on the receiving end of a pointed question-exclamation, first by Count Pusłowski greeting me:

"Mister Frank, what did you do?!"

It was echoed like a reproach by the "refugees" from Radio Free Europe and Voice of America (Jerzy Ptakowski and Tepa, Władysław Wańtuła) who began to flock to the Institute upon the election by the Board (on Prof. Z. Brzezinski's impasse-resolving recommendation) of Vice President Feliks Gross as the new Executive Director, who immediately used them on new projects (oral history and History of Polish Émigré Social and Political Thought), placing them in the room which until then had been my exclusive work place.

I soon realized that the chorus-like reproach was about that something I had said in my "Finest Hour" in the old *Rittersaal* in Wrocław, a statement which reporters had misquoted in the press (through ignorance or by design?) and which, when I protested, was to have been retracted, but wasn't because it reached New York in its original version, falling into the hands of someone who didn't wish me well, to put it mildly, and passed it on to the local Polish press which, not surprisingly, refused to print my correction. A misunderstanding became a weapon against me.

Unperturbed, I put my plans for the Institute on hold, including the wonder medicine (about which, however, I spoke to my doctor, who was intrigued by it), doing what I considered important at the moment. When Professor Gross became Executive Director (October, 1975), I started my new course, "Poles in America: A Bicentennial View," at NYU, with the Institute, except for L.K., distancing itself from it. Despite the enthusiasm and the sacrifices of the speakers (Archacki, Kusielewicz, L.K., Pinkowski, Podbielski), the course barely attracted the required minimum number of students, but I succeeded in persuading the Dean to repeat the course next semester, in the Bicentennial year itself.

Nineteen seventy-six was a banner year for Polonia as pointed out already elsewhere, and much of it had to do with my activities. The second course became a toast of Polonia, which provided tuition scholarships for students, and even some students (from a CETA program at the Polish and Slavic Center), to make it a very well-attended course, including the counselor of the Polish Mission to the U.N., (Bogdan Zejmo who, at my request, had secured the Dean's permission, in order not to rub some of the sponsors the wrong way). An important aspect of the course was the certificate ceremony making it "An Official Bicentennial Event," the only ethnic group study so designated.

By then the Polish Institute (and the Kosciuszko Foundation) became part of the "Event" with at least three members as guest speakers; one meeting, during the March 25 University Spring Recess, featuring Henry Archacki's talk, "Polish Free Masonry in America," was held at the Institute and followed by a reception, hosted by Francis Pusłowski, Assistant to the Executive Director.

Similarly, Dr. Eugene Kusielewicz, President of the Kosciuszko Foundation hosted the penultimate lecture and discussion of "The Image of the Polish American in American Fiction" by Rev. Walter

Żebrowski. Special guests included Senator Katelbach with his daughter Nina Polan, and Professor Robert Belknap, my former dissertation adviser at Columbia University. He contributed to the discussion and later took part in the planning meeting of the Literary Section for the annual meeting of AATSEEL (American Association of Teachers of Slavic and East European Languages) to be held in New York that winter, when the Literary Section would return to its source, where it had been first announced publicly.

I told the planning meeting that I was writing to Professor William Harkins, President of AATSEEL, to enter a panel the like of which had never been seen at an AATSEEL meeting. The panel, "Sienkiewicz's Triple Anniversary," would have a dozen speakers from all over America (and Poland) who would need not just the customary two hours, but the entire afternoon in the largest lecture room available. I was making these demands (which were granted) because I was speaking from a position of strength. The Literary Section was in its third year, and after the great successes of the first two years, was in the middle of the third with an unparalleled program. I distributed printed copies of it, prepared by me during the winter recess.

It was an extraordinary program. It listed 21 "Conferences, Lectures, Discussions" spaced out between January 14 and May 29, 1976. Literature was represented by 8 meetings, followed by History (5), Science (3), Culture (2), Communism (2), Music (1). Like Gorky, I had indeed created my own university, which was what I had been working on, even if, with the election of the new Executive Director, it had become an illusion.

What I was really creating, or building, was a reputation, which was considerable, and became even more so when, upon the conclusion of the "Bicentennial" courses, I embarked on the Bicentennial book and started promoting it.

My growing reputation was not something people in and around the Institute were happy about, as I found out when, picking up the phone to make a call, I accidentally overheard a telephone conversation about me. I hung up quickly but not before I heard the caller accuse me of planning to take over the Institute and staff it with my followers. He was obviously concerned about the few dollars he was able to get out of the Institute, poor man. But I had a greater shock when at a Board meeting I suggested that the Institute make even a token donation to the *Poles in America* publishing fund ($100) for the record, and heard President John Gronouski's insane remark,

"We don't support such projects."

This, with reference to a book that Polonia was waiting for aroused by the euphoria of the Bicentennial, from a man who was chosen, selected one might say, to guide that euphoria into a constructive future for the Institute on the threshold of a new era of a multi-ethnic, multi-cultural America.

No, John Gronouski was not the proper man for the job. Americanized to the core, he was an American political animal at his best as a domestic problem-solver, but not as head of a scholarly institution, even if his own academic credentials, including a doctorate, were satisfactory. The "American" aspect of his background, which was the main reason for selecting him, and which he even wanted to include in the name of the Institute, was of little use, running counter to the still traditional enclave.

That tradition was maintained by the new Executive Director, Professor Feliks Gross, the last, with L.K., of, if not the founders, then of their associates. The problem with the position was that there never existed a precise job description for it. With absentee presidents from the beginning, the executive directors ran the Institute in their name, but according to their own vision, favoring their own projects which, in the case of Gross, a Socialist, ran from oral history to social thought.

As for the third member of the Institute's upper echelon, the Secretary General, also without a precise job description, Thaddeus Gromada did a lot of improvising. A token board member as a Polish American in the Institute dominated by émigrés from Poland (a malicious observer referred to him jokingly but cruelly as a "house nigger"), he rose to Secretary General, a position he almost lost in a close vote to its previous occupant, the incomparable L.K. From the beginning Gromada set his sights high, very high, for himself and for the Institute which, as a Polish American "nationalist," he wanted to transform into a Polish American Institute, doing slowly but with a missionary zeal what Gronouski tried to do in a hurry, unmindful, unlike Gromada, that there were still many wartime Poles left.

All three were at that time following a common agenda—fund-raising. With Blanka Rosenstiel's glossy flyer bringing no results (I had thought of my own artistic concept, which would have), it fell to Ewa Markowska, office manager, to produce a typewritten one, as if that would matter (mine was hand-printed, and it would have). When I secured an early copy for *The Polish Review*, L.K. refused to print it, it was so awful. Only a weak Polish mind would conceive of writing something in English at the Institute without asking L.K., or me, for help.

It was then that the idea of a professional fund- raiser entered the picture, but for some reason Bolesław Łaszewski of Fregata Travel undertook the job. In a time-honored ritual Bolesław II (as distinguished from Bolesław I, Wierzbiański, a close friend) rolled up his sleeves and got down to work, using the speaker's table in the lecture room as his desk. I don't know how successful he was—his effort was short-lived—because by then something happened that filled me with disgust at the spiteful behavior and duplicity of some Poles in New York and had a great influence on my future decisions.

Maria Kuncewiczowa was in town, to promote her latest book, and I promptly invited her to give a talk at a meeting sponsored by the Literary Section at the Kosciuszko Foundation. The moment the announcement of the meeting was printed in the Polish American press, attacks on her began, starting with her love of caviar, a sure sign for her attacker of her pro-Russian sympathies. Only a paranoid Polish mind could construe such a relationship. The attacker went further, threatening to remove Kuncewiczowa from the lecture room (a threat which worried her) and calling on me to cancel the meeting.

My reply, co-signed (reluctantly) by Kusielewicz, was firm. I called Kuncewiczowa the "First Lady of Polish Literature" whom we should feel honored to see and hear, and any person trying to prevent that would be removed by me personally because I would be at her side at all time. When I showed Kuncewiczowa a copy of that letter, she was no longer worried and gave me an autographed copy of her book with a dedication "To my defender in..." with a few pointed epithets in the direction of her attackers.

The meeting was a great success. There were no intruders (fellow board member Zofia Borowska's brother, on a visit from Poland, had volunteered to look for them) except two boys passing out leaflets against Kuncewiczowa. My wife took care of them, taking their leaflets and sending them home with a message to their father not to use them for such purposes. She even got them a snack from the woman preparing the reception downstairs.

The Kuncewiczowa affair resurfaced at the annual meeting of the Institute two weeks later. Somebody made a motion to censure me for inviting Kuncewiczowa, to which I replied that I could invite anybody I liked as long as I cleared it with my Board, and I turned to Prof. Błaszczyk with a request to confirm my having discussed it. To my surprise and shock he "didn't remember" and I knew then that one of my closest associates was turning against me, as was also Dr. Ostrowski, my one-time partner, while Professor Wagner, presiding, a long-time acquaintance, maintained a discreet silence. In the hostile atmosphere nobody vouched for me until three women: the widows Gierat, Janta, and Wittlin took the floor in my defense, tearing into my critics and reminding them of all the things I had done for the Institute when it was practically inactive. Instead of censuring, the meeting should commend me!

I would always remember the meeting as a total waste, except for the inspiring stand by three remarkable women (one of whom cited the Crucifixion of Christ). Not a word was said at the meeting about the most vital unsolved problem facing the Institute: securing a clear title to the lovely building, a perfect seat of a respectable institute. As probably the best informed student of the history of the Polish Institute, I knew that title to the building plus an endowment from the Jurzykowski Foundation could have been secured 15 years earlier (instead of the three-year lease, renewable, for the symbolic one dollar per year) if only an accommodation had been reached with Alfred Jurzykowski on not insurmountable formal points, and more faith placed in Stanisław Strzetelski, the dynamic Executive Director (1955-1961), the only one capable, with the support of Jurzykowski who had confidence in him, of creating an intellectual stronghold of unlimited potential.

As I dwelled on this during the last stages of the meeting which didn't interest me, having coffee instead with Mr. Sierpiński, I told him I felt great affinity with Strzetelski, but that I was deciding to accept finally a teaching position in Chicago. He understood, and lowered his voice to a whisper that my plans here would be scuttled, just like Strzetelski's.

I spent the summer of 1976 working on the evolving book and on *The Polish Review* with L.K., while traveling occasionally to

Chicago. The university I was joining was a brand new modern branch of the University of Illinois, with excellent athletic facilities, which I liked, but no evening division, an absence I didn't like. My meeting with the Slavic department was a depressing experience, with low class instructors and professors, except for the poet Tymoteusz Karpowicz representing a new phenomenon in Polish academia, a poet-scholar, like Barańczak. These trips to Chicago deprived me of a chance to meet Cardinal Wojtyła when he visited the Polish Institute.

I had met His Eminence Karol Cardinal Wojtyła in Pittsburgh in 1966 during the Millennium celebrations, when I presented him with a much appreciated copy of the Polish Institute's "Register of Scholars..." Later that year I met his former secretary, Father Pajdzik, who had been driven out of Poland and became a parish priest near Pittsburgh. Father Pajdzik, whom I was helping to join the Philosophy Department at the University of Pittsburgh, told me something extraordinary: his conviction that Cardinal Wojtyła would become a Pope. I wanted to tell the Cardinal about it at the Institute, and about Father Pajdzik, but alas, I wasn't there. I wasn't there to tell him about Polonia, about my book with three religious authors in it, and to seek his advice on how I could best help Poland.

I wasn't there because I was in Chicago, helping to develop the biggest Polish program in America. My ties with the Polish Institute were tenuous now, mostly in connection with the Literary Section, no longer vigorous, and with the coming Sienkiewicz Symposium.

The Sienkiewicz Symposium was all I had said it would be in my letter to Harkins, and more. Joe Malik of AATSEEL couldn't get over the size of the panel and the caliber of the speakers: Jerzy Krzyżanowski, talking about his father, Julian, an outstanding Sienkiewicz scholar; Harold Segel, talking about Jeremiah Curtin, Sienkiewicz's American translator; David Welsch, the prolific translator; Tymon Terlecki, Mieczysław Giergielewicz, Joachim Baer, and others, with L.K. and myself taking turns as chairmen in view of the length of the proceedings. The audience, too, was quite substantial, and included many of my former associates; a few contributing authors to *Poles in America*, including Eugene Kusielewicz and Jerzy Maciuszko, with whom I discussed his essay, "Polish Letters in America," before he left for Cleveland. A surprise guest was the Director of the Polish National Library in Warsaw, who was impressed and told me that we were ahead of Poland, where so far there were just plans for the anniversary celebrations.

My last official appearance at the Polish Institute was a symposium celebrating the publication of *Poles in America: Bicentennial Essays*. It was the second such symposium (actually third, counting a presentation at the ACPCC convention at Orchard Lake), but while the first, at Loyola University in Chicago on Sunday, August 6, 1978, had three contributing authors (Lawrence Biondi, S.J., host; Anthony Kuźniewski, S.J., and myself), the one at the Polish Institute, co-sponsored by the Kosciuszko Foundation, had six (Leon T. Błaszczyk, Metchie J.E. Budka, Michael Budny, Edward Pinkowski, Theodore L. Zawistowski, and myself), with a seventh, Eugene Kusielewicz, absent, gone to Rome where on that same Sunday, October 22, 1978, was the inauguration of His Holiness John Paul II.

This was my third encounter, real or unreal, with Karol Wojtyła (actually fourth, counting my trip in 1972 to Wadowice, where part of his soul still lived). When someone pointed out the coincidence of the two events, adversely affecting the attendance at mine since the top echelon of the Institute had also gone to Rome, I had this to say:

> *There are two important events today, one in Rome and the other in New York, at the Polish Institute...*

and on that note my official ties with the Polish Institute came to an end.

• • • •

This is a personal view of the Polish Institute, as was that of the Polish American Congress, two entities with which I had close ties in the 1970s, a decade I like to call "my creative decade." What happened to them after 1978 and 1984, respectively, I know only from reading.

In front of me is a beautiful publication, amply illustrated and generously supported by advertisers, with a compound title next to and below a drawing of a house (strikingly similar to the drawing on my proposed booklet):

1942-1992
50TH ANNIVERSARY

POLISH INSTITUTE OF ARTS & SCIENCES OF AMERICA
*208 East 30th Street*New York*NY*10016-8202*

Inside red covers, between 14 pages of congratulatory letters and 36 pages of advertising is the story of the Institute, written in two parts: five double-columned large pages of "A Half Century Of Changing Mission Of The Institute," an analytical essay by Feliks Gross, President of the PIASA; followed by 50 double-columned richly illustrated pages of:

POLISH INSTITUTE
The First 50 Years 1942-1992: An Historical Survey
by Thaddeus V. Gromada [VP and Executive Director]

divided into chronological sections of various length: 1942-1945, 1946-1955, 1955-1961, 1962-1965, 1966-1972, 1973-1975, 1976-1980, 1981-1989, 1989-1992; followed by brief article-summaries on "The Polish Review" (67-68), "Alfred Jurzykowski Memorial Library and Archives" (68-69), "Branches and Circles of the Polish Institute" (69-70), "Sections of the Polish Institute of Arts and Sciences" (71-72); followed by lists of PIASA Presidents, Executive Directors and Secretary Generals (72) and the title page of the last part of the book, Benefactors*Advertisers*Sponsors (73) with four double-columned pages of benefactors (74-7), twenty-nine pages of ads (78-106), and one three-columned page of sponsors (107). The last page of the book (108) contains membership information in three categories: regular, sustaining, student.

It is a pleasure to behold this album-like book and leaf through its contents, testimony to the Institute's status in and outside the Polish American community.

It is one thing to admire a book's appearance and leaf through its well-organized contents and another to read them, specifically the essay by PIASA's President Feliks Gross and the "Historical Survey" by Vice President and Executive Director Thaddeus V. Gromada. With the staff at their disposal, led by the tireless Executive Assistant Jane Gromada Kedroń, one would expect that the two authors would subject their statements to rigorous editing in order to remove inaccuracies, omissions, and stylistic weaknesses as a courtesy to the readers of the book. Professor Gross at least explains his omissions in a *post-scriptum* as being due to editorial limitations even if his essay is loaded with names and ideas and needs only a little organizing to be a perfect example of a free wheeling scholarly ramble. As for Professor Gromada, he was in need of more help, beginning with calling his effort a "chronological" rather than "historical" survey because as a historian he knows that a survey so titled must be accurate. This writer found at least three inaccuracies pertaining to him and at least one important omission concerning his Literary Section. An even more important omission is one concerning the Natural Science and Technology Section, which was left out altogether, together with its founder, the once formidable Dr. Janusz Ostrowski.

To be fair, there are things worthy of praise in Gromada's narrative. One is the relationship between PIAS and PAU, Polska Akademia Umiejętności, which is rendered on a few occasions as "Polish Academy of Arts and Sciences," an inaccurate rendition because the noun is untranslatable into Polish (even Jacek Fisiak, the best specialist on the English language in Poland, trips on it, calling it "Skills" on some occasions, which is even worse). Gromada has the good sense to start using just the acronym PAU.

Another plus is the account of the circumstances surrounding the loss by PIAS of the beautiful building on East 66th Street, a calamity which could have been avoided. How the Institute survived its year-long homelessness is a testimony to the tenacity of its leaders, the generosity of the Jurzykowski and the Kosciuszko Foundations (neither could hardly be indifferent), and the help of the Polish American community with fund-raising and voluntary work. But the survival was not complete, there was a victim: Professor Ludwik Krzyżanowski, the famous L.K., whose death in the middle of the struggle brought another problem, how to replace the lifetime editor of *The Polish Review*, which he had personified for thirty years, determined to end his life and work at his old desk in the old building, his home. But even this painful departure had to be gotten over, and the Institute was able to find, and then move into its new quarters in time to prepare the celebrations of its 50th anniversary, which resulted in the book.

What the future holds for the Institute is a question which Professor Gromada asks at the end of his survey. It's a good question, even if not phrased in the same words. Reading about the scholarly conferences that now accompany the annual meetings helps to provide some answers, not easy to arrive at this point in time.

The old annual meetings were not all that stifling as the narrative seems to indicate. They allowed a free flow of ideas, which the conferences, dedicated as they usually were, to a specific topic, restrict. If the PIAS is to serve both Polonia and Poland, and if America continues to be the model for the world, which is likely to be the case well into the next century, the Institute should take a close look at what is happening here. The three big E's (Economy, Education, Environment) with which the Democrats came into power, are constantly addressing the question of how to improve the quality of life, while dealing with the most pressing problems, like health, for example. Universities and think tanks—and the Institute should strive to become one—are increasingly moving away from traditional scholarship, using education with an eye to the market, to provide students with marketable skills. Enormous strides are being made in the proper care of the environment (cleaning up of Lake Erie and the Hudson River, which is filling up with healthy fish and is soon to become a beach area) which is totally lacking in Poland, and the battle for better health care goes on, a problem which is assuming catastrophic proportions in Poland. This writer is pointing out Poland's problems to the Kosciuszko Foundation as a suggestion to bring grantees here to seek solutions, and the same goes for the Polish Institute.

One of the finest statements in Gromada's survey points to the apparent harmony within the Institute:

> Beginning with 1976 to the 1990's, a good enduring relationship and partnership developed between Executive Director Gross and Secretary General Gromada. They understood the concept of division of labor. Therefore, they were able to complement each other.

There is deep symbolism in this statement. On one side of this partnership Feliks Gross, the oldest and last of the wartime scholar-refugees, classmate of Ludwik Krzyżanowski and Karol Estreicher, both gone (here and there), and on the other Thaddeus Gromada, after John Gronouski probably the most successful of the *American born* Polish Americans, as he stresses, involved with the Institute. What's in store for it? In his early 90s (when one is in one's 90s, it doesn't matter whether they are early or late), Feliks Gross, from whom this writer had received a fine letter commending him for his appearance at the Kusielewicz memorial service, will not last forever. Who will succeed him to preserve the "partnership" between the Polish and American-born Polish Americans? Perhaps this time Zbigniew Brzezinski can be persuaded to accept the presidency of the Institute, bringing into it his knowledge and experience, and ending his brilliant career brilliantly.

D. THE JOSEPH PILSUDSKI INSTITUTE

This is the last of the four "other" organizations, sharing some features with the Polish Institute (wartime exiles) but without the Polish-born American-born dualism. As a matter of fact, prominent Polish Americans were instrumental in the founding of the Institute in 1943, but death and lack of successors reduced their numbers, while exiles from Europe became the core of the Institute. Its early history was written by one of the directors, Michael Budny, for the *Poles in America* volume in 1978. By then, the founding members, of the same generation as Halecki, a member of both institutes, began to pass away, just like him. The oldest and the last—like Feliks Gross at the Polish Institute—died in 1993, leaving behind him but a slim link with the past, as reported in a brief obituary in *The New York Times* of December 8, 1993:

WACLAW JEDRZEJEWICZ
Historian, 100

Waclaw Jedrzejewicz, a Polish émigré and historian, died Nov. 30 at the Cheshire Convalescent Center in Cheshire, Conn. He was 100.

Mr. Jedrzejewicz was a prolific author of books and articles on Polish history between the two World Wars. During that time he served in a series of military and diplomatic posts in the Polish Government.

He arrived in the United States in 1941 and two years later helped found the Josef Pilsudski Institute for Research in the Modern History of Poland which is now at 180 Second Avenue at 12th Street in Manhattan.

He is survived by a daughter, Ewa Beck of Cheshire, and a son, Tomasz, of Cupertino, Calif.

Ewa Jędrzejewicz Beck is married to Andrzej J. Beck, the son of Poland's prewar Minister of Foreign Affairs, Wacław Jędrzejewicz's colleague in the Government, hence the link with the past, which goes deeper, with Andrzej Beck serving as the current President of the Joseph Pilsudski Institute, while its Director is already a relatively recent arrival from Poland, Dr. Janusz Cisek. The rest of the management consists of Vice President Danuta Cisek (not related to Janusz), Vice Director Jerzy Światkowski, Treasurer Władysław Jędrych, and Secretary Halina Janiszewska, all of them also members of the Institute's Council. Other members of this body include representatives of old Polonia (Stanisław Blejwas) as well as of the wartime exodus (Zarema Bau, Jacek Gałązka, Janusz Krzyżanowski, Tadeusz Pawłowicz, Ludwik Seidenman, Stanisław Świderski, Piotr Wandycz) and of the younger generation (Andrzej Cisek, Danuta's husband, also not related to Janusz; Magda Kapuścińska, John Micgiel, and others).

What is in store for the Pilsudski Institute under the new management, with its book knowledge of Marshal Pilsudski, whom its predecessors had known personally, having served under him in war and peace, before their successors were even born and before they learned about him in school? It is a question that many in the Polish American community are asking with some misgivings.

To begin with, the Pilsudski Institute, under the old members, had beautiful quarters on Park Avenue South, where the members were busy building up and looking after its growing collections of books, maps, stamps, and coins. It was a cheerful place, but it was gradually growing empty of people. As the old members were no longer fit to serve as directors, young men from Poland filled the position. As in the Polish Museum in Chicago, there was considerable turnover, for reasons that are not very clear. Also, the splendid quarters on Park Avenue had to be abandoned, and the Institute moved, courtesy of the Polish National Alliance, to a building in need of renovation at Second Avenue and Twelfth Street, where a large long room became a gallery, one of the most beautiful rooms of that kind in Polish America. This was achieved with a great deal of work under the present director. Whether the other rooms were similarly renovated to accommodate the Institute's collections this writer is not in a position to say. Reportedly some rooms serve as the director's quarters and others are rented to students from Poland, allegedly at high prices.

Other than that, the Institute issues a Bulletin filled with membership lists (including honorary, lifetime, supporting, regular, domestic, institutional, close to a thousand entries), a list of donations, a statement of estimated revenues and expenditures, announcements and short pieces—biographical and obituaries. Announcements feature events organized by the Institute in order to stay in the community's and the media's eye. How successful the efforts will be, only time will tell. For now, judging by the brevity of the Jędrzejewicz obituary (by contrast, the obituary of Professor Lucjan Dobroszycki, a member, was far more extensive), it seems that the Institute was not able to summon more respect from the papers for a more important person, hence the efforts are not successful.

P.S. As a pragmatic Silesian, I do not join in the cult of Pilsudski, considering such veneration unnecessary. But I admire him as a man who had revitalized Poland after a century of captivity. What Kosciuszko failed to prevent, Pilsudski succeeded in undoing, and for this he deserves our undying gratitude and a place in the Polish Pantheon. The Pilsudski Institute should strive to keep him there. A visit to the Institute's 1997 Christmas Party, and the sight of the gallery filled to capacity indicate that the memory of Marshal Pilsudski shows no signs of growing less. Because of that, two meetings in connection with the present book were held there, the last one on June 27, 1998. Because of that, two meetings in connection with the present book were held there, the last one on June 27, 1998.

Nota Bene: The Kosciuszko Foundation

Just as I finished my sketch of Eugene Kusielewicz for this book, I received a call that he had died suddenly. I immediately called the Foundation with a reminder to have a memorial for him and a request to include me in it.

The program, under the name of "A Memorial Service," took place two months later (February 7, 1997), consisting of "Opening Words," 21 "Recollections," and musical "Prelude," "Interlude," and "Postlude." My participation was the 20th "Recollection," but my name was not included on the printed list of 22 "Participants," which did not surprise me, since this was not the first time that my materials or other forms of presence have been trifled with at the post-Kusielewicz Foundation. This remark should help end the dubious practice.

With few exceptions, among them the touching speech by young Christopher Kusielewicz, most of the "Recollections" were rather pedestrian, some speakers trying to inject humor into their remarks, with one mindlessly referring to the late Kusielewicz as a "controversial" person. I brought with me my sketch in which I call him a "Creative President" of the Kosciuszko Foundation, but the rest of it was taken from published materials, known to anybody concerned. In the last moment I decided to speak about a different Kusielewicz, largely unknown, one capable of rising above and beyond the duties of president, and I cited three examples of it.

The first was his selfless support of my book, *Poles in America: Bicentennial Essays* which, thanks to his support and the help of his assistant, Mary Van Starrex, became something of a catalyst in Polish America and a bestseller at the Kosciuszko Foundation. It was highly praised in Poland. The second also concerned a book, Stefan Kuczyński's *Litwin i Andegawenka* (*The Lithuanian and the Princess Anjou*) an excerpt of which I came upon in a Polish periodical *Poglądy* ("Views"), whose editor, Wilhelm Szewczyk, had told me that the publication of the book was unlikely because of its subject matter. I discussed it with Kusielewicz, and it turned out that not only was Kuczyński the Foundation's grantee when writing the book, but also a former student of Professor Halecki. I promptly received a grant from the Foundation to go to Poland, find Kuczyński, evaluate his manuscript, and prevail upon the publishers to print it. I described this odyssey in a different context but with the same conclusion that Kusielewicz's intervention resulted in the publication of the book.

But it is the third example that tells us most about the real Kusielewicz, and I am putting it under the heading "As Others See Us." While teaching in Chicago and working on a study program that would have created a new intelligentsia out of which would come new leaders of Polonia, I invited Kusielewicz for a meeting with the Dean, who invited us to lunch. The man was so impressed by Kusielewicz's knowledge, his articulate speech and force of argument that when we were momentarily alone he exclaimed: "He is tremendous! You have people like that in the Polish community?" How many people in the Polish community in America can one say that about? I am writing about it elsewhere, but suffice it to say here that my program failed when Kusielewicz left the Foundation and with him went the Foundation's support of my program.

• • • •

Dr. Eugene Kusielewicz's death, together with that of Dr. Walter Golaski, Trustee Emeritus, was mentioned in a brief note, A SAD LOSS, on the first page of the Winter 1996-1997 issue of the Kosciuszko Foundation's *Newsletter*, with a promise of longer remembrances in the next issues, with the promise duly kept.

The same issue on the same page contains another brief note, namely that the "Market value of endowment fund [of the K.F.] increased from $11.5 million in 1991 to over $18 million at year [1996] end."

This is an impressive figure as is also the figure in the title of the leading article of the *Newsletter* of Summer 1997:

KOSCIUSZKO FOUNDATION SCHOLARSHIPS
AND GRANTS TOTAL $1 MILLION

The $1 million figure appears as a goal, a target that allows the Foundation to be taken seriously, unlike the previously quoted $900,000. But is the figure justified in relation to the $18 million endowment?

How foundations spend their money is, or should be, public knowledge. One example of it is a report about the John and Mary R. Markle Foundation in a *New York Times* article of June 18, 1997. It is cited here because of the coincidence of dates with the Kosciuszko Foundation report, and because, like the K.F., the Markle Foundation was also 70 years old, another coincidence and, in yet another coincidence, was headed by a lawyer, Zoe Baird, remembered as the unsuccessful candidate, due to some irregularities, for the job of President Clinton's Attorney General.

The New York-based Markle Foundation, which has $150 million in assets, awards about $7 million in grants each year, mainly to nonprofit organizations, research institutes and universities. The ratio of $7 million in grants to $150 million in assets compares in favor of the 1 to 18 ratio of the Kosciuszko Foundation, with the cost of all the symposiums, lectures, concerts, and exhibitions presumably not falling under the category of K.F.'s grants and scholarships. Be it as it may, questions still remain how well the Foundation spends its money and what are the motivations for the spending?

In a recently introduced procedure, members of the Foundation's staff report on their respective activities, with the reports tending to become essay-type efforts, in which the writers use high-sounding words like "mission" (or "historic mission"), which traditionally has had a meaning or connotation of missionary work or high-level assignment in war and peace ("Albright mission to Israel"), but here it is being used lightly (one "mission" I even encountered in a letter to me from Maryla Janiak). This is not to denigrate the good intentions of the staff members, but professional language should be used professionally. A great "mission" is still to be discovered, like helping to save the environment in Poland or to restore family values (in collaboration with the Polish Women's Alliance?).

One more question came up after the remarks I had made earlier while analyzing the "Teaching Fellows" program and it concerns Mr. Rybicki at Rice University. It is not clear what his exact position is. In the *Newsletter* of Spring 1997 he is described as the current holder of the "Polish Studies Lectureship" which, in turn, is described as one of the Texas Chapter's most successful programs. Which is it, and why the confusion, which extends into listing the Rice program in Ms. Janiak's report as "Courses in Polish History?" There is not even a trace of history in Mr. Rybicki's activities, among which he teaches a class in Central European Cinema, "among others"; delivers "a talk presenting the highlights of Tadeusz Kosciuszko's biography"; and another on "The Art of Translation," concerning the reception of Shakespeare in Poland, early American translation of Sienkiewicz, "and other subjects." What we are dealing with here is either a case of a highly versatile man or of bad editing of the *Newsletter*.

These are cases that strain credulity about some of the programs. Mr. Rybicki is described simply as a "translator of English and American books into Polish," which means that he is not a scholar (that's the impression I had when I saw him on Polish television in New York), but there is also someone else listed, Andrzej Nowak, "Polish Studies Kosciuszko Foundation Lecturer at Rice University." Is he the "Teaching Fellow" or are there two? Mr. Rybicki's specialty is not really needed here. What is needed more is translation of Polish books into English.

If the Kosciuszko Foundation has problems finding proper candidates for its various grants, as would seem to be the case in renewing the grant to organize and catalogue the relatively small collection acquired by the University of Pittsburgh from Alliance College, a task now augmented by the addition of yet another grantee (a musicologist), may I suggest two outstanding candidates, Prof. Jacek Fisiak (Poznań), the best specialist on the English language in Poland, and editor of the new two-volume *Polish-English and English-Polish Dictionary (Słownik polsko-angielski i angielsko-polski)*; and Prof. Edward J. Czerwiński, retired now, but in retirement editor of the *Dictionary of Polish Literature*, both works discussed in this book.

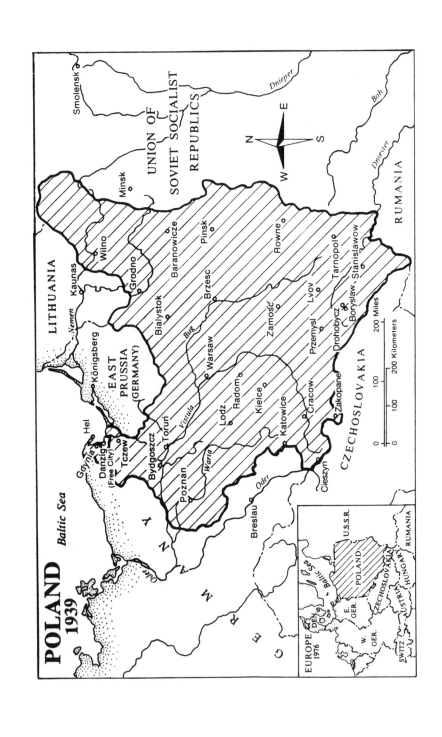

POLAND
1939

Baltic Sea

LITHUANIA

UNION OF
SOVIET SOCIALIST
REPUBLICS

RUMANIA

EAST
PRUSSIA
(GERMANY)

CZECHOSLOVAKIA

Smolensk

Minsk

Dnieper

Boh

Dniester

Königsberg

Nemen

Kaunas

Wilno

Grodno

Baranowicze

Pinsk

Rowne

Tarnopol

Borysław·Stanisławow

Białystok

Brzesc

Lvov

Bug

Zamosć

Przemysl

Drohobycz

Warsaw

Radom

Kielce

Zakopane

Cieszyn

Katowice

Cracow

Vistula

Lodz

Oder

Hel

Gdynia

Danzig
(Free City)

Tczew

Bydgoszcz

Torun

Poznan

Warta

Breslau

Oder

N
E
S
W

200 Miles

200 Kilometers

100

100

0
0

EUROPE
1976

U.S.S.R.

Baltic Sea

DEN.

E.
GER.

W.
GER.

SWITZ.

AUSTRIA

POLAND

CZECHOSLOVAKIA

HUNGARY

RUMANIA

6

Frank Mocha

INDIVIDUAL ACCOMPLISHMENTS

INTRODUCTION

This is the most difficult chapter in the book, because it calls first for establishing criteria for accomplishments and then making choices, always a hard task. There is only one criterion: how the accomplishment relates to Poland, the main concern of the book. This excludes strictly material accomplishments which, while strengthening the Polish presence in America, have no direct bearing on Poland and its most immediate problems: the care of the environment and health care, especially children's health, and the long-range demographic problem.

Having thus identified the most important problems facing Poland (aside from foreign policy), this chapter will nevertheless concern itself mostly with intellectual accomplishments as a proper background for everything else. The making of choices here is complicated by chronology. The founders of the Polish Institute, of the Kosciuszko Foundation, of the Pilsudski Institute, and of most of the Polish American press are all gone, and their deeds are history now. Gone are also their successors (Gronouski, Krzyżanowski, Kleban, the able assistants Pusłowski, Sierpiński, and others; presidents Jordanowski and [even] Kusielewicz; professors Giergielewicz and Weintraub), except Feliks Gross, remaining as a witness to history. Of the next generation Drzewieniecki; Pomian, Dziewanowski; Karski, Zawodny, Nowak Jeziorański, are all retired but still heard from, as is also this writer, the youngest.

It is the next generation, which begins with its oldest member, who was young enough to have avoided the disruption of his education by World War II, hence most prominent now, Zbigniew Brzezinski, that this chapter will concern itself with; but first, an important distinction. It is certainly an accomplishment when Thaddeus Radzilowski becomes President of St. Mary's College at Orchard Lake, but it is probably a greater accomplishment when

James Pula becomes Dean of Metropolitan College of the Catholic University of Washington, DC, and greater still when Stanley Blejwas becomes University Professor and successful organizer of an endowed chair of Polish Studies at Central Connecticut State University in New Britain. While it is important to strengthen Polish strongholds, as Radzilowski is doing at Orchard Lake, with a clear benefit to Poland through international conferences he is able to hold by having the academic know-how and the necessary mechanisms for it, it is equally, or even more, important to build or strengthen Polish presence at American institutions, as Pula (arriving with a new book on a most Polish of topics, Kosciuszko) and Blejwas (raising money) are doing.

These three, together with a few others (Thaddeus Gromada, at the Polish Institute after early retirement from Jersey City State College; Donald Pienkos, University of Wisconsin, Milwaukee; John Kulczycki and Alex Kurczaba, University of Illinois, Chicago, but rarely seen outside the university; Mieczysław Biskupski, St. John Fisher College, Rochester; and a very few others) are the new vanguard of Polish and Polish American Studies in America, replacing the wartime generation of which there are precious few left (Piotr Wandycz at Yale, Anna Cienciała at the University of Kansas, Zbigniew Kruszewski at the University of Texas, Andrzej Korbonński, border case chronologically, at the University of California at Los Angeles); all on the verge of retirement.

Who will replace the new vanguard, itself getting old? Although there are some new voices: John Radzilowski (Thad's son?), writing occasionally for *GP Light* (careful with the Polish nobility, John, it's not that simple) and Joanna Kot, perennial winner with her younger sister of the Polish Arts Club's literary prizes when a student at Curie High in Chicago, and author at present of a fine article in *The Slavic and East European Journal* (No. 4, 1996, pp. 649-666) as Assistant Professor of Russian at Northern Illinois University, there are not nearly enough of them, and the replacements will come from Poland, a process that has been going on now for some time, with mixed results, filling this writer, and his associates, with misgivings.

Why misgivings when we have really all come from, or derive from, Poland, and intellectuals or educators from Poland were never strangers for long to these shores? They were among the first arrivals here: the dissidents, at least one educator, the explorers, and the military men. Then came the priests and members of religious and teaching orders, with a task to hold together and educate the poor and illiterate masses which were arriving in the second half of the nineteenth century and at the beginning of the twentieth. They were successful beyond expectations: Polish American organizations were springing up and growing, followed by a constantly expanding network of schools. The outbreak of the Great War put an end to the mass migration, and when Poland regained independence, the main task of the limited number of Poles arriving here was to educate the leaders of American Polonia (the name began to be used in the interwar period, as in *Rada Polonii Amerykańskiej*—the Polish American Council, RPA) to support Poland's causes.

In other educational developments, the Kosciuszko Foundation, founded in the interwar period, initiated its exchange program with Poland. It was now possible for young Polish Americans to study in Poland and vice-versa. Young Dr. Ludwik Krzyżanowski of the Jagiellonian University in Cracow was probably the first grantee from Poland not only studying here (Chicago) but also teaching! Thus a tradition was started, which is now being questioned. In another significant development Wacław Gąsiorowski, writer of historical novels from the Napoleonic era, became head of Alliance College, which was carrying things too far!

With the exception of Arthur Coleman, Alliance College never had a first-rate president (insistence on PNA membership was a factor here) and that's probably a reason for its ultimate demise, but bringing in a popular writer from Poland and not an educator was not helping Alliance, which shows that even at an early stage of the replacement practice, it was counter-productive and even scandalous later (Polish at Columbia). But there is a more serious argument against it, mainly that if the replacement is temporary, it can result in the elimination of the post.

By now several professorships in Polish, or including Polish, are occupied by scholars originally from Poland, the most prestigious of them the Alfred Jurzykowski chair of Polish Language and Literature at Harvard, which Stanisław Barańczak took over after Wiktor Weintraub's retirement. This writer was deeply concerned about the fate of the chair ever since a controversial changeover at Wayne State, and asked Barańczak's former chairman in Poznań about him. When told that Barańczak was the "real thing," he was satisfied.

Barańczak's accomplishment are his writings, both poetry and prose. Published mainly by a major New York commercial publisher, the prestigious Farrar, Straus & Giroux, and reviewed in mainstream publications, his writings are not only well distributed but are receiving a high level of visibility, so far only achieved by Czesław Miłosz among Polish writers/scholars/poets in America, which is particularly true of Barańczak's latest book, *Laments*, a translation (in a bilingual edition) of Jan Kochanowski's *Treny*, which has two additional claims to distinction: it was accomplished in collaboration with Seamus Heaney, the Irish Nobel Prize winner, and reviewed, among others by, yes, Czesław Miłosz, a Polish Nobel Prize winner, in *The New York Review of Books* (February 1996).

For the sake of his writings Barańczak resigned his position of Editor-in-Chief of *The Polish Review*, for which, in a significant changeover, he had been allegedly designated by Ludwik Krzyżanowski before the latter's death, to be succeeded, in another changeover, by a native Polish American, Joseph Wieczerzak, with another native Polish American, Gerard T. Kapolka, as Assistant Editor.

The next most productive of the Poland-originating scholars in America (recent publications) after Barańczak, but, unlike Barańczak, with a doctorate from an American university (Brown), is Michael J. Mikoś, Milwaukee, listed after him not in any attempt at ranking but because, like Barańczak, he is also a translator of Kochanowski's *Treny*. In an excellent article in the Kosciuszko Foundation's *Newsletter* (Spring 1996), Harold Segel ably compares the two translations, including their respective levels of visibility inevitably favoring the Barańczak-Heaney effort, but still rejoicing over having *two* new translations which to this writer, who once taught the *Laments* to large Polish Literature classes in Chicago, is an "embarrassment of riches" in view of the existence of excellent translations in a book by George Rapall Noyes, used by this writer.

To this writer, also very much under the spell of the *Laments* since his school days (when at least one had to be learned by heart, with nobody complaining; traditionally it was No. 8), especially No. 7, the translation of which in the George Rapall Noyes collection couldn't possibly be improved upon, even by the formidable Barańczak-Heaney team, it's a mystery why Mikoś attempted their translation. The answer, provided by Segel's article, is that Mikoś' translation had previously appeared in his anthology, *Polish*

Renaissance Literature, and was simply reprinted and published separately by the "earnest and valiant scholar" as a "good pedagogical tool."

Mikoś' anthology, *Polish Renaissance Literature*, favorably reviewed by Samuel Fiszman of Indiana University in *The Slavic and East European Journal* (1996, No. 4, pp. 777-8); its forerunner, *Medieval Literature of Poland* (1992); and its sequel, *Polish Baroque and Enlightenment Literature* (1996), not so favorably reviewed by Gerard T. Kapolka in *The Polish Review* (1997, No. 1, pp. 114-117), together represent Mikoś' accomplishment. The same can be said of *Monumenta Polonica* (1989) a bilingual anthology covering the Middle Ages to the late eighteenth century, just like the Mikoś' anthologies, by Bogdana Carpenter (University of Wisconsin), another scholar/translator (with her husband, and probably because of that hers is more successful than Mikoś' undertaking, according to Kapolka), with a doctorate in Comparative Literature from Warsaw University. Another accomplishment, *The Adventures of Nicholas Wisdomseeker*, a translation—with the help of a grant from the National Endowment for the Humanities and an encouraging interview with *The Chicago Tribune*—of an eighteenth century Polish novel by Ignacy Krasicki, the century's best Polish writer, *Mikołaja Doświadczynskiego przypadki, 1776* [with the name misspelled in both *The Tribune* and the KF *Newsletter*], by Thomas H. Hoisington, a non-Polish holder of a doctorate in Slavic Languages and Literatures, and a one-time member of the Literary Section of the Polish Institute.

These translations from Old Polish literature are not only important as badly needed teaching materials, but also as sources of information for those ignorant of Polish literature and culture, and its western roots, who will discover that some of it is worth reading, indeed, as for example Kochanowski's "Lament 19" in which his late mother tells him in a vision how his little daughter is better off with her than on earth, where terrible things await a woman and she enumerates them—a must read for women's activists who would discover that some of the terrible things still exist for many women, but under different guises.

How deep the ignorance of things Polish is and how important that men like Hoisington undertake to clear some of it was demonstrated to this writer during a "Bookmark" television program moderated by Lewis Lapham, editor of *Harper's Magazine*. One of the guests on the discussion program, Lawrence Weschler, staff writer for *The New Yorker* (at that time covering Solidarity), tried to explain why there were many medievalists among Polish historians, with Lapham finding it incongruous, as an American would.

What other individual accomplishments are there worthy of writing about? What is Tymoteusz Karpowicz, the other scholar/poet with Barańczak, doing now that he is retired? After his inspired long poem "Wiatr od morza," dedicated to Solidarity and printed in parts, in this writer's translation, as "Wind from the Sea," in the September/December 1980 issue (No. 5) of the Chicago Polish students publication *Echo*, and after a successful spectacle on the 100th anniversary of the death of the poet Cyprian Norwid (1821-1883), there was another lament-like long poem as a reaction to another violence, "Moja Czecznia" ("My Chechnya") printed in the comet-like new publication *2B*, edited by Tomasz Tobako in Chicago. What next?

There is another new publication, *The Sarmatian Review*, with an intriguing connotation and potential, edited by Ewa Thompson of Rice University. This writer hasn't seen a copy yet, but the fact that Prof. Kamil Dziewanowski contributes to it is an indication that it could become an accomplishment as defined on these pages.

In "Letters to the Editor" in the last issue of *The Polish Review* (1997, No. 1, p. 121), there are challenging suggestions from Prof. Alex Kurczaba of the University of Illinois, Chicago:

> Kurczaba suggests lobbying, particularly by Polish Americans for more tax funding of courses at public institutions and a summit meeting of Kosciuszko Foundation, Polish American Congress and Polish Institute of Arts and Sciences representatives on endowments of chairs at a few key universities.

The funding suggestion is precisely the point made by this writer to the Kosciuszko Foundation in this book, namely that courses at public institutions should be funded, whenever justified, by public money. It is the opposite with endowments, and all the proposed summit meeting would accomplish would be to initiate a search for rich donors, like the late Alfred Jurzykowski, to provide the funds.

There already are such funds, a million-dollar scholarship fund in Chicago (left by a rich woman) for Polish American students, half of it at the Illinois Institute of Technology and half at Loyola University, where it had been sitting idle for several years, earning interest, and was about to be activated just at the time when this writer was preparing to leave Loyola and Chicago, mainly for health reasons, but also because of an ugly conflict with a Hispanic chairperson. Perhaps the summit meeting could delegate someone (ideally, Dr. Radzilowski) to find out how the fund was being used for best results.

There are also named professorships. One had been held by Dr. Raymond Mayer, retired (a Polish American with a Ph.D. from Illinois Institute of Technology), at Loyola; another by Dr. Andrzej Walicki (from Poland) at Notre Dame. Also, Piotr Wandycz holds a named professorship at Yale.

As for endowments, this is also already happening. Stanley Blejwas' accomplishment is one example, and Zbigniew Kruszewski's efforts in this direction at his university in Texas (El Paso) is another. But there is a third, a valiant campaign for the establishment of a Chair of Polish Studies at the University of Virginia which is progressing well under the leadership of Blanka Rosenstiel, President of The American Institute of Polish Culture in Miami, Florida, whose accomplishments will be discussed further in the next sub-chapter, "Polish Women in America."

Why not get behind this bound-to-succeed effort instead of starting new uncertain ones from scratch which, even if successful, would create problems of another kind? Where are the candidates for the endowed chairs to come from? Poland? Not from the domestic Polish Studies field which is still growing weaker at a faster pace than growing stronger due to natural attrition. At this point there is just nobody here qualified to be a candidate for an endowed chair in Polish, except for a few scholars who are already too old for it. Perhaps in a few years Radzilowski and Pula will attain the necessary academic reputation, the former on the basis of the accomplishments in his present position, and the latter partly from the critical reception of his present book. Academic reputation is not gained by overreacting to a "Polonophobia" article in *Chronicles*, it is gained by creating new knowledge in one's specialty.

The present writer's own accomplishments can be gleaned from this book, in chapters on the Polish American Congress, the Kosciuszko Foundation, the Polish Institute of Arts and Sciences, and his brief biography at the end of the book. The only information not to be found in the book are the titles of his first works, marking his evolution as a scholar, swift, to make up for time lost in the war.

After rebuking Arnold Toynbee for leaving Polish pilots out of the Battle of Britain ("Polish Heroes," *New York Times Magazine*); after reviewing Wiesław Kuniczak's *The Thousand Hour Day* ("History as Literature," *Polish Review*) and writing a well-received paper at Columbia University ("American Intervention in Russian Revolution," unpublished because of family in Poland), came the specialized works: an important article ("The Karamzin-Lelewel Controversy," *Slavic Review*), followed by the publication of both M.A. (*Pushkin's "Poltava" as a Reaction to the Revolutionary Politics and History of Mickiewicz's "Konrad Wallenrod" and Ryleev's "Vojnarovskij"*) and Ph.D. theses (*Tadeusz Bułharyn/Faddej V. Bulgarin/1789-1859: A Study in Literary Maneuver*), in *Antemurale* XVII and XIX (1974-5), followed by an article on a related topic ("Polish and Russian Sources of *Boris Godunov*," *Polish Review*) and a digression in 1976 resulting in three books, of which this is the third.

He considers his finest accomplishment his paper at Columbia University on the 50th anniversary of D-Day about Polish contributions to the battle of Normandy and W.W.II.

A. POLISH WOMEN IN AMERICA

There is a good reason why this sub-chapter should follow a discussion of Jan Kochanowski's *Treny* (*Laments*) in the "Introduction." In "Lament XIX," subtitled "Or Dream," a woman appears, a rare appearance of a Polish woman in Polish literature, up to that time full of foreign queens of Polish kings, but she too is no ordinary woman, she is the poet's late mother, a wise woman it seems, as she is holding her little granddaughter, Ursula, in her arms, and chiding her son for his inability to come to terms with his own grief. "Master, cure thyself," she advises him.

In his search for the beginnings of a responsible Polish woman-hood in order to relate it to our own times, this writer came across the Kochanowski connection a second time. He was very mystified when, on one of his trips to Poland, a fellow-Silesian—a judge and soon his biographer, who fancied himself something of a writer—introduced his wife to him adding proudly that her maiden name was the same as that of Kochanowski's wife (we see her in Lament VII), which he said was *Podlodowska*, and indeed there was something out of the ordinary about the judge's wife. Her sister, incidentally, worked for the Ossolineum publishing house, providing this writer with all kinds of good books.

These remarkable encounters had a surprising ending, if "surprising" is the right word for it. As he was scanning *The New York Times* for Polish names, as was his habit, a name hit him with all the force of memory. Reading a fascinating article, "Computer Age Millionaires Redefine Philanthropy," on the front page of Sunday, July 6 (exactly a year after "Silver Zlotys and a Dream of America"), he forgot about the Polish names until he turned to page 9 for the continuation of the article under an expanded title, "Microsoft's Wealthy Redefine Giving," and there, under one of the two photos illustrating the article was the name, TINA PODLODOWSKI, with a caption, "A Microsoft millionaire and Seattle City Councilwoman" and a quote, "You start thinking, 'How can we crank that safety net for other people?'" There was not much more about Tina Podlodowski except that she was 37, and although "not on the same scale of raw wealth" as Bill Gates, also from Seattle, she was "considered the political star among Microsoft retirees...who has championed neighborhood planning, gay rights and technological efficiency, saving the city millions in computer costs." Nothing about the Podlodowski name. Was it her real name? Was she aware of its significance? It was easy to get her address and write to her, to let her know what an illustrious name she carried.

If Tina Podlodowski is Polish, her skills and accomplishments are the latest testimony to the evolution of Polish womanhood in this century after centuries of backwardness and suppression. But if she is Jewish, her having the name would be a big discovery and set literary detectives on its trail to determine its real source. After a few futile tries to talk to her in the absence of a reply, I left the big questions on her answering machine.

"What's in a name?" asked the poet. In Poland, always a great deal, but perhaps it is ending now when interest in history is waning. There was relatively little excitement when a bearer of another famous literary name, that of the "Father of Polish Literature," Nicholas (Mikołaj) Rey, became U.S. Ambassador in Poland. But even in the Communist period, just as the judge was proud of his wife's maiden name, people would flock to the scene of a Radziwiłł marriage in Warsaw, proud of the name's great Polish-Lithuanian history; and the press would report to its grateful readers how a Potocki, having lost the family estate, would gladly work on it, taking care of what was left of its once famous herd of pedigreed horses. It would be good if Tina Podlodowski felt some of that pride.

When we talk about centuries of backwardness and suppression of Polish women, it applied to the 90% of the Polish nation which was not of noble birth, which means not privileged. Even impoverished gentry, while enjoying little privilege, felt entitled to it, and would not allow itself to slide too low socially and intellectually. Readers of Polish literature (Józef Korzeniowski—not to be confused with Konrad/Conrad—about the "gentry village") recall how women of that class wore gloves when working in the fields, to protect their hands; and veils, to protect their complexion. It wasn't privilege that made Maria Skłodowska (Curie) reach for the highest achievement of any Polish woman, dead or alive, but education, but by then women were already coming into their own because of strides in their emancipation. There was none of it in Kochanowski's time.

Jan Kochanowski came from a noble family, what Czesław Miłosz calls in *The History of Polish Literature* "the ascending middle stratum of the gentry class" (60). The poet himself enjoyed the patronage of the great Chancellor and Royal Hetman Jan Zamoyski, and of the king himself. As for the women in the family, in the Laments we see his wife and his mother in connection with the death of his beloved Ursula: in No. VII the wife laments the need to prepare her daughter's death bed (casket) rather than the bridal bed in future; in Lament XIX his mother reverses the two, with the death bed a blessing rather than grief, and the bridal bed more often than not a misfortune, along with other misfortunes, rather than a blessing.

There is another woman in the Laments, in a brief "Epitaph (*Epitafium*) to Hanna Kochanowska," the poet's other daughter, who had apparently followed her sister soon, thus also avoiding the pitfalls of marriage, against which Jan Kochanowski compiles a catalogue of evils, ranging from buying a master with the dowry; through pain in bearing children and speculating which is a greater pain, bearing or burying them; to becoming an orphan forcibly deprived of one's patrimony by a forced marriage or, much worse, of her freedom by marauding pagans (Tatars) and spending one's life in ignominious captivity. This fate befell women marrying old soldiers who received land for their years of service and settled near the unruly south-eastern steppes.

It's all true, but Kochanowski's harangue about marriage and children, voiced by his mother, raises some questions, considering that he was one of eleven children (like him, of literary disposition, Miłosz, 61). He married late, after passing forty, only fourteen years before his own sudden death, which means that his beloved Ursula would have indeed been an orphan, a fate she had avoided, just as she had avoided marriage, referred to figuratively and cruelly in these two lines:

> "And when a woman is called a wife,
> She had already been buried alive." (FM transl.)

But marriage and children were not the only destiny for a woman at that time. Since the Middle Ages, as Helena Goscilo points out in her Introduction to *Russian and Polish Women's Fiction*, "a woman in medieval Poland had two possible 'career' options, wife or nun" (26), with the latter becoming indeed a career if the woman brought her dowry with her and became the abbess or Mother Superior. Some of the religious orders the women entered were, or became, teaching orders, like the Felician Sisters who, when teaching became difficult or forbidden in Poland during the Partitions, left for America where, together with other teaching orders, they improved the educational level of the parochial schools, while at the same time starting the presence of educated Polish women in America.

One should know more about the Felician Sisters who first arrived here in 1874, especially about their background. From this writer's experience, not with the Felician Sisters but the Ursulans, who ran a secondary school for girls in the formerly German Silesia, in the same town as a boys' Gymnasium he was attending, the Ursulan Sisters were extremely well educated and excellent teachers, under constant supervision of the Mother Superior who was a superior woman indeed, with distinctly upper class bearing and manners. The few social events the boys' school shared with hers were instrumental in improving the boys' study habits and social graces.

By the same token one should know more about the founders and presidents of the Polish Women's Alliance, whose names point to upper class origin (Honorata Wołowska) and such organizations as the patriotic Legion of Young Polish Women (Grażyna Cioromska), founded after the Second World War. This was the time when a new type of Polish woman began to arrive in America, resourceful, enterprising and ultimately successful women, not living on the fringes and off Polish or Polish American organizations, as so many did and still do, just like many men, but following their own agendas, dictated by their talents and abilities. Among them three stand out, to be discussed here in chronological order of their arrival in America: RENA ROWAN, BLANKA ROSENSTIEL, and BARBARA JOHNSON. Beside success, they have another thing in common: all three, now divorced (Rowan) or widowed (Rosenstiel, Johnson) had been married to American men, and here an explanatory note is called for to explain this coincidental phenomenon.

If anything, this was the final stage in Polish women coming into their own, but that would be simplifying matters. Women in Poland, that is aristocratic women, began to act independently as early as Poland's decline and fall. In two of history's least explored liaisons, both Napoleon and Alexander I, his adversary, had Polish mistresses, Countess Walewska and Princess Czetwertyńska, respectively. Alexander's brother, Grand Duke Constantine, stationed in Poland, had a Polish wife, just like several high Russian officials, among them Admiral Shishkov, the Minister of Education. Since, after the fall of Napoleon, Russia was the most important continental power, in total control of most of Poland, it would seem that the Polish ladies were taking advantage of it for their own benefit. But, until the November 1830 Insurrection, Russian rule of Poland was rather liberal, and the inter-marriages were not frowned upon until later in the century.

After the Second World War America assumed a place in the world Russia had had in Europe until the Crimean War in the mid-1850s, and marrying an American was the best way to leave war-torn Europe after a war-disrupted childhood in Poland, as was the case with RENA ROWAN, who came to the United States as early as 1945 as the wife of an American officer according to the Kosciuszko Foundation *Newsletter*. Making clothes for neighbors to support her four children brought out her talent in design which led her to the fashion industry. Today she is one of the most successful business-women in the United States, serving on the boards of many charitable organizations, of the American Center for Polish Culture and, most importantly, helping Poland.

As for the two widows, they inherited great fortunes making them the wealthiest Polish women in the world, and LADY BLANKA ROSENSTIEL certainly behaves like one judging by the magnitude of her social and cultural activities in her capacity as Founder and President of The American Institute of Polish Culture, Inc., Miami, Florida. The Institute has its own magazine, appropriately called *Good News*, a periodically published and richly illustrated collection of topical reports, essays, and other pieces dealing with Polish history and culture. Its 90-page 1996-1997 issue contains on page 37 the story of the woman behind the "good news":

LADY BLANKA: EXCEPTIONAL COMMITMENT
TO AWARENESS OF POLAND'S RICH HERITAGE

by Gina Janiga

She was born in Warsaw, Poland. After World War II she studied art in Brussels, Belgium. In 1956 she moved to the United States and in 1967 married Lewis Rosenstiel, chairman of Schenley Industries and a great philanthropist and humanitarian. Widowed in 1976, she resides in Miami Beach during the winter season and spends the summer at her Blandemar Farm Estates in Charlottesville, VA.

Her creative skills are endless. She has sung throughout Europe, appeared on Belgian TV, been a model and a professional fashion designer. She loves to design, sing, paint; her sculptures are exhibited in major public institutions. She is involved in many institutions across the country, especially with the two organizations she founded, The American Institute of Polish Culture in 1972 and the Chopin Foundation of the United States in 1977. In 1984 she was elected President of the American Council of Polish Cultural Clubs (ACPCC), a national body with more than 40 member organizations, and she held the post for 2 years. She is widely recognized for her ability to launch meaningful programs: she had initiated the establishment of an American Center for Polish Culture in Washington, DC, and, recently, a Chair of Polish Studies at the University of Virginia.

She has an exceptional commitment to the promotion of distinct values of Poland's rich heritage. Her work has always been a labor of unique dedication, perseverance, and love; she keeps her responsibilities with honor. Countless people and organizations have benefited from her generosity and sincerity over the many years. "I am following in the footsteps of my beloved mother in her great love for Poland; my work of promoting Polish culture is done not only from my heart and love for Poland but also from the need to show to the world the glorious legacy of the proud Polish nation and to bring the treasure of Poland's rich heritage to the doorstep of many people and organizations," says Lady Blanka R. She is a brilliant and simply magnificent woman and her enchanting personality and distinct beauty fascinate everybody. Her genius, artistry, spirit and superb work are highly recognized. She does everything with a masterly touch of perfectionism. She made the "American dream" a reality. She loves life and lives every moment of it intensely. She is of enduring greatness and represents the very essence of the Polish and American way of life.

This enthusiastic biography is followed by photographs of Lady Blanka receiving the Polonia Restituta Order at the Polish Embassy in Washington, and the Ellis Island Medal of Honor in New York. Then follows a list of her other awards and honors (26), preceded by a list of institutions which benefit from her continued financial support (16) and of public benefit institutions in which she is active (34).

"Update on Polish Chair Project at the Univ. of Virginia," pp. 10-17 of *Good News*, contains letters of support from members of the Honorary Committee, including Lech Wałęsa, chairman, and nine distinguished co-chairmen, headed by Zbigniew Brzezinski; it ends with an impressive List of Donors, which leaves no doubt that Lady Blanka's most ambitious project so far will soon become a reality.

BARBARA PIASECKA JOHNSON, the third of the group, is the hardest to define, perhaps because being younger than the other two (and this writer, for that matter), she had no memory of independent Poland that to me was paradise irrespective of what it was to others. Born in 1937, she had just a vague memory of the war, which for Rena Rowan meant deportation and exile in Siberia before a lucky exit. All Piasecka's growing up and education was under communism which, whether one is aware of it or not, leaves an imprint on one's personality leading those fighting it into leaving the country as Barbara did in 1968, with a master's degree in Art History and $200, but promising to return in a Rolls-Royce, a prophetic promise and a belief in her abilities.

I knew next to nothing about her except what I saw in the papers about the nasty inheritance trial. But even then I was of two minds about her, was she a fortune hunter or a victim of her own good luck? All I could think of was what *I* could do for Poland and Polonia with even a fraction of the money she emerged with from Manhattan Surrogate's Court in June 1986 as one of the world's wealthiest women!

Just as with Tina Podlodowski, the Microsoft millionaire, when getting down to writing about the even wealthier Barbara Piasecka Johnson I found an article about her in *The New York Times*, not just a piece of reporting, but a well written and very well researched essay by David Margolick, "Basia Johnson Lech's American Angel," in the *Sunday Magazine* (October 8, 1989), with Basia (Barbara) and Lech (Wałęsa) on the front cover of what I had put aside as a collector's item. I read it with a renewed interest.

The author approaches his subject with a great deal of sympathy, which was also the attitude I developed. It appears that the marriage in 1971 to J. Seward Johnson, Sr., son of the founder of Johnson & Johnson and 42 years her senior, was nevertheless a perfect match during the 12 years of the marriage before his death from cancer in 1983. It was after his death that she turned into a tragic figure in what she called "my American hell" brought about by the 17-week-long will contesting trial against her. Surrounded by a pack of legal hyenas (no "legal eagles" they) whose firm almost lost her case that was all but impossible to lose; it was sued by her for malpractice, including an old friend, Nina Zagat, and her multi-million dollar legal fees while the rags-to-riches saga still had Basia as a "maid."

The whole brutal experience has left Basia feeling embittered toward her adopted land, according to Margolick, and disinclined to launch any major charitable initiatives here (which were reportedly legion before). Her subsequent involvement in the $100 million Gdańsk shipyard project was probably a direct result of her feelings, and its abandonment (*after* Margolick's article) was more likely the fault of the Poles and Lech Wałęsa than her own. Reading and thinking about it now I feel an overwhelming regret for failing to get her involved in my projects, which would have suited her personality, and were likely to increase her resources rather than deplete them.

What I perceive as Barbara Piasecka's single fault was her not following up on her resolve to attend New York University after she had left the Johnsons' employ. With a master's degree in Art History, getting a doctorate would have been easy. Seward Johnson would still have pursued her and even financed her studies as an investment to make her optimally prepared to assemble his art collection. All she needed was to perfect her English by taking English for Foreign Students courses at NYU or at Columbia University, just as this writer had done on the way to *his* doctorate.

The result would have been a rarity even in America: a holder of a Ph.D. and fabulously wealthy wife of Johnson & Johnson's largest individual stockholder rolled into one. Instead of being a target of the tabloids, she would have been sought after by the highest circles, even Jackie Kennedy who would have used her as a consultant on art. Since I was teaching at NYU at that time, our paths would have crossed, she might have even wandered into my class on *Poles in America*, which would have been a meeting of incalculable consequences, as this was also the time when I had brought from Poland samples of a honey mixture medicine which I considered miraculous (cure for cancer?) after a doctor in my hometown (Szymborska's uncle) who had concocted it, stopped my incipient pneumonia from flaring up by trying it on me. Since I had also brought with me the doctor's detailed notes, and would have had ready access to Johnson & Johnson's labs through Seward Johnson's wife, the rest would have been simple, but alas, it didn't happen that way, and hence my regret.

Instead, I was waging lonely battles, described in chapters on the Polish American Congress and the Polish Institute, not even aware that Barbara Piasecka Johnson was haphazardly giving money left and right, by helping Poland, trying to buttress the venerable Polish Library in Paris, helping to start the Institute for Polish-Jewish Studies in Oxford, and in America supporting the New York-based *Polish Daily News* (*Nowy Dziennik*); embracing the idea proposed by Miłosz of an institute on Central and East European studies and discussing it with Alexander Schenker of Yale, and Wiktor Weintraub and Stanisław Barańczak of Harvard, and talking about donating as much as $100 million [!], all plans delayed by the will contest and then abandoned, together with plans to endow a Barbara Johnson chair in Polish History at Yale, and to help that school purchase and catalogue its archives of Czesław Miłosz and Aleksander Wat, the late Polish-Jewish writer. It is as if she were giving up on America, after her "American hell" period. Has she also given up on Poland, after the Gdańsk shipyard episode? She reportedly resides mostly abroad, with her sister and a secretary taking care of her affairs here. Yet, this is a woman who could have been the First Lady of American Polonia, and have a statue in Poland (Gdańsk).

The once young and vibrant Basia is 60 now. Is that why she keeps out of sight in the two countries that really matter, or should matter? Even at 60, it is not too late for her to earn the recognition she deserves.

After these four, what other Polish women in America deserve mention? Two, to begin with, one born in America and the other in Poland.

BARBARA MIKULSKI, United States Senator from Maryland, has the distinction of having been elected to the Senate, which in itself is a considerable accomplishment. She is a strong voice in the Senate on matters pertaining to Poland and Polish immigrants (and refugees earlier), and she cooperates closely with the Polish American Congress on these matters, and with the Polish Women's Alliance on matters pertaining to women. She is the author of *Capitol Offense* (Signet 1997), a fiction about one 'Noric' Gorzak, a freshman senator in the nation's capital.

Ms. Mikulski lends her name and prestige to initiatives concerning Polish history and culture, as for example the recent drive led by Blanka Rosenstiel, President of the American Institute of Polish

Culture, to establish a chair of Polish Studies at the University of Virginia. Ms. Mikulski is a member of the Honorary Committee for this initiative, and her letter supporting it appears in the last issue of *Good News* (p.13).

MAŁGORZATA DYMEK (TERENTIEW)-ĆWIKLIŃSKA, editor and publisher of the weekly *Gwiazda Polarna* (*Pole Star*), published by Point Publications, Inc., in Stevens Point, Wisconsin. Although there was some controversy surrounding her taking over the venerable publication after its last managing editor, Alfons Hering (who had worked for it 32 years), she is trying valiantly to keep it alive in view of declining subscriptions due to natural causes and the shrinking number of people able to read Polish in America.

Among MD(T)-C's accomplishments one stands out, her launching of an English-language supplement to *Pole Star*, the monthly *GP Light*, the compound title consisting of the acronym of *Gwiazda Polarna* and of the adjective "Light," which was probably intended to denote the lighter contents of the publication as compared with the more conservative tone of its parent publication. A practical purpose of the new publication was no doubt to gain new subscribers to compensate for the losses by the old one.

How successful the new venture will be is hard to say. As a former Fulbright Scholar, the editor/publisher is a well-educated woman, and her command of English is good, so good as a matter of fact that this editor had entrusted her with the translation of Professor Aleksander Gieysztor's contribution to this book. But starting a new publication in America is not easy, most of them are short-lived, their life-span determined by their promotion and the amount of advertising they can attract.

As for the contents of *GP Light*, it is a mix of reporting, anecdotes, serious articles (as, for example, those provoked by the anniversary of the Warsaw Uprising) and debates, but mainly attempts at creative writing, mostly of a biographical nature, requiring good editing (not always in evidence) when it comes to quotes from Polish or facts from Polish history. Not helping matters is the monthly arriving late, and readers who complain are not happy about it. They must not be disappointed.

Polish women have been relatively well represented in American colleges and universities after World War II. Of those already retired or close to retirement the most prominent, and not just because of a famous father, is Helena Łopata Znaniecki, a well-known sociologist. Another woman with a well-known name connection is Maria Żółtowska Weintraub, Wiktor's widow; another is Elizabeth Valkenier Kridl, the late Manfred's daughter. There was Irene Sokol, the Polish American historian; the two Święcicki sisters, Danuta Lloyd and Maria Ziemianek, the translator of Pasek; Eleonora Korzeniowska, Regina Grol Prokopczyk, and others. Not a college teacher but a high school administrator and a scholar in her own right with a doctorate and at least two books in pertinent areas (East Europe and American Polonia) is Angela Pienkoś, who is also the mother of four sons! Another busy lady, too busy to get a doctorate despite a famous name connection, is Krystyna (Serejski) Olszer, for years the assistant of Ludwik Krzyżanowski on *The Polish Review*, and after his death realizing her dream of teaching Polish on college level and doing it at Hunter College as a grand-mother, proving that it is never too late.

Of a somewhat younger generation are three women who have reached the top of the academic ladder represented by tenure, full professorships, and chair of their respective departments at some point. None of them will set the world on fire but each has her own accomplishments that set them apart from the academic rank-and-file. MADELINE G. LEVINE, with Harvard degrees, a professor of Slavic Languages at the University of North Carolina at Chapel Hill, and translator of Polish poetry, has hosted Miłosz in her department which if anything shows her commitment to Polish poetry. She was one of the first respondents when a dictionary of Polish literature was being planned by the Literary Section of the Polish Institute, offering to write about Julian Tuwim.

The other two have something in common: both are married to American husbands and neither, it seems, has any children, which may, or may not, have something to do with their success. In the case of BOGDANA CARPENTER, who had blazed a trail from Seattle to Ann Arbor to Wisconsin, all the time translating Polish poetry with her husband, it was certainly a productive match in that sense, cul-minating in a major work, *Monumenta Polonica*, an anthology discussed in the "Introduction" to this chapter.

EWA THOMPSON is the most visible of the three, not for any scholarly reasons or excellent translations but because, having no more worlds to conquer nor presumably any family responsibilities, she is becoming a self-styled spokesperson on things Polish, as she had demonstrated recently by responding to the provocative

"Polonophobia," along with Alex Kurczaba, another seeker of a platform, both muddying even more the already muddy field of Polish-Jewish relations. The problem with people who came out of Comparative Literature is they are not Slavists. If they were, they would have plenty to write about. As for Thompson, she *has* a new world, *The Sarmatian Review*.

Two more women, of different generations and with vastly different motivations, have to be listed here, in order to make a point: Ewa Gierat and Elżbieta Wasiutyński.

EWA (KARPINSKA) GIERAT stands for all the women of the wartime generation—the Pope's generation—and there are still many left. It was in her "Domek" in Bethlehem, Connecticut, that the label "Pope's generation" was first used publicly at an intellectual meeting, one of twenty such meetings held there since 1971.

Widowed after the premature death of Stanisław Gierat, a perfect companion and a great Polish patriot, she filled the sudden void with what then became her main occupation: work for the Polish Scouting Organization—ZHP, Inc. The quarterly newsletter she edits is a gem full of uplifting information distributed in a dozen countries.

Recognition for all her noble work was long in coming, but it came, as the "Man of the Year" award at the Annual Dinner of the Polish American Congress, Connecticut Division, whose former president and the emcee at the dinner was the other woman, Elżbieta Wasiutyński, who honored this time a woman, Ewa Gierat, about whom it could be said that "she wanted nothing for herself."

ELŻBIETA WASIUTYŃSKI, daughter-in-law of Wojciech Wasiutyński, is a woman about whom it could be said that if Ewa wanted nothing for herself, Elżbieta wanted it all, specifically the presidency of the entire Polish American Congress. This writer felt at first uncomfortable about that ambition, but was gradually changing his mind, making it up after learning about the award for Ewa Gierat.

In making this award to Ewa Gierat, Elżbieta Wasiutyński tells us something about herself, about her ability to identify worthy people, an important attribute for a national office. There is more to it. Her education at the Sorbonne is well-known, and her working habits are legendary. This writer knows first-hand about her work for the Solidarity movement and on the *Studium* for Polish Affairs, edited, on top of his academic work, by the equally dedicated

Andrzej Ehrenkreutz at Ann Arbor before he moved to Australia for health and family reasons.

On top of her work at present in connection with the endowed chair of Polish Studies in New Britain, she is raising, like Angela Pienkoś in Milwaukee and Lech Wałęsa (another symbol) in Gdańsk, a large family, and this is her biggest asset as far as this writer is concerned.

Post Script: In my chapter, "The Big Fraternals," instead of counting dollars and cents, I recommended that they set up a quasi-Embassy in Warsaw: to educate Polish young people about America (Polish National Alliance); to help restore family values (Polish Women Alliance); to start a Pro-Life movement to avert threatening depopulation (Polish Roman Catholic Union); to introduce a cult of physical culture to schools, a sure ticket to children's health (Polish Falcons), all under the aegis of the Polish American Congress, whose current president rejected the idea! PAC clearly needs a president with pertinent assets and vision to see that my recommendation is a matter of life....

B. POLISH PUBLISHERS IN AMERICA

Books on and about Poland are published in America by main-stream commercial publishers, by university presses, by specialized academic publishers like *Slavica* and East European Monographs (the present book), and vanity presses. Shorter works (articles, book reviews) are published in magazines, journals (*The New York Times Book Review, The New York Review of Books*, and in professional quarterlies (*Slavic and East European Journal, Slavic Review, Polish Review*). The volume is small, except in unusual times, such as the rise of Solidarity and the martial law, since there is no such thing as a ready market for Polish books, as there is, for example, for Jewish books. But there are two publishers who strive, trying to create a market, one by publishing books in Polish only (Bicentennial Publishing), the other by publishing Poland-oriented books and making them a large part of its overall output (Hippocrene Books).

BICENTENNIAL PUBLISHING CORP. is a Polish American success story brought about by its founder and president Bolesław Wierzbiański, who was determined, after the demise of the Polish daily *Nowy Świat (The New World)* in New York, to start a new daily, and succeeded beyond expectations.

BOLESŁAW WIERZBIAŃSKI (born 1915 in Poland, came to America in 1956) was well qualified for the task. He is listed in *Who Is Who in Polish America* as a "journalist, publisher, Polish community leader"—a description which fits him well. A journalist with *Światpol (World...), Iskra (Spark)*, and the Polish Radio, Warsaw, in the 1930s, he was editor-in-chief, Polish Press Agency, Paris, in 1939-1940, and London 1940-1947; war correspondent, Polish and Allied Headquarters, London, and Allied Control Command (Germany), 1943-1948; commentator, Radio Free Europe and Voice of Am., London, 1946-56, and New York, 1956-65; finally co-founder, publisher, editor-in-chief of *Nowy Dziennik— Polish Daily News*, its weekly literary-social supplement *Przegląd Polski*, and a "Polish American Review" *New Horizon* in 1971.

It was a long uphill road to success. It is one thing to launch a publication in America—and a Polish one at that—and another to make it last. Without help, *Nowy Dziennik* would have probably shared the fate of *Nowy Świat*. Help came from many sources, among them Bolesław Łaszewski (vice president), owner of Fregata Travel; Dr. Kusielewicz, President of the Kosciuszko Foundation; Barbara

Piasecka Johnson, and others. A big help were subscribers from among the immigrants and refugees during the Solidarity and martial law dramas for whom the Polish daily was the only means of keeping informed about Poland. No wonder critics say that the paper caters to the new arrivals. The name "Bicentennial" was probably suggested by the success of this writer's courses at NYU on "Poles in America" from the point of view of the Bicentennial with Mr. Wierzbiański one of the guest speakers (on "The Polish American Press"). He was able to move his enterprise from New Jersey to larger quarters in Manhattan, add a bookstore and a "gallery" for lectures and exhibitions, while visitors literally from all over the world would call on him in his editorial office!

If anything is a measure of success, the visitors are, and their caliber is a sign of its degree. They range from an old loyal subscriber Wojciech ("Voytek") Fibak, the Polish once high-ranking tennis player-turned entrepreneur, on his infrequent visits to his residence in Connecticut from his other residence in Paris and his business ventures in Poland; and an old friend, Professor Andrew Ehrenkreutz, former editor of *Studium* now residing in Australia, to Lech Wałęsa, before and after he became President, and most recently, Prime Minister Włodzimierz Cimoszewicz after his talk at the School of International Affairs at Columbia University. It was the last visit which pointed to the seriousness with which the Polish daily is read by the most recent immigrants, who protested the visit to this writer (while changing the windows in the Columbia University house in which he resides!), because all they could think of was that the Prime Minister was a former Communist.

The visits have been growing in intensity (including American officials of various ranks) with Poland's attempts to become a member of NATO and to join the European Union. But the most frequent visitor was the soon to be recalled Consul General Jerzy Surdykowski, an old friend of Mr. Wierzbiański from the days (or years) of his working for him as a reporter during an extended stay here (to what extent he owed his consul's job to this fact is a good question and a sure sign of Mr. Wierzbiański's growing importance). As for this writer, Mr. Surdykowski struck him as a puffed up jack-of-all-trades fancying himself to be a writer of books about Polish Constitutions among other topics, when one look at it at the bookstore revealed a bad mistake (what audience was this book written for?), only strengthening the impression that the man talks about writing a "few more" books like a short-order cook at MacDonald's talks about frying a few more hamburgers. Let's hope the new Consul, Dariusz Jadowski, who had already paid a visit to the *Nowy Dziennik*, will be an improvement.

To this writer the best part of the Wierzbiański enterprise, next to the bookstore brimming with Polish books and the gallery staging art exhibitions and hosting significant speakers, such as the historian Norman Davies discussing his new book, *Europe: A History*, is the weekly literary-social supplement *Przegląd Polski*, a review which should properly be called literary-historical, there is so much history in it. Just one issue (July 6, 1995), has three historical articles: "A Ukrainian Historian about the OUN-UPA Crimes" ("Historyk ukraiński o zbrodniach OUN-UPA," Teofil Lachowicz); "Polish Underwater Kamikaze of the year 1939" ("Polscy podwodni kamikaze z roku 1939," Narcyz Klatka); and "Letters from Kamieniec Podolski" ("Listy z Kamieńca Podolskiego," Teresa Siedlarowa), the last one a special kind of history, with special allusions in which the author presumes the reader's close reading and good memory of Sienkiewicz's "Trilogy." One such allusion we encounter when the author talks about the town Bar and adds, in parentheses ("Bar, which was taken"), and we remember the almost exact words ("Bar wzięty") at very end of volume one of *With Fire and Sword*.

The historical tone of the *Przegląd* is underlined by frequent contributions to it by the historian Andrzej Pomian. This writer's acquaintance with him through the pages of the *Przegląd* is valuable for many good reasons. For one, it lets us know that he was a historian with a difference, not just a strictly factual scholar but one capable of unbounded love for what Halecki called the Polish eastern "borderlands" and of care for the Poles stranded in them, but also of anger. In an essay "Orchids in the Taiga" ("Storczyki w tajdze," July 20, 1995) on Danuta Mierzanowska's *This Was Yesterday. An Actress-Model Remembers* (*To było wczoraj. Modelka-aktorka pamięta*, London 1991), he shows movingly her lucky escape from the Soviet hell, but the question suggests itself what about those who were not so lucky, and his anger erupts (separated by asterisks from the essay) at those who would abandon them, anger provoked by Prime Minister Suchocka's spokesperson's insolent (*bezczelne*) statement in 1993 that Poles from those lands were citizens of those lands, not of Poland, therefore not subject to repatriation. "Insulting nonsense" ("*obraźliwa brednia*") he calls it and goes on justifying in firm language, citing precedents (interwar Poland, Israel and Turkey) the necessity, even the right to, repatriation. Even as a Silesian, and probably because of it, I totally share Pomian's resolve and have a solution to the problem, to be discussed in connection with Russia in this book.

The borderlands—the never forgotten *kresy*—are present in another of Pomian's essays (August 10, 1995) this time for strictly sentimental reasons, but first, my own encounter with the Poles from the *kresy*. At the Third (and last) Congress of Scholars of Polish Descent in Poland (in 1989), there were participants from the Soviet Union, among them two young professors from Grodno. They noticed I had a book with me, a copy of my *Poles in America*, which I used to illustrate my paper. They knew about the book and asked me to give them my copy for their Polish club. I told them I would give it to them just before departure. On that day they were outside my room in my hotel early in the morning. They insisted on helping me pack, carried my luggage to the waiting bus for the airport, then we had breakfast at which I asked them to whom I should dedicate the book. "To the fellow countrymen from *kresy*" they said unhesitatingly.

As for Pomian's essay, it was its title, "At the Beginning there was Kiev" ("Na początku był Kijów"), that had drawn my attention, but upon reading it I was in for a surprise. It was one man from the *kresy* (Pomian, it turned out, comes from Podole, same geographical area as memorable Kamieniec) writing with great feeling about another's book, *The World of My Memory* (*Świat mojej pamięci*, Warsaw 1992), dedicated to the memory of his Irish wife, Eileen Garlińska (d. 1990) "who fell warmly in love with the homeland of her husband and spread goodness around." The husband, and author, Józef Garliński, was the same Garliński whom I had known in London half a century ago as a fellow member of the tennis section of the A.Z.S. (acronym for the Polish Academic Sports Association), a fine postwar athletic body consisting of tennis, volleyball (I was a playing captain), basketball (led by a former Polish Olympian), swimming (I did some), fencing (surprisingly, was the least active), and cross country running (I won the traditional May 3rd race three times: 1948 (the Olympic year in London), 1949, and 1950, retiring the cup and leaving it with the Polish Combatants in London rather than taking it to America.

In all that time I met Józef Garliński only a few times at the
tennis courts. Even at that, there was some tension between us: for
some reason he questioned my high ranking (No. 2 in singles, No. 1
in doubles). Only before leaving London did I hear that he was
engaged in writing about Auschwitz and that it was to be his doctoral
work. The fact that he had been an inmate there did not impress me,
since almost everybody in our circle had been an inmate of one thing
or other, but I envied him the doctoral work, regretting too late that
I could have done the same with the famous Stalag XVIIB (the
graveyard of Soviet POWs), my story of which has not been told to
this day, to my regret. Reading Pomian's essay brought other
regrets. Garliński and I both had remarkable wives, it appears. The
Irish Eileen and English Doreen should have gotten along well,
making the husbands also get along well and probably work together,
taking advantage of his better academic know-how.

I did not see him again for almost a quarter of a century (he was
invisible during my five visits to London) when he came to America
on a book tour sponsored by the Pilsudski Institute. The late Wacław
Jędrzejewicz brought him to the Polish Institute to meet me, at that
time the engine of the Institute by virtue of my Literary Section,
admired by the Pilsudski people, and the *Poles in America* project.
We were both doctors now and authors of books, but I had no idea
how productive he really was. We talked about mutual acquaintances
in London, and this was the last time I saw him. I didn't meet him
during the Congress of Polish Culture in London in 1985. I am
meeting him now in Pomian's essay, which is excellent, especially his
thoughts about the centuries-long devastation of most of Poland by
Russia, and his conclusions on that subject for the future.

It is such essays that make the *Przegląd Polski* a valuable part of
Bicentennial Publishing, and Pomian takes much credit in that
respect for his honesty and sincerity. There is one more which
should be mentioned here because, like the previous one, it is about
someone I should have known more about but didn't, and it also tells
more about Pomian himself. The essay, "On the Trail of Struggle,
Blood and Suffering" ("Na szlaku walki, krwi i cierpienia," October
26, 1995), revolves around a story of, and by, a colleague, Jerzy R.
Krzyżanowski "Szpic"—*With Szaruga. A Partisan Tale* (*U Szarugi.
Partyzancka opowieść*, Lublin 1995). It appears that both
Krzyżanowski and Pomian were involved as members of the Home
Army in the first landing of an allied plane in occupied Poland, in

the spring of 1944 near Lublin, Krzyżanowski as a 21-year old soldier in a partisan unit of "Szaruga" providing cover for the operation ("Most I"—"Bridge I"), and Pomian as one of three emissaries of the civilian Underground to go on that same plane via Italy and Gibraltar to wartime Poland's high authorities in London. This was, incidentally, the same route I took to London in that same spring of 1944, except via France (after escaping from Austria) on foot to Barcelona, by train to Portugal, and by ship to England.

Pomian did not meet Krzyżanowski during the "Most I" operation, but he met other heroes of his book, among them Jacek Mościcki, nephew of Poland's prewar President, one of the few who were lucky to survive both the war and the persecutions of the Home Army in the so-called "People's Poland." To save them, and himself, "Szaruga" (pseudonym of Alexander Sarkisow) joined with them the new Polish "People's Army" the II Army of which was being organized in Lublin under the command of General Karol Świerczewski (of Spanish Civil War fame, where Hemingway had known him). The People's Army did not save them. Accused of attempted desertion, they were tried and sentenced to be shot. Under their applications for clemency Świerczewski, the "thug in general's uniform," wrote "Refused" except for one prison sentence. As for Krzyżanowski, arrested a year earlier, he did a few years in labor camps, but endured it, completed humanistic studies in Warsaw and emigrated to America where he had a rewarding academic/writing career at Ohio State University, Columbus. Our paths crossed when he entered a paper in my symposium celebrating three anniversaries of Henryk Sienkiewicz in 1976, basing the paper on the work of his father, Julian, a famous professor of literature and a specialist on Sienkiewicz. Pomian ends his essay with his own comments on the sad postwar reality in Poland.

Such comments are the strength of Pomian's writing. In them, he gives vent to his feelings, in this case his outrage at the criminal persecution of the wartime Underground by the regime, its members acting even after 1956 as agents of an alien ideology and of a foreign power and getting away with it even when that ideology had lost its grip on the country in 1989. By then there were just a few of the criminals left who could be proven guilty, but all members of security organs, judges in political cases, officials in political sections of the Ministry of the Interior, censors and their party/government supervisors should have been morally stigmatized, and deprived of citizens' honorary rights, particularly the right to be elected, according to Pomian. So far, nothing has come out of bringing the past regime to account, and Pomian cites evidence to the contrary: when running for President as candidate of the post-Communist Left, Kwaśniewski had allowed himself to declare publicly that he was not cutting himself off from the Polish Peoples Republic, and Jacek Kuroń, of the Freedom Party, called an anti-Communist stand a "wrongheaded stupidity" ("zacietrzewiona glupota").

A recent issue of the *Przegląd* (August 14, 1997) deserves to be singled out on account of its rich content. As if continuing Pomian's comments, it begins with Nowak Jeziorański's deliberations about present Poland, "The Lost Decalogue" ("Zagubiony Dekalog"), followed by yet another memory trip by Jerzy Krzyżanowski, "Z generałem 'Marcinem' w Rosji" ("With General 'Martin' in Russia"), which gives additional information to what was known about the fate of General Kazimierz Tumidajski, commanding officer of the Lublin District of the Home Army. This is followed by a disturbing article about the origins of the Curzon Line (Wojciech Rostafiński, "Jak powstała Linia Curzona"), and an excellent post-mortem essay by Kazimierz Braun on "The Third Anniversary of the Death of Wojciech Wasiutyński—*Polityk, Publicysta, Historyk, Moralista*").

There are two more pertinent articles in that issue, both by known historians not for the first time appearing simultaneously in *Przegląd* in slight opposition (the other time it was a look at the merits and demerits of the Polish uprisings). Andrzej Pomian, by now practically a house-writer for the *Przegląd*, paints a picture of the Polish Underground ("Obraz Polski Podziemnej") filling gaps left by Andrzej Kunert in his books about the war and the Underground. What emerges is the duplicity and treachery of Stalin and the Polish "patriots" serving him. Reading it, anybody who had any doubts about, even love, for Stalin (and there are such among distinguished Polish historians who wept when Stalin died) shall be cured once and for all. By contrast, Marian Kamil Dziewanowski's "Krechowce" (place name which, after a battle there, gave its name to a famous cavalry regiment, commanded by Bronisław Mościcki, another nephew of the future President—see Pomian, "Na szlaku..") is an optimistic, even romantic, account of some aspects of the formation of the Polish Armed Forces during the First World War and after, forces which, coming literally from all corners of the world, eventually numbered 900,000, and *this* was the real miracle of 1920, not the battle itself!

As Pomian often does, I will add my own comments to Dziewanowski's beautiful essay. He is right in saying that:

> ... in July of 1917 the [Russian] Provisional Government under strong pressure of the Western Allies, especially France and Great Britain, forced Russia to an offensive at all cost, to save the Western Front threatened with breakdown.

But the biggest pressure was exerted by the United States, whose President, Woodrow Wilson, wanted to keep America from entering the war, which would be necessary if Russia was defeated enabling the Germans to shift forces from East to West and win the war, but not if America came in. Wilson dispatched an envoy, Senator Elihu Root, to Russia with loan offers and a simple message: "No war, no money!" A hastily prepared offensive followed, ending with a total defeat resulting in demoralization, chaos, and anarchy, just what the Bolsheviks needed to start the Revolution.

I wrote a paper at Columbia University in 1959, "American Intervention in Russian Revolution," for which I thoroughly researched the above scenario. The paper was well received, but Prof. Hazard, editor of *The Slavic Review*, advised me against publication on the ground that my thesis about the Revolution being a result of an American blunder and not a historical inevitability was taboo in Russia, and could bring trouble, even to my relatives in Poland.

I visited Poland that same year (1959) and took the paper with me. The advice I got from friends and relatives was the same as Hazard's, but I was ultimately convinced by a friendly Russian intelligence colonel with whom my family and I shared a compartment on a night train from Warsaw to Silesia, where he was going to join the entourage of Nikita Khrushchev visiting Poland. He advised me to stay away from political science and stick to language/literature. I took the advice and the paper remained unpublished.

Compared with the excellence and marvelous connotations and associations of most of the *Przegląd* essays and articles, the *Nowy Dziennik* is uneven, and the new format is not an improvement. The reporting is good, but not free of inaccuracies, which are also present in the *Przegląd*. At times the reporters don't dig deep enough, as was the case with the 17-week-long probate hearing of

Barbara Piasecka Johnson, but this may have been influenced by her being a benefactress, as pointed out by a biographer in *The New York Times Magazine*. What both publications need is a good copy reader, but that's a common complaint in all publishing and journalism.

As for the personnel, Mr. Wierzbiański's assuming the role of an elder statesman becomes him, he is after all the holder of many awards. He still writes longer pieces, but increasingly sticks to the short editorials marked "b.w." or "bw" in which he criticizes (Wspólnota Polska, Poland, Polonia), exhorts (Polish American Congress), praises (the Kosciuszko Foundation, the Polish Institute, Hippocrene Books). In his criticism he names the illness but not the cure; there is little about the environment, which could keep Poland out of the European Union, but he does sound an alarm about depopulation, Poland's nightmare.

As for his top editor, "c.k." or "ck" has a long way to go before he becomes another Ignace Morawski, whose column, "Window on America," displaying an astonishing knowledge of, and familiarity with, America, was on a Pulitzer Prize level. But journalists like Morawski, who as a young man had seen both the last Kaiser (in Poznań) and the last Czar (in Kharkov) were few and far between even in his day, and we are not likely to see their like again. Czesław Karkowski is a hard worker, and he writes on many subjects, making the impression that he is at home in all of them, which is impossible without first knowing America well, not as simple a task as one might think.

It is a pity that Mr. Wierzbiański wasn't able, or didn't want, to hold on to Irena Dubicka, whose father had worked for him for many years, writing, among others, the "Sylwetki Polonijne" ("Polonia Profiles"), mine among them. I had known her on and off for many years, and used her in a key role in my Solidarity Symposium in 1982. Raised in a journalistic atmosphere and well educated, with a doctorate in Physiological Psychology from SUNY Albany, and thoroughly Americanized, yet perfectly bilingual as a former girl scout, she could have continued as editor of the *New Horizon, Polish American Review*, a singularly uninspiring publication in content and appearance now, raising its standards and the standards of the entire enterprise that is the Bicentennial Publishing Corp.

On my last visit to the "Galleria" for the Norman Davies' *Europe: A History* program, ably conducted by Barbara Nagórska,

Mr. Wierzbiański's wife and his Executive Vice President, I congratulated him on his success, to which he replied that it was a "temporary success," which reminded me of what Marshal Piłsudski is alleged to have said to his closest associates not long before his death: "There will be war, but I won't be here, and you will lose it" [appr.]. Why should Mr. Wierzbiański be so pessimistic about his accomplishment when only two years ago he was quoted in his own daily that *Nowy Dziennik* along with Kultura (Paris) and Hippocrene Books were the three great accomplishments of postwar Polish emigration? Since Kultura lies outside our immediate sphere of interest, let us look at the other publisher of Polish reading materials in New York, namely Hippocrene Books, but first a few remarks about what it was that created a fertile ground not only for Polish books and reading materials in America but for knowledge about Poland in general: it was the Solidarity movement and Lech Wałęsa.

Looking at my own chapter, "Solidarity—A Movement Unlike Any Other" in *Poland's Solidarity Movement* co-edited by me (Loyola University of Chicago, 1984), I give credit for the beginning of the trend to Flora Lewis who, in an excellent article, "Once Again Poland is Europe's Special Case" (*The New York Times*, August 31, 1981), written during the negotiations preceding the signing of the famous Gdańsk Agreement, gives convincing arguments "why the events in Poland were so important" and why Lech Wałęsa "has become one of the best known personalities in the world in our time, if not the best, and his country, Poland, is becoming, because of him, better known abroad than at any time in its 1000-year history...."

Better knowledge of Poland was becoming a fact. FM quote:

Gone are the not so distant times when an American President (Ford) could say...that Poland was a free country; when another President (Carter) had his remarks...mistranslated in Poland by an inept translator; when America's security advisor (Richard Allen) could state in a TV interview, sympathetically but inaccurately, on the eve of what seemed like an imminent invasion of Poland by the Soviet Union, that Poland had suffered "dozens of years" of partitions; and when a TV personality (Harry Reasoner), in a hastily assembled studio panel after the attempt on the Pope's life, speculated wonderingly and naively why a "Polish" Pope had been elected in the first place, putting the anchor man (Dan Rather) in obvious discomfort and compelling this writer to phone the studio immediately to provide some reasons why. This insistence on accuracy and truth about things concerning Poland has reached even Hollywood. Meryl Streep, playing a Polish refugee in "Sophie's Choice," had to learn Polish.... Aside from the main topic of that film, this is a far cry from Hollywood's earlier "Polish" films, such as "Miracle of the Bells," in which Frank Sinatra and Alida Valli ruin a beautiful Polish song ("O gwiazdeczko"—"Oh, little star") singing it in an incomprehensible language passing for Polish. Nowhere is the insistence on accuracy and truth about Poland more in evidence than in the mushrooming publications concerning Poland. To name just a few, John Keegan's *Six Armies in Normandy* (Viking 1982) is the first true and accurate account by a non-Pole of the Polish participation in the Allied invasion of Europe; Stewart Steven's *The Poles* (Macmillan 1982), beside being accurate on the whole, is the first work by a non-Pole to put the number of Poles world-wide at 50 million,...no "small" nation.

Among other books to come out at that time was one co-authored by Michael Dobbs, K.S. Karol and Desa Trevisan, *Poland: Solidarity: Walesa* (McGraw-Hill, 1981); Jadwiga Staniszkis, *Poland's Self-Limiting Revolution* (published in France and by Princeton University Press); James Michener, *Poland* (Random House, 1983), which led to an exchange of letters between the author and this reviewer, with the former expressing an opinion that "the book will stand for Poland in western circles for years" (Michener to Mocha, 12 February 1984); Bill Kurtis (CBS, Chicago), *Bill Kurtis: On Assignment* (Rand McNally, 1983); two books dealing with the attempt on the Pope's life, one by Paul Henze, *The Plot to Kill the Pope* (Scribner's 1983), coinciding with another book about the conspiracy, Claire Sterling's *The Time of the Assassins* (Holt), and a third, based on persistent rumors about the Pope's earlier meeting with Leonid Brezhnev, the Soviet leader, a meeting described by an Italian journalist, Luigi Forni, in his book, *The Dove and the Bear*, published by Hippocrene Books.

HIPPOCRENE BOOKS publishes a broad variety of books but has established a niche for itself in foreign language dictionaries and text books, travel guides, maps of cities around the world, and a strong Polish section, due to the fact that its two principal executives are both Polish.

GEORGE BLAGOWIDOW, born in Częstochowa, Poland, in 1923, of Russian parents who had arrived in Poland in 1920. Listed in *Who Is Who in Polish America* as "publisher and author" he was educated in the University of Cracow (1945); University of Munich, Germany, and Institute Superieur de Commerce, Antwerp, Belgium (1945-1950); MBA (1953), Ph.D. (1959), Graduate School, New York University, followed by a fine career in publishing: sales manager, Doubleday & Co. (1955-62); vice president, Macmillan & Co. (1962-66); president, Funk & Wagnalls (1966-70), when he founded his own publishing company in New York City, Hippocrene Books.

Immersed in my own projects (and teaching) in New York and Chicago, and in publications connected with them, I did not become aware of Hippocrene until my involvement with Solidarity, when I discovered that Hippocrene was a Poland-friendly publisher, even if by virtue of a single publication, as I thought then, *The Dove and the Bear*, by Luigi Forni. I made the same discovery about Charles Scribner's Sons, by virtue of another single publication, Paul Henze's *The Plot to Kill the Pope* which, as I was to find out, had been pointed out by Zbigniew Brzezinski to the then president of Scribner's, Jacek Gałązka, under whose aegis it was published in 1983. I visited Gałązka on my next trip to New York from Chicago, and over lunch he told me about Hippocrene Books, just a block away from Scribner's, and George Blagowidow, whom he recommended as publisher of my own writings. I did not get around to it until I left Chicago and returned to New York; by then Gałązka had already left Scribner's and was immersed in Wiesław Kuniczak's monumental translation of Sienkiewicz's *Trilogy* as publisher of Hippocrene Books.

JACEK MICHAŁ GAŁĄZKA, born in 1924 (another of the "Pope's generation" of which there are still many active) in Wilno, Poland, arrived in the United Stated in 1952. Listed in *Who is Who in Polish America* as publisher/editor. Educated at University of Edinburgh, Scotland, 1948 (B.Com. [Commerce? Communications?]) for a career, like Blagowidow, entirely in publishing: marketing director, St. Martin's Press (1955-63); Charles Scribner's Sons, 1963-1985: manager, Reference Department (1963-67), marketing director (1967-74), executive vice president, publ. (1974-83), pres. (1983-85); Macmillan Publishing Co., vice pres., publ. (1985-6); publisher, Hippocrene Books, Polish Heritage Publishing (1986-).

Like Blagowidow, Gałązka is also an author, but unlike Blagowidow, who writes fiction, Gałązka translates from Polish literature (Stanisław Jerzy Lec), authors an *American Phrasebook for Poles*, co-authors a *Polish Heritage Travel Guide to U.S.A. & Canada* and edits the yearly *Polish Heritage Calendar* since 1986, in other words, everything he does is serving the Polish American community.

The two men, president and publisher of Hippocrene Books respectively, are a good team. Exact contemporaries, separated by a few months only, they have no generational differences, but similar memories and backgrounds, which is of great help in selecting materials for publication. Here is what Gałązka says about these materials in a letter to *Nowy Dziennik* in answer to its reporter complaining about a "tragic" lack of books in English on Polish subjects:

> ... As it happens, at the Polish Institute's Conference where the interview had taken place, there was a stand of Hippocrene Books and Polish Heritage Publications which specialize in the area in which we have published so far over 50 items....

Among the items, in addition to Blagowidow's "Pulaski detour" (Leszek Szymański's biography *Casimir Pulaski: A Hero of the American Revolution*) and Gałązka's special projects, are Iwo Cyprian Pogonowski's dictionaries and his *Poland: A Historical Atlas*; Adam Zamoyski's excellent histories: *The Polish Way: A Thousand-Year History of the Poles and Their Culture* and *Forgotten Few: The Polish Air Force in the Second World War*; Ewa Kurek's *Your Life is Worth Mine*, with an introduction by Jan Karski; Richard C. Lukas, *Did The Children Cry? Hitler's War Against Jewish & Polish Children*; retold by F.C. Anstruther, *Old Polish Legends*; George Blagowidow, *The Last Train to Berlin*; plus Polish song books, love poems, cookbooks, herbs and folk medicine, and Jerzy Krzyżanowski, ed., *The Trilogy Companion, A Reader's Guide to the "Trilogy" of Henryk Sienkiewicz*. "The greatest literary undertaking in the history of Polonia produced the greatest success for a Polish book in America. The enormous eight-year labor of W.S. Kuniczak has brought a strong chorus of praise from book reviewers in America" [Hippocrene publicity]. This should be a good argument for the A. Jurzykowski Award.

This writer finds only one item below the high standards of Hippocrene Books, namely Józef Garliński's *Poland in the Second World War* (1985). Poor writing and editing obscure the meaning of this important project, which is a great pity, because in Chapter 1,

"The Outbreak of War," in the sub-chapter "German Proposals to Poland," Garliński discusses the possibility of Germany attacking the West first, a possibility unfortunately not explored sufficiently by Poland, as Garliński points out, and he seems to know what he is talking about and how important the German proposals were as a means for Poland to save itself or at least postpone the attack by not rejecting them outright, as was the case. These passages should have been written in the clearest language in order not to leave any doubt in the reader's mind as to their exact meaning.

C. DICTIONARY OF POLISH LITERATURE
Edited by E.J. Czerwiński
Commentary by Frank Mocha

The most remarkable thing about this dictionary is that it proves the wisdom of the old saying, "better late than never." Such a dictionary had been proposed twenty years earlier by the present reviewer who, as Chairman of the Literary Section of the Polish Institute of Arts and Sciences, wanted to start a publication program of needed texts, beginning with a Dictionary of Polish Literature. It was to be a paperback like the *Dictionary of Russian Literature* (Philosophical Library, 1956, reprinted in 1971 in hard cover by Greenwood Press Inc., Westport, CT) by Professor William Harkins, my one-time adviser at Columbia University; the incentive to go ahead with the project was an expectation that it would be as useful as the Russian dictionary. The expectation seemed justified when after an initial announcement of the project in *The Polish Review* there was an avalanche of letters from members of the Literary Section offering to write individual entries.

There was another incentive. Just around the time of Harkins' dictionary's second edition, a book landed on my desk from Poland, *Polscy pisarze współcześni, Informator 1944-1970* (*Polish Contemporary Writers, Informant 1944-70*), a new edition, expanded, compiled by Lesław M. Bartelski, published by Agencja Autorska (Author Agency), Warsaw 1972. The receipt of the book by me coincided with a visit to Columbia by Jarosław Iwaszkiewicz, one of Poland's better writers and a very productive one. I was already after my doctorate at Columbia, but I would always try and attend such meetings. This time I had a good reason: to show the book. The meeting was surprisingly small, next to me just a few graduate students and only one faculty member, George Shevelov, a Ukrainian professor of Slavic Linguistics (with a sound knowledge of Polish which he demonstrated in his course on the "History of Polish Language," offered once every two or three years taking turns with Russian, Czech, Ukrainian and Byelorussian). He also taught the history of Common Slavic (before it split into separate languages) and Old Church Slavonic, the literary language after the split, and a new course, "History of Russian Literary Language." He was an amazing scholar, and I don't think we will see his like again in the Slavic field. It did not surprise me to see him display a good knowledge of Polish literature in the meeting, and considerable interest in the book.

But the man who was even more interested in the book was our visitor, who wanted to know first of all if he was in it. When I showed him that his entry occupied two double-columned pages he checked them quickly complaining that not all his works had been included. His complaint and his earlier uncertainty about being included made me think and, returning home, I subjected the book to a close scrutiny. I soon noticed an exclusion, that of Czesław Miłosz, and I started reading Bartelski's introduction, looking for criteria for inclusion.

Bartelski goes to great pains explaining his book. In a typical official formula, the 3-page "Word from the Author" ("Od autora") begins with July 22, 1944 (the date of the establishment in Lublin, after its "liberation" by the Red Army, of the "Lublin Committee" acting as the Provisional Government of Poland), and how Polish culture had been enriched since then by many valuable works contributing lasting values to contemporary literature. He then goes on about the role played in that process by the writers, which is the reason why the book, appearing for the second time, is dedicated to them.

The first *Informator*, published in 1970, proved to be extremely needed, becoming in a sense a bestseller publication. The author had expected it, aware of the lack of this type of book broadening the knowledge of literature and of its creators. Hence the idea to publish it, without claiming for it the rank of a scholarly work, but important in everyday life as a source of information. After all, membership in the Polish Writers Union changed every year, in 1969-1970 alone 115 new members had been admitted (232 in the last five years), and there was also a considerable number of new works. Bartelski insists that the *Informator* has above all a practical purpose: to give the biographies and creative output in the years 1944-1970 of members of the Polish Writers Union—the only criterion for inclusion.

Bartelski goes to great pains explaining also why, having no possibility nor competence to widen the circle of writers, it was necessary to rely in the gathering of data for the book on materials from the ZLP [Polish acronym for the Polish Writers Union], which was also the advice of some critics after the first edition. He also assumes that since belonging to ZLP is a voluntary act governed only by statutory rules, he had no right, nor duty to include in his *Informator* people who were not members of ZLP. He was saying it to anticipate any misunderstandings arising—as he thought—from faulty reading of his remarks.

Then he goes on to say what the *Informator* is not. It is not a dictionary or an encyclopedia. It concerns itself neither with the characteristics of individual writers nor even more so with their evaluation. It gives concise names and full bibliographies, facilitating orienting oneself to the output of writers listed in it. But it should not substitute for such a publication as the *Dictionary of Contemporary Polish Writers* (*Słownik współczesnych pisarzy polskich*) prepared by the Institute of Literary Research whose goal and purpose must be a more comprehensive and fuller portrayal of Polish literature.

The 1972 edition consisted of 1200 names of writers (poets, prose writers, authors of stage works, authors of reportages, critics, and translators) who were members of the Union of Polish Writers in December, 1970, together with those who after that date resigned from the Union or whose names were crossed out by the Board for statutory reasons. But some were left in, and others added.

Bartelski decided to leave in the names of some outstanding writers, either fallen after July 22, 1944, or deceased after the war. In any case, in accordance with the postulates of the readers as well as critics, he broadened the list. It is difficult to imagine contemporary Polish literature without the works of Krzysztof Kamil Baczyński, Tadeusz Gajcy, Juliusz Kaden Bandrowski, Tadeusz Borowski, Władysław Broniewski, Maria Dąbrowska, or Zofia Nałkowska, and many others, he argued, deciding also to add to the *Informator* Polish writers living abroad, who are not ZLP members but publish their works in Poland [Kołakowski?].

The information about writers in the *Informator* is quite extensive. It includes: (1) first and family name (or literary pseudonym); (2) date and place of birth (or death); (3) education; (4) date of debut in periodicals; (5) year of first book and its title (for writers whose debut took place before 1944); (6) prewar activity and under occupation if it had a public character (resistance movement, armed forces, cultural underground, secret teaching, repressions from the occupant, and others). What the *Informator* did not include was public positions occupied by writers (except Sejm deputy) and state decorations received by them, but literary prizes and awards were included.

The information consists of two basic parts. The biographical data was based on personal questionnaires filled out for the Polish Writers Union and updated, while the bibliographic data was taken from the alphabetical catalogue of the Polish National Library, the most reliable institution in that respect. The bibliographic data was brought up to December 31, 1970.

How much simpler by comparison Professor Harkins' *Dictionary* is, a difference between free and controlled literature, no matter how well the control was disguised by statutory rules of the Polish Writers Union. Bartelski's extensive explanation of his book in the introductory essay differs from Harkins' brief "Preface" by the amount of detail and justifications of certain decisions, compared to the concise manner in which Harkins outlines the purpose of his book:

> The present work seeks to provide in a compact form essential information on the entire field of Russian literature, as well as much information on literary criticism, journalism, philosophy, theater, and related subjects.

This was exactly how I wanted to approach the Polish dictionary project except, unlike Harkins who, like Bartelski, did all the work by himself, I was going to rely to a great extent on contributions from members of the Literary Section, particularly of articles dealing with periods and genres in the history of Polish literature. As a matter of fact Harkins, too, had certain articles written by others: "Drama and Theater" (Martha Bradshaw Manheim); "Philosophy" (George Kline); "Literature, Soviet" (Rufus W. Mathewson, Jr.); "Criticism, Soviet" (Edward J. Brown); and general help from Rose Raskin and Leon Stilman.

At the next Board meeting of the Literary Section I announced my decision to follow the style and format of the *Dictionary of Russian Literature* for our dictionary. To my surprise, there was opposition, from a member who, as a recent arrival from Poland, had grandiose ideas to follow the style of the *Dictionary of Contemporary Polish Writers*, an extensive and broader work put out by the Institute of Literary Research. When I pointed out to him what an immense work it would have to be to cover the entire field of Polish literature, not just contemporary, he didn't seem to be aware of the problems involved, nor of the need to produce something smaller, and as useful as Harkins' dictionary, quickly. American ways were foreign to him, and he eventually returned to Poland, but while here he effectively blocked the project, which was at first postponed, to the great disappointment of those eager to contribute to it, and, as far as I was concerned, abandoned with the arrival of the Bicentennial and projects connected with it. Yet, it could have been done before that, one of my great regrets. With the Literary Section out of my hands after my departure to Chicago, the project was never resumed, until it was taken up, *independently*, by Edward Czerwiński twenty years later!

Looking now at Czerwiński's *Dictionary of Polish Literature* (Greenwood Press, 1994), and William Harkins' *Dictionary of Russian Literature* (reprinted in 1971), it is difficult not to notice the similarities. To begin with, the same publisher, same format and style, and similar general appearance, which lead one to think that Czerwiński was very familiar with Harkins' book and probably used it as a model to some extent, which is nothing to be ashamed of. On the contrary, it puts his book in perspective by establishing the only link between it and the project of 20 years earlier which was also to have followed Harkins' lead. After these similarities, everything else is dissimilar.

Czerwiński's book, very well funded (IREX, NEH, USIA and US Dept. of State), is superior in a physical sense. At 6 1/4" x 9 1/2" it is somewhat larger than Harkins' book, and its fine but slightly smaller typeface augments the superiority as do also the 464 pages of text proper versus 439. The cover of his book is more elaborate.

The differences in conception are spelled out in the 3-page "Introduction" which the Editor begins with a passage about the dramatic circumstances at the start of his book:

> Work on the present volume began in 1986, at a time when the entire population of Poland seemed to be on strike. Most scholars refused to collaborate on any project, even one as non-political as a *Dictionary of Polish Literature*, meant primarily for an English-speaking audience. They were, in a word, demoralized....
>
> The first draft of the *Dictionary* was completed in December 1989. Factual material was supplied by those scholars who contributed to the two-volume *Literatura Polska: Przewodnik Encyklopedyczny* (*Polish Literature: Encyclopedic Guidebook*), edited by Czeslaw Hernas and Julian Krzyzanowski.

Published in 1984-85, the encyclopedia, unfortunately, was dated long before it was published. Censorship prohibited an honest evaluation of many writers' work and the inclusion of controversial figures. It was not until the triumph of Solidarity that Polish scholars awakened from their lethargy. As a result the first draft of the *Dictionary* became obsolete and our efforts had to be redirected to an honest, open reevaluation of Polish writers and Polish literature and culture in general.

What remains of the first draft are the general format, the biographical and factual material, and the entries. Even in the original plans, of course, controversial authors were included. After 1990, however, critical evaluation was unhindered by censorship, and materials on banned authors became available.

The Editor was "fortunate in obtaining the services of outstanding specialists...who," together with him, "wrote the entries, supervised final revisions, and established contacts with numerous Polish scholars who contributed to the final draft of the book." Since no affiliations are given, these people are not listed here, for fear they might be confused with their namesakes. The Editor adds:

> No caveats were imposed on the work of these scholars, except a reminder that the book was intended for an English-speaking audience with a very limited knowledge of Polish literature. The editors also hoped that scholars would find the book useful. In order to effect this delicate balance the format of each entry includes information that will prove useful to both layman and scholar: in the case of authors, name, date of birth and death, a brief biographical review of the author's works, and in-depth discussion of the author's most important and most representative work, and a brief statement regarding the author's development, his or her use of themes, his or her place within the Polish tradition, and his or her importance in world literature.

It is not clear further what is meant by "bibliography for each section." There is a "General Reference Bibliography" at the end of the book, and "a great deal of information on each subject can be found in the primary bibliographical source given after each entry. The entry itself, however, was compiled and critically analyzed by the cited scholar (where appropriate) or by the Editor. The Editor takes full responsibility for changes made in submitted entries and for all critical analyses of literary works," but he admits that "without the earnest work of Polish scholars, past and present, this dictionary would have been impossible to complete within one's lifetime," a surprising admission meaning probably one's "remaining time."

The work also includes entries for literary periods, universities, individual works, major publications, and movements.

The Editor makes a point that "it has only been in recent years (post-World War II) that American scholars have contributed significantly to Polish scholarship," then starts listing them, and it turns out that they are all Polish scholars active in America, or in Poland and translated into English. He begins the list with a big name:

> Perhaps the most important figure in this regard is the Polish scholar Manfred Kridl, whose *A Survey of Polish Literature and Culture*, translated from the Polish by Olga Scherer-Virski (The Hague: Mouton and Company, Printers, 1956), and anthology of Polish literature provided young American students of Polish descent [only? *FM*] the opportunity to discover the riches of a country that was almost erased from the map of Europe.

The list includes the late "Wiktor Weintraub, Professor of Polish Literature at Harvard University, known especially for his work on Adam Mickiewicz (*The Poetry of Adam Mickiewicz* [The Hague, 1954]); Czesław Miłosz, the Nobel Prize recipient, Professor Emeritus of Polish Literature at the University of California at Berkeley (*The History of Polish Literature* [London and New York: 1969]); as well as scores [?] of excellent American scholars who are cited in this volume..." but excludes Wacław Lednicki for reasons unclear to this commentator but strong enough to alert him to look for other exclusions in the book.

The Editor includes two recent volumes of Polish criticism now available in English: Julian Krzyżanowski, *A History of Polish Literature*, translated by Doris Ronowicz (Warsaw: PWN-Polish Scientific Publishers, 1978), and Bogdan Suchodolski, *A History of Polish Culture*, translated by E.J. Czerwiński (Warsaw, Interpress Publishers, 1986). He also includes a hope that this volume [which? ambig. *FM*] will contribute to the further study of Polish literature. Then he voices his most important acknowledgements:

> The editor would like to express his sincere gratitude to Grzegorz Boguta, director of Polish Scientific Publishers (PWN), for permitting use of material from the two volumes, *Literatura*

Polska: Przewodnik Encyklopedyczny [*Polish Literature: En-cyclopedic Guidebook*], edited by Czeslaw Hernas and a core of Poland's finest scholars. Without the encouragement, scholarly guidance, concern, and interest of Professor Hernas, this book could not have been completed. I humbly dedicate it to my friend and mentor.

After these very sincere and humble words of gratitude and of generous dedication (p. ix), the book moves to the text proper listing in alphabetical order the entries (p. 1), of which, after checking the Index, there are about 1600.

Sixteen hundred entries is a somewhat disappointing number, if we recall that Lesław Bartelski's *Polish Contemporary Writers* has 1200 entries just for the years 1944-1970. The question arises of what were the Editor's criteria for inclusion, and how good were the "services of outstanding specialists...who, together with him, wrote the entries, supervised final revisions, and established contacts with numerous Polish scholars who contributed to the final draft of the book"? I can see leaving out Bartelski (he is only mentioned once, in a group of writers who *also* "published significant works" in the 60's and 70's), but not Lednicki! For reasons known only to the author, Lednicki is also absent in Miłosz's *History*, and so is Weintraub (left out in Czerwiński's *Dictionary* proper) and, for that matter, Kridl (very much present in the *Dictionary*, which would rule out the possibility of Czerwiński following Miłosz). But, just for argument's sake, why would Miłosz ignore what were undoubtedly three stars of Polish literature in America after World War II, before his arrival on the scene? Was he making a statement that he was the only star (his *History* came out long before his Nobel), or was it because the three had something he didn't—a doctorate? These are speculations I leave for others to dwell on. I am more concerned with the exclusion from the *Dictionary* of writers who appeal to me personally, as well as to others.

Among the writers I almost resent not seeing, eager to know more about them because they were my boyhood companions, is first of all Maria Rodziewiczówna. I can almost hear snickers about F.M.'s lowbrow literary tastes, but let us remember it is Polish literature we are talking about, in which Sienkiewicz-Mickiewicz reign supreme, not Przybyszewski, or Witkacy. When the "Polish Daily *Zgoda*" in Chicago ran the "Trilogy" in installments, the paper's circulation went up. It went up again when the "Trilogy" was

followed by the novels of Rodziewiczówna. I used to clip the install-
ments, bind them together, and give them to my best students of
Polish as prizes. The paper's editor at that time was Anna
Rychlińska, who had a master's degree in Polish literature and
certainly knew what the public liked to read. Later on, my neighbor
in New York, Dr. Edmund Osysko, a former school principal in
Poland and a writer, would call a large beautiful tree in Morningside
Park next to a bench we often sat on during our meetings on Fridays
"Dewajtis," that's how strong a hold Rodziewiczówna has on her
readers. I feel almost as strongly about Janusz Meissner (*Szkoła orląt*
[*The School of Eaglets*]), whose popular books about flying surely
had something to do with Polish pilots' successes in international
competitions before the war and their unmatched wartime combat
record in the Battle of Britain; and Wacław Gąsiorowski (*Huragan*,
Księżna Łowicka [*Hurricane*, *Princess Lowicki*], for his presentation
of history in a light manner, directing the reader to serious histories.
I regret not seeing in the *Dictionary* Kornel Makuszyński, another
boyhood companion, whose humor I found infectious, and even
Antoni Marczyński, whom I met in a POW camp in Germany, and
enjoyed hearing—a marvelous raconteur. Russian writers of that
caliber are present in Harkins' *Dictionary*, making it richer.

   An elitist in everything else, I have a democratic approach to
literature: it should serve the greatest number of readers, and that's
what the works of Sienkiewicz and Mickiewicz were written for and
dedicated to. Skill is the key element. Art for art's sake had been
denounced before, but there is room for it as long as it does not push
out popular literature. How inclusive should a *Dictionary* be?

   This commentator (*not* a reviewer) found the section on
universities (pp. 418-25 and elsewhere) rewarding but confusing,
mainly because of the placement of the entries either under the letter
"U" or by location. Thus we have the new Polish universities
(Gdańsk, Katowice, Łódź, Wrocław), together with the "old"
(Poznań, Warsaw, Lwów, Wilno) with the last two no longer in
Poland and two others, the Jagiellonian in Cracow and Catholic in
Lublin placed separately, as is the new Marie Curie in Lublin. But it
is the old University of Wilno which demands our attention because
it was the stage for the most important chapter in Polish-Russian
relations, with three of the most important figures in the history of
the relations, Prince Adam Czartoryski, the historian Joachim

Lelewel, and the poet Adam Mickiewicz, all involved in one way or another with the University and its subsequent demise.

A considerable part of this writer's doctoral dissertation on Tadeusz Bułharyn (Faddej Venediktovich Bulgarin), a Polish-born influential journalist and writer in Russia, and another figure in the drama as translator of Lelewel's criticism of Karamzin's official *History of the Russian State* (which, incidentally, became the material for this writer's article, "The Karamzin-Lelewel Controversy," in *The Slavic Review* and a chapter in his dissertation), deals with the Wilno drama. Although the entry in the *Dictionary* is sufficient for its purposes, the importance of the topic and the present absence of scholarship on Polish-Russian relations makes the inclusion of pertinent background passages from the dissertation mandatory.

> Wilno, once the capital of the Grand Duchy of Lithuania, became, in the period under review, one of the most important cities in the Russian Empire. Its new importance was the result of the reorganization of Russia in 1802, chiefly along the recommendations provided by Prince Adam Czartoryski, when eight ministries were formed. Czartoryski, beside heading the Foreign Affairs Ministry, became also member of the council for schools in the Ministry of Education (whose first head was the Polish-educated Zawadowski). The new ministry's model, in the absence of any Russian tradition, was the former Polish Commission for National Education, founded in 1773, the first modern Ministry of Education in Europe. ...Russia was divided into six school districts of which Wilno, with the densest network of educational institutions in all of Russia, was one. The Wilno district, very characteristically conceived under Czartoryski's influence, included not only all the provinces taken by Russia in the partitions, but also provinces which had belonged to Poland in the more distant past. Thus Wilno became a cultural center for an area much larger than before the partitions. The curator of the huge district became Czartoryski himself who held that position from 1803 until 1824, throughout almost the entire reign of Alexander I. The headquarters of his educational activity was the University of Wilno.
>
> Wilno's most important educational institution has also acquired a new importance. The former Jesuit Academy, founded in 1579 became, through a charter of 1803, the Imperial University of Wilno. With Czartoryski's guidance, and under the leadership of carefully selected chancellors, the University reached great heights, attaining the highest level in the Russian Empire and ranking with the best institutions in Western

Europe. Its professors were permitted considerable freedom in their work; their activities often extended beyond the academic subjects they taught. The University was also taking full advantage of the liberal winds blowing at that time in Russia. In a few years this would change, but meanwhile the University was like a magnet attracting the best minds in Poland and Lithuania.

The University's excellence became Czartoryski's special concern once his other official duties came to an end, and particularly when he realized that Poland was not going to be restored in its entirety in a union with Russia under Alexander which he advocated, nor would even the Lithuanian provinces be united with the Congress Kingdom [result of Karamzin's famous "Protest of a Russian Citizen" to Alexander]. Meanwhile the University, and other higher schools in the Wilno district, was producing intelligentsia far in excess of the local needs, and beginning to export the surplus into Russia proper. The long-range purpose of this policy was to make up through education what was lost at conference tables. The ultimate aim of this plan was to assure Polish intellectual and cultural primacy within the Russian Empire. This was precisely the accusation leveled against Czartoryski later by his Russian enemy, Senator Novosilcev, who went as far as to declare that the whole purpose of the huge enterprise that was the Wilno center of learning was nothing less than a Machiavellian-Wallenrodian scheme (reference to a poem by Mickiewicz with a Machiavellian theme) by Czartoryski to capture Russia from within. The accusation was not entirely without foundations.

The rest is history, with the *Filomats* receiving most attention, because of Mickiewicz, while Lelewel's attack on Karamzin, engineered by Bulgarin, and Prince Czartoryski's grand design are known only to specialists, but deserve to be made known to a wider audience, for obvious reasons.

A few technical points. The Editor had a fine idea of starting every letter in his alphabetical sequence of entries on an odd page number. This should have been carried further by ending each letter on an even page, in this way not leaving blank pages. I did this successfully with *Poles in America*, occasionally adding or editing out a line or two to accomplish it and give the book an orderly appearance and an air of efficiency. A case in point in the *Dictionary* is page 49, which has one "Bibliography" item consisting of two lines followed by two blank pages, looking as if there was a major break in the book. That item should have been accommodated on the previous page or a new name included for that letter to fill the blank page.

There is also the inevitable mistake, a little embarrassing but not unusual when dealing with languages. A little-noticed mistake of that kind can be seen in a book by a well-known Polish American scholar who had rendered "Panorama Racławicka" as "Panorama by Raclawicki," making two errors in the process. The mistake in the *Dictionary* is of lesser gravity, simply leaving a proper name in its Polish grammatical case, in this case the genitive plural in memoirs of the "Maskiewiczów" brothers, which should have been rendered "Maskiewicz" (p.16). This type of mistake is encountered frequently with street names in the growing number of reports from Poland, and it is excusable in that context.

As if to underline whose ultimate responsibility the *Dictionary* is, there is only one name at the end:

ABOUT THE EDITOR:

E.J. CZERWIŃSKI is Professor Emeritus of Slavic and Comparative Literature at the State University of New York at Stony Brook. His many articles have appeared in journals such as *The Polish Review, Comparative Drama, Modern Drama, World Literature Today.* His books include *Contemporary Polish Theatre and Drama, 1956-84* (Greenwood Press, 1988).

A gap in important materials for Polish Studies in America has now been filled and an earlier neglect at last made up. That's an accomplishment. Thank you, Edward Czerwiński!

D. POLISH PARTICIPATION IN THE BATTLE OF NORMANDY (D-DAY) AND IN WORLD WAR II

A 50th Anniversary lecture* given at the Institute on East Central Europe, Columbia University, New York, June 29, 1994.

* * * *

First, I want to apologize for my emaciated appearance, but I am recovering from a serious surgery and this is my first public appearance, so please bear with me. I chose today's date, three weeks after the anniversary, for two reasons: 55 years ago today we celebrated with my family in Poland my father's nameday *and* 50th birthday; we also celebrated my graduation from Gymnasium. The day-long festivities surrounding the double celebration—including father's hobby, the amateur orchestra that awakened us on that memorable Sunday—were clouded by a prevailing feeling that this would be the last family gathering and that, like the protagonists in Mickiewicz's epic poem *Pan Tadeusz* more than a century earlier, we too were experiencing many good things of life for the last time as we entered the summer of 1939, because almost everyone in Poland believed that war with Germany was inevitable, with all the sorrows and upheavals that wars bring.

The second reason for today's date is that around that time 50 years ago the First Polish Armored Division landed in Normandy from England, going immediately into action in the vicinity of Caen, and then Falaise. Units of the former Polish Navy had been active in the English Channel since D-Day, as part of the Allied Armada, and Polish pilots, both fighter and bomber, had been active over Normandy and beyond even before D-Day.

How did Poland manage to have such formidable forces, placing them fourth after American, British and Canadian in the Operation Overlord, and third over-all in the West if we count the remaining Polish units still in England (Polish Airborne Brigade and Commando units) and the Second Polish Corps in Italy, forces that dwarf

---

* The lecture, shortly after life-threatening oral surgery at the Memorial Sloan-Kettering Cancer Center, was a test whether I could still function as a scholar, writer, and lecturer. After speaking for an hour, and then playing ping-pong following a reception in my apartment, I was declared fit by all present. The lecture is reproduced here as it was delivered, which was an accomplishment.

the Polish Legions of the Napoleonic Wars (which gave Poland its national anthem)? The British historian of the Second World War, John Keegan, puts it well in *Six Armies in Normandy* when he says that "the Poles never give up," but there was more to it than that. To understand what it was and to set the record straight for the benefit of the younger generations, just as the American D-Day veterans are doing now, we must get a clear picture of Poland's role in World War II, which is the wider purpose of this paper.

The tragedy of the Second World War happening at all was what I would call leadership inflation. Great leaders of the previous world conflict, Wilson, Lenin (it is interesting to speculate how he would have behaved this time), Clemenceau and Foch, were either dead or politically dead (Churchill) or dying (Hindenburg, Piłsudski). When President Hindenburg died, Hitler became undisputed master of Germany, having already before (1933) been nominated its Chancellor. Marshal Piłsudski saw the danger and proposed to the French a preventive action against Germany, whose forces were still very small. But this was a different France, of ineffective military leaders, like Gamelin, while its best military commanders, Petain and Weygand, were posted abroad, and of civilian leaders who would rather appease than take action. Piłsudski's proposal was turned down. There is no documentary proof of the Polish proposal and French reply, but everybody in Poland was talking about it, based on what? At any rate, that same year (1934) Poland signed a non-aggression treaty with Germany to secure itself, but also giving Germany security from its only vulnerable border. Germany immediately entered upon a massive build-up of its armed forces and, with Piłsudski dead at the age 67 in 1935, started a series of occupations (the Saar and the Rhineland) and annexations (Austria, Czech Sudetenland, Memel). When the rest of Czechoslovakia was dismembered early in 1939, Germany began to make demands on Poland. Having learned the lesson of Munich the previous year, the French and British appeasers (Daladier, Chamberlain) backed Poland's resolve to reject German demands. Who knows how Hitler would have behaved towards Poland had Piłsudski still lived?

When the war came in September, it came with a violence unanticipated, especially by the young in Poland, who considered themselves invincible. Not so in the West, where England was taking out of Poland just before the war its excellent anti-aircraft guns for the defense of London (one can ponder on *that*) and Gamelin offered the only viable war plan he had, to abandon western and northern Poland, defend Warsaw at all costs and retreat in the direction of south-eastern Poland, there to create a bridge to Rumania through which France would supply Poland. This plan fell through when the Soviet Union entered Poland along its entire eastern border and began disarming Polish units unsure of Soviet intentions. In retrospect, one wonders if the Molotov-Ribbentrop agreement a month earlier had not been concluded just to prevent the Rumanian connection. The Germans were in a hurry to finish the Polish campaign in order to discourage the French and British, in a state of war with Germany since September 3, from attacking it. In this, they succeeded.

There began an evacuation from Poland of soldiers, sailors, and pilots, many of whom, five years later, would be in the Battle of Normandy, having survived other battles. It was not an exodus, or escape from Poland, it was an exit by trained men going to fight another day in a war which was evolving into a world war, to the surprise of Hitler who had not foreseen this evolution in a war, moreover, which was started in Poland.

In Poland itself, almost immediately after the September campaign, an underground army was started, which was to grow into the biggest underground army in occupied Europe. This army cooperated closely and was part of the Armed Forces of the Polish Government-in-Exile (formed on October 1) whose Prime Minister and Commander-in-Chief was General Sikorski, who broadcast over French radio an appeal to Poles all over the world to join him. His appeal was answered immediately, first by Polish soldiers interned in Rumania and Hungary, and then by volunteers who had heard it, and by Poles living in France who, as conscripts, had an option to serve in the Polish, rather than the French, Army. But it was not only soldiers who were arriving in France. A team of Polish mathematicians (and Poland was famous for mathematicians) started working on the German code "Enigma," and succeeded in breaking it. This was an extremely important accomplishment (for which Poland does not get credit, as seen on a recent *60 Minutes* television program), which was one of the decisive factors in the war.

As we can see, the September campaign was not a total defeat in a total war. And there was more, showing that somebody was thinking in Poland. An order was issued to the Polish Air Force and Polish Navy, neither a match for their German counterparts except in individual combat, to evacuate to England. While the war was still raging in Poland, some Polish pilots were allegedly arriving in England in their own planes, and those whose planes were destroyed on the ground at dawn on September 1, were speedily dispatched from internment camps in Rumania and Hungary to France and then to England, strengthening the Royal Air Force (RAF), on which so much depended. The evacuation of the Polish Navy is a story of hit-and-run, hide-and-seek and Polish bravado, all of which were needed in a highly dangerous operation resulting in some destroyers and other warships (submarines), some merchant ships, and even passenger ships, reaching English ports. Among the latter was the pride of Poland, the liner *Piłsudski*, the same ship which had carried the Polish Olympic team to Los Angeles in 1932, and was now put to service ferrying troops from Australia, and getting sunk by a German U-Boat off the coast of South Africa.

In France, Sikorski's army grew rapidly. Soon there were two divisions ready and two more forming, a motorized Brigade under General Maczek, future commander of the First Armored Division, and a mountain brigade under General Szyszko-Bohusz, which was sent with an Allied Expeditionary Force to Norway after the German invasion of Denmark and Norway, and landed in Narvik, from which it had to retreat after some fighting and return to France, where an imminent attack was expected after the German invasion of Holland and Belgium on May 10, 1940.

The danger produced changes in the Allied command structure. Chamberlain resigned and was replaced by Churchill, and Weygand was recalled from Syria to take over from Gamelin. But it was too little, too late. When Hans Guderian's tank columns broke through the Ardennes, they not only reached the English Channel, driving the French before them, but they cut off the British Expeditionary Force at Dunkerque. In this situation the Polish Army could not make a difference, since it was misused from the beginning, treated like the Americans in the First World War until Pershing put his foot down and used his Americans as he saw fit.

Sikorski did not put his foot down. Yet, his army, composed of battle-tested veterans and enthusiastic volunteers, was probably the best force in demoralized France. If augmented by the crack French mountain troops, wasted on the Italian border, and the always battle-ready Foreign Legion units, the Polish divisions could have been expanded into a powerful corps and, with support elements, into a force equal to an independent army. If that force was put into tanks, and France had plenty of tanks even if not of the best quality, and whipped in a hurry into a tank force by Maczek, then placed opposite the vulnerable and unprotected Ardennes gap, it would have crossed the path of Guderian's columns and at least slowed them down, giving Weygand a chance to regroup and start a counteroffensive in a classic maneuver which he had seen and probably advised in the Battle of Warsaw in 1920, as the head of the French mission during Tukhachevski's invasion of Poland.

Why didn't Sikorski do it? To spare his soldiers? He lost most of them anyway in France. Or did the French not allow it? If the latter is true, the French would have made the same mistake Napoleon did during his 1812 invasion of Russia, when he scattered the Polish Army among the various components of the Grand Armee instead of keeping it together like an iron fist, and lost the war because of that, as the French Resident in Warsaw reproached him for during the hasty retreat. We will never know.

It is hard to tell whether Sikorski's desperate stand would have saved France by lifting the spirits of the French who were demoralized further by another development. Anticipating an attack through Belgium, France had offered to place its troops on the German-Belgian border, a good move, but incomprehensibly not accepted by Belgium, which was having a try at appeasement, forgetting the scenario of World War I, with fatal results. Thus, another delaying tactic did not materialize and it was little Belgium which speeded and probably caused the doom of France.

Still, just as the campaign in Poland, the campaign in France was not a total loss for the Poles. When Sikorski gave an order to evacuate via the Atlantic and Mediterranean ports, only Maczek's Brigade made it, because it was on wheels. Of the two divisions, the First was almost totally lost. The Second, in south-east France, evacuated into Switzerland except for its Reconnaissance Group [this writer's unit], which escorted the division to the border and, while protecting its crossing, was cut off by the Germans. Some of its motorized elements managed to reach Grenoble, and then Marseilles. The division itself, commanded by General Prugar-Ketling, entered into extensive educational and military programs, producing engineers and legal experts, while also becoming a part of the Swiss defense network. Overall, the French disaster was highly depressing. France in 1940 was a "Fallen Idol" for the Poles, who cured themselves of the earlier infatuation. England was now the goal and, luckily for all concerned, elements of the Third and Fourth Polish Divisions, forming near the Atlantic ports, were able to evacuate by sea to England. There they were assigned to protect the North Sea coast, where a German invasion could be expected. But it was the pilots who entered into life-and-death struggle with the German Luftwaffe when the Battle of Britain began in August of 1940.

The Battle of Britain was the moment of truth for England, which was now reduced to only one ally—the Poles. The Polish pilots made the difference. Churchill's famous saying: "Never in the field of human conflict was so much owed by so many to so few," applies partially to them. The ratio of German planes shot down over England by the Poles was high, some say as high as 30%, due to a daring method of air combat. The Polish pilots attacked head on, like playing chicken, forcing the German adversary to swerve at the last moment, exposing a wider target and getting shot down. It is no exaggeration to say that without the Polish pilots the Battle of Britain would have been lost, and with it, the war. A veteran British pilot said as much at the ceremonies in Poland marking the 50th anniversary of the outbreak of the war: "Without your boys, we couldn't have made it," end of quote. But there is even stronger proof than a veteran's statement. By the time Göring decided to switch the Luftwaffe's attacks from military installations and airfields to civilian targets, the Royal Air Force had been reduced to such low level that it couldn't defend itself effectively another day, a fact the Germans would have discovered on that day. Without the Polish pilots, that day would have arrived earlier, with fatal results.

With Britain safe, the war moved to the Mediterranean, a British lifeline threatened by Mussolini's Italy and uncertainty about Franco's Spain vis-à-vis Gibraltar. In the huge struggle, helped quietly by America, Polish air and naval units were also active. The Polish Carpathian Brigade was fighting alongside the British in North Africa, the next theatre, where Italy was in position to threaten Egypt from Libya. There was also a little-known war theatre in East Africa, where Polish boys, probably evacuated sons of Polish officers interned in Rumania, and thus steeped in military tradition, were aiding the British to drive the Italians out of Ethiopia. Put in charge of battalion-size units of natives, they were given the rank of major or lieutenant colonel, due to the shortage of officers, and were instrumental in swift British victory. When the young warriors arrived finally to England, they did not relish the prospect of going back to school.

With the Soviet Union in the war since the summer of 1941, all kinds of problems arose for the Polish Government-in-Exile in London. At first, there were no disagreements. When Sikorski traveled to Moscow to meet Stalin, the latter even agreed for the Polish POW's, held in the Soviet Union since 1939, to leave for the West. Many officers were missing, but that would become a problem later. Both Britain, and America after Pearl Harbor, were overjoyed with the new ally, supplying him at great risk and with heavy losses through the U-Boat infested northern route to Murmansk, thus keeping the retreating Soviet armies alive (and, incidentally, giving rise to one of the countless myths of who, or what, won the war— American spam! "This prototypical American food saved the Soviet Army," according to *The New York Times Magazine* of June 3, 1994), until it was able to counter-attack before Moscow in December 1941. The counter-attack provides two more likely answers to the question of who or what won the war.

The first is a case of another small country misbehaving, with equally fatal results, but this time to the detriment of Germany. Little Finland had joined Germany in the attack on the Soviet Union, but its president, Field Marshal Mannerheim wanted only to regain territory lost in the unprovoked winter war of 1939-40. Had Finland acted as a true ally and moved beyond its old border, thus linking with the Germans and closing the ring around Leningrad, it would have made it impossible for the Russians to supply it across Lake Ladoga to keep it from inevitably starving. With Leningrad doomed and dying, the Germans could have diverted most of the besieging forces for a concerted attack on Moscow from the north, causing it to fall. But with the Finns not cooperating, it didn't happen and, instead, there was a Soviet counter-attack.

The counter-attack, for which fresh Siberian divisions had been diverted from the Far East, coincided with the Japanese attack on the United States at Pearl Harbor, leaving a strong suspicion that somehow the Soviet Union knew about the impending attack, freeing it from worrying about Japan. This is one of the mysteries of the war, but a costly one for Germany which, in a show of support for Japan but a height of stupidity in itself, declared war on the United States, expecting Japan to reciprocate by declaring war on the Soviet Union. This, of course, did not happen. Safe from Japan, and with the

Germans thrown back from the gates of Moscow, the Russians were able to shift their industry to Siberia, out of reach of the Luftwaffe, while increasing their demands for shipments from the Allies, demanding a second front, but also hardening their attitude towards Poland.

Because of that, and because Britain and America were increasingly accommodating the Soviet Union, the Poles in England lost their trusted and only-ally position, the more so when, beginning with 1942, Britain began to fill with Anglo-Saxons, or "English-speaking" as Churchill would say, soldiers and their machines, including the formidable VIII Air Force with its 3000 planes constantly replenished.

1942, moreover, was a year when the war began to turn around, with the two reluctant allies (like Belgium earlier spelling the doom of France), Finland and Japan, now beginning to spell with their action, or lack of it, the doom of Germany, this time without the Poles. The great American naval victory at Midway in June effectively stopped the Japanese expansion, allowing Roosevelt to turn his attention to Europe. The Casablanca Conference followed and, soon after, massive American landings in North Africa, synchronized with the Battle of El Alamein and the defeat of Rommel. Attacked from both ends of North Africa, the once formidable Afrika Korps ceased to exist. The Germans suffered another defeat when General Paulus and his V Army was trapped in Stalingrad and, forbidden by Hitler to break out, surrendered in early 1943. But the Poles were not totally idle, going ahead with the evacuation of their people (including women and children from detention camps) from Russia to Iran. When they asked about the missing officers, fearing that they may be among the victims uncovered in mass graves by the Germans near Katyn in Byelorussia, Stalin became offended and broke relations with the London Poles, while the Western Allies, not to antagonize him, kept their distance in the dispute. The subsequent death of the generally respected Sikorski in a plane crash in Gibraltar in the summer of 1943 while visiting with his daughter the Polish exiles from Russia in the Middle East, is a great mystery.

Yet another mystery was about to unfold and, by a strange coincidence, restore to the Poles their value as a trusted ally, rather than a source of friction.

Despite two painful defeats, Germany was not yet beaten. It was just the end of the beginning, as Churchill put it. The Germans started a new armament program dwarfing the earlier ones and compensating for the idle euphoria following early victories in the West. German factories filled with millions of slave laborers and French civilian workers, obtained from Vichy France in exchange for sick French POW's. Tanks and planes went back to the drawing boards, in order to produce a superior tank (the Tiger), to match the formidable Soviet T-34 (another claimant to have won the war), and maintain the Luftwaffe's superiority in the air in view of American mass production (yet another "winner"), and to mount the third invasion of Russia. In the first two the Germans had been stopped at the gates of Moscow and Leningrad, and beaten at Stalingrad. The third aimed at Central Russia, the Kursk region, from which it would be easy to continue either to Moscow or to Stalingrad or both. Hitler was very uneasy about this campaign, and he had reason to be, because somehow the Russians obtained his plans for the impending monumental tank battle (from the mysterious Miller?), and prepared accordingly. The German attack was blunted by six successive Soviet defense lines, and the Germans began to retreat, but *not* because of a Russian victory, which was in the making, but because, in the middle of the battle, Hitler received the news that the Allies had landed in Italy, and suddenly Russia became secondary and the German tanks were shifted to Italy.

With the best German tanks in Italy, it is no wonder that the Allied Italian campaign was so inept, despite the fact both the American V Army, commanded by Mark Clark who had replaced Patton, and Montgomery's multinational VIII Army, consisted of battle-tested veterans, including the II Polish Corps, which had been organized, under General Anders, out of the Poles evacuated from Russia. When the campaign came to a halt at Monte Cassino and several Allied attacks including an American bombardment of the monastery could not dislodge its German defenders, the Polish Corps took the mountain and the monastery in a frontal attack, at great losses. The 50th anniversary of the battle was celebrated a few weeks before the D-Day anniversary at the Polish cemetery at Monte Cassino, with the participation of Polish veterans from all over the world. Monte Cassino was one of the two Polish-fought turning point battles in the West, not counting the Battle of Britain and Enigma. The other one took place a few weeks after Monte Cassino, at Falaise in Normandy.

By now so much has been said and written about Operation Overlord, the code name for D-Day, that it is difficult to add to it, especially after viewing countless documentaries about it, and a semi-documentary full-length movie "The Longest Day," and reading Stephen E. Ambrose's richly illustrated and well-documented monumental D-DAY, published to coincide with the 50th anniversary of it (it includes, among other illustrations, the men, uniforms, and insignia of the First Polish Armored Division), except to agree with Eisenhower's decision, one of many decisions, to launch the invasion from England, and not from the south as Churchill wanted for various reasons. Only England had the logistics necessary for this type of operation. As for Ike's second decision, to launch the invasion on June 6th rather than wait for better weather, which was not expected within the next two weeks: in view of what happened in the middle of that period, Eisenhower's decision was a lucky one according to Pamela Harriman in a video statement deposited in the Eisenhower Library. She points out that on June 13 the Germans began to use the V-1's against England. Had the invasion not begun a week earlier, the entire invasion forces would have been within easy reach of the terrible rockets, called *Vergeltungswaffen* (weapons of revenge), with consequences that are not difficult to imagine. The entire south of England was one huge arsenal, and the ports were full of ships, reportedly one thousand, loading it and the men who were to use the weapons. To get it all out as soon as possible was Eisenhower's problem, and his decision was a stroke of genius. For some unknown reason, worthy to investigate, the Polish Armored Division did not cross the Channel until the end of July, and its first engagement did not come until August 8. Why so late?

It is just possible that somebody objected to it being used (Stalin?), but Field Marshal Montgomery, to whose army group the division belonged, remembered how well the Poles had fought just a few months earlier at Monte Cassino, and since he was facing another turning-point battle, he needed the Poles to win it for him.

That's how it was with the Poles in the West. They could have saved France in 1940, but they were not given the chance despite Gamelin's high opinion of their fighting abilities, or perhaps because of it. They never received credit for breaking the "Enigma" code and for their probably decisive part in the Battle of Britain. In Italy it was the Poles who won the turning-point battle of Monte Cassino after others in the multi-national VIII Army had tried and failed.

Yet, when it came to the Victory Parade in Rome, General Mark Clark is reported to have said concerning the Polish II Corps: "We don't need a fire brigade." But it was the "fire brigade" which had opened the road to Rome for Clark to speed on collecting road signs to Rome, to be shipped home to America (where he was to become commandant of the Citadel Military Academy after the war). And Lee, Montgomery's replacement, accused Anders of causing trouble when the latter complained to him about Poland not getting fair treatment in the war. Churchill went even further, telling Anders that the Allies had enough troops now, they didn't need the Poles any more. But Montgomery needed them.

Unlike the Battle of Britain, in the Battle of Normandy the Polish Air Force had the easiest time of the three service branches. The Luftwaffe was no longer a threat—there were only two German fighter planes in Normandy on D-Day—so the task for the pilots was to disrupt lines of communication, both road and rail, and generally bomb or fire from low altitude at anything that moved below. This bombing also included points of German resistance, and because of that some French towns in Normandy were totally destroyed (Caen). Americans were particularly ruthless in this type of destructive bombing.

The naval units had a more difficult task. Transporting and protecting two million men and an incredible amount of equipment in stormy weather was a task that at times seemed impossible, and there were many casualties, especially in the landings on the beaches. Luckily for the Allies, Rommel, who was in charge of the defense, was absent on D-Day, attending the birthday of his wife in Germany, and his plan to nail the invaders on the beaches the first day, "the longest day" as he called it, was not realized, mostly because of Hitler's refusal to commit the tank divisions into action which he did not think was the real invasion, expecting it at Calais. The Polish naval units, which by then included a cruiser, a submarine and several destroyers, had their hands full on two fronts: in the Channel itself helping with the invasion, and in the western end of the Channel, patrolling and keeping an eye out for German naval units which could come up from the Bay of Biscay ports (Brest) and interfere with the invasion. There were casualties in this duty, too.

But it was the land battle that was the costliest and bloodiest, and the Allies won it because they had numerical superiority, which was widening with each day. Had both sides been equal in numbers, the

Germans would have won, but they had only one million men in France.

Numerical superiority was not the case, as fate would have it, for the Poles. From the moment it landed and moved to the vicinity of Caen, the First Polish Armored Division was engaged in heavy fighting, especially after the German tank divisions started moving closer to the beaches. Montgomery, the overall commander of Allied land forces, had to destroy those divisions or at least neutralize them in order to proceed with the invasion. It was a difficult task in view of the better quality of the German tanks, but Montgomery succeeded in surrounding them with his own divisions, yet leaving one route of escape. To close the route or, in his words, to be "the cork" for the huge bottle the Germans found themselves in, he chose the Polish Division. To carry out the order the Poles had to reach Hill 262, a high ground dominating the plateau where the Germans were concentrating. It was a race. To this day one can see the tracks the tanks made on the soft ground while racing to Hill 262. The Poles got there just before the Germans who, after a short but bloody struggle, surrendered. This was the Battle of Falaise, which cost the Poles 542 dead, including several Polish Jews, all resting now in a beautiful Polish cemetery nearby.

The division itself, making up its losses from among the captured Poles serving in the Wehrmacht (this was becoming a new source of manpower for the Polish units both in France and in Italy), continued to fight, crossing the Seine on a memorable for the Poles September 1 and blazing a trail across northern France, crossing into Belgium at Ypres, liberating a few towns and taking part in the long (85 days) and stubborn battle for Antwerp, an important port city the control of which shortened the supply line for the Allies by 500 kilometers. The heavy fight for and liberation of Breda nearby but already in Holland was part of the battle, after which the division received a deserved winter rest to recuperate and make up its losses. The good relations at that time with the grateful citizens of Breda resulted in several Polish-Dutch marriages, among them that of this writer's childhood friend, Tadek, from our hometown in Silesia. Then it was across the Rhine and into Germany.

Entering Germany was for the Polish Division a memorable experience on many levels: military, taking a few towns (Aschendorf, Pappenburg) on the Frisian coast and accepting the surrender, virtually on the last day of the war, of Wilhelmshaven, the largest

base of the German Navy; emotional, the liberation of POW, concentration, and labor camps, in one of which Maks, another hometown
companion and volleyball teammate, found his brother Józef, a
farmer, doing what farmers do, cutting clover; and patriotic, the
liberation of a camp for women, Oberlangen, most of whose 1728
inmates were fighters from the Warsaw Uprising.

By a remarkable historical coincidence, while the Battle of
Falaise was raging in Normandy (August 1944, just a few months
after Monte Cassino in Italy), another battle was raging in Poland,
the Warsaw Uprising, one of the most tragic but also most significant
chapters in Poland's part in World War II and in its own history.
What made it so?

First, the coincidence, which could be called *Triumph and
Tragedy*. It didn't matter how many German fighters the Poles shot
down in the Battle of Britain, how many Enigmas they broke, or
how many turning-point battles they won, they were doomed from
the beginning, and there was something like a conspiracy to belittle
them in their finest hours, and the chief culprit was, and this will
surprise his worshipers, Winston Churchill who, at the Teheran
Conference criticized the Poles as "troublemakers" (Sikorski?) so
viciously that even Stalin defended them to the effect that they had
great scientists and were good soldiers, a brief but perfect capsule
reference showing that he knew the Poles better than Churchill. Re-
reading the latter's *The Second World War* memoir after nearly half
a century we find real gems. Next to a useful statistic in Volume II,
chapter 9, "The French Agony" summary (p. 177):

> A Hundred and Fifty Thousand British and Forty-two Thousand
> Poles Carried to Britain [from Dunkirk],

we read elsewhere that the war began on September 3 [after Britain
had declared it], and then find a real stunner:

> I had known Weygand when he was the right-hand man of
> Marshal Foch, and had admired his masterly intervention in the
> Battle of Warsaw against the Bolshevik invasion of Poland in
> August, 1920—an event decisive for Europe at that time (p. 57).

It is a scrambled passage but full of both questionable and useful
information. To give Weygand credit for the Battle of Warsaw when
he himself had disclaimed it (whether out of modesty or for truth's

sake we will never know) is what is questionable about Churchill, as is also not mentioning Marshal Piłsudski, whose "right-hand man" Weygand probably was (they were almost exactly the same age, 53 in 1920). But Churchill couldn't resist to be the global historian and unwittingly inserted two useful gems, first, the August coincidence of the battle and its decisiveness for Europe, and second, Warsaw, and it is Warsaw we are concerned with.

Warsaw became a sophisticated European city only in the second half of the eighteenth century, under Poland's last king, Stanisław August Poniatowski, before the lights went out to the great sorrow of those who had known and loved it, among them Prince Pyotr Andreyevich Vyazemski, a Russian poet and admirer of Poland, who begged Aleksander I to restore Poland so that the lights could go on again in Warsaw. They went on brilliantly but briefly during the residency of Prince Józef Poniatowski, the late king's nephew, in the Duchy of Warsaw, growing increasingly dimmer until independence in 1918, which was confirmed by the great victory in 1920. With Poland squeezed between two totalitarians, the lights went out again on September 1, 1939, just when Warsaw was again becoming a sophisticated European city and Poland itself a viable country, with a high birthrate, stable currency, a new Central Industrial Region and a new sea port, Gdynia, the last one giving the country a chance to escape or at least divert the war.

Just as the Central Industrial Region had been built to make up for the possible loss of industrial Silesia which was too close to the German border, Gdynia had been built to compensate for the possible loss of Gdańsk. When the Germans demanded it, it should have been given up, and even an access to it allowed from Germany, though not a highway, but a skyway to be built by the Germans over the narrow neck of the "Corridor" thus not violating the territorial integrity of Poland, with both concessions a relatively small price to pay for postponing the war as long as possible. The Poles were too quick to reject German demands without stopping to consider the alternative, nobody having an idea of what was meant by total war. Poland was being ravished, concentration camps being filled to capacity, and Warsaw being destroyed piecemeal, first in the September campaign, then by the liquidation of the Warsaw Ghetto uprising, and finally during and after the Warsaw Uprising.

In the midst of past and future disasters in Poland, the Warsaw Uprising seems like Polish bravado, without the slightest chance of success. But perhaps there was a plan, or plans, behind it. The Polish Government in London kept in touch with Warsaw through its radio unit near London; also, Warsaw was supplied through air drops from Italy, but only a few of the drops reached their destination, the rest falling either in German hands or, as the Varsovians claimed, to the Russians on the right bank of the Vistula. But there were no Russians there yet in significant numbers. Warsaw, together with all of Northern Poland, East Prussia, and Pomerania, was in the strategic sector of the First and Second Byelorussian Fronts ("Fronts" being the highest command units, commanded by Marshals, of the huge Soviet Army, of which the Germans faced four on the Eastern Front, including the First and Second Ukrainian Fronts, by then already entering Rumania and Hungary). The Byelorussian Fronts were to attack along the Minsk-Warsaw-Berlin axis, but at the time of the Warsaw Uprising the offensive was still in progress, with the Byelorussian Fronts having waited to hear whether the Normandy landing had indeed succeeded—another must for the Western Allies to succeed, otherwise who knows what Stalin would have been up to? The moment the landing succeeded, the offensive took off like an avalanche, inflicting heavy losses on the Germans, even heavier than at Stalingrad, and its forward units soon reached the Narev-Vistula line, its objective. But there was another Eastern Army in the vicinity of Warsaw, a Polish Army formed in the Soviet Union. What this army was up to in the vicinity of Warsaw is also one of the riddles of the Second World War and of the Warsaw Uprising.

When General Anders led out of Russia the soldiers that were to become the Second Corps, the Polish "patriots" in Moscow demanded a Polish Army. Since there were no longer any Polish officers in Russia except for a few Communists, Stalin agreed to the formation of just one symbolic unit, a regiment, "Tadeusz Kościuszko," but then changed his mind and ordered the formation of larger units, their officer corps to come from among Russian officers of Polish background, of whom there were a great many (with at least one Marshal among them, Konstanty Rokossowski, commanding at that time the Byelorussian Fronts): 19,000 such officers, including 50 generals, answered the call, to lead the new units and train junior officers. The future General Jaruzelski was probably one of the first Polish junior officers of the new army. To speed its growth it was moved from Moscow to Ukraine, where the regions of Zhitomir (Żytomierz), Berdyczew (Berdyczów), and Vinnitsa (Winnica) had strong Polish minorities even after Stalin's expulsions of the Polish population to Kazakhstan in the 1930's.

Soon two armies were formed, First and Second, and a Third projected. Was Stalin thinking of a Polish Front? The recruitment gathered further momentum when the armies entered Poland proper, where even deserters from German-occupied Poland came to join. The First Polish Army soon moved to Lublin, where the Polish "patriots" organized the so-called Lublin Committee (Polish Committee of National Liberation, PKWN) in July, 1944 (the date is important), which became the Provisional Government of Poland. The First Army commander, a Polish general, Berling, about whom one would like to know more, then moved to the suburbs of Warsaw on the right bank of the Vistula, probably establishing contact with the Polish Home Army. Did he meet with its leader, General Bór-Komorowski, and if he did, was the outbreak of the Warsaw Uprising soon after, the result of the meeting? We can only speculate.

What if Stalin used Berling as an instrument to deceive the Home Army and to destroy Warsaw in the process, leaving the willing Germans to do it? The two deadly adversaries facing each other across the Vistula had one thing in common: hatred of Warsaw. The Germans remembered who it was disarming them in Warsaw in November 1918, and Stalin remembered personally the crashing defeat of 1920. There was a tacit agreement between them of no interference in what was about to take place. Under these circumstances any thought that Berling had his own ideas about being a new Piłsudski is preposterous. He was nothing but Stalin's lackey dangling in front of Bór-Komorowski the bait of his help. The rest is history. When the great offensive of the Byelorussian Fronts ended on the Narev-Vistula line, there were no Soviet plans to cross it on account of the Warsaw Uprising. Soon, Warsaw was one great ruin, with only a few inhabitants after the capitulation and deportation of its defenders on October 3. Now the Soviets began their own deportations of the remaining units of the Home Army.

In this real and imagined scenario, the Home Army was not without fault in its ill-conceived decision to rise on August 1, but once it had been made, it should have been followed relentlessly. If it's true that a Hungarian Corps standing nearby offered to join the Uprising in order to improve Hungary's image, was it necessary to ask London's clearance for something that would have provided necessary help to clear larger areas of Warsaw for more accurate air drops and even for parachuting the Polish Airborne Brigade raring to go instead of being wasted at Arnhem? The Home Army had poets but no resolute leaders, who were all in the West, banging their heads against the wall of the growing indifference of the Allies seduced by the myth of Soviet invincibility. The truth, very skillfully guarded, was that if America stopped supplying the Soviet Union the myth would burst like a soap bubble. The Allies were blind not to see their strength growing opposite the Soviet power weakening. The process was reversed with the Western Allies demobilizing after the war, but until then the Soviet Union was running out of steam. Why did it take until January 1945 to resume the offensive? Even then Zhukov was complaining about high casualties, until threatened by Stalin with replacement by Konev. Resorting to alternate history, in any clash over Poland and Warsaw, and with the help of the Hungarians and the presence of the commando paratroopers, the Uprising would have had a real chance and the Russians would have found out that without American planes and trucks (because it wasn't just spam) their armies were not worth much, and that Patton, Montgomery, Anders, Maczek and their superior equipment were more than a match for Zhukov, Rokossowski, and company. But this was not to be.

The Western leaders had their individual agendas. Churchill wanted to end the war as soon as possible to save Britain from total bankruptcy, and Poland was becoming an obstacle. Roosevelt won the elections but was dying and all he wanted was to finish the war under his Presidency. And Eisenhower, the Supreme Allied Commander, notified Stalin that he was not interested in taking Berlin and turned his armies south instead, giving Stalin free hand to follow earlier agreements at the Teheran and Yalta conferences, a big mistake because both Western signatories were out soon and there was no need to be bound by their decisions.

The Polish Armies East had never become a Front, their role downplayed just as in the West, where at least the Russians were unable to deny the Armored Division its finest hour, but there was no victory parade for the Poles in the West. In the East they had joined the new offensive, and at the crossing of the Oder (Odra) river died in great numbers judging by the size of the cemetery at the site of the crossing, the officers side-by-side with their young charges. After that, the Armies were scattered, attached to groups of the Byelorussian Fronts, from Pomerania, to Berlin, to the Neisse

(Nysa) river, to Bohemia, as the war ended, leaving just its consequences, which for Poland had already been decided in Teheran
(1943) and Yalta (1945), with *all* of Poland, for the first time, in
Russian hands.

For the past 50 years the Poles have been complaining about the
way they had been treated by both their foes and allies. Every child
in Poland knows the Polish contributions to victory which place the
country among the top four. There is general agreement that it was
American production that won the war. To cite just one statistic, at
the height of the war, with the industry in high gear, America was
producing 250 planes a day, many of them going to Russia together
with other arms and supplies.

Field Marshal Rommel put it best after the Battle of El Alamein:

> From the moment American overwhelming capacity
> showed itself, there was no chance of victory.

But even American capacity would not have helped if the Battle
of Britain had been lost; or if there was no radar; or if the Enigma
code had not been broken by Polish mathematicians; or, for that
matter, if the Norwegian Underground had not destroyed the
German production capacity of heavy water. Everybody remembers
Quisling, he passed into our language and can be found in dictionaries under Q, but who remembers Norways's role in preventing Hitler
from building an atomic bomb, or France's for sending its supply of
heavy water to America as the Germans were entering? All these
examples predate the Battle of Normandy, where American capacity
was overwhelming and even then it was touch and go (What if
Rommel hadn't gone to his wife's birthday?) which shows that no
single factor can be credited with ultimate victory. There were many
more contributions, such as Yugoslavia's "No" to Hitler, leading to
an unplanned campaign, not only tying down large German forces in
the Balkans, but delaying the attack on Soviet Union by a crucial
month; and the Polish Underground smuggling out a complete
German flying bomb to the Allies for study. As a footnote, one
more, a quote:

> Frank Mocha spent the middle war years in a German
> prisoner-of-war camp in Austria (Stalag XVIIB) where, to keep
> his mind working, he became an expert bridge player (Polish
> Jews from Warsaw were his instructors) and, to keep his body fit,

he became a star athlete (the Germans encouraged sports to discourage escapes), winning many trophies which he always shipped to his family in Poland to be traded for whatever they needed most. The athletic ability was providential. When a new type of plane was sighted in flight over the camp, the camp elders determined it was a jet plane, and Mocha, the youngest and the fittest, was entrusted with the task of warning the Allies that the Germans had a jet plane, a new weapon which could influence the outcome of the war. A daring escape followed, leading from Austria back to France, then to Spain and Portugal, and finally Gibraltar. In London, after an extensive debriefing by a Captain Lisowski, who turned out to be a Polish-speaking British intelligence officer, and a highly secret report to Churchill himself, Mocha was told that every production site in the vicinity from which the plane had flown was destroyed by British bombers and that he had made a great contribution to the war effort. Talk about winning the war....

This is a page from my obituary which was never printed because, as you can see, I am still alive. Thank you!

* * * *

SPECIAL ACCOMPLISHMENTS

There are other accomplishments worthy of notice, some, like the Polish Supplementary (Saturday) Schools—a collective effort of great importance for the preservation of Polish values, thrive thanks to the good will of their participants, and because they are essentially a voluntary undertaking, belong among individual accomplishments. Their importance for the Polish American community and for Poland was underlined during the V Convention of Polonian Teachers and educational leaders (and Parent-Teacher Committees) which took place at Columbia University's Teachers College during a long weekend of May 23-26, 1997. There were about 150 participants in the Convention, including speakers from here and from Poland, among them Dr. Edmund Osysko, chairman of the Educational Commission of Polish American Congress; Mr. Jan Woźniak, president of the central authority of the Polish Supplementary Schools; Mr. Janusz Boksa, president of the Association of Polish Teachers in Chicago; and guests out of Poland, among them Professor Andrzej Stelmachowski from "Wspólnota," and Mr. Krzysztof Dąbrowski, representing Polish publishers of pedagogical materials. In the course of the debates a motion was made to establish a National Polonian Educational Fund, and to hold the next Convention in the year 2000 in Orchard Lake, Michigan.

Another unheralded accomplishment is that of ALBIN WOZNIAK as a tireless editor and publisher of *The Polish Studies Newsletter*, an 8-page monthly filled mostly with information about books and articles by Poles and about Poland, interspersed frequently with the editor's apt and well-meant comments, in other words, a gold mine. There is also information about jobs with western corporations in Poland, about Polish websites, and computer jobs for Polish nationals in America. In the "Tidbits – Iskierki" column of the November 1997 issue, Wozniak serves some controversial food for thought by claiming that "too much Polonian secular money has been going to the Roman Catholic Church" (for the construction of the John Paul II Center), to the detriment of worthy secular projects. Somehow he reasons that "at stake here is the survival of organized Polonia as an ethnic group," that "Polonia is being assimilated rapidly," and he asks questions, "Where is the Polonian identity here in America? How does it manifest itself?" I am not sure if the questions are well

taken, but perhaps the answers lie in the future of the Saturday
Schools.

Despite this biased intensity, Wozniak's fear of assimilation is
real. Just look at the media and the Polish names, both on their staffs
(Jim Miklaszewski, NBC, Tony Guida [?] and others, such as Judith
Dobrzynski, a writer for *The New York Times Television* insert, to
name just a few), and in the news (Wayne Gretzky, the greatest ever
hockey player; Tara Lipinski, the 14-year old figure skating
sensation and US national and world champion; Robert Kowalski,
advertising in a suave voice his book, *Evolve*, about cholesterol, on
the evening news; Joe Dudek, "the youngest of a Boston-area elec-
trician's seven children [who] transformed himself into a sports folk
hero" becoming "Thinking Fan's Vote for the 1985 Heisman
Trophy" (*Sports Illustrated* cover) and now enshrined in the College
Football Hall of Fame. There is one more name on that (partial) list
where Polish background is not even hinted at, which could mean
two things, one that Polish names are no longer a hindrance in
America, becoming rather an adornment (Zbigniew Brzezinski can
take much credit for that) and two, perversely, that if the bearers are
so good, why say they are Polish (everybody knew who Private
Slovik was, but then, the Unabomber Kaczynski is also getting a lot
of attention so it's hard to generalize), and this is probably the case
with the bearer of the last name to be listed, young Jonathan
Lipnicki.

Jonathan Lipnicki should be viewed in double capacity, as the
first successful child actor after Macauley Caulkin ("Home Alone")
and as a news maker on a new breaking news show, "Access
Hollywood," a strong rival of "Entertainment Tonight," the original
program of this type. One can't even say that Jonathan is assimilated
in the mainstream culture, he is (part of) that culture.

There are degrees of assimilation, the ideal situation being when
a child stays with one foot in the culture of its ancestors, and that's
where the Saturday Schools come in and why they should be cultivated, so that Mr. Wozniak does not lose sleep over "Polonia...being
assimilated rapidly." The Jonathan Lipnickis are here today, gone
tomorrow, cashing in on their ephemeral quality while it lasts, and
that's America, but there are others who are here today *and*
tomorrow, like the two candidates for New York City Council in the
recent elections.

Bill Murawski, in common with Seattle City Council member Tina Podlodowski, describes himself as a "community activist" which means that everybody around him benefits; one can't ask for a better description than that. Thomas N. Rudny, on the other hand, is a priest of the Polish National Catholic Church, deeply involved in Polish American affairs, but also East European generally, Jewish, immigration assistance, and neighborhood organizations, in keeping with his declared resolve to work hard for ALL.

Father Rudny provides a transition to a selected group of real achievers, for whom assimilation doesn't even exist. Comfortable in both cultures, they use both for private and professional reasons and are a credit to both, deserving separate treatments.

WITOLD RYBCZYNSKI, born in Scotland, the son of a Polish World War II officer, chose architecture as a means of expression, becoming a writer about ideal or unusual houses. His articles appeared frequently in the "Arts & Leisure" section of *The New York Times*, creating for him a widening circle of readers of his books, which he discussed on the television program "Bookmark," conducted by Lewis Lapham, editor of *Harper's Magazine*, and for which he received the Alfred Jurzykowski Award. His essay on *The New American Ghetto* by Camilo Jose Vergara, appeared recently *The New York Review of Books*.

RAFAL OLBINSKI, a world class graphic designer, as well as illustrator and painter. Educated in the Warsaw Polytechnic, he remains in close contacts with Poland, giving exhibitions of his art and attending professional meetings. Very successful in America (since 1981), has his own spacious studio in mid-Manhattan, where this writer visited him in connection with designing the cover of this book, when he also learned that Olbinski had just returned from a professional trip to London and Copenhagen. In New York he is connected with the School of Visual Arts and with the Polish Institute of Arts and Sciences which had nominated him one of its Fellows. Winner of numerous awards and prizes, his biggest success is probably the selection of his poster in the competition for the official Poster of New York—the Capital of the World. A talented and resourceful man, he is an ideal role model for young people arriving here from Poland, not only as an artist but also a family man and father of three children.

EWA KRZYZANOWSKI, daughter of the late Professor Ludwik Krzyżanowski, is in one respect the outstanding Polish woman in

America, as a trail blazer in television. Educated in Vassar College, she became involved early in television, doing special assignments, as for example her trip to Chicago to interview Polish American students in connection with the Popes's visit. It was then that this writer, teaching at that time in Chicago, met her for the first time and became impressed with her position at NBC and her professional manner, displayed while working, and her worldly ways displayed at the dinner table. Her father was very happy to hear a detailed report of her visit. He would have been even happier to hear of her success now.

New York Times Television, October 13-19, 1996, has a baby gorilla on its cover, with a caption, "Beyond Biology 101, PBS Frames Nature In an Unnatural Setting," by John Noble Wilford. Inside, it turns out the come-on illustration is part of "Eyewitness," a science series on the Public Broadcasting System that was just beginning its second season. In it, nature is framed in unnatural settings, like a science museum, and "the producers think of the unusual format they have created as a virtual reality museum, a magical place where anything can happen...and they advertise it as 'an entirely new concept in TV'." It's all very complicated, but this is what "the guiding spirit of Eyewitness," Eve Krzyzanowski, had to say about it:

> You have to be entertaining above all in this world of informa-
> tion overload and short attention spans. We think we have
> developed an engaging way to impart information with a mix of
> strong graphics, some myth and legend, facts and clear explana-
> tions. This seems to have appeal at a variety of educational
> levels and all ages.

The producer is Ms. Krzyzanowski, who is a BBC vice president for development and production in the United States. Her producing credits include several animated and live-action series, while all the time searching "for a whole new way of looking at natural history TV."

JOHN MICGIEL provides, by virtue of his position as the current director of the Institute on East Central Europe at Columbia University, a good transition in this book from American Polonia to Poland, especially now when Poland seems to be at last getting on the right track after the recent elections ending with the defeat of Communists. Micgiel has lately been a subject of considerable interest, having two interviews with *Nowy Dziennik* (A. Dobrowolski), chairing a meeting with Javier Solana, Secretary of NATO, and even co-hosting the Polish Teachers Convention in May. All this exposure also exposes some of Micgiel's personal history, namely that he is an American-born child of Polish parents driven out of Poland in 1941 to forced labor in Germany (the older children in the family were born, of all places, in Garmisch Partenkirchen, probably at the time when this writer was at a POW camp not far from Garmisch).

His road to the present position is a Polish American success story, described elsewhere in this book, in connection with the Kosciuszko Foundation in which he once worked and which had supported him with scholarships. Because of the strong family history, he is comfortable in both cultures, and even makes others comfortable by urging in one of his interviews not to be ashamed of Polishness!

This writer, who has known John Micgiel for over ten years now and had several readings arranged by him at the Institute, had some misgivings about the level of his knowledge and the soundness of his scholarship, but these misgivings are gradually disappearing, replaced by a growing conviction that he is the right person in the right job at the right time, and so is his soon-to-be-partner Mark von Hagen as director of the Harriman Institute (the two institutes are to be merged). The institute has much influence in Poland (at least, it should have) and it needs a strong leader. The air of reliability surrounding Micgiel and his healthy common sense are the right recommendations. The work ahead is mind-blowing....

...and that's just my point. With the stress on NATO lately, other problems in Poland (health, environment, demography, more important in the long-run than NATO) are neglected, or simply ignored, and a suspicion arises whether John Micgiel is aware of their importance. This suspicion is fueled by a certain arrogance in him concerning NATO. After a NATO Symposium at the National Defense University in Washington, Micgiel was interviewed by a Polish television program in New York, and when the interview turned to money, and a sum of one billion and a half was mentioned in some connection, Micgiel remarked: "That's no money!" ("To nie są żadne pieniądze!"). In a world short of money, in Asia, Europe, and America, to say that $1.5 billion is "no money" makes one wonder whether the person who said it can be taken seriously.

The person who can and must be taken seriously is EDWARD
PINKOWSKI, the grandson of a Polish immigrant, a native of
Holyoke, Massachusetts, a former magazine editor, newspaper
publisher, and author of a dozen books, who has made more major
discoveries of lost Polish bonds in American history than any
historian of his time.

Among them are the grave of Anthony Sadowski, the famous
Polish frontiersman who died in 1736; the last residence in America
of Thaddeus Kosciuszko (now the Thaddeus Kosciuszko National
Memorial); and, most recently, he was instrumental in finding and
identifying the remains of General Casimir Pulaski in Savannah. For
this, due to a fortunate accident of chronology, he became the last,
but not the least, entry among "Special Accomplishments" in the
chapter "Individual Accomplishments" in this book, closing its part
dealing with American Polonia. He is the only writer who is also in
its predecessor, *Poles in America: Bicentennial Essays*.

In Edward Pinkowski's own words to this writer:

> Never has one name intruded in my life as much as General
> Pulaski. If you want to write sixty lines on my contributions to
> the Polish past, it is important to realize that I am a few steps
> ahead of the encyclopedias in the biography of Pulaski.
>
> I have proven that Pulaski was born March 6, 1745, in
> Warsaw, where the family lived for at least the first ten years of
> his life, not Warka, and died on board a square-rigger, known as
> the Wasp, October 15, 1779. Because of a paper trail, I know
> where his body was from the time of his death.
>
> For leading workmen to Pulaski's skeletal remains in a brick-
> lined vault under the Pulaski Monument in Savannah, the mayor
> of the city, Floyd Adams Jr., editor of a black newspaper there,
> gave me a key and made me an honorary citizen of Savannah.
>
> No historian has received more awards since then as I have.
> In March, 1997, the Chicago Society of the Polish National
> Alliance gave me a glass vase with Pulaski's head etched on it.
>
> On May 3, the *Georgia Guardian*, a weekly paper, presented
> an award to me "in recognition of outstanding contribution" to
> Savannah in 1996.
>
> On July 12, the ACPC honored me in Toronto with its
> Distinguished Service Award "in recognition of his meticulous
> research on Generals Pulaski and Kosciuszko which resulted in
> establishing eminent shrines and correcting historic beliefs."
>
> On October 10, Anna Kornatek, director of the Pulaski
> Museum in Warka, Poland, honored me with the Pulaski Medal
> designed by Anna Jaruszkiewicz.

In November, the Polish Heritage Society of Philadelphia named me the Distinguished Man of the year, reported in *The Post Eagle*, November 26, 1997.

It means a great deal that I began the Pinkowski Institute shortly afterwards to remind others of my presence on earth and recognize my work.... The Pinkowski Institute wasn't even in existence ten days when you called on New Year's Day. You have a chance to list it as the newest body in Polonia. The headquarters of the Pinkowski Institute is at 9900 Stiring Road, Cooper City, Florida, and somewhere in southern Florida I hope to have a separate building to house my collection and expand on it.

Cordially, Edward Pinkowski,
January 13, 1998.

Part II

POLONIA AND POLAND

An (im)perfect jewel

7

Robert J. Bonsignore

"A STRANGER TALKS TO LADY POLAND"

who are you lady poland?
   where are you?

do you live in history? in the hearts of your people?
   in your language?   in your wealth?

i walked the streets of warsaw, of lublin, of krakow
      and i did not see you
         i a stranger in your midst

there at birkenau from the soil i picked the ash bones
      of all peoples
  there was maximilian kolbe
        edith stein
           russians
             jews
               gypsies
  you lived though eternal lady
    but you hide from us

your beloved poland has risen
    we look into the faces of our german
        and russian brothers
           knowing that cain killed abel

see
  i speak thus though not a pole
          why?

strangers look for you my lady
      and look at your children
         in wonder

consumed by hitler and stalin
offered in the holocaust of warsaw
noble hearts noble minds noble bodies

burning embers which rose to the heavens to become stars
looking down today at earth's theatre
this stage called earth
actors all called to perform
our ancestors our audience

lady poland show your true face
mother of us all future generations await

we are still at the dawn of human history
seedlings yet to grow into mighty oaks

i speak to your children hoping they will tell me where
you their mother reside

• • • •

June 27, 1998

On the Occasion at the Pilsudski Institute of the Book Presentation by Frank Mocha, Ph.D....a True Patriot, True American, and True Son of Poland.

Some fifteen years ago through a mutual acquaintance, I met Dr. Mocha. I had been a member and officer of The Edith Stein Guild, a Catholic Organization, which honors the name of this German Jewish philosopher and psychologist. She had been born in Breslau in the 19th century, was a nurse in the First World War, converted to Catholicism in 1922, became a Carmelite nun under the name Sr. Theresia Benedicta of the Cross, was arrested by the Nazis in Holland, and was murdered in Auschwitz August 9, 1942.

As part of a study group visiting Poland in 1985 I inadvertently became conscious of things Polish, and this consciousness-raising was enhanced by the good offices and efforts of Dr. Mocha. To him I am thankful.

Attached are excerpts from "Poems by Adam Mickiewicz"of Books of the Polish Nation portraying each Pole as a Pilgrim here on Earth.

8

Frank Mocha

WHAT'S WRONG WITH POLAND?

To answer the question, one has to determine first who is asking it, and whether it pertains to spiritual or material values, or politics, or all of the above, which is the correct answer. There was to be an introduction to this part of the book also asking a question, namely:

> What do Poles in America think of Poland and
> what can they do to help?

The question is not as aggressive as the title of this chapter, and because it was partially answered in the chapter on the "Big Fraternals," the introduction was dispensed with, leaving only the question in the chapter heading, seeking the roots of the ills the fraternals are being encouraged to try and cure.

What is wrong with Poland in general is the erosion of morals and manners caused by an unprecedented century of disruptions of which Poland, a beneficiary at first, became the main victim, and its people sustained losses second only to the Jews who, however, despite the Holocaust, by a strange logic benefited from the second disruption, by regaining their ancient home after almost two thousand years of expulsion and exile.

Poland had regained its ancient home after a much shorter wait than the Jews, and earlier, after the first disruption, which for Poland did not end until a great victory over a new deadly enemy, Russian Communism, in the Battle of Warsaw ("an event decisive for Europe at that time," according to Churchill) in August 1920. With Europe weak and ruined after the long war, and Poland flushed with victory, the reborn country became immediately a major European power, and its leader, Marshal Józef Piłsudski, a world figure. It was into this heroic euphoria that people of this writer's generation were born in the early 1920s (today it is often called the "Pope's generation").

To a young boy from a large family living in a comfortable apartment that came with father's job on the railways (with a garden

259

and pieces of reclaimed land to grow potatoes and vegetables) in a secluded mineral waters spa near the Czech and German borders, life was a paradise, only occasionally disturbed by echoes of strange goings-on in Warsaw. To him, Marshal Piłsudski could do no wrong, and any problems Poland had stemmed from the difficulties of bringing together people from different parts of Poland separated by partitions, as he was taught in school. It didn't matter that his father had different ideas. Living in a prosperous and well-run formerly German Upper Silesia, he was concerned with signs of unrest in the world, such as the Japanese invasion of China, the emergence of fascism in Italy and of national socialism in Germany, the latter event putting Poland in harm's way just as Piłsudski died.

The young man was caught in the wheels of war too early to ponder some of the domestic phenomena, as for example why the Silesians referred to the people in the rest of the country as "Poles," as if they were foreigners, and to the rest of the country itself as "Poland," as if it were a foreign country, and why there were in Silesia so many of those "Poles" occupying all important positions, as if Silesia were a colony, and that's just my point.

When I was drafting the chapter, I intended to place the breakdown of morality in Poland between two dates of reference: 1939 and 1989, the loss of independence and the regaining of it, with four different systems within the span of half a century: democracy, but in reality a semi-dictatorship; German occupation laws; Communist domination; and an evolving free market democracy. I was speculating which did more harm, German wartime occupation, since wars customarily contribute to the loosening of morals (but I rejected it, on the single ground that Poland was the only country in occupied Europe without a Quisling, and its stand against the occupant was exemplary) or communism, with the latter the obvious candidate, as I was able to see for myself when visiting Poland after the war. But Communist domination did not end with 1989, and the best proof of it is that a former communist is even now president of Poland. By the same token Poland was not a paragon of morality prior to World War II. There were questionable acts on the highest level, and the person responsible for it, based on my experience as a Silesian, was the highly admired and venerated Marshal Piłsudski.

Reaching into memory, I recall my father telling me about the answer given by Piłsudski to a delegation of Silesian Insurgents asking him for help in the Uprisings: "We don't need German

colonies!" a surprising statement on many counts, betraying ignorance of Silesia's history and mineral resources, without which
Poland would remain an agricultural country in an industrial world,
a fate Thomas Masaryk saw for it. Years later, when I repeated the
criticism of Piłsudski to one of the first members and avid supporters of the Pilsudski Institute, L.A. Kupferwasser of Chicago, he
exploded in holy anger and never forgave me the "blasphemy." Such
were the feelings Pilsudski inspired in people, but not in Silesia,
where my older brother wrote witty lampoons about him which cost
him a career in the police force. As for me, I cried when as an altar
boy I heard in church the news of Pilsudski's death on May 12, 1935,
but I was capable of laughing at my brother's wit and, reading the
opposition newspaper "Polonia" my father was subscribing to and
noticing the frequently confiscated issues, I began to realize that all
was not well in Poland run by Pilsudski's "colonels." There were
whispers of detention (concentration?) camps in Brześć and Bereza, I
even knew someone condemned to one of them, but since he was a
highly vocal member of the local German minority, as a patriotic
commander of the "Sons of the Insurgents" I was inclined to think he
had asked for it, not giving it much thought. It was only recently that
I learned more about some unsavory facts of life in interwar Poland.

In the November 13, 1997 issue of *Przegląd Polski* there
appeared a memoir-type essay about *Wojciech Korfanty* ("Family
Reminiscences") by his daughter-in-law Eugenia, who describes in
gruesome detail the persecution, including incarcerations, torture,
and death, probably by arsenic poisoning, of her father-in-law
because of his opposition, with others, to Piłsudski, mainly to his
May 1926 coup. To quote:

> Piłsudski was a man insanely ambitious and envious. He
> couldn't stand people who were his equals or superior to him.
> That's why he belittled the contributions to the emergence of
> free Poland by Ignace Paderewski, Roman Dmowski and others.
> He disregarded the date of the signing of the Treaty of
> Versailles on June 28, 1919, cosigned by Paderewski, Dmowski
> and Maurycy Potocki because he wasn't part of it.... During the
> struggles to make Silesia Polish he is alleged to have said:
> "What do you want to fight for? Silesia is German" [!]...

About the outstanding "German" Silesian, Eugenia Korfanty says:

> I remember Wojciech Korfanty as a truly superior man. He had
> prestige and aroused respect. He was a splendid speaker. When
> he spoke in the Prussian Parliament as a Polish deputy from
> Silesia, all those present listened with great attention.... When he
> marked on a map the future Polish borders, including Pomerania,
> Poznan province, and Silesia, there were offended voices from
> the floor: "Mister Deputy, please do not forget that you are
> speaking in the German Parliament!" He spoke beautiful literary
> Polish, and French like a Frenchman. Of course, German was his
> first language.... Residing in Czechoslovakia, he quickly
> mastered the Czech spoken and written language.... It can be
> sincerely said that Wojciech Korfanty sacrificed his entire life,
> completely, to the cause of Poland.... It was not until June 1997
> [on the 75th anniversary of Polish troops entering Silesia], that
> Korfanty's accomplishments were recognized posthumously by
> bestowing on him the Order of the White Eagle.

During the ceremony Eugenia was asked what was the cause of the
hatred between Piłsudski and Korfanty. She claims it was one-sided,
of Piłsudski for Korfanty, who wanted to cooperate with him, and
when Piłsudski was imprisoned in Magdeburg, Korfanty traveled to
the [German] authorities with a plea to have him released, but in the
meantime the prisoner had been freed and the future Marshal was
already on his way to Poland.

After a lifetime of service to Poland, this great Polish Silesian
spent the last years of his life in exile in Czechoslovakia, and when
the Germans entered Prague, was smuggled out by the French
Embassy to Paris. With war in the air, he returned to Poland, "to be
of use," only to be arrested again and die shortly afterward on the
eve of war.

What is one to make of the inability of the Poles to unite even in
the face of deadly danger to the nation, a fact which illustrates the
most disturbing aspect of Poland between the wars? And what is one
to make of the 6,500 Polish officers from the September campaign
spending six years in German prisoner-of-war camps (mostly
Murnau) not trying to escape to join the war effort? Were they
afraid that they would not be made to feel welcome by Sikorski, who
had his own detention "quarters" which the Germans knew about,
mentioning them while ridiculing the Polish Army in Scotland in
their propaganda broadcasts and "poison" press? Having their own

mini-cult of Piłsudski they knew just how to handle his partisans among the Polish officers, which means almost the entire Polish officer corps. Had the war gone differently for Poland, these men would have had to answer for their inactivity, which makes the Polish Army in the West and the Underground Army in Poland look like so many heroes. With both out of the way the communists had an easy job to dominate the nation. What forms it took and what results it brought is a subject for a separate study with only some aspects mentioned here, but first another digression about Silesia, which at any rate figures prominently in the communist mismanagement of Poland.

Except for scholars and specialists, few people know that Silesia was one of four original Polish provinces and dialects, but it was separated from Poland in the XIVth century and subjected to Germanization. There were ample opportunities subsequently to regain Silesia, but they were not taken advantage of, with Poland expanding in the opposite direction. This was a big mistake, because regaining Silesia would have also meant gaining a skilled and industrious population which Poland lacked and which would have been an important factor in reversing Poland's decline. Once Silesia became a Prussian province, its Germanization intensified and there no longer was a Poland to look to. When Piłsudski looked upon Silesia as German, he was expressing a prevailing opinion among people who did not know its history. In view of this, the three Silesian Uprisings were not taken seriously by Piłsudski, who was unable to realize that it was a miracle that there should still be enough Polishness left in Silesia to fight for the right to become part of Poland again, and win. Despite the victory, Silesia was looked upon as a kind of colony to be exploited, and there were rumors about full autonomy for Silesia. (This is an important point, because exactly the same rumors are circulating in Silesia now.) Despite, or probably because of the rumors, Silesians were making great strides, except in politics, where Korfanty was a victim. Strides were made in education, with the undereducated teachers from "Poland" being replaced by graduates from Silesian pedagogical schools, and Gymnasium graduates entering prestigious and practical university-level institutions, such as the Higher Commercial School in Warsaw and particularly the Polytechnic in Lwow, both important in creating a Silesian managerial class in Silesia and, in the case of the Polytechnic, a mini-brain trust investigating ways of saving Poland in the impending war by diverting raw materials to where it really mattered.

A well-researched and painstakingly documented paper was submitted to the Ministry of Defense and to President Móscicki, according to the young reserve officer of anti-tank artillery and graduate of the Polytechnic who told me about it (and of the absence of any reply) when I watched him (on my way to join the defenders on the first day of the war) commanding an anti-tank battery with great precision resulting in the destruction of two German tanks and quick retreat to another position before an inevitable air attack, because he had no anti-aircraft guns (most of them were in England by then) to defend and hold his position. The young officer was doing what the paper had proposed, namely reliance on anti-tank and anti-aircraft artillery at the expense of the navy and the air force.

Aware of the German build-up in the air and on the sea, next to expanding land forces, the young Silesians had reached a conclusion that the only way Poland had a chance to defend itself was to ring the country with a circle of anti-tank guns backed up by anti-air batteries, produced by diverting steel from ship and plane produc-tion, which was to be discontinued as of no consequence in the coming war. Within a few years (the paper was produced shortly after Piłsudski's death), enough guns would have been produced capable to inflict on the Germans casualties they didn't expect, and since they would know about the plan or at least suspect its existence, confront them with a choice.

There was more to the plan. Knowing from history how effective guerrilla wars were in Silesia under the first Piasts, the young planners recommended daring cavalry raids behind enemy lines (a specific one from Suwałki into East Prussia to threaten Königsberg) to cut communications, destroy supplies, and raise havoc generally. The reduced infantry would just back up the much expanded artillery, with the rest of the army defending Warsaw, where Silesian miners, brought for that purpose, would dig under-ground storage rooms for water, food, and even a hospital. Poland at that time still had plenty of daredevils for the raids, and enough unemployed miners to do the digging properly. It also had heroes of the Wołodyjowski and Ketling kind who, in the sad event that Warsaw had to capitulate, would stay behind, hidden, and blow up the underground structures during the German victory parade, burying the marching victors with their equipment and Hitler with his staff.

I listened to my informant, a local hero, with admiration and disbelief as I escorted him to a well-chosen new position. Disbelief not of the plan, but of it being ignored by the addressees. Barely out of Gymnasium, with just the equivalent of ROTC as my only military education, I nevertheless understood that the only way to fight the Germans with any chance of success was on our terms, not theirs. A year later, when in a POW camp in Bavaria, I was told by the Bavarians how they were afraid of Polish cavalry raids! So the plan was not entirely unrealistic. Who were the morons responsible for Poland's war readiness, declaring mobilization, then calling it off, and running in circles instead of accepting the only plan that made sense?

I once asked Wacław Jędrzejewicz whether he had known anything about the plan. Just rumors, he said, which means that somebody looked at it and rejected it, but why? Because it came out of Silesian minds, hence not to be trusted? Perhaps Korfanty had concocted it in exile? I rather think it was a simple case of envy of the glory to be won by the Silesians, and envy is as Polish as vodka.

I am dwelling on Silesia because in my mind it always had a special destiny of which Poland's neighbors were more aware than Poland itself. It was here where the Mongols were stopped by Silesian Piasts in 1241 and Europe was saved. But a hundred years later, in one of history's bitter ironies, the only king of Poland called "Great," (Casimir/Kazimierz), the last of the Piast kings, ceded Silesia to Bohemia as a price of the latter's neutrality in the expected war with the Teutonic Knights.

The Piasts' powerful successors, the Jagiellonians, could have reclaimed Silesia but, in their preoccupation with the North, the South, and the East, there was no time for Silesia. This was a bad mistake, because Silesia next passed with Bohemia under the tight control of Austrian Habsburgs. During the Swedish invasion of Poland in 1655 the then-Polish king sought refuge in Silesia, not as a sovereign but as a guest by the (cautious) grace of the Habsburg Emperor. Less than thirty year later (1683) the Emperor's capital, Vienna, was besieged by the Turks; another Polish king, Jan Sobieski, was passing through Silesia, not as a refugee but as the "Savior of Vienna," greeted in Polish by the Silesians and planting oak trees along the way. This was a golden opportunity, and the last, to reclaim Silesia. Not doing it was not just a bad mistake, but a fatal one. Sobieski was a great warrior ("The Lion of the North" the Turks called him), but he was not a wise ruler. The extent of his mistake became apparent during the rule of his successor August II, King of Saxony.

There has been much interest recently in XVIIIth century Saxony, stressing its wealth (based on porcelain) and culture (Johann Sebastian Bach). It was this kind of partner Poland needed after the "century of wars." Had Sobieski reclaimed Silesia, which was separating Saxony from Poland, the two countries would have been united not just dynastically, but territorially, forming a continuous land mass stretching from the heart of Germany to the heart of Russia. As it was, August II had to travel from Dresden to Warsaw through Habsburg territory. It is no wonder that he plotted the dismemberment of the Habsburg Empire, which would have been highly beneficial to Poland, restoring Silesia and ending the unproductive Austrian orientation (and removing a future partitioner). The Northern War spoiled the plans. Since Charles XII was a supporter of Stanisław Leszczyński for the throne of Poland, August II became an ally of Peter the Great of Russia, and Poland became an unwitting victim of a Swedish invasion, a second one within half a century. As for Silesia, it was Prussia which took it away from Austria in 1740, encircling Poland from the north and west and posing a real threat.

The tragedy of the loss of Silesia by Poland and failure to regain it was made more acute by the province's growing importance. There is a saying, originating in the XVIIIth century that whoever controls Silesia, controls Europe. And indeed, Frederick's Prussia, together with England, controlled Europe during the Seven-Years War, barely fifteen years after acquiring Silesia. Old Kutuzov, Napoleon's nemesis in 1812, understood it, and chased the invader to the outer limits of Silesia, dying there. With Napoleon out of Silesia, Russia was safe. As for Napoleon, after raising a new army, he intended to reach Silesia, there to meet Prince Józef Poniatowski with Polish cavalry reinforcements, but it was not to be, and he lost the campaign before reaching Silesia, in Saxony, with his last ally, Poniatowski, losing his life there.

With the discovery of coal as a source of energy, Silesia, with huge reserves of it and by then firmly a part of Prussian-led united Germany, became, along with the Ruhr and Saar, one of the most important industrial pillars of Germany, celebrated in song and contributing to Germany's industrial revolution and its rise as a leading economic power. The loss of the most vital part of Silesia after World War I was one of the causes of World War II, after which Poland was belatedly awarded the whole of Silesia, a fit, albeit controversial compensation for the pain of losing Wilno and Lwów. History has come full circle.

The marriage of Silesia and the rest of Poland was not a happy one in the period between the world wars, with pro-German sympathies ripe and a nostalgia among the older generation for German law-and-order. The brutal expulsion after the war of pro-German Silesians was too excessive, and the influx of expellees from eastern Poland led to conflicts between the two layers of population, frequently provoked by the use of the Silesian dialect by the native Silesians, causing further departures, this time of apolitical Silesians, who should have been cultivated and encouraged to stay. Instead, they were contributing to the German *Wirtschaftwunder*, while depriving blundering People's Poland, bereft of an educated leadership (except for the Church), of skilled and resourceful population.

For the sake of my own security, I did not visit Poland, particularly Silesia in order to see for myself, until 1959 when I already had an American passport. I lived at my brother's in Racibórz (Ratibor), a town which, despite its Piast history, had remained in Germany after World War I. The exodus to Germany was still on, I even had a sample of one of its reasons, when a group of drunken recent settlers started calling my family group, escorting me to a night train and conversing in the Silesian dialect, "!" These were fighting words, but on my insistence, to spare Teutonic Knightsmy relatives, it came to blows only between me and the hostile group's leader, who couldn't apologize enough when he found out I was American. To his remark that he thought I was one of "them," I screamed:

"I *am* one of them! I was born here!"

The incident ended with my giving the hostiles a lecture on Silesian history which they admitted they had no idea of. This, if anything, was a proof of how inept the communist regime had been in handling this most important problem. The exodus continued until 1989, when it slowed down, then stopped, and now a reverse movement is beginning, which is the best news from Poland since the end of World War II.

Another piece of good news, no less important, is that following the last elections to the Polish parliament a Silesian from Cieszyn (Teshen), Jerzy Buzek, became Prime Minister. In a recent interview with the German periodical *Der Spiegel* Mr. Buzek was being teased about his using the Silesian dialect, to which he replied that it was an old Silesian language which he was proud to have retained.

The two pieces of good news seem to indicate that, at least as far as Silesia is concerned, things are entering the right track. The return of the Silesians, whose exodus was motivated more often than not by economic rather than nationality reasons, means that there are opportunities for them in Poland, the lack of which had driven them out in the first place, but this applies to the later stages of the exodus, while the earlier ones were definitely motivated by reasons of nationality, and were badly mismanaged, and this is where the communist regime can be held accountable. Other than that, throughout the entire communist rule, Silesia was, because of its coal and money generated by the high wages of the miners, a favored province, and the miner a prince among workers.

But not everybody was a well-to-do miner in Silesia. For the others, like in the rest of Poland, the average wage in the artificially maintained full-employment economy was less than half of that of the miners, and here we enter the area of political witticisms which the Poles are so good at, and which accurately describe the economic reality in Poland at that time. The best of the dark humor,

> "Whether standing up or lying down,
> 2,000 [zlotys] is coming to you,"

depicts the guaranteed employment picture, and another of the witticisms describes the nature of the work and payment for it:

> "We pretend we are working,
> and they pretend they are paying us."

These were the self-made rules on which the economy of People's Poland was resting. How the worker was to exist on the ridiculously low pay, was up to him. Accordingly, absenteeism was rampant, with workers doing jobs outside their place of employment and, more disturbingly, stealing from it anything that could be used at home, or sold, with impunity. Some even built houses with materials stolen over a long period of time. A new morality developed, according to which stealing from "them" was not stealing but part of payment. Since the supervisors were also doing it, it went largely unpunished.

My visit in 1959 coincided accidentally with Nikita Khrushchev's visit in Poland, the first I think after the stormy "Thaw" of 1956, which had brought some loosening of Soviet control over Poland. This was lucky for me, because since there was also some (temporary) rapprochement between the Soviet Union and the United States, my American passport opened all doors for me. But there were some clashes: with a captain at customs in Warsaw, and with another in the Racibórz jail who did not allow me to visit a childhood friend incarcerated there. Both clashes placed me in eye-to-eye confrontations with sworn communists, but the first one was revealing.

Since my British wife and our three American children travelled with me, the bone of contention was the size of our luggage, which the captain was questioning. He objected first to the large suitcase-full supply of jars of Gerber's baby foods, cans of Similac formula, and plastic bags of powdered milk, as if Poland had no food for small children. In retrospect, I could see his point, since one of the few things the communists did well in Poland, was children's care. But my wife had worried whether the milk was pasteurized and the bottles sufficiently sterilized. The captain also objected to the quantity of luxury goods (purchased at the duty-free shops at Amsterdam airport): Danish liqueur (for women), scotch whiskey (for men), brandy and cigars (for father's 70th birthday), and as many as five cartons of Marlboro cigarettes (a rage in Poland). All the captain could think of was the corrupting influence of these and other goods (such as the children's stroller, a little marvel of American inventiveness, which I was begged to leave behind on departure, to be copied in Poland), but it all fell comfortably within the limits allowed by our combined tickets. The captain revenged himself by making us exchange a maximum amount of dollars for zlotys at a very unfavorable rate (the special rate for Polish Americans wasn't in place yet). As we were leaving the shabby airport we were surrounded by a crowd of people admiring our clothes, the children's casual summer outfits, and the stroller, which all three used simultaneously.

The hunger for Western goods was overwhelming in Poland; it lasted throughout the entire communist rule till the onset of the free market, when it was finally fed. It was this hunger for consumer goods that made the Poles compromise their once finest quality— love of country—by willingness to leave it even at the cost of denying it by claiming to be of German descent, because that was what was happening in Silesia (and the southern part of former East Prussia) right up to the 1980s, often willingly abandoning their houses, unlike their expelled post-war predecessors, in whose houses they probably lived. I met such a person when looking for the house my late mother had lived in as a girl, and the occupant immediately assumed that I came from the "Reich" to reclaim the house. When I realized what she was planning to do, I begged her to reconsider, that as a person illiterate in German, she would live on welfare in drab blocks on the outskirts of some town until she learned German, instead of living in her present cheerful home.

The impression I carried away with me from Poland was one of hopelessness, of people believing that nothing was going to change for them, that the only thing left for them was to go on with their lives and hope for the best. This was also my advice to those who asked me for it, which was all I could tell them in my circumstances except to add that the future of the world would be determined not by wars but by economy, which was exactly what Khrushchev implied in his famous battle-cry, "We will bury you!"

In the meantime there was church to fall back on, and its importance in those years cannot be overestimated. But there was also something else, another of the things that the communists did well in Poland, namely sports, in which Poland became a veritable superpower in track and field, fencing, boxing, weight lifting, and soon also in soccer and volleyball. On the last Sunday in Poland we watched on television the track and field meeting between Poland and Russia, which was very close right up to the last event, the 10,000-meter run. Since a Polish runner, Zimny, was a favorite, nobody was surprised to hear the announcement that Russia renamed its team Western Russia, with Poland immediately countering with Western Poland. As expected the Polish runners finished first and second, winning the meet for Poland by a comfortable margin of 7 points. The television room, which was full, exploded in applause with the spectators giving vent to their patriotic feelings. Watching them I knew that a nation that takes such pride in the victory of their national team is not defeated yet, especially if the opponent was Russia.

These were the good Poles, the core of the nation and its future, still in the majority, my relatives among them, who regretted my not being with them in Poland but glad I was in America, seeing in me a kind of security, not necessarily material. These church-going, family-raising, God fearing people were determined to outlast the evil that had enveloped them, raising their children in the same resolve, like the young student working the switchboard at the Marie-Curie University in Lublin who, during a summer I was a leader of a Kosciuszko Foundation student group, told me "loyally" that as of the beginning of the program the next day, all telephone conversations would be monitored and recorded. I told him that he restored my confidence in the youth of Poland, and asked him if he had a girlfriend. He had, and I handed him a twenty dollar bill to buy her a present in the hard-currency shop (an engagement ring).

There was another group of people in Poland who thought *they* were the future, still in the minority but growing in confidence. Some of the younger ones among them were ready to confide in me that they were Party members and I always told them not to tell me that, because I would remember it. Because of them, I was afraid that future leaders of Poland would all be Communists, because they had ready access to universities and career jobs. It was also they who occupied diplomatic posts abroad and received foreign scholarships, grants and fellowships, if the government had been entrusted with the selection.

In time, a third group evolved, the smallest but the most prominent in giving Poland a bad name. Among them were the new "Germans" who couldn't speak German and were trying Germany's patience with their shenanigans, but for reasons of its own Germany was hanging on to them. They are now beginning to return, and Poland should take them back, of course, to bolster its sagging population and in the hope that their children will grow up to be good Poles. And then there are the visitors to the border towns, like Frankfurt on the Oder, where there are reportedly thousands of Polish prostitutes operating. There are also swarms of Polish waitresses of dubious morals working for $2 an hour and tips in second-rate restaurants in New York and Chicago. And then there are the Polish car thieves in Europe....

There is another group, of Polish priests, who are present in every significant Polish community in the world. In America, they have an organization PAPA II (the Polish American Priests Association) with 10 members in Cleveland, and reportedly more in Brooklyn.

This diversity is reflected to some extent in the holders of the top positions in Poland, where the President is a former Communist; the new Prime Minister a (Silesian) Protestant; and the new Minister of Foreign Affairs a Jew. The Church's part in this diversity was present in the Christmas ceremony in the Royal Castle on December 23, when the Primate of Poland, Cardinal Józef Glemp, blessed the traditional Christmas wafer while delivering an invocation:

> I ask God that the wafer we are about to break in our hands would serve to renew peace and to strengthen the will to do justice; let it serve the desired moral and social order in our land.

It was with the Primate that the Prime Minister, Jerzy Buzek, began the time-honored Christmas ritual of breaking the wafer, followed by the others present, among them the papal nuncio, Archbishop Józef Kowalczyk; other dignitaries and politicians; representatives of the world of science and culture; and members of the new cabinet, with its most significant appointee, Professor Bronisław Geremek.

In a statement on that occasion Mr. Buzek remarked that the festive atmosphere of the approaching holidays was a reminder of the great summons uniting all Poles without exception, namely to complete the restoration of sovereign Poland, of repairing the state. He said, specifically:

> As a result of the realization of a political reform, there will emerge a strong state; strong through concentration of its energy on solving the most important tasks, among them assuring safety for citizens, guaranteeing justice and equality under the law, and assisting the weakest.

The key words in the statements were "moral and social order...justice" and "safety...justice...law...assisting." They tell us where to find what is wrong with Poland now.

It has been an unwritten rule among the Poles abroad to blame the Communists for every ill in Poland, but it's a faulty rule, because some of the ills existed before the Communists came to power.

Justice, for example, left much to be desired in the period between the wars, and there was no equality under the law in Old Poland, except for the nobility. The old saying, "a nobleman on a piece of land is equal to a governor" (*"szlachcic na zagrodzie równy wojewodzie"*) describes this "equality" well.

The devastation of Poland by Germany in the Second World War was far more extensive than in the First, and it left Poland ruined not only physically but also mentally. There were no national leaders this time and no great post-war victory to restore the nation's faith in itself. Instead, it was a defeated nation this time, with an invincible neighbor whom the Poles considered responsible for ·winning the war, Soviet propaganda playing down the extent of American help. This invincible neighbor, keeping armies large enough to overrun Europe after American withdrawal and demobilization, was the guarantor of Poland's Western border, thus tying the country to itself, with Stalin appearing as a father-figure to many Poles, including the present Minister of Foreign Affairs.

What saved the nation from sinking into total dependency on the Soviet Union was the task of rebuilding the country, particularly Warsaw, 80% destroyed, and the near-miraculous brick-by-brick reconstructing of the Royal Castle, a long-range project which attracted the attention of the world and much help from American Polonia, both great morale boosters. At the time of this writer's first visit to Poland (1959) whole sections of Warsaw were still roped off, not to be touched until the original blueprints had been found or duplicated, but the pride was already there on people's faces, of the hero-city returning, like winning another Battle of Warsaw.

Poland's rich history provided the next morale boosters when important anniversaries arrived, first the world-wide celebration of the 600th of the University of Cracow (the Jagiellonian—this writer had the pleasure of being asked by his Ukrainian instructor to announce it in his class on "Slavic Civilizations" at Columbia University and receiving, probably because of that, a grade of A+), and two years later (1966) the greatest anniversary of them all—MILLENNIUM OF POLAND'S CHRISTIANITY. It was the year also when Karol Cardinal Wojtyła visited Pittsburgh to open and bless a Marie Curie-Skłodowska wing of the University with this writer serving as one of the co-hosts in his capacity as the Polish professor.

By then scholarly exchanges with Poland, started by The Kosciuszko Foundation before the war and interrupted by it, had already resumed, and a two-way traffic began. To accommodate the American students (and to siphon off the dollars and marks held by the natives), hard-currency shops started opening in Polish cities. In retrospect, these developments mark the beginning of Polish consumerism.

Gradually a double-currency economy developed in Poland. By some estimates there were about 5 billion dollars held in Poland by private citizens: emigrants returning with their savings and those who had saved money sent by their relatives in America (some dollars may have come from air drops during the occupation). For the regime to lay its hands on even part of the money would be a boon. Hence the currency shops, little supermarkets in which one could buy not only Western consumer goods, mostly American, but also hard to get for local currency domestic products, like badly needed building materials (cement, tiles, nails) at reasonable prices, but no delivery (to be picked up).

But it was the American consumer goods (jeans, records, sodas) that were the rage. When we add to it other developments in the consumer field (American movies and Marlboro cigarettes produced on license in Poland), it all amounted to a growing Americanization of Poland.

It also amounted to a false image of America, as a land of unlimited purchasing power with which to buy the good things of life. Almost everybody's dream was to go to America and live like an American, having not the slightest idea of how to accomplish it, without the knowledge of the language and true knowledge of American realities, hence my proposal for Polonia to undertake to inform young people in Poland, where ignorance of America persists to this day.

A chance encounter with a shipyard worker in the 1970s in Szczecin underlined the need for such information. The man was operating a piece of heavy equipment and wanted to know how much a similar operator earned in America. When I told him probably $50,000 a year, he gasped, exclaiming next what he could do with $50,000!, citing immediately a bigger apartment and a bigger car. When I told him that a $50,000 man with a family in America probably also couldn't afford a bigger apartment and a bigger car, and that the American pay scale did not apply to Poland with a much lower cost of living, he was unconvinced, all he could think of was the dollar figure. It was the same in Gdańsk in 1980, when the

Solidarity union's striking shipyard workers were also citing in interviews the need for bigger apartments and bigger cars among their grievances. It would not surprise me to learn that the Barbara Piasecka-Johnson plan to buy the Gdańsk shipyard fell through over the men's expectations to be paid according to an American scale.

In their learning about America (mostly from movies) the young people in Poland were, and still are, mostly interested in the seamier and more exciting aspects (sex, violence, crime) to the neglect of positive aspects of America (work ethics, keeping appointments and meeting deadlines, courtesy in business and office), all in short supply in Poland, while uncontrolled sex, violence and crime are on the rise. Who is to blame for this situation? Communism, certainly, for the absence of work ethics and of courtesy; erosion of morals and manners, brought about by growing consumerism, for the bigger evil. But also to blame is the lessening influence of the church and of the family.

Some of us in America (unfortunately, not many) have been watching the developments in Poland with alarm, looking to the most recent arrivals for confirmation of our worst fears, and finding them, while also discovering a huge irony. While under Communism genuine emigrants were arriving "after bread," and genuine exchange students (with an occasional agent now and then) and young scholars (some with Fulbright Fellowships, given to candidates trusted by the government), there were only a few motivated solely by the greed for dollars (a surgeon who got a job cleaning big freezers in Chicago, at a risk of frostbite to his hands which would put an end to his career; a former *starosta* [county head], cleaning one of my student's Michigan Avenue advertising agency's equipment with cancer-causing chemical fluids, all for the great—to him—sum of $17,500 a year); and during martial law genuinely motivated Solidarity activists found themselves on these shores, some stranded (like the Fulbright scholar Jerzy Thieme), others leaving Poland by various means (like the computer scientist Andrew Targowski), both participating in this writer's well-funded International Symposium on "Poland's Solidarity Movement" with other scholars (Lawrence Biondi, S.J., Irene-Dubicka Morawska, Leszek Kołakowski, George J. Lerski, Władysław Majkowski, Frank Mocha) at Loyola University of Chicago in April of 1982), and others were arriving with perfectly marketable skills (like the graphic artist Rafał Olbiński) leading to successful careers here, an entirely different situation developed with the onset of the free market in Poland and its introduction by Leszek Balcerowicz, the Finance Minister, by his widely debated "shock therapy."

The huge irony of the new situation was that the long-awaited free market (which came with independence in 1989 turning Poland into a "market democracy"—a new term) brought with it unexpected hardships. The shops and stores filled with Western goods (not necessarily better than the domestic, especially food, but preferred) and new ones were opening, but there was no money, or not enough of it, to pay for the goods. Only the new entrepreneurs had enough money. As in African countries after independence (Kenya), when no manna fell from the sky and disappointment turned into anger, and the departing former colonizers were asked to turn around and return to restore order, there was a similar feeling in Poland, of nostalgia for the old system.

The disappointment was made even more acute when President Bush, visiting Poland on that occasion, offered only a modest $100-million grant, adding that America had its own financial problems. Here were the Poles, expecting that the world owed them so much that it would take care of their needs for ever, finding out that they had become, in effect, yesterday's news, and that their beloved America was brushing them off with an excuse of financial problems. Reporting on it, *Życie Warszawy* ("Warsaw's Life") commented sarcastically, *"We* should have such problems," a comment showing how little the Poles really knew about America, if a Polish newspaper didn't know about the $4-trillion U.S. foreign debt (dwarfing Polish indebtedness) and about the yearly problems with balancing the budget in America.

There followed what the Polish American Press called "wasted years" in Poland, which began at first on a good note, with the III Congress of Scholars of Polish Descent, symbolically marking the end of the old and the beginning of the new, since this time the Congress was taking place at the reconstructed Royal Castle, under the aegis of its curator, Professor Aleksander Gieysztor. I wanted to make it even more symbolic by using the place and the occasion to hand Lech Wałęsa a copy of the book from the International Symposium which had been dedicated to him. I had notified the organizers about my plan, and Dr. Miodunka, substituting for Hieronim Kubiak, told me they had a special meeting about it. I also asked Professor Gieysztor to schedule my paper, "The Evolution of Knowledge of

Poland in the USA" in which Wałęsa figures prominently, last in the afternoon session, in order not to disrupt it while honoring Wałęsa, but a priest whom I had asked to be a go-between in synchronizing Wałęsa's entry, cited various obstacles which made me doubt his sincerity and willingness to help bring a symbolic event to a conclusion. It did not take place, and I had a feeling that many good things in Poland would not be taking place for one reason or other.

To begin with was Lech Wałęsa's becoming President in 1990 after a compromise year of General Jaruzelski's Presidency, and *not* trying to become a meaningful national symbol but a strong President, a possibility the drafters of a new Constitution should not have allowed. But the drafters were in America, lecturing (Geremek) or teaching (Osiatyński) and collecting honoraria or faculty pay (and a computer from my Alma Mater in the case of Geremek), and not completing the drafting of the Constitution in time for the 200th anniversary of the May 3rd Constitution in 1991, thus causing Poland to miss a great opportunity to attract attention to itself by world-wide celebrations of a famous document, the way America celebrated its own in 1987 (with conferences, stamps, and commemorative medals which I had brought to show in Poland and left at the Consulate in New York to show Leszek Balcerowicz) and Poland its other great anniversaries, the Jagiellonian and the Millennium. True, Professor Geremek lectured about the Constitution, but that's just one lecture, and by a medievalist!

Lecturers from Poland descended like locusts on America at that time, not always bringing a good product, and even then acting as if dispensing great wisdom, and only so much of it, at that, as, for example, Professor Ajnenkiel, turning to his audience at the Institute on East Central Europe at Columbia with a curt question "Enough?" And then there was the group of young editors from the Polish media, including the Solidarity organ, receiving training at select publishers, television stations, and magazines (Lapham's *Harper's* among them), but spending as much time as possible doing something else, the Solidarity man dashing off to Washington, others working on the side and looking for bargains to take with them to Poland. True, they were enriching Poland indirectly, but they should have been spending every waking hour perfecting their skills to make Poland better prepared for the European Union.

Membership in the European Union became for Poland literally a matter of life and death. No longer a part of the Eastern bloc with its inefficient planned economy, artificial rates of exchange and a wastefully maintained full employment, Poland had to find a substitute for the system which, no matter how bankrupt, still provided an illusion of security and even well-being for people.

The (Western) European Union is a logical goal for Poland in view of the country's shift west following World War II and the imposed Bug-River Eastern border line which, despite the painful loss of Wilno and Lwów, became a de facto border between East and West Europe, with Poland returning to its Western roots. So much for theory. In practice other factors are taken into consideration.

In practice it means privatization of huge government monopolies, a slow process in the absence of investors, with the result that former well-connected communists were acquiring them. It also means proper financing of education and health care, both troublesome, especially health, where children are the victims. One of the biggest problems is the neglected environment made even worse in the western areas by the departing Soviet troops.

Without putting all these problems in acceptable shape, joining the European Union was out of the question. Meanwhile unemployment was rising, and so was inflation, while the earlier high birthrate was falling precipitously. Balcerowicz's "shock therapy" was taking its toll, and the last big wave of emigration started, legal (doctors and scientists) and mostly illegal (workers), with people leaving without a backward glance, unlike the highlanders in the now seemingly forgotten sentimental song,

> Highlander, are you not sorry to leave...
> (*Góralu czy ci nie żal opuszczać strony ojczyste*),

whose somber refrain "For bread" gave a name to the economic emigration of a century ago. This time it was for the dollar and no longer the lecture vultures, except for the likes of Janusz Onyszkiewicz, member of Parliament and former Defense Minister, talking about Poland and NATO (but not daring to talk about Kaliningrad); otherwise, low-grade workers, cleaning women, waitresses, and increasing number of live-in self-styled health-care "specialists" (often doctors) looking after infirm elder Americans. Some, when their "visits" ended in a fiasco, would volunteer to take valuable mail to Poland (like rare photos), without ever sending a proof of delivery (this writer resorted to this method in good faith, despite having his collection of rare materials rifled by earlier "visitors" from Poland).

I witnessed the erosion of traditional Polish values on my last visit to Poland to take part in the Combatants rally in Warsaw (and Częstochowa) in 1992 (I am still wondering why 1992?) and I was disappointed how few people turned out to witness what was a unique sight of old Polish veterans from all over the world still marching...

The direct result of Poland's difficulties in the early 1990s was the steady loss of popularity by President Wałęsa, who totally mishandled a chance of becoming a man of destiny in Poland, having been handed the chance on the proverbial silver platter, but completely misreading his role. Instead of surrounding himself with sycophants, he should have gotten himself a genuine mentor, who would teach him what to say and how to say it, and who would also translate for him what this writer had to say about him in his book on Solidarity (he must have a copy, because it was sent to him through Professor Geremek after his lecture at Columbia University). Failing to do that, it is no wonder that he was more popular abroad, where he kept his mouth shut, or spoke through a translator, than in Poland.

He was invited to the 50th anniversary of D-Day in Normandy in 1994, and arrived with a crack battalion of infantry (no doubt for the sake of NATO membership). That same year he participated in the celebration of the 50th anniversary of the Polish American Congress in Buffalo. The sequence and significance of the two events did not escape the attention of the participants, among them many Americans friendly to Poland, including Madeline Albright, the then-US Ambassador to the United Nations (and former student of Professor Brzezinski at Columbia) and a strong supporter of Poland's membership in NATO.

Next to President Wałęsa there were several other guests from Poland at the PAC's meeting in Buffalo, among them Prime Minister Waldemar Pawlak and the ubiquitous Jacek Kuroń, former Secretary of Labor. All of them had one thing in common: total ignorance of the English language. This writer, who started to plan the present book at that time, intended at first to start it on that note, but decided against underlining the linguistic poverty of Poland's leaders. Whether that poverty had anything to do with the results of the coming Presidential elections in Poland is a valid question.

President Wałęsa was not invited the following year (1995) to the celebrations of the 50th anniversary of the end of World War II in Berlin, for the simple reason that Poland was not invited, a decision for which Germany was criticized in many quarters, particularly in Poland. Whether this was the reason is hard to say but the fact remains that it was the last time Poland was snubbed by Germany since the end of World War II, which only shows the low level Poland was at that time, perhaps the lowest since the war, but the low level was ending, coinciding with the beginning of strong support of Poland by Germany, including membership in NATO and in the European Union.

Germany's support of Poland coincided in turn with another significant development, the defeat of Lech Wałęsa by Aleksander Kwaśniewski in the presidential elections in 1995. The fact that a former Communist became President of Poland did not raise many eyebrows, it was overshadowed by Balcerowicz's "shock therapy" beginning to succeed and Poland beginning to turn the economic corner.

The new President, whose popularity was high even before his election, endeared himself further to the nation by a commitment to lead Poland into the European Union and NATO. He was well received abroad thanks largely to his (and his wife's) facility in English. The couple is close in age and life style to the Clintons, which in Poland, in love with everything American, was important.

More important was the continuation of the economic reform. Gradually unemployment began to decline and so did inflation, and trade began to grow, with Germany the most important partner and investor. Privatization too was on the increase, and Poland was beginning to show the fastest economic growth in Europe. Also, the disturbing emigration slowed down, and a reverse movement started.

Communist influence began to decline, and in the parliamentary elections in 1997 a coalition of Solidarity and Freedom Union (Unia Wolności) won the majority of seats, allowing the leader of the majority party, Marian Krzaklewski of Solidarity, to nominate a Prime Minister, Jerzy Buzek, a chemistry professor from Silesia and, most significantly, a Protestant (Lutheran).

Poland still has a long way to go to meet the standards of European Union. It is still far behind even the Union's poorer members, but it is moving in the right direction. A most recent article in *The New York Times* ("Normal Poland," December 27, 1997) makes a point that today's Poland resembles more Spain or Portugal than its former neighbors from the Soviet bloc.

With unemployment at 10.6% on par with the average for the European Union, important highway construction is taking place, along a north-south axis by an American firm, and west-east with money provided by the European Union. As for NATO, New Yorkers had a look at the Polish military, when a 100-strong Polish Army band marched in the Pulaski Parade, with three generals leading: Army, Navy, Air Force.

The new Prime Minister has his priorities in high order. The fact that he is Silesian like Wojciech Korfanty, but unlike Korfanty a leader rather than a victim, speaks for itself in many ways. His Protestantism endows him with a pragmatic mind-set, different from the traditional Polish Catholic *Weltanschauung*. These departures bode well for Poland. How well will be a test of Poland's future.

9

Wieńczysław J. Wagner

IMPRESSIONS FROM POLAND

It is quite natural, for a person coming to Poland from abroad, to compare what he sees and experiences in that country to his own place of residence. Some of his impressions will be positive, some negative. In many respects, he will find no substantial differences between the two countries.

To someone who lived in Poland years ago and pays a visit to his mother country another comparison comes to mind: the Poland of yesteryear and that of today. When I was leaving Warsaw on October 3, 1944, to go to German prisoner-of-war camps after the collapse of the Uprising, the Polish capital was in shambles—or rather did not exist. Those few buildings that were still standing were being burned by the Germans after the city was subdued.

In the last days of the "Battle of Warsaw" the condition of the town was so miserable that proposals were advanced to abandon the old capital and either select another town as capital, or build a new city. In the editorial of a journal I was editing until the end of the Uprising, just before the armistice, I defended the idea that Warsaw must be rebuilt.

As we all know, the Old Town of the capital was completely annihilated during the battle, but rebuilt after the war soon after the hostilities ended, with the pieces of old stones and bricks used as building materials. Today, this part of Warsaw looks exactly as it looked years ago, and foreign visitors can hardly believe that half a century ago the Old Town was nothing more than a heap of ruins.

Yes, the disaster of war and the Uprising administered a death blow to the hundreds of churches, palaces, libraries, museums and other landmarks of Warsaw. However, on the positive side, the destruction of the town permitted its reconstruction in a more reasonable way that the dictates of modern times require. Some narrow streets have been considerably widened. In particular, Ulica Świętokrzyska, in the very center of Warsaw, became much broader than it was before the war. Remnants of some old buildings which were dilapidated in 1939 were removed.

However, until the "bloodless revolution" of 1989, the progress in building and reconstruction was not impressive. The few new buildings were constructed in the cheapest possible way from the most inexpensive materials, and soon after they were put to use various repairs were becoming necessary. Besides, the real estate having been appropriated by the communist authorities, the bureaucrats of the public administration did not care about the condition of the property they had to manage, and both the few pre-war buildings which were saved and the new structures were neglected. Half a century after the end of the war, traces of bullets are still visible on many walls.

The end of the "Polish People's Republic" in 1989 marked the beginning of a new era in the history of Warsaw. The town revived. With the gradual switch from a planned economy to the market system, the shabby shops where there was hardly anything to buy and where the saleswomen considered it to be a special favor to shoppers to serve them, were transformed into genuine and attractive buying places, with a great variety of items and personnel eager to satisfy the wishes of the clients. Previously grim faces, dissatisfied with the arrival of a customer who would disturb the employee who was quietly smoking or reading a newspaper, turned into smiling physiognomies, welcoming business-bringing guests. Even in public offices where the citizens used to be treated as nuisances to be rid of as fast as possible, people began to be treated with more consideration. Enthusiasm for the new system was such that some optimists would open huge stores, supply them with expensive wares and expect impressive profits, only to run into bankruptcy later.

However, business is picking up. In the last few years both Polish and foreign entrepreneurs have built many impressive buildings and quite a few hotels. Holiday Inn, Marriott, MacDonalds, Burger King and other American and West European firms have made appearances in Warsaw and quite a few localities in Poland. A visitor from the United States may feel at ease, the more so that many stores have English names, and the English language paper, *The Warsaw Voice*, can inform them of what is going on.

Again, if one turns on a TV set, there is a good chance he will see American movies, and if he would like to hear some beautiful Polish military or folk songs on the radio, in most instances he will be disappointed. Instead of local melodies he will have to listen to the hits or country music from the United States. The hatred towards everything that came from the East and the desire to be integrated with the West is so strong that hundreds of foreign words, particularly English, are being used by the mass media, and also by average people, polonized and replacing Polish terms. All this is shocking for someone who attended schools in Poland and, returning after many years, would enjoy immersion in Polish tradition and culture. Unfortunately, nobody seems to care, and institutions which should rise to defend the national heritage, such as the universities, the Polish Academy of Sciences, or professors of Polish, keep silent.

Fortunately, the music of Chopin, the incarnation of the Polish spirit, is cultivated in a few places. Every Sunday, during the summers, Chopin music is played in the beautiful public park Łazienki, one of the oldest in Europe, and concerts featuring the famous composer take place in Żelazowa Wola, his birthplace, and in the Ostrogski Palace, headquarters of the Chopin Society.

An outlet for Polish patriotism is offered by numerous anniversaries of important events from the Polish past, commemorating both happy and sad happenings, of which there were hundreds in the last fifty or sixty years. Recently, the most memorable celebrations were organized on the occasion of the 50th anniversary of the Warsaw Uprising and of the end of World War II, but hardly any week passes without some reason for digging into history and setting up a remembrance. Of course, beside national events there are local ones, to recall the death of a county hero executed by the Germans, the burning of a village by the Russians, or something similar. Most of these celebrations are carried out very well and attract hundreds of people. However, most of those who attend are older citizens. A substantial part of the young generation is more interested in making money than in displaying its Polishness. Quite a few of the energetic and enterprising middle-aged and younger persons, dismayed by the miserable state of the Polish economy during communist times and disappointed by the slow progress of the market economy, decided to look for a better economic future in foreign countries and left Poland either for good or for a temporary stay abroad.

At first glance, some old Polish customs seem to be surviving, such as the courtesy extended by men towards the fair sex including the kissing of hands. A foreign visitor is also favorably impressed by the eagerness with which younger people offer their seats to the older, or to mothers with babies, on public transportation. Again, the patience with which the Poles wait for green light before crossing a street is praiseworthy. In Italy or France most people do not care about such trifles, in accordance with the song: "The light is red, just go ahead."

On the other hand, the rise in crime is alarming. During communist times, everyone was afraid of the police who could arrest, beat up, torture and even kill anyone they wanted, criminals or political dissidents, practically uncontrolled by higher authority. At the present time, the fear of law-enforcing organs is over, human rights including those of the defendants and suspects are again respected (as a matter of fact, Poland began to enact relevant rules as early as the XIV century), and the law breakers count on their impunity. Car thefts became frequent, and citizens who did not hesitate to walk on the street of the capital at any time of the day a few years ago prefer not to leave their homes in the nighttime, and they may feel insecure even in their apartments or houses because of burglaries and break-ins.

Certainly, Poland entered on the road of economic progress and, as mentioned above, some foreign investors have tried to establish their businesses in the country. A number of them were successful, but many were discouraged by the bureaucratic formalities they were required to follow, and sometimes they were unable to surmount the obstacles and decided to go to some other country. As a matter of fact, the rules and regulations enacted during the Polish People's Republic regime, bordering sometimes on the absurd, have not been repealed but are being amended from time to time, sometimes in an awkward manner, and at other times ambiguously, so that it may be difficult to know what the law really is. It may be added that the employees administering the rules are, in the majority, the same who functioned during communist times, and they are accustomed to making simple problems complicated to make the customer feel how important their office is and what a great favor they bestow on those whose petitions are granted. Sometimes, positive answers are made dependent on the payment of a bribe. Of course, this happens in Italy and many other countries, but this is hardly a consolation.

To add to the confusion, re-privatization laws have not been enacted, as yet; they are being discussed all the time. Recently [before 1997—FM], the leftist-dominated parliament rejected bills aiming at the return of nationalized property to previous owners, and is working on other proposals, which would give the owners some bonds the value of which is questionable. It may be added that the property was taken over either by violation of standards respected in civilized countries, or contrary even to the rules enacted by the communist authorities. Thus, the owners of buildings in Warsaw were to get compensation for the nationalization of their property. However, they never received anything. Therefore, the status of real estate in Warsaw is not clear. In the country, some previous owners were able to recover some of their possessions, the decision being taken by local authorities. Frequently, persons claiming ownership (or their descendants) are required to purchase their own property, given priority over other prospective buyers. Often, persons interested in the purchase hesitate to enter into transactions because of the fear of a lawsuit. Anyhow, people go to court rather frequently, and the result of litigation is varied because of the lack of rules to be applied.

Another comment. The interest of most Poles in public affairs is great and they like to discuss politics. They are individualists and during the last few years established many, indeed too many, political parties. In the mass media, most space is devoted to interesting news, both from Poland and from abroad, usually presented in a professional and objective way. This constitutes a sharp contrast with the TV and radio in the U.S., where, just before leaving for Europe in March of 1995, all that I could hear was whether O.J. Simpson murdered his wife or whether Michael Jordan would return to basketball.

It is impossible not to mention the problem of responsibility of former Communist Party activists for all crimes and abuses they have committed. Of course, there is no question of vengeance against those who caused much suffering to individuals or enriched themselves to the detriment of the society, but just of administering simple justice.

Investigations should be geared in two main directions: against those who persecuted Polish patriots, political dissidents and other non-conformists; and those who in one or another way stole public money or took advantage of their positions to get unfair advantage for themselves or their families.

In one type of cases, the defense could consist of the fact that the perpetrator's acts were not prohibited by the Communist system under which the nation lived; but in other instances, this argument would not be possible because the very rules in force were violated.

The first post-Communist government, that of Tadeusz Mazowiecki, introduced the unfortunate policy of forgiveness to the former rulers of the country. This "gruba kreska" [untranslatable, "thick line?" crossing out?—FM] idea was understood to apply only to political decisions; but in fact, proceedings against suspects who should be subjected to investigation for their crimes were very rare, and if they were initiated, their result was in most instances: dismissal of the case. Such was the result of one of the most publicized trials with Generals Stanisław Ciastoń and Zenon Płatek as defendants, accused of masterminding the murder of Rev. Jerzy Popieluszko. Many other investigations had a similar fate. Either the witnesses could not identify their oppressors after many years, or they just "did not remember." At other times, the court found that the proof of guilt has not been established in a convincing way: "beyond reasonable doubt," to use the American formula.

In still other instances, the former Communist Party colleagues stand behind their friend and make the proceedings impossible. This was the case of Ireneusz Sekuła, an active Party member and former head of the Customs Office, elected as a member of the lower house of the Sejm (parliament). The Minister of Justice (Attorney General) accused him of embezzling a very important sum of money, but the leftist-dominated Sejm refused to agree to hear the prosecution's arguments and deprive Sekuła of his parliamentarian immunity. The majority voted against Sekuła, but the required 2/3 of the votes could not be reached.

If the case lands in court, the defendants use all possible means to extend the proceedings as long as possible. Because of the fact that there is no American rule of "one day in court" in continental procedure, the trials progress little by little, one session in the court following another two or five weeks later. Many defendants count on running out the statute of limitations which renders a conviction impossible. Fortunately, the lower house accepted a bill which would set the beginning of the running out the statute of limitations at January 1, 1990. This was confirmed by the Senate on June 30, 1990. However, Senator Ryszard Jarzembowski, leader of the post-Communist group in the Senate, declared that this decision was unconstitutional and should be declared such by the Constitutional Tribunal on the ground that the law cannot be retroactive.

Possibly, this approach will be supported by the "ombudsman" Tadeusz Zieliński, who is known for his anti-clerical and pro-leftist

ideas. A few months ago, a rare conviction in a political murder case
(the victim was a young dissenter, student Stanisław Pyjas, in
Cracow) resulted in a 10-year sentence. Professor Zieliński
petitioned the Supreme Court for a revision of this decision, deeming
it too harsh. The traditional function of the "ombudsman" is the
defense of citizens against the arbitrariness of public administration.
Professor Zieliński deemed it proper to express his dissatisfaction
with a judicial decision. However, the Supreme Court did not change
the judgment.

It is shocking that dozens of former police agents, prison
employees, and other oppressors who were able to enrich themselves
walk with impunity on the city streets, meeting with a smile their
victims—usually poor, and sometimes crippled for life by tortures
which were inflicted on them. The trial against the notorious sadist
Adam Humer and others who excelled in the sophisticated beating of
prisoners drags on for months as the defendants hope the delays will
save them by running past the statute of limitations.

Many protests expressed by individuals and organizations, such
as the General Okulicki Foundation of former members of the Secret
Army—A.K., were not successful and have little chance to be so as
long as the Ministry of Justice and the positions of prosecutors are in
the hands of former communists. On June 28, 1995, on the 39th
anniversary of the Poznań massacre when the police shot and killed
over 70 protesters, the chairman of the local "Solidarity," Marek
Lenartowski, appealed again for making the criminals of the Polish
People's Republic era accountable for their deeds and shouted:

> I warn you, Communists, who get back to power by different
> means, do not play games with the inhabitants of Poznań and
> the workers of that city. Stop making fun of free Poland.

and he continued:

> It is difficult to live in a country where until now no honest
> count of merits and demerits was made. And the June, 1956,
> requests are still timely we want freedom, law, and bread.

Another battle is being waged in the field of veterans'
privileges. The post-Communists induced the Sejm to grant the status
of ex-combatants to former policemen and members of various
formations who "cemented the People's Republic." President Wałęsa

vetoed the statute, and the parliament was unable to override his disapproval; but it appears that the fight did not end, as yet.

Along with economic disaster, communist rule brought about deep and unfortunate changes in the mentality of the Polish nation, similarly to that of other countries under communist domination. We have heard about the most difficult problem which West Germany had—and Germany still has—in making the East Germans' way of thinking similar to the Westerners'. For about 45 years the Poles had to live in a system where membership in the omnipotent Party rather than talent and hard work was instrumental in earning promotion, in traveling abroad, in taking part in political decisions, and even in being permitted to have an apartment or to buy a car. The fulfillment of basic needs, such as the purchase of a pound of meat or a dress was frequently possible only by virtue of "connections" or outright bribes or favors. Free expression of opinion was hindered by fear that the other party to a conversation may be a secret police informer.

The minds which had to adjust to this reality cannot be healed overnight. Frequently the approach to the problems of life of an average person is still to follow the previous pattern—a patient in a hospital feels that he will not get proper attention if he neglects to give gifts to the physician and the nurses; a person applying for any license is prepared to bribe the proper officer, etc. Most probably, it will take longer than the life of one generation before the thinking of the population, or at least a significant part of it, gets back to what we consider normal.

Another mention is due to the problem of returning Polish emigrants. After 1989, the government proclaimed its eagerness to see Poles in our "diaspora" re-settle in their country of origin. In fact, some people got back, and in a few cases even those who were born in other countries decided to settle in Poland. Unfortunately, most of them were disappointed.

In the first group were persons who were willing and able to serve their mother country by their experience, knowledge, contacts, education and mastery of foreign languages. Frequently they would offer their services—usually without compensation—to the proper authorities. In a few cases the offers were accepted; but in most cases their willingness to work met with rebuttal, unlike the handling of the same problem by most other countries which emerged from under communist rule. A separate study could be written on this

subject, with many examples cited. Let me just state that the country
which badly needs educated people, which lost more than 6 million
of its citizens (particularly from its "intelligentsia") during the war
and about one million of the most enterprising and active young men
and women who emigrated from Poland in recent years because of
political and economic reasons, refused an opportunity to improve its
human resources in a way which did not require any effort or outlay
of money.

Most probably the reasons for this sad state of affairs are:
primarily, the reluctance to have competitors who could be better
equipped, in many instances, to perform their duties than the local
people, and also, particularly on the part of employees in lower
positions who kept their jobs after the change of the government and
who were recruited from among Party members, bias against the
returning Poles who were staunch anti-Communists.

The second group was composed of retired persons who
intended to spend their last years in the country of their fathers.
They met with an unpleasant surprise: they would have to pay heavy
taxes on their retirement benefits, usually up to 45%. In foreign
countries old age benefits are not taxed, unless they reach a substantial amount. In Poland, where salaries are a fraction of those in the
United States, a modest income, according to American standards,
seems high and is subjected to high taxation. Thus, some people who
intended to settle in Poland realized that they just could not afford it.
During communist times, prices in Poland (and in other counties
within the Soviet "zone of influence") were artificially low; now in
most instances they match the American prices.

The fiscal policy of the Polish government is detrimental to the
interests of the country. The returning retirees would spend all the
money, obtained abroad, in Poland; but they cannot allow themselves
to be deprived of nearly half of their income from the very moment
they begin to live in Poland.

Because of all this, Poles from abroad had to reconsider their
re-settlement decision, and some chose to return to the foreign
country after they had moved to Poland. Sometimes, this decision
was prompted by a disgust with the bureaucracy and conflicting
information, e.g., recently my friend from Minnesota arrived in
Poland, considering settling in Warsaw. However, after a few days
he decided to return to the United States.

There is no need to describe all he went through during the short time he spent in Poland. Let me mention just one event. After landing at the airport, he went to an officer who took care of certifying the amount of money visitors brought to the country and declared one thousand dollars. The officer told him that such a small amount did not have to be entered on the declaration, the minimum sum being $2,500. But when my friend appeared in a bank with the intention to open a dollar account, his request was refused on the grounds that any amount brought by a foreign citizen needs to be certified. Explanations did not help. Some old rules, introduced during the Polish People's Republic, which render the life of Poles and foreigners miserable, have not been revoked or changed, and conflict with the new ones as well as with reason.

Another remnant from Communist times is addiction to alcohol and tobacco. To be sure, even before World War II many Poles had a liking for vodka; but the habit of drink became a scourge of the society during the time of the People's Republic. People used to drink in order to forget their everyday problems. Another consolation was smoking. Cigarettes begin to be used, in many instances, in the early teens. An anti-smoking campaign is being undertaken by the government only now. Statistics show that 100 to 110 persons die every day in Poland as a result of smoking; and that one and a half million Poles are addicted to alcohol.

Last comment: If a taxi is needed, the best idea is to call a company which will send a car with a courteous driver within minutes—and at a reasonable rate. If the tourist prefers a more democratic transportation, he will soon realize that the net of buses and streetcars is good, and that timetables posted at every stop are abided by most of the time. However, the drivers drive poorly. Very rarely do they go smoothly. Usually, the cars go fast and then slow down or stop suddenly, as if an unexpected obstacle appeared in their way. Passengers feel they are treated like bags of potatoes.

Trains make good progress. Twenty years ago they were slow, and often they would stop on the way in some field for any reason, usually because the electric current had been cut. Sometimes, such an interruption lasted for hours. Usually, there was no water or toilet paper, and the washrooms were dirty. At present, most trains meet Western standards, they run fast (from Warsaw to Cracow in 2 1/2 hours, to Poznań—in 3 hours) and on time. Maybe they will soon match the perfect functioning of Polish pre-war railways. They are improving steadily, and on important routes, such as one from Paris to Berlin, Poznań, Warsaw, Mińsk, and Moscow, they will be modernized and the trains will be running as fast as on the best West European routes.

The recently opened subway transportation (on one line, to begin with) met with genuine praise. The cars are comfortable, the stations—pleasing to the eye, and the speed of the trains—adequate.

Summer 1995

10

Jan Nowak Jeziorański

POLAND AFTER COMMUNISM

(Excerpts from a speech given in Polish in the Assembly Hall of Collegium Novum at the invitation of the Rector of the Jagiellonian University, Cracow, June 1995)

Thank you most cordially for inviting me back to this assembly hall. I spoke here once in 1989 and that meeting, extremely moving for me, has remained deep in my memory. I realize that it wasn't my private person that mattered then, but that the former Director of Polish Broadcasting in Radio Free Europe appeared before you at the beginning of the Third Republic, speaking no longer from the distance of Munich and through a barrier of jamming, but facing you and addressing you directly. That fact was a spectacular sign of a breakthrough that had just then taken place in Poland. And because it took place within the four walls of the Villa Magdalenka, and the Polish people actually did not take part in it, it seems to me that my appearance in the assembly hall of the Jagiellonian Alma Mater was a confirmation of the change that had taken place.

On my way here, I asked myself what I have to offer you six years later. I believe that I can simply offer a different view. A view not only from the prospect of my life's experiences, but above all from a distance, because I look on Poland both from afar and up close. For 45 years, the whole world was open to me with the exception of my native country, but since September 1989 I have made 26 trips here. I am therefore in a kind of swing movement between the United States and Poland.

I stand outside any political alignments, a position I have deliberately adopted in order to gain greater credibility for my mission. This mission is a continuation of what I did in my "Free Europe" years: an attempt to influence society in the spirit of my own concerns. My age no longer permits me to be interested in any office or position. Nor do I expect any decorations and honors because those I have already been generously given satisfied my ambitions entirely. I do not state my electoral preferences publicly and try to remain outside internal disputes. The fact that I reside in Washington, and not in Warsaw, undoubtedly makes this easier for me.

293

My view of present realities is completely different from the way the Poles see themselves. It seems to me that the last half-century, a time of very intense experiences for me even though I was abroad, will go down in our history as a praiseworthy chapter. Our fortunes had touched rock-bottom in 1945. It was difficult to imagine a greater defeat. Our expectations, our hopes and our trust in our allies had been utterly broken, and it looked as if there was no way out of the fall. And yet that society, which had lived through such terrible disappointments and which had been subjugated by a foreign power, drew on its own experiences and was able to construct unusually effective forms of resistance even though it had no staff of leaders or politicians who would point the way.

The fact that Poland was the only one of the vassal states where the Church maintained its unity and autonomy is enough to prove the effectiveness of this resistance. In a system bent on destroying it, the Church achieved the apogee of its influence, an apogee expressed in the ascension to the Throne of Peter of a Pope from Poland. The effectiveness of this resistance was also demonstrated by the fact that only in Poland did the peasants stave off collectivization, only in Poland did the intelligentsia gradually win for itself a relatively wide margin of freedom of speech, and only in Poland did the workers become a force that the system had to reckon with. What happened in 1989 was the last step on a road to freedom that led though 1956, 1970, and finally 1980.

But September 12, 1989 was a turning point not only on a Polish, but also on a global scale. There is no exaggeration in the words of Bronisław Geremek that I read recently in *Tygodnik Powszechny*—that it was Poland that overthrew communism. So it was! Thanks to Poland's courage and thanks to the fact "the king was naked" and that Moscow was no longer capable of stopping what was happening here. Face to face with the total collapse of the system, it could no longer intervene. Poland was the country that shattered the paralyzing barrier of fear of the Soviet Union, blazed the trail for others, and set in motion a whole chain of events: the fall of the Berlin Wall, the gradual liberation of the states of the Eastern bloc and later the Baltic countries, and the disintegration of the Soviet Union. It began here, and we can say that victory in the Cold War was won by two countries: by the American superpower that won the arms race and the economic race, and by the small country on the Vistula, powerless and defenseless in the face of foreign domination, that nevertheless knew how, in some miraculous way, to find the right road for itself. This road was at total variance with the established stereotype of cavalry charging tanks and of incessant insurrectionist outbursts always ending in terrible catastrophes.

It seems to me that I differ from most of the people in Poland in my opinion of the first non-communist government, the government of Tadeusz Mazowiecki. That government accomplished extraordinary things. The unconditional acknowledgment of the border on the Oder and Neisse and the reconciliation with Germany was in itself an event commensurate with the millennium spent under the German threat. Treaties of neighborly friendship were also patiently and wisely negotiated with all neighbors, not excluding difficult ones, like Lithuania. For the first time in its history Poland is free of conflicts, ethnic or territorial, with any of its neighbors. For the first time foreign armies withdrew from this land without a shot being fired, voluntarily. Rights have been restored to national minorities. All these are great accomplishments.

In the economic field, the successes have been, if anything, even greater. After all, Poland started from a position far worse than that of all the other post-communist countries. The mad galloping inflation, reaching 900% at the end of 1989, was pushing the country into total chaos; the budget deficit was reaching astronomical dimensions. The burden of debt was so enormous as to make Poland an insolvent country. There was grave danger of economic dependence on the Eastern bloc—trade with the East represented two thirds of our commercial transactions. Finally, shortages of basic goods were so acute as to threaten the country with a social crisis. Then, in one blow all subsidies, privileges and allowances for the state and agricultural sectors were abolished. Thanks to this measure, the budget deficit was radically reduced. Inflation fell from 900% to 50% on an annual basis. The *zloty* became, to a limited extent, a convertible currency. The introduction of free market mechanisms created a wave of basic goods to the shops. The unleashing of private enterprise and its spontaneous, dynamic growth was a milestone on the road forward.

The first danger came from the breakdown of the trade with the East, especially with Russia, which simply stopped being able to pay its bills. Poland's answer was a reorientation of its foreign trade from East to West in a record short time, along with an unprecedented intensive growth in commercial transactions. Today it beats all records, and foreign trade is the main driving force in the Polish economy. Poland's alacrity, determination and courage in introducing these reforms, together with how much the world owed Poland then, contributed to the reduction of our debts, first to other states and then to commercial banks, by half.

It was, of course, necessary to demolish the teetering structure of communist Poland in order to be able to erect this new edifice. It was an operation which entailed huge social costs. Production fell by at least 14% in 1990, and 10% the following year. Furthermore, living conditions deteriorated drastically in connection with this transition phase, the effects of which are still felt today. The average level of unemployment stands at 15%, but we know that in some regions of the country it reaches 30%. It is often forgotten, however, that it was a healing operation, necessary after 45 years of senseless planned economy, centrally directed.

There is an essential difference between the way Poles view their reality and the way we are seen from the outside. All the international financial institutions maintain that Poland excels and is a model for others, and that what has happened confirms the correctness of the road it had chosen, even if Poland was like a ship setting sail on an open sea without a chart or a compass. All signs herald improvement. At present the average Pole can barely feel the progress in the sphere of production and the growth of national product. But when I speak, for example, with an American official touring post-communist countries as part of his job of coordinating and distributing aid, he says that he has nowhere seen such vitality, such dynamism, so much initiative and momentum as in Poland. The difference in the assessment of the situation is striking.

As for myself, when I compare Kraków of September, 1989 with that of today—and a mere six years have passed—I see a completely different city. The Kraków of those days revealed itself as a dismal, terribly sad city. [?–FM] There was hardly any traffic, the shop windows were empty, the green spaces neglected, and the people—even if it was an era of a certain euphoria—looked bent down. The Kraków of the present defies comparison even with Innsbruck or Salzburg, because neither of those cities displays such vigor, such movement, so many young people. The changes for the better are striking.

Yet, when I mention this in Poland, the response I hear is,

"Well, you see only the facade, and not what hides behind it. Things are bad, and getting worse."

I can understand that half the people feel that living conditions are worse than they were under communism. But I cannot understand that 58% say that they will be worse. This pessimism is paradoxical, because Poland's whole strength lay in the fact that even in the worst situations it never lost hope and the will to fight. And it is precisely now that this hope is being realized. According to the unanimous opinion of all experts, if Poland continues on the same road it is now, within twenty years it will catch up with the advanced Western countries. And just at this moment, there appears suddenly a general pessimism which seems like a paradox, because it is in total contradiction not only with what I have seen, but it also flies in the face of statistics, the findings of foreign experts and the opinions of financial institutions.

I am convinced that the mass media play a major role in spreading this pessimism, or rather in shaping a poor morale of our society. They do it rather unconsciously since there is a tendency to show Polish reality from its worst side: a tendency which is not intentional, nor is it planned, but it particularly strikes a viewer observing this reality from the outside. The press, radio and television are commercialized to the extent that they have lost the sense of a mission. Yet a newspaper or a radio station in a democratic system can set itself a goal not only to gain the greatest possible number of listeners or readers, and therefore advertisers, but above all to fulfill its mission. Radio Free Europe had a specific mission. The independent press movement had a definite mission—it fought a system, it fought a government. Unfortunately, at the moment when it reached its goal, its momentum carried it on to attacking the new authorities and presenting the post-communist realities in an extremely one-sided way. I can see this, for example, in reports by certain correspondents. Some meeting, of which I am a participant, is presented in such a negative way that I am uncertain if this is really the same meeting that I saw.

This also applies to scandals, abuses of power, and so on. I am not suggesting the introduction of selective news. Competition in the press and radio does not of course permit one paper to cover up something that another would uncover. I am rather thinking of the way information is presented, about headlines and the emphasis on certain events. If people imagine that abuses and scandals are an exclusive element of the present reality, let them read the secret report of the Grabski commission on the abuses uncovered by the Supreme Court Commission in the late seventies. It makes terrifying reading, except that no one was permitted to write about such phenomena. They were covered up, making it impossible to fight them.

Today, any sort of scandal is publicized immediately. This leads to the impression that abuses are linked with democracy. I am a man of the mass media. For six years a campaign, however unconscious, but intensive, has been drumming into people's heads that everything that has been happening is one big failure. This must have a highly destructive effect on people's minds.

The next problem is the massive frustration that the Polish people still feel. This too needs to be understood. Since we talked about the achievements of the Mazowiecki government, we must also say something about the original sin committed then, which is still revenging itself. The fact of the matter is that a system can be changed very quickly; laws can be changed, economic reforms can be introduced. But to change human consciousness shaped by half a century in specific conditions is extremely hard.

Mazowieck's error was, in my opinion, his failure to take advantage of the "honeymoon." He did not take advantage of the moment that accompanies every revolution: the euphoria, the extremely high expectations, the hope that reigned here for the first two or three months. He did not use the period to carry out decisive, quick political reforms. I can understand that the deal made in Magdalenka was necessary. There was no other road to sovereignty and democracy. But that deal lasted too long.

Instead of being held in an atmosphere of euphoria and hope, when "Solidarity" was still united, the Polish parliamentary elections were the last to take place in the entire former Eastern bloc. The order was reversed. If, as in the other post-communist countries, the elections had been conducted immediately after the Berlin Wall was torn down and while "Solidarity" presented a consolidated social movement, the basis would surely have emerged for stable policies of a government which would have a lasting character. It staggers belief that after six years Poland still had no constitution. After six years it continued to be governed according to the principles of a hastily put together "Small Constitution" which is full of loopholes, legal ambiguities and is, because of that, dangerous. ['95]

In the former Czechoslovakia, for instance, events took an entirely different turn. The Czechs put through an act of restitution of the Czechoslovak Republic, as if closing and repudiating the past and making a clean break between the Czechoslovak People's Republic and the sovereign Czechoslovak Republic, which later divided into two states. In Poland events did not even move to the point where the army would take a new oath, since the old one was a pledge of loyalty to the Soviet "ally." There was no spectacular break with the past. I am not talking about mass purges, but it seems to me that the judges and prosecutors, for example, who handed down sentences in political trials—political, I emphasize—should not so much be dismissed as forbidden to hand down sentences in this type of cases. After all, we can hardly demand that these people sit in judgment of themselves or that from one day to another they change the false criteria of justice that were dictated by the party and by ideology.

Because of all this, Poland lacks stability today and governments change constantly. This in turn hinders the continuity of reform, because it entails changes of officials, experts, and policy makers. Also, this lack of stability undercuts our exceptional international position. Naturally, the phenomena I am discussing are not confined to Poland. It is the same in many parts of the world: excessively magnified hopes give way to frustration, disappointment, disillusionment and longing for what was. This can be observed everywhere, except, perhaps, in the Czech Republic. Only in Poland this phenomenon presents itself in a heightened form.

When I was Director of Radio Free Europe it seemed to me that brainwashing had failed completely in our case and that Poles were immune to any form of indoctrination. As it turns out, I was mistaken. Certain schemata are still encoded somewhere in people's subconscious after 50 years. I am thinking above all of the yearning to return to the cage. There is a paradox lurking here. No country in the world has demonstrated such dedication, such a willingness to make sacrifices and such tenacity in the fight for the regaining of freedom. And then, just at the moment when it won that freedom, it acts as if freedom no longer mattered. One symptom of this is the disastrously low voter turnout that manifests alienation not just with respect to this or that government or system but with respect to the state itself. This phenomenon threatens the foundations of democracy. A craving for the security provided by the cage is embedded in the human subconscious. It is safe in the cage, because the bars afford protection. There is no need to worry about food in the cage, because there are keepers in charge of feeding. The only limitation is on freedom of movement. But creatures brought up in a cage feel uneasy in freedom. They have a sense of danger because they are suddenly left to their own devices and are responsible for their own fate. The longing for the cage is quite apparent today. It is seen, after all, in voting for the elites that built the cage and played the role of the keepers. Also encoded in the people's consciousness, or in the subconscious, especially among the former elite, is an aggressive attitude toward the Church, a desire for some sort of religious war, going well beyond a reasonable separation of Church and State.

All of this constitutes a threat to our new democracy, since it leads to the return of the former elite. Not to the return of the system, for that system was so irrevocably bankrupted that even representatives of the former authorities know that an attempt to renew it would end as before. If, however, we reach the point where the three most important organs of the state find themselves in the hands of a party with a tradition of one-party rule, if that party controls the government and the office of the head of state while also commanding a majority in the parliament, then the system of what the Americans call checks and balances, which means the mutual overseeing and limitations of the organs of authority, will be violated. Then, without doubt, the temptation will arise to make that authority permanent, even by legislative means, because there will no longer be any brakes, any power of veto, which would control and limit such aspirations.

If we talk about the economic prospects for Polish democracy, they are bound up with the fact that the course laid out at the beginning has not only proved itself to be correct, but has also been followed consistently. We can talk about slowdowns, about a slackening of the tempo of change, but there is no switching to another track. And it is not my conviction but that of Western experts that, if Poland sticks to that course, the time will inevitably come when an improvement is felt by the average citizen.

I have already mentioned that for the first time in history we have no external threats and conflicts with our neighbors. This is also our chance. The greatest threat comes from ourselves, from our own society. That is why we need a movement of renewal that would set for itself the goal of restoring true values and transforming people's consciousness, still not keeping up with the changes.

Not everything however depends on us. The present hopeful tendencies of development will not hold if Poland and the other countries of our region continue to be barred from the world's greatest potential market, the European Union. Poland will never catch up with the countries of Western Europe, which are entering an era of tempestuous economic expansion, if the Polish economy fails to be fully incorporated in the European Union's integral processes....

[The speaker devotes the rest of his paper to the problem of Poland's future security, beginning with Russia's ability, under a charismatic leader like General Alexander Lebed, to renew its offensive military potential (while reminding his listeners that it took Hitler just a few years after 1933). Then he moves to the problem of Poland's membership in NATO and lists five points of alternative policy for today:]

1. Don't falter regardless of the prospects in order not to be excluded from further dialogue between NATO and Moscow and risk being manipulated by the great powers, together with the other countries lying between Russia and Germany.
2. It is a also a must to elaborate a vision of collective security that is not aimed against Russia and that does not exclude Ukraine, the Baltic States, Romania and Bulgaria.
3. Do not succumb to the fetish of alliances (like 1939). The assurance of security depends on raising the cost of any aggression so high that it no longer pays (1980).
4. Others will not defend us if we are not determined to defend ourselves (Brzezinski's answer to Havel's question; Tito's resolve; Poland's need to organize its forces).
5. Do everything to forestall any agreement between Russia and Germany directed against Poland. Search for cooperation with Russia (taking advantage of our few Russophiles) and closer ties with Germany (no longer the eternal enemy).

We must not give Russia an excuse to brand us as implacable Russophobes (creating a political center for the Chechens on Polish territory) to hinder our NATO admission. NATO for Poland will be decided in America, but unlike 1944 when Roosevelt managed to fool five million Polish voters, no American president can ignore eighteen million votes from a coalition of twelve ethnic groups supporting Poland.

P.S. To this writer, by far the most disturbing aspect of Nowak-Jeziorański's paper is the cage syndrome in Poland; the most important task for *all* Poles is to fight it.—FM

Part III

POLAND AND POLONIA

COLLINS

SŁOWNIK
ANGIELSKO-POLSKI

pod redakcją
PROF. DR. HAB. JACKA FISIAKA

POLSKA OFICYNA WYDAWNICZA

COLLINS

ENGLISH-POLISH
DICTIONARY

EDITOR-IN-CHIEF
PROFESSOR JACEK FISIAK

[We need to better communicate—F.M.]

POLSKA OFICYNA WYDAWNICZA

Frank Mocha

INTRODUCTION

A few months after Nowak Jeziorański's speech in Cracow, presidential elections took place in Poland and his worst nightmare began to materialize—the three most important organs of the state found themselves in the hands of a party with a tradition of one-party rule. But there was a difference: the presidential election was close to the last moment, and only poor judgment and bad advice caused Lech Wałęsa to lose to Aleksander Kwaśniewski. Also, there was now no longer one-party rule in Poland. There was spirited opposition from Marian Krzaklewski's Solidarity and Leszek Balcerowicz's Freedom Union.

This part of the book, just like the previous, was to have a questioning introduction, but reversed, namely:

What do Poles in Poland think of Polonia
and what do they expect from it?

This is a deceptive question, not easy to get an answer to without first knowing who the respondent(s) would be. Fortunately, the presidential elections in Poland took place during the planning sessions for the book, providing the editor, in view of the large number of presidential hopefuls, with a veritable cross-section of Polish society. We will look at the candidates and try to gauge what they think of Polonia and what they expect from it. We will not look at all of them (28 at the beginning, mostly without a valid opinion one way or another), focusing instead on a few selected names.

Of great help in this quest was a questionnaire prepared by Jolanta Szaniawska for *Przegląd Polski* (October 12, 1995) and her personal interview in the same issue of Jan Olszewski, one of the candidates and former Premier.

QUESTIONS OF AN EMIGRANT-VOTER

1. What's emigration to you—let's call it here "Polish Community."
   Any ideas to deepen its ties with Poland?

2. Is Poland capable of becoming a "presence in the world?"
   What do we have to give? If so, what's your program for it?

3. What should people of Polish descent living in the USA and Canada give their homeland? What is expected from them?

4. What is the place of the Community at home—economic, political, cultural? What could Poland do for it as a democratic, modern state?

5. Can the Community be a political entity, for example, in the coming elections?

Only questions 3 and 4 are in keeping with the main question of this chapter, but others are also worthy of answers, as will be seen in the interview with Olszewski.

11

Frank Mocha, Ed. & Comm.

EXCERPTS FROM STATEMENTS BY PRESIDENTIAL CANDIDATES

A. JAN OLSZEWSKI, born 1930 in Warsaw in a railroading family with socialist traditions. A lawyer.

"Politics Is Not Only A Game" ("Polityka to nie tylko gra.")

Active in the Committee for the Defense of the Worker (KOR) and in the Movement for the Defense of the Rights of Man and Citizen; active defender in law suits in 1976 (Radom, Ursus). Co-author of the "Solidarity" statute, and the union's adviser. Co-chairman of National Citizens' Committee, and co-author of Citizens' Constitution Project. Deputy in the first term of the III Republic. Prime Minister 1992. Married, father of one son.

1. One third of the Polish nation (or people with some Polish ties) lives abroad (statement first advanced by this writer at the II Congress of Scholars of Polish Descent in 1979). This defines the character of the Polish Community which must be reflected in the Constitution. Its Citizen's Project adopted an idea of Poland as a state for all Poles.

2. Poland is already a "presence in the world" by the sheer fact of its geographical position, and by the numerical strength of that part of the Polish nation which inhabits the country, almost 40-million strong. Moreover, it is a national organism biologically unbelievably resilient. It is estimated that if Poland enters the European Union in the first decade of the next century, Poles will make up one fifth of those entering productive age in the Union. What Poland has to offer is the high level of education and training of these people. (This is true, but the biological resiliency is no longer true because of adverse demography brought about by declining birthrate, with Olszewski a good example of it, with one child only. Poles will still be one fifth, or even more, of those entering productive age, only because other countries have even lower birthrates. But this is a crisis of Western civilization, to be discussed in greater detail in the last part of the book.)

3. Olszewski would rephrase the third question by asking first what Poles abroad have a right to expect from Poland before they start giving,

namely to be treated as partners and not ignored, dismissed, or even isolated. And what can they give? In the past, after the war, it was 40 years of charitable giving, to meet the country's most pressing needs, which at present Poland can take care of by itself, and the giving can take a different form, namely as a gift of knowledge and experience, which in Poland is worth its weight in gold, but all offers of it, mostly free, to help in the rebuilding of Poland, have so far not been taken advantage of, to Olszewski's (and Wagner's) regret. What he would also like to see is for Poles abroad to channel their former charitable giving to the part of the Polish diaspora beyond Poland's Eastern border, to place on the Western national Community the burden to rebuild economic, cultural and biological Polishness in the East!

4. Poland should strive to finally create for Poles abroad a situation such as, for example, the English and the French have. They have behind them their state, which is a significant one, with international prestige. Irrespective of that, wherever its citizens may be, they can always appeal to this institution, their common creation. Just as in the Jewish diaspora. Irrespective of that, wherever Jews live, Israel is the object of their pride. I am not in favor of imitating that community. Poles and Polish tradition are somewhat tied to another type of reaction to their surroundings. Poles are in that respect considerably more open and partnership-like with relation to other people and communities. I am convinced that there are elements in the Jewish diaspora worthy of adopting. An example of it in the United States is a strong Jewish lobby which has an influence on the politics of the state. This fact is of particular significance when the United States is a superpower which will decide the balance of power in the XXI century, while we are still situated...fatally.

5. It is my belief that the Community should be a political entity. The participation of Polish environments is of course marginal and the size of this electorate limited. But its votes count morally, because it is the position of a group having at this time the right to vote. But it's not just that. These votes have real influence in parliamentary elections because they count as votes in the Warsaw election district. I urge all who want and can, to take part in the elections. It is a direct form of influence. The future of Poland is not clear-cut, although I have hopes that history will go favorably for us and we will return as a rightful member to the European cultural, civilizational and political community. This does not at all mean that there is no danger. In former Soviet Russia there is taking place some gigantic process of forming a new political-economic system. I would be very cautious with optimistic assessments of whether what is happening there sooner or later must fit into and find a common language with the rest of the Western world. This is not at all something one can count on. We may be dealing with the rise of a new system, perhaps just as threatening as the Soviet. Here

I mean mafia capitalism. This is a danger, rising just across our border. And now a question: are we going to be pulled into it, shall we break free from it, and will we be able to lead out of the system the territories in the East which were once in the circle of civilizing influence of the old Commonwealth? As can be seen, it is essential to take part in the political life of Poland—a part which will spare one the choice of undesirable political forces.

In his brilliant analysis, Olszewski doesn't once mention Kaliningrad, geographically the closest danger to Poland.

There were other interviews with candidates in the Polish American press, but none with the sweep of Olszewski and with very little about Polonia, showing typical ignorance. There were also two articles by publishers, B. Wierzbiański in New York, and Adam Michnik in Warsaw, both interesting.

B. WALDEMAR PAWLAK, leader of Polish Peasant Party, Prime Minister twice, farmer.

"Let Us Take Care Of Poland" ("Zaopiekujmy sie Polską"),*Nowy Dziennik*, October 20, 1995)

This interview tells us a great deal about the Polish Peasant Party (*Polskie Stronnictwo Ludowe*—PSL), which in 1995 was celebrating the 100th anniversary of its existence, but nothing about its attitude toward American Polonia (which has, or had, numerous "Peasants" in its ranks), and nothing about the attitude toward Polonia of Poland in general, which is surprising in an interview with the former Prime Minister of Poland.

The young leader of the PSL seems to be a well informed man except when he talks about Poland as "one of the biggest [countries] in the world" which, however, cannot be held against him. When he was in school under communism children were taught that Poland was among the ten leading industrial powers in the world and the Soviet Union was soon to be No. 1, hence some of the bigness syndrome must have rubbed off on him.

He is more modest and closer to the mark when says that "[Poland] has a chance to occupy a place that counts and be a leader in East Central Europe." He probably knows that both in area and in population Poland already *is* a leader in that region, but in Europe as a whole it ranks lower than in the period between the world wars (because of the emergence of an independent Ukraine) and *much* lower than before the Partitions. But it is agriculture that Pawlak is best informed about because this is the environment from which he comes and from which he derives his support. He is not afraid of competition with the agriculture of the European Union, but only if Polish agriculture has the same financial rules, which is not yet the case, with Polish agriculture still far behind when it comes to defense mechanisms in which the European Union is very effective.

Pawlak does not say so but one of the conditions of Poland's entry into the European Union is reduction of its agriculture, a hard condition if one considers that agriculture could be an important bargaining tool in Poland's relations with Russia. On his 1995 visit to America, where he was concerned about Poland's entry into NATO, he should have probably been interested in American agriculture and its grain elevator technology.

Polish agriculture needs an enlightened leader, not as prime minister or president, but as Minister of Agriculture, who by his enlightened policies would lift the peasant from the derisive level of a boor (*cham*) in which he had been traditionally, and even with the help of the Bible, placed, to the level of a modern farmer, as in France, for example. If, in the process, the farmer became prosperous, it would keep his children on the farm, keeping the family structure intact, for the benefit of Poland.

C. HANNA GRONKIEWICZ-WALTZ, president, National Bank of Poland (*Nowy Dziennik*, September 12, 1995).

The syndicated Polish American journalist, Robert Strybel, reported from Warsaw (*Naród Polski*, September 21, 1995):

> A woman President of Poland has become a distinct possibility since National Bank president, Hanna Gronkiewicz-Waltz, threw her hat in the ring. In a recent survey, among potential hopefuls, she came in second only to ex-communist front-runner Aleksander Kwaśniewski. Gronkiewicz-Waltz, an expert in economic law, has wide vote-getting potential because she projects the image of a successful female professional. Unlike radical feminists, however, she is also a devoted wife and mother fully supporting the Church's teaching on the family. Her chances would increase if President Lech Wałęsa, who has yet to officially declare his candidacy,

decided against running for re-election next autumn. In 1993, Poland became the first ex-Soviet bloc country to have a woman prime minister, law professor Hanna Suchocka.

This portrait of Gronkiewicz-Waltz is followed by another revealing paragraph which indirectly also concerns her:

> An Institute in Defense of Poland's Good Name has been set up by the Christian National Union (ZChN or Zjednoczenie Chrześcijańsko-Narodowe), Poland's main Catholic political party. It's purpose is to combat anti-Polonism throughout the world by encouraging the media to truthfully portray Poland's history and current events. "We cannot allow Swedish newspapers to call Polands president 'a boorish dictator' nor permit the spreading rumors in America about alleged 'Polish concentration camps'." ZChN leader Ryszard Czarnecki said. The Institute has branches in Britain, Germany, Norway and Sweden. The address of its main office is: *Instytut Obrony Dobrego Imienia Polski*, ul. Twarda 28, 00-853 Warsaw; phone: (48-22) 24-33-60; fax: (48-2) 642-9352.

The interview itself, reprinted from *Polityka* for which it was ably and penetratingly conducted by two interviewers, Janina Parandowska and Jerzy Baczyński, gives a disturbing picture of the infighting and alliance-forming which had resulted in no fewer than half a dozen Prime Ministers in the first five years since 1989 (Mazowiecki, Bielecki, Olszewski, Suchocka, Pawlak, Oleksy), and produced as many as 28 would-be presidents. This writer was genuinely impressed, and touched, by Gronkiewicz-Waltz' election slogan, which gave the title to the interview, and whose message was *exactly*, in his opinion, what Poland needed then, and still needs.

There was not a word about Polonia in the interview, but shortly after it there appeared in the *Nowy Dziennik* a paid announcement connected with Polonia, if indeed it was a Polonia initiative. The text of the very professionally composed announcement (in Polish) was:

HANNA GRONKIEWICZ WALTZ
"Let Us Take Care Of Poland"

There comes into being a Polonian Committee of Social Support of Hanna Gronkiewicz-Waltz. Persons interested to join in the work of the Committee and participate in the meeting-lunch with the candidate for president on October 9, 1995 in New York are asked to contact:

New Jersey, fax/tel.: (201) 836-2424;
Boston, tel.: (617) 721-9174;
New York, fax (212) 581-7370)

or in writing:

Election Committee of Hanna Gronkiewicz-Waltz
c/o ARC Communications
P.O. Box 777, Times Square Station, New York, NY 10108

This writer took advantage of the invitation and wrote to Hanna Gronkiewicz-Waltz, c/o Election Committee, sharing with her his ideas about her fine election slogan, never receiving a reply to his letter or an acknowledgment.

Returning to the interview, the candidate's declaring herself an enemy of re-communization, which she views as "concentration of all powers within one political option," is worthy of note, because it runs along the lines Nowak Jeziorański outlined at about the same time.

On the domestic front, Hanna Gronkiewicz-Waltz is the mother of one child, like Kwaśniewski and Olszewski having a prominent one-child family, which is apparently becoming a pattern in Poland. One-child families may be good for China, but not for Poland, not now.

D. THE CANDIDATES

BOLESŁAW WIERZBIAŃSKI, "Kandydaci," *Nowy Dziennik*, 7/21/95.

Wierzbiański's sober analysis provides some answers to the problems of the election spectacle, but also raises some additional questions, chief among them one not without importance to the Polish American community, namely who would in the coming years represent us in the world and that includes the United States?

The second question, prompted by the large number of candidates, invites comparison with the splintering of Parliament in the II Republic, leading to the authoritative rule of Piłsudski and the present apprehension that the history of the early 1920s and 1930s would repeat itself in the III Republic, to which Wierzbiański tends to answer "No."

The first candidate to declare himself, **JANUSZ KORWIN-MIKKE**, leader of the Union of Real Politics, visited Polonia and *Nowy Dziennik* without making, in the words of Wierzbiański, an "earthshaking" impression. It was quite different with the candidate of the Freedom Union, **JACEK KUROŃ**, member of Parliament and ex-Minister of Labor.

The Freedom Union, despite considerable loss of ground in the earlier parliamentary elections, had probably half a dozen viable presidential candidates. Among those Janusz Onyszkiewicz, married to Pilsudski's granddaughter and a frequent visitor to America, was a serious candidate, putting out Hanna Suchocka but stepping aside for Kuroń, a surprising move in view of some of Kuroń's statements.

Yet, Kuroń was a popular figure. In Polonian circles it was believed that as long as he didn't get in a clash with **LECH WAŁĘSA**, he had a good chance. But there were others. The candidate of the ruling coalition of the Alliance of the Democratic Left and of the Polish Peasant Party was **ALEKSANDER KWAŚNIEWSKI**, leader of the Alliance.

Among other candidates who counted we must include **ADAM STRZEMBOSZ**, First President of the Supreme Court; **TADEUSZ ZIELIŃSKI**, Citizens' Rights ("ombudsman"); **ANDRZEJ OLECHOWSKI**, ex-Finance Minister and Foreign Affairs; as well as Jan Olszewski, Waldemar Pawlak, and Hanna Gronkiewicz-Waltz, discussed earlier.

Wierzbiański's estimate did not exclude a final battle between Kuroń and Kwaśniewski. But he qualified it:

> As far as we are concerned, from this side of the ocean and among émigrés, we do not cross out the very shrewd Lech Walesa, still by far the main anti-communist leader in Poland.

It didn't happen, and Communists were back in power just as Nowak Jeziorański and Hanna Gronkiewicz-Waltz feared, to huge disappointment in Polonia, but not in Poland.

E. WHAT KIND OF PRESIDENT DOES POLAND NEED?

Adam Michnik, a brilliant historian even if, like Arthur Schlesinger in America, he is without a formal doctorate; Editor-in-

Chief of the very successful *Gazeta Wyborcza*, he formulated the question thus ("Jakiego prezydenta Polska potrzebuje?" *Nowy Dziennik*, October 13, 1995), and not what kind of president citizens of the Republic want to elect:

> Our problems will not be solved by a president appointed by the so-called Right dominated by a nationalist and populist platitude. Nor by a candidate of the post-communists, because when they take over the totality of power, Poland may change into a 'republic of corrupt comrades'. Nor by a man from nowhere, elevated by an accidental constellation of stars. What we need is someone with a credible and undisputedly democratic biography; a person of dialogue and compromise.

An additional problem is the lack of a new constitution. Without it, it is not very clear what the purpose of the elections is. With the constitution still not passed, the extent of the president's competence is not defined. There exists therefore a legitimate concern that the deputies and senators will pass the new constitution for a specific person and not out of concern for a political order.

Michnik formulates the next important question: "What is the condition of Poland and of the Poles today?"

He justifies the question by his belief that it is sometimes worth going beyond every day reality, beyond daily quarrels, beyond shortsighted decisions and short-lived alliances. It is sometimes worth looking into the mirror of history to see Polish politics from a wider perspective in order to find the sense and senselessness of our own elections in the long line of accomplishments, struggles and misfortunes of many Polish generations. Perhaps then we will discover another measurement of responsibility for the past and future. Perhaps today's dangers and hopes will be seen more clearly.

Michnik makes a good point when he maintains that (the last) 200 years of our history explain well why Poland has such a magnificent tradition of liberty and such a weak democratic tradition. He is too hard on the Saxons when he says that Poland's greatness, its international position and internal power broke down finally in the Saxon period, forgetting that it was the great Sobieski who ruined Poland at the end of his reign, and the unfortunate intervention in Poland's internal affairs by the adventurous Charles XII of Sweden that completed the ruination (including Sweden's own, when the Cossacks crossed the frozen Gulf of Bothnia north of Stockholm), making it impossible for August II to avoid a by-then unequal alliance with Peter the Great of Russia, and for Poland to benefit from the potentially very advantageous union with the wealthy and ambitious Saxony. From then on, Poland went downhill by its own momentum.

The slogans which Michnik uses to describe certain phenomena in Poland are always apt, especially the one about how the Poles were "stubbornly standing out for independence" ("wybijali się na niepodległość") while other nations were creating their wealth and building democratic institutions, underlining the sources of Polish complexes and the roots of specific Polish tardiness. The Poles were reasoning in categories of "freedom and nation" and not "state and law" because they had neither state nor law.

Polish Romanticism especially was not a good school for thinking about the state. It "measured strength according to task," appealed to "feeling and faith," despised "intentions measured according to strength," and mocked the "glass and eye" (of science).

The resurrection of the Republic in 1918 brought also the resurrection of the idea of the pre-Partitions Republic—a European power of the [XV?] XVI and XVII centuries. And with it, the resurrection of "dreams of power."

The balance of the II Republic's 20 years is not clear-cut. Much was accomplished, but there was from the beginning an internal conflict leading to a systematic destruction of the authority of the parliamentary democracy and the violation of the constitution together with a tendency to dictatorial government. That Michnik is not evading a critical duty to subject the epoch of the II Republic to a final analysis is suggested by a clear conclusion that the Poles were not able to build at that time a democratic order; they built an imperfect system of half-democracy and half-dictatorship. Whether this imperfect system, terminated in 1939 and replaced after the war by the post-Yalta doctrine of "limited sovereignty" which lasted until 1989, can now evolve into something more perfect, will be discussed in the last part of this book examining far-reaching measures and asking for stronger resolve than the "successes" Michnik lists so far.

Describing the condition of Poland, Michnik talks about the success of people from Tadeusz Mazowiecki's government, who "set in motion the logic of Polish success which is still in place" and he lists, next to Mazowiecki, Balcerowicz, Kuroń and Skubiszewski, followed by the next governments, of Bielecki, Olszewski, Suchocka, adding that it is also possible to talk about the success of Wałęsa. Since this is a rather exclusive list, one can assume that these people are the best Poland has to offer, the builders and architects of a future perfect system. Yet, most of these people are guilty of serious mistakes, beginning with Mazowiecki's mistake (mentioned prominently by both Nowak Jeziorański and Wagner in this book, but not by Michnik), and we don't know how much credit for Balcerowicz's "success" belongs to Jeffrey Sachs. Reading Michnik's reasoning is a depressing experience, especially his easy dismissal of certain facts as "nonsense" (the government of post-communist coalition and recommunization), a facility in which Kuroń also excels as when he calls an anti-communist stand "wrongheaded stupidity" ("*zacietrzewiona głupota*")!

We must never forget that *all* people of any importance in Poland were educated under communism, and there is no escaping its corrosive influence in one way or other. For these people to build a perfect system in Poland is an impossibility. At least a generation must pass before Poles can even think of perfection for Poland. To echo a Russian XIXth century thinker (Chernyshevski), "What is to be done" in the meantime?

The nation has to be educated to think of the common good, starting from kindergarten, and this makes **EDUCATION** the most crucial among the three big E's, since the second one, **ENVIRONMENT**, depends on it, and the third, **ECONOMY**, seems to be doing well in the market democracy in Poland, well enough for the country's early admittance to the European Union. A well-functioning economy will furnish the funds necessary to make education an attractive career option. This should not be difficult, as the reportedly overcrowded schools at present (the result of a high birthrate not so long ago) will soon start emptying as the now plummeting birthrate will result in fewer children in schools. It is a Polish irony that a threatening demographic catastrophe should work constructively to improve the educational problem, hopefully of short duration, since both problems have to be reversed if Poland is to avoid depopulation. To avoid it, family values should be stressed in schools, with the family presented as a cornerstone of society. In this, the help of American Polonia, a repository of family values, could be crucial.

It is surprising that in all his arguments Michnik does not once mention American Polonia, as if it did not exist. Yet there is in its midst the brilliant Zbigniew Brzezinski, whose ideas had earned him a global reputation. There is also a man who knows Poland better than any of Michnik's "success" claimants, and cares for it more than most of them, having spent a lifetime in its service. That man is Jan Nowak Jeziorański, a household name in Poland whom Michnik should have considered in his search for president, just as he should have considered the last President of the Polish Government-in-Exile in London, Ryszard Kaczorowski, if for no other reason than as a symbol of Poland's continuity as a nation and as a state.

The presidency should not be a political football. It should be a seat endowed with dignity and history, occupied by an elderly gentleman-scholar, in possession of both endowments. In his obsession with current politics and compromises, Michnik fails to see that such people exist in his own country, but he would probably label them as coming "from nowhere" (no party affiliation?). This would probably be true for Jan Szczepański if he were still active, but certainly not for Adam Strzembosz, the "candidate of families" supported by five political groups of the right and Aleksander Gieysztor, curator of the Royal Castle and host of the III Congress of Scholars of Polish Descent in 1989 and, because of that, speaking for Poland about Polonia in this book, in the most suitable manner possible—as needing a give-and-take relationship.

12

Aleksander Gieysztor

POLES IN POLAND LOOK AT POLISH AMERICANS (REFLECTIONS)

The image of America in the eyes of Poles living in Poland has petrified to the point where it has almost become a myth. It changes little, if at all, despite all the new developments on both sides of the Atlantic.

Equally rigid is the place American Poles occupy in that picture. Regarded by Poles in Poland as citizens of the United States or Canada, Polish Americans and Canadians are—or, as the Poles see it, should be—fully at one with their respective societies. The Poles do distinguish between, on one hand, those Polish Americans who were born in America many years or several generations ago and, on the other hand, those who came with successive immigration waves during the past half century, particularly in the last fifteen years. But in general it is believed in Poland that those waves too have already joined and reinforced the community of Polish Americans who are part of mainstream America. (Temporary stays of varying length that Poles undertake to study or work in America are outside the area of vision of the whole picture beyond the ocean.)

Poles in Poland generally suppose that Polish Americans in the United States or Canada participate with full rights, duties and benefits in the economic, societal and political activities of their countries and in their civilizations. As for culture, Polish Americans seemingly have a double membership in it: American and Polish. They maintain and cultivate national traditions that were once brought over from the old country and are now reinforced by all kinds of contacts with it. The Polish language belongs with that heritage, albeit in a diverse way, as does its own form of Catholic faith. And so do, in varying degrees of faithfulness, customs and traditions that have been either inherited from immigrant ancestors or preserved since one's own arrival not so long ago. Ditto various forms of participation in the Polish spiritual and artistic culture, in the awareness of one's roots and separateness, and in one's sense of "myself" and "ourselves" within American society.

318

This commonality or community of culture, this sense of one's values, in the realm of the spiritual above all, manifests itself in various symbolic forms, in creative expression in the arts, literature, music, in intellectual pursuits related to cognition, information, and learning, as well as in the receptive process of availing oneself of the accumulated and constantly augmented wealth of one's own social culture. Certainly the Polish language belongs here as a means of communication and as a culture-making tool, even as Poles both in Poland and America have become aware that standard Polish is no longer the sole vehicle of Polish cultural values, which can also be transferred through language variants, or trends. From this perspective, the Polish community throughout the world is the object of mutual pride of Poles in Poland and of Polish Americans.

Participants in this community are concerned about its cultivation in the face of various developmental incommensurabilities in today's rapidly changing world. On one side there is the overwhelming competition of American English commanding all fields of education, coupled with the innovation-restricting insistence on tradition. On the other side, in Poland, there is accelerated social transformation accompanied by the sprawl of mass culture with its limited ideological horizon. It is worth noting that these processes, visible as they are in Poland, are also shared by much of Europe at the end of the XX century.

What do Poles in Poland expect when they see Polish Americans? Certainly, just as it was before, and still holds true, the Poles in Poland expect American Poles to show solidarity, which they understand as a national unity manifested not just at the time of historic trials but at all times. It is easier now to fulfill this expectation at all levels because the accessibility of communication is incomparable with anything that previous generations experienced. Translated into the language of everyday activities, beginning with economics, this solidarity has ceased to be relief aid extended individually to families and communities, beautiful examples of which we have seen throughout the previous decade; the framework for activity now is different. Now each Polish lobby in the United States, if indeed such lobbies exist, should adopt an open-minded attitude toward Poland's coming into the free market: internal, external, and intercontinental. Banks and industrial investors, and the economic policy of the federal government as well as local and state initiatives—these various fields of activity are better known to Polish

Americans. In these fields it is no longer a question of helping a poor relative but helping a country that, after only a few years of transformations, is not just beginning to stand on its own strong feet but also achieving a level of economic growth that the rest of Europe acknowledges with a certain dose of astonishment.

This is related to a deeper phenomenon stemming from the transformation taking place in the most recent years. The participation of enlightened Polish Americans, and sympathizing with Poland, in the formation, reconstruction and, partly, in the development of civic and democratic society in Poland (the development that, I might add, is still moving too slowly and is threatened by many political obstacles) may prove to be of high value. This participation may be articulated as dissemination of knowledge about Poland and as promotion of the belief that each citizen is responsible for the wellbeing of the locality, township and the whole country, and that local initiative is a value to be developed in conditions of internal freedom.

The differences between Poland and Western Europe are considerable but they do not prevent Polish regional governments from adapting management models from France and Germany. The Polish-American participation in propagating those truly democratic models would be a natural expression of our solidarity.

In the cultural relationship between the Polish diaspora and the old country it is education, directed both ways, that is a civilizing factor which at present decides the quality of life of states and nations. In its newly found freedom, Poland is now also free to offer Poles abroad its substantial educational resources for activities ranging from refresher courses for the youth of Polonia in the Polish language and in the values of Polish intellectual and artistic culture, to advanced studies at graduate and post-graduate levels in many fields of international standing and granting recognized diplomas.

What kind of hope do we Poles direct towards American Polonia? Our hopes are trained towards the point where its national culture meets and intersects with the American culture. In addition to cooperating with Polish institutions and outposts in America, we are counting on access to the United States' leading scientific research centers and educational institutions for constantly rotating scientific cadres from Poland. We are hoping for the participation of American experts, of Polish descent and others, in Poland's academic life.

In this way a cultivated domain of culture can be extended to intellectual and artistic activity in many fields. For many years the exchange of talent (scientific and artistic) between the old country and the Polish diaspora has followed the rather one-way road described by the unfavorable (to Poland) name "brain drain." Bilateral (two-way) free flow along the Polish path would make it possible for all concerned to participate in the world's circulation of values, which includes not only the creative process but also its study—a different condition for raising the quality of human cultural life in general, and Polish across the ocean and in the Old Country in particular.

In the human dimension, as usual, the most significant and the most valuable factors are acquaintanceship, intimacy, and friendship. Each trip to Poland, whether a tourist trip, a family visit, for business or study, creates or strengthens the trans-Atlantic bond which we are reflecting on here. Accordingly, Poles in Poland are looking forward to welcoming Polish Americans and American Poles in the old country, many and often.

(Translated by Małgorzata Dymek-Ćwiklińska and F. Mocha)

13

Frank Mocha

POLISH "WSPÓLNOTA" AND AMERICAN "POLONIA"

Stowarzyszenie "Wspólnota Polska" (roughly translated as "Polish Community" [Commonality] Association) is a new mechanism replacing the old "Polonia" Society after 1989. Called into being without consulting American "Polonia" (by far the biggest of all the Polonias at about half the population of Poland—using Polish descent as the only criterion), the new entity's sudden arrival rubbed the American behemoth the wrong way, as the saying goes. This writer, for one, having spent half of his productive years studying American Polonia and its huge but largely unknown potential, voiced his puzzlement in a civilized way—by Airmail—initiating an intelligent correspondence with "Wspólnota"—his letters always promptly answered by its Secretary, Senator Bogucka-Skowrońska, a charming lady judging by her letters, and a grandmother by 1992—good news I received with mental congratulations in her direction the last time I personally visited the Association. I miss her no longer being its Secretary!

My last, and only personal visit to "Wspólnota" coincided with my last visit to Poland, as a participant in the Combatants' rally in Warsaw and Częstochowa. On that occasion I brought with me a quantity of the first part of my memoir, published early so I could take it with me; because it concerned my education in prewar Poland, and since education was undergoing a crisis in Poland at that time. The book, copies of which were to be distributed to English-speaking teachers in Poland (it was subtitled, *The Education of a Polish Schoolboy*), was to serve as a reminder of better times. Taking a receipt from a certain Mr. Górski, I left the books in the "Wspólnota" bookstore and inquired about their fate after returning to America. By then Senator Bogucka-Skowrońska was no longer Secretary and my letter remained unanswered. But the books were in the basement bookstore, because sometime later I asked Prof. Wieńczysław Wagner, in Poland at that time on an academic assignment while offering his services (*free*) to the new government (his unsuccessful attempts, described in a letter to *Nowy Dziennik*, are a sad testimony to Poland's inability to take advantage of available human resources), to get a copy for himself. He did, but only after a lengthy search because, in a fit of what at first I called Polish stupidity, Mr. Górski had the books repacked from an easily identified sturdy American box (with my name and title in green printed on the outside) to an indistinguishable cheap box. I was well known in Poland then, as seen by the way Prof. Gieysztor had greeted me at the III Congress in 1989 ("Profesor Mocha, mityczna postać!"—"a mythical figure"). What Prof. Gieysztor of my generation knew, and meant, Górski of the young generation profited by. In a profit obsessed market society, the box was a valuable commodity. I had no time to dwell on it, having to undergo surgery, after which I wrote to Prof. Stelmachowski.

Professor Andrzej Stelmachowski was something else again. All I knew about him was that he was president of "Wspólnota" and that he did not answer letters gladly. My letter remained unanswered, perhaps because he didn't think I would recover. A more likely explanation was my having asked him to write this chapter for my book; writing it would have put him in an uncomfortable position in view of his low opinion of Polonia voiced in a meeting at Green Point the details of which I was informed about.

My informant described him as a large well-fed man with a condescending attitude toward his Polonian audience. He was vague about the goals, and about the accomplishments of the Association so far, stressing that its main concern was Poles in the East, both in formerly Polish territories of Ukraine, Belarus, Lithuania, and in Russia, Siberia, and Kazakhstan. As for American Polonia, he criticized it for not keeping up with the Jews in America, or something belittling of that sort, and I was surprised to hear that nobody in the audience had pointed out to the professor that he was woefully ignorant of American realities.

It was this meeting more than anything else that made me write to Prof. Stelmachowski again (after my 1996 interview with *The New York Times*), sending him some data about me and trying to get him interested in my book. I wanted his views on the Polish Community, to see how they compare with those of Prof. Gieysztor or the former Prime Minister Jan Olszewski, who visualized the Western Polish Community taking up the responsibility for the part of the Polish diaspora beyond Poland's Eastern border. This time a correspondence developed which ended the following year with the

professor regretfully declining to "help" write the chapter concerning statements or comments from Poland because of "numerous
official duties" but promising to make available individual articles in
his possession about American Polonia should I want to see them,
which I wanted, receiving a brief reply with wishes of energy in the
writing, and of getting enough strength in the vacation season, which
I acknowledged equally briefly with a comment on how some of us
in America spend our vacations—working. Both the brief communications took place in July, 1997.

What was one to make of it? Was the professor apprehensive
about committing himself to writing and then being quoted? There is
still much of that apprehension left from the pre-1989 years. When I
sent the "Silesia" publishing house two of my articles in *Modern Age*
about prewar Poland with a view of having them published in Poland
and there was a typographical error in the date, I was accused of
"disinformation" and discovered that it still wasn't easy to correspond with most people in Poland. Was the professor in that
category? But then, why not send the promised articles? I think that
because they were other people's comments, other factors were
involved, which was just as well because the comments would probably just be a set of platitudes, as most comments from Poland about
Polonia are. I was more interested in learning the nature of the
professor's "numerous official duties."

The best source of information was an article in *Nowy Dziennik*
of July 28, 1995, with a revealing title, "A Specialist of Small
Matters" ("Specjalista od małych spraw"), based on a 'special interview' by Elżbieta Ringer with Professor Stelmachowski, a guest at
the Third World Forum of Polonia Media at Tarnów in June of
1995.

From the beginning of the interview the stress is on the professor being much in demand ("rozchwytywany") by all, an impression
he obviously wants to maintain while wondering why "an elderly
gentleman with a cane" would be so popular. And every day somewhere else. "Yesterday I was in Poznań and Włocławek, today I am
in Tarnów, and now I am scampering away farther to take care of
official matters."

The "scampering away" was done in a car already waiting
according to his secretary urging him on. Reading this and realizing
that this President of "Wspólnota" and former Marshal of the Senate
[a Polish Senate rank] was traveling in style, I thought of the late

Attorney Aloysius Mazewski, President of comparable entities (Polish National Alliance and Polish American Congress), traveling by public transportation "to take care of official matters."

The official matters involve a great deal of travel, which the professor greatly enjoys judging by his description of a trip to Petersburg to attend Polish Culture Days combined with a conference about the fate of Poles in northern Russia. Meeting some of them from the furthest corners of Russia resulted in incredible stories.

Among his more interesting remarks was one about his preference for events to take place in smaller centers, such as Tarnów, and his belief that it is in the smaller localities of regional Poland that a new political class is beginning to grow—new managers who will be heard from in ten, perhaps twenty years. It's they who will be the Polish political elite which today consists of various amateurs in most cases only accidentally part of it. Amen to that!

The professor answered some specific questions in the interview. He wasn't much worried about the political situation in Belorussia or elsewhere, where "in big matters they shout that they love Moscow, or like or don't like something or somebody, but in small they are accommodating," for example opening a Polish Consulate in Grodno and building two Polish schools (in Grodno and Wołkowysk). It is in the "small matters" which are happening that the professor became a "specialist" by his own admission, hence the title of the article, "A Specialist of Small Matters."

Among his other immediate plans was bringing 100 Polish families from Kazakhstan as part of "Wspólnota's" difficult but continuing work on behalf of that republic's many Poles, some of whose children and grandchildren, dreaming about Poland, this writer had met during his summer IREX exchange study in the Soviet Union in 1971. In his opinion, repatriating Poles in Kazakhstan is a high priority plan.

But his "one more most important goal" is the professor's extraordinary idea of creating what he calls a "feeding zone" of Wilno. He dreams of developing vegetable and fruit-growing in the vicinity of Wilno where, as we know, Poles constitute a majority of 60 or even 80 percent of inhabitants. He is careful to stress that his idea has no nationalistic overtones, since Lithuanians living in the "zone" will also benefit. Wilno has appalling deliveries of vegetables and fruit, and the plan would fill the stalls with them, while at the same time helping the Polish farmers, who had received land after the dissolution of the kolkhozes, to get on their feet. The problems in making this "dream" come true are enormous, and he lists them, allowing the possibility of failure. He would like to get access to some European assistance funds for this and other projects (summer camps for children from East and West), some of which sound more like daydreams than reality, like the one about activating a special Vladivostok-Warsaw train to collect the young campers! Ms. Ringer calls him a story-teller ("gawędziarz"), and this sounds like one of them. Is the man an optimist or is he just having fun?

This uncertainty about the professor is more serious when he talks about his trying to coordinate the efforts of Polish organizations scattered in various countries. He calls it "niewdzięczna praca" ("unrewarding work"), especially in Germany, without the slightest mention of America. Yet, a month before the Stelmachowski interview, the Polish American Congress held its 120-strong Council of Directors meeting (June 22-24, 1995) whose agenda included Poles in the East, particularly Kazakhstan, and a report by the Charitable Foundation of the Congress, which brings aid after 1989 to Poles in the East, saying:

> ...between October 1994 and May 1995 that aid amounted to somewhat over 200 thousand dollars in medicines and medical equipment for hospitals; food and clothing for compatriots in Kazakhstan and other states which had emerged after the break-up of the Soviet Union.

(Reported by Bolesław Łaszewski, *Nowy Dziennik*, June 29, 1995.)

Is it possible that "Wspólnota" didn't know about the meeting, widely reported in the Polish American press? And about the Charitable Foundation's aid for Poles in the East? If that is indeed the case, then Stelmachowski has nobody but himself to blame for his "unrewarding" attempts at coordination. But there are even more serious doubts about the effectiveness of "Wspólnota's" work.

In the same issue of *Nowy Dziennik* (June 29, 1995) there was a disturbing article about Poles in Ukraine, the special part of it around Berdyczew that always had a large Polish minority (perhaps even a majority in some segments triggering Stalin's deportations to Kazakhstan in the 1930s). Those who remain, whose families survived Stalin and the Soviet Union and saw Poland independent again, feel neglected by it, undervalued and underestimated even by Wspólnota Polska. They feel particularly hurt when they hear about cynical statements in Poland about them like:

"Now they remembered that they are Poles."
~Teraz przypomnieli sobie, że są Polakami,

which provided the title for the article, but also caused some reflections. How could Poles say that about other Poles, and what could the other Poles say, but didn't, about the Poles in Poland, many of whom are also now remembering that they are Poles, and not communist stooges? What is happening to Polish solidarity, and what is "Wspólnota" doing to counteract such abominations when they reach its own field? And, finally, what about former Prime Minister Hanna Suchocka's mindless statement that the Poles in the East were citizens of other states (and, presumably, not our responsibility)? Of what states were the Poles citizens during the Partitions? Did anybody ask her that question? Did anybody reprimand her or castigate her the way Andrzej Pomian did in *Nowy Dziennik*, showing that when it comes to care for Poland and cultivating Polish values, American Polonia is way ahead of Poland?

Perhaps this is what Professor Stelmachowski at last understood, judging by his relatively recent visits to these shores, inevitably courting official Polonia. Perhaps his withdrawal from my book project is an indirect result of his new attitude toward Polonia, because the book is not the voice of official Polonia, but my own.

In the fall of 1996 Professor Stelmachowski visited at least three Polish American institutions, one after another, beginning with the Polish American Congress. which had invited him to its meeting as an honored guest. He acknowledged the invitation as a perfect opportunity to meet with representatives of American Polonia, but also as a manifestation of support by the Polish American Congress for the work of the Polish "Wspólnota."

While in Chicago, the professor visited the Polish Roman Catholic Union for the first time (Oct. 24), touring also its offices and the Polish Museum of America. In his talk there he made no secret that he was counting on establishing contacts which in the future would turn into cooperation consisting above all of varied exchanges. For example, in exchange for financial help which keeps flowing from the American side, "Wspólnota" could supply textbooks for Polish history and language, of which, in the guest's opinion, there are not enough on the American market. An example of help from the American side to the Polish is, among others, sending medicines to Poland, the transport of which in Poland (and distribution in other states where there are Polish centers, mainly in the former Soviet Union) is done by the Polish side. More attention should be paid to Polonia in the East, towards which both Poland and American Polonia have a joint duty. This was a new, surprising statement, and together with some other questionable ones, calls for a comment.

Professor Stelmachowski, former Minister of Education, strikes the pose of a mentor when in reality he comes here to secure financial help without having all the facts straight. Starting with the books in exchange for financial help, most Polish history books date to communist times, and Polonia does not and should not want them, for obvious reasons. Besides, for the relatively small number of students of Polish history, there is a growing number of books in English, starting with those by Oskar Halecki (out-of-print now) and Piotr Wandycz, as well as Norman Davies and other non-Polish authors. As for language textbooks, there are probably too many now, for the simple reason that Polish language teachers publish their own to match their level of preparation while ignoring the best book, by Alexander Schenker of Yale, published with the help of numerous grants by the Office of Education and calling for a good knowledge of linguistics. (Because of that, Professor Jacek Fisiak's new bilingual dictionary would go well with Professor Schenker's book.) And what is one to make of Stelmachowski's advice to pay great attention to the "problem" of the Polonia mass media, particularly television in Polish which should reach the audience "stronger," whatever that means?

The professor thinks that to trigger the need of organizational entities to come closer together will result in increased interest on the American side in Polish matters and vice-versa and, what follows will be better cooperation. This cooperation includes help from the American side. How this help is used and distributed should not be left entirely to the Polish side. Just as Professor Stelmachowski is sitting in meetings with Polish American organizations, their representatives should sit in meetings with "Wspólnota," especially concerning the Poles in the East, towards whom both Poland and Polonia have now a "joint duty." What Jan Olszewski had only suggested, became a reality, with Polonia assuming part of the burden. The problems connected with the Poles stranded in the East were described by Professor Stelmachowski in his third meeting, in the editorial office of *Nowy Dziennik*.

The resulting article by Andrzej Dobrowolski, "The Road Through Torment" ("Droga przez mękę"), November 14, 1996, quotes the professor about the magnitude and difficulties of the task. When it comes to educational matters in Belorussia and Ukraine, for example, there is a pattern in which it is difficult to come to any agreement on the governmental level in Belorussia and relatively easier on local level, while it is exactly the opposite in Ukraine. We learn with a shock that there is a border problem with Ukraine, with post-World War II expellees wishing to return to their former localities, now settled by Poles, being persuaded to remain where they are and have their own schools built for them. It is a different story for Poles in Kazakhstan, where repatriation, which two former Polish governments were afraid of, is finally taking shape. The professor also discussed schools in Silesia—a different problem, and even Polish taxes for returning emigrants.

Despite this seemingly successful visit, the next time "Wspólnota" was discussed in *Nowy Dziennik*, it was a criticism of its alleged shortcomings (May 27, 1997), including an allegation that important representatives of "Wspólnota" were bypassing New York while visiting America. This makes sense. "Wspólnota," whose activities are financed by the Association itself and other organizations, with additional subsidies from the Senate, was interested in the big Polish American organizations in Chicago, as potential donors. But on the same day the article appeared in *Nowy Dziennik* (it was an editorial), there was another one reporting on the V Convention of Polonian Teachers at Columbia University, with Professor Andrzej Stelmachowski participating on opening day with a long speech about the role of education in upholding the ties between Poles spread over the world and the home country, followed by Frank Milewski, President of the Polish American Congress, New York Division, and others.

This time the "important representative" did not bypass New York but made it his destination while being in touch with the Polish American Congress through Milewski. The sheer coincidence of the two articles was probably a bid by the editor, Bolesław Wierzbiański, for another courtesy visit by the professor, and a desire to show him how well Polonian journalism works, with reference to mutual criticism—the professor's in Chicago and the editor in his article. Whatever it was, it showed the man's popularity and respect for his labor (the Convention opening was delayed to enable him to get to it directly from the airport). As for this writer, he can rise above his disappointment of having only two important co-authors from Poland instead of three, and admit that Professor Stelmachowski, all things considered, is the right man for the right job in Poland.

14

Edited by Jacek Fisiak
Commentary by Frank Mocha

ENGLISH-POLISH AND POLISH-ENGLISH DICTIONARY

Just as Edward Czerwiński's *Dictionary Of Polish Literature* was seen by this commentator as filling a gap in Polish Studies materials in America, so also should Jacek Fisiak's *Polish-English and English-Polish Dictionary* be seen.

The two works have another thing in common: both were produced in Poland—one by a Polish American professor but a frequent resident of Poland, with the cooperation and help of his Polish colleagues; the other by a Polish expert on the English language with the help of his assistants.

That's where the similarity ends, except that both works have been selected for this book for similar reasons: as examples of works meant to help where help is needed.

Here is what Professor Fisiak, Director of the Institute of English Philology of the Adam Mickiewicz University in Poznan has to say about the Dictionary (letter of April 24, 1996):

> Many thanks for your letter of March 30, 1996.
> Under separate cover I am sending you with pleasure our new dictionary [...]
> Concerning the dictionary and the questions which you ask in your letter, I would like to inform you that the idea to publish our dictionary arose in 1991. One of main reasons was that dictionaries attainable on the market until now were obsolete. The idea to publish it was inspired by a colleague Jerzy Kulczycki, an migr London publisher, who suggested while visiting me in Poznan to publish a dictionary with the cooperation of the Polish publisher BGW with one of the British publishers. The final choice fell to Collins, the most reputable publisher of bilingual dictionaries in the world.
> The second reason for the decision to take up work on a dictionary was the fact that the pay of young research workers fell considerably in the year 90/91 and I wanted on the one side to secure for a group of my assistants additional earnings in a specialty which they represent, and on the other side

simultaneously ambitious research work. The dictionary was drawn up by a team. We ultimately began work with a team of 16 in 1993. Collins gave us an English framework in electronic form.

Our original input were Polish equivalents as well as a Polish framework for the Polish-English dictionary. As you can see we acted very fast, since the dictionary was handed over on diskettes to the publisher in January of this year. Because the dictionary is in electronic form we can reduce it and prepare derivative smaller dictionaries.

We are preparing such a dictionary and it will be ready to print on May 15 (30,000 entries). This is briefly the fate of producing the dictionary and of the work on it.

When I received the dictionary (two volumes, by regular mail), I was pleasantly surprised and impressed by its physical appearance. Slightly larger than the Kosciuszko Foundation's dictionary, which is the old dictionary the new one will be compared with, but still of convenient size at 9 1/2" x 6 1/2", with a snugly fitting colorful dust jacket (red, blue and yellow, with the wording in white), with the colors and wording repeated on the sturdy cover (a good idea), good paper and relatively large type (larger than in the Kosciuszko Foundation's dictionary), all adding up to a dictionary both inviting and easy to use. The fact that I started to use it immediately, because when it arrived I was in the midst of work requiring a dictionary, was its first recommendation.

But I noticed some drawbacks immediately. Mostly they pertain to missing entries, in both volumes or in just one, as for example "framework" in the English-Polish volume has no equivalent in the Polish-English, an absence I have noticed only now, when translating the letter above ("siatka" in the letter has no "framework" equivalent). Other drawbacks concern ambiguities, making me consult the Kosciuszko Foundation dictionary. When the "consultations" became frequent, I began making notes of them, for the sake of future editions, but mostly to look for a pattern. I didn't find one, but I discovered that the old dictionary was much larger: 1037 vs. 521 pp. for the English volume and 772 vs. 505 for the Polish. The larger size of the new dictionary, allowing for wider columns, and the narrower upper and lower margins allowing for longer pages, make up for some of the disparity in the total number of pages, and so does the great number of long entries (which include derivative vocabulary) in the old dictionary, as opposed to the generally shorter entries in the new. For reasons that are not clear to me the disparity in the total number of pages is greater in the English-Polish volume (2:1).

In the present essay I am commenting only on problems encountered while using the dictionary in writing and not while examining it systematically, which is not necessary in order to determine its usefulness—the purpose of this essay. Perhaps because in my work I am using the Polish-English volume less frequently, I am encountering fewer problems than with the English-Polish, but this probably reflects reality. Among the missing entries are:

diaspora	kołchoz
krajan	rampart
leki	starosta
pędrak	szyldwach

There are also entries missing for derivative words and expressions. The entry "wiadomo" has half a dozen of them, but "jak wiadomo" is not among them, yet it is one of the most frequent fixed expressions in the Polish language.

The English-Polish volume has numerous omissions, as is probably to be expected in a dictionary produced in a non-English speaking country. I am listing the omissions as I have "encountered" them, and not in alphabetical order:

diaspora	kolkhoz
troglodyte	bucolic
legerdemain	palimpsest
to stash	womanhood
logjam	sophomoric
canard	obstreperous
harbinger	equability
prescience	periwig
pesky	swain
anthropomorphic	clarion (call)
obstreperous	hinterland
vassal	detox
interpolation	succor
endorsement	caveat
polymorphic	mendacity
calisthenic(s)	lacuna
obfuscate	jurist
maw	firecracker
cabbala	verisimilitude
autobiography	Godspeed

As in the Polish-English volume, the English-Polish also has its share of omissions among derivative words and expressions. The entry "sky" has half a dozen derivative words but listed as separate entries, some hyphenated ("sky-blue"), some written as one word ("skylark") and some missing ("skyrocket").

Both volumes have what looks like an innovation in Polish dictionaries, namely a category called individually "KEYWORD" (*Słowo kluczowe* in Polish), consisting of various parts of speech, entered in alphabetical order but set off by brackets, listing all possible uses of the given words. Among these words we find, in the English-Polish volume, the indefinite article "a(an)"; the adverbs "about" and "anyhow"; the adjectives "all" and "any"; the pronouns "anyone" and "anything"; auxiliary verbs "be" and "have"; the "conjunction "but" and so on. In the Polish-English volume we find fewer of these words, beginning with the pronoun "co" ("what"), the preposition "do" ("to"), and going on to the interrogatives "gdzie" ("where"), "ile" ("how many"), "jaki" ("what"), "kiedy" ("when") and so on.

The "keywords" concept is a highly productive device, not only for the sake of the vocabulary, but as a language teaching tool. Together with the introductory material at the beginning of the English-Polish volume, and the "Guide to the Polish Grammar" at the end of the Polish-English volume, they make the dictionary a proper companion to the best Polish textbook in America (*Beginning Polish*) by Professor Alexander Schenker, reputedly the best teacher of Polish in America, a distinction the present writer enjoyed in his teaching days. These considerations are the dictionary's second recommendation.

There is a third recommendation, of a different kind but no less important to mention. It is the fact of Professor Fisiak presenting a set to Her Majesty Queen Elizabeth II of England on Her visit to Poland, thus establishing a distinguished pedigree for his dictionary.

Here is what its editor tells its users in the bilingual "Introduction" ("Wstęp") to both volumes:

> We are delighted that you have decided to use the Collins BGW English-Polish Polish-English Dictionary and hope that you will enjoy it and benefit from using it at home, on holiday or at work. This introduction gives you a few tips on how to get the most out of your dictionary—not simply from its comprehensive word list but also from the information provided in each entry. This will help you to read and understand modern Polish as well as communicate and express yourself in it.

The Collins BGW English-Polish Polish-English Dictionary begins by listing the abbreviations used in the English-Polish part of the dictionary, followed by guides to both English and Polish pronunciation. Next come English irregular verbs, plus numbers and expressions using time and date. The Polish-English part of the dictionary begins by listing the abbreviations used in it and a style and layout section for that part of the dictionary. At the very back of the Polish-English part you will find a brief guide to Polish grammar and tables with irregularly declined and conjugated words.

• • • •

NOTA BENE: A suggestion was made in the preceding essay that Polish "Wspólnota" should, within its exchange plans outlined by Professor Andrzej Stelmachowski, supply Professor Jacek Fisiak's dictionary to American "Polonia" (ideally to users of Professor Aleksander Schenker's *Beginning Polish* textbook, possibly with the cooperation of the Kosciuszko Foundation).

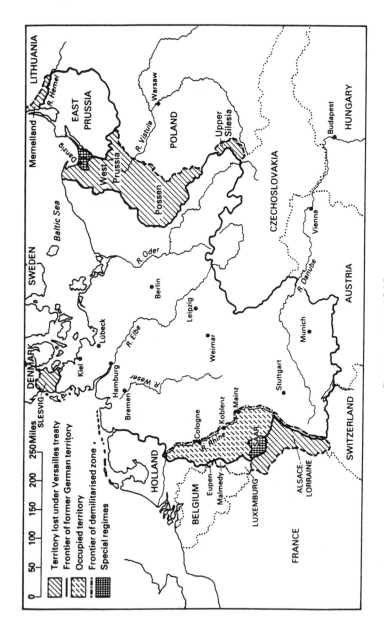

GERMANY, 1919

Legend:

- Territory lost under Versailles treaty
- Frontier of former German territory
- Occupied territory
- Frontier of demilitarised zone
- Special regimes

0 50 100 150 200 250 Miles

LITHUANIA

R. Memel

Memelland

EAST PRUSSIA

Danzig

West Prussia

R. Vistula

Warsaw

POLAND

Upper Silesia

Budapest

HUNGARY

Possen

Baltic Sea

SWEDEN

R. Oder

CZECHOSLOVAKIA

Vienna

R. Danube

AUSTRIA

Berlin

Leipzig

DENMARK

SLESVIG

Kiel

Lübeck

R. Elbe

Hamburg

Bremen

R. Weser

Weimar

Munich

Stuttgart

SWITZERLAND

Cologne

Koblenz

Mainz

R. Rhine

SAAR

HOLLAND

BELGIUM

Eupen

Malmedy

LUXEMBURG

ALSACE-LORRAINE

FRANCE

Part IV

THE GOAL:
THE MOST PERFECT POLAND IN A
THOUSAND YEARS
A DREAM?

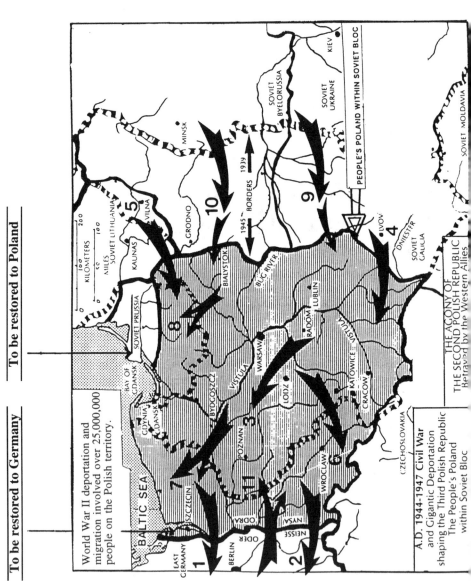

To be restored to Germany

To be restored to Poland

World War II deportation and migration involved over 25,000,000 people on the Polish territory.

A.D. 1944-1947 Civil War and Gigantic Deportation shaping the Third Polish Republic The People's Poland within Soviet Bloc

THE AGONY OF THE SECOND POLISH REPUBLIC Betrayed by the Western Allies

Movements of People

1. Aug. 2, 1945, Allied decision in Potsdam. Oder-Neisse border closed. 5,000,000 German war refugees not allowed to return.
2. Allied decision to transfer 3,500,000 Germans out of Poland, west of the Oder-Neisse border.
3. Return home of Poles deported east out of areas annexed to Germany.
4. Departure of Poles from Lvov and Soviet Galicia.
5. Departure of Poles from Vilna, Soviet Lithuania, and Byelorussia.
6. Migration of Poles to Silesia.
7. Migration of Poles to West Pomerania.
8. Migration of Poles to Mazuria.
9. Return of Poles from USSR immediately after the war.
10. Return of Poles from USSR after 1956.
11. Return of Poles from the West
12. Emigration to Germany postwar and later.

Map labels:
EAST GERMANY, BERLIN, BALTIC SEA, BAY OF GDANSK, GDYNIA, GDANSK, SOVIET PRUSSIA, KAUNAS, SOVIET LITHUANIA, VILNA, GRODNO, MINSK, SOVIET BYELORUSSIA, KIEV, ODRA, ODER, NEISSE, SZCZECIN, BYDGOSZCZ, POZNAN, WROCLAW, VISTULA, BUG RIVER, BIALYSTOK, WARSAW, LODZ, RADOM, LUBLIN, KATOWICE, CRACOW, VISTULA, LVOV, SOVIET GALICIA, DNIESTER, SOVIET UKRAINE, SOVIET MOLDAVIA, CZECHOSLOVAKIA, PEOPLE'S POLAND WITHIN SOVIET BLOC

1939 BORDERS, 1945 BORDERS

KILOMETERS 0 100 200
MILES 0 100

15

Frank Mocha

INTRODUCTION: THE CASE FOR PERFECTION

"The most perfect Poland in a thousand years" is a dream, never to become a reality, Polish national character being what it is, and two seemingly insoluble problems (DEMOGRAPHY, KALININGRAD) standing in the way, but it is worth considering and to dwell upon.

There is an important recommendation to be worked out, based on my experience and other factors and arrived at with the help of two personal dates falling at the beginning and end of the last stage of writing this book, thus carrying its personal bias to the end. The first is my birthday on February 18, my 77th, which I was never to celebrate according to a prophecy by an old family friend and local sage in my old hometown in Poland during my first postwar visit in 1959 (described in my unpublished volume, *Working and Raising a Family in America in the 1950s*) when, at the age of almost 38 and a half, I had lived half of my life, as the man gravely told me (it had something to do with the timing of my visit). I took his words seriously, thinking of 76-plus as not too early an exit in view of my stormy life, but my thinking changed with the approach of the date and the realization that there were many projects I had not completed; I lived in a half-hope that this prophecy, like an earlier one (also described elsewhere), made by a gypsy and concerning an earlier exit (66), would also not come true, allowing me to complete my tasks.

The second date, May 3rd, is by contrast a joyful one. I looked forward to it after greeting the fateful 77th birthday in the early morning hours while watching on television another joyful event, the XVIIIth Winter Olympic Games broadcast from Nagano, Japan, and seeing the ice hockey "Team U.S.A." losing to the Czech Republic (a loss attributed by one of the players, Tkachuk, to the fact that "Americans are soft," a comment this writer will return to at some point), a loss which did not detract from the double significance (personal and patriotic) of the two dates. May 3rd marks the anniversary of the famous Polish Constitution (1791). In Poland, and in Polish communities abroad, it has been celebrated as a national holiday, in which part of the celebration was the National Run (*Bieg Narodowy*), a cross country race for a prize (a cup), which this writer had won in his hometown in 1939, the last time it was held before the war. What's more important, he had also won it in London in the Olympic year 1948, the first year it was revived after the war, *50 years ago* (winning it also in two following years), when the Games were resumed, too. These coincidences, and May being the favorite month for the Poles since 1791 (celebrated in song and verse), gave him an idea to hold a Symposium, a meeting of generations, one passing, others ascending, triggered by another coincidence: the coming out of his book. Where to hold the Symposium? Preferably in the Kosciuszko Foundation, named after the defender of the Constitution.

The idea of the "important recommendation" was suggested to me by a fine Polish American, Mr. Walter Lasinski, who is an archivist of the Polish National Catholic Church and a Polish patriot, a dying breed apparently. In a conversation about the progress of my book, he told me how dismayed he was about the Poles, in Poland and here, imitating American lifestyle while abandoning traditional Polish values, especially family values. I couldn't agree with him more, adding that while acquiring all the bad habits, the Poles ignore the good things they could learn in America, namely work ethics, punctuality, efficiency, and courtesy in personal and professional relationships, as pointed out elsewhere in this book. But there is one special area, to be spelled out in the "recommendation," in which Poland, as a country, must not imitate America, because it concerns DEMOGRAPHY.

The Polish imitations of American lifestyle are reflected in a variety of ways, including sports, and it is a helpful coincidence that the XVIII Winter Olympic Games were taking place when the book was still unfinished, because they provided several valid points about America, Poland, and American Polonia. The point about America, voiced by Tkachuk, probably of Ukrainian descent, is that Americans are not tough enough in competitions that call for lengthy preparation and intensive training, such as long-distance cross-country races and relays, finishing far back and out of medal contention. Even the highly promoted ice hockey team, consisting of NHL players, managed to win against Japan and Belarus only, losing to Canada and Sweden, and finally to the Czechs in an elimination quarter final. Of the six gold medals America won, four were won by women, including women's ice hockey and the most prestigious competition, women's figure skating, won by the incredible Tara Lipinski, at 15 the youngest and probably the best gold medalist since the legendary Sonja Henie in 1932. The rest were medals in competitions won by brief bursts of energy, as in the free style moguls and snowboarding. But even that compares favorably with the Polish team which was nowhere, a fifth place in the biathlon 4 x 7.5 km relay its best showing. The weakness of the team was underlined by the fact that it was not even seen in the opening parade of nations, its spot taken by a commercial, and any complaints for being slighted would be ill-advised in this case.

Yet, Polish names abounded in the Olympics. Next to the history-making Tara Lipinski, who received 6 first place votes out of 9 judges (a Polish judge voted for her rival, Michelle Kwan), there were two Polish names on the victorious hockey team, Carol Mleczko, one of the better players, and Blahoski, and there was "the great one," Wayne Gretzky, on the Canadian hockey team, whose link with Poland is through his Polish grandmother. Gretzky's finest hour was spoiled by his not being selected for the shoot-out to break the tie with the surging Czechs, the bad decision probably responsi-ble for favored Canada's loss, and the return of hockey's dominance to Europe, and it is there, on the old continent, allegedly dying, that we must seek answers to not only Poland's, but also Polonia's future.

What are the lessons of the Olympics, a traditional yardstick of nations' physical (and mental) health? These are very difficult and complicated points to make, since we are dealing with the Winter Olympics only, but it seems that Europe is (re)asserting a superiority in sports (with Poland absent from that trend, but sharing with America the tendency to do well in short-effort sports only, as seen in the Atlanta Games in 1996 and pointed out in Poland, and by this writer in the essay on the Polish Falcons) at the expense of America, this trend taking place at a time when the world is entering a crisis of Western Civilization at its source, in Europe, brought about by who knows what. Let us look at the general background.

Since the end of the Cold War, instead of entering a golden age of peace and prosperity, the world has been in a state of continuous crises (Palestine, South Africa, Iran, Afghanistan, Poland, Soviet Union, Armenia, Georgia, Chechnya, Ethiopia, Somalia, Iraq, Kurdistan, Rwanda, Bosnia). Even the Olympic Games, with the time-honored tradition of cessation of all hostilities, had a threat of war hanging over them. These were essentially local crises, yet they are probably responsible for a certain weariness in Europe and conviction that after a millennium filled with conflicts—religious, ideological, or simply territorial—the old continent, responsible for the world until recently, was not able to restore order on the eve of the new millennium. While the world is going through the motions, resetting its computers for the year 2000, and Juan Antonio Samaranch, President of the International Olympic Committee is "calling on the youth of the world to assemble in Salt Lake City on February 8, 2002," there is an air of resignation that the next millennium will be no different from the present one, a feeling reflected in such books as Zbigniew Brzezinski's latest, which is a call for the United States to take action to prevent global anarchy.

The book, *The Grand Chessboard: American Primacy and Its Geostrategic Imperatives* (New York: Basic Books, 223 pp., maps), ably reviewed, even if with some restraint, by Bernard Gwertzman under a title "Endgame: Zbigniew Brzezinski's latest blueprint for American foreign policy" (*The New York Times Book Review*, Nov. 16, 1997) is not his first to discuss the theme of anarchy. About a decade ago it was the similarly titled *Game Plan: A Geostrategic Framework for the Conduct of the U.S.-Soviet Contest*, and four years ago it was one even closer to the mark, namely *Out of Control: Global Turmoil on the Eve of the Twenty-First Century*, which was probably an answer to the view of the future in Francis Fukuyama's *The End of History and the Last Man*. To paraphrase Gwertzman, the idea of global anarchy facing an inactive United States is a theme that also has been put forth by Richard N. Haass in *The Reluctant Sheriff*, and Samuel P. Huntington has inveighed against Fukuyama in *The Clash of Civilizations and the Remaking of World Order*. All these topical books have either an American or global focus. It is the most recent of them, *A History of Europe*, that focuses on Europe.

A History of Europe by a distinguished Oxford historian, J.M. Roberts (New York: Allen Lane/The Penguin Press, 628 pp.), reviewed by a Yale Professor of History and Classics, Donald Kagan, under a telling title "Continent No. 1: The hegemony of Europe has expired, a historian says, but its tracks still repay examination" (*The New York Times Book Review*, Dec. 28, 1997) is a book whose appearance is timely and welcome, according to its reviewer, because, as the matrix of Western Civilization, Europe has long been attacked by multiculturalists and others riding the wave of hostility to the West currently favored in much of the academic world. For the most part, these attacks reveal an astonishing ignorance of and indifference to the realities of European history, and of world history as well. A good deal of their success comes from the decline of the study of the past in our schools, especially that of Europe, leaving too many listeners unequipped to evaluate the arguments. There is, in fact, good reason for a broad discussion of the remarkable experience of Europe and its offshoots, particularly in comparison with the world's other civilizations and cultures, but to be of any use it must rest on an accurate knowledge of what has taken place and on informed, well-supported interpretations of what that experience means.

It is these interpretations that take up most of the book, and the author tells the story well, providing his readers with a "guide" that can help them discern what it was that left Europeans "with a sense of shared experience." Many readers will learn with surprise that by far the greatest impact on European civilization was made by the Arabic world of Islam and that even the few innovations reaching Europe from distant Japan, China and India, such as Indian math, had undergone refinement in the "Arabic crucible."

Most of the influence, in any case, ran the other way. From the dawn of the modern era in about 1500, it was Europe that increasingly gave shape and character to everyone else. By that time the author discerns new processes at work in Europe that were to "transform the lives of people round the world." The new Atlantic civilization with Europe at its heart was "radically unlike any other, including its own tradition-bound agrarian-based and geographically confined predecessor. It was to be innovative and secular minded, industrial and urban in its material nature and worldwide in its influence." This is how the author describes this "arrival" of America:

> By 1900 this dynamic and disruptive civilization had moved far toward global hegemony. "It was a unique moment in world history; for the first time one civilization among many was accepted universally as a model. [...] European values went round the world on the powerful wings of aspiration and envy."

A century later, the author believes, things have changed. By the end of World War II the history of Europe could no longer "be

separated comprehensibly from the history of the rest of the globe."
And with the conclusion of the Cold War, he thinks, the history of
Europe as an independent entity may well have come to an end, in
the same way that the Holy Roman Empire came to an end during the
Napoleonic wars.

Another manifestation, next to World War II and the Cold War,
of the decline, or perhaps even the end, of European history as an
independent entity and, with it, the decline of European strength and
vigor, is the steady decline of European emigration to America,
which is music to the ears of the multiculturalists here, but bad news
to the earlier European emigrants and their descendants, who owned
America for 200 years and whose dominance, both numerical and
cultural, will come to an end when the dominant group becomes a
minority, which is expected to happen by the middle of the next
century. The reason for it is DEMOGRAPHY, which Roberts'
reviewer discusses in a different, but not unrelated context:

> Fully aware of recent trends in a different direction, Roberts
> wisely emphasizes the subjects that have traditionally been the
> center of historical interest: politics, international relations, the
> history of religions and important secular ideas. Economic and
> social questions are given their due, but treated in relation to
> the great public movements and events that have always been
> the main attraction of historical writing for most readers. The
> one novelty here is an unusual attention to DEMOGRAPHY
> (caps mine–FM). This is welcome, for the immense importance
> of the rise and fall of populations is too often ignored.

It is not ignored in this book, nor in recent writing by other
people. Patrick Buchanan, for example, sounds the alarm in an
article, "Low birthrates: Suicide of the West," a commentary on
another alarm, Nicholas Eberstat's in the fall 1997 issue of *The
Public Interest*:

> Using recent demographic studies, Eberstat writes that there is a
> high probability that world population growth will level off by
> the year 2040 and then begin gradual decline. But if demogra-
> phy is destiny, the West appears about finished.

He then cites some facts and figures showing that while in 1950 five
of the 12 most populous nations on Earth were Western (the United
States, the United Kingdom, West Germany, Italy, France), by 1995
only the United States and Germany remained among the 12, with

Germany only because of unification of West and East; and on a chart of projected "Top 12 in 2050" there is only one Western country, the United States, fifth at 272 millions behind India (1,231), China (1,198), Pakistan (306), Nigeria (279); and followed by Indonesia (251), Brazil (188), Bangladesh (178), Ethiopia (176), Zaire (146), Iran (143), and Mexico (127).

> What do these demographic numbers tell us? That the Western hour in world history is ending, that by its hedonistic embrace of the sexual revolution—of birth control and of abortion— Western civilization, that great vibrant part of the world once called Christendom, is marching merrily along toward civilizational suicide. God is not mocked.

A conspicuous absentee on the chart is Russia, once co-equal (as the Soviet Union) with the United States in population, whose shrinking and aging will put it, together with all other European countries, behind the Philippines.

But the prime example of Buchanan's alarm is Italy. This writer remembers then-fascist Italy, while a schoolboy in Poland, as the most dynamic country in Europe, passing ailing France in population and, as an early ally of Nazi Germany, bent on conquest. Now, according to Buchanan, after Eberstat (both of whom must have read Roberts):

> Consider Italy. Today, an Italian couple has on average 1.2 children, the lowest birthrate in Europe. This means that for every eight young Italians today, there will be five children, three grandkids, and one or two great-grandchildren. If these birth rates endure, the Italian people are headed toward extinction.

Eberstat:

> In Italy…barely 2 percent of the population in 2050 would be under the age of 5, but more than 40 percent would be 65 or over.

Eberstat, who is a demographer with the American Enterprise Institute in Washington, voiced similar dire predictions a few years ago about the eastern German state of Brandenburg is seeking to stem a drop in birth rates that may be the sharpest in modern world history (*New York Times*, Nov. 27, 1994):

Eastern Germany's adults appear to have come as close to a temporary suspension of childbearing as any large population in the human experience.

The article claims that demographers say such precipitous declines have never before been seen except in times of war, plague or famine. This time the astonishing drop in birth rates, which has been attributed in large part to economic uncertainty, seems to be a byproduct of German unification that no one predicted. This attribution was confirmed by a spokesman for the Brandenburg government:

This problem of falling birth rates, which you can really call dramatic, goes beyond Brandenburg and beyond the eastern states. [...] All over Germany people are feeling insecure, especially young people. They are thinking about studying and working, not about families. Naturally you see this more in the east, but it has spread westward and is now a serious national problem. We have to confront it.

There is a hint here, and in at least one of the earlier statements that the birth rate problem is a temporary one, as was also this writer's fear of the decline of Europe's vigor. Otherwise, how can we explain the chain of European successes at the just-ended Olympic Games? If the problem was dramatic in 1994, it should have been even more so in 1998. Instead, three European countries finished on top, the supposedly dying Germany first, followed by Norway holding on to its all-time superiority, and the ailing but still strong Russia; ahead of the former North American winter sports powers, the United States and Canada (home of ice hockey), with the allegedly terminal Italy not far behind, along with Holland, Austria, Switzerland, France, and even England, definitely not a winter sports nation, on the list with one medal (bronze).

Poland, always unpredictable, is a special case. Never a winter sports power, its all-time medal count at a modest four (including one gold for a freakish ski jump), behind Liechtenstein and new-comer China, it showed medal potential in the 4 x 7.5 km relay and in Alpine skiing, where young Andrzej Bachleda is bound to become a medal contender, like his father before him. In what sounds like a Polish joke but isn't, Poland finished ahead of such winter sports "powers" as Jamaica, the Virgin Islands and Australia, and still landed close to the bottom in the 4-man bobsled competition, doing what the Olympic motto stresses: that it is not winning but taking part that counts. And it is participation in international systems that Poland craves most, be it the European Union, NATO, or the Olympic movement. But it would have been good to win, if only to help dispel the perception of a dying Europe because of DEMOGRAPHY.

In Poland, too, demography took a wrong turn. But Poland is a special case in this respect because the wrong turn was totally unexpected. In a now classic article by Michael T. Kaufman, the Warsaw correspondent of *The New York Times*, "Poland's Mixed Blessing: Its Many, Many Babies" (Oct. 16, 1986) this factor is brought forth by citing a Polish demographer at the Institute of Work:

> By the late 70's we started to see a leveling off in the [postwar–FM] birth rate, and we were all predicting that the same thing was happening that happened in West Germany, East Germany, Belgium, Hungary, where the reproductive rate stabilized or even dropped. Then came 1981, and all predictions proved wrong and the birth rate of some 700,000 shot up by some 60,000 more than expectations.

As a result, Poles were having more children than Government demographers thought they would, and more children in relation to population than any country in Europe. Average family size also appeared to be inching up from 2.3 children per family, and as a result one out of every five people added yearly to the population of Europe, not counting the Soviet Union, was a Pole.

Kaufman's article brings out another impressive statistic. A country that lost one out of every six citizens in World War II and that reached its prewar population only in 1981 (actually 1979, as reported in *Trybuna Ludu* ["The People's Rostrum"], the official organ of the Government, and included in the present writer's paper at the Congress of Scholars of Polish Descent in 1979), was expecting a further growth in population of 5 to 10 million by the end of the century, according to a study by the Polish Academy of Sciences, bringing the total to well above the 40-million mark, instead of barely reaching it (if at all) in 2001, according to present estimates.

Such fecundity, Kaufman continues, is often a matter of pride and joy, but in Poland at that time it would necessitate a 40 percent growth in agricultural production, while farm productivity had risen only slightly in the previous decade, and meat was still rationed. Was that the main reason for the drop in the birth rate, which eventually assumed such catastrophic proportions as to lead editors of the Polish American press to wonder whether Poland was a dying country? This was 1986, yet, as late as 1995, Jan Olszewski was still talking (*Przegląd Polski*, Oct. 12), of a Poland 40-million strong, "biologically unbelievably resilient," making up one fifth of those entering productive age in the European Union if Poland enters (the one fifth is possible, since other European countries had even lower birthrates). At about the same time (June 28, 1995), *Nowy Dziennik* cited some findings of the United Nations Development Program to the effect that Poland belonged to the demographically most dynamic societies and that in the years 1991-2001 [?] the increase in its population of productive age will amount to 57 percent of that increase for the whole of Europe. The only way to interpret that information is to assume that it is false, that the increase in Poland refers to people born in the years of still-high birth rates, and that we are indeed dealing with a crisis of Western civilization.

What about America? In his commentary on Eberstat's report, Patrick Buchanan predicts some changes concerning the major countries, including America. The Russian Far East will likely pass to China, with the sick and shrinking Russian population unable to hold the Chinese (Buchanan forgets that Russia has a healthy reserve population, useless now because isolated in the KALININGRAD region). The next change pertains to India's rise as the dominant power in South Asia and the Indian Ocean, though the Hindu nation will have hundreds of millions of Muslim citizens and find herself surrounded by populous Muslim neighbors. Indeed, demography today appears to be a mighty ally of Islam, according to Eberstat/ Buchanan. As for America, Buchanan goes beyond Roberts' book:

> America too will change. As Bill Clinton happily observed last summer, at our present immigration rates and birth rates, the United States by 2050 will cease to be a Western nation, either in the composition of her population or in her culture.

It is a strong, bitter statement, but coming from President Clinton's political adversary it is not strong enough. It does not even mention the illegal immigration from non-European countries, especially across the Rio Grande, and the warnings of its implications for the United States from such organizations as the American Immigration Control. Following reports in the media of uncontrollable crossings of the Rio Grande by the illegals accompanied by devastation of private property on the American side along the border, and of calls for a two-year moratorium on all immigration, there is relative silence on the subject, as if the media have had enough of it. But there are other reports, such as the recent *60 Minutes* program on CBS about the giant Tyson Foods of Arkansas, Clinton backers since his early years, importing 4,000 Latin American workers into a small town (Raymond) and disrupting its homogenous character, while eliciting concerned expressions about the future of the United States.

To all appearances, the emerging "multiculturalism" in America is likely to be more disruptive than unifying. There are ethnic rivalries. In the past, they manifested themselves in low-level ethnic jokes, witty more often than mean, at the expense of the latest ethnic group, with the Poles, the last of the European waves, the last target of the jokes, which today are things of the past, judging by the Olympic Games where Polish names abounded without raising an eyebrow. (On the contrary, the most successful bearer of a Polish name became the most popular person in the Games.) Today the rivalries go deeper, and on higher levels, as experienced by this writer in the biggest Jesuit university in America, where a new chairperson set about dismantling an innovative and inclusive modern languages department by systematically eliminating or not allowing languages spoken by half of the world in order to expand Spanish and leave just three other "traditional" languages. What does that say for "multiculturalism" in America?

This example can serve as an omen of things to come and, since one of the languages to be eliminated was Polish—a part of "an experiment that didn't work" (Polish, in Chicago, the biggest "Polish" city outside of Poland!)—a warning and advice to the Polish American community, also voiced elsewhere in this book, to monitor such abuses. Furthermore, since the perpetrator of this particular abuse was a Hispanic, a member of the fastest growing community in America, estimated to reach 25 percent of US population sometime in the next century, it pointed to a polarization taking place in America. Aware of the polarization and trying to account for it, this writer developed a theory that it had more to do with climate than with nationality, namely that people deriving from different climatic zones cannot live side by side harmoniously. In his mind, this was probably one of the causes for the failure of colonialism, and even for the Civil War in America. But his theory was not entirely his own, it came to him after reading a man who knew more about such things than he, the excellent social studies scholar then at Columbia University, Dr. Amitai Etzioni.

Dr. Etzioni claimed in one of his statements that America was turning into what he called a "siesta republic." I agreed with him, comparing the well-kept and harmonious "European" neighborhoods of people deriving from temperate climatic zones with the spreading Hispanic slums with their littered streets and a high incidence of crime.

Even more disturbing, although not germane to the main gist of this discussion, is the report by the National Census Office that every fourth (legal) immigrant to the US comes from Mexico, articles about "Border Vigilantes" (*The New York Times Magazine*, Oct. 11, 1997), and statements about the border between the two countries by the Mexican writer Carlos Fuentes in books (*The Crystal Frontier*, Farrar, Straus & Giroux, 1997, in which he regards the border as "a wound that refuses to heal over") and articles (Richard Rayner, "What Immigration Crisis?" in *The New York Times Magazine*, Jan. 7, 1966, in which Mexicans coming to California feel to this day that they were cheated when Mexico ceded it to the United States in 1848, and "in coming to California they are asserting a historical right; with each payday and welfare check they claim revenge. It's a scar, not a border," notes Carlos Fuentes. There is also the alarmist column by Thomas L. Friedberg (*Foreign Affairs*), "Que Pasa Aqui?" (*The New York Times, Dec. 17, 1995*) about an unfolding Mexican drama:

> This drama is only unfolding in a country on America's doorstep, with the world's 11th-largest population, 13th-largest economy and 100 million people, half of whom will want to come north if things go bad.

If they do go bad, there is a 2003 United States invasion of Mexico to install a provisional government, as imagined in a series of "Worst-Case Scenarios" by Caspar Weinberger and Peter Schweizer in a book *The Next War* (Illustrated, 470 pp. Washington: Regenery Publishing. $27.50).

This discussion, in which nobody talks about the American poor: the Native Americans (meaning the Indians) and the poverty in Appalachia, in both cases the "real" Americans, concerns Poland only indirectly, to the extent that it concerns American Polonia, but there are some common traits, for which some parallels can be drawn. Just as America has a Mexican problem, which multiculturalism is rather aggravating than helping and which seems insoluble, and Russia a Chinese problem, for which remnants of Soviet multiculturalism are of no help and which also appears insoluble, Poland *had* a centuries-long Ukrainian problem going back to the multicultural Commonwealth period, which ended in disaster; the problem turned into a war when it returned with independence after World War I and was, in a height of irony, terminated by the Molotov-Ribbentrop Pact on the eve of World War II, to reappear briefly after the war with painful lessons for both sides. With these lessons, Poland, a faithful imitator of American ways, must not imitate one of them, multiculturalism, and that's the "important recommendation" mentioned at the beginning of this Introduction.

Polish multiculturalism? Now? Let us look at the background, dealing with DEMOGRAPHY. In the March 1997 issue of *Wprost* ("Directly"), a telling article "The End of Poland for Poles?" ("Koniec Polski dla Polaków?") subtitled "Rzeczpospolita wielu narodów" ("A Republic of many Nations") begins in a clear expository manner:

> An ethnically homogenous Poland was to be the biggest benefit we carried out of the Yalta and Potsdam Agreements. As late as a few years ago this was considered a plus, pointing to the war in Yugoslavia and the conflicts in the former Soviet Union as chief arguments against an ethnic mosaic. Meanwhile we will soon be joining the European Union and the settling down in Poland of thousands of German, Dutch, French and English people will be a certainty. But already there are 300-500 thousands (about 1 percent of the population) of illegal immigrants, who treat our country as a second homeland. Every year more than 30,000 obtain the right of permanent residence. In towns there come into being enclaves of Vietnamese, Armenians, Chinese [and other Asians and Africans–FM]. One must not forget the old Polish minorities—Ukrainians, Belorussians, Lithuanians, Germans or Jews. Shall we then in the next dozen or so years evolve from a one-nation state into a Republic of many nations?

This is the direction Poland is moving in, and which in its own best interest it must abandon before it is too late. A homogenous Poland, a nation-state, perhaps the only example of it in Europe, is still possible and, because of its uniqueness, it is Poland's strength.

The reasons for an open-door policy, practiced in Poland in the past mainly to compensate for population losses sustained through wars and invasions and while erecting a Commonwealth of Nations, no longer exist, and the new Poland, still evolving, must rely on Poles in order to grow and radiate strength and perfection like the Poland of Casimir the Great.

What's to be done? The open-door policy should be maintained only for returning Poles, both from Western Europe and the Americas, and from the East, descendants of countless deportees to Russia, Siberia and Kazakhstan, and from sizable Polish enclaves in Ukraine. The returning Poles will help Poland accomplish what the vanishing birth rate will not, to reach and pass the by-now mythical 40-million population, an important milestone needed if only to lift Poland from junior status in the Weimar triangle with Germany and France, and make it indeed one of the "engines of Europe" together with them.

As for the old minorities, remnants of sizable prewar communities (almost one third of the total population) and result of postwar population shifts (some extremely brutal) they will remain, amounting to less than a million all told, with not a single one amounting to 1 percent of the total population of Poland.

There is little likelihood that sizable numbers from member countries of the European Union will settle in Poland once Poland becomes a member.

That leaves the new minorities, and the question of how they found themselves in Poland in the first place? The truth is that Poland was not their destination, but Germany, where they were attracted by the legend of the German "Economic Miracle." But the "miracle" was a distant memory, and Germany was stuck with millions of foreign workers (7.3 at present) and has been trying in vain to unload them, even offering high premiums to make them go back to their countries (mostly Turkey); Germany also had millions of unemployed (5 at present) and had no room for any new arrivals. They were expelled, but not to their countries of origin, but to the last country from which they crossed into Germany, and that meant Poland.

What's to be done with them? Most of them know that Poland will soon become a member of the European Union where borders are virtually non-existent, and it will be easier to cross from Poland to Germany. Meanwhile they claim refugee status and are directed to refugee centers, where they are taken care of by the government, which does not have a clear immigration policy to handle the problem.

And what to do with the immigrants who on arrival choose Poland as their destination and start settling down and even open businesses? And what about the Russians, Ukrainians, Belorussians, who come for temporary stays and decide to remain and bring in their families? Without clear policies, the situation could easily get out of control.

Some commentators in Poland argue that it was the immigrants who built America, a statement which again shows ignorance of America and its evolution, as expounded in Roberts' *History of Europe*. Times have changed and patterns of immigration have changed with them, with the Europe-originating immigrants who built America no longer arriving in meaningful numbers. Today America is facing an immigration problem that Poland is only entering and has a chance to avoid, but must find a way.

With unemployment in Poland at 11 percent, on par with Western Europe but twice that of America, Poland must in future accept only immigrants who have skills which are in short supply in Poland. While it is impossible to shut the country off entirely from arriving foreigners, as the experience of France, Germany, Great Britain or Austria shows, tighter border control must be introduced to stem the flood, while threading a thin line between European Union's guidelines and Poland's policies. The fact that foreigners feel comfortable in Poland, flattering the notoriously vain Poles, should be of no account, but another is, DEMOGRAPHY. The almost Zero Population Growth, a mere 20,000 in 1997, if not reversed, could make the increased presence of immigrants not only acceptable, but necessary. Help is needed, and this is where American Polonia comes in, as outlined earlier in this book.

Despite unjustified criticism by its more recent members and a generally low regard in Poland based on ignorance, and some decline in its organizational structure since the heyday of the Bicentennial, American Polonia is still, in the eyes of some other groups, the best organized ethnic community in America. It is no surprise then that outsiders see it in stronger terms than Poles themselves, as in a recent article in the London *Economist* pointing out the political clout of a "10-million strong" Polonia in discussing Poland's chances to join NATO.

This high opinion of American Polonia is still too modest. This writer's estimates, as pointed out earlier, put the number of Americans of Polish descent as 20-million strong, a figure obtained by projecting the Kennedy family count of the strength of the potential Polish vote in 1960, and supported by this writer's scanning the mainstream media for Polish names and discovering that among the multitude very few were part of organized Polonia, but the names are there, ready to be harvested or just be aware of, which in most cases it is impossible not to be.

During the Winter Olympic Games, and even before and after, Tara Lipinski's face and story appeared on the front page of *The New York Times'* "Sports Sunday" and "Week in Review" sections and in many other publications, as did also Wayne Gretzky (*The New York Times Magazine*), sharing an article with Mark Messier ("Elders on Ice," March 23, 1997) in an issue dedicated to Nelson Mandela. The name that became almost as prominent, if for other reasons, is that of the "Unabomber" Theodore Kaczynski, to the extent that the Foreign Affairs columnist Thomas L. Friedman drops it off-handedly ("Ted Kaczynski could be my mailman") in an article on Saddam Hussein on Feb. 24, 1998. But it is not this unsavory connection but deep analysis of Kaczynski's mind that two articles on the front page of *The New York Times* of May 26, 1996, undertake under a joint title, "The Tortured Genius of Theodore Kaczynski."

Then there are names that one would wish were not Polish, especially Monica Lewinsky, probably the best known name in 1998, reflecting America's preoccupation with scandal. Another name reflects America's preoccupation with sweepstakes, with a sticker including the name, and a message, pasted on the envelope containing the sweepstakes announcement, usually from a charity (National Park Trust, National Children's Cancer Society, Easter Seal Society). The multi-colored stickers are either oval or rectangular, and their message is a variation of: "Congratulations MELINDA CHELMOWSKI, The NEWEST $1,000,000.00 Prize Winner." One would like to know who Linda Chelmowski is and by what magic she is the "newest" winner in three different sweeps? One would also like to know who is "The BIG LEBOWSKI," a name in the title of a movie announced in a one-page ad in the "Arts & Leisure" section of *The New York Times* of March 1, 1998. The following Sunday (March 8) brought a review, actually two, of the movie itself, "Down Mean Alleys With

John Goodman," and of the genre, "Neo-Noir's a Fashion That Fits Only a Few," and yet another Polish name. Lebowski turns out to be the name of a ruthless millionaire (fictional?) which also happens to be the name of the character played by Jeff Bridges, the star of the movie. But it is the co-star, John Goodman (Roseanne's television husband), who plays a character with the other Polish name, Walter Sobchak, harking back to earlier noirs. The connections, as explained by the critic Stephen Holden, are fascinating, but not germane to the points being made about Poland. All these and other names mean only one thing, that Polish or Polish-sounding names are becoming household words in America, for whatever it's worth. But their bearers are of no use for Poland, except one, Marta Kostyra, who goes under her married name of Martha Stewart.

MARTHA STEWART, a one-woman multi-corporation, is a success story so spectacular that *The New York Times* gave her front-page coverage in its "Money & Business" section of February 8, 1998. Titled "Master of Her Destiny" and subtitled "For Martha Stewart, A One-Woman Show With Many Flourishes" by Robin Pogrebin (an altered Polish name Pogrzebień?), the article lists them as, among others: Books (22; first, *Entertaining*, in 30th printing); *Martha Stewart Living* magazine (circulation 2.3 million); "Ask Martha" syndicated column (in 212 newspapers); "CBS This Morning" (weekly magazine, in Japan during the Olympics); Martha Stewart Everyday bed and bath goods at K-Mart (1997 sales $500 to $700 million); Martha Stewart Everyday Colors paints (Estimated 1997 sales $16 million); "Martha Stewart Living" TV program (Top-rated new syndicated program; on 197 stations); "Ask Martha" radio feature (on 135 stations); Web site (300,000 visits per week). In the world of Calvin Kleins and Ralph Laurens she is perhaps the country's pre-eminent female brand name. What a role model to enterprising women everywhere, including Poland!

To this writer Martha Stewart goes beyond being a role model. Even after reading about her, he did not really get interested in her until the Winter Olympics when, watching the Morning News for results, he noticed her blending with the News and smoothly switching into her own 9 AM "Martha Stewart Living" program, with stress on "living" and "good thing" when discussing and demonstrating the day's topics, be it cooking (in the kitchen), decorating plants (in the living room), fruit (in the garden), she was always in total but gentle control, even with a guest-expert on the day's topic, under her watchful eye, her soft but precise remarks falling with the delicacy of rose petals, her seemingly favorite flower.

Martha Stewart's cult-like persona should be part of my proposal to the fraternals on how to help Poland, perhaps by acquiring the tapes of her "Living" programs at first. With her blond hair, friendly smile and still good looks at 56, she would be very popular, on three counts: being American, Polish-born, and an expert. The Poles need some of the Martha Stewart optimism (which is rare even in America) because with the all-consuming stress on NATO and the European Union the quality of life is suffering and some important problems have been lost sight of or ignored, something we read about in letters from Poland.

We, Poles in America, must do everything to help Poland become a perfect country, but it is not happening. Here is an excerpt from a letter by a trustworthy man:

> There is much new in Poland, but we are unable to take care of the old, because the nation is poor and there are too many pensioners, and not only political, at that. The government and Solidarity are constantly assuring us that it will be better the moment we join NATO and the European Union takes us in. But how to get out of poverty nobody clearly knows since we are increasingly dependent on the West and in a state of war with the East. How long that will last nobody knows and the whole nation in fact lives from day to day.

A woman:

> I am glad you are better after a thorough check-up with instruments. They know now how to cure. Here too only money counts. Without money one can die. Already one has to pay for everything. Free medicine has practically ended. It is still on paper, but you end up paying everywhere. And in hospitals there is such poverty that when I needed help I had to go first to the drugstore to get a bandage because in the out-patient clinic they had none. Medicine you must also bring with you.

The man talks also about the difficulty of changing the mentality of people who for half a century were led by the hand in the previous system, and how large areas of the country are idle and full of unemployed while in the cities foreign capital is doing business. This is echoed by the woman, complaining that while some have made millions, others live in poverty, and the homeless are seen in the stations (railway?). All the bad things come from America, which probably also includes the absence of family in both letters, except for the man living alone with his widowed daughter (there is no family in Ms. Stewart *Living* either).

Concern for family is not entirely absent in Poland, as can be seen in a recent book by Father Władysław Majkowski, *Factors of Disintegration of Contemporary Polish Family* ("Czynniki dezintegracji współczesnej rodziny polskiej"), published in Cracow and reviewed appropriately in *Naród Polski* in Chicago (Nov. 20, 1997). Fr. Majkowski, graduate of the Gregorian University in Rome and Loyola University in Chicago (where he participated in my Solidarity symposium), and at present a lecturer of Sociology at the Academy of Catholic Theology in Warsaw, subjected to deep analysis the macro- and micro-structural factors lowering the stability of the marriage-family life in contemporary Poland. In the first category he included: the Marxist marriage ideology imposed by the Communist regime in Poland after World War II; accelerated process of industrialization and urbanization; legal secularization of marriage. The second destabilizing category includes: lack of social-personal resources of spouses and of satisfaction with one's life style, as well as lack of gratification arising from forming a marriage-family community. These factors lower the quality of marriage-family life and, with the simultaneous lowering or lack of social control, inevitably lead to the disintegration of marriage.

The book contains a post-sociological supplement in which the author postulates pro-family activities to help the contemporary Polish family. Among them are: preparation for marriage and family, help for families; suitable pro-family policy of the state; creation of a network of family counseling centers and help for the divorced. This is the area where Polonia could be of help.

The family must be restored to the center of life in Poland. Too much depends on it, perhaps everything: the future of Poland and its destiny. To put the family back where it belongs may take a long time, but there is already a growing agreement (echoed by the gentleman letter writer) that Poland needs at least one generation to put its house in order. Like the ancient Israelites, those who remember the previous system will not see the Promised Land.

The Promised Land will be one in which children are born freely without worrying how to provide for them and what domicile to raise them in, because they will be Poland's most important natural resource, solving the country's DEMOGRAPHY problem and bringing it closer to its more populous neighbors, especially Germany, Poland's future partner, with a similar but more advanced problem of demography ("We have some feeling that the tree of life may be falling") which the Germans feared but which, however, they said, "We are confronting."

In the article, quoted above and earlier, about the German problem, Ralph Kinzer's self-explanatory "$650 a Baby: Germany Pays to Stem Decline in Birth," sub-titled "Demographics," "The Disappearing Germans," there is also a mention about Poland:

> Some countries, including Hungary and Poland, provide payments to families that have newborn babies, but they are much smaller than the payments Brandenburg will now make.

This was November 27, 1994. Three years later, an article, "Like It or Not, Germany Becomes a Melting Pot" (*The New York Times*, Nov. 30, 1997) underlined Germany's predicament apparently unaffected by the payments (limited, to be sure, to the Brandenburg state). Another, in the same week, Sunday's *The New York Times Magazine*, Ben Wattenberg's bold "The Population Explosion Is Over" (one of Pat Buchanan's sources), underlined it and, indirectly, Poland's, further.

Yet the more recent report, in *The Week in Germany* (a weekly publication of the German Information Center, New York) of February 20, 1998, "More Babies, Fewer Weddings," reporting on the success of the payments in Brandenburg, adds:

> Germany as a whole welcomed 810,000 newborns to the world last year, 2.7 percent more than in '96. Although modest, the increase in the number of babies born in the western states (2.1 percent) is noteworthy. The birthrate there has been steadily declining since the 1950s, but has begun to rise again in the past two years.

This means that Germany is doing better than Poland (whose birthrate is perilously close to the ominous ZPG—Zero Population Growth) despite the fewer weddings, but, for better or worse, is stuck with 7.3 million foreigners.

To this writer, "left with" is a better verb than "stuck" and "for better" a preferred comparison. The "foreigners" are after all, mostly Turks, children of workers who had helped Germany bring about its liberating "Wirtschaftwunder" after a disastrous war, just as Polish workers helped reconstruct America after the Civil War. The comparison is not as far-fetched as it may seem, just as it is not far-fetched to see the Turks as deriving from a country which, after centuries of bloody strife ending with the fateful Battle of Vienna (1683) became Poland's friend, a century too late, beginning the friendship by allowing sanctuary to Casimir Pulaski's Bar Confederates (1768-1772) when the two countries still shared a border, and never recognizing the Partitions which followed. These are ponderables worth retaining, especially by this writer who, while criss-crossing Germany in 1988 in search of a wartime past, found the Turks very helpful as guides, and surprisingly knowledgeable about common Pole/Turk history.

This digression is necessary to establish links with the new Germany that is here to stay after integrating the Turks (about the other "foreigners" I have no opinion). These links go back a thousand years, to the year 1000, to the meeting in Gniezno, revived by John Paul II a thousand years later, of the young visionary German Emperor Otto III and the newly crowned (by him) King of Poland, Bolesław the Brave, both with a dream of new Europe, the dream shattered by the Emperor's untimely death and renewed hostilities. The Pope's initiative to revive the dream points to a future in which the year 1000 will be celebrated in Poland on the same scale as the advent of Christianity: 966.

While pondering roads to perfection for Poland, another meeting caught my attention, this one here and now, March 13 (1998) in Chicago, a high-profile banquet "to greet Poland in NATO" (prematurely?). The guest of honor was MARIAN KRZAKLEWSKI, leader of the majority party in the Polish Parliament and, as yet unofficial, candidate for President of Poland ("anointed" by Edward Moskal, President of the Polish American Congress, according to Albin Wozniak of "The Polish Studies Newsletter"). Before we return to the Krzaklewski question, let us add that Colonel Ryszard Kukliński is also expected at the banquet, leading to a digression: why Kukliński? Because Brzezinski had called him a hero? There is a literary precedent in Poland for his action, it's called "Wallenrodism" after a poem by Adam Mickiewicz, "Konrad Wallenrod," parts of it being sad songs and a famous hexameter; but nobody ever called

Konrad, Kukliński's literary ancestor, a hero. Mickiewicz himself was unhappy about the poem and its Machiavellian message.

Despite heated disagreement by Albin Wozniak in another issue of his "Newsletter" (Jan. 1998), Krzaklewski makes the impression of a man who would be the President Poland needs, to be elected not along the criteria in Michnik's diatribes, but because of support by the Polish American Congress. This support is the wisest action the Congress has taken in connection with Poland in years.

A presentable man, in an age when appearance means a lot, reasonably young at 47 with a long life ahead, Marian Krzaklewski is, because of that, a better candidate than the elderly professors stipulated earlier on these pages. Time is on his side, because on the long road to perfection, as already pointed out, only those who don't remember the previous system will reach the Promised Land, with Krzaklewski, the Polish Moses, leading them.

In a country in search of meanings and symbols, names mean a lot, and Krzaklewski's demands an analysis. With Lech Wałęsa only the first name was significant, LECH being the name of the legendary founder of a Slavic tribe out of which Poland was to evolve more than a millennium ago. In my book, *Poland's Solidarity Movement*, dedicated to Lech Wałęsa, I included the pre-Christian legendary history, adding some imagery from the poet Cyprian Norwid, and entrusting a copy for Wałęsa to Professor Bronislaw Geremek returning from a lecture at Columbia University. I was hoping that the book would help Wałęsa to develop a different persona from the one he was displaying in Poland, but he apparently never received it, to my sincere regret.

With Krzaklewski, both names are significant, and he does not need a new persona, he already has a good one, shaped by his professional and political experience: Doctor of technical sciences, underground activist briefly jailed, Wałęsa's successor in 1990 as leader of Solidarity, founder of AWS (Solidarity Election Action), member of Parliament, he stepped aside for Jerzy Buzek for Prime Minister. As for his names, Marian, a Christian name par excellence, reflects his conservative orientation, with a wife and 3 children. The family name is a miracle of symbolism, consisting of two words and a Polish ending -ski. The first part "Krzak" means "Bush" and brings the "Burning Bush" Moses symbolism to mind (there is nothing wrong with being partially also a namesake of President Bush). The second part "lew" means "lion" and there is no name a man would rather be called, especially a man gearing up for a fight. Krzaklewski's election to the Presidency should be in the interest of all Poles, at home and abroad. With his experience and education he is aware of Poland's vital problems, and his political-ideological orientation makes him a natural for solving the biggest problem—DEMOGRAPHY. But there is another problem no less important—KALININGRAD, the solving of which is a condition for Poland's perfection in the next century. It will take a man not only with the name of a lion, but with a heart of a lion, to stand up to the Russians and demand: "Get out of Kaliningrad! What's your price? Surplus grain? Our membership in NATO?"

How to go about it? Kaliningrad has been a taboo subject since the end of World War II when the Soviet Union annexed northern East Prussia, and renamed Königsberg Kaliningrad, giving its name to the enclave, which became the most "armed" piece of land in Europe. Following the break-up of the Soviet Union, the enclave remained part of the Russian Republic, although separated from it by 500 km and an uncertain future, yet in effect holding the new independent countries of East and Central Europe hostage.

The story (and "pre-history") of the region is told in a separate essay in this book but suffice it to say that its future is now a matter of certain urgency: should Belarus enter into a federation with Russia, we will next hear about a need of a "corridor" through Polish territory to connect the new Russian federation with Kaliningrad. Even more ominous are "German dreams about East Prussia," reported in an article, "To Return to Königsberg," by Roman Żelazny, a knowledgeable German correspondent of the *Nowy Dziennik* (Jan. 27, 1998) discussing "re-Germanization" of Kaliningrad. Suddenly we have the specter of a corridor stretching from Szczecin (Stettin) to Gdańsk (Danzig) as if World War II had never happened. If we add to it a recent statement by US Secretary of State William Cohen that he had "no desire to die for Danzig" we are back in 1939 and a "Polish" problem of the first magnitude. That's why Poland needs a strong President to confront the problem, because it is too big for a mere Minister of Foreign Affairs.

The current Minister, Bronisław Geremek, is a highly qualified individual, but his communist past renders him unfit for a high government post, although there is nobody better for this particular one. This writer, a struggling soldier-scholar in the free world, read with envy about Geremek's easy academic progress under communism when that information became public. After 1989 Geremek's frequent statements were like a chameleon's skin, changing with the landscape: when still immersed in medieval history he was warning Poland about having grandiose designs; then (1993), when chairman of the parliamentary Committee for Foreign Affairs, he spoke about the end of ancient threats, about the German dilemma ("German Europe or European Germany") and about the shadow of Russia, which should be treated as a neighbor, and not just because of the Kaliningrad enclave (his *only* allusion to it); in 1995, on the sixth anniversary of the 1989 events in Poland, he spoke at a meeting with New York Polonia in the gallery of *Nowy Dziennik* about Poland's "historical chance"; and on his last visit in New York, and first as Minister of Foreign Affairs, in February of 1998, while mostly involved with Poland's admission to NATO and a dialogue with American Jews, in meetings with Polonia in *Nowy Dziennik* and in the Polish Consulate he would refer to Poland as a "Central European power." At some point he claimed it was Poland that overthrew communism. Such progression shows a growing confidence and faith in Poland's potential, but it does not show in meetings with foreign dignitaries, as seen on television from the Department of State in Washington, with Geremek constantly bowing and scraping, and in the Moscow meeting with his Russian opposite number Yevgenii Primakov.

The Moscow meeting calls for a comment. The photo in *Nowy Dziennik* (March 6, 1988) shows the two men facing each other shaking hands, with a third, presumably an interpreter, between them; all three smiling, with Geremek's smile a conciliatory one, and Primakov's, one with a hint of condescension. That's how it was between the two countries during the entire postwar period and still is, never with complete equality, with the exception perhaps in the Gomułka-Khrushchev and Jaruzelski-Gorbachev eras. The meeting concerned the recent changes in border controls (very much needed to stem the illegal immigration—FM), with Geremek assuring his host that the changes do not herald the closing of the Polish border because of Poland's determination to join NATO and the European Union; that even as a member of NATO Poland will be interested in the best possible relations with Russia, and this was the intention of the Polish government.

That's just it. Would Geremek, within the "best possible
relations," be able to articulate Poland's claim to northern East
Prussia (the Kaliningrad enclave) as historically part of Ducal
Prussia, Poland's dependency, and would President Kwaśniewski,
another "stained" Polish "statesman," authorize such a claim, and *do
it now*, as both a signal to Russia (and Germany) to abstain from any
plans in that area and an announcement of Poland's long-range
foreign policy objective before membership in NATO submerges the
country's foreign policy in the alliance's overall policies? The
answer is "NO" (old loyalties, or whatever one can call it, die hard;
also, Geremek himself admitted "humorously" on his last visit to
New York that he had obtained his new function "quite by accident,"
and that something similar could cause him to lose it). The best one
can hope for is at least some statement from Geremek, presumably
an "ally" of Krzaklewski who, unhampered by a damaging past,
would be able to articulate such a claim. But so would Lech Wałęsa,
and here lies my "quarrel" (for lack of a better word) with Professor
Bronislaw Geremek.

For lack of any receipt, or confirmation, it must be assumed
that he did not deliver my book to Lech Wałęsa. Had he done so (and
as a scholar read beforehand another scholar's opinion of a man he
was advising), discovering that it was by far the best portrait of
Wałęsa in all the books about him (a conclusion which, as a percep-
tive scholar, he would have reached on his own) and conveyed it to
him, Wałęsa would have learned things about himself he didn't
know, and the new perception would have affected and transformed
him to the extent that he could have been salvaged for Poland, continuing to generate for it more goodwill and help than anybody in it
entire history, while serving a second term, putting Russia in its
place, and stepping down for Krzaklewski just like a decade earlier.
That none of this happened and is not about to, is due to the fact that
Professor Geremek is an egghead, member of a small coterie of like-
minded people in Poland who think even when they shouldn't, not
what's best for the country but what *they* think is the best, like what
kind of President Poland needs. Wałęsa was abandoned.

As a result it will all fall on Krzaklewski who, in a height of
irony, could be defeated if Wałęsa decides to run, taking votes away
from him. Now it's Krzaklewski's turn to be salvaged, and the only
way to accomplish it is to come to an agreement with Wałęsa,
perhaps with the help of what this writer had said about him in both

books. If there is one thing in Wałęsa that's useful now it is his common sense, and it is needed now. But beware of the eggheads! Luckily, Krzaklewski is their match: at least they cannot accuse him of speaking bad Polish.

Krzaklewski should run on a platform of getting the Russians out of the Kaliningrad (Königsberg or Królewiec) enclave. It should be his mandate, never to be forgotten. Just like the indomitable Roman, Cato the Elder (Cato Major) reminded the Senate after each session that in his opinion Carthage should be destroyed, using the same memorable sentence (that every child in Poland learned in his Latin classes and remembered),

Ceterum censeo Cartaginam delendam esse,

Krzaklewski should remind the Parliament about Kaliningrad.

Poland's claim is an old one, going back to 1466, when after a long-drawn war the Teutonic Order was divided between Poland and a revised Order, which became a vassal of Poland, with a new capital in Königsberg. It is the only historically justified claim next to a German, which is just as unthinkable today as the Russian presence is, but Poland should make a good-will gesture toward Germany. That's why the next chapter is "POLAND AND GERMANY".

(See map on page 338, and following page)

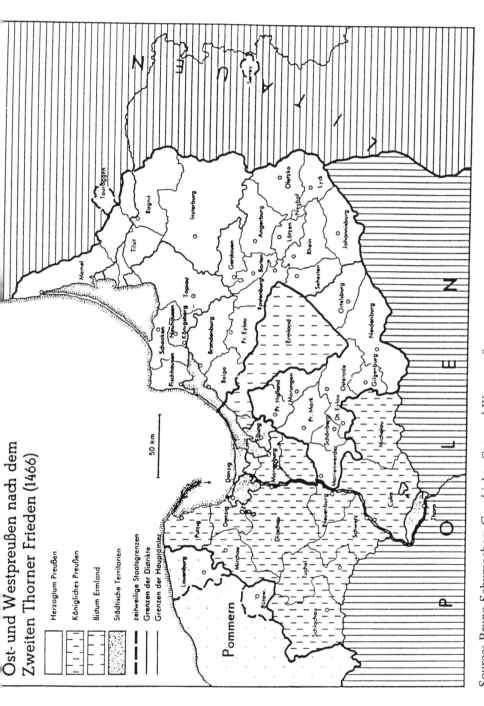

Ost- und Westpreußen nach dem Zweiten Thorner Frieden (1466)

	Herzogtum Preußen
	Königliches Preußen
	Bistum Ermland
	Städtische Territorien
	zeitweilige Staatsgrenzen
	Grenzen der Distrikte
	Grenzen der Hauptämter

Source: Bruno Schumacher: *Geschichte Ost- und Westpreußens.*

16

Frank Mocha

POLAND AND GERMANY—
PAST AND FUTURE

The proper way, and a perfect transition, is to start this highly personal chapter with a gesture toward Germany. It concerns the Polish-German border on the Oder-Neisse (Odra-Nysa) rivers. While it was a painful border for the Germans to accept, it was no more painful than for the Poles to accept the Bug River as the border in the East, both dictated by the Yalta and Potsdam agreements before and just after the end of World War II.

This writer, a volunteer in the war from Day One in Poland (literally) to V-E Day, was apprehensive about the Polish borders when reaching England from still-occupied Europe just before D-Day. A visit with his debriefing officer to the Headquarters of the Polish Government-in-Exile in London, revealed a map in Major Galinat's office showing Poland's border in the East intact except for some minor adjustments in favor of the Soviet Union in the Novogrodek area in the North and Dubno in the South. The Western border had the whole of Upper Silesia within it, up to the Nysa (Neisse) River, the Klodzko Nysa, not to be confused (as Churchill apparently was) with the Lusatian Nysa further West. The new border was much straighter, and this straightening was also in evidence in Pomerania in the North, resulting in a border that was fair and straight, with the Odra River marking it only in sections of its middle and upper course. East Prussia was marked for Poland in its entirety, up to the Niemen river.

I accepted the borders with full satisfaction and, worrying about my family in Poland and making up for time lost in the war, I did not give the borders another thought until after the war when the Oder-Neisse line became an issue, as was also the Eastern border, and news reached me about the huge population shifts from East to West, the confusion and disruptions caused by them I could see for myself still in 1959, my first visit to Poland (Upper Silesia). I interpreted the new borders as a piece of Stalin's Machiavellian scheme of not only robbing Poland of almost half of its territory (and helping himself to a piece of Germany), but rewarding Poland by driving a wedge between it and Germany that would tie Poland closer to the Soviet Union as the only "guarantor" of its Western border. The plan worked, and gradually the Western powers and even West Germany recognized the Oder-Neisse line (how much the recognition had to do with a desire to loosen the ties between Poland and the Soviet Union is a good question, as is also the Soviet Union's true attitude to the recognition). But the bitter memory remained in Germany, as I was to find out.

When I was teaching in the mid-sixties at the University of Pittsburgh, one of my colleagues was Dr. Gert Miller, a visiting German professor of social sciences. Dr. Miller, a veteran of the battle for Stalingrad and an inmate for a few years of POW camps in the Soviet Union, just like me in Germany, became for me a barometer of future Polish-German relations, as exemplified by our if-not friendship, then a relationship developing into one. We dined together almost every day in the Faculty Lounge on the 14th Floor of the Cathedral of Learning, as the main building of the university was called, taking a table for two, reserved for us by the charming black American hostess by the window, out of which we could see Forbes Field, the stadium of the Pittsburgh Pirates baseball club ("World Champions 1960" on, incidentally, Bill Mazeroski's famous home run) and, while having our dinner watch a game whenever the Pirates played at home. When there was no game, which means on most days, we talked, about the university and its Germanic tradition (seen in the way the staff addressed the professors by "Doctor" without the name) in what was then a Slavic ethnic city, with the Poles and Slovaks predominating; about our respective experiences as POWs and, inevitably, about Poland and Germany.

We both possessed considerable knowledge about each other's countries (and the late war in which we were on opposite sides, a fact which did not make much difference), gained in my case at home in Upper Silesia, which had been under Germanic (Austrian and Prussian) domination for several centuries, and in school where German was a required foreign language; in his case probably also in school and possibly during the war, a possibility I did not pry into. I was amazed to discover I could learn from him about Poland, about German traditions and influences in Cracow (due to colonization) before Queen Bona arrived from Italy with her retinue, and about Poland's considerable minority problems, including the German. In our talks we inevitably reached the Oder-Neisse line, a topic which he felt very strongly about.

While Gert Miller understood the strong political reasons for the Oder-Neisse border line between Poland and Germany (the historical were not as strong) and could see the implications of it as a stumbling block in relations between the two countries, he strongly objected to the sliver of land awarded to Poland on the other, German side of the Oder river close to its mouth right up to the Baltic coast. This was news to me, but I recalled reports about a delay in fixing the border, and surmised that this must have been it. Gert drew a map for me, and I could see his point. Unlike the Russians who can chop up the landscape while marking a border with only one consideration on their mind: acquisition of territory (look at the Russian-Finnish border), the orderly Germans are guided by many justifying factors: history, demography and geography among them, the latter present in a line of their national anthem:

"Von der Maas bis an die Memel"
("From the Moselle to the Niemen")

which gave me an idea to follow the German example, with the Niemen River now justifiably serving as a Polish border river of the most perfect Poland in a thousand years.

This new perfect Poland, stretching like the old imperial Germany from river to river (except that it is two rivers in Poland's case, from the Oder and Neisse to the Bug and Niemen) and from the Baltic Sea to the Carpathian and Sudeten Mountains, with three "gates" to fill three gaps in the natural borders: the Lithuanian-Belorussian Gate (Brama Litewsko-Białoruska) between the Niemen and the Bug; the Ruthenian Gate (Brama Ruska) between the Bug and the Carpathians; and the Moravian Gate (Brama Morawska) between the Carpathians and the Sudeten. This new perfect Poland's "arrival" depended on the willingness of its two big neighbors to honor its claim: Germany and Russia.

To make the Germans sympathetic to the Polish claim based on history and geography in formerly-their East Prussia, and to compensate them for giving up their own ideas for the area, the sliver of land on the German side of the Oder river should be restored by Poland to Germany as a GESTURE OF GOOD WILL, but also as a signal to Russia to do likewise for Poland with the Kaliningrad enclave (see map on page 338).

At the University of Pittsburgh there was another German professor interested in Poland, who sought my help in preparing a German bibliography of Joseph Conrad. I was glad to oblige, checking and editing the Polish entries and again learning something I didn't know, namely what a great writer Conrad was to command a huge bibliography in a country other than England or America and in a language other than the one Conrad wrote in, English.

Speaking of language and literature, no German has done more for Poland in those fields than the venerable KARL DEDECIUS, for many years Director of Deutsches Polen Institut, founded by him after the war with the support of a German countess, Marion Denhoff, its president (and, with Helmut Schmidt, publisher of *Die Zeit*) who, even after she had lost a huge estate near Königsberg, supported projects serving Poland and Germany. Having survived the war, it was inevitable that the two Polonophiles would meet eventually. And they did, but it was a long and perilous road for Dedecius. A member of the pre-war German minority in Łódź, he had just graduated from a prestigious Polish Gymnasium when war broke out in 1939. Drafted into the Wehrmacht, he participated, like Gert Miller, in the Stalingrad campaign, paying for it with seven years in a Soviet P.O.W. camp, which means that he did not arrive in Germany until the early 1950s, starting in Weimar in East Germany, then on to Frankfurt, and finally Darmstadt, where the Institute is located in a charming little palace (reminding one of the old seat of the Polish Institute in New York), which had survived the pounding of Patton's III Army to become an institution. Reading about Dedecius on the front page of *Przegląd Polski* of February 20, 1998, one is struck by the man's industry and knowledge. On a visit to the Institute in the summer of 1988, this writer was impressed by the shelves of books translated from Polish, one of which Dedecius displayed with a special pride: a leather-bound volume of *Letters, Speeches, Orders* ("Pisma, mowy, rozkazy") by Piłsudski. To my question whether he had met Gert Miller in the Wehrmacht, the answer was "no."

Next to being recognized as the greatest and most productive translator of Polish literature into German, his translations of Wisława Szymborska paved the way to the Nobel Prize for her. Since the Swedish Nobel jury reads above all in English and German, and Dedecius was the first to translate Szymborska on a large scale, her works were known and available to the jury in Stockholm. On their basis it was possible to form an opinion about Wisława's poetry early. Later there were also English and even Swedish translations. It had been the same with Reymont, who was read in German, and Sienkiewicz had all his works translated into German (his "Collected Works" incidentally, had been published 24 times in Germany).

Poland is fortunate to have friends like Dedecius, who brings her alive for the German people and whose translations are read by the Nobel jury with happy results. It wasn't always like that, a sign that times have changed. Early in this century a German-reading Nobel jury prevented a deserving Polish writer, Stefan Żeromski, from winning the Nobel Prize because some of his works were allegedly considered anti-German (*Wiatr od morza—Wind from the Sea*)?

Poland is indeed lucky to have a friend like Karl Dedecius, even if one of his assistants, Andreas Lavaty, did not deliver a promised map of the division of Prussia in the Peace of Toruń (Thorn) in 1466, but neither did Prof. Fritz Stern of Columbia University; but he at least sent an explanatory letter. Luckily, this writer found good maps, including the one in question, in Halecki's *History*. Only then did a letter arrive from Dr. Lavaty in Darmstadt notifying me that he was still looking, this time in Toruń itself. I am sending him a copy of Halecki's map.

You can't have everything (unless you try very hard, as I do), otherwise there would be paradise on earth, and that's too much to ask. All I want is a notch lower and less inclusive, PERFECTION FOR POLAND, too much to ask?

Seeking perfection, we should perhaps take another look at some aspects of Polish-German history, especially the much abused "*Drang nach Osten*" (Push to the East) which, according to some historians, was started by Pepin the Short (c.714-768), first Carolingian King of the Franks (751-768), son of Charles Martel (Old French = Charles the Hammer) (688?-741), who halted the Moslem invasion of Europe by his victory over the Moors of Spain in the Battle of Tours or Poitiers (732)—one of the decisive battles in history—and, like a king, divided the Frankish lands between his sons Carloman and Pepin the Short, father of Charlemagne (Charles the Great or Charles I [Old French = Charles the Great], 742-814, Emperor of the West 800-814). It was under this legendary Emperor, the first in the West since Rome, idealized in *Chanson de Roland*, that what we can call a "Christianizing mission in the East" begins. The forced conversions and wholesale massacres of the still-pagan Saxons and as far east as Pomerania left no doubt of things to come. But it had nothing to do with Germany and Poland, which didn't exist yet except as Germanic and Slavic tribes out of which the respective countries were to emerge.

For Germany, the process began in 843 with the Treaty of Verdun, a crucial moment in European history (EUROPEAN UNITY DESTROYED FOR THE NEXT ELEVEN CENTURIES), partitioning Charlemagne's Empire among his three sons, with Louis the German receiving the eastern part (later Germany); and culminating with HENRY I or Henry the Fowler ("Ptasznik" in Polish) 876?-936, precursor of the emperors and German king, 919-36, the first of the Saxon line of kings and emperors, and recognized in his own lifetime as the founder of a new realm—GERMANY.

Henry's army, rebuilt following an invasion by the Magyars, not only defeated them after a truce, but expanded his frontier at the expense of the Danes, and took from the pagan Slavic Wends Brandenburg, which, along with Saxony, would be, for a thousand years, the western neighbor of Poland, soon to embrace Christianity, but via Bohemia.

Henry was allowed by the Saxon nobles to designate his son Otto as his successor. There was a new development: OTTO I or OTTO THE GREAT, 912-73, German king 936-73, is regarded as the founder of the HOLY ROMAN EMPIRE, which he created by uniting Germany and Italy, and being crowned by Pope John XII in 962. This development had considerable bearing on Poland, whose first documented ruler, Mieszko, while embracing Christianity (966) and thus removing the danger of forced conversion, found himself in the position of a vassal of the Empire, a relationship which his son, Bolesław, succeeded in restoring to the level of equality in the famous meeting with Otto III in the year 1000, with Poland approaching perfection, even surpassing it with the acquisition of Slavic kin Lusatia along the river Spree beyond the Neisse (Nysa), a remnant of an ancient culture with an ancient capital Budziszyn (Bautzen). But there was one sore spot: hostile pagan Prussia, place of martyrdom of St. Adalbert (Wojciech, a Bohemian, member of the christianizing mission, whose relics were one reason for Otto's visit, pointing to another community of interests).

The perfection, or the drive for it, was gone, first with Otto's (1002) and then Bolesław's death (1025), with Poland entering the new millennium under cloudy skies. Every imaginable calamity descended on her, starting with a long-drawn war with Otto's successor, Henry II, a foe of his predecessor's designs, and continuing with a total disintegration under Bolesław's inept successor, Mieszko II (the "Old"). There was a massive pagan revolt, accompanied by some ancient clans, enemies of the ruling Piasts, abandoning Mieszko. In the resulting civil war, Mieszko's heir, Kazimierz (Casimir), sought refuge with his German mother in Germany, where he remained until he reached manhood, when the Emperor, in a fine gesture too easily forgotten by Polish Germanophobes, gave him 500 knights and sent him back to restore Poland, which he did with much spilled blood (the "Vistula turned red" with it in Mazovia) and help from the Kievan rulers. History rewarded him with a title, "Restorer" ("Odnowiciel"), and the drive for perfection returned with his successor, fittingly another Bolesław (the "Bold"), a warrior like his namesake but also the cause of the most unfortunate Polish tragedy.

Bolesław's prolonged absences in Kiev, probably encouraged by the Pope on account of Eastern Orthodoxy, were the cause of much disorder in Poland, fueled by criticism by Bishop Stanisław from the Cathedral's pulpit in Cracow, by then the capital of Poland. An example of this disorder is the story in Mickiewicz's ballad "Lilies" about an unfaithful wife's murder of a husband returning after a long absence. In real life, the roles were reversed, and it was the king who murdered the culprit bishop (1076), hacking his body into pieces and throwing it into the Vistula where, as the legend has it, it miraculously grew together, starting a cult resulting in sainthood. Suddenly Poland had its own "Murder in the Cathedral" but what really happened was that church-state relations got out of hand, with both the Emperor and the Pope involved. The latter had no choice but to excommunicate the king who, not wanting a civil war, went into exile in Hungary, leaving his son behind.

But Poland's drive for perfection did not end with the murder. Another Bolesław emerged (the "Crooked-mouthed" *Krzywousty*), the king's nephew (the son had been removed), a warrior as astute as his two namesakes. He fought a long war with Germany by successfully using guerrilla tactics, but arrived in time to lift the siege of Głogów (Glogau), to save children taken hostage, and fill the field of battle with so many dead that it was afterward called "Dog Field" on account of the packs of foraging hungry dogs.

It was as if there was a curse on the Bolesławs, destroying their life work. Like the Treaty of Verdun (843) destroyed European unity for 11 centuries by partitioning Charlemagne's Empire among his three sons, Bolesław's dying will (1138) unwittingly destroyed Poland's unity for two centuries by dividing the country among his five sons. Like the Empire, which eventually split into 300 separate units and became increasingly ineffective in the process (which was lucky for the rest of Europe), Poland too was dividing into smaller and smaller principalities of little strength, which was needed in both cases, to ward off the biggest calamity of them all, the MONGOL INVASION.

By 1240 the Mongols set out on Genghis Khan's dream, the conquest of the world. Under Batu Khan they blazed a bloody trail across Asia, subjugated both Russias (Kievan and Moscow) and entered southern Poland the following year, looting and burning. Western Europe was shocked but unable to help, with the Empire and the Papacy locked in a struggle, and England, gravely concerned, too far away. The Mongols crushed the knights of Little Poland and reached Silesia, where a hastily gathered army of Poles and Germans faced them under the command of Henry the Pious (Pobożny), the son of the would-be king Henry the Bearded (Brodaty), the Duke of Breslau who was, incidentally, the grandson, son, and husband of German princesses, showing how well Germans and Poles lived side-by-side in Silesia. The battle at Lignica was lost, but the Mongols retreated, Poland escaped the Tatar yoke, and Europe was saved. Among the participants in the battle was a small detachment of Teutonic Knights, a new presence in Poland.

The saga of the Teutonic Knights, members of one of the great orders of chivalry, originally founded in the Holy Land to fight the infidels, is a historical marvel, and a key, together with its successors, to the history of Poland and Germany from 1226—their arrival in Poland, to 1945—the ultimate end of the German *Drang nach Osten.*

The man who invited them to Poland was Konrad, Duke of Masovia who, with Henry the Bearded of Breslau, was then one of two leading contenders for the Polish crown. He needed help in his continuous war with the pagan Prussians on the northern frontiers of his Duchy, and the Teutonic Knights seemed ideal for the job. They were available, their project to establish the Order for a similar purpose on the borders of Hungary having just fallen through with their real intentions having been discovered there, but not perceived by the less discerning Konrad; hence he is remembered as having committed the most disastrous mistake in Polish history.

The Teutonic Knights' arrival in Poland coincided with other developments, all detrimental except one: the permanent weakening, as a result of external and internal troubles, of the power of the Empire (weaker, but free to make political designs, of which the Teutonic Order was an instrument). Then there was the German colonization which, although of a purely pacific order, represented a danger scarcely less grave to Poland than the earlier military expeditions of the Emperors. These expeditions, resulting in the acquisition of Lusatia and deep incursions into Western Pomerania and Lower Silesia, brought the frontiers of the Empire close to the cradle of Poland and Polishness, Great Poland, where the expansion stopped, and a frontier was developing which lasted until the Partitions of Poland. But the Empire found a way to jump over the obstacle, with the help of the Teutonic Order, later called NEW GERMANY.

All these developments, *and* the Mongol invasion, were taking place when Poland was becoming a veritable mosaic of duchies whose number was increasing unceasingly. If that subdivided Poland did not at that time disappear from the map of Europe is due to several circumstances: first, this divided Poland of the thirteenth century still remained the common patrimony of only one family (PIAST) whose members, even while fighting each other, were still conscious of their ties. In spite of their individual titles, they all (including the Silesian princes, who were the most numerous) remained dukes of "Poland." (This writer's grandfather, a famous locksmith and descendant of a line of gunsmiths stemming most probably from Lusatian nobility, took care of the locks of Prince Ratibor's [Racibórz] special room containing Piast family insignia.) Poland was also an ecclesiastical province. Being at different periods the subject of the Holy See, she kept for that reason a unity in the whole extent of her territory that was recognized by the highest authority of the Christian world. In Rome, even the provinces lost by the Piasts were always regarded as forming part of the Poland which belonged, in all its entirety, to the patrimony of the Church, and which paid Peter's pence.

What happened next in Prussia is shrouded in controversy. According to Halecki (p. 35),

The conquest of Prussia took the Teutonic Knights more than fifty years. They had to break the resistance of each tribe one after the other, and subsequently organize a completely new life. A vast German colony was created [stretching] from the mouth of the Vistula to that of the Niemen, where a German population, crowding in from all parts of Empire, superimposed themselves upon the natives, and even replaced the latter, who were either enslaved or exterminated. They finished by usurping the very name of the former Prussians.

The controversy surrounds the degree of the extermination, which some historians claim was total. Yet, according to linguists, there were still speakers of the Prussian language in the 1500s. This writer feels that it was the valor of the Prussians which none of the three Bolesławs was willing to test and Konrad was unable to overcome that was responsible for the assumption that to conquer Prussia you had to exterminate the Prussians.

Another controversy surrounds the intentions of the two contracting parties. While Konrad fully intended to keep sovereignty over the territory of Chełmno, offered to the Order for its base of operations, and to maintain ducal authority over any of its conquests in Prussia, the Grand Master Hermann von Salza's conception was totally different: Chełmno and the whole of Prussia were destined to form a new state of ecclesiastical character, governed by the Teutonic Order, a state completely independent of Poland and recognizing only the authority of the Holy See and that of the Empire. The Emperor (Frederick II) hastened to confer upon the Order an imperial charter, in which this point of view found its first confirmation.

The rest is history, properly recorded and reflected in international treaties and developments among which three stand out as far as the "New Germany" and Poland are concerned:

1) The spectacular rise of the Teutonic Order to power status. After conquering Prussia, the Order directed its attention to its immediate neighbors: Danzig Pomerania in the West, Lithuania in the East, and Poland in the South.
   The independent Danzig Pomerania, an extremely important province in divided Poland, was geographically separating the Order from the Empire. This was clearly understood by the Duke of Pomerania, who from the beginning helped the Prussians in order to avoid being surrounded on two sides by Germanic conquests, which was exactly what happened. When next Brandenburg threatened him, the Poles

appealed to the Teutonic Knights, who did, in fact, check the advance of Brandenburg, but only to seize the province themselves, beginning with Danzig where, in 1308, they massacred the royal garrison and a great part of the population.

2) It was the same with Lithuania. It supported its Prussian kin, for the same reason as Danzig Pomerania, not to be surrounded on two sides by Germanic conquests, in this case by the Teutonic Knights and the Sword Bearers, another German Order, who had founded a somewhat similar colony at the mouth of the Dvina in Livonia, and with whom the Teutonic Knights had federated in 1237. When next the Teutonic Knights conquered Samogitia, a Lithuanian province situated in the center of the Baltic populations, the federation was complete, and there was a formidable "New Germany," loosely connected to the Empire via Brandenburg and Danzig Pomerania, and stretching from Danzig to Riga, controlling three great rivers (Vistula, Niemen, Dvina), and threatening Poland, Lithuania, and the Old Russian Republics of Pskov and Novgorod (the latter threat depicted in the classic Sergei Eisenstein movie *Alexandr Nevski*). All this was happening when Lithuania was on its way to becoming the largest country in Europe under its legendary founder, Mendog, who had accepted Catholicism (and a royal crown from Pope Innocent IV in 1253) to avoid the "religious" aggression of the Teutonic Knights in order to put better resistance to the Tatars and, by attaching the Old Rus lands to Lithuania, put a limit to the Mongol conquests. This work was followed by the Grand Duke Gedymin and his successors, whose policies were turning the still pagan Lithuania from a former raider of Poland into an ally facing a common threat.

3) It was fortunate for Poland that with the end of the perilous XIIIth Century, a man emerged in the long line of would-be restorers of Poland, who did just that. Władysław Łokietek (the untranslatable nickname is best rendered as "Short"); of Kujavia (Kujawy) devoted his entire life to what Halecki calls in a separate chapter (5) of his *History* "The Reconstruction of the Kingdom" leaving it to his only son, Casimir, who was able to restore Poland to the rank of a European power in every sense, and earn for himself the title of "Great"—KAZIMIERZ WIELKI (1333-1370).

It was a long road for father and son. Despite two additional factors not mentioned before in connection with the unifying process, namely the canonization in 1253 of Stanisław, Bishop of Cracow, stressing the religious aspect of the country but also the traditional role of Cracow, and also, not unrelated to it, the steadily growing national consciousness, both as a reaction against Germanism, protested by the clergy becoming increasingly recruited from among the Poles, and by the knighthood showing its indignation against princes surrounding themselves with foreigners, there were other factors working against it. In the end it was the leading Polish families, the future Polish nobility, lining themselves in the name of the new patriotism behind the strongest and the best candidates, which proved decisive when spurred by the appearance of a powerful foreign candidate on the stage. Of the domestic candidates two remained, the first of whom, Przemysł II (Przemysław), Duke of Great Poland and inheritor of Little Poland, was crowned King of Poland in 1295 in the Cathedral of Gniezno, despite and probably because of, the occupation of Cracow by Venceslav (Wacław) King of Bohemia.

The other domestic candidate was the indomitable Władysław the Short. When the following year (1296) Przemysław was assassinated in a plot hatched between the margraves of Brandenburg and some discontented lords of the young king, it fell to Władysław to carry on the unification process, which became a matter of urgency when Venceslav occupied Great Poland in 1300 and, a foreigner, had himself crowned with the crown of the Piasts King of Poland, which thus became a mere appendage of Bohemia, together with which it would have been easily incorporated into the German Empire.

Władysław, the national candidate, exile as he was, did not waste time. He succeeded in gaining, on one hand, the moral support of the Pope, Boniface VIII; on the other, the help of the Hungarians. Aided by favorable circumstances in Bohemia (death of Venceslav in 1305 and assassination of his successor, Venceslav III, the following year, ending the Premyslides dynasty and beginning an intense rivalry between candidates for the Bohemian throne), Władysław reappeared in Little Poland in 1305 and in 1314 became the master also of Great Poland, his success obtained despite the opposition of the German burghers, who went as far as to revolt against him, but to no avail. Finally, taking advantage of the dynastic quarrels in the Empire and of the good will he still found at the Curia, in Avignon as formerly in Rome, he had himself crowned King of Poland in 1320 in Cracow itself.

This time the restoration of the kingdom of the Piasts was "definite" in Halecki's words, even if it only included at first the provinces of Great Poland and Little Poland. But they were the primary provinces, the first the cradle of Poland and its fortress, with its ancient capital, Gniezno, and its Cathedral; the second,

Poland's early expansion, with the new capital Cracow and its Wawel (Vavel) Cathedral as the new center of Polishness. True, in the restoration process Poland had lost one province of the greatest value, Pomerania, in 1309, its only access to the sea, but the king never reconciled himself to the loss, waiting only for his coronation to take steps to regain it without even waiting for the reunion of all the other duchies of the Piasts. Accordingly, in 1320, a tribunal of the Holy See recognized the rights of Poland to Pomerania. But action on the verdict was delayed by problems with Bohemia, whose new King, John of Luxemburg, an enemy of Władysław and a friend of the Teutonic Order, not only put forward claims to the crown of Poland but succeeded in exacting homage from nearly all the Silesian princes and even from one of the dukes of Masovia who, like himself, had also ranged themselves on the side of the Teutonic Order. As a result, it was the Order which entered into open war against the king, launching two invasions, in 1331 an 1332, of which the first ended in a Polish victory, albeit incomplete, at Płowce, but both brought devastation to the northwest of the kingdom and, what was even more serious, left the king's patrimony, Kujavia, and the territory of Dobrzyń, in the hands of the enemy. In a prudent move, Władysław had his son, Kazimierz, taken out of the battle, a move derided by the Teutonic Knights, who had no way of knowing that not risking the life of the wise young man was another move by the hard-pressed king in his plans to defeat the Order.

The marriage of his daughter, Elizabeth, to Charles Robert of Anjou in 1320 had cemented his alliance with Hungary, while starting far-reaching dynastic ties, and his alliance with Gedymin of Lithuania was also aimed against the Order.

When Kazimierz succeeded his worn-out father in 1333, the year after the second Teutonic invasion, he, as the saying goes,

> found Poland wooden, and left it in stone
> (*"zastłl Polskę drewnianą, a zostawił murowaną"*)

and that describes his long rule accurately. The highlights of his extraordinary reign are many, all beneficial to the mutilated and menaced country. But before he set to work rebuilding it physically and codifying its laws, he had to remove the danger of another war with which the Teutonic Knights were threatening him by saying that this time they would chase him all the way to Cracow. Seeing that a new war offered no chance of success if fought simultaneously against both the Teutonic Order and Bohemia, Casimir found a solution. A passage in Halecki shows his ability:

> Casimir decided to negotiate a compromise. The terms were fixed in 1335 at the Congress of Visegrad in Hungary, where he went to meet his father's implacable enemy, John of Luxemburg, at the court of his brother-in-law, Charles Robert. Taking into account the actual situation created before his accession, young Casimir recognized the suzerainty of the King of Bohemia over the Silesia Piasts who had rendered him homage. It was at this price that John at last renounced his pretensions to the throne of Poland. (p. 53)

As a Silesian, this writer always held it against Casimir that he handed Silesia over to Bohemia (which was the beginning of a separation that lasted six centuries), but changed his mind after more study of the circumstances surrounding the compromise. For one, Silesia was not yet part of Casimir's kingdom, and isolating the Teutonic Order from Bohemia was more than worth the price. Between them, they were quite capable of destroying Casimir's kingdom and dividing it among themselves before it had a chance to grow bigger and stronger. Besides, Silesia had not been abandoned without reservations, and Casimir seized every chance to formulate claims that could prevent the rupture of traditional ties between the Kingdom of Poland and Silesia, where he supported the last independent Piasts. It is quite possible that he would have found a way to terminate the compromise after the death of John of Luxemburg, had he himself not died prematurely. In the meantime, if the great king had not been able to regain all the territories that the country had lost on its western side, he immediately found compensation on the eastern side, where he opened almost unlimited vistas for Poland, beginning with the region of Halicz and its increasingly flourishing town of Lwów (remnants of an old Ruthenian kingdom of Daniel, whose descendants had perished), not germane to this chapter except to say that for their ultimate loss six centuries later Poland was "compensated" with Silesia!

The isolation of the Teutonic Order and the removal of the threat of war enabled Casimir to proceed with his program for Poland. In 1339 he organized a new canonical process in Warsaw against the Order. But unlike the earlier one under his father, it was no longer the Polish bishops who were nominated as judges, but two impartial eminent French prelates as representatives of the Holy See, and it was no longer twenty persons but a hundred and twenty-six representatives of all classes of the population serving as witnesses to answer a long interrogation investigating the whole relations between Poland and the Teutonic Knights.

The judgment which accorded to Poland all the disputed territories, including Danzig Pomerania, as well as reparations for the losses she had suffered, was unconditionally rejected by the Order, but all the same the judgment retained its moral force, and thanks to this initiative the whole Polish nation emerged for the first time as conscious of its unity and rights. As for the Order, it was possible to reclaim from it in the Treaty of Kalisz in 1343 Kujavia and Dobrzyń for the price of temporary renunciation of Pomerania and Chełmno. It was characteristic of Casimir to envelop his treaties with the "temporary" reservation, thus making clear his intentions.

At the same time, despite frequent conflicts with Lithuania concerning the Polish acquisitions in the East, Casimir continued his father's policy of closer intercourse with Gedymin's successors, for the sake of common antagonism against the Teutonic Order, but also thrusting back the Tatars from the Ruthenian territories. Therefore he encouraged every project of at last winning Lithuania over to the Christian faith, not by the sword of German Knights, but by pacific means with active participation of Polish missionaries and clergy. In this, he was assisted by Louis of Hungary, his nephew, who had succeeded his father, Charles Robert, in 1342. Also, Charles Luxembourg, King of Bohemia since his father John's death, and at the same time Emperor, took a lively interest in the plan of converting pagan Lithuania, and associated himself with Casimir's efforts. It was thus that the extension of the frontiers, and of Polish influence in eastern Europe, became one of great importance for the Christian world.

Whether it was due to Poland's growing importance and strength or the prospect of Lithuania embracing Christianity from other sources than the German Knights, they turned their attention from Poland to Lithuania, bent on conquering it before Casimir's efforts became real, a possibility attested to by his diplomatic talent, enabling him to place his relations with both Bohemia and the Empire on a peaceful footing, maintaining an increasingly close alliance with Hungary, making Poland participate in the policy of the whole of central Europe, and fixing the western frontiers of Poland which were to undergo no modification until the epoch of the Partitions, except from the Teutonic Order.

But nothing is better proof of the change that had been effected in Poland's international position during the reign of Casimir the Great than the political congress which assembled in Cracow towards the end of his reign in September 1364. Here is what Halecki says about it:

> This congress had been convoked to facilitate the proposal of the King of Cyprus, Pierre de Lusignan in favour of a new Crusade. In the capital of Poland he found, as guests of the king, renowned for his campaigns against the infidels, the Emperor Charles IV, who had just married a granddaughter of Casimir, the Kings of Hungary and Denmark, as well as many other princes, naturally including those of the House of Piast. The receptions were sumptuous and, in addition to the discussions devoted to the eastern question, which was considered no longer possible to treat without the co-operation of Poland, Casimir, in the character of arbitrator, decided the differences between Louis of Anjou and Charles of Luxembourg. What a difference when we remember the Congress of Visegrad at the outset of his reign! But what a difference also between the Poland which his father had left to him, and that which he had succeeded in creating during thirty years! Among the Piasts who surrounded the head of the dynasty, even the Duke of that Masovia which had nearly become a Czech fief, and which, thanks to Casimir's patience, had again become an integral part of the kingdom of Poland, was not absent.

The Congress of 1364 coincided with the foundation of the University of Cracow. The creation of this first Polish university—following that of Prague, the second to be opened in the whole of Central Europe—bears witness both to the high level of culture which Poland had reached, and to Casimir's desire to raise it higher still.

The year 1364 ranks with 966, 1000 and 1791 in Polish history and culture, and Casimir the Great has no equal except, perhaps, John Paul II (Copernicus and Marie Curie is something else), a comparison strengthened by the fact that both men came out of times of deep troubles for Poland, and both had outstanding predecessors and teachers, King Łokietek and Cardinal Wyszyński, respectively, a comparison which makes us also want to compare the XIVth and XXth centuries. But while Casimir had his work cut out for him with the road of reconstructing Poland mapped out for him by his father, the work of renewal was uncertain for Karol Wojtyła, who could only support and inspire it as Pope from outside, with Poland still largely a cultural desert with no accomplishments to be proud of except Solidarity, and reduced to celebrating old accomplishments, of which 1364 was the first (and 1000 the last, inspired by the Pope as if to remind the Poles of 2000, the proper year to celebrate it and the new millennium).

Just as the old millennium began in the spirit of Polish-German community, so could the new millennium, but here the comparisons break down. For one thing, there is no new Otto III (the old one was just a short-lived comet), and there is also no new Bolesław Chrobry (Krzaklewski?). The centuries-analogy also breaks down, but not entirely. While Casimir still had the inherited unsolved problem of the Teutonic Order, present Poland has two, DEMOGRAPHY and KALININGRAD, the latter harking back to Casimir.

But Casimir had another problem, though not of the same magnitude, succession, which brings the comparisons back. Here is what Halecki has to say about Casimir's problem:

> Unfortunately, providence withheld from him that collaborator whom he most ardently desired to continue his work. Although he married three times, Casimir had no son. He was haunted for a long time before his death by his anxiety to find a successor. No one among the Piasts of the collateral lines seemed to him worthy of the crown. He therefore destined it for his nephew, Louis of Hungary, and this promise of the succession, often formally stated, was, at the same time, the price of the Hungarian alliance. But Casimir was counting very reasonably upon the eventuality of Louis also leaving no son. He therefore considered in advance what would happen after the Polish-Hungarian union, which he foresaw would be temporary. He had a favorite grandson who bore his name, born of the marriage of one of his daughters to a prince of western Pomerania. This part of Pomerania round Stettin, subject to the Empire, still kept its Slav character under a local dynasty. By a slight, but important, modification of the frontier, Casimir established an immediate contact between this duchy and his kingdom, at the same time separating the New March, an annex of Brandenburg, from eastern Pomerania, occupied by the Teutonic Order. A glance at the map is enough to enable us to grasp what the elevation of a prince of western Pomerania to the throne of Poland would have brought about. Casimir the Great intended to pave the way for it by adopting Casimir of Stettin and by bequeathing to him in his will the Polish provinces adjacent to the two Pomeranias, as well as territories in the very centre of the kingdom.

Immediately after the premature death of the king in 1370, Louis of Hungary took care to frustrate these plans. Thus the ingenious project of Casimir the Great concerning his succession was not realized. He left, however a far more important legacy to Poland.

> The real successor of Casimir the Great, that last king of the national dynasty, was the whole Polish nation, which after the ordeal of so many dynastic crises had been prepared by his clear-sighted guidance to shape its future lot by itself. The last Piast likewise prepared the Polish nation to collaborate with other nations in the framework of a common state, even were it under a king of foreign origin. This explains how the end of the epoch of the Piasts was, at the same time, the starting point of the epoch of the Jagiellos.

It is easy to speculate on an alternate history if Casimir had lived longer. The possibilities are mind-boggling and should guide the present and future stewards of Poland.

From the point of view of the Poland-Germany topic, the Jagiellonian era, part of Poland's three centuries long period of greatness—started by Casimir the Great and lasting until 1648—was one of mishandling the Teutonic Order problem. Other problems had to be solved first, among them the most difficult one, of succession, complicating and even spoiling Poland's domestic and international situation in an otherwise favorable climate, especially with regards to the Holy Roman Empire.

Thanks largely to Casimir's diplomacy, the Teutonic Order was becoming increasingly isolated, and the Empire, after initially conferring on it an imperial charter (Frederick II, 1212-1250), descended into a state of impotent anarchy, after a last show of strength when Frederick I, one of the most energetic German medieval rulers, broke up the power of Henry the Lion of Saxony and Bavaria by partitioning his domains (1180) and destroying the last great German duchy. This affected Poland directly, removing Saxony as a potential aggressor for centuries. German campaigns of the XII and XIII century had instead concentrated on conquering the Slavic Wends (whom Poland, deep in its own anarchy, was in no position to protect), bringing about tremendous eastward expansion in what was then the last manifestation of the *Drang nach Osten* (not counting the Teutonic Knights), resulting in the emergence of the margraviate of Brandenburg (founded as North March, or Mark, by Henry I). But it was not an Emperor of the German Hohenstaufen dynasty who confirmed the margraves of Brandenburg as Electors of the Holy Roman Empire, a new Germanic entity on Poland's border, but Charles IV of the line of Luxemburgs of Bohemia, where the Empire shifted with beneficial results for Poland at first (to be followed by the Habsburgs, marking the return of the Empire to, if not German, then a Germanic dynasty, a development not favorable to Poland from the beginning). It was amidst such past and future developments that the transition from the Piasts to the Jagiellonians was taking place.

The process of solving the succession did much to undermine Casimir's great work. It was as if the curse that seemed to follow the three Boleslavs' reign followed his, too. The agreements concluded before his death only recognized the right of succession as accruing to the eventual sons of Louis. Having no sons, he spent the rest of his life with one purpose only, how to secure to his daughters the succession to his kingdoms. As a result, under a king who in Hungary was Louis the Great, in Poland the "Hungarian Ludwik" brought about a marked regression as he plotted to make the Polish nobility accept a change of the succession agreement. Assisted by his mother, who was Casimir's sister, as well as by the faithful partisans he possessed in Little Poland, Louis at last triumphed over opposition, but at what price? The new agreement reached at Koszyce in 1374 gave him the right to name one of his daughters to the Polish throne in return for a charter guaranteeing for the first time, and even extending, all the rights and privileges of the Polish nobility. Koszyce marks the beginning of "Polish Nobles' Republic."

But it was these "bribed" nobles, especially those representing powerful Polish families, who succeeded in making the best out of a bad situation, while displaying statesmanship of the highest order. When Louis' choice, his eldest daughter Catherine, betrothed to a son of Charles V of France, died before her father, he then destined Poland for his second daughter, Maria, betrothed to Sigismund of Luxemburg, son of Emperor Charles IV. Immediately after Louis's death in 1382, Maria was raised to the throne of Hungary, but as the Polish nobles were no longer interested in maintaining a personal union between the two countries, and had no liking for Sigismund, then Margrave of Brandenburg, the Queen mother (Elizabeth of Bosnia) proposed to them her youngest daughter, Jadwiga.

Poland's great centuries are inaugurated by the remarkable history of a princess of fleur-de-lis, who was raised to the throne of the Piasts when scarcely eleven years of age, and died fifteen years later in the odour of sanctity. This life, so short, but entirely devoted to a great cause, marks, like the life of Joan of Arc in the history of France and the west, the most decisive turning-point in the destiny of Poland and eastern Europe.

This ode to Jadwiga by the clearly worshipful Halecki must be read in the context of the Polish nobles' master-plan, which while readily accepting Jadwiga, rejected not only her fiancé, William of Habsburg, for obvious reasons, but also an authentic Piast, Ziemowit of Masovia for Jadwiga's husband, in favor of a candidate who represented a program for the future in the traditions of Casimir the Great. This candidate was Jagiełło, Grand Duke of Lithuania, oldest son and successor of the late Olgierd and nephew of Kiejstut, the successors of Gedymin. That such a marriage did not make out of the resulting union of Poland and Lithuania a lasting European power stretching from the Oder to the Volga, and from the Baltic to not just the Black Sea but to the gates of Byzantium as saviors of the weakening Eastern Roman Empire (all objectives within reach), was due to many factors, not the least of them the unsettled problem of the Teutonic Order.

To understand the background of this amazing marriage fully, the personal sacrifices it demanded from both spouses and the problems it created, we must go beyond Halecki's *History* into his other writings, and into the rich literature, both historical and belletristic about Jadwiga, probably the most written about Polish historical figure. Among these works one is particularly informative, Stefan M. Kuczyński's well-researched *Jadwiga i Jagiełło*, sub-titled *Litwin i Andegawenka* (The Lithuanian and the Princess Anjou), published in 1974 as a result of personal intervention with the publishing house "Silesia" by this writer while on a research trip in Poland, after reading an excerpt of the historical novel in a Polish periodical, as pointed out elsewhere in the present book. The most germane to this chapter is Kuczyński's view of the Teutonic Order's reaction to the impending Christianization of Lithuania.

One of the purposes of the royal marriage, and Jadwiga's agreement to enter into it, was the conversion of the still mostly pagan Lithuania, the last stronghold of paganism in Europe. This was enough to cause the Order deep concern, but there was more, beginning with the death in 1382 of King Louis, who was considered, contrary to the best interests of Poland and Casimir's unwritten testament, a friend of the Teutonic Order, by Jagiełło, among others. It was the latter who was causing the Order even deeper concern when his uncle Kiejstut died under suspicious circumstances in that same year (Olgierd, Jagiełło's father, had died five years earlier), leaving him in control of all Lithuania and its huge possessions, but to the detriment of his cousin, Vitold, Kiejstut's son, who took refuge with the Teutonic Knights. When, still in that same year 1382, the Golden Horde under Tochtamysh took revenge for an earlier defeat (1380, at the Kulikovo Field, Moscow's first victory over the Tatars), by burning Moscow, razing it to the ground, killing most of its inhabitants, and breaking the rising power of Grand Duke Dimitri, Jagiełło's rival in the East, the latter's power seemed unlimited, but it was still not equal to the concentrated power of both Orders, and Jagiełło needed an ally.

These were the factors that made the Polish nobles decide on Jagiełło as Jadwiga's spouse despite her expected rebellion because of her devotion to Wilhelm. Jagiełło accepted readily the Polish proposals, his acceptance made easier by yet another death in that fateful year 1382, the poisoning of his beloved fiancee, Pojata (engineered by and intended for Jagiełło by the Teutonic Order, according to Kuczynski). The Order sought to frustrate and scuttle the plans with all the means at its disposal.

Once the decisions were made, events moved in an orderly fashion. Young Jadwiga arrived with her retinue in Cracow in 1384 and was crowned "king" of Poland. In 1385 Jagiełło's ambassadors appeared in Cracow and Buda to ask for her hand, concluding the marriage agreement on August 14 of that same year in the important Treaty of Krewo ("most important...in Polish history," according to Halecki). On February 18, 1386, when Jadwiga had reached the age of twelve [a date important also to this writer for more than one reason], Jagiełło came to Poland with several of his brothers (and his cousin Vitold, with whom he had been reconciled), was baptized (Władysław) and, immediately after, he married Jadwiga; a fortnight later his coronation was celebrated with Jadwiga a co-ruler whose influence increased with her years. One of her first acts was to restore to Poland the region of Lwów and Halicz which had been detached by her father. Other signs of the new state's influence was the homage to the Polish crown by the Voivod of Moldavia, and the request by the great republic of Novgorod for one of king Jagiełło's brothers to be its 'governor'. In February of 1387 Catholicism was officially introduced to Lithuania, after a dangerous invasion by the Teutonic Order, to coincide with the time when Jagiełło and the princes were being baptized in Cracow. The invasion was repulsed, but it was a warning.

The fact that the Order was able to organize a coalition against Lithuania speaks about its determination. It continued its subversive work, taking advantage of every chink in Jagiełło's thickening armor. One such chink was his own sister who, as the wife of the Duke of Mazovia, was being showered with presents by her neighbors, the Teutonic Knights, becoming their unwitting spy on her brother, until Jadwiga, during a visit, caught on to what was going on and informed the king. Another chink, a serious one, was Jagiełło's fatal mistake of downgrading his cousin Vitold, probably the most politically talented among all the princes, by not letting him have a privileged position he deserved and aspired to. Unable to change the situation by his proven loyalty, in 1390 Vitold again took refuge in Prussia, compromising gravely the interests of his country. This was precisely what the Order was waiting for.

Again the Teutonic Order seized the opportunity to organize "crusades" against Lithuania, questioning the validity of the conversion (and even declaring the marriage invalid by virtue of Wilhelm and Jadwiga having allegedly consummated theirs—*consummatio matrimonii*—earlier on his secret visit to her rooms in the Vavel), thus imposing upon the good faith of many western knights who came, even from France and England, to fight beneath its banner. For two years the situation was extremely critical, and only the reinforcements sent from Poland saved Lithuania, notably Wilno, which was twice besieged. The Polish reinforcements were crucial, not only saving Lithuania proper, but letting Jagiełło reach his goal of having a powerful ally while increasing his own power in Eastern Europe. To make sure that Lithuania would never be threatened again, he took steps to undo his earlier mistake: through the intermediary of the Piasts of Masovia, whom he had rapidly conciliated, he offered Vitold such important concessions that the latter once again abandoned his German protectors. In 1392 he was reconciled with the king, becoming a virtual ruler of Lithuania and all its possessions, and beginning a long and fruitful collaboration with

Jagiełło, made possible largely through the good offices of Jadwiga, who was also mediating between him and the Teutonic Order.

The latter was clearly in retreat. Having failed in its attempt on Jagiełło's life, then having lost the services of his naive sister, and probably because of it the last campaign (Jagiełło was reportedly a master of disinformation), and now the collaboration of Vitold, the Teutonic Knights realized that the agreement between Vitold and Jagiełło put an end to all possibility of conquering a Lithuania supported by Poland. It could be accomplished only with Poland out of the way, defeated or conquered.

Thus Poland became a primary target in what was to be a decisive battle. The Grand Master entered into negotiations with Sigismund Luxemburg of Hungary and a scheming Silesian Piast, Władysław of Opole, both with grudges against Poland going as far as to talk about partitioning it. It was Jadwiga who personally met the Grand Master—an honorable knight, after all—and averted an armed conflict which was abhorrent to her and for which Poland was not prepared.

Poland was not prepared because of Vitold who, in spite of the success of Polish diplomacy (thanks again to Jadwiga who was able to make Sigismund, her brother-in-law, leave the Grand Master's anti-Polish coalition), weakened Poland by engaging, against Jadwiga's advice, in ambitious campaigns, in which many Polish knights accompanied him, to bring the Tatars under his control. This obviously suited the Grand Master who, despite Vitold's earlier "treachery," entered in 1398 into a separate peace treaty with him, but at the price of the province of Samogitia; it is possible that some of the Teutonic Knights accompanied Vitold and, like their predecessors at Legnica, took part in the bloody battle on the river Worskla against Tamerlane in 1399.

Here a little digression is in order. Tamerlane or Timur (also called Timur Lenk [Timur the Lame], or Tymur Kulawy in Polish) was a new Mongol invader out of Asia, who in the early 1400s abandoned his conquests in Eastern Europe to return to Samarkand, just as Batu had in 1241. In the sources this writer consulted, there is no mention who it was that stopped Tamerlane, just as Batu's invasion is described as directed against Hungary and Germany, with no mention about Poland (or Polish knights) in either. Yet, both Legnica beyond the Oder and Worskla beyond the Dnieper were decisive battles, even if lost, just like the victory of Charles Martel over the Moors at Poitiers on the Loire in 732. After each of the battles the enemy withdrew, and Europe was saved, but one doesn't get that sense from the sources with reference to the Mongol invasions, and here is a task for the Polish Institute: correct the sources, and let the world know about the history of a country that's now reduced to knocking at the doors of the European Union and NATO.

The battle on the river Worskla saved first of all Moscow, which Tamerlane allegedly was planning to destroy, with great future benefit to the Polish-Lithuanian union. Since this didn't happen, the battle was counter-productive in more ways than one, including possibly speeding Jadwiga to her early grave that same year, without finishing work renovating the Cracow University, neglected by her father. Instead, until her death she looked after the widows and orphans of the knights fallen in the battle. The entire nation mourned her deeply, most of all Jagiełło.

Conventional wisdom tells us that the passing of Jadwiga removed the last restraint on Jagiełło *and* the Grand Master to start a war, and it did start almost immediately over the Order's harsh rule in Samogitia, but a treaty of 1404, while not settling all disputed questions, put off the inevitable clash, for which both sides prepared very carefully. *This was the last time* many knights from all the western countries believed it their duty to fight with the Order against the "infidels" and their allies. It was also *the last time* Poland would fight on the side of the "infidels" against the West. From then on, the situation would be reversed for Poland, and the continuing hostility with the Order would lose its religious aspect. It was to be another decisive war; the final provocation was provided by a general insurrection in Samogitia.

The warlike Grand Master, Ulrich von Jungingen, who had succeeded the cunning and treacherous Winrych von Kniprode, was not mistaken when he accused Vitold of complicity with the insurgents, for the Grand Duke had at last realized that he could not sacrifice an essential part of his country and his people, who were being slaughtered like their Prussian kin before them. (Sacrifice of and disregard for life in Lithuania is probably the reason why the Lithuanians never grew into a sizable nation. Had they done so, they would have subjugated Russia and changed history.)

Instead of putting down the insurrection, the Grand Master decided to attack Poland. Facing his Knights and volunteers from the western countries was an army consisting of Poles, Lithuanians,

Ruthenians, some Czechs and even Tatars, the importance of the latter greatly exaggerated by the enemy in order to scandalize European opinion. The opposing forces were about equal, the numerical superiority of Jagiełło and Vitold's warriors made up by the Grand Master's technical advantage. The famous battle of Grunwald was ultimately decided by the greater physical condition of the Polish nobility, whose formation absorbed the offensive of the enemy's entire power after an initial rout of the Lithuanians, the Czech detachment perishing to the last man helping to fill the breach, and Vitold's Lithuanians, Ruthenians and Tatars returning to help finish the job. Victory was decisive and many prisoners taken, especially among the western volunteers who probably did not wear the white coats with the black crosses of the Teutonic Knights, and thus were easily identified. In a fine gesture Jagiełło set them free under condition that exactly a year hence they would appear in the Vavel castle with the customary ransom. They all came, having created much good will for Poland abroad while ruining the prestige of the Order in the West, which was practically the only advantage Poland carried out from the battle. Just as Grunwald marked one or two *last* things in Polish history, it was the first among other decisive victories which really didn't decide anything for Poland.

This writer had the opportunity to visit and study the Grunwald battlefield, including the exact spot, marked by a rock, where Ulrich von Jungingen fell. The breath of history is strong there, making it easy to wonder about lost opportunities and Poland's penchant for them. What was the reason, exactly, for Jagiełło not taking the easy step of capturing Marienburg, the then almost defenseless capital of the Order, and the rest of its possessions, in which there was much bad feeling against the Order, dismiss it as no longer needed, and take advantage of the favorable situation to reclaim Silesia and perhaps also reach for Western Pomerania, two tasks left unfinished by Casimir the Great? It was all within reach, to make Poland a Baltic power with a firm western border, making the union with Lithuania simpler, but would it suit Jagiełło and Vitold (especially Vitold who, after the 1413 Union at Horodło became Grand Duke with grandiose plans for Lithuania)?

It is a sad testimony to Poland's inability to finish a task that the Teutonic Order escaped annihilation after Grunwald. Henry von Plauen, under whose command the Order rallied, boasted about its luck and resourcefulness at the Vavel meeting the following year.

The Order not only regained its losses but was capable because of that to drive a hard bargain at the first Peace of Toruń in 1411 with only minor concessions. The struggle was resumed three times over the concessions until the Order was forced in a new treaty in 1422 to at least renounce Samogitia.

The return of Samogitia was important, because it not only brought back the separation of the two Orders, but restored Lithuania's westernmost province, giving Vitold a free hand in the East, which suited the Teutonic Knights as it gave them a free hand on Poland's border. Despite this irritant, because that's all the Order amounted to after Grunwald, Poland was acquiring a growing importance in Europe, beginning with the Council of Constance which had started even before Grunwald and became the stage for the famous anti-Order theories of Paweł Włodkovic, to the offer by the Pope for Poland to undertake the pacification of Bohemia, torn by the Hussite movement, and culminating in Jagiełło having at last two sons born to him by his fourth wife, a Lithuanian princess, with the dynasty thus secured.

All this was happening during the fifteen years of perfect harmony between the two cousins after Grunwald and Horodło, with Vitold becoming a virtual master of Eastern Europe, expanding Lithuania's possessions to the Black Sea and further east than ever, arbitrating in interminable conflicts between the Tatar khans, maintaining the ancient Lithuanian pretensions to the great republic of Novgorod in rivalry with Moscow where, moreover, his grandson, subject to his tutelage, had been reigning since 1425. But he did not cut himself off from Polish influences and affairs, using Poles in great numbers to serve in his court and to take part in his military campaigns, and himself appearing at the side of the King in his relations with Hungary and Bohemia, with Brandenburg and Denmark, even with France and England. This authority had a great climax, according to Halecki:

> The authority which they enjoyed in Europe, and with the Emperors of the Greeks and the Turks, an authority which increased, above all, after the Council of Constance, manifested itself with the greatest splendor at the Congress at Łuck in Volhynia in 1429. There, surrounded by their eastern vassals, Jagiełło and Vitold solemnly received, together with a papal legate, the Emperor Sigismund of Luxemburg, who some years since had added the crowns of Germany and Bohemia to that of Hungary. Despite treaties of alliance renewed on several

occasions, Sigismund's attitude to Poland had always remained equivocal. An ally of the Order at the time of Grunwald, he had subsequently tried to arbitrate in its conflict with Jagiełło and Vitold. But these two soon had occasion to learn the Emperor's duplicity.

Although the Łuck Congress of 1429—a high point in the Union and the highest in the history of Lithuania, due mainly to the great political talents of Vitold and his collaboration with Jagiełło, the two princes complementing each other in an extraordinary manner—can be compared with the Cracow Congress assembled by Casimir the Great in 1364, the same cannot be said about their respective guests of honor, the Emperors, with the scheming Sigismund a total opposite of the wise and benevolent Charles IV. Clearly perceiving that Vitold's official position did not at all correspond either to the role he was actually playing or to his ambition, he suggested raising him to the dignity of King of Lithuania, doing it not out of a desire to do the right thing, as his grandfather would, but to break the solidarity of Poland with Lithuania and her Grand Duke. In this he succeeded beyond expectations.

The Emperor's suggestion ran contrary to the articles of the Union which considered the Grand Duchy an integral part of the Kingdom of Poland. As the Poles immediately entered into an irritating discussion of the interpretation of these articles, even Vitold who, at the outset had hesitated before so delicate a proposition, became exasperated. Jagiełło's own attitude complicated the situation. The old king was, in principle, favorable to the creation of a Lithuanian kingdom which his sons should inherit after the death of Vitold, who had no sons. In this way their subsequent election to the Polish throne would be a pure formality. Consequently, while trying to avoid an imperial intervention dangerous to the Union, Jagiełło was quite prepared to authorize the coronation of Vitold, but the latter died in 1430, before the cousins had a chance to iron things out and restore their cordiality.

The conflict which then broke out bears all the marks of the curse following successful Polish rulers (this includes Jagiełło, soon to die too), destroying their work. Jagiełło had appointed his still-living youngest brother, the turbulent Świdrygiełło, as Vitold's successor. The new Grand Duke was immediately seized by the idea of modifying the legal conditions of the Polish-Lithuanian Union; the Poles on their side claimed the cession of Podolia and Volhynia, having allegedly been only administered by Vitold as a personal right. In the civil war that ensued grave mistakes were committed on both sides. Świdrygiełło allied himself with the Teutonic Order, which broke the treaty of 1422 and invaded Poland; the latter opposed another Grand Duke to Świdrygiełło in the person of Sigismund, Vitold's brother. Despite a final victory that was compared, very erroneously, to that of Grunwald, and despite the renewal of the Union of Horodło by the Grand Duke Sigismund, these fratricidal struggles were prolonged in a deplorable way and were still going on when Jagiełło died in June of 1434.

It is regrettable that Jagiełło died in the midst of final shocks which he had not succeeded to prevent, and that both the Emperor and the Order were part of them. His old age (84) made it impossible to punish both: the former in Bohemia by taking up the Pope's offer, and the latter in Prussia, by finishing the Order for good. It had to wait.

It had to wait because Jagiełło's older son, also named Władysław (the younger was named Casimir), was only ten years old in 1434, and it was necessary to institute a regency. There was no doubt that real power would fall to the eminent Zbigniew Oleśnicki, the Bishop of Cracow, Jagiełło's page at the Battle of Grunwald, where he had allegedly saved the King's life, and entered on a career counterbalancing even the influence of Vitold.

> To this day we see nearly the whole of the Polish history of this epoch through the eyes of this great statesman, because the illustrious contemporary historian, Jan Długosz, was his disciple and passionate admirer as was also Halecki–FM. And he was not wrong. We may even add that the imposing figure of the first Polish cardinal belongs indisputably to general history.

This writer would like to add to the admiring testimony of Halecki in which he admits only one defect (a doctrinaire) that just as an earlier Bishop of Cracow had been the cause of an earlier hero-king's downfall, Oleśnicki would be the cause of a hero-king's death, only because their respective perceptions of events differed at a crucial point in time.

These were eventful times calling for bold actions and not doctrines. True, during the childhood of Jagiełło's sons, Oleśnicki did put an end to the civil war which was at the same time a new war with the Teutonic Order, and at the end of 1435 the latter was obliged to sign a "perpetual peace" guaranteed by its own subjects in

Prussia, who thus began to play a part, soon to be a decisive one, in the Order's relations with Poland. At the same time the Order abandoned Swidrygiello, and even though he still held out in the Ruthenian territories, the different parts of the Duchy were united and pacified under the rule of Vitold's brother. It was a different story elsewhere.

Poland faced grave problems south of the border: Sigismund of Luxemburg had died in 1437 and his son-in-law, Albrecht Habsburg of Austria, was to succeed him not only in Germany but also in Bohemia and Hungary. The Poles, however, knew that the accession of the Habsburgs was not looked upon with favor by the national parties of these two kingdoms, and they therefore aimed at gaining at least one of these crowns for their own dynasty. Here an almost five-centuries-long Habsburg involvement in Polish affairs began, completely mishandled by Poland, beginning with Oleśnicki. A Jagiellonian candidature to the throne of Bohemia, already considered earlier, seemed particularly opportune, the more so as Silesia was part of Bohemia then, never reclaimed by Casimir the Great or his successors.

The Bohemian project suited, above all, a fairly large group of the Polish nobility which allowed itself to be won over by Hussite influences. (These influences were still part of folklore when this writer was growing up in Silesia in the 1920s.) For Oleśnicki, on the contrary, this was precisely the reason to oppose it, and without his support of young Casimir's candidacy, the project failed. Was this prince of the church acting in the best interest of Poland?

Oleśnicki was more determined with the second kingdom, Hungary, and with good reasons, the first of which was the death in 1439 of Albrecht Habsburg of Austria without a direct heir. This time Oleśnicki decided to put Władysław himself on the throne of Hungary, not just to re-establish the union with that purely Catholic country (important consideration with Oleśnicki) under conditions more favorable to Poland than with Louis of Anjou, but to go much further in an ambitious plan whose goal was the defense of the Christian world against the Turks.

Little noticed by Poland and Lithuania absorbed by their Union and by the Teutonic Order and Tamerlane, was the Turkish danger. Neither Sigismund nor Albrecht had been able to repulse the Turks who, having crossed from Asia to Europe and conquered the Balkans after vanquishing the southern Slavs in the Battle of Kosovo in 1389, were looming ever more menacingly on the frontiers of Hungary:

> What glory for Poland should her king place himself at the head of a new Crusade, save Hungary, deliver the southern Slavs, and go to the help of Constantinople!

In his ambition and pride, Oleśnicki had no conception of the difficulties that awaited Władysław in Hungary. He was at first elected without dispute, but the Queen Dowager Elizabeth of Luxemburg, after having given birth to a posthumous son of Albrecht Habsburg of Austria, also named Władysław, showed herself firmly resolved to secure for him the whole of his paternal heritage. From 1400 to 1442 Hungary was torn by a civil war between the two Władysławs, both crowned and each supported by his own party. And when at last an agreement, at least provisional, ensured the throne to the young Jagiełło permitting him to turn against the Turks, Poland, after much time and money wasted, lost patience, and Oleśnicki was ill pleased at the compromise with the Habsburgs having been concluded under the auspices of a legate of Pope Eugenius IV who formed a league against the infidels, when it was his, Oleśnicki's, design.

What happened next is a page from the history of Polish heroism. Not receiving reinforcements from Poland but reiterated appeals demanding his return,

> the king remained faithful to the idea that had led him to Hungary. In his first Balkan campaign in 1443,...without any support from the Catholic west, with just his Hungarian army led by John Hunyadi, as well as with a group of Polish knights he achieved extraordinary successes, such as the Christian world, assailed by the Ottomans, had never known, and was for centuries not to know....

As a victor he crossed Serbia, penetrated into Bulgaria, and only the advanced season forced him into a withdrawal which was marked by new exploits. The following year the Turks offered him a ten years' truce. But the king refused to ratify the treaty and proclaimed that he would take up the struggle until the Turks were driven out of Europe.

He didn't drive the Turks out of Europe. The fleet provided by Pope Eugenius IV, his fellow Venetians, and by Philip of Burgundy to occupy the Straits and prevent Sultan Murad II from transporting fresh troops from Asia to Europe failed in its task, and it was near Varna on the shores of the Black Sea that Władysław flung himself into a hopeless battle. In a heroic charge this 20-year-old king died with the greater part of his Polish knights and the papal legate. Hungary was saved from destruction by Hunyadi, but the fate of the Balkans was sealed for centuries.

One is tempted to engage in alternate history. What if Oleśnicki had sent Władysław reinforcements and the latter won the Battle of Varna? The Bishop of Cracow would have been revered and probably canonized, like his distant predecessor, instead of being blamed for the king's death, at least by this writer; while the king, instead of having just a statue in Varna, would have grown into a giant, surpassing the boldest dreams of Casimir the Great and Władysław Jagiełło, becoming a new Charlemagne wearing half a dozen crowns including the imperial bestowed on him by the grateful Pope Eugenius IV taking it from the Habsburgs, whose scheming inactivity in 1444 was almost fatally punished 239 years later, when the Turks besieged Vienna in 1683 until another Polish hero-king saved Austria in the famous Kahlenberg Charge, becoming the "Savior of Vienna."

As for 1444, an easy date to remember for every pupil in the Balkans and in Poland, instead of being one of the decisive dates, like Poitiers (hard to think of others like it: Legnica 1241, Worskla 1399?), it became a date of mourning (another "curse"?), soon to be supplanted by another: 1453, the world-shaking and epoch-ending fall of the 1000-year Eastern Roman Empire (whose emperor had sent despairing appeals to the king), with its ancient capital, Constantinople, becoming the new capital of the Ottoman Empire, inching ever closer to the frontiers of Poland.

In Poland people refused to believe the death of the hero of Varna, but if his absence was severely felt, there was also the wish to replace him as soon as possible. Yet it was not until 1447 that his younger brother Casimir, since 1440 the Grand Duke of Lithuania after Sigismund, was crowned in the Vavel Cathedral. The new king had none of his brother's mystic and confident enthusiasm, but was destined like his father to reign for half a century; like him he distinguished himself by his long patience, while surpassing him by his energy and the clearness of his political conceptions. Resolved to avoid a new internal conflict, he put Lithuania on an equal footing with Poland, made the Lithuanians renounce the institution of a

Grand Duke, thus removing a source of personal ambition and, finally, divided the contested provinces equally, with Volhynia remaining in Lithuania, and Podolia with Poland. He also reined in the oligarchy of Little Poland, including Oleśnicki, despite his recently obtained Roman purple, for the benefit of the gentry and representatives of Great Poland, doing the same with the Wilno Palatine. All he needed to cement the Union was a great common task.

The task was the reintegration of territories lost in the past by the two nations and the extension of the federated state to its natural limits: the Baltic and the Black Sea. As regards the latter, while the disaster of Varna did not encourage the resumption of any project of a risky nature, for the moment the seaboard between the mouth of the Dniester and of the Dnieper remained beyond dispute subject to Casimir, as formerly to Vitold. On the other hand, as long as the Teutonic Order still kept the mouths of the Vistula and Niemen, the Baltic was accessible only by a small corner of Samogitia. This had to be rectified.

Casimir therefore followed closely the internal crisis through which the Order was then passing. The discontent that was increasing among its subjects had led them to create a "Prussian League" which began by defending the rights of the nobility and the towns and which finished by open revolt. Having seized nearly all the strongholds of the country, the insurgents had recourse, in 1454, to the King of Poland, spontaneously placing the whole of Prussia, including what had once been Polish Pomerania, under his sovereignty. It looked like the end for the Order.

Casimir, who had just spent six years regulating Polish-Lithuanian relations, did not hesitate to accept so tempting an offer. True, this time it was Poland who was breaking the latest treaty ("perpetual" 1435) of peace, but she did it at the request of the population concerned, who turned to her, attracted by liberties unknown under the rule of the Order. No one foresaw that the resistance of the latter would impose upon Poland a war of 13 years, the results of which would fall far short of the initial hopes.

What happened was so extraordinary and so full of disquieting weaknesses in what was the largest and, all told, the most powerful country in Europe, that the account will follow the objective narration in Halecki's *History*:

Neither the Prussian League nor the Poles had reckoned with
the international relations and the material resources [...] still at
the disposal of the Teutonic Knights. A victory that was fully
unexpected, gained over the Polish nobility at Chojnice at the
outset of hostilities enabled the Order to gain time and organize
its defence. On the other hand, King Casimir at once experienced a severe disappointment in the discovery that the
Lithuanians, misjudging their own interests, did not intend to
bring in all their forces. The Samogitians alone attacked Memel
[Klajpeda–FM] and cut communications between Prussia and
Livonia from which the Order was trying in vain to draw
reinforcements. The army of the Order consisted chiefly of
mercenaries, better disciplined and more accustomed to
prolonged operations than the mass of the Polish gentry [no
longer reliable–FM] whom, following tradition, the king had
chosen to use. However, Casimir was soon obliged to resort, on
his side, to mercenary troops or to hire those whom the Order
could no longer pay regularly and who, in 1457, sold the capital,
Marienburg, to Poland [!]. Even then the war was far from being
decided. Dreary and ruinous, it no longer had the character of a
conflict between two nations as at the time of Grunwald. The
German element which predominated in the Prussian League
was especially enraged against the Order, and Danzig, in which
the majority of the population was at this epoch already German,
rendered the most signal services to the king by providing him
with large sums of money and by successfully undertaking the
naval war against Denmark, the ally of the Order.

At last, from about 1462, Poland redoubled her efforts, both
military and diplomatic. Her army, better commanded, gained
successes which effaced the deplorable impression of the
Chojnice battle, and thrust back the troops of the Order towards
East Prussia. Laborious negotiations, in the course of which one
European power after another attempted to play the part of
mediator, prepared the compromise which served as the basis of
the treaty of 1466. This *Second Peace of Torun* was infinitely
more advantageous for Poland than the first in 1411. This time
Danzig Pomerania, with the territory of Chelmno, was after a
century and a half of alienation restored to her, together with a
part of Prussia proper, including the port of Elbing, Marienburg,
and the bishopric of Varna or Ermeland. All this territory, which
secured the kingdom extensive access to the sea, and was called
henceforth Western or Royal Prussia, remained in the possession
of Poland until the first partition [see maps of Partitions and
1466].

But the rest of Prussia, with Koenigsberg as its new capital, remained under the rule of the Order, which Casimir in vain endeavoured to transfer to the Turkish or Tatar borderlands where it could have resumed its original vocation. However, this East Prussia was no longer to be an independent state but a fief (vassal) of Poland. According to the treaty each Grand Master was to pay homage to the king and provide him with reinforcements in case of necessity. In addition, the Order was to renounce its exclusively Teutonic character. It undertook to receive Polish knights to the number of half of its members.

The Teutonic Order problem, by then over two centuries old, was mishandled again by Poland, when it could have been settled for good, given the unique conditions for a final solution, including a wise and determined king and a German population of Prussia opting for Poland, attracted by its liberties, among which the *neminem captivabimus* (no arrest without due cause) must have been a strong factor in view of the Order's harsh rule; the financing of the war, always a weakness in Poland, by Danzig, should have been decisive in making it the final clash, but it wasn't final. WHY?

Was it the influence of the foreign mediators, some of whom did not wish to see the end of the Teutonic Order in Prussia? Perhaps it was the influence of Frederick of Brandenburg, who was rumored to have been a potential candidate at the time of Casimir's election to the Polish throne? More likely history was repeating itself, and (just like Jagiełło, and Oleśnicki after him, were unable to finish the Order for good when it broke a peace treaty after Vitold's death, and had to be content with a new, "perpetual" treaty because of regency and problems south of the border) Casimir was facing the same problems, urging him to conclude the long war with a new treaty and no time to profit from lessons of history, as we should profit now; hence, the lengthy account of the saga.

Casimir must have known that the treaty would not be strictly respected, thus the compromise settlement of the problem put an unsatisfactory end to the almost perfect first half of his long reign, somewhat like the end of the long Jagiełło's reign. Casimir's switch from the national, serving the vital interests of the people, to dynastic policy in the second half is not viewed well by historians, but he was only following the example of other monarchs of his time, with the dynastic interests even more natural in his case, since he had 13 [!] children, six of whom were growing sons, all born of his marriage with Elizabeth of Austria, concluded on the eve of the Prussian war.

The "Mother of the Jagiełłos" or "Mother of Kings" as she is also called was the sister of Władysław the Posthumous (former rival of Władysław of Varna, as he is known) who, since 1444 had been the undisputed sovereign of Hungary as well as Bohemia. It was his premature death in 1457, in the midst of the Prussian war, that demanded Casimir's attention, since Władysław's Austrian possessions naturally returned to the younger line of the Habsburgs, whose head was then the Emperor Frederick III. But the two kingdoms which Władysław had inherited through his mother could now be considered the inheritance of his sister, the Queen of Poland, and her children, Casimir's sons. This was an excellent opportunity to re-establish the Jagiellonian dynasty in Hungary, and also in Bohemia, or even in both at once. But before taking any steps in that direction Casimir was obliged to wait for the end of the Prussian war, hoping to end it as soon as possible. This shows how detrimental the Order was to Polish-Lithuanian interests, even in its enfeebled state after losing its capital, Marienburg.

With his hands tied, Casimir raised no objections when the elections, carried out both in Hungary and Bohemia after the death of his brother-in-law, summoned native kings to the thrones: Matthias Corvinus, son of John Hunyadi, and John of Podiebrad, respectively. Casimir even allied himself with the latter in 1462, and also interested himself in the vast design of perpetual peace and European organization that the King of Bohemia propagated with his French collaborator, Antoine Marini. But it was Podiebrad's religious attitude, favoring (moderate) Hussitism, that disquieted the Holy See and made Casimir move with caution.

When Pope Paul II was asked by Casimir to confirm the Peace of Toruń, he demanded in return that the Polish King advance against the Hussite King. But it was not by force of arms against the national King of Bohemia that Casimir aimed to obtain the throne in Prague for his eldest son Władysław. It was through Podiebrad himself that he won the promise and indeed, upon that king's death in 1471, Władysław was elected King of Bohemia.

But the religious aspect of Bohemia came to haunt Podiebrad's legacy and Casimir's policy. There was another candidate for Bohemia in the person of Matthias Corvinus of Hungary, who, unlike Casimir, had been the instrument of the pontifical policy against

Podiebrad, and now claimed the price for his efforts. There followed, until his death in 1490, a 20-year struggle for Bohemia and Hungary showing the advantages and disadvantages of Casimir' dynastic plan.

First, Casimir attempted to stop an intervention by Corvinus in Bohemia by sending one of his sons, young Casimir, a future saint, into Hungary. The expedition was a complete failure and only pushed Corvinus into a war with the Jagiellos in which he allied himself with the Teutonic Order (which viewed it as an opportunity to break the Peace of Toruń) and which ended in 1478 with a precarious compromise: Władysław kept Bohemia proper, but Moravia and Silesia remained in the hands of Corvinus, who also claimed the title of King of Bohemia. This equivocal situation lasted until his death in 1490 when Casimir was again able to claim the throne of Hungary for one of his sons. This time he obtained his object, but after a prolonged struggle between two Jagiełło brothers: John Albert (Olbracht), who was originally supported by his father, and Władysław of Bohemia, who won and thus united the two kingdoms, also restoring to Bohemia the provinces which had been detached.

Thus, unlike Jagiełło who died in the middle of fratricidal struggles in 1434, Casimir's dynastic plan was completely realized on the eve of his death in 1492 (the date, incidentally, of the discovery of America). To quote Halecki:

> The triumph of his house was manifest. It had united under its rule so extensive a territory—from the gates of Moscow to the waters of the Adriatic—as to surpass by far that of any other European Power. The immense Jagiellonian federation seemed a valued element of equilibrium and peace in Europe, as none of the Jagiellos dreamt of war, unless it were to oppose the advance of the infidel, against whom an apparently insurmountable barrier was now raised.

Halecki's hymn to the Jagiellonian Commonwealth is apt, even if not entirely accurate chronologically. By 1490, when Bohemia and Hungary came into the Jagiellonian federation, marking its furthest expansion, that expansion and influence had already been shrinking, but only recently and only because engagement in one area (Prussia, Bohemia), led to neglect in others (Moscow-Novgorod, Crimea).

The double neglect, the first of which indirectly tied in with the Teutonic Order and the House of Habsburg, concerns two areas in the east soon to become a twofold danger. The agreement of 1478 had forced the Grand Master to pay the homage to the King of Poland which had been long withheld—the Order questioning the conditions of 1466 because of newly regained support from the Empire. The House of Habsburg, the seat of the Empire since 1437, never regarded the success of the Jagiellos in Bohemia and Hungary with favor, and Maximilian I, far more energetic than his father Ferdinand III, had also been a candidate to succeed Corvinus. Unwilling to renounce it, he entered into relations with the adversaries of the Jagiellos, but did not limit himself to the enfeebled Order: he took into consideration a more formidable enemy that was threatening Casimir—Moscow, since the fourteenth century a rival of Lithuania. In 1449 a treaty between Casimir and Basil II had fixed the spheres of their respective influence. But Basil, who had exhausted himself in long internal struggles from which a strongly centralized state had emerged, was in 1462 succeeded by Ivan III (Severe), who soon married the daughter of the last Eastern Roman Emperor (Constantine XI) and was determined to extend the domination of Moscow, the "Third Rome," over all the Russias. A few years, the same that Casimir had devoted to the Bohemian war, were enough for Ivan III to put an end to the Republic of Novgorod which, after having counted in vain on Lithuanian help, was crushed and annexed by Moscow, which thus increased its wealth and power immeasurably, to the detriment of its neighbors. This was the first warning to Casimir, but he was not able to prevent further successes on the part of Ivan who, towards the end of Casimir's reign, when the latter was preoccupied with the Hungarian question, begun in time of peace to appropriate one after another the many Lithuanian Grand Duchy's frontier districts.

However humiliating these losses, so far not very extensive, they disquieted the king less than the complete change of the situation which was taking place in the direction of the Black Sea. First, the "insurmountable barrier." It's true that Hungary, stretching at that time across the Balkan Peninsula all the way to the Adriatic, formed a formidable barrier, but that barrier was not insurmountable, because on the other side Hungary did not stretch all the way to the Black Sea. Here warnings also had not been wanting. Following Vitold's example, Casimir had established good relations with the Tatar khanate that was the nearest to his frontiers, that of the Crimea where the Gerai family reigned, benefiting by the support of the Jagiellos and, in general, remaining faithful and devoted to them.

Moreover, the rich commercial city of Kaffa, an old Genoese colony in the Crimea, had placed itself under the protection of the King of Poland. This protection did not prevent the Turks from taking possession of that city in 1475, and the Khan Mengli Gherai, whom they made prisoner, soon returned to the Crimea as vassal of the Sultan. Not extending protection to Crimea was probably a bigger mistake than not protecting Novgorod, because as vassals of the Sultan the Tatars constantly raided south-west Poland.

Neither was failing to protect Moldavia, that had often recognized the suzerainty of Poland, which supported it in the desperate struggle it waged against the Ottomans, especially since the accession of Stephen the Great. In 1484 the Turks tore from her two ports of great importance: Kilia at the mouth of the Danube, and Akkerman at the mouth of the Dniester. Thus they had reached the frontiers of the Polish-Lithuanian state which was almost imperceptibly losing its access to the Black Sea, the steppes between the Dniester and the Dnieper having become the field of action for the Tatars of the Crimea, vassal of Turkey.

With these preventable setbacks it began to look like another curse after an otherwise brilliant reign. All of a sudden the Jagiellonian federation was surrounded by enemies, all growing stronger: the Ottoman Empire expanding north with the help of the Tatars; Moscow, now beginning to call itself Russia after absorbing other principalities, and its Grand Duke—Tsar of All Russias and because of that a threat to Lithuania; the Habsburgs growing stronger with the Empire and viewing the Jagiellonians as rivals and obstacles to expansion, for the sake of which the Teutonic Knights were supported and employed in various ways, making it again harder for Poland to deal with them. Casimir was aware of all this, and while dreaming about victories over the infidels as the best way to heighten the prestige of the Jagiellonians and to avenge the death of his brother, he was preparing the defense of the Polish-Lithuanian frontiers, bequeathing it to his sons and successors, none of whom was his equal, except the youngest (Zygmunt). He prepared for them an excellent team of collaborators in Poland and Lithuania, but while great names to rival, if not surpass, Oleśnicki and Vitold, were still to come in Poland, they were already emerging in Lithuania; to mention just one, the Radziwiłłs, who were always to occupy one of the first places—if not the first—in Lithuania.

All the time there was a constitutional evolution, fertile in consequences, mostly limiting the power of the king, which enables us to understand better the critical years which followed the death of Casimir in 1492. It did not prevent the members of the dynasty from occasionally preparing their common political action in secret meetings, such as a family congress held in Hungary, Władysław's home, in 1494. This is why the definite result of that action, the expedition to the Black Sea in 1497, remains enveloped in a mystery which historical research attempts in vain to pierce. After having proclaimed that he was marching against the Turks to recapture Akkerman, Kilia, and perhaps even Kaffa, King John Albert suddenly turned upon Stephen the Great of Moldavia. We are ignorant how far this fatal decision was justified by Stephen's actions, but be that as it may, he inflicted a sanguinary defeat on the Polish nobility in the forests of Bukovina. His success was aided by the Turks who in the following year penetrated far into Polish territory, and by the connivance of the Hungarians, who, in spite of dynastic ties and a friendship that elsewhere was traditional, were always Poland's rivals on the soil of Moldavia. This writer has another theory.

The Bukovina disaster is a rare blot on Poland's honor, and perhaps the researchers should go back to work to explain it if only because generations of Polish school children had learned of it in the following lines in their books:

> Za króla Olbrachta
> Wyginęła szlachta.
> (Under the Albert King, the gentry perished),

which is not entirely true, since the king's younger brother, Alexander, advancing at the same time towards the Black Sea from Lithuania, had some success over the Tatars and prevented a complete annihilation of John Albert's army. The third brother involved, Władysław of Hungary, had to confine himself to subsequently reconciling Stephen the Great with the Jagiellos. But is this all there was to it?

There were reportedly reinforcements from the Teutonic Order taking part in the Black Sea expedition, an obligation stipulated by the Treaty of Toruń. But why would the Order carry out this obligation if it entirely ignored another, a more important one, to pay homage to the king, as neither John Albert, nor his successor

Alexander, succeeded in making the Grand Master pay the vassal' homage that was due to them? Was the Order's participation due perhaps to the also stipulated presence of Polish knights in it? It would be worth knowing how large the presence was, if there was one at all, but it doesn't seem likely that it was a factor in the Order's participation. Rather, it was a chance to harm Poland, either by conniving with Hungary, where there was always friendship for the Order, which the proverbial weakness of Władysław's rule would not be able to prevent, or with Stephen himself. An opportunity was there, and the Order was quite ready to take it, since the decline of the power of the Jagiellos on the eastern side encouraged at the same time their western adversaries. The Grand Master who did not pay the vassal's homage was a prince of the Empire, Frederick of Saxony, whom the Knights had elected in order to react more forcefully against the Peace of Toruń, an election which started a trend.

The Bukovina defeat put an end to the active policy of the Jagiellos in the eastern question. This defeat was, in addition followed immediately by another which most directly affected Lithuania, and it is at this point that Lithuania becomes a part of the "Poland and Russia" topic in this book.

Alexander, attacked by Ivan following the death of Casimir, under whose rule the Poland-Russia problem really begins according to the Russian imperial historian Nicholas Karamzin, was no match for the aggressor, who recommenced the war with an aim to wrest from Lithuania all the Ruthenian provinces. His victorious campaign in 1500 enabled Ivan to conquer in one blow one third of these. The frontier of the two states which formerly approached Moscow was thrust back to the gates of Kiev. Alexander's weakness was to be seen in his unsuccessful alliances.

With the intention of repairing the losses, and unable to count on reinforcements from Poland after the Bukovina disaster, Alexander allied himself on one side with Sword Bearers, marking the last time Lithuania was involved with a Germanic Order, and on the other with the last Khan of the Golden Horde, but he was not able to support at the opportune moment the efforts of his allies, the latter of which was, because of that, crushed by Mengli Gherai of the Crimea, the ally of Ivan of Moscow.

A truce concluded in 1503 ratified, at least provisionally, the situation created by the aggressor.

Even after the death of Ivan, Alexander did not succeed in his retaliation, and before his own death the following year he had to content himself with seeing one of he most dangerous invasions by the Khan of the Crimea repulsed. Otherwise, even if the decline of the power of the Jagiellonian dynasty so close after its zenith was painful, its most damaging aspects in the long run were the inability to offer protection to proud Novgorod and the new ally the Sword Bearers in the North, where their help in turn would have been sufficient to not only check Ivan's advances but to drive him back to Moscow, there to await an invasion from the South instead of help from Mengli Gherai. Had Poland offered the Crimean Tatars its protection, it would have turned them against Moscow instead of itself, and against Turkey, along with Moldavia, which should also have been protected, and was about to be if not for the turn of events cooked up probably by the Teutonic Knights.

These four areas on the peripheries of the Jagiellonian federation would have made it—if we resort to alternate history—impregnable in the East, surpassing even the dreams of Vitold and enabling the last two Jagiellonian monarchs to settle problems in the West (and South).

It must be remembered that John Albert, who died shortly after the disaster of Bukovina; Alexander, the least gifted of all the Jagiellos and the best argument for Poland to incorporate Lithuania (opposed once by Jadwiga) as unable to defend itself; and the indolent Władysław, the eldest who survived them, were not the only representatives of the family. It is true that their brother Casimir had died young, giving his family a saint, for he was soon canonized by the Church. It is also true that another brother, Frederick, archbishop and cardinal, had passed away in 1503 without having rendered the services that were expected of him. But the youngest of the six princes, Sigismund the Old (Zygmunt Stary), who had waited for a position equal to that of his brothers, had matured in the course of these years and was able to undo, as a sign of the vitality of the country, some of the damage brought about by his inept brothers. His high qualities, which showed themselves on several occasions, and which ushered Poland into the "Golden Age," also called the "Golden Century" (the sixteenth century), nearly half of which (1506-1548) under his reign, made him, with good reason, the hope of his dynasty and of Poland.

Sigismund I, first elected Grand Duke of Lithuania and then King of Poland, where he surrounded himself with remarkable statesmen, at once occupied himself on parallel lines with the two main problems for these two countries, the Muscovite danger and the situation in Prussia.

In the east it was necessary to put a final stop to the conquests of a neighbor who, under Alexander's reign, had been able to advance almost with impunity. A first war, undertaken by Sigismund in 1507 under conditions sufficiently favorable, was complicated by the rebellion of Prince Michal Glinski who, for reasons of alleged loss of his old influence, ranged himself on Basil of Moscow's side. However, this problem belongs in the Poland-Russia topic of the book, but suffice it to say now that the Grand Duke Basil broke four years later the peace of 1508 with the definite objective of seizing the important stronghold of Smolensk which, despite sizable Polish reinforcements (a must by then in every Lithuanian war), fell to the enemy in 1514, mainly because of Poland's absorption in the situation in Prussia, where the Grand Master had died.

Poland's absorption in interminable efforts to force the Teutonic Order at last to put into execution the stipulations of the Peace of Toruń, was renewed when the Grand Master Frederick of Saxony, who had refused to pay homage as a vassal, died in 1511. The Order nominated as his successor another prince of the Empire, a development which continued to bring the Order increasingly closer to the Empire, this time in the person of Albert of Brandenburg, of the younger line of the Hohenzollern-(an ominous ring on two counts)-Ansbachs. Although his mother was the daughter of Casimir Jagiełło, the new Grand Master followed with regard to the King, his uncle, the hostile policy of his predecessor, bringing to nothing the projects of agreement that were under negotiations at frequent intervals, and, more serious still, entering into relations with Sigismund's other adversary, Basil of Moscow.

But there was yet another link between these two enemies of Poland and Lithuania. They were both encouraged in their uncompromising attitude by Emperor Maximilian I. In regard to the question of Prussia, he styled himself as the defender of the long-since obsolete rights of the Empire; but why, in the critical year 1514, did he send an ambassador to Moscow who was won over to an alliance against the Jagiellos? It was because the Habsburgs never forgot their pretensions to the crowns of Bohemia and Hungary, and if the Emperor now exercised such a strong pressure upon Sigismund, it was to make him abandon the interests of his dynasty, and to secure to the House of Austria the right to succeed his brother Władysław.

Always closely united, the two Jagiellos decided in these circumstances on a meeting, first with the Emperor's plenipotentiaries who came to Pressburg, then with Maximilian I himself. The Treaty of Vienna, signed in the summer of 1515, did not recognize any formal rights of the Habsburgs to the succession in Bohemia and Hungary.

But the double marriage contracted on this occasion between the children of Władysław and the grandchildren of Maximilian naturally gave a new basis to Austrian influence in the two coveted kingdoms, and to the pretensions that Ferdinand of Austria raised eleven years later. The negotiators at Vienna could not have foreseen that the only son of Władysław was to die early, leaving no children.

The reconciliation with the Emperor in 1515 brought to the Jagiellos and, above all, to Sigismund, indisputable advantages, for Maximilian loyally kept his promise no longer to support the Grand Master in his opposition to Poland and to undertake nothing with Moscow against Lithuania.

It is true that the change which resulted held nothing decisive, the more so as Maximilian died in 1519, and the Jagiellos did not succeed in exercising a definite influence at the time of the election of his successor. In the conflict between Sigismund and Basil, Charles V, like Maximilian I, made attempts at mediation, but the question of Smolensk prevented any lasting peace. The truce, concluded in 1522 and periodically prolonged, was interrupted (by Lithuania?) after the death of Basil and during the minority of his son, the future Ivan the Terrible, by a third war which restored only a small part of her lost territories to Lithuania.

As for the Teutonic Order, a fundamental change was going to occur concerning it and having to do with the Reformation taking root at that time in Germany. At first, after what Halecki calls "The First Congress of Vienna" in 1515, Albert the Grand Master had no intention of yielding, even when abandoned by the Emperor; the armed intervention upon which Sigismund, losing patience, decided in 1519, resulted in no solution. The one which was at last found in 1525 was of a nature to evoke the greatest astonishment throughout the whole of Europe. To quote Halecki:

Albert accepted Poland's conditions, but it was no longer the Grand Master of the Teutonic Order who knelt in person in the great square of Cracow to pay homage to the King. It was the secular and hereditary prince, the first Duke of Prussia. For he had adopted the doctrines of Martin Luther, and the Order, whose religious mission had for long been pure fiction, was secularized. With it an implacable enemy, who, even though weakened, had remained a veritable nightmare to Poland, vanished from her vicinity. As had been the case with the Congress of Vienna, it was difficult to foresee the consequences of the new state of affairs.

It is true that East Prussia thereby became the appanage of a German dynasty, but the right of succession was strictly limited to the direct descendants of Albert and his brothers, so that the elder line of Hohenzollerns, that of the Electors of Brandenburg, found itself excluded. As for Albert himself, placed under the ban of the Empire, with which he seemed to have definitely broken, he found the best guarantee of his power in the suzerainty of Poland.

Albert's newly acquired reliance on Poland, which included gaining friends and extending personal influence, was in reality little liked by Sigismund I, despite the disappearance of the earlier nightmare, which was frankly speaking illusory because of the Knights constituting a kind of standing army ready to act at a moment's notice, but without the reserves that a normal nation had at its disposal. Hostile or not, the Knights were co-religionist. Extending Poland's suzerainty to a Protestant principality offended the religious feelings of this profoundly Catholic king, who was at the moment repressing the beginning of the Lutheran movement in the territory of western Prussia, and notably in Danzig, both Polish. If, notwithstanding, he decided on the agreement made in Cracow, it was because, like his father before him, he was increasingly uneasy about the situation south of the border, namely that of his young nephew Louis, who had succeeded his father Władysław on the thrones of Bohemia and Hungary.

Hungary was more than ever threatened by the Ottoman power, and while the King of Poland, occupied with simultaneous grave developments in Cracow, was counseling his nephew to avoid, at all cost, a new war with Sulayman the Magnificent, the influence of Austria was impelling the Hungarians to the conflict which ended in the catastrophe of Mohacs. In 1526 (a year after the Cracow homage), as in 1444, it was a Jagiełło king who died in vain, abandoned by the Christian Europe he was defending; the Hungarian army, to which Sigismund had only been able to send very feeble reinforcements (that's when a ready standing army would have made a difference), was annihilated.

At the same time, the question of the succession once more came forward both in Hungary and in Bohemia. We know that the treaty of 1515 had not prejudged it. But the King of Poland, who had felt sufficiently strong to ensure for himself the succession to the last Piasts of Masovia and at length to incorporate this old Polish province in the kingdom, hesitated before the crushing task of assuming power in the two great countries which were escaping his dynasty. Therefore, Ferdinand of Austria met with no opposition on the Polish side when he was elected, first, King of Bohemia, and then also of Hungary.

For two promises of little value—since the Russians would abide by mediation only if and when it suited them (the minority if Ivan IV), and since there was no question of collaboration between Protestant Prussia and Catholic Austria—the Habsburgs displaced the Jagiellos as a dominant power in East Central Europe!

The process could have been frustrated or at least delayed in Hungary, where Ferdinand was the candidate of only one party, while another party had previously elected a national candidate, John Zapolya (like Corvinus before). Zapolya, whose sister had been Sigismund's first wife, counted on the support of Poland, where he had won many supporters, but officially Polish policy remained strictly neutral, in spite of several attempts at mediation.

Having not succeeded before the Battle of Mohacs in allying himself with the King of France against the House of Austria, Sigismund hesitated still further before making common cause with the Habsburgs' new adversary, who was openly protected by the Sultan. An extremely delicate situation arose for Poland, a situation which was prolonged for many years and was further aggravated towards the end of the old king's reign. For, although he had given his daughter in marriage to John Zapolya, he could neither definitely reconcile the two parties which were contending for Hungary, nor prevent the Turks from occupying Buda in 1541, shortly after King John's death, under the pretext of supporting Zapolya's son who was a minor and, at the same time, the grandson of the King of Poland!

These complications, germane to this chapter only insofar as the Jagiełło-Habsburg relations are concerned, must nevertheless be understood as caused mainly by the need to organize the defense of the vast and threatened borderlands which the king had done more efficiently than his predecessors, but which were still, like the old curse, clouding the approaching end of his reign. The problem was the disproportion of the military and financial means at the disposal of the king to the size of the state and the place it held in Europe. Reforms were needed which, while solving other problems, would also ensure a permanent army to the kingdom. Such an army, had it existed earlier, would have defeated the Turks at the battle of Varna, thus removing the Mohacs follow-up; it would have made short work of the Teutonic Knights, while all the time keeping the Muscovites and the Crimean Tatars at bay.

Reforms had always been on Sigismund's mind, and new efforts, launched by the court, appear in the second half of his reign. But then the initiative emanated less from the king himself than from his second wife, the very beautiful Milanese princess Bona Sforza, whom the king had married in 1518 on the advice of Emperor Maximilian who, struck at the Congress of Vienna (1515) by finding in his rival as distinguished a humanist as himself, and the prelates and lords accompanying him, whatever may have been their political leanings, without exception penetrated with that Renaissance culture which was then taking possession of Poland and appearing even in far-off Lithuania, found what looked like the ideal wife for him, but turned out to be a serious disruption for the Jagiellos. According to Halecki:

> Recent researches have brought to light the truly superior intelligence and prodigious activity of this queen, whose ideas, dictated by the interests of the dynasty, also agreed in great measure with the interests of Poland. Nevertheless, we remain convinced that the methods applied by Bona, no doubt in conformity with the political doctrines of the Renaissance, departed in a deplorable way from the Jagiellonian traditions. Contrary to the king, who always respected the existing laws, his wife, whose influence was on the increase, cared little for the legality of the means chosen, even stooping to corruption, and when, towards 1531, the tried collaborators of Sigismund began to disappear, she saw to it that her docile but often unworthy protégés were nominated to the highest offices. The grievances which accumulated against the court were, therefore, in great part justified, and in 1537 the king himself had to acknowledge it after violent discussions with the nobility, whom he had inopportunely mobilized. From then on it was clear that any constitutional reform had, for the moment, become impossible.

It is just possible that Maximilian, realizing Sigismund's potential and the Polish nobility's love of privileges and liberties, had
arranged the royal marriage to an ambitious and reform-minded
woman to wreck the king's position by putting him on a collision
course with the nobility. If this was indeed the plan, it succeeded, but
it could have just as easily misfired. Even more recent research than
that alluded to by Halecki tells that Queen Bona's activity went in an
unexpected direction. Realizing Lithuania's situation as a minority
nation controlling huge territory, she thought of altering it by
making it possible for the Ruthenian population to earn a patent of
nobility through service in the army, thus creating an invincible
standing army out of Polonized natives. But it didn't happen.

In this respect, therefore, the reign of Sigismund the Old, whose
authority emerged impaired from this internal crisis, marks a
decided halt in the historical evolution of Poland. But by a happy
compensation this same reign continued one of the most brilliant
stages in the development of Polish civilization; with the University
of Cracow retaining its prestige of the previous century, soon its
most illustrious student, Nicolas Copernicus, would cover with glory
the school where his genius had been formed. On the other hand,
numerous distinguished members of the nation frequented foreign
universities, some of them producing works of literature. Side by
side with works of Polish inspiration but Latin in language, the first
small works to be written in the language of the country were also
emerging from the first printing presses (1543). Naturally, the
Italian queen, by intensifying the relations of Poland with the land of
her birth, contributed on her part to this movement. That is why her
forced departure from Poland was a grievous loss in more ways than
one, plus a curse for Sigismund, and a victory for the Habsburgs.

But Bona left something behind that compensated for the loss,
her son (born 1520) and the only son and namesake of Sigismund.
The second Sigismund, Zygmunt August in Polish, had many things
in common with the first, but he surpassed the first by his diplomatic
talent and his spirit of initiative, which he probably inherited from
his mother, who had him crowned in his father's lifetime, the
queen's intention being to make the cherished right of the nobility to
free elections of the King of Poland an empty illusion. Like his
father, he also had a dramatic marriage, having married, while Duke
of Lithuania, Barbara Radziwiłł, a brief marriage much opposed by
the nobility (and Bona).

From the point of view of the Poland-Germany topic, the reign of Sigismund II, marking the end of the Jagiellonian era, marks also the end of two Germanic Orders in the vicinity of Lithuania and Poland, the Sword Bearers in Livonia, and (symbolically), the Teutonic Knights in Prussia. The closing chapters of both Orders came amidst other problems Sigismund II inherited from his father. Like him, he only intervened in the conflicts between the Habsburgs and the Zapolyas—his sister and his nephew—as a mediator, without, however, losing his concern with what went on in Hungary; also like his father, he was determined to avoid a rupture with Turkey. He had no love for the family of his first and third wives, the Habsburgs, whom he accused of trying to dominate the world. He mistrusted his cousin Albert of Prussia, whose ambitious intrigues he divined. But the real enemy, to whom he indignantly refused his sister's hand, was, in his eyes, Ivan the Terrible of Moscow:

> It is, in fact, impossible to imagine a more absolute contrast than that between *the last Jagiłło*, thoughtful and refined, and *the first tsar*, a despot with revolutionary tendencies.

But it was a case of more than personal antipathies. The threat of a new Muscovite invasion weighed incessantly upon the Ruthenian provinces of Lithuania, but Sigismund soon perceived that the dreaded attack this time could come not only from the east, but also from the north, Livonia.

On this side, Lithuania had as her neighbor Livonia, where the Order of the Sword Bearers, formerly affiliated with the Teutonic Order, still held out. Fallen into decadence, like the latter, the Livonian Order was no longer capable of resisting the tsar, who was determined to cut free access for himself through its country to the Baltic Sea. His threats, followed by cruel invasions, forced the isolated country to seek efficacious help, which only Sigismund Augustus could provide. He began, in 1557, by settling on his own account without striking a blow the differences there had been between himself and the Knights. Two years later he entered into his first agreement in regard to protection against Moscow. Finally, in 1561, the last Master of Livonia, Gothard Kettler, ceded the entire country to the king, contenting himself with the Duchy of Courland which he received in fief, like Albert in Prussia. The secularization of the Order was followed by that of the archbishopric of Riga, and that town also placed itself under royal protection, obtaining, moreover, like the whole of Livonia, privileges which guaranteed the autonomy of the new province.

It is superfluous to insist upon the importance of this acquisition, which made the Jagiellonian Federation a great Baltic power. But this was the very reason why it at once provoked the rivalry of all the other interested powers. The House of Brandenburg had hoped to profit by the secularization of Livonia, as it had formerly done by that of Prussia, the more so since a brother of Albert had been the last Archbishop of Riga. Here is what happened:

> Sigismund Augustus succeeded in dismissing these [Brandenburg's] pretensions, but at the price of a concession that the future proved to be disastrous:
>
> > *he extended the right of succession in East Prussia*
> > *to the elder, electoral line of Hohenzollerns.*
>
> This was, however, the only mistake with which his policy can be reproached amidst all the complications of the first "war of the north" [Northern War], which broke out soon after the submission of Livonia and lasted until the Congress of Stettin of 1570,

but which is not too germane to this chapter. What is germane was something much more serious which on a dynastic level can be considered a curse persecuting the reigns of otherwise successful rulers in Poland (double in the case of the last Jagiellonian, Sigismund II who, like the last Piast, Casimir the Great, waited in vain for an heir).

Equally serious was the Muscovy part of the war which did not go well for Lithuania and resulted in the loss of Polock in 1563, a loss even more grievous than that of Smolensk (a glance at a map will show why), precisely because, despite valuable Polish reinforcements, as always in similar cases, it was essentially a Lithuanian war until final Union was concluded defining, among other agreements, Poland's responsibility for Lithuania and ability to wage a war avenging the loss and subjecting Russia to the Union's sovereignty (a formidable avenger was already available). The famous final Union was concluded in Lublin in 1569.

But even this success, paving the way to Russia's near-destruction, must take a back seat to what was taking place in connection with the new reality in Prussia after Sigismund's death in 1572. Because of the king's uneasiness with the secularization, we should consider his passing as the ultimate end of the Teutonic Knights' saga in Prussia (they still have an office in Vienna) and the beginning of a new Prussia. Suddenly East Prussia (Ducal Prussia) became an important piece in Central European political realities. They are part of modern European history and, as such, known to its students, and there is no need to go into great detail as with the Teutonic Order, which was an important lesson for both Germany and Poland, except to outline important stages; but a few remarks are in order.

Unlike Austria, which from an obscure March (Ostmark) evolved through lucky successions and dynastic marriages into the House of Habsburg which inherited, revived, and energized the Holy Roman Empire until it nearly dominated the world (Sigismund August's fears), Poland had no such luck; two of its dynasties ending without an heir, forcing the country to search for a new ruler under conditions of uncertainty in which to start building a new power base, with surprising results, and putting it into conflicts with old and new neighbors.

With the end of the second dynasty, a new House was already firmly established in Poland's vicinity, the House of Brandenburg, with a history very much like that of the Habsburgs. Founded by Henry I at the beginning of the tenth century on the land of the pagan Slavic Wends as the North March (or Mark), the Slavic *Brennabor* was conquered in an eastward expansion in the XII century by Albert the Bear, giving its name to the margraviate, and province, of Brandenburg, about the same time as the Teutonic Knights' arrival in Prussia (1226). Later it made great gains at the expense of Poland in the 1278 war of Ottokar II of Bohemia against Rudolf Habsburg. The Margraves of Brandenburg were made Electors of the Holy Roman Empire by Charles IV.

Poland's relations with Brandenburg were minimal except in connection with the threatened Danzig Pomerania (despite the massacre in 1308 it was better for Poland that Danzig Pomerania was seized by the Teutonic Order, from which it could be reclaimed in the Toruń Peace of 1466), and Casimir the Great's plans for Western Pomerania. They became closer with the secularization of the Teutonic Order (1525), when the Grand Master became Duke of Prussia, and East Prussia thereby became an appanage of a German dynasty, but the right of succession was strictly limited to the direct descendants of Albert and of his brothers, so that the elder line of

Hohenzollerns, that of the Elector of Brandenburg, found itself excluded. The name Hohenzollern did not have a strong ring yet, but it returned with a stronger one during the Livonian war almost half a century later when, to keep Brandenburg out of it, Sigismund II extended the right of succession in East Prussia to the elder, electoral line of Hohenzollern.

The saga of the Teutonic Knights came full circle. The "only" mistake of the last Jagiellonian, and a curse on the otherwise almost perfect reign of this sad and solitary man, was comparable to the probably also "only" mistake of Konrad, Duke of Masovia. The seed planted by the Teutonic Knights and the first Duke of Prussia, and cultivated by Brandenburg, was bearing fruit. All that the Dukes of Prussia in Koenigsberg and Electors of Brandenburg in Berlin had to do was to wait patiently for an opportune moment to advance their common cause. Such a moment came in 1621 with the death of the son and last heir of Albert of Prussia, when his duchy passed into the hands of the Elector of Brandenburg in conformity with the concessions made to the Hohenzollerns. As Duke of Prussia, the Elector paid homage to the King of Poland in 1621; but the fact that Koenigsberg and Berlin, separated from each other by Polish territory (Danzig Pomerania), now belonged to the same prince, naturally held great danger for the future.

The saga of the House of Brandenburg, with a history very much like that of the Habsburgs (a collision course?) and an evolution, like the Teutonic Knights' a historical marvel, producing its own Hohenzollern dynasty culminating in two Kaisers and ending, like the Teutonic Knights, in disaster. Below are stages of the evolution connected with, and at the expense of, Poland.

Though it suffered terribly in the Thirty Years War (1618-1648) Brandenburg emerged as a military power under Frederick William, the Great Elector. The end of that war marks the beginning of the Polish "deluge" in the middle of a "century of wars," periodically resumed with: RUSSIA, which survived near-extinction at the hands of a worthy successor of the Jagiellons, King Stephen Bathory (Stefan Batory, a Transylvanian), and a chaotic "Time of Troubles" following the death of Ivan the Terrible; SWEDEN, a largely dynastic war (1600-1660) waged by Sigismund Vasa, and his sons Władysław and John Casimir; TURKEY, provoked by Sigismund's closeness to Habsburgs; *all* started by a revolt of mishandled Ukrainian Cossacks.

The Great Elector, like a loyal vassal of King John Casimir, participated in the great Beresteczko battle against the Cossacks, Crimean Tatars, and allegedly Turks in 1651, probably because it was a decisive battle which, like many other Polish victories, was not followed up, thus bringing Russian intervention in 1654. Exploiting Poland's vulnerability, he was helping the Swedes when they invaded in 1655, determined to take this unique opportunity to free himself from the bonds of vassalage which tied East Prussia to Poland, eventually consummating his disloyalty by allying himself with the Swedish King (Charles Gustavus) and declaring himself his vassal as Duke of Prussia (Sweden was mostly interested in Royal Prussia). Brandenburg troops were reportedly of crucial importance in the 1656 Battle of Warsaw. But with Sweden losing the war despite the battle, the Elector of Brandenburg, kept in play by the Habsburgs, found it convenient to become reconciled with John Casimir:

> But his [the Great Elector's] alliance with Poland had to be paid for by the Treaty of Wehlau in 1657 which put an end to Polish suzerainty over East Prussia, with the result that a veritable foreign wedge dependent on Berlin was established between Polish West Prussia [Royal Prussia] and Lithuania.

As part of the alliance, Polish troops under the famous commander, Stefan Czarniecki, Sweden's nemesis remembered in the Polish national anthem, marched across the Elector's territory to help the Danes, new allies, fight their own war against the Swedes. It would have made more sense to fight and punish the treacherous Elector, but with another invasion mounted, this time from the south, Transylvania, and the suspended fighting resuming in the east, with the Cossacks temporarily abandoning Russia and helping to defeat it, thus opening an opportunity, wasted on both sides, for reconciliation, it was beyond the strength of the worn out and devastated, but still victorious Poland.

The hour of reckoning with the Great Elector arrived with the accession to the Polish throne in 1674, following a great victory over the Turks, of the already famous (and with a name to become more popular and better known abroad than any other in the history of Poland) warrior-king, Jan Sobieski, who immediately entered into an alliance with France. According to Halecki:

> This Franco-Polish alliance was directed, in the first place, against the Great Elector, Frederick William of Brandenburg,

with the definite object of recapturing East Prussia, which was in fact very discontented under the absolutism of Berlin.

There is no alternate history more tempting to ponder than to wonder *what if* Poland had acted on this alliance. Even Halecki muses:

> This plan, which would have redeemed a long series of Polish political mistakes reaching as far back as Conrad of Masovia, preoccupied John III for several years. In 1677 he concluded a new alliance to this effect with Sweden by a treaty signed at Danzig. But soon a complete and sudden change seemed to come over the king's foreign policy. The king who had supported Hungarian insurgents against Austria and had even thought of reclaiming Silesia which had so long been lost, gradually approached the Emperor, and instead of pursuing the project of a coalition against the Elector of Brandenburg he took the initiative in forming a Christian league against the Turks. This new policy, which began in the Diet of 1678-9, ended in 1683 with the memorable campaign which was to save the capital of the Habsburgs [Vienna].

Despite the relief of Vienna, which holds so considerable a place in universal history, a great opportunity was lost by not acting against the Great Elector, since a victory over him would have allowed Sobieski to deal with the Turks *before* their Austrian campaign, by not relying on uncertain leagues but stirring up the Balkans, where he was already a legend, and the Hungarians; but most of all by employing the Cossacks, who had a great affection and admiration for him (a Ukrainian scholar told this writer that ten thousand Cossacks were rushing to Sobieski's side at Vienna).

The situation in East Prussia, because of its discontent, was similar to that of Casimir Jagiellonian, but was more favorable because of Sobieski's war record. Victory there, followed by a crusade generated by him against the Turks would have won for him the same honors Władysław of Varna would have received had he won in 1444.

The problem was that a war designed to occupy East Prussia would have had the appearance, at least, of a war of aggression and conquest, and consequently would never have gathered the whole nation, which had little knowledge of Berlin's diplomatic intrigues. Sobieski was aware that the danger from the Hohenzollerns might in future become still more disquieting. But the Great Elector succeeded, in 1679, in himself forming an alliance with Louis XIV, and found French diplomats to help him in upholding the opposition directed in Poland against the king. At one point John III had wished to march against Brandenburg without waiting for the approval of the Diet, and to take possession of East Prussia for his family as a basis of a dynastic policy, which would have been the best solution.

One detail should be mentioned here as throwing light on the Elector of Brandenburg. When the huge Turkish army, commanded by the Vizier Kara Mustafa, laid siege to Vienna in the summer of 1683, the King of Poland responded to the appeals of the Pope and the Emperor, proceeding immediately to mobilize, and rapidly lead an army of thirty thousand men into Austria. The Austrians had also obtained reinforcements from most princes of the Empire, *with the exception of the Elector of Brandenburg*.

Apparently the Duke/Elector was not going to risk an army which he would need to defend East Prussia in case of an invasion by Sobieski. He need not have feared. After Vienna, instead of returning to the East Prussian project, John III spent the rest of his life, losing his military reputation in the process, trying to conquer Moldavia, and even Wallachia, in order to make a sovereign principality for his son, who could then succeed him as King of Poland. He did not succeed, did not reap any benefits for Poland from his great victory which appeared as a useless gesture, a *beau geste*, as far as Poland was concerned which, neglected by Sobieski, was sliding into decay. When he died in 1696, to quote Halecki,

> the hero of 1683 departed with the mournful presentiment that nothing could now avert the ruin of the Republic.

Five years after Sobieski's death, in the midst of election promises by a Saxon candidate to succeed John III, Elector Frederick III, the son of the Great Elector, took the title "King in Prussia" (1701) as Frederick I. The later history of Brandenburg is that of Prussia.

The Saxon period which has been compared to a night which fell on Poland and, in the words of one of Poland's most distinguished historians, the end of the epoch of Polish independence, surely belongs to the topic of "Poland and Germany," with two Germanic kings, August II ("unscrupulous and lacking in greatness") and August III ("revolting indolence") reigning for over sixty years. But in at least one respect these two kings were an answer to what Poland needed. For Poland, ruined in the "century of wars" (just like

Germany in the Thirty Years War earlier and France in the Hundred Years War) these wars had internal consequences more disastrous than territorial losses. Fought out in great part on the still very extensive territory which remained to Poland, they ruined her economically. Absorbing the flower of the nation, they made the Poles pay for even their victories, not only with their best blood, but also with a halt, if not a backward step, in the development of their civilization.

Under these conditions the Poland whose regeneration by her own strength Jan Sobieski had not succeeded in effecting, had imperative need of support from another state. This support could not come to her from any of the neighboring countries, which were only too happy to profit from her weakness. Against this there was another state, distant France, and failing that, Saxony.

Saxony had certain advantages for Poland. To begin with, it was not a neighboring country in the sense of Russia, Prussia, Austria, but this seeming advantage was really a disadvantage, if one considers that the province of Silesia, separating Poland and Saxony since the XIVth century, was a prized area that any Polish king should want to restore to Poland, especially a king from Saxony. If we add to it that a considerable part of Saxony's population consisted of Slavic Sorbs (whose remnants still exist today west of the Neisse [Nysa] river), out of regard for whom and recognition of, every Saxon king had to undergo the swearing-in ceremony in German and in Sorbian, a language similar to Polish, we can conclude that on linguistic grounds alone Saxony was closer to Poland than Lithuania, and as close as the latter's Ruthenian components, an important consideration when entering an expanding union.

But this was not the way Poles viewed the Saxon candidacy. Ignoring the fact that Saxony was wealthy, an important factor mentioned earlier in this book and the main reason for seeking a foreign candidate, all they understood was that the Saxons were German, and a German or Germanic candidate for the Polish throne was anathema to them. In addition, this candidate, supported by Poland's neighbors not wishing her well, beat out in an illegal election a highly desirable and popular French candidate, Prince Louis de Conti, who was probably Poland's last chance of saving itself, as an ally of powerful France. His election was already proclaimed when a minority opposed him with a last-minute candidate, Frederick Augustus I,

Elector of Saxony, who hastened to have himself crowned King of Poland under the name of Augustus II.

The misgivings, which is a mild description of the feelings in Poland about the Saxon candidate, proved more than right when he became king. At a time when Poland had imperative need of peace, Augustus II dragged her against her will into a new war, which completed her ruin. Totally oblivious of Poland's interests and new realities which made Sweden an ally rather than an enemy, he attacked that country in concert with Denmark and Russia, with Tsar Peter the Great his intimate ally. There was nothing to gain for Poland except possible recovery of Livonia, but much to lose in the form of territorial and other compensation to Peter of Russia, Frederick of Prussia (soon a king), and Austria. The great (second) Northern War began in 1700 with the defeat by Charles XII of all the allies, and it was Poland which paid the price by becoming occupied again by the Swedes and devastated, including the destruction of the fortifications of proud Lwów. The only winner was Peter, whose decisive victory at Poltava (1709) sealed the fate of Poland by removing one potential neighbor-ally, Sweden, with a second, Turkey, where Charles sought refuge, in decline. The new King of Prussia suggested a partition, but Peter preferred a slow decline, starting by reduction of the army to the low figure of twenty-four thousand men. Of the three former powers declining simultaneously, Poland was in the gravest danger, surrounded on all sides, with no exit, like a king in a chess game, by hostile powers.

Whether it was personal ambition, sudden care for Poland in view of the Prussian King's suggestion, or just plain envy, Augustus II had had enough of his Russian ally. The prodigious success of the Tsar, who was preparing to assume the imperial title was, moreover, beginning to arouse considerable uneasiness in Europe. In 1719 Augustus was consequently enabled to enter into an alliance against the Tsar with the Emperor Charles VI and even with England, under conditions very favorable to Poland. Considering the indignation which roused the whole country against the Muscovite designs, the hour seemed at last propitious for an understanding between the king and the nation, inspired this time by the vital interests of the Republic.

The moment, unique in the long reign of Augustus, was unfortunately lost. The king could scarcely be surprised that he met with no confidence, for until now he had done nothing to deserve it.

But he was assuredly not wrong in reproaching the Poles for the shameful weakness which in 1720 led them to renounce every effort that could have delivered them from the domination of the Tsar. The latter, on his part, concluded with Prussia the first treaty directly aimed against the existence of Poland, and designed to prevent in advance any project of recuperation.

It is no wonder that Augustus II dedicated himself to trying to secure absolute power for himself in Poland and Saxony, and transmitting it to his son Frederick August. He succeeded in his son getting elected after him, not because of absolute power but by Russian cannon making sure of it by protecting a minority in an election which prevented Stanisław Leszczyński, father-in-law of Louis XV, from becoming a legitimate King of Poland. This was the last chance. After it, life in Poland, under the most unworthy sovereign Poland has ever had, took this form:

> *Za króla Sasa,*
> *Jedz, pij i popuszczaj pasa.*
>
> Under the Saxon King,
> Eat, drink, and loosen the belt.

Under the impression of the dreary monotony which those thirty years reveal, we almost end by asking ourselves whether Poland, condemned to a more and more passive role, had indeed at that time any history of her own. The former rampart of Christendom became a roadside inn, serving, above all, Russian armies which were thus enabled to make their appearance on the battlefields of Central Europe.

Poland was absent from those battlefields, of which there were many in the mid-XVIII century, some of them concerning Poland, like the unprovoked attack by Prussia's Frederick the Great on Austria (1740) and annexing Silesia, thereby outflanking all the western provinces of Poland. It was comforting to see Poland's neighbors at war, which was also the case in the Seven Years War (1756-63) when Russia almost wiped out Prussia, but a new Tsar switched sides and enabled it to become the chief continental military power.

The famous switch of sides produced an alliance between the two "greats": Frederick II and Catherine II. This was a danger sign for Poland which, with the almost simultaneous death of Augustus III began to wake up from its lethargy. The military pirate Frederick was the chief danger, and not just in military matters: he was ruining Poland by flooding it with false currency and hurting it by kidnapping big Polish peasant young men for his regiments, while ridiculing the Poles in every way he could (a witty man, he is probably responsible for the Polish jokes). Yet, when next he engineered what was later called the First Partition of Poland, he took the country by surprise. There was shock and disbelief. The popular saying until then that

> *Polska nierządem stoi*
> Poland exists because it
> doesn't have a government

was exposed for its idiocy, and a veritable race was set in motion to save the country. Luckily, Poland had a new king (about whom it was later said that "He lost and saved Poland"), Stanisław August Poniatowski, who knew what was needed: education and a constitution. One year after the partition (1773) the National Committee for Education (the first Ministry of Education anywhere) was already in place, and political literature, a tradition, was flourishing. Also, the Prussian evil genius Frederick II was soon dead.

Frederick finished what the Teutonic Order's Grand Masters had started (due to an unwitting mistake by Konrad of Masovia); what the Dukes had continued; what Albert had made possible; what Zygmunt August with another mistake had confirmed; what the Great Elector had emancipated; and what Frederick III (I) had crowned. All that remained to be done was to unite the two parts of the "New Germany" and it fell to Frederick II, and that is probably why he is called "Great." What is the true nature of his accomplishment?

The stages should be clarified by their background which shows Brandenburg's acquisitions in the Thirty Years War, and explains how, after 1701 for the following century and a half, German history was largely dominated by the successful struggle of Prussia for hegemony over Germany in order to unite it, a struggle facilitated after the long Northern War by acquiring the eastern part of Swedish Pomerania (1720) by King Frederick William I, who took advantage of the general European peace to create a unified state and to build up the most efficient army in Europe. It was left for his son, Frederick II (the Great) to test the instrument his father had made; with him, Prussia entered on its career of ruthless conquests, of which Royal Prussia and (Danzig) Pomerania (without Danzig) were the most important (1772). A glance at a map will show why.

Prussia underwent a period of eclipse due to the French Revolution, which was indirectly responsible for the Second and Third Partitions of Poland, in which Prussia took the cradle of Poland, the province of Great Poland, and, in a height of greed, Poland's capital, Warsaw, with Austria taking the entire south of Poland, with Cracow.

Poland was gone, and the bright lights went out in Warsaw, as a Russian poet in love with the city lamented. A race to save Poland did not succeed; it probably could have (the defenders of Warsaw had repulsed both the Russians and the Prussians in its first siege in 1794) but its goals had been met: a virtual revolution in education, and a constitution, without a chance to be tested. A crime had been committed without parallel in history, with punishment for all three perpetrators when it was almost too late. An early punishment was in the making during the Napoleonic Wars, when Poland was partially resurrected (in the form of the Duchy of Warsaw, 1807) out of portions of Prussian Poland, but the Poles were misused (especially in Russia in 1812) with fatal results. A face-saving Congress Kingdom was established out of the Duchy of Warsaw (with the Tsar as King), but Prussia succeeded in getting part of its losses back, as it was regaining its former stance.

Poland was gone, but Germany was never far away, it was *in* Poland, but in the form of Prussia. There is no hatred of Poland such as felt by the Prussians. The treatment of Polish Napoleonic veterans returning from France to Poland in accordance with Napoleon's wishes after the Battle of Waterloo is a good example of inhospitality and hatred. Another example is the treatment of Polish soldiers interned in Prussia after the November 1830-31 war with Russia. On the other hand, there is the enthusiastic reception of veterans and civilians, among them Adam Mickiewicz, who wrote some of his works in Dresden, Saxony. There was also some sympathy for Poland in Germany during the Spring of Nations, but the March Revolution of 1848 was put down by force. An example of the official Prussian attitude toward Poland can be found in Iwo Pogonowski's book:

> As early as 1856, the [future] German Chancellor Otto Bismarck (1815-1898), Berlin's ambassador to the all-German Parliament in Frankfurt, wrote that the Polish minority must be exterminated.

As Prussia was regaining its former stance, there were certain parallels with an earlier period. Just as Frederick the Great's Prussia had entered on a career of ruthless conquest, so did Bismarck's Prussia a hundred years later. In 1861 William I (regent since 1858) became king, and in 1862 he appointed as chancellor Otto von Bismarck, who was to direct the destiny of Prussia and (after 1871) of Germany until 1890. Bismarck effected the elimination of Austria from German affairs and the union of Germany under Prussian hegemony (after a struggle of a century and half) by means of three deliberately planned wars. The first (1864) was fought in alliance with Austria against Denmark over Schleswig-Holstein. Its settlement furnished a pretext for the Austro-Prussian war of 1866, in which Prussia quickly and thoroughly defeated Austria and its allies and gained additional territory by the annexation of Hanover, Hesse-Nassau, Schleswig-Holstein, and the free city of Frankfurt. The German Confederation was dissolved, and the Prussian-led North-German Confederation took its place. Finally, in the Franco-Prussian War (1870-1871) the North German Confederation overwhelmed France (recruits from Great Poland fought well in the Prussian army, having been exhorted by their officers that Emperor Napoleon [III] was *their* enemy), and in 1871 William I of Prussia was proclaimed Emperor of Germany. In its main features the subsequent history of Prussia was that of Germany, just as, in another parallel, the later history of Brandenburg was that of Prussia (when Frederick I became King of Prussia).

Whether it was the rising importance of Prussia or its relatively liberal constitution, the Prussian nobility, which had supported King Casimir in the Thirteen Years War and was receptive to Sobieski's plan of recapturing East Prussia, became the most loyal of Prussia's citizens. As mostly members of the conservative Junker class, sitting in the upper chamber, they held immense tracts of generally poor land east of the Elbe, particularly in East Prussia, under semi-feudal conditions. Endowed with little money and much pride, they formed the backbone of the army. As for the Poles, deriving from neighboring Masovia, they were working the land or owning farms in southern East Prussia.

There was considerable Germanization going on in the formerly Polish provinces of Prussia, often leading to school strikes and some violence. The "Iron Chancellor" as Bismarck was called, wanted nothing less but complete Germanization, but it was all legal, within his *Kulturkampf* which, although directed against the Catholic Church, was also concerned with schools. Excesses were protested by Polish members of the Reichstag and depicted in literary works, which were flourishing in view of the relatively high level of literacy prevailing. Two examples stand out, both by the Positivist poet Maria Konopnicka (1842-1910):

> During the height of Bismarck's "Kulturkampf," Kononicka wrote a hymn-like poem, *Rota*, which is an assertion of the Polishness of the lands under Prussian rule and a readiness to fight to preserve it. Set to music, the song has power and majesty (literally, since Konopnicka speaks of the "Royal Piast tribe" as ancestors) unequaled in the annals of hymnology, except, perhaps, for the American "Battle Hymn of the Republic." Although strictly forbidden, or perhaps because of that, the song almost became the national anthem. But it was another of Konopnicka's poems, the heart-rending "The Prussian is Torturing Polish Children," which proved even more pointedly that the pen is indeed mightier than the sword. Written and set to music in Italy, the poem became another battle hymn, protesting the mistreatment of Polish children in Great Poland on account of school strikes against the forcible Germanization of Polish schools. Translated into European languages, the poem shook the throne of the Kaiser, embarrassing him in front of Europe. For this writer, studying it in school in Upper Silesia in the 1930s, it uncovered the depth of Polish-Prussian enmity and, by extension, the Polish-German problems looming ahead.
>
> (Quoted from *Between The World Wars: The Education of a Polish Schoolboy*, Frank Mocha, 1992.)

The problems passed the test of time but, in the final analysis, Poland was saved by the two world wars (one a continuation of the other) which came just in time to prevent the Germanization (and Russification) of the country if continued and with harsher methods used (like the Russian mass deportations). Both wars have been discussed in various parts of the book in various contexts, and will not be gone into here. Suffice it to say that their end had opened up a possibility of Poland and Germany coming together, not just to coexist, but to cooperate as partners in the new Europe that is still taking shape.

A clear signal for this was a meeting in Gniezno in 1997 of Presidents of East Central European countries, called by the Pope in early celebration of the meeting of King Bolesław the Brave and

Emperor Otto III in the year 1000 in Gniezno, the first capital of Poland. In the millennium that passed since the first meeting there had been other instances of Polish-German cooperation and community of interests, beginning with a German Emperor helping young Casimir Piast to restore Poland; Wit Stwosz, creator of the famous altar in the Cracow *Mariacki* Church; many outstanding German wives and mothers of Polish Piasts; Emperors Charles IV, V, and VI cooperating with Polish Kings; alliances with and final settlement of the German Order of Sword Bearers in Livonia and Courland, a Polish dependency; Princess Izabela Fleming-Czartoryski; a plethora of Polonized German scholars (Brückner, Estreicher, Stieber, and so on); Karl Dedecius and the Deutsches Polen-Institut in Darmstadt; and ending, hopefully, with another Congress in the year 2000.

What can Poland bring into the Polish-German partnership? According to United Nations estimates, and some Polish spokesmen a few years back, "Poland belongs to the demographically most dynamic societies" and that it will account for most of the natural increase in Europe, while Germany, on the basis of reports quoted on this book, is becoming, like it or not, a melting pot with 7.3 million foreigners at the latest count and, according to an article in the May 1998 issue of *Deutschland*, a population likely to decline and the percentage aged over 65 to increase. This has to do with the crisis of Western Civilization affecting Europe, and if the adjective "dynamic" describes Poland correctly (Poland is rumored to be also becoming a melting pot, and it is a purpose of this book to avert it), it could revitalize the ailing continent, starting with Germany, and put an old saying to rest as no longer apt:

> Jak świat światem,
> Nie będzie Niemiec Polakowi bratem.
> As long as the world turns,
> A German will not be a brother to a Pole.

LAST REMARK: In 1947 the Allied Control Council for Germany formally declared Prussia out of existence. This action not only confirmed an accomplished fact; it also was intended against the spirit of German militarism, aggression, and imperialism, of which Prussia, rightly or wrongly, has been held to be the chief instrument for the last two centuries.

THE HISTORY OF NATIONS

HENRY CABOT LODGE, Ph. D., LL. D. · EDITOR-IN-CHIEF

RUSSIA AND POLAND

BY WILLIAM RICHARD MORFILL, M. A.

OXFORD UNIVERSITY

REVISED AND EDITED BY

CHARLES EDMUND FRYER, Ph. D.

INSTRUCTOR IN HISTORY, McGILL UNIVERSITY

VOLUME XV

ILLUSTRATED

P · F · COLLIER & SON

PUBLISHERS ∴ NEW YORK

1907

17

Frank Mocha

POLAND AND RUSSIA—
PAST AND FUTURE

This is a special chapter and, because of it, it is being written from the first person point of view. In the German chapter, despite, or probably because of, my partially German background and a childhood spent in the shadow of Germany while being brought up in a Prussian-type discipline, I tried to maintain a third-person distance in order not to appear more conciliatory than I already was. I spent my early adulthood—the war years—as an adversary and prisoner-of-war of the Wehrmacht, when not a hair fell from my head, and the most frequent command, or request addressed to me from the first days of occupation to when taken prisoner by a young fellow-Silesian Wehrmacht officer and possibly a not-so-distant relative, until quite late in the war (1943, when I finally left German-occupied Europe) was:

"Kom mit uns!"

("Come with us!" or, closer, "Join us!")

Russia was never that close except once, briefly, in 1971.

On the contrary, on a descending line of closeness and significance Russia has always been the most distant in Europe. From the Pyrenees (Spain is not in that line simply because, like India, it is a sub-continent, referred to by geographers as "Little Africa") to the Urals, France looked down on Germany, Germany on Poland, and Poland on Russia. Russia twice succeeded in reversing the direction, but only briefly, both times the sudden ascent was followed shortly by a descent: 1812 and the Congress of Vienna followed by the Decembrist Revolt; Stalingrad and Berlin followed by NATO. On both ends of the line there was almost continuous struggle for primacy: of Western Europe between France and Germany, and of Eastern Europe between Poland and Russia.

Poland's case was a function of the German "Drang nach Osten." Under German pressure, which would have turned Poland into one of the numerous components of the German Empire but for its deterioration, Poland was shifting East where a vacuum opened up after the destruction of the Old Kievan Rus by the Mongols in 1240. With a new Russia rising around Moscow, the territories of the old were taken over first by Lithuania, and then by Poland. After Moscow freed itself from two-centuries of the "Tatar yoke," it began to claim the ancient lands, and a struggle broke out with Poland for their control, and the control of East Europe. The struggle survived the Polish Partitions and re-emerged after World War I with a "decisive" victory by Poland over Russia's successor state, the Soviet Union in 1920, but it ended twenty-five years later, in 1945, with all of Poland under Soviet control. Of the many defining moments of the struggle none is more revealing than the "Time of Troubles" in Russia, which this writer was drawn to by a plaque in the Zagorsk Monastery northeast of Moscow in 1971.

THE ZAGORSK MONASTERY PLAQUE

THE ZAGORSK MONASTERY PLAQUE
Transcribed by Eugene Beshenkovsky, Russian archivist:

Злоключение было от поляков. По злокознен ному коварству Римскаго Папы с Езуитами вымыслив они лже-Димитрия, и под его имекел довели было Россию до края бедствий. Обитель сия ко избавлению всеми образы не токмо спомоществовала, но всех сынов Отечества действия, предприятия, ревкования совершении, духом своим оживляла. И хлебом во время глада снабдевала, многими деньгами нуждам Отечества служила. Даже жертвовала и самими церковными драгоценными утварями. Но и долговременную выдержала осаду и тем северныя страны, а через них и саму Столицу и всю Россию предохранила.

The literal translation is mine:

There was a mishap [misadventure] from the Poles. After a perfidious craftiness [insidiousness] of the Roman Pope with the Jesuits having invented a False Dimitri, and under [in] his name they had brought Russia to the edge [brink] of disaster. This cloister not only helped toward salvation in all ways but revived [revitalized] with its spirit the deeds, the undertakings, the zeal, [and] the accomplishments of all the sons of the fatherland. [It] also provided bread in time of hunger, [and] served the needs of the fatherland with much money. [It] even sacrificed the precious church vessels themselves. But it also sustained a siege of long duration and in this way protected the northern lands and with them the capital itself and all of Russia.

It was only after finishing the translation that I realized I was reading a different plaque from the one I had seen in Zagorsk in 1971. The contents of both are similar, but the differences are important. The plaque I had seen does not mention the Pope and the Jesuits, but refers to Polish and Lithuanian riders (*vsadniki*). Also, to think of it, it was rectangular, not oval, which is how I described it to Prof. Mark von Hagen, Director of the Harriman Institute at Columbia University, when I asked him to get me a photo of it on his trip to Russia, not thinking that I was returning to some defining moments of my own connected with Zagorsk.

At this point, a few digressions are in order to throw some light on the training of Slavic specialists in America, culminating in my case in an American-Soviet exchange, and my experience in both, including Zagorsk.

I had applied to IREX (International Research and Exchanges Board) for an "Exchange of Language Teachers" program when teaching at the University of Pittsburgh and at the same time completing my doctoral dissertation at Columbia (on a Polish-Russian topic), but mainly to round out my knowledge of Russian and of Russia in general. My opinion of Russia had not been much different from the one described earlier and carried out of a Polish school, with Russia a backward country, an opinion reinforced by the stories about the Russian (Soviet) troops entering Poland in 1939, a mob, both in terms of personnel and equipment. This explains easy German victories until American help (massive) and Hitler's mistakes (sacrificing Rommel in North Africa and Paulus in Stalingrad, with colossal losses in men and material) turned the tide in 1943. Except for a look at the border guards in East Poland just before the war, the first time I met Russians was in a prisoner-of-war camp in Austria, victims of the early German victories—a self-destructing isolated mob—totally abandoned by Stalin, including his own son, and all probably perishing there in one of the still unexplained war dramas. Afterwards it was observing them from a distance, heading the gigantic Soviet Union as one of its by-far the largest republics (the other ones also no midgets, with Kazakhstan as large as all of Western Europe, and Ukraine, fattened on parts of Poland, as large as France), and the Warsaw Pact, including Poland.

It was not until 1959, when already married (in England) and settled with my family in America (New York), becoming a citizen (a security factor) that I ventured to visit Poland, armed with an American passport. By then I had already returned to school (after

Sputnik in 1957), to continue my university studies begun in England, and to be of use in the Cold War. It was with this on my mind that for my term paper in an American Literature course I had selected a challenging topic, "American Intervention in the Russian Revolution," finishing it just before my trip and, in order to work on it as a future M.A. essay (my adviser's suggestion), taking it with me. This step proved fateful. In Poland we had the good luck of being there when Nikita Khrushchev was paying an official visit. The night train from Warsaw to Silesia, our destination, contained some of Nikita's relief security detail and was full, with the only compartment fit to accommodate our family group occupied by two Russian colonels. To my and the stationmaster's surprise (this was turning into an international incident), they offered us the compartment (in the name of Soviet-American friendship), saying they would be smoking in the corridor and taking short naps in turns in the one seat next to the door, which was all they asked. When I joined one of them, with a Polish-sounding name, for a smoke, and we talked about America, I told him about my paper; I was amazed at his reaction, when he told me that my paper would be considered anti-Soviet and I should not publish it.

The encounter with the Soviet intelligence officer (because that's what he was) is described in great detail in *One Man's Saga*. Suffice it to say here that what the man objected to was my conclusion that the Russian Revolution was an accident of history brought about by US President Wilson's miscalculation of Russia's true needs, and *not* the historical inevitability which is a credo in the Communist canon. The officer, admitting that he was indeed of Polish descent, advised me to leave political science alone and to concentrate instead on language and literature, if for no other reason than my family in Poland. He had a point; I thanked him and we parted on the best of terms. I had to admit I was impressed by the new type of *homo Sovieticus*.

Back in America, I declared "Polish and Russian Literary Relations" as my area of concentration, and worked on the language while filling gaps in the literature, which I had read widely in excellent Polish translations in the Gymnasium before the war. Professor John Hazard, the then-Editor of the *Slavic Review*, coming out of the Russian Institute of Columbia University, was at first puzzled when I didn't submit my paper, which he had read and praised, for early publication, which would help me make a name for myself and gain an easy admission to the Institute. But I stayed away from that, too, studying instead exclusively in the Department of Slavic Languages and Literatures.

The department was then filling up with young American professors teaching the large classes, booming as a result of the National Defense Education Act passed by Eisenhower after the scare following the launching of the Sputnik. These young professors, attracted by the sudden openings in universities all over the country, were slowly replacing the aging native professors (Manfred Kridl at Columbia, Gleb Struve at Berkeley, Vladimir Nabokov at Cornell) of Polish and Russian (Czech and Serbo-Croatian were also offered, on a smaller scale) and making swift progress on the academic ladder. They would do their servitude by teaching one or two terms of elementary Russian and then move to literature courses which they taught in English, using for reading assignments the many translations that were becoming available. In effect, students were learning Russian (and Polish) in English, and here a problem arose for the few students whose native language was Polish or Russian but who were deficient in English, or were often barred from advanced degrees because of that. A kind of tyranny of English developed with the departure of the native professors, who had been deficient in English, and it was now the native students who were considered deficient and being victimized for it. To redress the situation there was a constant search for native professors of Russian, and that was how Nabokov had become one. At Columbia, a Russian jurist [!] Leon Stilman was imported from Paris, put through a rush doctoral program, becoming in quick succession chairman of the department and was soon creating Columbia's first Ph.D.'s in Russian. He proved to be a great teacher, and his wife Galina a great instructor of advanced Russian and co-author of a text. Both had considerable influence on my progress.

Beside using native speakers for language teaching Columbia would also hire them for literature, but on a per course basis. I was lucky (and unlucky) in both areas. My first luck was enrolling for a course on Pushkin taught by Professor (a courtesy title) Yershow, a cultured Russian émigré from Odessa, probably the most interesting city in Russia, as I was discovering. Yershov's upper class Russian was what I needed after completing the available language sequence. It was Yershow who introduced me to Pushkin in depth after a survey course with Harkins on the "History of Russian Literature." He also, for my sake, included in the course Pushkin's translations of

Mickiewicz, thus pointing me in the right direction in my area of concentration.

A course with another of the native instructors was revealing in different areas. The course, "Soviet Russian Literature," was both interesting and necessary for me, but it was the instructor, Adamowicz, who turned out to be a real mine of information, all of it important. First, I noticed that his Russian was similar to mine by virtue of the so-called "Polish accent" manifesting itself mainly in the pronunciation of hard consonants after the "soft sign." When I pointed it out to him, he told me that like most members of the intelligentsia in his native Minsk, the capital of Belorussia, he spoke Polish, and that there were still strong pro-Polish feelings there which he shared, asking me to keep it to myself. This shed some light on the ancient Polish-Russian struggle in Eastern Europe, expanding my knowledge of the problem. Having by then completed two degrees at Columbia (the first *magna cum laude*, making me a member of the prestigious Phi Beta Kappa fraternity), I was preparing an outline for my Ph.D. dissertation, dealing with a Polish-born writer in Russia at the time of Mickiewicz and Pushkin, Tadeusz Bułharyn (Faddej Bulgarin), stemming from the same general area as Adamowicz, and I asked him to read it for me. What happened next fills me to this day with sorrow, wonder, and doubts about America, its educational institutions and resolve, doubts that would be increasingly strengthened.

Adamowicz read my outline and, familiar with its subject, was highly supportive, but warned me not to make it known in the department until it was in a shape hard to turn down because, in his opinion, the department's young professors were liberal, even pro-Russian, that they were enthusiasts of new criticism and Freud, to the exclusion of history, biography, and even geography. What were they doing in a Slavic department funded to a large extent by the National Defense Education Act? Then I remembered a lecture by Wacław Lednicki, "Tolstoy in War and Peace," except that it was not about Tolstoy's masterpiece, but about the great writer changing his attitude from hostile to sympathetic toward the Poles, based on one short story. One of the young professors felt cheated and took time at his next class to vent his anger and disappointment, going so far as to declare that such a lecture had no room at the university, showing a total ignorance, or disregard, of who Lednicki was, as if he had not been present at Stilman's lengthy and most enthusiastic introduction of him.

Adamowicz who, like Yershov, felt uncomfortable and subdued in the office he was allowed to share in the department, asked me to visit him on Saturday morning when he was free and so was his old father, whom he would like me to meet to continue the conversation in strict privacy. When my wife dropped me off on Saturday morning, there was a crowd of people in front of the house in which he lived on the Upper East Side just below Harlem. Touched by a bad premonition I inquired about the reason for the commotion, and was told that a big black car had arrived earlier, two men had gotten out and entered the house; they had been seen afterwards dragging the Adamowiczes, shoving them into the back of the car and taking off. Had anybody called the police? In the by-now New York tradition, nobody had! Just then a police patrol car pulled up, attracted no doubt by the crowd, and I volunteered to tell the police what had happened. They asked me to follow them to the small apartment upstairs, easy to find because of its open door and signs of a thorough ransacking inside. It was a small two-room apartment with a kitchenette with unwashed breakfast things in the sink. The front room, which also served as an office had papers scattered all over the floor, with one sheet, my outline, overlooked on top of the typewriter. The police kept it, took my address and phone number, told me they felt it was a political kidnapping, and that was the last time the name was mentioned, except when I told the story to Stilman, who refused to do anything about it.

With Stilman and Galina I was lucky *and* unlucky. Lucky, because when he once took over Yershov's class ("Turgenev and Goncharov") before the latter's death and asked for the summary of the second quarter of the 19th century, I astounded him and the class with its brevity:

> "The Decembrist Revolt. End of Alexander I rule.
> The reign of Nicholas I. The Crimean War.
> End of Nicholas I rule."

The statement, in faultless Russian, probably earned me Stilman's support for the National Defense Foreign Language Fellowship which, covering all expenses, including the care of children, permitted me to give up a promising career in printing and advertising, finish all my courses and even audit some, including Stilman's famous Pushkin seminar.

The seminar produced some more revelations, good and bad. It showed the depth of Stilman's knowledge which, despite his recent heart attack (which, incidentally, deprived me of Galina's superior teaching while she tended to Leon), was on full display. Taking cognizance of my presence, he seized on it to broaden the seminar to include Mickiewicz, to shouts of protests of the large but small-minded class. To Stilman's question of who wanted Mickiewicz included, there was only one other student (the brilliant Marina Ledkovsky, once allegedly a fiancée of a Radziwiłł), but that was enough for Stilman, and it became a seminar for me and Marina, and a real education in my chosen specialty, with Stilman arriving with an armful of books to every class, frequently relying on me, as when he asked me if the Andrusovo Treaty border between Russia and Poland was fair.

Next to the opposition to the inclusion of Mickiewicz as additional work, there was one more incident at the seminar when Polish literature was rejected by the supposed "Slavists," who were not even convinced of its merits when Stilman told them that Mickiewicz was the most important Slavic poet. Next, it was Sienkiewicz's turn.

A colonel, on leave from the Army or Pentagon to get a degree at Columbia and insisting on special treatment when there were no grounds for it, like many others of his kind in other universities behaving as if America owed them something even in peacetime, objected to my statement during a break that Sholokhov did not write *The Quiet Don*. He strongly objected to my argument, which Adamowicz had accepted, that there were influences of Sienkiewicz in another of Sholokhov's novels, but not in *The Quiet Don*. He considered it unthinkable that Sholokhov would be influenced by Sienkiewicz, meaning that Sienkiewicz was an inferior writer, to which I replied "If that is what you think then you are not a Slavist and don't belong here."

It was incidents like this that made me doubt the effectiveness of the Slavic programs and the future of the Polish part of them, especially at Columbia, where the man hired to fill Kridl's place was only an Assistant Professor dividing his teaching between Polish literature and 18th century Russian. He knew neither Polish nor Russian well enough to teach in them, yet Stilman claimed the department was lucky to get him, and he would have been right had the qualifications been a little stronger for an Assistant Professor at Columbia, even one filling two spots. Was there perhaps a little Jewish solidarity in it? I rather think not. A budgetary coup is a better answer in view of filling the Russian 18th-Century spot. Polish language continued to be taught by Ludwik Krzyżanowski, and here one can't avoid blaming him for neglecting to take a doctorate like Stilman, when Kridl was still alive to sponsor it.

The new man was a sight to behold when I first met him. Stocky, with a large head, wearing a British Army officer's overcoat, and indulging in a habit of clicking his heels to everybody in sight. But the clicking stopped once he became a tenured Associate Professor, which was rather soon, he had only a few articles published in *The Polish Review*. It was at that time that I took his required 18th-Century Russian literature course, which for me was an extraordinary experience. The first two-hour lecture was an inspired performance, taking everybody by surprise, but there was a cancellation the following week and a repeat of the first lecture the week after that, and from then on a rather limping performance, leaving everybody in the unusually strong class wondering. Things picked up a bit with the mock-heroics and then Derzhavin, when I discovered that he was getting the many allusions solved from an excellent Polish multi-volume textbook, which I also had. I never told him that, afraid that it would embarrass him for not listing the book on the reading list, and spoil my chances to get an "A" from a man who was *ex officio* my adviser. I got a "B+" and the insulting question why wasn't it an "A"?

While the Russian course put me on guard against the by now self-assured man, his Polish courses were worthless, and I didn't learn a single thing from them, which was a pity, because having completed my secondary education in different schools, with different schedules, I never had a continuous sequence of the "History of Polish Literature," in which there were gaps I needed to fill, and had to do it on my own. When the man took too long reading the chapters of my M.A. thesis, I realized he was delaying me on purpose, and I asked one of the new professors, who read the entire thesis in one weekend; all I had to do was to make a few corrections, retype, and hand it in.

There was a nasty clash between us the following summer when Columbia hosted a well-funded National Defense Polish Language program in which I was to be one of the faculty, according to the chairman (Harkins by then, who wanted me to get the experience), but the Polish professor cheated me out of it, when I really needed the money. When I pointed out to him that I had three children, he replied brazenly that children were not the responsibility of the university, to which I retorted that they were everybody's and that I did not want him to continue as my adviser. This was O.K. with Harkins. Also okay were (temporarily) my money troubles when three young Columbia Fulbright scholars going to Poland and needing a crash course in Polish asked me to be their instructor, handing me the Fulbright checks for that purpose and some satisfaction and recognition.

Recognition was what I craved and which, despite being cut off from the NDEA program, I was getting at Columbia. Of the three young scholars one was a no-show, for reasons unknown to me, and I felt badly about accepting his Fulbright check which the other two had pressured him into handing over to me, and I asked them to let him know he could make a separate arrangement with me, at my and his convenience. I was in a good position to accommodate him, as I was fortunate to secure, as an outstanding alumnus of the School of General Studies, a job in its newly opened building, where with flexible hours, I was on duty on its fourth floor, the foreign languages faculty floor, setting up appointments and generally controlling the traffic on it while having much free time for myself, especially at night when I decided to have my meetings with the two remaining Fulbright scholars. My wife made it a habit to send one of our children with a thermos of hot coffee, and that's how my creative coffee hour was born, because I soon discovered that I had two future stars on my hands, and that I was having something to do with their evolution, as one of the resident faculty, observing us at work, pointed out to me.

Of the two, Fran Millard, a brilliant English student, came to Columbia by way of Yale, where she had studied history with Piotr Wandycz and Beginning Polish with the author of a good textbook by that name, Alexander Schenker, whom she praised highly making me want to try harder to help her. She returned from Poland fluent in Polish and ready for a doctorate in history and Certificate in the newly established Institute on East Central Europe.

Stanley Blejwas, the other student, was not so lucky with his language background. From a Polish American family, which I was pleased to find out, he had studied Polish with Ludwik Krzyżanowski and was bitter about the experience. That's when I was sorry to learn that Ludwik was not a good language teacher, which was regrettable on account of the NDEA program which, if I were allowed to team up with him for its second part (the first belonged to Harold who supplied an assistant, a woman friend, for both) would have helped.

Stanley did not return fluent in Polish, like Fran, but he was admirably determined, and he took some more Polish with me, this time with his wife and in my apartment during the day. Later he was director for the Kosciuszko Foundation of a student group in Poland, and had more exposure to the language. Today he is fluent, and he is the founder and head of an endowed Polish Studies program at the University of Connecticut, New Britain. At some point he confided in Radzialowski that I was the best Polish language teacher he ever had, and Tad, who was then resident at the NEH, placed the statement in its file.

Further recognition came when Professor Joseph Rothschild, Political Science at Columbia, former student of Polish in Ludwik Krzyżanowski's classes, asked me to give him a refresher course before his own research trip to Poland as a Fulbright scholar.

But the best and most revealing recognition came when Ludwik asked Harold to fill in for him in his second year Polish class. Inexplicably, Harold asked me to do it, for reasons which became clear to me the moment I faced the class. This was no ordinary class, but a teacher's dream that doesn't come often in his work. About a dozen strong, consisting mainly of doctoral candidates in history, political science, and literature, my wife completing the second year of her foreign language requirement among them, surprised, with all eyes turning in her direction with smiles as I entered, it was a class the memory of which I was to cherish for a long time. Without a scrap of paper or a book with me, with little bows to a few acquaintances, I first gave them a talk about Polish as a Western Slavic language, about the nature of its difficulties, and then proceeded to isolate the difficulties, remove or reduce them, or simply put them in their place, while filling the blackboards with little tables and graphs explaining, for example, the complicated but capable of being made simple, relationship between direction and location in Polish, finishing with the most frequent mistakes, in using numbers (citing an iron-clad rule) and words for teaching and learning, all the time making brief pauses to check whether the class comprehended and kept up with me. When I finished, thanking the class for attention, which was rapt, there was loud applause (with my wife blushing) and then Ira Mendelsohn, whom I knew as a tennis player at Riverside Park courts, soon to get his doctorate and depart to teach in Israel, stood up and made a statement which I count among those I remember and treasure for ever:

"Why don't *you* teach Polish at Columbia?"

Years later I met Professor Mendelsohn when on a Sunday morning, having arrived from Israel for that purpose, he was chairing a Jewish conference on the top floor of the International Affairs building at Columbia University. He stopped when I arrived, a little late, gave a wave of recognition and pointed me to an empty chair right in front of the rostrum. After the extremely interesting program we reminisced, about his fine statement, which he remembered, too, and about Polish-Jewish relations, which we both agreed left much to be desired. I told him I had many ideas on the subject, and suggested he should invite me to Israel to discuss them, bringing my Jewish grandchildren with me.

Mendelsohn's statement voiced what I was dreaming about and aiming at, and the possibilities were seemingly limitless. Not taking advantage of them was the deliberate fault of the person in charge of the Polish program, who instead of making it a stronghold of Polish culture in America, had turned it into a secure little personal preserve. I was determined to change that perception.

Not long after the Mendelsohn class, which was the last great Polish class at Columbia, I came across another one only slightly less significant when Ludwik Krzyżanowski asked me to administer the final examination in his first-year course. Putting the students in an office next to my control desk, I noticed that there were among them several younger than the usual graduate or adult evening students. They also finished the examination quicker than the rest and came out to hand them in. Out of curiosity I asked them what they were studying. They replied that they were first-year students at Columbia College. I invited them in, treated them to my coffee, and we had a chat.

I asked them if they were aware of what a fine college they were in? They were. Why were they taking Polish? They came from Polish American families, mostly from Long Island, and there were about twenty of them who kept in touch by sharing a table in the cafeteria. Why then so few in the class? The others had listened to an adviser who told them Polish was not on par with the Core Curriculum. This was the man who a few years later, after Ludwik was gone, advised my son Paul to take Polish. Would the others register for Polish if the level improved? All of them, and maybe more. I asked them to keep that in mind at the Polish table where I would visit them soon.

The next evening I stopped in Ludwik's class when he was giving the final examination in his second-year Polish. To my chagrin, there were only three students (a fourth one was absent.) I noticed how abusive he was with them, especially one, a giant postal clerk, whom Ludwik made look like a fool. But he finished the exam first; I asked him out for a smoke and apologized for Krzyzanowski's treatment. He said he didn't learn much in the classes, and would gladly repeat them (the New York Post Office was apparently paying his tuition) if someone else was teaching and then, like an echo, he repeated Mendelsohn's statement:

"Why don't *you* teach Polish at Columbia?"

Ludwik, just then leaving the classroom with the other two students, heard the postal clerk's exclamation, but took it well. After bidding the students good night, I handed L.K. the exams from his first-year Polish and offered to walk him along his usual route, down Morningside Drive, past my 115th Street to the No. 4 bus stop on 110th Street. We talked as we walked. I told him about the Polish American students in the College and the potential they promised. He agreed, adding that like the superior Mendelsohn class (it was this quality that had stopped Harold from visiting the class, Ludwik suspected), the College students needed someone like me, who would give them proper attention, which he was unable to, occupied full-time with *The Polish Review*. I said that with twenty Columbia College students registering for Polish, there could be a beginning class of 30 students, out of whom with normal attrition at least half a dozen would reach third-year advanced level, with one or two declaring a major in Polish to start with, all this adding up to a full-time job in Polish for someone. The prospect excited him, and he urged me to think of myself in this role, promising that at his retirement at Columbia in 1971 he would strongly recommend me to take his place, and build on it. He would do it not just for the good of Polish at Columbia, but also for the sake of the Polish Institute, which he wanted me to join the moment I received my doctorate, and *The Polish Review*, for which I was already writing the "Chronicle of Events," and would, he was hoping, take up other responsibilities.

For me, this frank and honest conversation with a respectable person opened up a window of opportunity, but it also put my area of specialization in scholarly research in the desired perspective, just as I had spelled it out: "Polish-Russian Literary Relations," with Polish first and Russian second.

But this was not to be. The number of students taking Polish was decreasing under Krzyżanowski's routine teaching, with only the few doctoral candidates who had selected it as their minor Slavic language taking it, and Harold not making any efforts to attract the Columbia College students, perhaps even starting them off himself in a beginning course separate from Ludwik's course, which would make sense and, in addition, all told, Harold was good at beginnings. But why should he when he could offer a variety of "graduate" Polish literature courses (survey, the Novel, the Romantic Drama) to two or three students, courses as routine as Ludwik's language courses, and as detrimental to the future of the Polish program, while spending the free time on awful translations of Fredro's comedies and a controversial concoction (suspicion of plagiarism) of Russian 18th century literature, all this time Polish sliding to minor status not only in name but in contents? This worried me, making my chances grow less, while preparing for my orals and having serious problems making the family's financial ends meet, with no Fulbright scholars on the horizon augmenting my income, and the once productive General Studies job losing its worth with its chief benefit of tuition exemption no longer a factor.

I needed a teaching position, and Harold, for his own reasons, kept urging me to seek one, but I wasn't going to accept anything which did not include Polish, and because of that I bypassed an opening at St. John's in Queens, and another one at Lawrence in the Midwest, both excellent schools, except that I didn't know it at that time. Just as I was beginning to think of returning to the printing and advertising industry, which was booming then, promising to make me some real money while putting academia on a back burner, what looked like a real academic opportunity came along from the University of Pittsburgh, where Polish, as at Columbia, was part of the appointment.

I liked hilly Pittsburgh when I came for an interview, and I could see myself living and working there. The town's rich ethnicity (mostly Polish and Slovak) and robust athleticism (football, baseball, hockey), the Frick and Mellon mansions, two great rivers joining to produce the mighty Ohio, all this was very inviting. The university itself, the imposing Cathedral of Learning with its famous National-ity Rooms around the marble ground floor with its confessionals, was at that time passing through financial problems resulting in state-related status, but I was more concerned with the problems of the Slavic Department, which were likely to turn into more bad luck for me. This time it was a Polish Ukrainian who was the problem, having become acting chairman when the regular chairman, Charles Bidwell, a fine linguist and a World War II veteran with whom, because of that, I was expecting to have a good rapport, became ill with leukemia just before my scheduled interview. The acting chairman gave me only a one-year "visiting instructor" appointment with the excuse that it was all he could do in view of Bidwell's illness. I accepted it only because I believed that Bidwell, who struck me as a valiant man, would recover. Also, there was another valiant man in the university, Carl Beck, who was director of a similar institute as Columbia's but with a stress on Communism; and a great fundraiser, who urged me to accept the imperfect appointment until the completion of the doctorate, by which time he would have plans for me.

Back in New York I immediately sat for my orals, and here the not totally unexpected happened. Having passed linguistics with flying colors and Russian literature adequately, I became involved in an argument with Harold about the real ending of Zeromski's *Ashes* which Harold was apparently ignorant of. William Harkins, the chairman, sided loyally though reluctantly with Harold, declaring that I should repeat that part of the examination, letting the department know when I would be in New York next.

Harold's risky argument was part of a pattern of consistent belittling me, triggered probably by an incident in his survey course when, announcing a new period with the name of a king in Polish, WŁADYSŁAW IV, he had not used the ordinal numeral but the cardinal, a bad mistake. He noticed the shocked glance of my neighbor, and likely heard him say:

"Why don't *you* teach Polish literature at Columbia?"

There was a purpose to Harold's hostility. He never tired of telling me how the aging prominents in Polish literature (Folejewski, Giergielewicz) were accepting him (typical Polish kowtowing to foreigners, but Weintraub considered him his "biggest mistake"), hinting outrageously that he would succeed them, but he knew that he could not fool me. In my rising stature despite a lack as yet of an academic position he saw a threat to his imagined future primacy, hence he would go to great length to show off his alleged fluency in Polish (it was his mother who was fluent), in Russian (repeating ad nauseam "Ya govoriu po russki"—"I speak Russian," a standard sentence known to everybody), and piling up, and boasting about, what turned out to be worthless translations. Even the object of his pride, the article on Jeremiah Curtin, Sienkiewicz's first American translator, is full of holes. One cannot but wonder at the man's chutzpah in not just undertaking translations from Polish but in teaming up with a woman of big street-smarts but small language culture. Teaming up with me, a proven though reluctant translator, would have resulted in no mistakes and probably a prize, instead of the 145(?) by Giergielewicz's count in Fredro's *Zemsta* alone, including such beauties as the renditions of "karabela" and "mara." This is not to denounce the man, it's a free country, but to make a statement about the Poles, whom he once called the biggest anti-Semites, but who nevertheless lionize him, even making him a trustee of the Kosciuszko Foundation!

But why am I writing about it in a chapter on Poland and Russia? Because it was happening after my visit to Poland where I saw the Russian presence and made an important decision to stick with language and literature and within these limits to concentrate on Polish-Russian literary relations, expanding it to include history in order to arrive at its last chapter, taking place now. To what extent will Poland need Polonia's help to stand on its own strong feet is the purpose of the book, and everything I do is subject to it. A strong Polish presence at a good university with necessary mechanisms and a strong student body was an important factor in such an under-taking.

My acceptance of the Pittsburgh appointment should have suited Harold, yet he continued hurting me (annoyed, I once threatened to take him behind the proverbial barn). The Polish examination mishap became known in my department in Pittsburgh, relayed by Harold's female teammate to her friend who was a member of my department's faculty. These are methods that are foreign to me, but it wasn't the first or the last time that I was the target, of Poles, Jews, Ukrainians, Russians, and even a Serb and a Hispanic woman. I don't care about the foreigners even if they are American now (America has always been a refuge of the refuse), but the Poles worry me, in Poland and in America. How can Poles in America help Poles in Poland, whom they consider soiled by Communism, when they are no better themselves, worse in some respects because they are full of capitalist vices? The result is an erosion of traditional Polish values which has already been touched on in this book and will be further discussed in this chapter, the last in the book.

I arrived in Pittsburgh well equipped with books. I brought with me Stilman's excellent historical report, written after his famous trip to the Soviet Union and to be used as a companion reader in advanced language classes. It included the early, Kievan period, with good maps and enough information I needed to get started on Russian history, in Russian. I had used it in my own reports on Russian history in Dmitri Grigorieff's and Galina Stilman's language classes, intermediate and advanced, respectively.

Among the books I brought was a remarkable volume, *Russia* * *Poland*, the 15th and last of *THE HISTORY OF NATIONS*, a collective work edited by Henry Cabot Lodge, Ph.D., LL.D., published by P.F. Collier & Son, New York, and contributed to by numerous associate editors and authors, including William Richard Morfill, M.A., Professor of Russian and other Slavonic Languages, Oxford University, author of Volume 15. The remarkable thing about that volume is its title and date, 1907, which means that as late as 1907 Poland, out of existence for over a century, was still discussed on the same level as Russia, in a joint volume. And even though the Preface by Charles Edmund Fryer, Ph.D., Harvard University, states that "the discussion of Poland is intended to be more or less supplemental," the fact remains that because Poland's history is very much a part of the history of Russia, and was remembered as such, it is discussed with amazing detail on the same level with it, in the same volume, and justifiably so, permitting us to draw certain conclusions and engage in some productive and rewarding speculations strengthening Poland's case.

The Scotsman Patrick Gordon, for many years in the service of Tsar Peter as a trusted adviser and friend, wrote in his diary quoted in the volume that:

> "Russia must either disappear from among European
> nations or adopt western ideas" [still true today]

telling us that Peter was doing precisely that and succeeding by traveling and learning in Western Europe, bringing foreigners into the Russian service, and sending young men to study abroad (like Boris Godunov before him). But Gordon died too early (1699) to see how uncertain Russia's situation was despite Peter's successes in modernizing it and a great victory over the young Swedish warrior-king Charles XII in 1709 at Poltava, "a battle which has always been reckoned one of the decisive battles of the world," with Russia assuming the place of Sweden as the leading power of northern Europe. Yet, just a year later, in the middle of the long Northern War, Peter was trapped in Moldavia in the disastrous Pruth expedition in the war with Turkey, and had he not talked himself out of it with the help of his second wife, the resourceful Martha Skawron-skaya [Skowrońska, Polish?], and had the Turks not consented to allow him to escape from his dilemma, the great victory of Poltava would have been just another battle, with Peter agreeing to return all his conquests and not to interfere in the internal affairs of Poland. The consequences of such a reversal are not hard to imagine.

Warned of Russia's potential by the example of the Poltava victory, the three erstwhile adversaries, Sweden, Turkey and Poland would form an alliance, actually just confirm it, since the former two were already acting for the benefit of the latter, with Sweden's Charles having forced August II, the Saxon King of Poland and Peter's ally to abdicate and make room for the reform-minded Stanisław Leszczyński, with Peter having to agree to it, and Turkey making him agree further not to interfere in Poland's internal affairs. The alliance would form a barrier along a continuous border with Russia running from the Arctic Ocean down to the Black Sea (a barrier similar to but much more formidable than the one against the Bolshevik Soviet Union two centuries later), with Poland, the centerpiece of the barrier, its biggest beneficiary. Poland's decline would be halted and reversed under an enlightened king, and so would its inactivity, starting with renewing the Franco-Polish alliance, directed once against Brandenburg but abandoned by Sobieski, to be directed now against Prussia plotting a partition of Poland, and joined by Sweden, which would regain the power status it was losing to Russia. Isolated behind the formidable barrier, Russia would suffer what Gordon feared for her, but what conservative circles and the clergy, opposed to Western ideas, wanted, the old ways. But the biggest beneficiary of the reversal would be Europe and not because of Russia's disappearance from the European family of nations, but Prussia's, and here again Poland would be the biggest beneficiary.

Another important book I brought with me from New York would be useful to me in more ways than one. DeBray's *Slavic Civilizations*, not much in use today because of the shortage of real

Slavists in favor of narrow specialists, was much sought then. Because it contained sections on all the Slavic nations, large and small, it would give me an idea how Poland and Russia fit in the mosaic (about equal). In practical terms it would be the basic text for a course on Slavic civilization I was designing in view of the rich ethnicity of Pittsburgh. Other than that I brought enough materials for the three courses I was going to teach in the first term: a three-volume set of Pushkin for a course I was to teach in Russian (the Ukrainian Acting Chairman was making sure I would have no time for my dissertation after spending it on preparation for the course three times a week); three of the four big novels of Dostoyevsky in the still good English translation by Constance Garnett, plus *The Notes From the Underground*, for a course on Dostoyevsky; 12 copies (a good guess) of Patkaniowska's *Beginning Polish* (no Schenker yet until I determined the level of the class) which was a mistake because in the first class I discovered that the book had in the back the translations of each lesson's exercises, and there was no honor code at Pitt.

Other than that I brought a copy of Mirsky's *History of Russian Literature*, Kridl's *History of Polish Literature*, and all the notes I had made so far in connection with my doctoral dissertation. I arrived at the Cathedral of Learning straight from the bus station and the secretary, a Russian Jewish lady fluent in Polish and Russian, greeted me and told me that my Dostoyevsky class was waiting for me.

I took the elevator from the 4th to the 12th floor and started walking down a hall until I reached the proper room, glanced in and, without losing a beat, kept walking toward a water fountain I noticed at the end of the hall. What I had just seen took my breath away and made my mouth dry: a mid-sized classroom filled to capacity, with some students standing or sitting on the windowsill. This was a twice a week class (Tuesday and Thursday) of one hour 15 minutes each. I was drinking water and thinking, how am I going to keep a class of that size interested for over one hour? I had expected a much smaller class, which I would have taken either to my office or the cafeteria for an informal first meeting, but this crowd? Luckily, I had a class roster which the secretary had given me and a dozen copies of my reading list. I started toward my classroom, noticed an empty one on my way, entered mine, said "Good Morning!" receiving an uneven reply, looked the class over, noticing that it was evenly divided between men and women, congratulated myself for having such a

fine class and the class for having me! Then I asked those without
chairs to go and get them next door, and a volunteer to go to the
office and make forty xerox copies of the reading list and get about
fifty small (3X4) lined index cards. While waiting I turned to the
blackboard, wrote my name on it preceded by a "Mr." (form of
address) and invited questions.

Immediately a hand shot up and a lovely young lady in her early
twenties got up from her chair over which a luxurious fur coat was
draped and asked aggressively:

> Why are you teaching the most prestigious course
> in the university without having a doctorate?

I told her the course was assigned to me by the department probably
because my application showed that I had studied Dostoyevsky at
Columbia with one of the finest specialists on him in the United
States. That made sense to her. At that moment the volunteer arrived
with the materials and I asked him to distribute a copy of each to
everybody. On the index cards I wanted name, address and telephone
number (optional) on top, and beneath, literature courses taken,
including Russian, and knowledge of foreign languages, including
Russian. The index cards filled, I had them collected, then turned to
the reading list. I told them they could read about Dostoyevsky if
they wanted to, but they didn't have to, all they needed to know
about him would be written by me on the blackboard over the span
of the course. What they had to read was two of the three novels (the
fourth, *The Possessed*, was omitted as too political). My personal
choices were *Crime and Punishment* and *Brothers Karamazov*, but
The Idiot was acceptable, too. As for *The Notes From the Underground* they could consider the book supplementary. There would be
a paper to write and final examination, but no midterm. I would
keep office hours immediately after both meetings, starting that day,
so if anybody had any questions or problems, please remain behind
after class and we will address them immediately. By then the class
period ended. There were some applause before the students
dispersed, while a few remained behind.

When I reached the office the secretary told me excitedly that
several students had stopped by on their way from class and spoken
enthusiastically about the course. She handed me a key to a spacious
office two doors down the hall and next door to the university's
ROTC office, which I immediately visited, introduced myself to its

occupants, a Colonel, a Lieutenant Colonel, and a Captain, fine officers who were pleased to hear that like the two senior ones, I too was a World War II veteran. They offered me a cup of coffee, adding that the coffee pot was on all day and I would be welcome to help myself to a fresh cup any time I felt like it. This was good news saving me the effort of going down to the cafeteria every time I wanted a cup of coffee, which in my case was very often. We talked about NATO and the Warsaw Pact and I told them about my trip to Poland in 1959, about the Soviet intelligence officers, and about the generally improved appearance of the Soviet uniformed men, which they were very interested to hear. They asked me if I would like to travel with them when they were taking their cadets to visit military bases by plane. The invitation came from Colonel Watkins and I accepted.

     I rewarded myself for a busy morning with lunch in the Faculty Lounge on the 14th floor. When I stopped on my way at the reception desk to pay for the buffet lunch which included a hot dish ($1.50) I noticed that on the plate for the money there were several silver dollars, which guests were apparently paying with. I asked the hostess, a black American lady, whether I could buy the silver coins from her, and when she agreed, I immediately bought the few she had, considering it, in view of my passion for coins, a bonus, like the coffee before. A third bonus on my first day awaited me when, having filled my plate, I took a seat at a table by the window and discovered that I was sitting above the Pittsburgh Pirates Baseball Club's stadium, Forbes Field, and that an afternoon game was about to begin. Not really a baseball fan, I nevertheless enjoyed watching the game when there was nothing better to do, and watching it while having lunch was a real treat, like having a ringside seat at a boxing match, especially when watching someone like Bill Mazeroski at bat. I felt that living and working in Pittsburgh was not going to be a hardship, except for the separation from the family, but weekend bus trips to New York would help in that respect.

     In the afternoon there was a departmental meeting presided over by the Dean of Humanities, Walter Evert, a gregarious man who greeted me effusively congratulating me on the Dostoyevsky course which nobody dropped after the first meeting and students were still signing up for; he inquired about the status of my dissertation whose completion would result in a promotion and removal of the "visiting" label. Before leaving, he urged us to make do without Bidwell who was recuperating at home after a hospital stay, and wished us a good semester. I was at last able to get to know my colleagues, a Russian Professor of Literature (the friend of Harold's friend), a Ukrainian Professor of Linguistics (the acting chairman), and a part-time instructor from Chatham College, a sincere young Slavic woman who wanted to sit in on my Dostoyevsky course.

My general impression of the department was on the whole good. There were two native speakers-graduate students teaching Russian, another teaching Serbo-Croat, and the Polish was certainly in good hands. But there was the hint of a feud between the Ukrainian and Bidwell, two full professors of Slavic Linguistics, too much for a small department that didn't even have a Pushkinist, a specialty that the Ukrainian seemed to be pushing me into, but why? I understood why when he told me about my predecessors whom he apparently had been also pushing into Russian courses.

Incomprehensibly, there had been three of them in the past few years: Tadeusz Gasinski, Edward Czerwinski, and Magnus Krynski. I know very little about the first two in Pittsburgh, except that Gasinski's baby (he was married) died there of pillow suffocation, which was probably the cause of his leaving and blazing a trail of teaching jobs in Alaska, Hawaii and, finally, South Africa; Czerwinski ended up in Stony Brook, Long Island. As for Krynski, the Ukrainian told me that Krynski had promised him to let him teach Polish Literature. I laughed when I heard that, but cried when I saw through the scheme. The Ukrainian was a graduate of a pre-war Polish Gymnasium (a good one, judging by his still considerable grasp of Latin) yet he couldn't tell the difference between Mickiewicz's "Lilije" and Słowacki's "Lilla Weneda," but as a tenured professor he could teach anything he wanted in the depart-ment as long as someone showed the need for it, and that would have been Krynski's role. The Ukrainian would have killed two birds with one stone: the Poles would have fallen on their face in the Russian courses, while Polish, just as at Columbia, would not have amounted to anything except to provide a job for a superfluous linguist. Was that why Krynski had left, not to be a party to the scheme once he perceived it?

It is no wonder that upon realizing it, I put my future in Pittsburgh in the hands of Bidwell (and Beck). But Bidwell died soon (and, symbolically, the departmental secretary, who looked after me so well), a death that I genuinely lamented not just for professional reasons, but because he was one of us—the World War II veterans (later Prof. Treadgold, editing my article for *The Slavic Review*, recalled Bidwell as his World War II comrade-at-arms), but there was no gain for the Ukrainian (except that he was now securely the sole linguist in the department), because a new chairman was appointed, a Russian nationalist with whom, however, I had an excellent rapport at first, as a result of which he secured for me a promotion to Assistant Professor (a rarity before the doctorate, but still leaving the "visiting" label), and a substantial raise in pay. Most importantly, immediately upon arrival, he asked me to introduce a second Polish language course, taking away the Pushkin, probably a calculated move, but highly acceptable to me for several reasons: frustrating the Ukrainian's wily scheme; letting me unload a course taking too much of my time (despite my fondness of Pushkin); getting deeper into Polish which, from the first day, with the first class of exactly twelve students, half graduate, half community, was becoming a success to be nurtured in Pittsburgh.

My Dostoyevsky course was also sacrificed, probably a calculated move too on the part of the new chairman, but again, acceptable to me, and understandable. After all, he had brought two faculty members with him, and several graduate students, and they all needed jobs. As for me, I had a replacement course ready, which was to become my star course, *Slavic Civilizations.*

Pittsburgh at last had the makings of a strong Department of Slavic Languages and Literatures, in which Russian would dominate, but not to the submersion of the others, which were in evidence in the new course as a beginning, with more to come, particularly in Polish.

Simultaneously with my arrival, Polish received a strong shot in the arm because of an important anniversary in 1966: THE MILLENNIUM OF CHRISTIANITY, celebrated in a big way in Pittsburgh, including the university. The centerpiece of the celebration was the opening of a new wing, the MARIE CURIE SKLODOWSKA wing, in the University's Science Building. The ceremony, which coincided with my afternoon class, was to be performed by Cardinal Karol Wojtyła, who was visiting America at that time. There was to be a meeting with Pittsburgh Polonia afterwards in the Webster Hotel under the aegis of a Polish cultural club, the Polish Arts League, with which I had established contact earlier. I told the Arts League people that I would come to the meeting after my class and bring the Cardinal a gift. I came and handed him a copy of the just published *Register of Polish Scholars in the U.S.*, which contains 2,000 names. The Cardinal accepted the gift with gratitude and a simple expression, "That's what I wanted!" greeting me with equal simplicity: *The Polish Professor.*

"The Polish Professor" was becoming a household word in Pittsburgh. Playing tennis on the university's courts with his students, including the department's new secretary and her husband, a brilliant biology scientist of Nobel Prize potential; playing touch football on Sunday mornings before breakfast with young executives in a parking lot opposite a local drugstore while waiting for the arrival of the Sunday *New York Times*; swimming with teenage swimmers practicing before the 1968 Mexico City Olympic Games; involving his students in the activities of the Polish Arts League, including naming winners for its prizes (the Kosciuszko Foundation's Polish-English and English-Polish Dictionary) for the best of them (in 1968 an Israeli student Tova "Tosia" Wild, escorted by her husband, an Israeli Army Lieutenant); and every evening late into the night typing in his office, with a coffee break the courtesy of a black Polish-speaking (from "Polish Hill") foreman in love with the ceremonial swords in the ROTC office and called, because of that, "Czarniecki" in a cruel pun ("czarny" means "black") by the Poles in his crew and using the name, finally succumbing to the temptation and "borrowing" the swords carrying them out in his trouser legs, only to be stopped by the guard when one of the swords slipped to the marble floor, and losing his job despite a great defense by the Colonel and the Professor.

Every day the graduate students and the secretary would peek at the current page number in the typewriter and comment on the rapid progress made on the first draft of the dissertation made possible in large measure due to the presence in the department of the legendary Elizabeth Hill, a perfectly bilingual Mellon grantee from Cambridge University, where she had, among other things, trained the entire British diplomatic service in Russian, and was now eagerly aiding me with supervising and evaluating our department's teaching fellows, and with difficult problems of Russian history, with special attention to the Time of Troubles and the marriage of False Dimitri and Marina.

All this activity came to a sudden halt in the middle of 1968 when student protests in connection with the controversial war in Vietnam exceeded "the allowable limits of civil disobedience" (Telford Taylor) especially at Columbia University where they seriously disrupted not only the university but also the immediate neighborhood. Concerned about my family, particularly the safety of my wife, a Columbia employee, I left Pittsburgh immediately after the Spring semester to find Columbia in total disarray and chaos. Afraid for its future I called my chairman in Pittsburgh to ask whether, in view of the uncertain situation, I could finish my dissertation there. His negative reply left me no choice but to wait for some solution of the impasse at Columbia, while availing myself to help my Alma Mater. The solution arrived soon, with New York police intervention, entering student-occupied Hamilton Hall through underground passages and attacking the protesters from within (getting even for the spitting and verbal abuses endured), which shocked some people.

Amid the chaos and fright, there were some light moments. In one, the construction workers finishing work on the International Affairs Building hanged out during the lunch break a white sheet with the following inscription in bright red: "Try to take **THIS** building!" One look at these beefy men munching on huge hero sandwiches and washing them down with cans of beer was enough to make the would-be occupiers change their minds. In another, Professor Zbigniew Brzezinski came out of his already functioning office of Communist Affairs to answer the protesters' questions. When none were forthcoming, he turned to them and said sarcastically: "Since there are no questions, let me go and plan some more genocide."

With the "uprising" over and students being taken by ambulances to St. Luke's Hospital amidst shouts of "Beasts!" at the police, I was able to turn to my academic priorities. Having already cleared the Polish examination, I settled with the department the important matter of my dissertation sponsor by having the good luck of being assigned to Professor Robert Belknap, a neighbor on 115th Street and, like me, a family man. I gave him all the pages I had typed so far and was told to check with him in two weeks. Then I went to Butler Library to see the Slavic Bibliographer, Anna Stuliglowa, a former fellow-student, and discuss the problem of getting a few still needed sources.

I was surprised to see Anna as a bibliographer, an important position but not what I had thought she wanted. We both had taken a Polish literature course with Harold (Romantic Drama) and I remember her correcting him gently when he tried to apply Hegel's dialectical logic, based on the triad of THESIS, ANTITHESIS and SYNTHESIS, to a work at hand to which it did not apply. Harold ignored it lightly, but knowing him I was sure that he wouldn't forget and forgive. Was that the reason that Anna ended up in Library School instead of a Ph.D. program in Polish where I would have liked to see her? A daughter of a Polish World War II officer, a graduate of Barnard, with native fluency in Polish and functional knowledge of Russian and probably also French, at home with Hegel, she was a perfect doctoral candidate, but it was also good to have someone like her as Slavic Bibliographer at Columbia. She would soon be leaving for Cornell, and would be hard to replace, but before that happened she would take care of everything I needed.

First she put me in touch with Sergei Jacobson (Roman's brother), the Slavic Librarian at the Library of Congress in Washington, who informed me that any Russian books and periodicals up to 1917, not available in America, were in the Helsinki Library which, as one of the deposit libraries in the Russian Empire, of which Finland had been a part since Peter the Great, used to get a copy of every publication in Russia. Because of deterioration of the huge collection, a Swiss firm had microfilmed it, and copies could be ordered from it. He gave me the address and a confirmation that the two periodicals I was interested in, published by F. Bulgarin, the subject of my dissertation, were among the microfilmed materials and could be ordered. I immediately phoned the information to Carl Beck at Pitt, who promised that his Institute would order the two items right away, to be shipped express to my New York address, as well as pay for my research at Yale Library, where there was another old source deteriorating (as reported by a former classmate doing summer research at Yale), to be read before it was taken out in preparation for microfilming. To make it official, Carl asked me to send him a formal application before the end of the current fiscal year. I did that, writing also to my chairman, asking him to order a portable microfilm reader, just on the market, a Polish typewriter, and a demographic German map of Europe, showing the extent of pre-World War I German colonization, including the outline of the Jewish Pale of Settlement in Russia, and I included a page from the firm.

This was not all. Anna had discovered that there were already two dissertations on Bulgarin, both completed in 1966, one at Harvard and one in Berkeley, which could be obtained on Inter-Library loan, and that there was, in the library of the University of Wisconsin, the only copy in America of a key source in my research, Bulgarin's four-volume historical novel, *Dimitrij Samozvanec*, and she ordered it for me on Inter-Library loan, to be read in the library. The book arrived almost overnight and, until the Belknap date, I spent my days in the library reading it and finding it incredible, but invaluable for my research.

By the time of my appointment with Belknap, the microfilms had already arrived from Switzerland, and I had something to show him as well as tell him about my other successes with Anna Stuliglowa, adding up to all my sources being in place. It was just as well because for a moment I had the uneasy feeling that I was being cross-examined by two young assistant professors (there was a colleague with Belknap) about my ability to write a dissertation (these were the American "New Critics" talking), until I exploded saying in not so many words that my concern was whether there was anybody in the department (except the by then inactive Stilman), knowledgeable enough about Russia and Poland to sponsor it, that all I really needed was a cooperating adviser. That did it, and after the other man departed, Belknap and I reached a very productive agreement consisting of honest cooperation and iron-clad schedules.

He liked the draft and was pleased with the new materials which would fill the gaps left in the text. As they were being filled, I would start typing a new draft, and as each chapter was completed, in line with the agreed upon table of contents, I would bring it in on my periodic trips to New York, leaving it in the office upon arrival on Friday morning and picking it up Monday afternoon, allowing for an hour's conference. This sounded very efficient, and was adhered to faithfully, except somehow the title had changed from "Making It" to "A Study in Literary Maneuver," no doubt the influence of the other man, overlooked.

The completion of all my arrangements coincided with the end of the childrens' school year, and we all needed a vacation. A friend of my wife's at work was renting a secluded farm in Bucks County near the Delaware River and asked us to visit on the nearest Saturday. Just in case, we loaded our old station wagon with extra clothing and sports equipment and had a pleasant drive to Frenchtown, bypassing Princeton, and then climbing up along a country road, suffering a flat tire on the way, taking a dip in a pond on the way to cool off, and arriving at the farm in early afternoon, just in time for a picnic on the grass. It was a lovely place, but perhaps too isolated for the friend, and she decided to pass on the second week, inviting us to use it up, while she would leave with her visitors, confirmed city dwellers like her. After they left, while Doreen was looking the place over and cleaning, as was her habit to do at all new places, with just Jane keeping her company, I took the boys on a sightseeing tour, starting with the pond, which was water from a little stream casually dammed to form a little pool. We strengthened the dam by piling some flat rocks laying around and saw the pond rising and growing longer. Next to the pond was a flat meadow and on it a section of concrete pipe, which made me immediately guess that the flat meadow was really a neglected tennis court, which the examination of what looked like a big tool box on the side away from the pool confirmed, containing a net, two poles, and a few tools useful around a grass court. We were going to have our own tennis court! we announced to Doreen who, having finished the cleaning was preparing a light supper.

By unanimous agreement, we were beginning what was to be our best vacation, which our children still reminisce about and dream of repeating, this time with their own children, if the farm still exists. I mention it in this chapter because it was such a stark contrast to my reading throughout about the Time of Troubles (Anna, trusting me, let me take the books out of the library) and because Russia and Poland were never far out of my mind for the next eight years, and on and off later, and **NOW**.

The smell of coffee woke me up early next morning. After a cup (with the rest in the thermos) for me, tea for Doreen, and chocolate drink for the children, we set off in our station wagon. Something made me stop Doreen (she always did the driving when children were in the car, and I never objected). I ran up to the pond and, sure enough, a snake was swimming on top. I threw a rock at it, and it vanished under. For Jane's sake I would run ahead every time to scare it, but checking with the owners first.

The owners of the farm were having breakfast in their house below and, after having us admit we had just had coffee, invited us to join them in a sumptuous American Sunday breakfast, during which we talked. They were medical scientists, with grown-up children away; they would show us the location of their lab in case of emergencies and, yes, the lady stopped on her way to tell them about us; and then they stopped to show the children an old swing outside, and continued in their absence about the possible emergencies: snake bite from occasional copperheads sunning themselves on the rocks, hornet stings, raccoons not to be played with, and black bears, harmless, but not to be encouraged by leaving food or garbage out. What about the snake in the water? Harmless water snake, best to come first and scare it to go under for the girl's sake, and perhaps enlarge the pond a little. I told them that's exactly what we had done, while thinking also about restoring the court. They were all for it, even promising help and, if it was a good job, an extra week's stay on the farm. Before we left, they showed us on the map which was the best store to shop for groceries in Frenchtown, how to find their lab, gave us some ointment to apply immediately in case of bites, and told us that there was a rope on the branch of the tree for swinging over the pond like Tarzan but it was hidden in the tree to discourage uninvited guests.

Shopping in a little New Jersey town was a novel experience for us. The brands were different, and the prices, lower, on account of sales tax being lower than New York's. We made monumental shopping, including buying the Sunday *New York Times*, and were glad to return to our secluded farm waiting for us undisturbed, with only a big bird (an eagle?) circling above keeping a silent watch.

After lunch, climbing the tree we loosened the rope tied to its biggest branch stretching over the pond. The trick was not to let go of it but weigh it down with a rock otherwise it would hang over the water; another trick was to jump off nimbly after the return swing in order not to hang over the pond or fall in as the arc got shorter. Yet another trick was not to jump off or drop on the other side, which looked inhospitable, full of dry thorny bushes hiding probably a nest of snakes or some nasty insects. After a demonstration by me with a full-throated Tarzan yell and the children's squeals, their turns came, ending frequently with being stranded over the pond and requiring help involving me climbing the tree and putting the swing in motion by hand. But soon dropping in the water and swimming ashore became more fun than calling for help and real fun began, with the children never tiring of it.

It was no fun for Paul and me restoring the court, but it was nevertheless a labor of love. First we started clearing the surface of all kinds of debris left over from parties or from the field being used for other games, and piling up the refuse near the inhospitable side of the pond separating it from the court but letting us keep an eye on Jane and Mark until Doreen arrived. While the grass was sparse, there were tufts of it in clusters over the court. These had to be trimmed or even carefully uprooted as the wrong kind of grass. There was a sickle in the tool box, and a whetstone, which I soon put to use, having learned it from my father when helping him on our own plot of land to control unruly grass and weeds. All we needed now was some rain to give the trimmed grass some nourishment and to seal the holes after the uprooted and leveled tufts. And the expected rain came, making us rush back for shelter, and protection from the sudden thunderstorm and lightning.

The rain stopped just as suddenly as it had started, refreshing the air and the parched ground, and leaving behind a huge rainbow on the horizon. Since we were still wearing our swimsuits, we went back (with me a little ahead, again scaring the snake), amazed to see how big the pool had become, overfilled with water from the swollen stream, the excess spilling with a splash over the dam. The water too was fresher and softer as we found out by taking low jumps now into it from the rope and then swimming back.

As for the tennis court it began to look like one, the trimmed grass now reviving and glistening with drops of rain which would cause it to grow into a real grass court, in need of drying first and then being rolled over with the concrete pipe section for lack of a steamroller.

On our way back at sunset, to take advantage of the refreshed air we decided to fry some hamburgers in a little fireplace we just noticed in the back of the house, opposite the kitchen. Approaching it I noticed, too late to hide it from Jane, several furry brown spiders crawling about, probably washed out of the fireplace by the rain. As Jane screamed, I started killing them, by running them down and slapping them with the palm of my hand, with Doreen sweeping them into a neat little pile on top of the classified section of *The New York Times* to start the fire with. Even then some crawled out, unless they were ones that never left, which meant that they were all dead now, as I reassured Jane. Soon we had our hamburgers on rolls, with a big salad, and plenty of coffee for me, over which I read some more about Russia in the Time of Troubles.

First thing in the morning, after a good but quick breakfast, we went to the tennis court, finding it inviting for the first time. With Doreen taking the younger children to the pond, Paul and I set to work. We took the net out of the tool box, spread it out on the ground to straighten out, and then took out a little shovel to dig out the dirt from the concrete hollow piles in the ground that held the net posts. Then we started rolling the concrete pipe section on the court, but found it a hard job. It was then that the owners drove up, to offer help when they somehow figured it would be needed, and how right they were, to our and their amazement. Together, we rolled the court over several times until we were satisfied that it was the best we could do, even the children who came over marveling at its flatness and asking whether they could play, too. Of course! Then came the important part, marking the lines. Although I knew the correct dimensions, there is a method to marking them, and the owners brought a book with instructions, a tape measure and a long wooden contraption to pour the powder between its two slats. Then we inserted the net poles; they fit and we attached the net to them on both ends, and turned the handle at the toolbox side to stretch the net tight. Then the owner and I measured and marked the lines with special markers, and the two wives put down the contraption and moved it along while Paul was carefully, and to the envy of his brother and sister, pouring the white powder between the slats. When it was done, we all stood back, looked at the court in its full dress and clapped our hands. It was beautiful! One has to see a freshly marked court to know what it feels like, especially deep in the wilderness.

All that was needed was to test our creation, which was to be properly christened, at the request of the owners, in a mixed-doubles match in late afternoon. For now, Paul and I just hit a few balls to test the bounce off the court, but standing way behind the baselines, and we were pleased with it, with the owners watching and nodding. Before they left, I told them about the brown spiders, and they were interested, and how I had killed them to calm Jane, which distressed them, saying they hadn't known about the spiders which could have been a rare species that I may have destroyed. Not quite, I told them, I had had a similar apprehension and captured one alive which, judging by the slowness of its movements, was probably a female carrying eggs, and here it was, and I handed them a matchbox with the spider inside. Scientist to the core, they thanked me, took a peek at the prisoner, put her away safely, and left.

After a well-deserved lunch we filled our canteens with refreshments and went to find the source of the stream while the water was still cascading strongly. We climbed steadily and soon found ourselves in real wilderness, with only the stream as our guide. Jane was getting worried, especially after we spotted a snake sunning itself, saw two raccoons racing after something, and heard some branches breaking possibly by a bear, with still no sign of the stream nearing its beginning. We turned back, the boys reluctantly, the girls eagerly, with just enough time to put on our best tennis whites and set off again.

When we arrived at the tennis court, the owners, also in tennis whites, were already there, setting up a picnic on top of the tool box.

In their spacious station wagon they also brought a few friends and a few old beach chairs. We sat around the tablecloth-covered tool box, had some refreshments and talked. The friends couldn't get over the restored tennis court and estimated its market value. Our host told me that I was wrong suspecting the spiders of being poisonous (reason for killing them) but right about the survivor being a female. She was now in safe seclusion laying her eggs and would soon be transferred with her progeny to the fireplace which was to be their preserve as a rare species (I was right) for which I deserved credit.

It was time for tennis. Our hosts, like college grads of that era, were quite athletic and good tennis players, but not quite up to Doreen and me who were, in addition, considerably younger. But it was an enjoyable game, arranged chiefly as a symbolic celebration of the restored court, and in this sense it was a great success. The real game was between me and Paul who, almost fifteen, thought it was time for him to take a set from me, but it was not to be, not on that occasion, anyway, but he was clearly the spectators' favorite. Darkness was descending when the celebration ended, and we parted in good spirits.

Such was our bucolic existence, including a nasty hornet sting suffered by Mark, on this memorable vacation. Its isolation was good for the family, strengthening ties that bind while also acting like a balsam in a stormy year. As if on cue, we departed on a Sunday which was to turn into a stormy one, in more ways than one. But before that, I was able to finish my reading, expanding my knowledge of Russia in the Time of Troubles, giving much thought to the matter of to what extent the Polish intervention in Russia at that time was a factor later in the century in Poland's own time of troubles known as the "Deluge" sparked by the Cossack revolt when Russia in turn intervened.

When we departed, with the children saying a fond good-bye to the happy surroundings, we took with us some old farming implements, true period pieces like hand-made sieves, now long discarded in the farm's shed, and as we took at first a different route from arriving, we saw many such pieces in charming souvenir shops and well-attended garage sales in quaint little towns along the Delaware.

We ran into a violent storm as we turned into central New Jersey, and our car stalled in the middle of the highway in ankle-deep water. Paul and I took our shoes off, got out and pushed the car to the side, when a lone passing car stopped to help, and its occupant, a student, discovered that we had run out of gas. He took a piece of rubber hose and siphoned some gas out of his car into ours, but having swallowed some, went into shock. I drove him in his car to the nearest town, and noticing an M.D. shingle had to almost break the door down to get him help. He did get it, and we soon rejoined my family. The young man was America at its best; its worst, we were about to see.

There was a demonstration with racial overtones in a town further down the road where we stopped to get gas. A police officer trying to break it up was knocked down and stomped (fatally, according to the late news). With Jane screaming, "Daddy, help him!" I was about to, but thought better of it with my family in harm's way. It was with thoughts like these, and the new knowledge, that I returned to New York and soon proceeded to Pittsburgh.

In Pittsburgh the news was also disturbing. The secretary, who had been invited with her husband to lunch by the chairman, told me that he harped about my popularity. A good friend, she warned me that he felt threatened by it, and suggested that I should shun it a little for a while. Carl Beck also had something disturbing to say, namely that the chairman had casually remarked that I was giving Poland more attention than Russia in my *Slavic Civilizations*. If that were the case, it was because except for language, there were no courses on Poland yet at the university, as there were on Russia, and I used the civilization for a background in Polish history and literature. This was quite logical for Carl, even desirable, but he urged me to speed up my progress on the dissertation, which I assured him I was doing, by starting the Yale research project, which his institute was funding, before the beginning of the term.

The Yale project was work and vacation combined. Every Friday morning I would take an early local plane to New Haven, make a courtesy call in the Slavic Department to see Alexander Schenker (he was pleased to hear in my first visit about Fran Millard's high praise of him), then go to the library to work until closing time at midnight, with a short break for lunch (usually with a colleague), and again Saturday until noon, by which time my family would have arrived from New York, and we would spend the afternoon in New Haven and vicinity, exploring and sightseeing; spend the night in a motel, have breakfast next morning, Sunday, in the children's favorite Dunkin' Donuts, then drive to New York, where I would stay until Monday night, returning by a late plane to Pittsburgh, to be at work on Tuesday, where, by my first return the microfilm reader had arrived.

The chairman called the whole department for my demonstration of the reader, which gave me a chance to not only try and display the microfilm of Bulgarin's "political and literary newspaper" *The Northern Bee* (*Severnaja pchela*, 1825-1859), but also a microfiche (small rigid rectangles kept in a special box, thus no need to wind and rewind) of his "Literary Pages" ("Literaturnye listki" 1823-1824), a "literary supplement" to *The Northern Archive* (*Severnyj Arxiv*, 1822-1828, a "journal of history, statistics and travel"), finding everything in perfect condition and absolutely indispensable to my dissertation. My audience was duly impressed and I was satisfied that I could now proceed with greater speed, having located and secured all the sources and acquired a reader enabling me to work in the comfort of my office, with coffee available next door. Students again began to peek over my shoulder, and also this time to watch me use the reader, but not for long.

One day when I was deep at work with the reader, the chairman's busybody student and general factotum arrived with a request that the Ukrainian professor needed the reader. Knowing that the man wasn't doing any research I saw in the request a contemptible attempt to hamper me, and I told the students that I was using the machine. In a huff he rushed over to the chairman who came over saying something about seniority and generally speaking highly of the man whom only recently he was contemptuously referring to as *Galichanin* (roughly translated, somebody from Galicia but this is only one variation of a Russian's condescending reference to a Ukrainian). He repeated the request. I said nothing, removed the microfilm, put the reader in its box for the student to take away, placed the microfilm in my briefcase and left for the library, where there were many readers, but not always available. On that day one was, and I made an arrangement with the Slavic librarian, a fine Russian lady for a change, that I would always call before coming, not to waste time, because it was a race now.

There was an unexpected irony in this situation. A few days later as I was leaving my office on the way to my evening Polish class, I heard the Ukrainian, who was still in his office after his afternoon class, calling me in a hoarse voice. Knowing that the man had a weak heart, I knew something was wrong. For a split second I thought of ignoring it, but this is not my way of settling things, and I went over, found him clutching his chest and gasping hoarsely, made him comfortable by loosening his tie and belt, and even carried him to the next office which had a carpet on the floor and laid him on it placing his folded coat under his head. By then the secretary arrived who, taking my course and not seeing me in class, thought I had forgotten the time, called his wife, her own husband, and the ambulance. They all arrived almost simultaneously, taking over (the medic wanted to know who had taken care of the stricken man, and when I told him he said I had saved his life) allowing me and Carol, who gave me a long knowing look, to go to class, which was waiting for me.

While tending to the stricken man I had noticed that the microfilm reader was not in his office which made me think that it was gathering dust in the chairman's.

The dissertation was turning into a colossal job and I was beginning to worry that I wouldn't be able to finish it within the allowed five years, for which I was regularly registering (for library research) at Columbia. Luckily for me Robert Belknap, with whom I faithfully kept up the Friday-Monday arrangement after each chapter, after the VIIIth told me to stop there, write the Introduction, Conclusion, compile the Bibliography, have them checked, and start typing a clean manuscript for reproduction in five copies. This was to be a labor of love, but a student in my Polish class talked me into having his wife, an alleged expert, type it, and it was she who almost made me miss the deadline. I spent more time rushing her than I would have typing it myself. She farmed part of it out, and ended up with a typo in the title, but it was finished!

Looking at it now, even with its botched-up and faded typing (corrected in the published copy) in an impressive volume bound for my wife in imitation-leather with golden lettering by the Columbia University Library, I still wonder how I did it while teaching full-time, while looking after the Polish Club as its faculty adviser, and seeing my family throughout the work as often as I did. The last-minute race, of correcting overlooked mistakes (but still missing the unfortunate typo) with the typist, a disorganized and burdened with little children but decent Filipino woman helping her husband as a typist (how many rice meals I had with her while checking on her progress?), putting the five defense copies in special blue boxes provided by Columbia, placing them flat in a canvas bag in the back seat of her husband's car, and dashing to the bus station and barely catching the Friday night Greyhound bus to New York, with the husband waiting in case I missed it.

When Doreen picked me up at the bus station in New York, she was excited to see the five blue boxes, and when I delivered them to the Slavic Department, I was officially a new expert in Polish-Russian literary relations. Only the defense remained, but I expected no problems there. It would be scheduled to give its committee time to read.

Back in Pittsburgh my students were excited, having heard the news from the typist's husband, and started calling me "Doctor" in a traditional fashion there, but I asked them to wait. The ROTC crew gave me a little party, at which Colonel Watkins, who was receiving a Brigadier's star (hence it was a double party), confessed that he felt the doctor's title to be more prestigious than a general's to which I replied that I felt the opposite to be true since there were more doctors than generals. Carl Beck congratulated me, pleased that the help of his office had been a factor in my success, and he called my chairman after I had told him that the Russians and the Ukrainians in the department had greeted me with a stony silence, including a new secretary, a Russian (what else?), who had succeeded Carol, pregnant with her first child.

Then disaster struck, from the least threatening sides, from allies as a matter of fact. It turned out that Carl Beck's phone call to my chairman started a chain of events that proved a defeat for me as far as the University of Pittsburgh was concerned. (Incidentally, the chairman's ignorance was so great that he asked me whether Carl was Poland's prewar Minister of Foreign Affairs, in which case he would have to be close to 100 years old, while Carl was in his early forties.) The chairman of course knew that I still didn't have the degree, and he wrote to the chairman at Columbia asking when it was expected, and Prof. Harkins allegedly (I never saw the letter, nor the reply) replied that he wasn't sure, thus betraying a lamentable ignorance about the real status of the degree or simply not being helpful. Knowing nothing about it, I was called, just before Christmas recess (1969) to the Dean of Student's office, expecting another celebration and a discussion of my future, but the message I received was disastrous.

To this day I don't know what really happened. It wasn't the Dean (a brilliant biologist whom I had met once when Elizabeth Hill voiced to him her regrets for picking the Russian chairman for his present job) who was receiving me, but the Associate Dean, a hatchet man in this case. He knew I was going to New York for Christmas and asked me whether I was planning to attend the MLA yearly convention meeting immediately after Christmas in New York. Impressed by his knowledge about the conventions, I told him I always did. He asked if I would inquire about job opportunities in my field. I always looked at them for various reasons, but why was he raising it? Because the university had learned, through my chairman's exchange of letters with the Columbia chairman that my dissertation wasn't completed yet (not defended) leaving the degree still in doubt of being awarded in this academic year. I exploded, almost shouting that I still had another year after this within my time limit, which left plenty of time and, besides, the defense would take place early in the spring, and I expected the degree in the summer. I was right about the extra year and was entitled to take advantage of it, he said, but the university had its guidelines and had to act on them without relying on expectations. He was genuinely sorry, he assured me, because as a family man himself, he knew what it meant to me, and wished me luck.

On my way out I stopped at Carl's office. He was of a better mind. He knew the Associate Dean to be a good man, dedicated to the good of the university, but he was acting under instructions. All I had to do was to get the degree in the summer, before the beginning of the 1970/71 academic year. Then he invited me to lunch, but not in the Faculty Lounge, which had ears, as he put it, but in the expensive Webster Hall, adding that he had money for such lunches from his Institute, and this would be, anyway, an overdue celebration of my dissertation.

Over lunch he confided in me that he had a good relationship with the new Chancellor, a scholar and a West Point man (with an opera singer for a wife), hired finally after a long search, which should count for something. I, in turn, confided in him that I had heard rumors about his health, something of the kind of the late Bidwell illness, except lungs (he was a chain-smoker, with little help from me he went, over lunch, through almost a pack of a special brand, *Sobranie*, which he was getting from a tobacconist in New York, and when I told him I was getting English cigarettes there occasionally, for sentimental reasons, he asked me to get him a fresh supply, insisting on giving me money for them) but he assured me that things were under control, but that one of the reasons he wanted me to stay in Pittsburgh was to be there if things got out of control.

The moment I arrived in New York I went to the department to confront Harkins, catching him before he, too, left for Christmas. I asked him about the letters and he answered somewhat indignantly that I didn't have to know what one chairman writes to another, but corrected himself, "I shouldn't have said that." We agreed on early defense.

At home I discussed the matter with Doreen who, as Personnel specialist, knew about such things. She told me the key word in such cases was "accountability" but that the authorities usually had their way, as long as they acted within reasonable guidelines to protect themselves from a lawsuit, which I would never resort to, anyway.

We both had a problem understanding Harkins' motives, if there were motives, considering Belknap's excellent cooperation, but Belknap was just an Assistant Professor and Harkins was Associate and the new chairman after Stilman. He already had a name in the profession which was the reason my chairman eagerly invited him for a lecture when I included him on the list of my suggestions. The lecture was on Slavic folklore, his specialty. It was this lecture, incidentally, when the Ukrainian confused two Polish poems, from one of which Harkins quoted a key line, "Pani zabiła Pana" ("the Lady killed the Lord") in such atrocious Polish ("Pany zabyła Pana") that I was embarrassed for him, as Elizabeth Hill was embarrassed for his Russian. It just may be that the Russian chairman's having been a witness to this poor performance gave him some leverage, or probably Harkins just wanted to be invited again. Things would clear somewhat at the defense, the nearness of which I reported to Carl Beck when I returned to Pittsburgh after the holidays, having first ascertained at the MLA meeting that the Slavic field was near saturation point, with just a few jobs, a good reason to fight for the job in hand.

In Pittsburgh itself there were factions and alliances, all turned against me, except Carl Beck, my students, and the Polish community. It was Carl Beck's intervention that made the chairman keep my *Slavic* course, my stronghold, which in his view attracted good students. He was right: I had some of the best students in the university, from all ethnic backgrounds except the Russian, an absence which I later compared to the Spanish at Loyola. There was an intellectual called Benesh, a lovely girl by the name of Cyrylla, and a student who wrote an excellent paper about one of his Polish ancestors shooting the tycoon Frick on his mansion verandah at Sunday breakfast and Frick not pressing charges but mending his baronial ways by donating, among other things, the Frick collection to the University. But the best paper was about Polish-Jewish relations which was so well researched that I suspected the author of plagiarism, except for a rather poor style, which for me was a good reason to give him an A+, because it meant that he wrote it independently. I collected such papers, telling the student that I would publish them under their names. When I noticed their absence later, I reached the sad conclusion that my filing cabinet had been pilfered at the university during my frequent absences, but by whom?

The chairman or his Russian secretary was a likely suspect, because the man simply did not want me to pass him as a scholar, which I had already done, anyway. He had one badly reviewed book on Nikolai Berdyaev (his dissertation?) and I had a publishable (by definition) dissertation, a few installments of "Chronicle of Events" and a review article.

What first put me on notice was when the chairman forbade Carol to type the review article ("History as Literature," based on W. Kuniczak's *Thousand Hour Day* about September, 1939). She expressed surprise, saying she enjoyed doing it because it was so well written. This was also the opinion of scholars in America and even in Poland, which must have reached the envious man, making him feel threatened.

The more likely candidate was the Ukrainian, a little man with the narrowest of horizons and the broadest of inferiority complexes covered up by nastiness and envy. Totally ignorant of literary and historical terms he viewed Marx as a dangerous word not to be uttered within earshot for fear of being overheard and denounced. A native of Brody (on which he did an article—his only one, I think—proving that the name was not the plural of "broda" [beard] but of "brod" [ford, as in "to ford a river"] and showing where it occurs in such a context) in Volhynia, he was of course not the "Galichanin" the chairman thought him to be, betraying his ignorance of the Russian Empire's geography, since Volhynia was not Galicia, but a part of the Russian, not Austrian, partition of Poland. The Ukrainian never expressed any gratitude for the Gymnasium education he had received in prewar Poland, no simple matter, since there was no open admission to it. It did get him admitted to an Austrian university, in Graz, but he did not tell me when and under what circumstances. Despite the advantages he had had in Poland, he was hostile to everything Polish, and this hostility was transferred to me and my Polish program.

He was a great admirer (worshipper is a better word) of another Ukrainian, but who was a friend of Poland (he once told me that at an international conference of Slavists in Italy they had no common language to conduct it in until they discovered that they all spoke

Polish!), George Shevelov, one of the foremost Slavic linguists in the world and an excellent teacher, whose course notes, especially from his star course, "History of the Russian Literary Language," I had brought with me to Pittsburgh, with the intention of showing them to Bidwell. But the Ukrainian was also interested in the notes, and began badgering me about how Shevelov taught his famous courses. I recalled this persistent pestering when, much later, when already back in New York, I looked for the notes and could not find them. Missing also were the excellent papers from the *Slavic Civilization* course and, felt most painfully, my paper on "American Intervention in the Russian Revolution," of which, luckily, I still had the final draft, enabling me to reconstruct the paper. But the others were lost. When I realized it, I also realized that the man had good reasons to want me out—before I discovered the missing items.

It's true I had great students, but students were only just beginning then to play a part in university life. If anything, they could harm a professor by their excessive devotion. And so it was with me. The students' insistence on having a Polish Student Club did not sit well with the Russian chairman, who viewed the Club just like the Tsars, and later Communist bosses, viewed and treated Poland.

As for the Polish community, I began to find out how helpless it was in protecting its group interests in America. The president of the Polish Arts League, a very successful businessman Tony Tabak, talked about "weathering it out" when my most devoted student, the energetic Helen Gaida, talked me into paying him a visit. It was even more disappointing when we, in turn, visited the Polish Falcons, who should have been a powerhouse in Pittsburgh but were one in name only. Located in something that looked like a renovated barn, whose ground floor was filled with memories and memorabilia of a glorious past, and whose upper floor, ascended by an insecure stairway, contained, among other rooms, a well-stocked bar, it looked full of activity, but I was fed too many drinks to even get a chance to find out if I could enlist the former fighters in my fight.

Yet, Pittsburgh's Polonia was well organized. It had the reverently referred to so-called "Centrala," which was the central authority of the Polish organizations, and it seems that "Centrala" once spoke up in a big voice when the Bishop of Pittsburgh kept referring to all the Slavs as "hunkies" and having to explain himself for it in Rome ("in harmless jest") after which he was transferred to Boston, ending his career in Rome itself. Rumors had it that he was being penalized which, if true, would point to an amazing fact of the

Poles being capable of challenging the Church hierarchy (a challenge which had resulted in the past in the formation of their own church, the Polish National Catholic Church) but not the educational ones, which were looked upon as part of official authorities which, for the Polish immigrants had retained a foreign, even hostile, memory. This was probably the reason why the Poles started their own schools in America, even higher schools, instead of handing their children over to "foreign" authorities. Who were the authorities at the University of Pittsburgh?

There was a whole pyramid, starting with chairmen of departments, in my case of the Slavic Languages and Literatures, to the Chancellor and the Board of Trustees. Carl Beck, a director of what was really an auxiliary institute made up of faculty from other departments, was not really part of the pyramid. The real power, as far as faculty appointments were concerned, was the Dean of Faculty, popularly referred to as Jerry. Jerry may have had his own long-range plans to settle the conflict in the Slavic department. There was a temporary instructor of Russian in the department, like me a doctoral candidate at Columbia, who came to Pittsburgh with her husband after he had received an appointment in the History department at the university. The first time I saw her in Pittsburgh was before the Harkins lecture, when she came to talk to him about her status at Columbia, just as I did after. When next her husband received a grant to do research in Russia, she needed faculty status in order to go with him. As coordinator of language teaching, I assigned her a section in Elementary Russian, visited her in class, and wrote a positive evaluation. She spent the next year(s) in Russia, which must have been beneficial to her because when I heard of her next she was the head of the department.

Meanwhile the wheels were turning for me. Early spring in 1970 I sat to the defense of my dissertation, with the committee consisting of Harkins, Belknap and Marina from the department, and two professors recently arrived from Poland, a young historian, who was soon to instruct my son, and a highly positioned former Communist, who was soon to succeed Brzezinski upon the latter's departure to Washington. The former Communist questioned my reliance on encyclopedias, until I had to point out to him that they were mostly German encyclopedias which often contained information not encountered in Russian ones. Then he turned to secret police, about which there was little in the dissertation but the interrogator obviously knew a lot, until Marina practically exploded, telling him it was not a dissertation about secret police. The young historian was more to the point asking me why, having mentioned the historian Nikolai Karamzin, I did not say more about him. Harkins ruled that it wasn't necessary, adding that if I wanted to add a sub-chapter, it would be a valuable contribution, but that it was up to me. I said I would, and I spent most of the summer working on it, having it accepted and incorporated into the dissertation, to the great satisfaction of the historian who, I suspected, wanted somebody to do research that he needed himself after reading Richard Pipes. The sub-chapter, expanded, became an article in *The Slavic Review*, my most important publication up to that time.

With all the requirements for the degree of Doctor of Philosophy, in the Faculty of Philosophy, Columbia University, thus fulfilled, I received from the Registrar a few cards stating it in lieu of the diploma itself, which was not to be given out until the next commencement, and I returned triumphantly to Pittsburgh, feeling a great deal of satisfaction in completing one of life's major tasks not only on time but almost a year ahead of the deadline, while working, supporting a larger than average family, giving it memorable vacations (the one before the farm was in Woods Hole, among oceanographers) and living a full life.

I had a rude awakening from my euphoria the moment I reached my office. A student, the husband of the Filipino dissertation typist, had apparently been laying siege to my office for the past week to tell me that Carl Beck had been calling Columbia throughout the summer to find out about my doctorate, without any luck. Something was wrong and, to put the record straight, I gave the student one of the little cards (very pretty cards, with a red border, and the student could not take his eyes off it) and told him to take it to Carl and give it to him. He returned in a few minutes with a message from Carl that the decision reached in my case before Christmas was binding, but that he would keep the card for a meeting with the Chancellor. But I knew better. Although a novice in the academic field, I knew that the Chancellor would not overrule the decision reached by the Dean without risking his resignation, as was the case with his predecessor who had come into conflict with Mrs. Frick about the proper use of the Frick collection by the Arts Dept.

There was a silver lining in the failed Pittsburgh appointment. The same student who had caused considerable grief by talking me into having his wife type my doctoral dissertation, talked me now into making the acquaintance of his friend (from his army service?),

Daniel Matuszewski, who was working in the New York Office of International Research and Exchanges Board (IREX), with a view of getting a grant. On my next trip to New York I visited the office on the East Side (it's in Washington now) and found Daniel a reasonable young man, who advised me to apply for the State Department sponsored Exchange of Language Teachers with the Soviet Union, with the Russian side taking place in the summer of 1971. I took the application and started getting the necessary recommendations, from Harkins and Belknap, and from Carl, who gladly obliged when my chairman refused (to think that it was he who not so long ago said how lucky the department was to have me as coordinator of language teaching—the man was obviously in the wrong profession, or was it me, mixing with the academic cockroaches). My application was duly approved.

My forthcoming trip meant a lot to me. It was to round out my education as far as Russia and the Soviet Union were concerned, and I was preparing accordingly, without neglecting my teaching and my students. One, a graduate student in the Department of Education, was going to Cracow on my recommendation. Another one, a young priest and former secretary of Cardinal Wojtyła, forced out of Poland to annoy and harass the Cardinal, wanted to study philosophy in the university's excellent department, and I was able to make it possible for him by accompanying him to an interview with the department's chairman. This young priest was telling everybody who cared to listen that his former superior was going to become Pope one day, and some reporters picked it up and wrote about the prediction, reminding its author about it when it, indeed, came true.

Yet another student decided to go for a Junior Year in Cracow, having taken all the available Polish courses with me. It was Helen Gaida, whose proud retired steelworker father I was pleased to meet in his own house, to tell him how proud he should be of his daughter. Helen chose to go to the Kosciuszko Foundation to settle all the formalities at the same time as I was leaving Pittsburgh, and since she was driving, she gave me a ride, taking also my books, maps and notes. There was going to be a scholarly conference of the Polish Institute at Columbia University at that time, and she wanted to take part in it, too, and she did, making a very valuable acquaintance with Mary van Starrex, Ludwik Krzyżanowski's assistant, which led to friendship and eventually a job at the Kosciuszko Foundation under Eugene Kusielewicz, only to be dismissed later by his unworthy successor. I only regret that, through my own bad luck, I couldn't do more for her. She was clearly the model of what, twenty years later, I was trying to create in Chicago, the new Polish American intelligentsia, but this project was torpedoed, too, by the same unworthy man. Otherwise she would have been in the book not as a memory, but leading other women in individual accomplishments.

The year 1971 was an important one for me and for my family. I wasn't the only one receiving his degree officially, our son Paul was graduating from a private school nearby and entering Columbia College, which meant that a family tradition had been established. To make it more memorable, I decided to take part in the commencement exercises at Columbia, and later in our son's at the Cathedral of St. John the Divine. Both ceremonies were duly recorded in many family photos, with only Jane, in a rebellious mood at her age (14) a reluctant participant, but they were nevertheless sensational in Russia and Poland because that's where both the celebrants were going, I to the IREX-sponsored program at Moscow State University and Paul to a summer program at the Jagiellonian University in Cracow, to meet afterwards at our relatives' in Poland and return together, both richer and wiser for the experience.

I was looking forward to the experience, not just for personal reasons but also to see first-hand how useful the exchanges were. The group briefing at Kennedy Airport revealed that there were 25 participants, of which only one (myself) was taking along any athletic equipment, and quite a few were so apprehensive, judging by their questions, as to be unfit for the program (one was sent home later from Moscow). I was wondering about the selection process, which apparently did not take into consideration the physical and mental condition of the candidates, the latter aggravated by the ground rules, including one that had the effect of scaring some fainthearted soul by forbidding any activity that could be interpreted as engaging in intelligence work, as if such work would even enter the minds of members of this group which was probably par for the program.

The flight itself was an experience for me. On the first leg, to London, a fencing team from West Point was flying with us on its way to Rumania, and I made the acquaintance of its coach who, on hearing that my son Paul was interested in fencing, suggested he apply to West Point, and meanwhile take fencing lessons at the Athletic Club in New York as a future cadet. This interested me.

After familiar London I began to feel a little tense watching the landscape from a window seat. This was the Soviet Union we were approaching, and about to enter from the Baltic above the green flat land of Lithuania or Latvia. Everything we saw now from above had been soaked in Polish blood in centuries of Polish-Russian strife that had been refreshed in my memory by recent reading. It was the land of the ancient enemy we were entering, and I, too, began to feel apprehensive, but for different reasons. I was convinced I would find traces of that ancient enmity.

The Moscow Sheremetev Airport was surprisingly efficient, perhaps because it was run like a military airport. There was a captain eyeing the passengers as they were descending the portable staircase from the plane. Last to descend I exchanged a cold glance with him. Former efficiency vanished when it came to checking the passports, and meticulous checking of proofs of required vaccinations. It turned out that there was an epidemic of typhoid in Soviet Central Asia and there were fears that it might reach Moscow, hence all arrivals needed to be vaccinated. I took a stand and refused to be vaccinated at the airport, pointing out that I had all the vaccinations required of passengers going to the Soviet Union in America and I showed the appropriate notation in my passport. I took another stand when it was discovered that my big bag was missing and probably was on the London plane continuing to Teheran and I was blamed for it. They would contact Teheran and I should come back tomorrow. As a result, when everybody was settling down in the huge university dorm (in identical sections, easy to get lost in, on purpose?), I was given one of the university's two cars and a driver to go back to the airport and, luckily, get my bag. On our way back the driver showed me the well-marked place where the Germans had advanced, virtually on the outskirts of Moscow, in 1941. He invited me to call on him whenever I needed a car, an offer I appreciated and followed up.

The next day was the formal opening of the program in the Humanities building. The Dean of the University (who during the war had been stationed in Poland, as he told me, where he had experienced the tragic accidental killing of all the inhabitants of his quarters, leaving him to live with a guilty feeling, and now meeting someone to unload it on in a very Russian act of expiation) called on all the participants in alphabetical order, letting them introduce themselves including position and place, but left me out until the end when he called on me in his own way:

> "And now a special guest,
> a former front soldier (*frontovshchik*)
> who helped us beat the Germans.
> Frank Pavlovich Mocha."

Two things stood out in this introduction. The respect for the soldier, who "helped" *them*, not the Allies as a whole; the other was the patronymic, which startled me, never having been addressed in this fashion, and not recalling having filled out the name of my father on any form, which could mean one thing only: they had gotten it from Poland. To make my Polish presence known to the press, I replied in my way:

> I am Professor of Slavic Languages,
> particularly Polish.

Later my fellow participants reproached me for specifying Polish in a program for Russian, but the Dean praised me for it, and the reporters and guests were eager to talk to me. One of the latter, a musicologist, was an enthusiast of American rock music, a liking he admitted to in a whisper, since officially rock music was not accepted in the Soviet Union. I asked him what he thought of Krzysztof Penderecki, the Polish composer very highly thought of in the West. The musicologist was stingy in his praise, even suggesting that Penderecki was perhaps overrated. But that same day I heard on the radio a program about the Polish weight lifter Waldemar Baszanowski, who was praised highly.

The two examples point to a certain pattern in Polish-Russian (Soviet) relations at that time, according to which Soviet (Russian) primacy had to be maintained. Since the Soviet Union had no composer of Penderecki's stature, praising him would amount to recognizing Polish primacy in an important cultural field. On the other hand praising Baszanowski was safe, even encouraged, since he excelled in just one weight class of a field in which the Soviet Union held overall primacy, sports. But even here there were surprises, such as the Polish victory in track and field which I witnessed during my visit in 1959, when the Soviets immediately renamed their team "West Russia" in order to lessen the impact of the defeat.

Following the formal opening, the program began. The group was divided into four language sections of 6, based on ability and compatibility (I was in a section of Ph.D.'s from prestigious universities with teaching record in university colleges), the sections joining for lectures or excursions. The workday lasted from 8 in the morning til 4 in the afternoon, with an hour's lunch (dinner) break in the Professorial Dining Room near the Humanities building in which all classes and exercises were held.

Despite vacations for regular students, the building was very busy with adult students, mostly officers from the armed services. These were not the officers I had heard about in Poland, and seen in the Austrian POW camp, but a new breed of well-behaved, polite young (mostly) men, well dressed in their light summer uniforms and beaming with confidence. Observed mostly at mealtime, their table manners were also correct, and they did not sit in clusters but wherever there was an empty seat, showing themselves to be perfectly agreeable table companions. I would run into them in my frequent afternoon excursions to the *Druzhba* (Friendship) Bookstore on Gorky Street, where all the satellite countries had their separate stores in which well subsidized books could be purchased and, in my case, sent home from the university post office in the basement of the dormitory building. The bookstore was usually crowded, and I was quite astonished to see the number of officers buying books in the Polish store, and finding out, after striking a conversation, that they were Polish or of Polish descent, just like the intelligence officer on the train in 1959.

The dining room and the bookstore were my two main observation posts, with a third the cafeteria (if one could call it that) in the basement of the dormitory building (in a different section from the post office). A cavernous low ceilinged room with wooden tables and chairs and a counter with a very limited menu, the best on which were fried eggs served in their little frying pans smelling of some awful grease, to be eaten with as much bread as one wished because it was free and in great supply in baskets on the tables (the free bread was something that impressed me, and I took advantage of it by taking a supply of it to my room for a late snack to be eaten with an occasional piece of sausage or, even less often, fruit purchased, with tea, in one of the small canteens on the various upper floors.

But my most important observation post was my own room which, in a very clever design serving many purposes, was one of two side-by-side with a little foyer and a small bathroom, with the other room occupied by a compatible host (or roommate), a student spending part of his vacation on this assignment, usually a highly intelligent and discreet student, who could be of great value as guide, helper, and informant. Mine was Kolya (Nicholas), a Russian germanist from Kazakhstan, who soon steered in my direction a variety of interesting students, resulting in a veritable stream of visitors turning my room into an exciting meeting place, including refreshments purchased by me on frequent quick trips (courtesy of the university driver) to the well supplied small supermarket in the American Embassy.

History was repeating itself in an extraordinary way, and I was becoming as popular at Moscow University as before in Pittsburgh or at Columbia, except that I wasn't teaching, not in the strict sense, anyway. It all began when, instead of spending the entire hour in the dining room, I would use the second half to hit tennis ball against a practice wall nearby. Soon there would be a crowd of spectators, and the prettiest assistant on our staff, who once had boasted to me about playing tennis, having brought a racket and put on shorts and sneakers, left after seeing me hit, saying with some indignation that she was not going to make a fool of herself hitting with "the first racket of the USA," and that I should play with Olga Morozova and Alex Metrevelli (national champions) and she set about contacting them. On my way from class, still wearing shorts and sneakers, I ran into a group in the yard playing with a volleyball. A tall woman player suddenly lobbed a high one in my direction. I dropped my briefcase and the racket, did my customary three-step routine learned in Stalag XVIIB and hit a spike so ferocious that the ball bounced off the ground to the second floor windows of the dorm. "I knew you could hit," she said, and from then on whenever they were playing there she was, at my door inviting me to join them in practice.

But it was the individual students that interested me most. There was the Polish girl, Ewa, from Toruń, who had not gone home for the summer, despite her mother's plan to camp together in the Masurian Lake district. I told her what I thought of her neglecting her mother, but she said she felt very comfortable in the dormitory, and it was easy for her to arrange to stay on, the authorities actually encouraging foreign students to stay, and I could understand the students liking the hot-house atmosphere of the dormitory, since it was beginning to work even on me.

Then there was the Ukrainian from Kiev, Vladimir, who was passing himself off as a Finn to escape Russian condescending treatment, but he was also buying dollars from me, paying four rubles for a dollar, and that's when I knew the real value of the ruble, rather than the artificial one of $1.67 for a ruble. I could spend the rubles in the American Express store, no questions asked, since we were getting a stipend in rubles.

There were two other Ukrainians, as different as if they were from different areas. One, a very aggressive Poland-hating Ukrainian nationalist who tried to insult me by laughing at my Polish accent in Russian and then Poland by saying that there was nothing of value in it, that it was a nothing country now, and that it was Ukraine that was going to stretch "from sea to sea." This was dangerous talk in Moscow, and even Kolya tried to stop him, while glancing involuntarily at the ceiling, but I caught the glance and Kolya caught the catch and knew that I knew about the mike. I decided to shut the foolish Ukrainian up by ridiculing him, telling him that Ukraine already went "from sea to sea," and when he looked bewildered, I added, "from the Black to the Azov," and the room doubled up in laughter, with Kolya and Vladimir the loudest, while the hapless fool moved threateningly towards me. I slapped him lightly across the face to "wake [him] up," told him to get out and not to come back to make trouble, while the other Ukrainian told us how he came by his Polish name, when mothers were giving them to their children after the war upon hearing that "Galicia" was going to be restored to Poland. This was news to me and I asked him what part of Galicia he came from? "Ivano-Frankivsk" he replied, then added "Stanislav" and I finally understood he was talking about Stanisławów.

Among the welcome visitors was a young girl who looked Polish and when I asked her whether she indeed was, she said no, but that her grandmother was, having arrived with others from the Ukraine into Kazakhstan where many of them were settled in the vicinity of the capital Alma Ata. I, of course, knew about Kazakhstan from Kolya, about its apple orchards and particularly its worrisome border with China from the vicinity of which Russians had allegedly been moving away lately (Kolya had taken me to take a look from a distance at the ominous looking Chinese Embassy from which not a sign of life emerged, and had been telling me how the Chinese students in Moscow, who often came to the Embassy in a group, and also lived in a close-knit group in a section of the dormitory, saved money from their small [but larger than the Russian students'] stipends, to make huge purchases in Moscow, mostly rice, to take with them to China on visits or when returning, which reminded me about the Filipinos in America), but I didn't know about the Poles in Kazakhstan, and this was news to me. Only much later did I learn that there had been a mass deportation of Poles from the Ukraine by

Stalin in the 1930's (an early example of "ethnic cleansing") and here
was this girl.

Central Asia was much in evidence in Moscow, as I remembered
from Stilman's illustrated narrative showing it as a magnet attracting
exotic Central Asians wearing their native garb with intricately
embroidered little caps on their heads. They were also in evidence in
my room, when one evening a door burst open and a dark-skinned
girl with jet-black long hair and shiny black eyes literally jumped
into the middle of the crowded room exclaiming loudly:

> "Ya Shakhridze! Ya dikaya!"
> (I am Sheherazade! I am a savage!)

By the end of the first week I was a confirmed Muscovite
which, surprisingly, pleased me, but also worried me on account of
Russia's apparent facility to attract like a magnet, seen primarily in
what I perceived as hot-house atmosphere of the University, where
elites were collected. When I pointed it out to students from Africa,
who were also among my visitors, they pointed out that the reason
they were here was because they had been turned down by American
schools, which was a sobering thought, but possibly prompted by the
fact that the Patrice Lumumba University was not the success it was
intended to be, and that there were instances of racism in Moscow,
where racism had been eradicated according to communist propaganda. But I was primarily worried about the Polish students, like
Ewa who felt at home, literally, in Moscow, and another one who
was making it a home by marrying in Moscow, but at least in the old
Saint Ludwik church overflowing with Moscow Poles every Sunday
(even when the priest had to be away on rare occasion and the faithful would go on with the service, minus the rituals), and also on the
Sunday of the wedding.

History is full of Polish assimilation in Russia, but it was time to
stop it because more was at stake this time, during a global contest
which, in this writer's opinion, hanged in the balance, with the new
adversary making headway despite occasional setbacks. It was lucky
for the West that the clash at the Fulda Gap had not taken place so
far, because it would have been fatal, and new setbacks were already
at work, making the clash less likely with every year, with Poland
emerging as the catalyst for change. This was the time of the coastal
strikes there, leading up to a fall of a government and the rise of
KOR (Committee for the Defense of the Worker), with the strikes

eliciting a grudging but admiring comment from a Russian to this writer, "Tol'ko Poljaki..." ("Only the Poles..."), indicating that there was room also in Russia for change. All these implications were totally lost on the other participants in the exchange who, if interested in anything at all outside of it, would be interested in American domestic news about Watergate, which had no bearing whatsoever on the larger issue.

Trying to make the best of my stay, and regretting not being able to have Paul visit me for at least a weekend, I purchased a Russian calendar-diary and made entries in it of everything I thought worth remembering. The visit to the Polish church was the first, and the fruit and vegetable market nearby where one could buy expensive produce flown in by farmers from Georgia and Armenia. Another was my surprising rapport with the local people. A woman working in the Professorial Dining Room noticing her little daughter watching me hit tennis balls against the wall asked if the girl could stay with me for half an hour while she took care of something. Of course! Just then the little girl asked me to give her one of the balls, and very touchingly addressed me by the familiar *dyadya* (uncle) very much used in this part of the world by children to strangers, but I have never heard it used in America, even in ethnic neighborhoods, and of course I gave her the ball.

The next two entries were of a more serious nature. One described a vicious fight I witnessed on my way to the "Friendship" bookstore, about something so trite as to make me wonder about the pent-up anger in the Russian soul. One man had inadvertently put his hand on another man's shoulder when passing him on a crowded sidewalk on Gorky Street slightly soiling his white shirt. One word led to another and soon fists were flying and blood flowing, with the shirt turning into a torn bloody rag. Always an enemy of unnecessary violence I stepped in and stopped the fight, with loud support from the onlookers, mostly women. The man with the shirt pointed to it with a mute question, what now? I said that I was a visiting American (this was greeted with some applause) and that in America in such cases we take a collection for the aggrieved party, and I took my beret off, put a ruble in it, and handed it to the most vocal woman, who soon made the rounds ending with the shirt man and handing him the money from the beret. It all ended up amicably, to everybody's satisfaction.

It was too late for the bookstore now, and I proceeded to the Belorussian railroad station, prompted by a recent movie with the same title. It seemed to me that part of the movie had been shot at the station as it looked just as dreary. The tea I had in the cafeteria was served in a chipped cup, and the wooden tables were dirty. Walking around the station I noticed a group of men in the back congregating around something. When I asked one of them what it was, he replied, "The best vodka in Russia," and pointed to a metal bucket on the ground, into which men were dipping tin cups and paying a man next to the bucket. When I approached him, he handed me a cup and stretched his hand on which I saw several ruble bills. When I took just a small dip, he pointed out that I had paid for a full cup. I told him that I wanted first to disinfect the cup with a little vodka. This was apparently something new to them, and they all stopped, watching me. A man with an empty cup asked me what was I going to do with the vodka after rinsing. When I said pour it out, he insisted that I pour it into his cup instead of wasting it. After sloshing the vodka around a little in the cup, I poured it into his, then dipped my cup in the bucket, filled it about half way, and told the vendor to give the rest to the thirsty man. He drank it in one powerful gulp, exhaling vigorously, which made me think it was so good. One swallow convinced me that it was a devil's brew, and my face must have shown it, judging by the general laughter. I looked at my man watching me and handed him my cup. He bowed deeply and said,

"Dyakuyu, Pane!" (Thank you, Sir),

startling me. This thank you formula I had never heard, and was to hear only once more, on leaving one of Moscow's best restaurants, when a liveried attendant, an Emil Jannings' look-alike, thanked me in exactly the same words after he helped me into my coat, and I gave him a ruble. In this type of language, a mixture of Polish (the garbled title) and Ukrainian, but mostly old Slavic was refreshing to hear the old politeness surviving, even on this level.

But it was the next entry that I particularly enjoyed making, going beyond the proper date box into the blank pages in the back of the diary. It was a Sunday excursion to Zagorsk, an old monastery town with cathedrals and churches containing old sculptures and frescos, and old XVI-century defense walls with towers. The town was filled on that particular mid-summer Sunday, and the pilgrims, whom I was surprised to see, arriving on foot and by bus, gave it a festive air. As we were entering the monastery compound through its wide-open gates in the wall, something on the right gatepost caught my attention: it was a metal rectangular plaque with raised writing on it. I moved closer and started reading, slowly because it was in what looked like Old Russian. The group stopped, waiting for me, but our instructors and the monastery guides, realizing it would take me long to read the writing, decided to go on, with just one instructor and one guide staying behind with me to help me catch up with the rest. The moment I realized what the writing was about, I took out my diary and started copying, with the instructor looking over my shoulder and marveling at my knowledge of Old Church Slavonic, which required very little help on her part, unless the letters were worn out and hard to read. The copying done and the instructor giving a quick check for omissions, we caught up with the group as it was admiring the frescos of Andrei Rublev in one of the churches. The rest of the excursion I spent reading and re-reading the text and looking at the walls imagining what it was like to defend the monastery in the Time of Troubles in Russia.

By then our instructors knew about my insatiable curiosity about everything historical, and when on the return trip by train there was an educational record about the intricate network of canals connecting the local rivers in order to supply Moscow "occupied by the Poles," and I started to take notes again, the record was repeated to let me catch everything I wanted and needed. Others in our group would have preferred other records, musical, but our Russian escorts were firm in accommodating me, by giving anything educational or historical a high priority. It was the same when visiting St. Petersburg and I stopped the bus to examine the markings of the Flood of 1824, and the Bronze Horseman statue (Peter the Great) as an inspiration for Pushkin's poem of the same title, based on that flood.

My background and work in Russian (and Polish) literature, without a doubt the highest in the entire group (if one considers work with and under Harkins, Stilman, Yershov, Adamowicz and Belknap in literature, and Leda Berryman, Grigoriev and Galina Stilman in language), was now becoming extremely useful and important. Without it, I would not have been able to make certain discoveries as, for example, finding the house in Moscow once belonging to Princess Zinaida Volkonskaya, the site of the famous meetings of Pushkin and Mickiewicz; and the Taras Shevchenko museum in Kiev. With this background, the new findings (the Zagorsk plaque particularly) and new knowledge (details of the Polish occupation of Moscow, for example), were falling in their proper place and helping to make me an expert.

But scholarly discoveries and adventures were not my only goal in Russia (officially, they were not even a part of the program, which was specifically an exchange of language teachers between the United States and the Soviet Union), which for me was to get to know the country as well as possible, because there was no guarantee that there would be another chance for me to do it. On the contrary, my plans to be the group leader the following year were shattered from the beginning by my breaking most of the ground rules and overstepping the guidelines.

I was lucky to enjoy a special relationship with the Dean, who asked me to call on him after the ugly scene with the Ukrainian (he knew about it), assuring me that the man would be properly penalized (I was hoping it would not be expulsion), and asking me how he could make my stay even more productive. At that time I still smoked a pipe on occasions, and since the Dean was a pipe smoker, I brought mine along with a tin of fine Dutch pipe tobacco, which he immediately asked to try and marveled at its taste and aroma. I made him a present of the tin, which he called a "royal [tsar's] gift." I asked him whether it was possible for me to get a car and the driver who was a veteran to visit the field of the Battle of Kursk, which was of special interest to me, and on the way visit the site of Kulikovo Pole. He smiled at the range of my interests, promised to do what he could, and reminded me of the short range of our independent excursions, which I was aware of.

My battlefields excursion was disallowed, as was also the application by a friendly Ukrainian to take me to his cabin on the river Ob, beyond the Urals, which was just as well as both would conflict with the group's scheduled excursions which I did not want to miss. Among them was one to a charming recreation spot in the upper reaches of the Volga, still unpolluted at this point but already wide. Our instructors soon found a place to rest (my companions were always in need of one), where I changed into shorts and sneakers and proceeded in the direction of what sounded like a volleyball game. It was the same group that had been practicing in the university yard, practicing on an outing. They immediately invited me to join them. The girl who had first recognized me as a spiker proposed a match between a team consisting of her, me, and a blond Teutonic giant (an East German from Rostock, I later found out) and the rest. We were outnumbered, but between my and the giant's spikes and the girl's excellent set-ups, we had too much power and won. The loud booms of the spikes attracted a crowd of spectators, which was not unusual in this sports obsessed society, where sports served not only propaganda purposes, but also as a distraction from life's hardships, which could not be entirely hidden or ignored.

To cool off after the game I decided to take a swim in the Volga. After crossing it, I was caught in a strong current on the way back, probably because I was tiring. By then my group was already walking to the train, except for Lydia Polyushkina, a young Russian instructor from Queens College in New York, who stayed behind for me.

Lydia was closest to me in the entire group, mainly because she was interested in sports, and actively, too, by getting to know Olga Morozova during the latter's stay in Queens for the US Open Tennis Tournament. Like me in Warsaw in 1959, she was as emotional in Moscow in 1971, caring for the city to the extent that when I once threw a butt on the street near the Kremlin she had me pick it up. On that occasion she had another shock. Passing a statue, I named the two men in it, Minin [Kuzma] and Pozharski [Dmitri], without even stopping to look at them. But Lydia stopped, turned around, ran to the statue and came back asking "How did you know it?" "It couldn't be anybody else" I explained. Impressed, she remembered it, and at the water's edge did the right thing trying to help the man, even wading into the water and moving towards him, but he waved her back, unwilling to place her in danger with him. Instead, he tried again, this time dropping to the bottom, swimming under the strong current and emerging in a weaker one, near where Lydia was waiting with his things.

Surprisingly, this little incident points to the complicated problem of Polish-Russian relations. It became clear to me when there were no applause from onlookers on shore, as is the custom in Russia in such cases. They looked disappointed that I had come out from a brush with danger. Lydia noticed it, and asked if I could explain it. This was already after the Zagorsk excursion and the incident at the statue of Minin/Pozharski. I told Lydia that the statue depicted the organizers of an uprising against a Polish garrison in Moscow, and Zagorsk had been besieged by the Poles, while the upper Volga region had made Russia's last stand during the *smuta* (Time of Troubles). People here knew it, because they learned it in school, as part of history. They also knew that I was Polish, because they watched the volleyball game and heard the Russian girl call me "a Polish friend."

There was another discovery I made in connection with the incident and the preceding excursions, namely that it was possible to compare the Moscow uprising against the Polish garrison in 1613, with the Warsaw uprising against the Russian garrison in 1794, simply because just as one of the Russian organizers, Minin, was not a nobleman but a merchant, one of the Polish organizers, Jan Kilinski, was a shoemaker (later made colonel by Kosciuszko), pointing to the popular nature of both uprisings. Of course, the final results were entirely different, but that's another story.

For me, the 10-week stay in the Soviet Union was of enormous value, providing me with knowledge and insight I would have otherwise not obtained and not only in Moscow, but also in the former capital, St. Petersburg, renamed Leningrad after the Revolution, and the ancient capital, Kiev, where I had chosen to go rather than Tbilisi in Georgia, regretting that it was not possible to go to both.

In Moscow, an event of great importance was the visit to the Lenin Library, and observing how a Soviet library worked, with entire areas out of bounds, and some materials allowed only to be read under supervision of a librarian, in order to prevent making notes or photocopies.

The crowning part of the visit was a meeting with the chief librarian, a well-educated woman, in the spacious special collections room. After showing us wonderful old manuscripts, beautifully bound, frequently encrusted with gold or jewels, she produced what she called a "special" item that the library was proud of, the first edition of Nicolas Copernicus *De Revolutionibus Orbium Caelestium*. Seeing it took my breath away, and my first thought was what Polish library it had come from, and to the great annoyance of my American companions I voiced the question. Caught by surprise, the woman went red in the face, unable or unwilling to answer. I took pity on her saying that it was probably from the magnificent library of Bishop Joseph Andrew Zaluski, while thinking that he had been one of the Senators whose deportation in 1767 was the cause of the Bar Confederacy. His great library was loaded by the order of Catherine the Great after the Third Partition onto peasant carts and transported to St. Petersburg and there left to the mercy of the elements until a sufficiently large house was built for it. Even then some of the leather bindings, and parchment, were cut into strips to bind other volumes, later to be found by scholars and laboriously restored. I didn't say any of this, but I was determined to report what I had seen to the Polish National Library in Warsaw.

One of my colleagues, Joan Delaney, a former nun and, after Lydia, the closest to me, was an avid researcher of Bulgakov, of whom I had only read so far his Civil War play *The Days of the Turbins*. Joan got me interested in his masterpiece, long out of print and not reprinted, *Master and Margarita*, a Polish translation of which I immediately bought in the "Friendship" store and read in two evenings, becoming thoroughly captivated by its mysticism and supernatural and was, strangely, affected by it on at least three occasions; equally strangely in the three "capitals" in succession. The first one occurred not in Moscow itself but some distance from it at Leo Tolstoy's "Yasnaya Polyana," where I was pleasantly surprised, when shown the great writer's sparsely furnished bedroom which included a piano, to hear that he played on it "his favorite composer, Chopin." But this was not the Bulgakov-induced strange experience, which occurred in the huge filled-to-capacity gazebo outside.

This was tea-time, for which I was sharing a small table with Joan and two other American participants and, this is important because he was witness to all three of the occurrences, a Russian-American by the name of Savyeli. As Joan was entertaining us with her own experiences with Bulgakov, I suddenly heard behind my back the clinking of glasses as if several were hitting against each other. I remembered seeing earlier a girl carrying a huge tray of glasses full of boiling water, resting it on her shoulder and supporting it with the other hand. I realized that the girl was now near our table—right behind me. Without turning around I stood up as if in slow motion in a film, put my left hand under the tray and steadied it just as it was about to crash onto our table scalding the women and Savyeli, and with my right hand lifted a glass already leaning to one side and spilling its contents, scalding me, and sat down to a burst of standing ovation by all.

This was Russia at its best, grateful and appreciative, especially the servant girl, who couldn't find words to thank me while sobbing, overcome by emotion. I told her it was not her fault, that there were too many glasses, and I reached in my pocket and handed her a small American compact (of which I had several) to "powder her nose" which produced another round of applause followed by Joan's intricate efforts to explain this via Bulgakov, and Savyeli's looking at me with undisguised wonder.

It was Savyeli who was not only a witness but almost an unwitting victim in the second occurrence which took place on a busy street in Leningrad. We were waiting to cross the street to where the bus was to pick us up, with Savyeli just starting to move and me still carrying on a conversation with a talkative Russian and waving back to some girls in the upper windows of a building opposite when behind me I heard the loud roar of a car. Without turning I reached, grabbed Savyeli by the collar of his coat and pulled him to the sidewalk just as the car whizzed by leaving a smudge on his coat. All the terrified man could say was "You didn't even see the car" to which I said that I had heard it and seen the expression in the eyes of the man I had been talking to who was facing the street the car was coming from. Both men gave me long, wondering looks.

Leningrad was also the scene of an encounter which, while having nothing to do with Bulgakov, disturbed me, especially in its aftermath. The hotel our group had booked happened to be a favorite watering hole of alcoholic Finns who checked in for short stays, bought great quantities of vodka and drunk until they passed out, at which time the militia would be called to deliver them, like so many logs, to the nearest border crossing. I tried to find a reason for this arrangement, but it was most likely dictated by hard currency. Since I don't suffer drunks gladly, I would stay out late, taking advantage of the northern evenings' "daylight," visiting the "Bronze Horseman" and rereading its dedication which is very snappy in Russian:

> "Petru Pervomu, Yekaterina Vtoraja"
> (To Peter the First, Catherine the Second).

Returning one evening later than usual, when it was already dark, after stopping in a crowded restaurant and accepting an invitation by a young Armenian farmer loaded with rubles after having sold his produce (his date, a young Russian from Kaliningrad, a fact which interested me greatly, was a devoted Stalinist, rejecting my and the Armenian's accusing him of murdering the Polish prisoners in Katyn, saying at this late date that the Germans had done it), I missed the hotel stop, and found myself suddenly in a strange part of town, and got off immediately. A young Russian approached me offering help. He guessed from news reports that I must be an American staying in the hotel I had just missed. We walked back and talked. He had something important to tell me, and asked if I would I meet him early the next evening in an abandoned cabin, and he gave me detailed directions, leaving me near the hotel, out of sight of the doorman.

The "doorman" expressed mild surprise at the lateness of my return, adding that he had left some hot tea and sweet rolls for me on the table in the sitting room, and while checking it out asked me politely what I had seen interesting tonight. When I told him the "Bronze Horseman" he smiled approvingly. In the sitting room I found Lydia and Savyeli, still up and drinking tea and vodka (courtesy of the Finns) of which I also had some, telling them about the dinner with the Armenian and his Kaliningrad date, and how amazed I was that someone in Armenia should know about the Katyn Forest massacre.

The next day was some kind of day of mourning, and we visited the well-landscaped cemetery of World War II defenders of Leningrad, rows upon rows of huge rectangular graves containing 500 bodies each. I had to admit that this was an even greater sacrifice of human lives than Warsaw's except, again, the end results were different. Perhaps it was because of such thoughts that I decided to keep the date with the young Russian. After an early supper I filled my thermos with coffee (a welcome courtesy of the kitchen manager in exchange for a souvenir pin of the Kosciuszko Foundation—the Russians are avid collectors and go for such things), put also some American candy in my briefcase (I had some in reserve from the Embassy store) and set out. The doorman was on the verge of starting a conversation but I pretended I didn't notice and kept going at a fast pace which soon brought me into a swampy area with boards thrown over pools of water beyond which was a dilapidated cabin in which I found the Russian sitting at a rickety table eating apples. He was very happy to see me, offering me some of his apples and some stale bread, with me sharing some of my coffee (a rarity in Russia) and candy, and we had a modest late supper during and after which the man told me his story.

As a young boy after the war he had lived in Poland with his father who was stationed there briefly in some legal capacity but was soon recalled to Russia when it was felt that his heart was not in the prosecutor's work. His son was admitted to an engineering school and, afterwards, employed in the production of rockets and missiles, but his and his father's stay in Poland was always held against him and when he received a postcard from some philatelic club with a stamp showing some aspect of the American space program, he was accused of being a spy and, since there was nothing else against him, reduced to the low-grade job of driving a garbage truck. It was then that he decided that the Soviet Union was an evil system aiming to dominate the world. He began to give me production figures for rockets and missiles proving that if the pace of production continued, the West would have no choice but to capitulate or face annihilation. When I started taking notes he stopped me, saying that I would have to memorize the figures. I told him I didn't have a good memory for figures and it would have to be somebody else who would take them; I was determined to do something about it, knowing that there was a person at the Embassy whose job description suggested that he was in intelligence work. It wasn't that I trusted the Russian man implicitly, he had a personal grudge that was likely to affect his credibility but he was quoting vital figures that should be checked. We agreed that if someone came to meet him, that someone would be standing under a clock in the Leningrad railway station next Sunday at noon, checking his watch against the clock, and was to be approached with a question about the correct time, when the appropriate figures could be quickly given orally. That settled, we parted company, with the Russian guiding me across the water pools.

It was back to Moscow the same day by night train to my regret, with no chance to make a stop at Novgorod, or even see it from the window. I long suspected that the trips were arranged in such a way as to afford the visitor as little chance as possible to view the countryside. But I insisted on at least setting foot on Novgorod soil, and of course my instructors had the door of the carriage open for me to take a lonely short walk and think of Alexandr Nevsky and his times. When I told that to the conductor who followed me to take me back to the train, he asked how I knew about Nevsky. "It's history," I told him, made a Novgorod entry in my diary, had some of my coffee, freshly refilled in the hotel, and slept the rest of the way.

The next day, while my colleagues were resting after the Leningrad "exertion" ("bednye" or "poor souls" our ever caring women instructors called them),I took off to the Embassy, requesting to see whom I thought to be the proper person. Aware of how well the Western outposts were infiltrated in the Communist countries, I refused to fill out a file card stating my name and the reason of my visit. But I was admitted into what looked like a sound-proof room (padded) and received by a reasonably young man behind a clean desk with an American flag next to it. We shook hands and sat down, he cast a quick look up toward a heavy light fixture on the ceiling (like Kolya in my room), pointed to a blank file card on his desk, nodded, and started a small talk about the baseball season in America while jotting something on a clean sheet of paper and passing it to me. I was commenting on the pennant races in America while reading his message, which was an invitation to a baseball game at the Luzhniki Stadium between the staffs of the American and Canadian embassies, and to come ready to play if they were short a man. He was the captain, and he knew about my athletic prowess. Was there anything he could do for me? the small talk continued. Yes, he could advise me who to see to change the itinerary of my return trip, since I want to meet my son who is in summer school in Cracow, and visit my war-time comrades-at-arms in London. He thought the agency that arranged the trip was my best bet, since they must have an office in Moscow, and as for my son, a letter from him arrived today from Poland, and he handed it to me, saying it should help me in my plans, and wished me good luck. I was eager to read the letter.

Paul was informing me that on July 13th, his 18th birthday, he received a summons from the American Embassy in Warsaw to present himself personally in the Embassy to register for the military draft, and he was now registered.

Paul's information, not totally unexpected, introduced a new element into my existence, putting all else on a back burner, because America was still at war in Vietnam. I had to admire American efficiency in reaching its citizens even abroad when they were needed, but this need was a misunderstanding and a result of miscalculation for which the young of the country were paying with their lives, crippling the nation in the process. This was not a war I wanted my sons to be involved in. There was no glory in it, because it was a dirty war, cruel and merciless, fit for mercenaries but not innocent and idealistic youth. Who were the morons in Washington who were willing to send 18-year olds to certain death? I often thought that the war could have been won if all the American soldiers were above the age of 25. A loyal citizen, while I didn't want America to lose a war, I was going to do everything to spare my son the trauma of this particular one, even if it meant taking his place, a solution I had thought about. A different solution suggested itself while in Russia.

I was aware that there was a large group of Vietnamese students in the dormitory a few floors above mine, and that, like the Chinese, they kept to themselves, even doing their own cooking, mostly mutton and rice, judging by the smells reaching my room in the evenings. After reading Paul's letter, I decided to pay them a visit. To my surprise, some of them knew who I was, having seen me practicing volleyball in the yard, or hitting tennis balls on the wall, and they invited me to join them in the meal. We conversed in French and Russian, depending who knew which better. As a rule I don't accept chance invitations to meals, unwilling to embarrass myself or the hosts in case of disagreeable food, but there is not much wrong you can do with mutton and rice. As a matter of fact, it was very good, even the sauce I am always wary of, and there was good wine to wash the fat down with. There was something else, excellent coffee, served in beautiful French china, and a glass of cognac, served only to me and another guest of whom I became fully aware when he raised his glass and proposed a toast to Ho Chi Minh. When I drank it, he said, in very good French, that drinking it speaks well of me, and that I must therefore be an opponent of the war. He was putting me on the spot, and I had to be careful what I said. All eyes were on me.

I told them that before I became an American citizen I was a Polish soldier, and Poland's motto is "For Your Freedom and Ours," which means that we will not be free until everybody is free. As a loyal American citizen I don't criticize America, but I am very unhappy about the war, especially now, when my son could be drafted into it, and be killed unnecessarily. He won't be killed if he is careful, the man said, but he could become a prisoner of war, in which case not a hair will fall off his head, because he is my son, and they like my attitude, and he asked for Paul's picture. I gave him one from the graduation, and he gave me an address that I immediately entered into my diary to notify him if and when Paul should indeed end up in Vietnam.

I wrote to Paul congratulating him on his ability to move freely in Poland (he made the trip to Warsaw on his own, getting a lot of fatherly advice from a Consul) and his progress in Polish, judging by his letter. Otherwise I advised him to think in terms of getting a deferment, by which time the war in Vietnam would be over. I also wrote him about the Volga swim, about volleyball, and tennis.

Tennis on a high level became a reality on Saturday, after the Embassy baseball meeting. The man was already at the stadium when I arrived, after some problems entering, in which he did not intervene, for obvious reasons, but my University ID was sufficient, as he thought it would be. I gave him all the details, some of which he asked me to repeat, and by his questions I could tell that he had been trained well. He spoiled the impression when I reminded him that the rendezvous was tomorrow and he said that unfortunately he was beginning his vacations in Crimea on that same day. I was disappointed with the American intelligence work in Moscow, but perhaps I was too hasty under the influence of Paul's letter, in which the Warsaw Embassy seemed to function so well. Discussing the matter later with a former Ambassador in the Soviet Union, I was told that the man, for his own protection, would not tell me that he was going to follow up on my story.

Since there was no need for me on the baseball team, and I had my tennis things with me, I went to the tennis stadium nearby, remembering that it was semifinal day in the Russian nationals. Both Morozova and Metrevelli were in, both reaching the finals, and both beating Polish opponents, which only confirmed my earlier theory about Polish-Russian relations in sports.

There were other pertinent revelations. During the other semifinal, between a second-rate French player and a Rumanian (not Ilia Nastase) a young woman approached me and, knowing somehow who I was, asked me to use my influence and get us a court. I looked at her as if to say "This is your country!" but I spoke to an official and a side court was assigned to us. It was a good red clay court, the young woman was unbelievably fast on her feet, it was my favorite surface, and pretty soon we had more spectators watching us than the semifinalists. After a set which I won 6:2, I asked her whether she was a sprinter, and she replied indignantly, "Don't you know who I am?" and then I recognized in her the fastest woman in the Soviet Union, just returned from an athletic meet in Los Angeles. I asked her, curious of her reply, who was the fastest woman in the world, and without the slightest hesitation she replied "Shevinskaya" (Irena Kirszenstein-Szewinska, a Polish sprinter voted once the fastest woman of all time).

This was the answer I expected, and I was pleasantly disposed towards her and when she invited me to tea at her home I accepted, only to be called a spy by her father and sister (a *candidat*, Ph.D. candidate in science, earning, as she boasted, 260 rubles a month), like every foreigner in Russia, according to the IREX briefing.

The excursion to Kiev was another revealing experience eroding my opinion of the Soviet Union and its prospects. A small plane without air conditioning and refreshments except hard candy was a veritable torture chamber. When the stewardess rolled out her trolley in the aisle with its meager offerings, there was a race towards her rather than waiting in one's seat, and the plane tilted dangerously to one side, causing the pilot to shout that if passengers don't return to their seats we will surely crash.

The Kiev (Kiiv) landing was an exercise in pilot daring and airport inefficiency. Things settled down when we were met by Kiev University representatives and taken to a welcome luncheon. The university, painted in shocking red, was not the most cheerful place, and its Dean, an obviously political appointee, was saying all the wrong things in his welcoming speech, that Kiev suffered the most in the war, as if Leningrad and Warsaw had been in another war, and what a great school it was: exchange with Cracow.

I found Kiev a beautiful and warm city, even more than Moscow and Leningrad (whose name I never got used to), all three embedded in my memory through history and literature, the latter more pervasive in the two northern cities, with Kiev having already the smell of the south (in that respect I would have liked to visit Odessa). In my mind there were the inevitable, but rather improvised comparisons with American geography, with Leningrad and Moscow (perhaps reversed?) standing for New York and Boston (Chicago?), and Kiev (Odessa?) for New Orleans (perhaps Washington?), with only Kiev having a great (big) river.

Great river distinction (Dnieper) is something Kiev shares with foreign capitals (and great cities) such as Vienna and Budapest (Danube) and, to a lesser extent Cracow, Warsaw, and Gdansk (Vistula), Paris (Seine), London (Thames), Berlin (Spree), Hamburg (Elbe), Washington (Potomac), New York (Hudson), but not Moscow (few people know that it has a navigable river of the same name) or Leningrad (St. Petersburg, whose Neva is only known from history and literature), and the quintessential Russian river, the Volga, with its great tributaries Oka and Kama, is really on the peripheries of European Russia, almost bordering its lower reaches with Kazakhstan.

Unlike Moscow and Leningrad, Kiev is marred by too many statues. Next to the magnificent one of St. Vladimir, the Christianizer of Old Russia in 988, overlooking the Dnieper and bearing a cross, there is the less magnificent one of Bohdan Chmielnicki, Ukrainian hero of dubious fame, on horseback in a less prominent location, and then the countless likenesses of Lenin, one directly in front of our hotel, displaying a text consisting of 99 words. Savyeli and I counted the words, to the great interest of onlookers and discovered that 50 of them were of Polish origin and 49 of Russian, corresponding with the linguistic ratio in Ukrainian cited by Professor George Shevelov at Columbia. The statue became a meeting site and the chocolate-colored Lenin a butt of jokes about Kievans licking it.

The highlights of the Kievan excursion included a visit to the Taras Shevchenko Museum, where this leading Ukrainian Romantic poet, who had placed its literature on record during this rich period in Slavic literatures, is on display. Among the still poorly catalogued materials, I found, to the surprise of our instructors, references to a Polish companion of Shevchenko from their Siberian exile days, who later took care of the ailing poet until his death. It is regrettable that this chapter in the history of Polish-Ukrainian relations is little known, with most Ukrainians dwelling on the unproductive might-have-beens of the Battle of Beresteczko in 1651.

For me personally another highlight was a symbolic swim in the magnificent Dnieper flowing through the city's lower grounds, when after crossing the river I was greeted by Polish-speaking onlookers with the customary, "How is the water?" which, if anything, told me that there still was a Polish presence in Kiev left after a century-long (1569-1667/86) Polish reign and subsequent Russian rule. Another was a field trip to the junction of the Dnieper with Desna, its biggest left bank tributary, and another swim, almost as perilous as the Volga earlier.

Otherwise there were visits to old churches and dinners with the hosts, in intimate atmosphere since there were only 8 of us (10 with the two instructors) on this trip, the others having gone to Tbilisi (as supposedly *bona fide* Slavists, they should have come to Kiev). My meeting with Ukrainian dissidents, allegedly arranged by Vladimir with a literary circle, did not materialize, since nobody approached me in the agreed upon church. It was a pity, since I wanted to talk to them, among other things, about my third and grimmest Bulgakov-induced experience, which is, however, not germane to this narrative. I left Kiev with mixed feelings about the future of Ukraine.

Back in Moscow I was putting my affairs in order. There were still three experiences worth mentioning, with the first one quite extraordinary and very Polish-Russian. A group of young doctoral candidates in history visited me with the expressed desire to "apologize for the Partitions of Poland" [!] but insisting that they had been engineered by Prussia. I was in total agreement with them on that, even pointing out that just as Lithuania, then the Polish-Lithuanian Commonwealth and Poland itself in the XIV-XVIIth centuries were filling a power vacuum in the East, Russia was doing it in the West in the XVIIIth when Sweden, Poland and Turkey declined simultaneously, with Poland having the additional problem of centuries-long rivalry with Russia for the control of their border-lands. They liked that, but they didn't like when I told them I couldn't forgive Russia its XIXth century Russification in trying to make of Poland a province of Russia, with all the persecution it entailed. They maintained that the Poles had brought it on themselves by always looking down on the Russians, considering them inferior, even the horses they were riding, and they cited appropriate passages in literature. They were right about that and I made a careful note of the passages in my diary.

Before the young scholars left, I showed them color pictures from the summer commencement at Columbia, which they admired and begged for copies of which I let them have and which are now gracing their living rooms, as they said they would, for better understanding in the future. Also, harking back to our earlier debate, and the horses, I recommended that they read Leonid Leonov's *The Thief*. Finally, I asked them if they knew the location of the former house of Zinaida Volkonskaya. They knew and even why I wanted to find it. This was my second experience.

Princess Zinaida Volkonskaya's house was near where the "shirt fight" had taken place on Gorky Street. I must have seen it, but looking for it I still couldn't find it. Not one to give up, I asked two building workers. They burst out laughing and pointed to a little metal plaque on the side of the house near the one they were working on. On it, the Pushkin-Mickiewicz meetings were clearly recorded.

My last day in Moscow was spent, at her request, in the company of Sheherezade. Just as the fast runner had used me to get a court for us, I was now using Shakhridze to open doors for me. Her energy was inexhaustible. When my companions were preparing for the farewell ceremony, which I was going to pass up except for the meal ("bring a date" the lady-director suggested), Sheherezade and I were criss-crossing Moscow taking care first of the travel agency (difficult, but not with her), purchasing some gold-plated bargain glass holders; buying something for her in the American Embassy store (all she wanted was raisins and corn flakes), and at noon stopping in a Polish boutique.

This was the third experience, an oasis of Polishness in Russia, not the traditional patriotic one but a harbinger of a free market. The two young ladies running it were epitomes of good looks, good fashions and good manners. Soft music was playing the latest numbers of Stan Borys while elegant Russian women were making their purchases. One of them, sensing that I was a foreigner, asked me how this place compared with similar ones in the West. I said very well, except perhaps in interior design, which was not the most important thing at this stage here. I noticed how the owners listened, coming over to the little table we were sitting at and offering refreshments. Coffee, perhaps? It was excellent, coming from the hard currency store. Where were they getting their products? Made in Poland in an arrangement with local dressmakers and designers, all of high quality. Would Sheherezade like something (what a lovely name, shall we play it for her? when I nodded, Nikolai Rimski-Korsakov's plaintive tune filled the room)? The Russian woman offered to help her pick something suitable, a pair of laced-up light leather sandals, very exotic, and highly appreciated, adding that everything she wears comes from Poland, including underwear, and then she said something that made the experience real:

"What Paris is to Warsaw, Warsaw is to Moscow."

It was with this thought on my mind that I left Russia.

• • • •

On the first day in New York, to get reacquainted with it, I took an evening walk with my wife on Broadway. On our way back on College Walk we passed Prof. Brzezinski carrying a briefcase, probably on his way home after late evening work. I was about to call after him to tell him about my trip which I was sure would interest him when I thought better of it. I felt it would result in a meeting or a class visit calling on statements from me about the Soviet Union which, in view of my experiences, would become known in the university, especially since I had intended to criticize the laxity of American intelligence. In view of my earlier decisions, I decided to stand by them and occupy myself instead with putting my notes in order.

In line with those decisions I was to concentrate on language and literature, the first of which was about to materialize with Ludwik Krzyżanowski having retired that year and designated me his successor. Our earlier designs were also revived regarding Columbia College students, since I was going to have at least one of them in my class, for starters, my son Paul. Because of that, I was going to make

Polish the best language course at Columbia, and the best Polish course in America. Accordingly, I also selected the best textbook, Schenker's, and began to study it, while working on my notes and waiting for a call from Columbia.

The call never came. Instead, Paul came after the first class and told me that Polish was being taught by a certain Mr. Aleksander Minkowski, who was writing a book about New York and amusing the class with his adventures, including stories about cockroaches. I listened to it with dismay turning into disgust. What kind of people I was dealing with? When Paul next told me he was dropping the course as a waste of time I agreed with him, but I almost wept. What a waste! With his summer course in Poland and practice with our relatives there, he would have been a star in my class, but to waste time with a minor writer? I was aware that there were such scribblers, the name Olgierd Budrewicz comes to mind, even supported by the Kosciuszko Foundation, writing uninformed books because of poor grasp of English and misinforming Poland about America and Polonia, but that the head of a Polish program in a major university should use scarce funds for a Polish course as a financial aid to a useless writer? And at what cost, and what loss! I literally ran to confront Harkins. This was the second time he was harming me, but this time it really hurt, and I told him so, and that the department was losing a student! His reply was that Harold was in charge of the Polish program. "A plague on both your houses!" and I meant it.

On my way out I ran into a former fellow-student who had been translating Russian scientific articles for the Museum of Natural History, but was starting a teaching job, giving up the Museum job, for which he had promised to recommend a replacement. Within half an hour I was there, met the Dean of ichthyology, accepted the job at 10 cents a word, took an article to do overnight and became an expert and fast translator with my improved Russian, spending an increasing amount of time at the Polish Institute.

My work at the Polish Institute and in connection with the Polish American Congress (*Poles in America*) is described elsewhere in this book, as is also my progress in becoming the leading expert on Polish-Russian literary relations, for which I was to be funded by the Lanckoronski Foundation whose representatives in London were aware of my works, as were also Slavists in Poland who were using them.

In some aspects of Polish-Russian relations I was able to move ahead of the field, in others I demolished certain stereotypes hurting those relations, for example the one I neglected to tell the young historians in Moscow that Poland was not a highway for attacks against Russia, because the only time that Poland participated in an attack on Russia, in 1812, that attack came from East Prussia.

In my research I developed a novel approach to the history of Russia, underlining the element of luck in it, absent in Polish history, hence its tragic course.

The most outstanding example of Russian luck was the premature death of Stephen Bathory (Stefan Batory, whom Halecki ranks among "the most glorious of our kings"), about whom a Russian chronicle said (in paraphrased words): "Batory died in Cracow...some Poles are glad...the fools... had he lived another year there would have been no room in this world for Russia..."—that year needed for a third and last campaign against Russia, "for everything" as he said.

Other examples of this good luck included Vitold stopping Tamerlane before another destruction of Moscow; the fall of Constantinople at the most opportune moment for Moscow (1453); the small population of Lithuania; the carelessness and immaturity of Charles XII; Peter talking himself out (with the help of his wife, Catherine) of the disaster of Pruth in 1711; Napoleon splitting the Polish army in 1812; Germany losing in the West in World War I; Hitler declaring war on America in World War II.

As pointed out to the young Russian historians in Moscow, Polish-Russian history was one of rivalry for control of the East European borderlands, as Halecki calls them (and as it is reflected in the literature of both countries), which ended with the victory of Russia in 1945, and the end of Prussia, but the victory became empty with the fall of Communism in 1991 when the borderlands became independent states. But one area remained untouched:

> Prussia was gone but, like an indestructible nightmare, it left behind a new reincarnation, the RUSSIAN KALININGRAD ENCLAVE, and a new problem. A remnant of an old Polish fiefdom, among other reincarnations, it has to be dealt with before it, too, becomes a nightmare.

WHAT IS TO BE DONE WITH THE
KALININGRAD ENCLAVE?

September 15, 1991

One of the benefits of the current upheaval in the Soviet Union is that we are at least learning history and geography or, more to the point, historical geography. This new knowledge helps us to understand the reasons behind the historically inevitable disintegration of the Soviet empire. History has a long memory that no amount of manipulation or justification will erase, especially if, as in the case of the Baltic states, the justifications ("window on Europe," security) are no longer valid. The same applies to other Russian-Soviet land grabs, particularly the one tacitly forgotten but at last beginning to attract attention, namely the obscure and increasingly isolated enclave called Kaliningrad oblast, so named after being carved out of the once formidable East Prussia by Stalin himself in 1945.

The enclave is part of the Russian Republic, whose President, Boris Yeltsin, intends to keep it that way, even if the oblast is separated from Russia by two republics, one of them already an independent state, Lithuania. Yeltsin's early recognition of Lithuania was allegedly in exchange for guaranteeing the civil rights of Russians living there and assuring the economic survival of the isolated Kaliningrad enclave. Looking at a map, and here geography helps, one wonders, how can tiny Lithuania, with economic problems of its own, assure the economic survival of an area inhabited by almost one million Russians, especially since the two territories are separated by a natural barrier, the Niemen River? We are obviously dealing here with the never-say-die Russian-Soviet-Russian manipulation. Otherwise why wouldn't Yeltsin address his concern to Poland, which has a long open border with the Kaliningrad oblast and whose economy is slowly but determinedly getting on track? If he did, he would cause the unmentionable to become known, that the entire former East Prussia once belonged to Poland, and here history is of enormous help.

Neither of the two countries now discussing the economic welfare of the Kaliningrad region have any historical right to it. The Russians "visited" East Prussia three times: during the Seven Years War, during the Napoleonic Wars, and towards the end of the Second World War, when they remained. There is a story how

Stalin, by then the undisputed master of Eastern Europe and then some, proposed to the members of the Polish Provisional Government before the Potsdam Conference how he planned to divide East Prussia between Poland and the Soviet Union. He took a pencil and asked how he should draw the dividing line on the map, from North to South or from West to East—as long as Königsberg (Kaliningrad) was in the Soviet part. The Poles chose the West-East line and that's how it is to this day.

As for the Lithuanians, if they had any tribal ties with the Baltic Prussians who inhabited the area in question in medieval times, these ties came to an end in the thirteenth century, when the Teutonic Knights not only conquered and colonized the whole of Prussia from Vistula to Niemen, but in the process wiped out and colonized the native pagan Prussians. Only the name remained. The Lithuanians still managed an occasional foray across the Niemen into Prussia, but the roles gradually switched, and it was the Teutonic Knights who were crossing the Niemen, conquering neighboring Samogitia in Lithuania proper, linking with another Germanic Order, the Sword Bearers, in Livonia (present-day Latvia), and creating a Baltic power stretching from Gdansk (Danzig) to Riga and threatening not only Lithuania but the Russian republics of Novgorod (defended by Aleksandr Nevsky) and Pskov as well. As for Lithuania, which had in the meantime filled the void after the receding Mongols and occupied the former Old Rus' lands stretching to the Black Sea (some Russian historians call this period the Russo-Lithuanian state), it was squeezed on two sides and cut off from the Baltic Sea, with its very capital, Vilnius, under siege. It was at this dangerous point that Poland came up with a solution, at first unofficially, by helping to defend Vilnius, and then on a monumental scale.

Ever since Christianity arrived in Poland in 966, the conversion of the troublesome pagan Prussians was a top priority. Adalbert, the Bishop of Prague, undertook the task for the Polish King, Boleslaw the Brave (his mother, a Bohemian Princess, brought Christianity into Poland), but was martyred by the Prussians. One of the reasons for the visit to Poland in the year 1000 by Otto III, the Emperor of Germany, was to pray at the relics of the holy martyr. Subsequent conversion attempts were equally unsuccessful, especially during the feudal division of Poland, when the neighboring province, Masovia, could barely contain the Prussians, let alone convert them. Exasperated, the Duke of Masovia, Konrad, invited the Teutonic Knights to help him with the task. The Grand Master of this knightly order, which was no longer needed in the Holy Land and not wanted in Hungary, readily accepted, and from then on Prussia became the battleground of Polish and Germanic interests. The year of the invitation, 1226, is considered one of the most fateful years in Polish history, when a mistake was committed that Poland was not able to erase, until it took two world wars, and still it is not done entirely satisfactorily.

It took the Teutonic Knights fifty years to conquer Prussia, but they did not conquer it for Masovia, but for themselves, forming a new state of ecclesiastical character, governed by the Teutonic Order: a state completely independent of Poland, and recognizing only the authority of the Holy See and that of the Empire. This "New Germany" as it was later called, began to devour its neighbors. The following century was critical. Luckily, Poland was coming out of its feudal division and began to solidify. The last king of the Piast dynasty, Casimir the Great, named as his successor his nephew, Louis of Anjou, King of Hungary, also the Great, who, having no sons, entered into an agreement with the Polish nobles that one of his three daughters succeed him on the Polish throne. In a stroke of genius, unique in Polish diplomacy, a great marriage was arranged in 1386 for the 12-year old virgin queen, Jadviga, perhaps not an ideal marriage to a man three times her senior, but the man was the Duke of Lithuania, Yagiełło, and because of that a perfect partner in a union that not only introduced Roman-Catholic Christianity into Lithuania, but was to turn the history of that part of the world around. (I wonder, as a footnote, whether the trip to Vilnius General Jaruzelski took during the Communist Party meeting in Moscow in February of 1386 was not to mark the 600th anniversary. If so, it would say much about this needlessly maligned man and about the royal wedding.) Suddenly Poland had a Queen *and* a King, whose cousin, Vitovt, another Great, perhaps the greatest Lithuanian of them all, was in the King's stead ruling Lithuania and controlling the East European world as far as the Volga Tatars. Together, the two cousins waged war on the Teutonic Knights and at Grunwald in 1410 inflicted a defeat on them from which the Order never fully recovered. It was an East-West battle, the only time Poland led the East against the West (the Knights came from almost every West European country). It is commemorated in a fine statue, commissioned for the New York World's Fair of 1939, and now standing in Central Park on a little hill at the back of the Metropolitan Museum.

For reasons that are not clear to this day, the King did not follow up the victory by taking Marienburg, the defenseless capital of the Order, sending the few survivors back to their own countries, and annexing all of Prussia. His younger son, Casimir, also had an opportunity to terminate the Order when the Prussian towns rose against it and asked the Polish King for protection, placing the whole of Prussia under his sovereignty. A long war with the Order ended in 1466 with a compromise treaty dividing Prussia into Royal or West Prussia, which henceforth remained firmly with Poland until the Partitions, and the rest, with Königsberg as its new capital, Unable to transfer the Order to the Turkish or Tatar borderlands, where it could have resumed its original vocation, the King resigned himself to its continuing presence, but on new conditions. This East Prussia was no longer to be an independent state, but a fief of Poland, paying homage to the king and providing him with reinforcements in case of necessity.

The Order, no longer a threat, continued to be an irritant, allying itself with enemies of Poland, whoever they might be at a given moment, and refusing to pay homage to the King. Exasperated, the youngest son of King Casimir, Sigismund I (The Old), was about to take decisive action when in 1525 an event took place that astonished the whole of Europe: in the great square in Cracow the homage was paid, but it was no longer the Grand Master of the Teutonic Order who knelt in person before the king, it was the secular, hereditary prince, the first Duke of Prussia. The former Grand Master had adopted the doctrines of Luther and the Order, whose religious mission had long been pure fiction, was secularized. With it an implacable enemy who, even though weakened, had remained a veritable nightmare to Poland, disappeared. The great event was celebrated in art and literature, the stone plate on which the homage took place was not to be touched, and is still there, and the nation rejoiced. Nobody paid much attention to the fact that the first secular Duke's name was Albert of Brandenburg, of the younger line of Hohenzollern, a name that would resound louder and louder.

The post-treaty East Prussia became Ducal Prussia, whose rulers, although vassals of Poland, were nevertheless an appanage of a German dynasty. When, through Poland's neglect, the right of succession passed to the elder line of Hohenzollerns, that of the

Elector of Brandenburg, Poland was suddenly faced with a rising power north and west, separated by Polish maritime provinces, the Royal Prussia. Through a skillful change of alliances during the Swedish "Deluge" of Poland, the "Great Elector," the most outstanding of the new rulers of Ducal Prussia, was freed from vassalage, and Poland's sovereignty over him ended in 1660. His successors soon became kings in the former Ducal Prussia, and when they next invaded and annexed formerly Polish or Bohemian and then Habsburg Silesia, Poland was suddenly encircled by its former vassal, who soon began to plot its downfall with Russia and Austria. The partitions of Poland followed, and after them two world wars, which annulled the partitions except for East Prussia, which escaped the consequences after the First World War, but after the Second fell victim to the famous pencil of Stalin, who wanted a piece of Germany.

Should this be allowed to stand? Shouldn't this be a matter for the International Tribunal? Should not the Kaliningrad enclave, in all fairness, be restored to Poland under its Polish name, *Królewiec*? Can we ignore history? Judging by some irresponsible statements by a Lithuanian group claiming the area under the name "Lithuania Minor" it would seem so, sadly. Frankly speaking, Lithuania is already larger than it was before its loss of independence; why start the new era with aggrandizement schemes in the style of the overburdened old Grand Duchy? Finally, what about the Russians living in the enclave? On linguistic grounds, at least, they would be more comfortable in Poland than in Lithuania. And once a Russian economic miracle occurs, and this is bound to happen, they might want to return to Russia to partake of the bounty and make room for the Poles who might want to leave Russia. As for the Kaliningrad naval base, it could be leased, in the same way that the United States leases its bases around the world.

What is to be done with the Kaliningrad enclave?

Eliminate it!

P.S. Latest reports in the EIR (*Executive Intelligence Review*) indicate that the Russian economic miracle is receding at an alarming pace.

18

Frank Mocha

THE FORMIDABLE UKRAINE

March 12, 1992

It was only a matter of time before informed thinkers, not just newspaper reporters and commentators (including self-styled "pundits") took up the case of Ukraine, potentially the most disruptive region in the post-Communist world. Dimitri K. Simes's [not so] recent "Get Tough with Ukraine" is such a welcome if harsh departure, even if it discusses only one explosive point of disruption, the Crimean question, but it is a useful beginning if one allows that Ukraine is still in the process of inventing itself, as a state and as a nation.

It is impossible to discuss Ukraine, one of the most abused regions in history, without delving into its distant past, when it was a borderland on the periphery of the Roman Empire, and a highway for the Scythians and the Sarmatians (both tribes strongly rooted in East European literature, folklore and pseudo-history) and other invaders who laid the region waste whenever they passed through it.

It was a no man's land without a name (Roxolania?) when it was chosen as an alternate route to Byzantium by Scandinavian princes, who in the process established a state along a Dnieper River, *their* highway, around 862. This so-called Old Rus, or Kievan Rus, the political ancestor of the Eastern Slavs, became christianized a little more than a century later (988), attaining a high level of civilization, but it was from the start threatened by new waves of nomads from the East, the Pechenegs and the Polovtsians, followed by the Mongols, who put an end to the state in 1240. But even before, the dynastic Rurik princes began to migrate northeastward, taking the patriarch with them and founding new political centers, Rostov, Suzdal, Tver, and the emerging Moscow. They, too, fell under the sway of the Mongols, and remained under the "Tatar yoke" for two centuries, throwing it off about the time of the fall of Byzantium in 1453, when the Dukes of Moscow, promoting themselves to Grand Dukes and later autocratic "Tsars of All the Russias," began the centuries-long process of reclaiming the lands of Old Rus they considered their patrimony under the newly developed political

505

theory of the "Third (and last) Rome." (Present-day rallying efforts by Moscow bear resemblance to this one).

With the exception of the short-lived "Kingdom of Galicia" in its western extremities bordering on Poland, the territory of the former Old Rus never experienced statehood after 1240 until now, as independent Ukraine and Belarus. During the intervening 750 years Old Rus changed rulers many times. The warrior Grand Dukes of Lithuania wrested it from the Tatars, who retreated into the Crimean peninsula. In 1569 the southern part of Old Rus, increasingly called the "Ukraine" was ceded to the Polish kings, when Poland and Lithuania transformed a dynastic union—initiated in 1386 in order to christianize Lithuania as a defense against the Teutonic knights— into a Commonwealth capable of stopping the westward expansion of Tsarist Russia. Russia had the upper hand for a few years, but the brilliant campaigns of Stephen Bathory and the ill-advised but over- whelming Polish intervention during the Time of Troubles, both with Cossack participation and both almost putting an end to Russia, showed Poland's potential to be *the* dominant East European power, a potential spoiled by an unfortunate Cossack rebellion in 1648 leading to a vicious civil war and a Russian intervention in 1654, which ended with Russia again on the brink of disaster and the Cossacks temporarily again on the side of Poland. Internal problems and the threat from the Ottoman Empire in Ukraine prevented Poland from gathering the fruits of the victories and settle the differences with Ukraine, especially under the popular King Jan Sobieski under whom Poland had its finest hour and last hurrah— Vienna 1683, when reportedly 10,000 Cossacks were rushing to his aid which, if true, would have been the last joint action unless one counts the ineffective initiatives by Ivan (Jan) Mazepa, after which Ukraine passed under permanent control of Russia.

In the following century the battle between Poland and Russia for control of Eastern Europe, so poignantly depicted by Pushkin in his "patriotic" odes (which include an allusion to "Bohdan's [Chmelnicki] heritage,") led to partitions (1772-1795), when Russia gained all the lands of the former Old Rus, except Galicia, which was annexed by Austria, and *never* belonged to Tsarist Russia. It returned to Poland with independence after the First World War, together with part of Belorussia. Both areas were seized by the Soviet Union in September of 1939 and incorporated into the Soviet Republics of Belorussia and Ukraine, in accordance with the

Ribbentrop-Molotov Pact a month earlier and remained within these republics after the Second World War, and are now within independent Belarus and Ukraine.

The nationalistic euphoria of independence ignores many facts which are not in the least euphoric. First, in the decisive Battle of Beresteczko (1651) over which the Ukrainians still agonize, they allied themselves with the Crimean Tatars, what does that say for a Christian people? Next, Ukraine (*and* Belarus) owes its western border to the Ribbentrop-Molotov Pact of ill repute, allowed to stand by the Yalta Agreement of equally ill repute, in disregard of the Treaty of Riga in 1921 after the Polish-Soviet war of 1920. Poland, the injured party but ruled by Communists after Yalta, never complained, just as it never claimed the northern part of former East Prussia, annexed by Stalin on a whim, while on another whim later (1954, on the 300th anniversary of Russia's intervention) Khrushchev gave Crimea to Ukraine, although the peninsula had never been part of it. Both leaders would turn in their graves if they saw what they have wrought. By robbing the neighbors of the Soviet Union (and Russia in Khrushchev's case), they were mostly fattening Ukraine, creating an albatross hard to drop. There is the matter of access, but in the case of the Crimea it is a simple one by using, like the retreating Germans in 1943, the Kerch peninsula route from the Kuban.

A map of the formidable Ukraine "equal to France," unlike France shows four protrusions: west into Poland, Czechoslovakia, Hungary and Rumania (the protrusions resemble a big tit suckled by a small brood); east into Russia (Donbas); and south into eastern Rumania and the Black Sea (The Crimean peninsula). Much blood was spilled by the Ukrainian Cossacks fighting the Crimean Tatars, but there is much Russian and Soviet history in the Crimea itself, including famous Sevastopol and infamous Yalta. But before Soviet and Russian history in the Crimea, there was Tatar (and Ottoman) history, with the rich merchant city Kaffa, an old Genoese colony, and fabulous Oriental slave markets, a history not to be ignored, if only because the national poets of Poland and Russia paid homage to the Tatar heritage while themselves exiles in the Crimea: Mickiewicz with a cycle of his "Crimean" sonnets; Pushkin with one of his "Oriental" tales. How many peninsulas, countries for that matter, can boast such honors?

The Tatar history in the Crimea was terminated by two acts of violence, the Russian conquest in the XVIIIth century and the Soviet deportation in the XXth. The best of all solutions for the Crimea would be to make amends for the violence and restore the sunny peninsula to the unfortunate expellees and their descendants after half a century of exile, not so long if one considers the return of the Israelis to their ancestral home after nearly two millennia. 166,000 Tatars have reportedly already returned to the Crimea from Central Asia. Membership in the Commonwealth of Independent States would be the next step.

Would the formidable Ukraine agree to such a solution?

Everybody else would!

But, surprisingly, this was not the consensus at a book party (*The Tatars of Crimea*, Return to the Homeland, 1998, Edward A. Allworth, Editor) at Columbia University, 3/5/98.

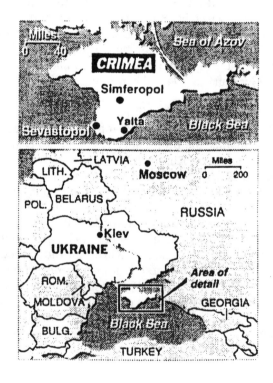

19

Frank Mocha

CONCLUSIONS

In my concern for Poland and search for perfection with American Polonia's help, I have listed from the beginning two seemingly insoluble problems, KALININGRAD and DEMOGRAPHY, listed at first in a reversed order, which is of no consequence because both are of equal importance and each, in its own way, a condition for perfection.

The solution of the first, left behind by Prussia, taken over by the Soviet Union, and inherited by Russia, would make Poland, in its geographical shape, "the most perfect Poland in a thousand years," removing or at least lessening its vulnerability vis-à-vis her two powerful neighbors which was present from the day of Independence in 1918 and proved fatal twenty years later; and also solving other problems and putting some Old World customs to rest.

Among the other problems is one of being Russia's neighbor, which never did anybody any good, as neighbors from the Baltic to the Pacific know only too well, Poland especially. That's why it is good that there is now a buffer zone between Poland and Russia consisting of independent states created out of the formerly contested borderlands—except that by virtue of the unfortunate KALININGRAD enclave Russia is still Poland's neighbor, a situation which could be aggravated further if one of the independent states, Belarus, keeps trying to enter into a union with Russia, bringing it right to Poland's doorstep on a wide front and next demanding access to KALIN-INGRAD, a "corridor" of ill-repute creating a nightmare for Poland.

This is a Polish problem and nobody will solve it for Poland. Raising it could conceivably affect Poland's chances for NATO membership, which in itself could be a bargaining chip, that's how important the problem is. To hear William Cohen, US Secretary of Defense say publicly and thoughtlessly that he has "no desire to die for Danzig" tells us what the West thinks of Poland's problems. To solve this one, Poland must become a viable economic force capable of offering inducements, like surplus grain, for example, or by building grain elevators and improving the lot of the Polish peasant in the process, but the problem *must* be solved, otherwise Poland will become Russia's hostage. To begin with, it must be the future President's mandate.

As for putting some Old-World customs to rest, this is closely connected with the big problem at hand, namely helping oneself to a former adversary's territory, without a clear justification for it, as Russia's neighbors know only too well. The Kaliningrad enclave is the last example of this heavy-handed outrage, and it is time to do away with it, Poland becoming the instrument for change.

Another custom, not directly connected with the big problem is letting soldiers have their way in a conquered city, a custom allegedly invoked for the last time by Suvorov after taking Warsaw in 1794, which showed what it meant to be Russia's neighbor. The time has come for Poland and Russia to have normal relations based on trust and mutual respect.

The problem of DEMOGRAPHY is closely connected with the crisis of Western Civilization, which in Europe is reflected in an alarming drop in birthrates even, or perhaps especially, in such formerly fertile countries as Italy, which is declared to be dying by some alarmists (Patrick Buchanan quoting demographers). Poland, although still cited by domestic (Olszewski) and foreign observers as "biologically unbelievably resilient," no doubt as a result of one of the highest post-war birthrates in the world, has been experiencing since independence a declining birthrate, which is reaching alarming proportions, and if not reversed will turn Poland into a demographic midget and a haven for immigrants shattering the dream of perfection.

In America the European demographic crisis is reflected in the decline of immigration from Europe with an accompanying decline in the percentage of Europe-originated population which, from a large majority not long ago, is likely to become a minority soon, passed by non-Europeans, mostly Latinos, whose growing numbers are turning America into an uncertain multicultural society heralded by Bill Clinton, and already seen in wasteful bilingualism and the rise of Spanish seen everywhere, especially in voting instructions. What the long-range effect is likely to be is hard to say, but this writer has doubts, already expressed about the problems arising when people from different climates live side by side.

As for the Spanish language, some people worry about its progress, others call it "the language of today," while still others talk about the "Spanish peril." There were a spate of articles in 1996 commenting on those opinions and providing additional reports, the most remarkable of which, James Brooke's "North Dakota, With German Roots, Adopts Spanish as Second Language" (*New York Times*, March 2, 1996) has the following comments, "Where German heritage defers to 'the language of today'," and subtitle, "Preference Reflects Trend Among Students Elsewhere in the U.S." The decline of German in America, caused also in no small measure by two world wars, is the more remarkable in view of the fact that as late as the Bicentennial every fifth American was of German origin. As for Poles in America, I estimate that more children and young people in that group are learning or studying Spanish than Polish. I am sure that nobody else is aware of that.

The German phenomenon in America must surely have its roots at home. There are fewer visitors from Germany among faculty and students in American universities, which means they are needed at home, which in turn means there are shortages in certain professions, which further means there is a decline in ethnic German population (there are still plenty of foreign-born, not too readily accepted). For someone familiar with Germany, and concerned about Poland, it is of some significance that the greatest population crisis has occurred in the State of Brandenburg, Poland's closest neighbor, where lively exchanges have been going on across the Oder (Odra) river, including university level, producing what could amount to dual citizens.

Here is a chance for Poland, together with Germany, its biggest investor and supporter, to reverse the European DEMOGRAPHY crisis by creating a new type of European in the "heart of Europe" (historian Norman Davies' name for Poland, Chancellor Kohl's name for Berlin), near the cradle of Poland and one of the cradles of Germany, as part of the European Community's priority programs. But to do it, Poland would have to first cure its own DEMOGRAPHY by restoring the family to the center of society, providing help and clinics for unwed mothers, and cash payments for having children, and it is in these areas that Polonia's help could be crucial, as expounded in the "Big Fraternals" chapter.

There is one more important problem. To accomplish any worthy project, the nation must first cure the erosion of morals and manners, and here is where schools come in, since it is too late to educate mature citizens, but perhaps evening classes could be held, where in the good old days men's choirs had been practicing. Pursuit of happiness must replace pursuit of money, which is easier said than done. Among the young people from Poland I have been encountering in America I met alcoholics, liars, and thieves. The thieving was often done not for material gain (but who knows?) but rather out of spite or simply envy. I am not sure whether to blame Communism for that, because these vices existed before, but the stakes were much lower then. Today there is no standing still, or one is left behind, which explains the rise in crime in Poland, for which education could also be blamed. But it is the petty crimes that are most disturbing, because done by people supposedly educated yet unable to tell right from wrong.

Just one or two examples. An old wartime partner and companion had found me through the Polish American Congress, and a nice young man on duty phoned me from Chicago with particulars of how to contact him. I happened to have a valuable photo with the friend on it, and sent it by somebody who very much wanted to deliver it personally. I even gave him a silver dollar (worth 20) to make sure. I never heard from him again, or from my friend.

A more painful loss. Those who read my chapter about Russia must have wondered why I never quoted from my Russian diary. A young "scholar" from Poland who stayed in my apartment (1981/82) saw it once, and I could not find it afterwards. With the diary several very interesting articles also disappeared, one about the death of Prince "Jarema" Wiśniowiecki when escorted by the hetmans to the Dnieper crossing after Beresteczko (probably poisoned by them), and the other about the rescue of Henryk Dąbrowski in 1812 by his young wife in Russia, both important contributions to what I knew about these men, and that's why they were stolen, for no reason known to a normal man.

"Normal" is the key word here, because it is the return to some kind of normalcy that is at stake. It is not normal to aspire to a Western lifestyle on an income that is only a fraction of American, and buying on credit is the way (J. Perlez, "Joy of Debts: Eastern Europe on a Credit Fling," *New York Times*, May 30, 1998). This is the greatest danger to Poland leading to a nation of bankrupt consumers, and the way out is a return of family values, with geographical perfection, the first in a thousand years, a perfect uplift.

POLSKA TO WIELKA RZECZ

IN MEMORIAM

After much thought I have decided to do away with
an extensive section, selecting only two examples:
one, a Polish American woman of distinction;
the other, an unheralded but significant Polish
American scholar. Both were role models.

Others who passed away are mentioned in the book.
From Bronisław Malinowski (1884-1942) to Wacław
Jędrzejewicz (1893-1993) and in between a legion of
heroes, activists, teachers, scholars, writers, businessmen
or women, but mostly ex-servicemen, whom it would
take a volume to list and describe, turning the book into
one huge obituary detracting from its main purpose,
concentration on the here and now and the fate of
Poland.

Marilyn R. Komosa,
Cook County Judge, Passed Away

Reprinted from *Naród Polski*, May 21, 1997

Chicago, IL—Judge Marylin Komosa, 65, passed away on April 2 at Lutheran General Hospital in Park Ridge. IL. She was the first woman of Polish descent elected to a judicial position in the county and served as Cook County Circuit Court Judge from 1964 until her retirement in 1996. She also had the longest tenure of any female judge on the trial level in Cook County, and in the State of Illinois.

Ahead of her times, Judge Komosa was one of 15 female judges out of 338 judges in Cook County, yet she won the admiration of her colleagues. In 1983, Judge Harry Comerford said of her: "She has the warmth and an understanding that transcends beyond the bench to the litigants and attorneys who appear before her. Along with her legal knowledge, this combination creates a tremendous atmosphere in her courtroom."

A resident of the Edgebrook neighborhood of Chicago, Judge Komosa graduated cum laude from Loyola University Law School and was a Phi Beta Kappa graduate of Northwestern University. She worked in private practice and as a public defender before serving on the bench for 31 years.

She also studied Spanish at the University of Mexico and Polish at Alliance College in PA. More recently, she spent several summer vacations at the Jagiellonian University in Cracow, Catholic University in Lublin, and the John Paul II Center in Rome improving her knowledge of the Polish language and culture.

Judge Komosa was the first woman to serve as President of the Advocates Society, a group of Polish-American attorneys. From 1985-1994, she chaired the Law Day Reception for new citizens. She was Vice President of the Illinois Division of the PAC, a Crown Honorary Member of the Knights of Dąbrowski, and was active in other Polonian organizations such as the Polish Women's Alliance, Polish Arts Club, and the Polish Women's Civic Club. She belonged to PRCUA Society #1000.

Judge Komosa's family was also noted for their leadership in the Polonia in Chicago and nationwide. She was the daughter of Charles Rozmarek, President of the Polish National Alliance for 28 years and the Polish American Congress for 24 years, and Wanda Rozmarek, a noted author, educator and philanthropist.

She was also a member of the Women's Bar Association and Federal Bar Association and a Past Director of the National Association of Women Judges. She was listed in "Who's Who in the Midwest," "Who's Who of American Women," and in 1973 she was chosen by Loyola University as one of four women graduates to be included in a special publication entitled "Our Leading Ladies—The Alumnae."

Judge Komosa was the wife of the late Edward J. Komosa, and mother of four: Edward S., Cathy, Atty. Marilyn (Andrzej) Rogalski of Bethesda, M.D., and Charles A.; grandmother of Alexandra Rogalski; and sister of Elaine (Jorge M.D.) Tovar.

The Mass of Christian Burial was held at St. Hyacinth Parish on the northwest side of Chicago and she was buried in St. Adalbert's Cemetery, Niles, IL. She always gave us her "best." Now, may she rest in eternal peace.

THANK YOU NOTE — "On behalf of the Rozmarek-Komosa Family, we would like to express our sincerest thanks to all who remembered our dearest mother, Judge Marilyn Rozmarek Komosa, through donations and kind words."

Sincerely, The Komosa Children —
Edward, Cathy, Marilyn and Charles.

NOTA BENE: Here is a significant footnote, quoted to the best of my recollection. If my memory serves me right, Rozmarek's granddaughter—I call her a Polish-American "princess" the way Jews call their special young—wasn't able to take Polish in my scheduled summer 1982 course at Loyola, because the class was canceled before late registration, and for all I know she was talked into taking Spanish. Her mother, Judge Komosa, was one of "Our Leading Ladies — The Alumnae" of Loyola University. This is the "Spanish peril" discussed in the CONCLUSIONS, and it is **REAL**.

METCHIE J.E. BUDKA
1917 – 1995

Metchie (Mieczysław) Joseph Edward Budka who contributed the article entitled "Pulaski and Kosciuszko: Heroes Extremely Apropos" to the first edition of the collection *Poles in America* was born in Salem, Massachusetts, the younger son of Joseph and Bogumiła (Budczynska) Budka. His first undergraduate year was in Science at the Massachusetts Institute of Technology. Then, seeking a broader background in the Humanities, he transferred to Harvard College where, after completing all the Science degree requirements, he was permitted to transfer to Slavic Languages and Literatures. The characteristic features of his future work and development as a Slavic scholar were to reflect this initial duality of interest and training. They echo his background in the two disciplines with their diverse and complementary demands for precision in observation and documentation, for rigor in criticism and interpretation.

Immediately after graduation from Harvard, Class of 1940, Budka's main interest in continuing Slavic, most particularly Polish, Studies was subordinated to other concerns and responsibilities following the death of his father in 1941. He took a teaching post in science. When war came in December 1941, he tried to join the Navy. Because of his chemistry background however, he was sought out and called to join that laboratory at the Harvard Medical School, where, in response to wartime needs and battlefield conditions, an extensive research and development program was devoted to the preparation of usable protein fractions. As a member of this group, Budka worked on problems in protein purification and characterization. His first three publications were therefore in science. In spite of two full-time appointments in teaching and research he continued Slavic Studies at Harvard and was awarded the M.A. degree in 1949. Henceforth, Polish Studies were to be his prime interest. In 1950 he married Barbara Low, a scientific colleague at Harvard. Remembered here principally as a Polish scholar, writer, and translator, Budka remained throughout his life both gifted teacher and scientist.

Metchie Budka is perhaps best known for his widely-praised translation of the American travel diaries of JULIAN URSYN NIEMCEWICZ (1758-1841), poet, playwright and writer. Budka's first major work, it was to symbolize his life long interest and explorations of the many bonds and bridges in Polish-American relations. In 1956 he visited Warsaw, at the invitation of Warsaw University. He had chosen to work on Niemcewicz's memoirs and began to search in the libraries there for unpublished material on his life in America. He learned then that Niemcewicz's manuscript American diaries, unpublished in his life-time and thought to be lost, had recently been found. For Budka this finding was the pivotal event in his life as a Slavic scholar. He promptly decided to devote his doctoral dissertation to work on these manuscript diaries alone. Seven notebooks, three written in French, four in Polish, cover the period 29th August 1797 to 8 November 1799. An eighth, in French, describes his journey to Niagara in 1805. Budka prepared the first critical annotated edition of these journals with the Polish text of the 1797-1799 notebooks translated into English and the French text left essentially untouched. He translated the French of the "Journey to Niagara, 1805" into English. In 1962, Budka was awarded the doctoral degree at Harvard in Slavic Languages and Literatures. Two years later, in 1964, he won the first Kosciuszko Foundation Doctoral Dissertation Award.

Budka early recognized the lively grace of Niemcewicz's engaging account of American life in the immediate post-Revolutionary period and of even greater significance the role of these travel diaries as prime documents in American history. To make the Niemcewicz diaries more readily accessible, Budka then translated the complete French text into English, and rewrote the detailed introduction of his dissertation to provide a more general biographical account of Niemcewicz and his place in Polish literature and history. He sought out contemporary illustrations to enhance the text. The title Budka gave to the English edition of Niemcewicz's diaries *Under Their Vine and Fig Tree; Travels through America in 1797-1799, 1805* (The Collections of the New Jersey Historical Society, 1965) was inspired by words in a letter George Washington wrote to Niemcewicz "...if my vows...could have availed, you [the Polish People] would *now*, have been as happy under your own Vine and Fig Tree, as the People of these United States...under theirs."

The Niemcewicz diaries teem with life. Their range is almost limitless: from agriculture to mining, from prison management to the institution of slavery, from a Shaker dance to the manners of American children, from cameos of persons to landscape views. Niemcewicz had an insatiable curiosity, and a keen eye for the telling detail. He used a multiplicity of detail as a deliberate technique, explicitly acknowledged. A painterly device, he employed it in all his writings, to define a man or a place to illuminate a scene or a state of mind. In what was to provide the key to the documented importance of the Niemcewicz diaries Budka adopted a parallel construct. He scrupulously investigated and verified every allusion, every detail. His notes record the evidence—facts and data proved reliable, observations and judgments found to ring true. Budka also made extensive comparative studies of other famed travel accounts of the period, and he thus clearly established Niemcewicz as the pre-eminent chronicler of life in the post-Revolutionary United States.

Nowhere is the assurance of well-established reliability more important, or the details more telling, than in Niemcewicz's account of his two week stay at Mount Vernon as the guest of George Washington. From that account—the whole tenor of George Washington's life in retirement, his habits, his occupations, his concerns, and his views—there emerges in sharp focus a unique likeness of the man himself. His record of the most minute details of life at Mount Vernon has greatly aided the work of restoration there. Further, Niemcewicz's description of the slave quarters at Mount Vernon has been of central importance in restorations at Colonial Williamsburg. Elsewhere, the American diaries have proved a resource invaluable to historians of the period.

If Budka's scholarship established the documentary value of the diaries, his translation recaptures, as Wiktor Weintraub wrote in his Preface "the easy grace, the abandon of Niemcewicz's Polish and French." *Under Their Vine and Fig Tree* was applauded as "...an exemplary piece of literary-historical scholarship." For this achievement Budka was honored with two awards: In 1965 he received the Award of Merit from The American Association for State and Local History and, in 1979 the Miecislaus Haiman Memorial Medal from the Polish American Historical Association. As Weintraub observed, these diaries are "one of the earliest and most important documents in the complex, fascinating and still largely unexplored story of American-Polish Relations."

Budka's research on the life of Niemcewicz led him inevitably to TADEUSZ (THADDEUS) KOSCIUSZKO, hero of the American Revolution and legendary hero of Poland's struggle for independence. In the Kosciuszko Insurrection of 1794, Niemcewicz, adjutant-general to Kosciuszko, was taken prisoner with him after his defeat at the battle of Maciejowice. After their release in 1796, Niemcewicz accompanied Kosciuszko on his second visit to America. Kosciuszko's service in the American Revolution had begun twenty years earlier in October 1776 when he was appointed engineer with the rank of Colonel. To mark the Bicentennial of the American Revolution The Polish Museum of America decided to publish photocopies of autograph letters held in their Kosciuszko Archives. Appointed editor of this project, Budka recommended a unified theme: publication limited to those letters and documents related to Kosciuszko's years of service in the American Revolution. This critically annotated collection entitled *Autograph Letters of Thaddeus Kosciuszko in the American Revolution...*, provides a remarkable biographical sketch of this period in Kosciuszko's life. Budka acknowledged that the publication was unlikely to affect those committed to Kosciuszko as legendary Romantic Hero, rather, he insisted that the letters give us a deeper measure of the man: an outstanding human being, greatly concerned for the welfare of his men, angered by injustice, a good friend.

The biographical accounts in Budka's article "Pulaski and Kosciuszko: Heroes Extremely Apropos" once again echo the dual themes of Poles as heroes of the struggles for Independence in both Poland and the United States. The personal valor and military prowess of CASIMIR (KAZIMIERZ) PULASKI, were already legendary in Europe when he arrived in America in 1777. In Pulaski, Budka saw the soldier of conscience. He recognized Pulaski's total commitment to American Independence for which he fought as fiercely as earlier he had fought for Poland's Independence. Pulaski sought always to be in the thick of the fight and in his last battle (1779 Savannah, Georgia) he died fighting for American Independence. In writing about Kosciuszko's life, Budka emphasized that, in the fight for Independence and Liberty, Kosciuszko's concern for the common man, and his devotion to the cause of justice never faltered. He fought for Independence and Liberty in the United States and saw them prevail and flourish. He fought later for them in Poland and, though the battle was lost, he emerged as a symbol of freedom and democracy.

Budka returned to translating when asked to provide an English language text of the twentieth-century Polish work by Prime Bishop Francis Hodur of the Polish National Catholic Church entitled in English, *APOCALYPSE or The Revelation of the XXth Century.*

Written in highly idiomatic Polish, the nuances of Hodur's style reflect his ecclesiastical background. Later, Budka also accepted the primary role in translating into English a second twentieth-century Polish text of a unique sociological study by Hieronim Kubiak, entitled in English, *The Polish National Catholic Church in the United States of America from 1897 to 1980.*

Budka's writings all serve to bridge two cultures, American and Polish. Thus his work on the Niemcewicz diaries has proved the paradigm of his major contributions as both scholar and translator. Budka's particular triumph was to add the name of Julian Ursyn Niemcewicz to the honor roll of those who belong to both countries. He lectured on both Kosciuszko and Niemcewicz to both lay and academic audiences. Budka contributed articles and reviews to many professional journals. His unpublished studies in eighteenth and early nineteenth century Polish history and literature ranged widely. Budka's passion for facts, for the unembellished truth as a sure base for understanding, was evident in all his writings: A just reflection of the man himself.

REMEMBRANCES

At the Memorial Service, held to honor and celebrate Metchie Budka's life, Joseph E. Gore, President of The Kosciuszko Foundation, rounding out the span of Metchie's life as a Polish scholar, spoke of his volunteer work as the Foundation's Resident Scholar. Gore said of him: "The title was most fitting. For above all, Metchie was a scholar and a teacher...mentor to many...He was unselfish in giving of himself to anyone in need—whether student, scholar or Foundation President." In their memories of him, all Metchie's colleagues recognized a man of the Enlightenment, one who looked for reason, who was skeptical of unexamined authority and tradition.

What then of Metchie Budka the man? That openness of spirit which dominated his life as both scholar and writer found echo in the dominant theme of his life as a man. This was his love of life itself, of people and their boundless variety, of harmony and counterpoint.

Metchie's friends all recognized his pleasure in the uniqueness of people. Patricia Koechlin, friend and former colleague, remembers Metchie's joy in people as truly universal. He understood, she wrote, and was at ease with all manner of men as they with him. Joel

Blum, friend and former student, wrote 36 years later "He touched us with his warmth, ...with his capacity to accept us. We *knew* that he found something very special in each of us and we knew that was not an easy task. He touched us with his humility. He never took himself too seriously." Joel Janicki, friend and colleague, remembers him; "Metchie possessed a style that was all his own. His pithy insights into Polonia [and] Russian Poetry...all expressed with distinctive vigor were delivered in his trademark Bostonian cadences."

Metchie had an immense and open pride in his Polish ancestry matched only by his deep love of America. This sense of dual heritage, of place, and of belonging, were rooted in his strong sense of family. He and his mother were always very close. He was deeply moved when, on his first visit to Poland in 1956, he met his grandmother, then nearly 100 years old. He saw her strength and resolve as an inheritance.

Metchie had an old French medal, A L'HEROIQUE POLOGNE, inscribed on the reverse with the words "Tu ne meuras pas." In celebration of his life we may say, "Metchie, tu ne meuras jamais." Metchie Budka will live on not only in the hearts and minds of all who loved him but in his works.

The Metchie J.E. Budka Award has been established at the Kosciuszko Foundation to honor nationwide outstanding work by young scholars in Polish Literature, Polish History and Polish-American Relations. The first winner of this annual Award was named in 1997.

Barbara W. Low (Budka), M.A., D. Phil., Metchie Budka's widow, is Professor Emeritus of Biochemistry and Molecular Biophysics, Columbia University, New York, NY.

HONOR ROLL

World War II veterans, still living at the writing of the book, known personally to this writer or his associates:

Banasikowski, Edmund
Drzewieniecki, Włodzimierz
Dziewanowski, Marian
Ehrenkreutz, Andrzej
Gałazka, Jacek
Gawełczyk, Maksymilian
Jurewicz, Jan
Kajkowski, Aleksander
Kaniecki, Edward
Karski, Jan
Kobylański, Zenon
Koczor, Henryk
Krzywicki, Jerzy
Krzyżanowski, Janusz
Krzyżanowski, Jerzy
Łaszewski, Bolesław
Maciuszko, Jerzy
Massalski, Tadeusz
Michniewicz, Stefan
Mocha, Frank
Mostwin, Danuta
Mostwin, Stanisław Bask
Niedużak, Janusz
Nowak Jeziorański, Jan
Olfinowski, Józef
Pogonowski, Iwo Cyprian
Pomian, Andrzej
Ptak, Józef
Sawicki, Wiktor
Sułkowski, Edmund
Świderski, Stanisław
Tomaszewski, Karol
Wagner, Wieńczysław
Wandycz, Piotr
Wierzbiański, Bolesław
Winowski, Ryszard
Wróbel, Czesław Bolesław
Zachariasiewicz, Władysław
Zawodny, Janusz

523

BIOGRAPHIES OF CONTRIBUTORS

FRANK MOCHA

Frank Mocha was born in formerly German Silesia from which the family moved after plebiscite to newly Polish Silesia, where he received his elementary and secondary education (1927-1939). A WWII veteran from Day One in Poland to V-E Day in England (including 3 years in POW camps: in Alsace, Bavaria-Stalag VIIA, and Austria-Stalag XVIIB); he reached England on the instructions of the camp's Polish elders to inform the Allies that the Germans had developed jet planes, seen in flight over Stalag XVIIB. Rejoining the Army, he was sent to an Officer School, graduating just before the war's end. He matriculated and entered the Polish College of the University of London, studying economics and history, with the help of a British Government scholarship. As an ex-serviceman, he was eligible for emigration to America.

Arriving in New York with a British wife in 1951, he entered the printing industry and started raising a family. The birth of his third child in 1957 coincided with the Soviet Sputnik, which marked a turning point for him. As America feared to be overtaken in technology and lacked specialists on East Europe, Mocha decided to return to school, at first part-time, helped by a tuition grant at Columbia University, and then with a National Defense Fellowship. He left printing and became a full-time student, graduating *magna cum laude*, Phi Beta Kappa and, while teaching at the University of Pittsburgh (1966-1971), earning a doctorate in Slavic Studies at Columbia, followed by a 10-week study at Moscow University under a grant from IREX (International Research and Exchanges Board) in 1971. Later he was active at the Polish Institute of Arts and Sciences in New York, chiefly as chairman of its Literary Section and Associate Editor of *The Polish Review*, and taught at NYU (New York University), publishing his M.A. and Ph.D. theses, and numerous articles.

The year 1976 was another turning point for him. While teaching at NYU, he offered a course, *Poles in America: A Bicentennial View*, the only one of that kind in America. It became an official Bicentennial Event in New York City and the subject of an article in *The New York Times* (Tom Buckley, "The Revival of a Heritage"), but also the germ for a book of essays, *POLES IN AMERICA: Bicentennial Essays*, 1978), widely supported by all segments of American Polonia, as a summary of Polish contributions to the USA.

By then, Poland itself had begun to stir, indicating the beginning of crisis in the Soviet bloc, and his training had come full-circle. As an expert on the area and frequent traveler to Poland as director of summer programs in Lublin he was given a Mellon Grant by Loyola University of Chicago to organize an International Symposium on Solidarity (1982). This too became the germ for a book of essays, *POLAND'S SOLIDARITY MOVEMENT* (1984) which, smuggled into Poland, had some bearing on the fall of communism there.

The present book, *AMERICAN "POLONIA" AND POLAND*, also the subject of a *New York Times* article (David Gonzalez, "Silver Zlotys And a Dream of America"), is part, with the other two, of what he likes to call his "Trilogy," to be left behind as a testimony to his work in the last 20 years. *AMERICAN "POLONIA"* is more than a sequel to *POLES IN AMERICA* because it includes Poland now, an impossibility then. It is an apt ending of his labors during what was really a digression from his post-doctoral research (which was to have been a biography of Boris Godunov, and a study of the Time of Troubles in Russia) which he can now return to, while at the same time working on a companion volume to *AMERICAN POLONIA—ONE MAN'S SAGA*, which he intends to dedicate to his three children and six grandchildren.

MAŁGORZATA DYMEK

Earning graduate degrees from the University of Pennsylvania and the University of Warsaw, Małgorzata Dymek has been, since 1990, the editor and publisher of the oldest independent Polish weekly newspaper in the United States, *Gwiazda Polarna*, as well as *GP Light*, its more recent English-language monthly supplement, both headquartered in Stevens Point, Wisconsin, where she makes her home. Prior to her present position, Ms. Dymek worked as an executive producer for the Polish Television Network in New York and as an editor and executive editor of *Nowy Dziennik*, the largest Polish daily newspaper on the East Coast, published by Bicentennial Publishing Corporation. In addition, she has worked as a freelance writer for various publications, including *Commentary*, as an editor, and as a translator.

Małgorzata began her professional journalistic career in 1973 as a translator for the Polish Press Agency in Warsaw, quickly becoming an announcer on Polish Radio there. In 1981, she wrote for and edited *Congress Post*, covering the first Solidarity Congress in Gdańsk; writing and researching additional reports for Reuters and the Associated Press.

Between 1976 and 1981, she worked as a reporter and producer for Polish Television in Warsaw, writing and directing short films; and producing a weekly news program covering cultural events and hosting interview shows with artists and celebrities ranging from Erskine Caldwell, Mercer Ellington, and Billy Graham to Peter Ustinov, John Mayall, and Liv Ullman. In 1981, she was named editor-in-chief of the Polish News Bulletin of the U.S. Embassy in Warsaw.

Ms. Dymek came to America as a Fulbright Fellow in 1982, and afterwards worked as executive editor of *New Horizon Polish-American Review*, an English-language monthly supplement to *Nowy Dziennik*, in addition to fulfilling her duties with Bicentennial Publishing.

Ms. Dymek's excellent command of English, both written and spoken, acquired in Poland and England (Norwich College), is her best recommendation. Her mastery of English makes her superior to other Polish immigrants who arrive here with insufficient knowledge of English, or functionally illiterate, and discover too late that the only jobs available to them are low level jobs without health insurance and other benefits.

It would not be an exaggeration to consider Ms. Dymek a role model for other Poles contemplating settling in America. She is also a living proof that it is possible to shed earlier communist influences and function successfully in the American market democracy.

EDWARD JOSEPH CZERWIŃSKI

Edward Joseph Czerwiński was born on June 6, 1929 and graduated from Grove City College in 1951, entering the U.S. Air Force in July of that year. He was discharged in September 1953 with the rank of Second Lieutenant and immediately began graduate work in English and American Literature at Pennsylvania State University. He received his Master's degree in January 1955 and began work on his doctorate in English and American Literature at Emory University in Georgia. He passed his doctoral exams in December 1957 and completed the first draft of his dissertation, *Eloquent Phantoms: The Role of Women in the Novels of Joseph Conrad*, in 1959. He began graduate work in Russian and Polish literature in 1960, without completing his dissertation on Conrad.

After a year at Indiana University, he entered the graduate program at the University of Wisconsin, completing his Master's degree in 1964 and his doctorate in 1965. He spent two years in Poland, 1962-64, the first scholar to be awarded a fellowship from the Kosciuszko Foundation after World War II. He completed his dissertation, "Dialog and the Polish Theater of the Absurd and Its Effects on Russian and East European Theater and Drama."

His teaching experiences include the following: instructor of English at Georgia Tech, 1957-59; assistant professor of English and Drama at McNeese State College, Louisiana, 1959-60; associate professor of Russian and Polish Literatures at the University of Pittsburgh, 1965-66; SUNY at Buffalo, 1966-67; associate professor of Russian and Polish at the University of Kansas, 1967-70; professor of Russian and Comparative Literatures at SUNY at Stony Brook, 1970-93; professor emeritus, 1993 to present.

He is founder and director of the Slavic Cultural Center and was instrumental in presenting the following groups and artists to American audiences: Józef Szajna's Studio Theater productions, *Replika* and *Dante;* the Olsztyn Theater of the Deaf; the Warsaw Mime Company, Izabela Cywińska's production of Suxovo-Kobylin's *The Death of Tarelkin* (with her husband, Janusz Michałowski, in the lead role); Kazimierz Braun's American Premiere of Tadeusz Różewicz's *White Marriage*; etc.

As an editor and translator, his publications include *The Soviet Invasion of Czechoslovakia: The Effects on East Europe* (with Jarosław Piekalkiewicz), 1972; *Pieces of Poland: Four Polish*

Dramatists, 1983; *The Dramaturg and Dramaturgy* (with Nicholas Rzhevsky), 1986; *Chekhov Reconstructed: New Translations of Chekhov's Plays*, 1987; *Satire Cum Poesis: Three Bulgarian Plays*, 1987; *Contemporary Polish Theater and Drama (1956-84)*, 1987; *A Dictionary of Polish Literature*, 1994; and numerous articles and reviews.

He is a member of the editorial boards of *Books Abroad* (now *World Literature Today*), 1968-; *Twentieth Century Literature*, and *Comparative Drama*. He is the founder and editor of *Slavic and East European Arts Journal*, 1982-; and the Polish Literary Section of the *Encyclopedia Brittanica*, 1975-78, 1988-1995.

Professor Czerwiński is the recipient of numerous awards including the Distinguished Alumni Award from Grove City College (1973), the Chancellor's Excellence in Teaching Award from SUNY (1973-74), Distinguished Professor Award of the New York State Teachers of Foreign Languages (1975), Man of the Year in Culture and the Arts by the Polish Cultural Clubs of America (1986), and the *Amicus Poloniae* Award from Poland.

In addition, he is listed in *Who's Who in America* and *Who's Who in the World*. He resides in New York City.

WIEŃCZYSŁAW J. WAGNER

Wieńczysław J. Wagner, born on December 12, 1917, is married and has three children. He received his L.L.M. in Warsaw in 1939.

During the war he was a member of the A.K. (underground Home Army) and the secret Polish government. He was a junior judge (aplikant), legal counsel at the Zieleniewski factories, and editor-in-chief of the "Warsaw National Voice," first during the Warsaw Uprising, then in German prison camps.

In Paris, France, 1945-48, he became Dr. en Droit at the University of Paris; president of the A.K. Association in France; chairman of the first convention of Z.P.U.W. (Związek Polskiego Uchodźstwa Wojennego)—Polish War Refugees in France; and vice-president of the Polish Catholic Students Association.

In the United States since 1948, he taught Polish language and literature at Fordham University (1948-49); co-founded (with Prof. Domaradzki) the Paderewski Foundation, and organized the first chapters of the A.K. in the U.S.

He settled in Chicago in 1949; organized the Association of Polish Federalists; and received the degrees of L.L.M., J.D. and S.J.D. at Northwestern University.

Wagner began his teaching career at Northwestern, then moved to Notre Dame (1953-62), Indiana University (1962-71), the University of Detroit (1971-89), the Jagiellonian University in Cracow (1990-92), the Catholic University of Lublin (1991-93), and the Copernicus University (1993-94). He was named "Outstanding Educator of America" in 1973 and 1975. Member of the Indiana Bar.

While holding positions at the above institutions, he was also a visiting professor at universities in France (Paris and Rennes (1959-60); at Cornell (1961-62); Nice, France (1968-69); Warsaw (1979-80); "Distinguished Visiting Professor" at Seton Hall (1980-81); London (1986-87).

In summers, he lectured at various institutions in France, Luxembourg, Germany, Greece, Italy, the Caribbean, Guatemala, Bolivia, Chile, Argentina, Uruguay, Brazil, Algeria, Morocco, Senegal, Rhodesia, Zaire, Togo, Burkina Faso, Cameroon, Egypt, Jordan, India, Cambodia, Pakistan, and Korea.

Prof. Wagner is the author of more than 250 books and articles in English, French, Polish, German, and Portuguese.

He is former Chairman, Comparative Law Section, Association of American Law Schools; Vice-President, American Foreign Law Association; Chairman, International Meetings Comm. (American Comparative Law Association): Vice-President, International Movement of Catholic Lawyers; President, Council of the Polish Institute of Arts and Sciences in America; member, Executive Council of World Federalists; President, American Council of Polish Culture; Knight Commander, Order of Malta; member of about 30 other organizations (American, Polish, French and international). Decorations: Commander's Cross, Polonia Restituta; Golden Cross of Merit; military decorations.

Dr. *honoris causa*, Copernicus University.

JAN NOWAK JEZIORAŃSKI

Zdzisław Jeziorański, whose conspirational pseudonym was Jan Nowak, was born in Warsaw on May 15, 1913. A graduate of the Adam Mickiewicz Gymnasium in Warsaw, he studied in Poznań University, where from 1938 until the outbreak of the war he worked in the Department of Economics headed by Professor Edward Taylor. Following the German attack on Poland, he took part in the September '39 campaign in which he was captured but managed to escape after a few weeks, and early in 1941 became active in the clandestine Union of Armed Struggle (*Związek Walki Zbrojnej*), organizing the distribution of subversive publications in Germany itself. From April 1943 he maintained direct contact between the Polish Government-in-Exile in London and the Home Army in Poland. He was the last envoy from the Polish Supreme Commander in London to reach Warsaw before the outbreak of the Warsaw Uprising in August 1944 and the first emissary of the Commandant of the Home Army to arrive in London after the fall of the Uprising.

In London, in 1948 he began working in the Polish Section of the BBC, and later (1952-1976) he was director of Polish Broadcasting in Radio Free Europe, and also a consultant to the United States National Security Council (1979-1992). He now lives in Washington, having served as national director of the Polish American Congress since 1979.

Jan Nowak Jeziorański is the author of following books:

63 Days: The Story of the Warsaw Uprising (1945)
Russia and the Warsaw Uprising (1947)
The Polish Road to Freedom (1974)
Courier from Warsaw (1978)
Poland Has Remained Itself (1980)
War on the Air Waves (1986)
Poland from Afar (1988)
In Search of Hope (1993)
Discussions about Poland (1994).

Jan Nowak Jeziorański has received wide recognition for his work, as attested by these precious decorations and awards:

Cross of the Courageous (*Krzyż Walecznych*), 1943
Virtuti Militari, 1944
King's Medal for Courage, 1949
Gold Medal of the Polish Combattants Association. 1967
London *Wiadomości* Literary Prize, 1979
The monthly's *Puls* (Pulse) Literary Prize, 1980
Honor Roll, Simon Wiesenthal Institute, Los Angeles, 1988
Grand Ribbon of the Order of Polonia Restituta (Poland
    Reborn) awarded by the Government of the Polish Republic
    in London, 1990
"Victor" Polish Television Prize, 1991
Commander's Cross with Star of the Order of Merit, 1993
"Golden Microphone" Polish Radio Prize, 1993
Order of the White Eagle, 1994.

Jan Nowak Jeziorański was awarded a doctorate *honoris causa* by the Adam Mickiewicz University in Poznań, his old Alma Mater, in 1991.

JACEK FISIAK

Born 1936, M.A. (Warsaw), Ph.D. (Łódź), D. Litt. (Poznań), Professor of English and Director of School of English at Adam Mickiewicz University, Poznań, since 1965. Rector (= Vice-Chancellor/President) of Adam Mickiewicz University (1985-88). Minister of National Education of Poland (1988-89). Chairman of Committee on Modern Languages and Literatures of the Polish Academy of Sciences (1981-1993). Honorary Doctor, University of Jyväskylä, Finland (1983). Member of the *Academia Europaea* (1990). Member of Academy of Finland (1990). Member of Norwegian Academy of Sciences and Letters (1986). President International Association of University Professors of English (1974-77). President *Societas Linguistica Europaea* (1983-84). President International Society for Historical Linguistics (1981-83). Secretary General FIPLV (1980-83). Fulbright scholar, UCLA (1963-64). Visiting Professor University of Kansas (1970), University of Florida (1974), SUNY (1975), University of Kiel (1979), The American University (1979-80), (1990-1991), University of Zürich (1984), University of Tromso (1985), University of Jyväskylä (1987), University of Saarbrücken (1990, 1993), University of Bamberg (1994).

Research and teaching interests: English linguistics, history of English, historical linguistics, contrastive linguistics, language contact and lexicology. Member of numerous professional organizations. Editor of three professional journals, *Folia Linguistica Historica, Studia Anglica Posnaniensia*, and *Papers and Studies in Contrastive Linguistics*, and member of numerous editorial boards in Poland, England, USA, Holland, Canada, Russia, Italy, France, Austria, Ireland, and other countries. Lectured at over 100 universities on five continents.

University medals: Jyväskylä, Abo, Helsinki, Louvain, Heidelberg, Amman, Yarmouk, Salzburg, Brno. Decorations: Commander's Cross of the Order *Polonia Restituta*, Commander's Cross of the Order "Lion of Finland," Officer's Cross of the Order "Palmes Academique," and others. Numerous awards for achievement in the area of research, training of young scholars and teachers, and academic administration. Polish Prime Minister's Prize for research (1996). Consultant of Swedish Ministry of Education, Austrian Ministry of Higher Education, IREX, Pergamon Press, and Ford

Foundation. Over 120 scholarly publications, including books. Supervision of 47 completed Ph.D. programmes.

Listed in 17 "Who's Who" publications and encyclopedias in Poland, the United Kingdom and the United States, e.g., *Who is Who in the World* (Chicago) and *The International Who is Who* (London). He should certainly continue his work on the English-Polish and Polish-English dictionaries, for which there is a definite market in American Polonia and among friends of Poland.

ALEKSANDER GIEYSZTOR

Born July 17, 1916, married, son (d. 1989), daughter. Studied at Warsaw University (M.A. 1938) and in Paris. Platoon (*plutonowy*) reserve Officer Candidate 1938. Served during the September campaign of 1939 at the Information and Propaganda Headquarters, also in the Warsaw Uprising, Lieutenant of the Reserve 1940-44, POW camp 1944-45.

Doctor of History in the underground Warsaw University, 1942 (promoted 1945). Assistant Professor (*docent*) of Warsaw University 1946, Associate Professor (*profesor nadzwyczajny*) 1949, Professor (*profesor zwyczajny*) 1970, retired 1986 but lectured part-time; Vicerector (*prorektor*) 1956-9.

Head of research of the beginnings of the Polish State 1949-53, Director of the Institute of History at Warsaw University 1955-75, Director of the Royal Castle in Warsaw 1980-1991, Chairman of the Council 1991-.

Member of the Polish Academy of Sciences 1971, President 1981-83, 1990-92. Member of the PAU (Polska Akademia Umiejętności) 1989-; of the Warsaw Scholarly Society 1952-, President, 1986-91. Board member of the International Committee of Historical Sciences 1965-, President 1980-85. Deputy chairman of the Council for the Preservation of the Memory of the Struggles 1992-.

Associate Professor, College de France 1968, Visiting Fellow All Souls, Oxford 1968-9; Dumbarton Oaks, Washington D.C. 1987; Visiting Professor, Harvard 1977-78.

Foreign member, Medieval Academy of America, British Academy, Royal Historical Society, Academie des Sciences et Belles Lettres, and others. Doctor *honoris causa* Budapest, Moscow, Oxford, Sorbonne, Poznań. Decorations: White Eagle, Virtuti Militari Class V, Polonia Restituta Class III, Golden Cross of Merit with Swords.

Medieval history, supplementary studies to history; bibliography in two commemorative volumes: *Cultus et Cognito*. Studies in the history of Medieval Culture, Warsaw 1976. Studies dedicated to A.G. on the fiftieth anniversary of his scholarly work, Warsaw 1991.

INDEX

APPENDIX

No 5

September - December 1980

A Publication of Polish Student Clubs in Chicago

Editorial Staff

Managing Editor
Robert C. Bramski

English Editors
Monica Brzezinski,
Christopher Mizera

Polish Editor
Dr. Tymoteusz Karpowicz

Sponsoring Clubs

Polish American Students Assoc. (UICC)
Polish Club at DePaul University
Polish Club of Loyola University

Campus Representatives
Richard Owsiany/**DePaul University**
Mark Sokolowski/**Loyola University**
Bruno Mikolajczyk/**Polish University Abroad**
Zbigniew Wytaniec/**U of I–Chicago Circle**
Joanna Kot/**University of Chicago**
Dr. Zofia Werchun/**Wright College**

Advisory Board

Production Director
Alicja Adamczewska

Graphics Consultant
Mirek Rogalewicz

Student Affairs
Andrzej Tokarz

Academic Adviser
Dr. Frank Mocha

Dictionary of
Polish Literature

Edited by E. J. Czerwinski

GREENWOOD PRESS
Westport, Connecticut • London

ADDENDA

1) Letter to PRZEGLĄD POLSKI—unpublished (a fragment)

Words of praise are due the editor of Przegląd Polski for, despite occasional careless errors, raising the level of each succeeding issue of the weekly. The best, in my opinion, is the issue of October 19, because it contains not only interesting articles, begging for a comment or even a polemic, but mainly because they are written by or about people of the wartime generation who will soon be absent from our community, and because of that it is important to know about them and to read their statements.

The first article, by Professor Jan Kott, "Blaski i cienie pracy tlumacza" (The pros and cons of a translator's work), is written in a language so fluent and precise, and with such knowledge of the subject, that one reads it in one breath. I was initially puzzled why the author of the article dedicated it to Professor Jerzy Krzywicki, but towards the end it became clear that the article was an appeal to Polish foundations in America to undertake patronage of Polish books in general and that Professor Krzywicki was connected with the Alfred Jurzykowski Foundation. I support the appeal wholeheartedly, albeit with a dose of pessimism dictated by personal experience.

But let's return to translations. Professor Kott writes that "poets translate poets, because translating for many of them is part of creativity." But a factor more important than creativity in translation is its language difficulty. Hence we have had translating teams: Krzyżanowski-Gillon, Kryński-Maguire, Carpenter-Carpenter, and more recently Barańczak-Heaney, an ideal team in view of the latter's Nobel Prize (at first I questioned, but not publicly, Barańczak's initiative to translate the "Treny"—Laments, since there already exists an excellent translation in an anthology by George Rapall Noyes). An exception to the team concept is Wiesław Kuniczak as a single translator of Sienkiewicz, but nevertheless fulfilling Kott's condition that writers translate writers, because he is the author of the best and hence singled out (for a Book-of-the-Month Club selection) novel about the September campaign. But just as with Kochanowski's "Treny," there also exists an earlier translation of Sienkiewicz's "Trilogy," by the American linguist Jeremiah Curtin, who introduces something not done by other translators of the "Trilogy," namely separating its individual parts with lengthy digressions explaining what was happening in Poland in between.

It is a sad history which Sienkiewicz for various reasons ignores, with the exception of small allusions. Thus, after the undervalued-by-historians great battle of Beresteczko (1651) Poland was in position to impose on East Europe a "Pax Polonica" and throw Russia to the mercy of the Tatars (who were anyway planning an attack on Moscow even before Beresteczko) and Cossacks, but the fruits of the battle were lost by the incompetent hetman Mikołaj Potocki who, after a foolish adventure ending with a humiliating defeat, lost a Crown army in Ukraine for the second time, opening the way for a Russian intervention.

A similar opportunity presented itself after the Swedish "Deluge" when the war with Russia was resumed and the Polish troops, this time with the Cossacks and Tatars as allies, were approaching Moscow following brilliant victories in Ukraine and Belorussia. An incomprehensible decision to retreat had fatal consequences: the revolt of the army, Lubomirski's mutiny, new restlessness in Ukraine.

Going back to Kuniczak...

2) Reply from TINA PODLODOWSKI (see pp. 189-190):

November 10, 1997

Dear Mr. Mocha:

Please accept my apologies for having not called and returned your call more quickly. This has been a particularly busy time in Seattle's city government. ... My family is the other priority for me. A two-year-old and a five-months old keep both parents busy quite handily.

Thank you again for the information regarding my family name. It's wonderful to have the connection to family and ancestors reinforced. Your book, when finished, will provide an important connection to Poland for many, many people. I regret that at this time I will be unable to assist you in your project. My family has made its philanthropic commitments to other areas at this time. I would like to emphasize that I think your book and work on behalf of Poland are very important. Thank you for the opportunity to become involved.

Sincerely,

Tina Podlodowski

Nota Bene: Tina Podlodowski's name was placed on a short list of individuals and institutions to receive a copy of the book as a gift.

* * * *

Photo on opposite page: Testing a Warsaw Pact weapon on a Polish military training ground in the mid-1970s with Polish officers looking the other way.

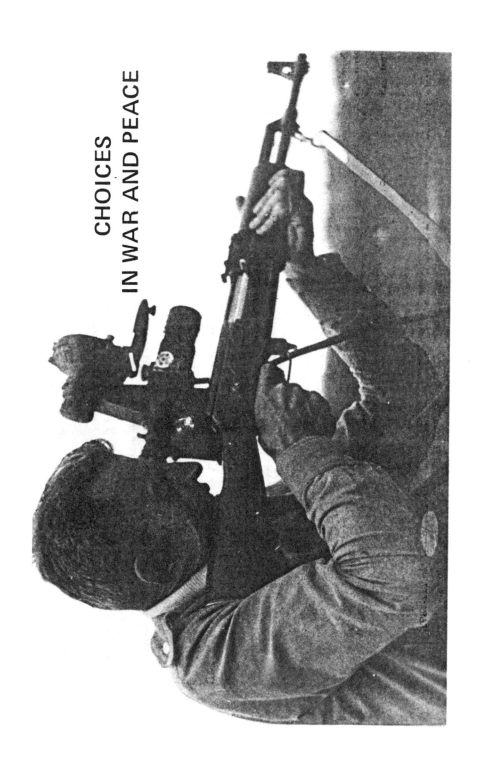

CHOICES
IN WAR AND PEACE

FAREWELL LUNCHEON

for

Dr. Frank Mocha

Professor of Slavic Philology and Dean of Humanities, Polish University Abroad (PUNO — Chicago Branch).
Adjunct Professor of Polish Culture and Civilization, Loyola University of Chicago
Faculty Adviser, Polish Club of Loyola and Pre-Professional Fraternity Pi Omicron Lambda (POL)
President, Polish American Educators Association (P.A.E.)
Past President, Polish Arts Club of Chicago (P.A.C.), sponsoring organizations

at

STATE ROOM, MERTZ HALL, LOYOLA UNIVERSITY (LAKE SHORE), 6525 N. SHERIDAN ROAD

on

SATURDAY, JUNE 30, 1984 AT 12 O'CLOCK

The Program will include:

Master of Ceremonies—Hon. Thaddeus L. Kowalski, Associate Judge, Circuit Court of Cook County
Keynote Speaker—Marion V. Winters, Ph.D. Cand., University of Illinois at C.C.
Hostess—Mrs. Doreen C. Mocha, Columbia University, New York

Nomination of a successor in Humanities at PUNO (Dr. Z. Wygocki)
Designation of a successor for Polish at Loyola (Mrs. Cz. Kolak, Ph.D. Cand., University of Chicago and outside of Loyola Izrael Taubenfligel)
Installation of a new Board of Officers of P.A.E.A. (K. Gill—President; K. Jesuit—Vice-President; Cz. Wolfe—Rec. Secretary; S. Strand—Treasurer; E. Pietraszek—Membership Chairman; M. Pietrzak—Publicity)

Dr. Mocha's New York address: 411 West 115th St., Apt. 42, New York, N.Y. 10025. Tel. (212) 222-3893

СССР
МИНИСТЕРСТВО ВЫСШЕГО И СРЕДНЕГО СПЕЦИАЛЬНОГО ОБРАЗОВАНИЯ

МОСКОВСКИЙ ордена ЛЕНИНА и ордена ТРУДОВОГО КРАСНОГО ЗНАМЕНИ
ГОСУДАРСТВЕННЫЙ УНИВЕРСИТЕТ имени М. В. ЛОМОНОСОВА

СВИДЕТЕЛЬСТВО

МОХА ФРАНК

(фамилия, имя, отчество)

гражданин Соединенных Штатов Америки

являлся слушателем Курсов русского языка для иност-
ранных граждан в Московском государственном университете
с 15 июня по 20 августа 1971 г.

/ Проректор
Московского государственного
университета

/Демидов В.Г./

Заказ 5338   Типография Издательства МГУ. Москва, Ленинские горы   Тираж 1000

POLONIJNE CENTRUM KULTURALNO-OŚWIATOWE
UNIWERSYTETU MARII CURIE-SKŁODOWSKIEJ
i TOWARZYSTWA ŁĄCZNOŚCI z POLONIĄ ZAGRANICZNĄ
„POLONIA"

KURS METODYCZNY NAUCZYCIELI POLONIJNYCH
W LUBLINIE

DYPLOM

NINIEJSZYM STWIERDZA SIĘ, ŻE PAN

F R A N K   M O C H A

UKOŃCZYŁ KURS METODYCZNY PO WYSŁUCHANIU 100 **GODZIN**
WYKŁADÓW I ĆWICZEŃ Z NASTĘPUJĄCYCH PRZEDMIOTÓW:

WIEDZA O JĘZYKU POLSKIM	18 GODZ.
METODYKA NAUCZANIA JĘZYKA POLSKIEGO	28 GODZ.
WYBRANE ZAGADNIENIA Z LITERATURY I KULTURY POLSKIEJ	24 GODZ.
OGÓLNE WIADOMOŚCI O POLSCE WSPÓŁCZESNEJ	10 GODZ.
ORGANIZACJA IMPREZ ARTYSTYCZNYCH I ROZRYWKOWYCH	20 GODZ.

DYREKTOR
POLONIJNEGO CENTRUM

W Kucharski

doc. dr Władysław Kucharski

PRZEWODNICZĄCY
RADY NAUKOWO-PROGRAMOWEJ
POLONIJNEGO CENTRUM

prof. dr hab. Wiesław Skrzydlo
REKTOR UMCS

KIEROWNIK KURSU

doc. dr Zbigniew Sobolewski

NR 14/79

LUBLIN, DNIA 6 SIERPNIA 1979 R.

$\Phi\iota\lambda o\sigma o\phi\iota a\ B\iota ov\ Kv\beta\epsilon\rho\nu\eta\tau\eta\varsigma$

To these two diplomas a third should have been added, from the Polish Combattants Association in London for winning the cross-country "National Race" in 1948 celebrating the May 3 (1791) Constitution. Unfortunately, the diploma was lost in the hasty sorting out of my papers in connection with what looked like a terminal illness. Documenting the breaking of the final tape, as depicted by the photo on the back cover, it is probably just as well that the diploma, with its connotation of finality, be not included. Another candidate for inclusion, Henry Archacki's drawing of and tribute to Ignace Morawski, Polish American journalist not equaled to this day, was lost too and cannot be included, which is also just as well because of the same connotation of finality, as both of the gentlemen are no longer living. But I am, and selected my most apt diploma, of membership in the Phi Beta Kappa chapter of a premier university.

Abandoning old associates was not an easy choice, but a logical one, helping to end the book on the same note, by stressing the scholar persona of my life. The two earlier ones, that of a soldier and an athlete, depicted in the two photos in the Appendix and on the back cover respectively, belong in the past, as part of history, while the scholar aspect is still ongoing, and, as Dmitry Chizhevsky, the respected Slavic scholar had said in not so many words, it is the process that counts, not the final result (because presumably we never know what it will turn out to be). The process is prominent in some parts of the book, such as the chapters on Poland and Germany/Russia, which are a search for understanding and solving mutual problems because (to paraphrase another scholar, Isaiah Berlin, with reference to philosophers), what scholars do in the privacy of their studies can change the course of history.

P.S. The cross-country diploma, if and when found, will be printed in the Polish American press, where it belongs — F.M.

Phi Beta Kappa

Founded December 5, 1776

This Writing Certifies That

Frank Morha

Was made a member of ΦBK by action of the
Delta of New York
at Columbia University

June 5, 1962

in recognition of high attainments in liberal scholarship

In Witness Whereof, the President and the Secretary
of the Chapter have hereunto affixed their signatures

Φιλοσοφια Βιου
Κυβερνητης

ΦBK

_____ President

_____ Secretary

MODERN AGE
A QUARTERLY REVIEW

O. Box AB
bllege Park, Maryland 20740

Dr. George A. Panichas
Editor
(301) 779-1436
(301) 779-6894

11 June 1987.

Dr. Frank Mocha,
411, West 115th Street (Apt. 42),
New York, New York. 10025.

Dear Frank:

<u>Magnificent!</u> That venerable adjective stayed consis-
tently in my mind as I read "In Sight of Crisis" from beginning to end with increasing admiration and sympathy. The revised manuscript, now reduced to a manageable and advantageous
length, will be a distinguished feature (as a memoir) in the
thirtieth anniversary issue of Modern Age, dealing with the
theme of "The Crisis of Modernity."

You speak of the "painstaking job of trimming" your
paper, but, my dear Frank, that effort has given to your com-
position an excellence, an astuteness, a compassion, a rele-
vance of meaning that, in their combined unity of value and
discrimination, heighten dramatically and deepen historically
your "remembrance of things past."

An entire world, at an epochal point of history --
"in sight of crisis," comes momentously alive to speak and
gesture to us, to teach us something of importance about our
selves and our destiny. Your memoir is, in this respect,
prophetic and poignant, moving and humane, warm, tender,
evocative, profound, frightening (in an inspired sense, of
course) -- and truly <u>Magnificent!</u>

I applaud you, Frank Mocha, and shake your hand
humbly and warmly in honor of your achievement.

Yours most faithfully,

George

GAP:mes

Back cover photo: Crossing the finish line in a traditional cross-country race revived after the war in the Olympic year 1948 in London commemorating the anniversary of the Polish Constitution of May 3rd (1791).